EIGHTH EDITION

SUPERVISION

Concepts and Practices
of Management

Raymond L. Hilgert

Professor of Managment and Industrial Relations
John M. Olin School of Business
Washington University, St. Louis, Missouri

Edwin C. Leonard, Jr.

Professor of Business Administration
School of Business and Management Sciences
Indiana University Purdue University Fort Wayne

South-Western College Publishing
Thomson Learning™

Australia • Canada • Denmark • Japan • Mexico • New Zealand • Philippines
Puerto Rico • Singapore • South Africa • Spain • United Kingdom • United States

Supervision: Concepts and Practices of Management, Eighth Edition by Raymond L. Hilgert and Edwin C. Leonard, Jr.

Publisher: Dave Shaut
Acquisitions Editor: Pamela M. Person
Developmental Editor: Tina Edmondson
Senior Marketing Manager: Joseph A. Sabatino
Media Development Editor: Sally Nieman
Media Production Editor: Robin K. Browning
Production Editor: Amy S. Gabriel
Manufacturing Coordinator: Sandee Milewski
Internal Design: Liz Harasymczuk Design
Cover Design: Michael H. Stratton
Cover Image: Index Stock Imagery
Photo Manager: Cary Benbow
Photo Researcher: Susan Van Etten
Production House: WordCrafters Editorial Services, Inc.
Compositor: Publishers' Design and Production Services, Inc.
Printer: Quebecor World–Taunton, MA

Printed in the United States of America
1 2 3 4 5 03 02 01 00

For more information contact South-Western College Publishing, 5101 Madison Road, Cincinnati, Ohio 45227 or find us on the Internet at http://www.swcollege.com

For permission to use material from this text or product, contact us by
• **telephone: 1-800-730-2214**
• **fax: 1-800-730-2215**
• **web: http://www.thomsonrights.com**

Library of Congress Cataloging-in-Publication Data
Hilgert, Raymond L.
     Supervision; concepts and practices of management / Raymond L. Hilgert, Edwin C.
Leonard, Jr.—8th ed.
          p. cm.
     Includes bibliographical references and index.
     ISBN 0-324-01389-2
     1. Supervision of employees. 2. Personnel management. I. Leonard, Edwin C., Jr. II. Title.
HF5549.12.H55 2000
658.3′02—dc21
                                                                                    00-038776

This book is printed on acid-free paper.

Preface

———o———

TO THE INSTRUCTOR

If there is one constant in today's business world, it is change. Wholesale changes in technologies, in organizational and competitive structure, and in the social, economic, and political environments all seem to be accelerating more rapidly than ever before. To operate successfully in the changing environment of this new millennium, organizations need supervisors with the managerial skills and creativity to turn uncertainty into opportunity. We prepared this eighth edition of *Supervision: Concepts and Practices of Management* to equip students with the knowledge and skills they need to become and succeed as supervisors in the present and future business world.

A TEXT THAT IS SKILLS-FOCUSED

The eighth edition has been thoroughly revised and updated from its predecessor, while retaining its thrust as a comprehensive single source and leading textbook on supervisory management. We have focused the text on helping students develop supervisory skills they can really use. While learning important supervisory management concepts, they will also learn how to be supervisors—namely, how to apply the principles of management in the real world.

The text is introductory in that it assumes no previous management knowledge. However, it presents challenging material in language that students can understand. The concepts are presented in direct, practical terms. It is not intended as a book for academic theoreticians.

A major goal of the book is to help the student, the potential supervisor, or the newly appointed supervisor analyze the many problems that confront supervisors, and the book offers practical advice for their solutions. For experienced supervisors, the text is intended to refresh their thinking, widen their horizons, and challenge them to examine how they are relating to employees, other supervisors, and higher management.

Materials for this text have been drawn from writings and research of scholars in management, leadership, and the behavioral sciences and from reported experiences of many supervisors, managers, and administrators. In addition to the authors' own experiences in management, the text reflects our backgrounds in teaching supervisory management courses, in participating in many stimulating discussions in supervisory development programs, and in consulting for numerous organizations.

TEXT FEATURES

Current/New Topics and Concepts

All chapters have undergone appropriate revisions and updating, which in part reflect suggestions of reviewers and adopters of previous editions. In particular, we have extensively updated material on organizational structure, motivation, communication, ethics, supervisory leadership, positive discipline, supervision of a diverse workforce, performance appraisal, and group dynamics and work teams. Among the many current/new topics and concepts discussed in the eighth edition are:

- the impact of technology and constant change
- strategic and operational planning
- the contingent workforce
- dealing with difficult people
- ethical tests in decision making
- employee empowerment
- knowledge empowerment
- participative management and the collaborative workplace
- self-managed (self-directed) work teams
- supervising a diverse workforce and compliance with applicable law
- the supervisor as mentor and facilitator
- time and stress management
- resolving complaints and alternative forms of conflict resolution
- workplace spirituality and wellness programs
- workplace violence
- relationship management
- no-fault attendance policies
- equity theory in compensation
- strategic business partners
- managing meetings with the boss
- coaching

An Integrated Teaching and Testing System

The text and all supplements are organized around learning objectives to develop a comprehensive teaching and testing system. Each text chapter begins with a series of learning objectives covering the key concepts. The objectives then appear in the text margins, identifying where each objective is fulfilled. The key concepts are reinforced at the end of the chapter, where they are summarized as related to their learning objectives.

Organization based on learning objectives continues into the supplement package, including a test bank, and integrated lecture outlines in the Instructor's Manual with transparency masters. The supplement package is covered in more depth later on in this preface.

"You Make the Call!" Opening Vignettes

To stimulate student interest, we begin each chapter with an opening scenario entitled "You Make the Call!" Each scenario presents a real-world supervisory situation that students will learn to handle from studying the chapter. These caselike scenarios, written in the second person, draw students personally into a problem situation and ask them to decide what to do. At the conclusion of the chapter, a section entitled "What Call Did You Make?" appears just before the chapter summary. Here we show students how to approach the problems in the scenario applying the concepts they just learned in the chapter. Students can then compare their own approaches and decisions to those suggested by the authors and perhaps also by you, their instructor. By applying chapter concepts to these opening problems and then comparing their results to those provided, students are also learning how to tackle the end-of-part cases.

Contemporary Issue Boxes

To better comprehend today's business world, students need to recognize and understand complex issues facing supervisors now and in the future. In our "Contemporary Issue" boxes within each chapter, we present issues and debate surrounding selected current management and supervisory topics, such as:

- the "emergent" and "migrating" workforce (Chapter 1)
- management by wandering around (Chapter 3)
- employee decision making (Chapter 5)
- strategic planning (Chapter 6)
- tips for better time management (Chapter 7)
- concentrating on people rather than structure (Chapter 9)
- electronic meetings and videoconferencing (Chapter 10)
- the escalation of the labor/management "war" (Chapter 11)
- innovation in employee recruitment (Chapter 12)
- inequities and disparities in compensation (Chapter 14)
- spirituality in the workplace (Chapter 15)
- harassment and incivility at work (Chapter 16)
- the "comeback" for dress and behavior codes (Chapter 18)
- employer reactions to employee abuses of electronic communication systems (Chapter 19)

Our "Contemporary Issue" boxes are often controversial in nature and include areas of contention concerning application of supervisory principles in current business practice. A majority of these boxes cite specific company examples.

Skills Applications

To develop skills, students need practice. Therefore we have increased the number of skills applications projects at the end of each chapter. Each chapter has at least four such projects, which are rather straightforward tasks that enable students to apply what they have learned. Some projects ask students to compare their own experiences with those of practicing supervisors. Others provide opportunities for small group work within or outside of class, or require self-assessment, library research, interviews with practicing managers. and other interesting applications.

INTERNET ACTIVITY

At least one skills applications project in each chapter has an Internet activity designed for students to seek out current information on designated Web sites. Internet-related projects are designated by an icon in the margin as shown here.

Cases

Instructors throughout the country have told us that our case studies are excellent tools for teaching and learning supervisory skills. In response to this feedback, we have increased the number of cases in the eighth edition, and we revised some of the previous cases in light of recent issues and trends. Of the total of 71 cases, 13 are new to this edition. Because the cases involve concepts from more than one chapter, they appear at the end of each major text part. To help you identify when to use each case, the lecture outlines in the Instructor's Manual suggest case choices next to the chapter coverage where they most apply.

Most of the cases are short—some are less than a page each. Yet they are challenging without being overwhelming for students. The cases are based on actual experiences of supervisors in numerous work environments. End-of-case discussion questions help students focus their thinking. For this eighth edition, we have extensive commentaries on the case questions in the Instructor's Manual to provide helpful guidance in implementing the cases and evaluating student responses.

INTERNET ACTIVITY

As in the previous edition, *optional Internet assignments* are attached to at least one case for each of the text's six parts. These optional assignments provide opportunities for students to search the Internet for current information that may be associated with or included within the concepts of the case. These are identified by an icon in the margin. For ease of recognition, this is the same icon used with skills applications that utilize the Internet. Students are thus urged to further apply their critical thinking and analysis of the case toward broader aspects of current business information.

You can use the cases in several ways: as fuel for class or seminar discussions, as written homework assignments, or as examinations. Case assignments are an excellent way for students to practice their skills on real supervisory problems and to assess their ability to apply what they have learned.

Skill Development Modules Video

SKILL DEVELOPMENT VIDEO

Today's students like the stimulation of visual presentations. To meet this need in the eighth edition, a Skill Development Modules video is available free to adopters. Eight video topics are included on this easy-to-use videotape. Each segment is only a few minutes in length, and each depicts an "ineffective" and a "more effective" way of handling a particular supervisory situation. The Skill Development Modules are identified by an icon at the margin as shown here.

The video segments are as follows:

Module 3:1   Communication
Module 4:1   Motivation
Module 5:1   Decision Making
Module 7:1   Planning and Time Management
Module 10:1 Meeting Management and Facilitation
Module 12:1 Employee Selection and Interviewing Protocol
Module 13:1 Coaching
Module 14:1 Delegation

Questions for discussion are provided directly within the student text, which require students to integrate the text material into their answers. The Instructor's Manual contains a complete description of each module, including running time, plus all the information you need to integrate the Skill Development Modules into your class presentation.

Other Pedagogical Features

In addition to the features previously described, the text provides a number of other features to enhance student learning. Among these are:

Marginal Definitions. In an introductory supervision course, students need to learn the language of business. Therefore, we have placed concise definitions of all key terms in the margins of the text, where they are first introduced. The key terms and their definitions are also compiled in a glossary at the end of the book for quick reference.

Summary Points. The major chapter concepts are summarized at the end of each chapter with reference to the learning objectives. By reviewing these summaries, students can quickly identify areas where they need further review. Then, using the learning objective number in the text margins, students can easily locate the discussion of the concepts they want to review.

Questions for Discussion. The end-of-chapter discussion questions are designed to help students check their understanding of chapter material.

Key Terms. All key terms are listed at the end of the chapter, with page numbers to make the explanations of the terms easy to find.

SUPPLEMENTS TO EASE THE TEACHING LOAD

As stated earlier, the integrated learning system extends to the supplementary package of the text. The Instructor's Manual with transparency masters is organized by learning objectives, so you can easily customize your lectures to emphasize the concepts that you feel your students need most. The extensive lecture outlines in the manual identify the materials that fulfill each objective, so that you can be sure your lectures cover the key concepts.

The comprehensive test bank and the PowerPoint® presentation slides are also keyed to the learning objectives for instructor convenience. All of these materials can add measurably in presenting your classroom lectures and discussions.

Instructor's Manual with Transparency Masters

Instructors always have more to do than there are hours in a day. To make your class preparations easier, we have developed a comprehensive Instructor's Manual with transparency masters. First, the manual contains extensive lecture outlines which form the core of the integrated teaching system. These outlines provide ample materials for faster and easier lecture preparations, including references to supplementary materials next to the chapter concepts to which they apply. You will be provided suggestions for when to show each PowerPoint slide or transparency master, use the cases, bring in the discussion of the chapter's boxed features, and more—all organized around the learning objectives.

In addition to the lecture outlines, the manual includes:

- Summaries of key concepts by learning objective.
- Solution guidelines for all end-of-chapter discussion questions.
- Commentaries on the Skills Applications, including suggested solutions and follow-up approaches.
- Commentaries on all cases, which will help you guide discussions or evaluate students' written analyses.
- Commentaries on the Skill Development Module video cases.
- A collection of transparency masters—approximately four per chapter—which can be utilized by instructors who prefer transparency acetates for classroom presentations.
- A bibliography of additional published resources.

PowerPoint® Presentation Slides

New to this edition is an extensive set of over 350 PowerPoint presentation slides, available on disk. All of these have been developed to correlate closely with text materials and learning objectives. The slides are easy to read and apply, and instructors should find them very helpful in adding focus to classroom lectures and discussions.

Test Bank

As in previous editions, the test bank continues to be keyed directly to the learning objectives. A grid at the beginning of each chapter correlates each test bank question to a learning objective, and also designates it as a definition, conceptual, or application type question.

For each chapter, the test bank contains 50 or more true/false and multiple-choice questions with answers. The eighth edition of the test bank now includes short essay questions, also keyed to learning objectives, to further expand your testing possibilities.

ExamView® Pro

The test bank is also available in ExamView® Pro computerized testing software. ExamView Pro enables you to quickly create printed tests, Internet tests, and online (LAN-based) tests. You can enter your own questions using the word processor provided, as well as customize the appearance of the tests you create. The QuickTest Wizard allows you to use an existing test bank to create a test in minutes, using a step-by-step selection process that gives you exactly what you want. It's simply the easiest test generator you've ever used.

Web Site http://hilgert.swcollege.com

The text now has a brand new supporting Web site, which includes all of the Internet Skill Applications complete with live links to Web sites, downloadable ancillaries for your use, and more. Visit our site often.

ACKNOWLEDGMENTS

In developing this text and supplementary materials, we are indebted to so many individuals that it is impossible to give all of them credit. Special thanks go to those organizations, supervisors, and managers who provided materials for the cases, exercises, applications projects, and certain illustrations. We appreciate the contributions of the following professors who reviewed the previous text and who offered numerous helpful suggestions and comments:

Amy A. Enders
Northampton Community College

Charles R. Jones
Oregon Institute of Technology

Pam Jones DeLotell
Lindenwood University

Karen Heuer
Des Moines Area Community College

Kris Sperstad
Chippewa Valley Technical College

Timothy A. Elliott
San Jacinto College Central

Charles O. Blalack
Kilgore College

Richard W. Foltz
Roane State Community College

Jacquelyn Blakley
Tri County Technical College

Bruce L. Conners
Kaskaskia College

George Kelley
Erie Community College-City Campus

We especially thank Tina Edmondson, our Developmental Editor at South-Western College Publishing, and Laura Cleveland of WordCrafters Editorial Services, Inc., for their outstanding roles in guiding our work on the eighth edition. This edition also reflects the work of Amy S. Gabriel, Production Editor, and Pamela Person, Acquisitions Editor, both of South-Western. Our appreciation also goes to Susan Carson of Last Word, who wrote an additional Internet activity for each chapter.

Thanks for coordination and additional work on the supplementary package goes to Shelley Brewer for the Instructor's Manual, Tom Lewis for the Test Bank, and D&G for the PowerPoint Presentation Slides.

We recognize also the prior contributions of academic colleagues and numerous former students who provided ideas, case materials, and suggestions that were included in prior editions and retained in this current edition. We particularly wish to recognize the following students at Indiana University Purdue University Fort Wayne (IPFW) whose classroom-prepared case materials were adapted for inclusion in this eighth edition. Rewritten as "You Make the Call!" opening vignettes were contributions from Mark Pepoy (Chapter 6), David Storey (Chapter 9), and Michael Kish (Chapter 18). The following case studies were developed from materials contributed by: Margaret Setlack (Case 2-1, "The Micro-Manager"); Mark Dankow (Case 2-7, "Break Time Is My Time"); Denise Quance (Case 3-4, "A Rose Has Its Thorns"); Sharon Spelt (Case 5-7, "A Woman's Place"); and Kevin Mason (Case 6-9, "Fear? Or Exaggeration?").

We gratefully acknowledge the word-processing services of Karen Busch of the Washington University staff and Louise Pruse of the IPFW staff. Their efforts contributed greatly to keeping this project on schedule.

Finally, we acknowledge the support of our spouses, Bernice and Ginger, who have become good friends while we prepared this and previous editions. Their encouragement and patience during these periods have been invaluable.

Raymond L. Hilgert
Edwin C. Leonard, Jr.

About the Authors

Dr. Raymond L. Hilgert currently is Professor of Management and Industrial Relations at the Olin School of Business of Washington University. He graduated from Westminster College, Fulton, Missouri, with a Bachelor of Arts Degree, and received his Master's and Doctor's degrees from Washington University. His business experience includes management positions at Southwestern Bell Telephone Company and a market research position with an advertising company. Dr. Hilgert has taught at Washington University for over 35 years, and he has served as an Assistant Dean and Director of Management Development Programs. He has published some 90 articles in management, business, and academic journals and has authored or co-authored five books on human resources management, supervision, and collective bargaining, three of which are in their sixth, eighth, and ninth editions.

Dr. Hilgert is a member of the Academy of Management, the Industrial Relations Research Association, the Society for Human Resource Management, the American Compensation Association, and the American Management Association. He has participated in or directed numerous management, supervisory, and business ethics programs and seminars. Dr. Hilgert is an arbitrator certified by the Federal Mediation and Conciliation Service, and he has decided over 550 grievance-arbitration cases. Dr. Hilgert holds the Senior Professional in Human Resources (SPHR) accreditation from the Personnel Accreditation Institute. He has received a number of teaching awards from students at Washington University.

Dr. Edwin C. Leonard, Jr., is Professor of Business Administration at Indiana University Purdue University Fort Wayne. He received his Bachelor's, Master's, and Doctor's degrees from Purdue University. Since joining the faculty some 35 years ago, he has held a variety of faculty and administrative positions, including serving as chair of the Management and Marketing Department in the School of Business and Management Sciences. Dr. Leonard has designed and conducted workshops and seminars for thousands of supervisors and managers. These programs often are customized to meet specific organizational needs. Dr. Leonard currently serves as academic advisor and coordinator of Do-it-Best Corp's Retail Management Training Course; this comprehensive program is for management personnel of one of the nation's largest hardware and building materials retailers. Dr. Leonard additionally is associated with a major full-service training and consulting firm.

Dr. Leonard's primary research interests are in the areas of employee involvement, teaming, organizational climate and leadership, human resource management interventions, and case development. He has published in a variety of academic and professional journals, instructional supplement manuals, and proceedings. His professional memberships include the American Evaluation Association, the Midwest Society for Human Resources/Industrial Relations, the Society for Case Research (SCR), and the Organizational Behavior Teaching Society.

Dr. Leonard was the recipient of the National University Continuing Education Association's Service Award for Continuing Education for the Professions, and he received the Award of Teaching Excellence from the Indiana University School of Continuing Studies. Dr. Leonard has received several "best paper" and "distinguished case" awards from various organizations.

Brief Contents

———○———

Contents

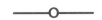

Part 4:   Staffing

Part 6:   Controlling

Chapter 18 Fundamentals of Controlling   618

Chapter 19 Positive Discipline   649

Supervisory Management Overview

Chapter 1

After studying this chapter, you will be able to:

1
Explain the demands and rewards of being a supervisor.

2
Describe the contributions of four schools of management thought.

3
Identify and discuss the major demographic and societal trends that will affect supervisors.

4
Explain why supervisors must continually grow and develop as professionals.

The Supervisory Challenge in the 21st Century

You Make the Call!

Every chapter in this book begins with a personalized short case section titled, "You Make the Call." After reading each case, mentally or otherwise decide what decision(s) or course(s) of action you would make as the person described in the case. As you read each chapter, think about how the concepts apply to the opening problem. Then, after you finish each chapter, check the "calls" you made by reading the suggestions in the section called "What Call Did You Make?" This section appears just before the summary for each chapter.

You are Charlotte Kelly, evening shift admitting services team leader for Pine Village Community Medical Center. Pine Village is a 240-bed facility located in a small southern city approximately 70 miles from its nearest competitor.

When you graduated from nursing school some 30 years ago, nursing jobs were plentiful. You began as a cardiac care nurse at a hospital in Greenville, South Carolina, where you met your future husband and began a family. Shortly after your youngest child graduated from high school, your husband was tragically killed in an automobile accident. You moved to Pine Village to be near your sister and her family. At that time nursing jobs were scarce, but Pine Village was looking for someone to be the admitting department's evening shift team leader, which you accepted. As a shift team leader, you assumed some supervisory responsibilities but you had limited authority and were not part of hospital management. The admitting department's supervisor was Pat Graham.

Shortly after arriving at Pine Village Community Medical Center, you began attending classes at the local community college. You received a certificate in medical records technology and decided to pursue an associate's degree in supervision and organizational leadership. With work requirements, you were able to take only one class each quarter. The supervision classes were taught by experienced instructors with relevant work experience. Your favorite instructor was Bernie Ray, a middle-aged supervisor at a local company, who incorporated many personal stories into his classes. Mr. Ray usually started each class with a current problem or issue that required students to interact and expand upon their supervisory perspectives. You liked this "team" or "collaborative approach" to learning, because your fellow-classmates brought a variety of experiences to the class and you learned from each other.

Late Wednesday afternoon, your boss, Pat Graham, summoned you to her office. To your surprise, Bob Murphy, vice-president of administration, was also present. Murphy began the conversation. "Charlotte, we are very pleased with the job you've done as a team leader on the evening shift. You are an excellent role model and a good listener. You have a reputation as being someone who expects a lot and gets positive results because you expect no less from yourself. You encourage your associates to get involved and to understand how their jobs affect patient care and relate to the functioning of the entire medical center." After Murphy had paused briefly, he continued. "Charlotte, we want you to become the ER (emergency room) supervisor effective Monday morning to replace Amy Talmadge. You've earned this promotion into management, and we know you will be able to handle this new assignment, even though you haven't worked in the emergency services department previously." Pat Graham then said, "Charlotte, because you've done such a good job of cross-training your associates, we'd also like you to recommend your replacement."

When you returned to your department, you were both exhilarated and a bit sobered by this event. "Wow," you thought to yourself. "This is the culmination of a five-year odyssey. It's been hard, but I knew right from the beginning that I wanted to be a supervisor. Pat Graham has been a great mentor. She shows interest in each employee and in increasing their skills, knowledge, and ability. I learned a lot from her, but I wonder if I've got the same right stuff to be in a supervisory management position. And do I really want all of the headaches, responsibilities, and pressures that a supervisor has to deal with?"

It is now Friday afternoon as you reflect on the events of the past two days. You have learned that Amy Talmadge was fired as ER supervisor. The ER department had become the butt of many employee jokes, and turnover has been extremely high. You also have learned that Amy Talmadge had the reputation of being an autocratic, demanding, and insensitive person. She expected her employees to do as she demanded, and at times she was known to have criticized and embarrassed people in public. The ER department consisted of a very diverse group of employees, which apparently had added to Amy's difficulties.

You are sitting at your desk contemplating your situation. "I know some things not to do, but I'm not certain that I can make the move from team leader to supervisor. Where should I begin?"

You Make the Call!

WHAT DOES IT MEAN TO BE A SUPERVISOR?

Explain the demands and rewards of being a supervisor.

Virtually every aspect of contemporary life has undergone major changes during the past several decades. There is little doubt that major changes will continue to take place in our society during coming years, and continuing change will be a challenge to every organization. Like all aspects of modern life, organizational concepts and managerial practices are also undergoing major changes, as illustrated in the "Contemporary Issue" box. Managers at all levels will be at the forefront of planning and coping with trends, factors, and problems requiring attention and more effective management if they and their organizations are to survive. This book will focus primarily on the first tier of management, which generally is referred to as the supervisory level, or supervisory management. **Supervisors** are first-level managers who are in charge of entry-level and other departmental employees.

Supervisor

First-level manager in charge of entry-level and other departmental employees.

From various economic, political, geographical, and sociological perspectives, recent decades have been a time of turbulence in U.S. business. Current critical commentaries on the U.S. business system indicate that traditional notions of getting a job done through power and positional authority are no longer effective. Today's managers and supervisors, whether they are in factories, nursing care units, business offices, retail stores, or government agencies, realize that reliance on authoritarian direction and close control usually will not bring about the desired results. Managers everywhere will continue to expect supervisors to obtain better performance from their human resources and do so in an environment that is constantly shifting and changing in nature.

Working supervisors

First-level individuals who perform supervisory functions but who may not legally or officially be part of management.

In many organizations, much of the supervisory work is performed by individuals who may not officially or legally be considered to be part of management. These individuals perform many of the supervisory functions to be discussed in this book, but they usually have limited authority and are typically referred to as **working supervisors.** Other designations for these types of individuals include *foreman, team leader, lead person, coach,* and other terms. For purposes of brevity, we will generally use the all-embracing term *supervisor* to identify first-level individuals who carry out supervisory functions among rank-and-file employees. The concepts and principles to be described and discussed in this text generally are applicable to all such individuals, and we will consider all of them to be "managers," even though officially or legally they are not part of the recognized management structure.

Supervisory work has become more complex, sophisticated, and demanding, and it requires professional and interpersonal skills.[1] As depicted in Figure 1-1, the job of the

contemporary issue

Is Loyalty Dead? The "Emergent" and "Migrating" Workforce in a World of Change

Driven by competitiveness in a global marketplace and in order to provide greater returns on company equity, the accelerated pace of change in organizational structure is likely to continue for the foreseeable future. Downsizing, restructuring, mergers and acquisitions, and expansion of new products into new markets mean that companies and organizations are likely to shift directions more frequently than ever before. Because of constantly changing priorities, many companies find it necessary to frequently shed employees, add new employees, outsource, and do whatever it takes to meet corporate needs without much concern about the longer-term consequences of the lack of stability in the workforce.

Professor John J. Clancy, Associate Director of American Culture Studies at Washington University in St. Louis, writes that, "Most American corporations are sending a clear, if tacit, signal that investments in loyalty are no longer warranted. More and more companies seek only an instrumental relationship with their employees and shy away from creating long-lasting bonds. We see this in the virtual disappearance of the informal employment contract that promised lifetime employment for good service; we see it in the increased use of outsourcing, often a cost-effective move but one hardly designed to build loyalty and trust among employees. We can only conclude that American management, despite its protestations, has accepted the social changes and no longer tries to recover lost loyalty."[1]

It appears indeed that employee attitudes about work have been shifting as we enter the 21st century. A major national survey of working adults conducted by Interim Services, Inc., and Louis Harris Associates revealed that 22 percent of workers held what were defined as "emerging" attitudes. These are employees who view loyalty in terms of working hard for a company today but not staying there for long periods of time. Emergent workers say they want pay based upon performance, and they are not interested in longevity. Although they want mentoring to help them grow, they do not care strongly about having specific career paths outlined. Further, emergent workers do not see anything wrong with changing jobs frequently in order to achieve their personal objectives. Almost 50 percent of the same survey respondents held attitudes that were called "migrating," that is, their attitudes incorporated some traditional views of work as well as emergent ones. These employees' attitudes appear to be shifting in the direction of emergent workers, particularly those with college degrees and annual salaries of more than fifty thousand dollars. Ray Marcy, president and CEO of Interim Services, Inc., commented that employers must be willing to move toward accommodating the attitudes of an emergent and migrating workforce. In particular, workplaces should be flexible in scheduling work hours and providing opportunities for employees to receive mentoring concerning their careers and career choices. According to Mr. Marcy, "Companies can also attract more emergent employees by granting workers more independence, encouraging debate, and limiting the need for memos, especially those that workers and bosses use for covering their tracks."[2]

In the minds of many observers, the concept of corporate loyalty reflects a "social contract" of the past that more or less has disappeared along with confidence in institutions, government, and other parties to our social fabric. Professor John Clancy comments that "it is pointless to try to motivate people with vision statements and appeals to corporate traditions." However, Professor Clancy believes that the energies and best performance of today's employees can be realized by an approach that is responsive to the attitudes of emergent and migrating workers. Professor Clancy states, "I see an untapped reservoir of loyalty to the work of people's own hands, the products or services they produce and of which they can and should feel proud. Therefore, management's words and actions should be aimed at this natural pride and handiwork, and organizational design and reward systems must capitalize on that."[3]

Sources: (1) John J. Clancy, "Is Loyalty Really Dead?" *Across the Board* (The Conference Board, June 1999), pp. 17–19. (2) Dave Murphy, "Generations Close Gap Concerning Attitudes about Work," (article originally appearing in the *San Francisco Examiner,* reprinted in the *St. Louis Post Dispatch,* June 7, 1999) p. BP18. (3) Clancy, p. 19.

FIGURE 1-1   The "Pluses" and "Minuses" of Supervision.

THE SUPERVISORY POSITION IS SATISFYING AND REWARDING

- A promotion to supervisor usually means more status and a higher salary that is not based on an hourly wage.

- Supervisors find considerable satisfaction when they work with motivated employees and assist in developing their abilities and potential.

- Supervisors have numerous opportunities to make their own decisions and to manage their departments with some degree of authority.

- Achievement of challenging goals and objectives provides great satisfaction and usually is rewarded in various ways by higher management.

- Being a supervisor provides opportunities for professional and personal growth and possible advancement.

THE SUPERVISORY POSITION IS DIFFICULT AND STRESSFUL

- If a supervisor has been promoted from his/her work group, the supervisor often finds the transition to supervision to be confrontational and difficult as former peer relationships change.

- Supervisors generally work longer hours; if part of management, there usually is no overtime premium pay for the extra hours spent on the job.

- Supervisory work is constantly characterized by interruptions, crises, problems, and complaints from various sources.

- Supervisors usually are under considerable pressure from the often-conflicting demands of higher management, customers, and employees; the constant shifting of priorities is particularly stressful.

- Supervisors who are part of management easily can be terminated for a variety of reasons; they do not have the job protections afforded by labor unions and contractual seniority provisions.

supervisor is both rewarding and stressful. The ideas presented in Figure 1-1 are not all-inclusive, but they give a feeling for the "pluses" and "minuses" of being a supervisor.

Although the supervisory management position is one of three primary levels on the management hierarchy (see Figure 1-2), it is the level where most people obtain their first management experience. Many higher-level managers have achieved their positions after obtaining practical experience and performance in first-level supervisory positions.

Today, the study and practice of management have become more formalized, and many practicing and prospective supervisors and managers also learn management concepts and principles in classroom settings. Although the systematic study of management has largely been a 20th-century phenomenon, the authors believe that some knowledge of the past is helpful in looking to the future. Further, a brief overview of the major schools (or approaches) to management theories and practices can provide some foundation and perspectives for the supervisory concepts and practices to be presented and discussed in this book.

As previously stated, this book is intended for both practicing and potential supervisors, especially students who are studying the field of management as one of their career choices. As an Appendix to this chapter, we include a section on "getting into supervision" which will help identify and discuss some of the important factors that one

The supervisory or team leader position is where most people begin their management careers.

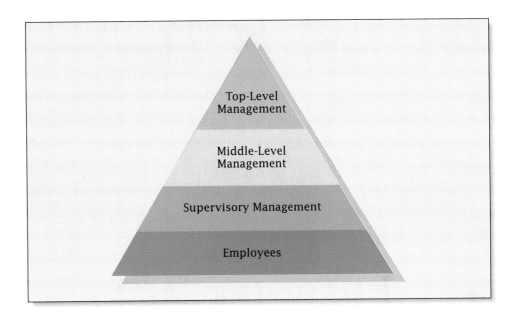

should consider if he or she is seeking a supervisory or management position. The Appendix also includes a number of "career tips" that are essential for those aspiring to be supervisors, and which probably are vital to almost any type of career planning irrespective of one's final choice of position or organization.

SCHOOLS OF MANAGEMENT THOUGHT

2
Describe the contributions of four schools of management thought.

Management practices can be traced throughout history, beginning with the Bible. The Great Wall of China, the Pyramids of Egypt, the Roman Coliseum, the Eiffel Tower, and the Statue of Liberty all resulted from the application of management principles. While there is no universally accepted theory of management, there is a common thread among the various theories. Each attempts to answer the question, "What is the best way to manage the task at hand?" Many of the early schools of thought still influence the way people approach the supervisory task. While there is little agreement on the exact number and nomenclature of the various management theories, we believe that four are deserving of mention here.[2]

Scientific management approach

School of management thought that focuses on determining the most efficient methods to achieve greater output and productivity.

Scientific Management

One of the first approaches in the 20th-century study of management was the **scientific management approach,** which focused on determining the most efficient methods to achieve greater output and productivity. Frederick Winslow Taylor, the so-called "father of scientific management," believed that managers should plan what, when, where, and how employees should produce the product; that is, a manager's job was to perform the mental tasks such as determining the "one best way" to do the job. The employees' jobs then would be to perform the physical tasks. To this end, Taylor developed certain principles to increase productivity.

Taylor believed that many workers did not put forth their best efforts, and as a result production often suffered. While observing workers in a steel plant, Taylor was shocked at the lack of systematic procedures, output restrictions among groups of workers, and the fact that ill-equipped and poorly trained workers typically were left on their own to determine how to do their jobs. Taylor believed that principles of engineering could be applied to make people perform somewhat like machines, that is, efficient, mindless, and repetitive. By eliminating choice, operations could be standardized. In brief, his principles of scientific management include the following:

1. Analyze the tasks associated with each job. Use the principles of science to find the one best way to perform the work.
2. Recruit the employee best suited to perform the job; that is, choose the person who has the skills, aptitude, and other attributes to do the job.
3. Instruct the worker in the one best way to perform the job.
4. Reward the accomplishment of the worker. Taylor believed that workers were economically motivated and would, therefore, do the job the way they were instructed if rewarded with money.
5. Cooperate with workers to ensure that the job matches plans and principles.
6. Ensure an equal division of work and responsibility between managers and workers.

Other leaders within the early 20th-century scientific management movement similarly focused upon determining ways to improve productivity through systematic studies and application of engineering principles. In particular, Frank and Lillian Gilbreth pioneered the use of time and motion studies of job operations through which efficient ways to perform a job could be determined and time standards could be developed. These then would be used for improving productivity and for purposes of compensation related to an employee's output.

The Functional Approach

In the early 1900s, Henri Fayol, a French industrialist, identified 14 principles of management that he believed could be applied universally. Some writers have referred to this as the concept of *universality of management,* which suggests that basic functions, principles, and their applications in management are similar regardless of the nature of an organization. A number of Fayol's more widely accepted principles will be introduced in subsequent chapters. In general, Fayol believed that each manager's authority should be co-equal with responsibility, and that there should be a unity of direction and authority flow throughout the organization.

Functional approach
School of management thought that asserts that all managers perform various functions in doing their jobs, such as planning, organizing, staffing, leading, and controlling.

More important, Fayol introduced the **functional approach** to the study of management. This approach defined the manager's role and proposed that managers do their jobs by performing various functions. He identified five functions as being critical for managerial effectiveness:

1. Planning: setting down a course of action.
2. Organizing: designing a structure, with tasks and authority clearly defined.
3. Commanding: directing subordinates in what to do.
4. Coordinating: pulling the organizational elements together toward common objectives.
5. Controlling: ascertaining that plans are carried out.

Other writers have built upon these ideas. This textbook is organized around the more current version of the functional approach to the study of management: planning, organizing, staffing, leading, and controlling.

Human Relations/Behavioral School

The contributions of Taylor and others gave rise to the notion that (1) if managers would use the principles of scientific management, worker efficiency would increase and, thus, productivity increases would follow; and (2) if managers would strive to improve working conditions, then productivity increases would follow. The studies at the Hawthorne plant of Western Electric provided some of the most interesting and controversial results in the study of management.

Elton Mayo and Fritz Roethlisberger, leaders of a Harvard research team, conducted a series of experiments from 1924 to 1932. In their illumination experiments they hypothesized that if lighting improved then productivity would increase. Contrary to expectations, productivity rose in both the control group (no changes made in working conditions) and the experimental group (working conditions varied). Numerous variations in working conditions were introduced, and no matter what change was introduced, productivity continued to rise until it stabilized at a relatively high level. The researchers concluded that the workers performed differently than they normally did because the researchers were observing them. This reaction is known as the **Hawthorne effect.** Other phases of the Hawthorne studies will be discussed in Chapter 15, particularly the studies that emphasized the attitudes and behavior of workers in small informal groups, and how these significantly can influence performance and productivity in either positive or negative directions.

The experiments at the Hawthorne plant gave rise to what was known as the **human relations movement** and later the **behavioral science approach,** which focuses study upon the behavior of people in organizations. Contributions from psychologists, sociologists, and other behavioral disciplines have provided numerous insights concerning individual and group behavior in work settings, and the impact of supervisory practices and procedures on employee motivation and work performance. Chapter 4, which discusses employee motivation in relation to supervisory approaches, mentions various social and behavioral scientists and their contributions toward understanding and managing human behavior in organizations.

Quantitative/Systems Approaches

While somewhat beyond the scope of this text, **quantitative approaches** to management had their origins in operations research approaches developed by the British dur-

Hawthorne effect
The fact that when special interest is shown in people, this may cause them to behave differently.

Human relations movement/behavioral science approach
Approach to management that focuses on the behavior of people in the work environment.

Quantitative/systems approaches
Field of management study that uses mathematical modeling as a foundation.

ing World War II. Quantitative approaches to management rely heavily upon mathematical modeling. Models are developed that attempt to quantitatively describe the interrelationships of variables through data which can be manipulated and outcomes predicted. Quantitative approaches have increased with the development of computers that enable processing large quantities of data and the use of probability models that quantify various aspects of problems to be decided. Quantitative approaches are often closely connected with systems approaches in which mathematical models are developed as a series or collection of interrelated variables or parts that can be analyzed and utilized in decision-making situations.

Quantitative/systems approaches are frequently found in large organizations where sales, costs, and production data are analyzed using computer technology. Mathematical modeling typically is used to build "what if" situations, for example, what would be the effect on sales if the price rose 10 percent, 20 percent, and so forth? A number of planning concepts to be introduced in Chapter 6 rely on these types of approaches.

FACTORS AND TRENDS AFFECTING THE ROLE OF THE SUPERVISOR

3

Identify and discuss the major demographic and societal trends that will affect supervisors.

Throughout the foreseeable future, supervisors will have to understand and deal with many complex environmental factors and trends. Therefore, we will examine some major demographic and society factors and trends that are likely to affect the supervisory management position. Figure 1-3 illustrates many of the challenges faced by a supervisor. While every supervisor is responsible for managing numerous resources, unquestionably the most important, overriding aspect of supervision is the management of people. Therefore, the nature of the workforce should be of vital concern to the supervisor who plans for the future. Finding and developing qualified people have always been among the most important supervisory responsibilities. However, the traditional challenges of attracting and retaining the most qualified employees may be superseded by the more acute challenge to supervisors of leading and motivating an increasingly changing workforce. The most significant characteristic of this changing workforce will be its **diversity.** Work groups will be composed of employees who differ on cultural, ethnic, gender, age, educational level, racial, and lifestyle characteristics. The supervisor will need to get people from many different cultures to work together.

Diversity

The cultural, ethnic, gender, age, educational level, racial, and lifestyle differences among employees.

Population and Workforce Growth

Despite the rather low birth rate of recent decades, both the population and the workforce will continue to grow. It is estimated that the U.S. population will grow at a modest rate from a 1999 level of about 272 million people to nearly 295 million people by the year 2010. The 1999 workforce of about 139 million is also projected to increase by about 20 million during the same time period. From these estimates, it would appear that a slightly higher percentage of the total population will be employed in the workforce, a continuation of a trend that began over two decades ago.[3]

FIGURE 1-3

Effective supervisors must be adaptable and be able to maintain their perspective in the face of rapidly changing conditions.

Immigration has and will continue to account for a considerable share of the nation's population and workforce growth. In particular, there has been a major increase in immigration of Asian and Pacific Island immigrants, many of whom are highly skilled professionals and information technology workers. Some employment analysts advocate that there should be an increased number of immigration visas granted in order to meet the growing demand for information technology workers and other high-skilled occupations.[4] The growth in the number of new immigrants may expand certain

In spite of the low birth rates in recent decades, both the population and the workforce are growing.

interracial and intercultural problems that have faced many supervisors in managing a diverse workforce.

Managing a diverse workforce does present some difficulties, but it also presents numerous opportunities for supervisors to build upon the strengths of individuals and groups of individuals. In the following sections, our intent is not just to create an awareness of the differences to be expected, but rather to accomplish some "consciousness raising." Supervisors must understand the rights of both their employees and their employers, irrespective of the many workforce differences that exist. Supervisors will need to recognize the value of a diverse workforce and their own need to become more adaptable to changes. Further, perhaps more than ever before, supervisors will have to be scrupulously fair in supervising diverse groups of employees through nondiscriminatory and progressive actions.

Changing Age Patterns

Both the population and the labor force are getting older. As of the late 1990s, about half of the workforce was between 35 and 54 years of age. The fastest growing age group during the next decade will be workers between 45 and 54 years of age, which will grow by some 9 percent by the mid 2000s. The median age of the population will go from about 35 years of age in 2000 to age 38 by 2025. The growth in numbers of people in these mature age categories will provide an ample supply of experienced individuals who are promotable to supervisory and other management positions. At the same time, because there are so many of them, there may be "a glut" of younger employees waiting for opportunities to develop. This possible "mismatch" in many firms between the number of employees desiring advancement and the number of opportunities available may lead to dissatisfaction, causing younger workers to leave and seek positions elsewhere.

Various descriptions of categories of workers have been provided by placing them within several major groups. Ann Clurman and J. Walker Smith define the population in three major categories: "generation Xers" are those born between 1964 and 1981; "boomers" are those born between 1946 and 1963; and "matures" are those born between 1920 and 1945. Members of the generation X group are those who will be replacing those in the mature categories, but generation Xers have fundamentally different ideas about work, loyalty, and commitment. In general, generation Xers have far less concern about staying with companies for long periods of time; they tend to want more personal and leisure time and have considerable skepticism about management's values and management's concerns for employees.[5] There can be little question that the success of supervisors will depend to a considerable extent on their abilities to tap the interest and motivations of all the members of the workforce.

Women in the Workforce and Related Issues

Perhaps the most dramatic change in the last several decades has been the increase in both the number and percentage of women in the U.S. workforce. Currently, some 60 percent of adult women are employed, and women constitute almost half of the U.S. labor force. In recent years, women have assumed many jobs formerly dominated by men. Women now hold close to 40 percent of the nation's administrative, supervisory, and other managerial positions. During the first decade of the 2000s, about 60 percent of the new entrants to the workforce will be women.

The movement of women into the workforce, however, has brought with it a number of problems that have impacted employers and are likely to continue. Nearly 60 percent of employed women are married, many of whom are raising children. Further, the number of families headed by women has steadily increased to the point that almost 20 percent of U.S. families are headed by women. Substantially higher percentages of African-American and Hispanic families are headed by women, and many of them are single working mothers.

Employees may bring their family problems to work. Supervisors need to understand that their employees' work performance may be negatively affected by a conflict between job and family obligations, which often impacts women employees more than men. In order to attract and retain qualified employees, more employers will be providing quality child-care facilities or assisting employees in making suitable child-care arrangements. Employees will continue to experiment with different types of workdays and workweeks, such as **flextime** (in which employees choose their work schedules within certain limits), **job sharing** (in which two or more employees share a job position), **telecommuting** (in which the employee works at home and is linked to the office by computer and modem), and the four-day, 10-hour-a-day work week. Given the increasing numbers of single working parents and the concern over the quality of child-care services, many firms are likely to implement these types of working arrangements.

Flextime
Policy that allows employees to choose their work hours within stated limits.

Job sharing
Policy that allows two or more employees to perform a job normally done by one full-time employee.

Telecommuting
Receiving and sending work to the office from home via a computer and modem.

Recent studies indicate that the typical two-income family hasn't figured out yet how to balance jobs with kids and housework. And despite efforts by many employers to provide child care and elder care, employees voice frustration with the juggling act. Efforts to help employees balance the responsibilities of home and job will require better supervisory coordination and planning skills.

Interestingly, the image or myth of "superwoman," a title that was in widespread use in earlier years to describe a woman who "did it all," seems to be disappearing. In particular, professional women are now looking for more balance in their lives as they try to juggle career choices and raising a family.[6]

Another major challenge for supervisors will be to ensure that sexual harassment does not occur in the work environment. Sexual harassment has been perpetrated against both men and women, but most attention has focused on the latter. Recent court decisions have reiterated the implications for supervisors, who are obligated to take action to prevent harassment and to take steps to remedy reported incidents of harassment. The topic of sexual harassment will be explored in greater detail in Chapter 16.

Racial Minorities in the Workforce

To what extent racial minorities will enter the workforce is an educated guess at best. Figure 1-4 projects changes for the major racial classes of the U.S. population. If one assumes that the workforce will mirror the general population, we can expect dramatic changes in workforce composition in future years.

Census data reveal that one out of seven residents of the United State speak a language other than English at home. Winston Churchill once said, "It is a good thing for an uneducated man to read books of quotations. . . . The gift of a common tongue is a priceless inheritance, and it may well someday become the foundation of a common cit-

---

FIGURE 1-4

The United States' changing population.

Projections of Racial Classifications of U.S. Population (by percentages)				
	YEAR			
RACE	**2000**	**2010**	**2025**	**2050**
Asian	4.0%	5.0%	6.6%	8.6%
Hispanic*	11.4	13.7	17.6	24.5
Black (African-American)	12.9	13.4	14.2	15.4
White	82.1	80.5	78.3	74.8

*Persons of Hispanic origin may be of any race; consequently, the overall percentages exceed 100. Native Americans and other racial classifications are not shown.

Source: U.S. Bureau of the Census as included in the *Statistical Abstract of the United States—1997* (U.S. Department of Commerce, October 1997), p. 14.

izenship."[7] But in the future, it will probably be more common for supervisors to find that many of their employees are natives of different countries and that the common English tongue has been replaced by other languages. The challenges for supervisors will be to learn about the cultural, racial, and language differences and to develop strategies for promoting cooperation among racially and ethnically diverse groups.

On the other hand, there are some futurists who believe that the increasing use of information technology will to some degree erode cultural and language distinctions. English is likely to become the dominant language of technology, although there will be many different languages and dialects spoken in the workplace.[8]

Opportunities for Women and Minorities

Glass ceiling
Invisible barrier that limits advancement of women and minorities.

Glass walls
Invisible barriers that compartmentalize women and minorities into certain occupational classes.

Progress in upgrading the status of women and minorities has been mixed. Some firms still seem to relegate women and minorities to lower-skilled and lower-paying jobs and have not fully utilized the potential contributions that many have to offer. While positive strides have been made, many women and minorities are concentrated in lower-level jobs. There appears to be an invisible barrier—a **glass ceiling,** that limits advancement. To compound the problem, many organizations have placed women and minority employees in certain specialized occupations such as human resources, accounting services, and so forth. These **glass walls** that segment employees can deny them the opportunity to develop the variety of skills necessary for advancement. For example, a 1999 survey of Fortune 1000 companies revealed that women comprised only 2.7 percent of the senior executives in those companies, although the glass ceiling problem was not as apparent at some high-technology firms.[9]

A survey in the mid-1990s conducted for a major consulting firm found that women were evenly divided between being fairly satisfied and not too satisfied with the overall status of women in business. By comparison, men perceived higher satisfaction levels among women in general. Other findings of the poll included:

- More than two-thirds of the women believe that a woman needs more experience or a higher degree than a man does to be considered for the same job.
- More than half of the females believe that women work harder than men.
- Men and women agree that the presence of women in the workforce has had positive effects on business. The effects most commonly cited by both men and women are "a greater importance placed on families" and a "greater awareness and acceptance of different styles and viewpoints."
- While both men and women see a male-dominated corporate culture as a major barrier to women succeeding, both genders also see that women have a tendency to be excluded from the informal communications network.
- Women who work for smaller companies express higher levels of satisfaction and are more likely to be ahead of their own expectations for their career. The authors conclude that this may be because many smaller companies afford women the opportunity to impact decisions and take control of their own careers, better balance work and family life, and make a difference in the lives of others—all of which are important motivators for both genders.[10]

Two recent studies found that minority professionals left their jobs at rates two to three times higher than did comparable Caucasian men and women. The primary reason cited for high turnover rates among minority professionals is that they left because they didn't feel recognized as valuable resources. According to this study, many minority professionals asserted that their organizations were publicly claiming support for promoting diversity, but in reality the minority professionals were excluded from many relationships, mentoring assignments, and other situations, which impeded their progress. Minority professionals usually resent the notion that they were hired because of affirmative action, and that many of their companies do not really concern themselves about enhancing a minority person's career. Interestingly, a number of minority professionals candidly acknowledged that they moved from their current positions to other positions because companies looking for qualified minorities were willing to pay higher salaries in order to obtain their services.[11]

Minority and women employees will continue to need an effective combination of educational and job-related experiences to provide them with opportunities to develop their talents. Organizations will be expected to design programs to attract and develop women and minority employees and provide them with the full range of opportunities open to everyone else.

Educational Preparation

Accompanying the changes in the racial and ethnic composition of the workforce are educational preparation factors that also will challenge supervisors in the future. Statistically, in the late 1990s some 9.4 million students under age 25 were enrolled in colleges and universities, a record high. About 48 million students were enrolled in U.S. elementary and high schools in the late 90s. These enrollments, too, were near record high levels, reflecting the fact that these essentially are children of the parents who themselves were children in the immediate post-World War II era and who were classified as "baby boomers."

Some forecasters believe that we may soon encounter problems with an overeducated workforce. That is, more and more college-trained employees will compete for jobs that do not necessarily require a college education to perform. For example, according to government data, about 70 percent of the occupations expected to have the most job openings in the first decade of the 21st century will involve skills that don't require a college education.[12]

Underemployment

Situations in which people are in jobs that do not utilize their skills, knowledge, and abilities (SKAs).

The competition for jobs and increase in lower-level service industry jobs probably will create underemployment. **Underemployment** occurs when employees bring a certain amount of skills, knowledge, and abilities (**SKAs**) to the workplace and find that the job lacks meaning and/or the opportunity to fully utilize their SKAs. A challenge for many supervisors will be to enhance workplace environments that can be satisfying to the underemployed. The current abundance of college graduates gives corporate recruiters a distinct challenge to select the best candidates available.

SKAs

Skills, knowledge, and abilities that a person has.

Yet we must keep in mind the other side of the picture; namely, that millions of young workers entering the workforce will not have completed a secondary school education. Of those who complete high school, many will receive an inferior education because their schools do not offer the variety or quality of classes that other schools offer. Thousands more will not have completed grade school and thus will not be educationally prepared to compete for better jobs. In addition, many individuals entering the workforce will have had considerable formal education, but this education will not have prepared them with specific skills that are directly applicable to the job market.

Competitive advantage

The ability to outperform competitors by increasing efficiency, quality, creativity, and responsiveness to customers and effectively utilizing employee talents.

An organization seeking to obtain a **competitive advantage** can do so by hiring qualified and adaptable people, training them thoroughly, and then appropriately using their skills. Unfortunately, many job applicants lack proper workplace attitudes and skills. To this end, companies will be required to spend more time and effort in training employees, particularly those who are unprepared and unskilled and who need to have their latent talents developed if they are to be successful and motivated to work. Supervisors will be required to allocate more time for on-the-job training for employees, and also to make sure that employees are given encouragement to utilize all available opportunities for continuing education. According to one estimate, American businesses currently spend about one percent of their payroll costs on training. During forthcoming years, it probably will require two or three percent of payroll expenditures for training if companies wish to maintain their competitive edge.[13]

Occupational and Industry Trends

Occupational and industry projections are that there will continue to be a steady need for people in business-related services such as computer services, retail trade, health care, transportation, and banking and financial services. The U.S. Bureau of Labor Statistics forecasts that there will be many opportunities for those with managerial and supervisory skills for the early part of the 21st century. Further, there will be strong demands for skilled and experienced people with technology backgrounds and professional specialties. Those who have both a technological background and who also are capable of managing and supervising products, relationships, and people will find themselves of particular value to their organizations. At the same time, however, low-paying jobs also will be on the rise. Millions of new service workers will be needed, such as cashiers at campus book stores, servers and washers at local restaurants, and home health care workers. Unfortunately, many of these service workers will find themselves in low-paying jobs, which in the late 1990s averaged only around $7 per hour.

At the same time, many of the nation's largest industrial corporations have eliminated thousands of jobs annually since the early 1980s, and this trend will probably continue in the future. Many companies are outsourcing certain functions or major departments to trim their budgets. Departments or services such as data processing, human resources, public relations, and accounting are especially vulnerable to being outsourced or downsized. Interestingly, a rather high percentage of persons who are displaced by outsourcing tend to be absorbed by the company that is providing the newly contracted services.[14]

While the media tends to focus upon large-scale businesses, small businesses and midsize firms are expected to create most of the job growth in the coming decade. Currently, only about 15 percent of the workforce is employed in firms that have 1,000 or more employees, and statistically more than half of the workforce is employed in enterprises that have fewer than 100 employees. Analysis of U.S. Bureau of Labor Statistics projections suggests that the biggest growth in supervisory and management positions—and jobs in general—will be in smaller and rapidly growing organizations, especially technology-based companies. Many small businesses can provide unique opportunities for new college graduates, and many supervisors have found that they can gain broader and more diverse experiences in smaller firms rather than in large companies where they may be assigned to specialized areas.

Changing Technology and Business Conditions

Many business organizations have been completely revamped because of technological advances, computers, robotics, automation, changing markets, and other competitive influences that demand both internal and external adaptations.

As implied in the previous section, computer skills are a must for those seeking careers in management. Computers now give managers access to a tremendous amount of information—information that is necessary for making effective decisions. Information technology allows people to be no more than a few seconds away from anybody else in communication terms. This may alter the traditional mode of face-to-face communication and the way things are done. The "computer revolution" will continue to be apparent throughout most organizations. Supervisors will have high-powered notebook-style computers. Advances in hardware, software, and communication technology require supervisors to learn how to operate computers as part of their day-to-day responsibilities.

A major problem that is likely to worsen in the future is that of "information overload," also referred to as "infoglut." With the growth of communication capabilities—including e-mail, voice mail, fax, as well as telephone and other devices—supervisors are being inundated by an estimated two hundred or more messages sent and received every day. Many individuals have difficulty with the extra work generated by the flow and volume of messages, many of which are time wasters. The ability to properly manage the flow of information will be another of the many demanding responsibilities of supervisors both now and in the future.[15]

Since it is difficult to forecast specifically when and how technological change will impact a supervisor's position, every supervisor will have to be broadly educated. Supervisors will have to prepare themselves and their employees, both technologically and psychologically, for anticipated changes. Supervisors who keep up to date with changes unquestionably will be more valuable to their organizations.

Global Challenges

Global challenges will continue to impact the supervisor. Substantial investment has been made in U.S. firms by the British, Germans, Swiss, Canadians, Japanese, and others. Identifying the various cultural/value system and work ethic differences is beyond the scope of this text. However, the supervisor must recognize that management practices differ culturally and structurally in these firms compared to U.S.-owned and -operated firms.

Computers and information technology will be an ongoing part of supervisory responsibilities.

The production facilities of numerous U.S. firms may be drawn to Asia, Eastern Europe, Korea, South America, Africa, Mexico, or other locations by the attraction of low wages and other factors that can be used to gain a competitive advantage. Management consultant Tom Peters said in *The Pursuit of WOW!* that the "it's not important unless it happens here" attitude has become a problem. To be successful in foreign countries, U.S. firms must make a strong effort to understand the cultural customs in these environments. Over half of the world's population lives in Asia and a majority of that population is under the age of 25, which is dramatically different from the rest of the world. As the new entrants to the Asian labor force become more literate, everything will change.[16]

To understand the potential of global competition, consider the case of General Motors (GM). General Motors has become Mexico's largest private employer with 75,000 employees. In Juarez, GM provides on-site education and volleyball courts, organizes Mother's Day parties, and sponsors a Mexican folk-dance troupe. The employees are provided free transportation and two meals a day. In return, management has been able to run the plants almost exactly as it wishes, with virtually no work rules. On the other hand, the impact of GM's relocation can be seen most visibly in Anderson, Indiana, where two factories employing about 5,000 people remain. This is in sharp contrast to the days when Anderson could lay claim to being the capital of GM's parts empire, as headquarters to two entire parts-making divisions employing more than 23,000 people. As of the late 1990s, both headquarters are gone, vacant lots stand where there were once factories, and many of the jobs, union leaders charge, have ended up in Mexico. GM's Mexican operations pay the equivalent of $1.65 to $3 per hour, plus benefits.[17]

While Mexico, for example, has a wage rate advantage, its workers may not be as well prepared as U.S. employees, nor will it have as many skilled supervisors to lead employees. International opportunities for technically competent U.S. supervisors will increase. However, transplanted U.S. supervisors will need to learn about cultural differences and find ways to adapt to nontraditional management styles.

Work Scheduling and Employment Conditions

General working conditions have changed and will continue to evolve. Only about one-third of employed Americans over age 18 still work a traditional Monday through Friday workweek. In the future, even fewer Americans will be working a standard 9 to 5 day shift because of the projected growth in jobs with evening, night, and weekend requirements.

Another phenomenon that is likely to continue is the **contingent workforce.** The contingent workforce primarily consists of part-time and temporary or contract employees; these employees were roughly 25 percent of the total employment base in the United States in the late 1990s. This is a type of "interim" workforce consisting of peo-

Contingent workforce

Part-time, temporary, or contract employees who work schedules dependent primarily upon employer needs.

The increase in the number of temporary and contract employees in the workplace presents a challenge to supervisors who must motivate a transient workforce.

ple who can be called in and sent home depending on the employer's needs. Employers have used these types of workers in an effort to reduce the wage and benefit costs that usually are paid to full-time employees. Temporary or contract employees often are supplied to employers by temporary agencies. Temporary workers who are registered with temporary agencies grew from about 1 million persons in 1990 to almost 3 million individuals in 1998. It is likely that temporary and contract employment will continue in the future because of the economic advantages to employers who use their services. Recruiting, training, and other associated costs are minimal even though the per-hour cost of contract labor may be higher than that for regular employees. When a project is finished or a business necessity dictates, the contract or temporary employees can easily be dismissed.[18] Supervisors often encounter difficult situations when trying to help motivate temporary employees who consider themselves as transients; that is, they will work at the firm only until something better comes along. A number of studies have further indicated that lower productivity and increased accidents can occur when employees are not fully committed to their jobs, which of course is complicated by the contingent workforce situation.

Two-tier wage systems
Paying new employees at a lower rate than more senior employees. (Also used to refer to disparities associated with high executive compensation.)

Other factors of employment are likely to complicate the supervisor's job in the future. Rapid turnover of employees is statistically documented by the fact that, on average, employees stay at their jobs only about 3.6 years, a figure that has decreased during the 1990s.[19] Work-scheduling problems because employees demand greater flexibility in work schedules to attend to family needs are likely to accelerate during the foreseeable future.[20] Still another thorny issue is that of **two-tier wage systems,** where companies pay new employees a lower wage than more senior or experienced employees. In some situations, this means that supervisors are challenged to motivate a workforce that includes employees who are compensated differently for doing essentially the same work. In recent years, another element of concern has been the growing disparity in executive compensation as compared to the income of most employees. In the United States recent surveys have indicated that compensation for major corporate CEOs has been several hundred times the income earned by average workers. Robert Reich, former U.S. Secretary of Labor, claims that this type of disparity of income between executives and employees is creating a "two-tier workforce" within companies that can have a negative effect on morale and performance. Mr. Reich believes that new types of compensation systems are needed to adequately reward employees for their contributions, and these will be more widely adopted in the future.[21]

Corporate Culture and Ethical Conduct

Corporate culture

Set of shared purposes, values, and beliefs that employees hold about their organization.

Corporate culture is the set of shared purposes, values, and beliefs that employees have about their organization. Top-level management creates the overall vision and philosophy for the firm. For example, when Hewlett-Packard was formed, David Packard and William R. Hewlett formulated a vision that was later stated in the Hewlett-Packard (HP) Statement of Corporate Objectives:

The achievements of an organization are the results of the combined efforts of each individual in the organization working toward common objectives. These objectives should be realistic, should be clearly understood by everyone in the organization, and should reflect the organization's basic character and personality.

Bill Hewlett frequently described the "HP Way" as follows: "I feel that in general terms it is the policies and actions that flow from the belief that men and women want to do a good job, a creative job, and that if they are provided the proper environment they will do so." This philosophy has been prominently communicated to every employee and as such becomes a way of life at Hewlett-Packard.[22] Co-founder Packard, when asked to reflect on his greatest achievements, said, "I think you get the most satisfaction in trying to do something useful. After you've done that, you ought to forget about it and try to find something better to do."[23]

Figure 1-5 (see page 22) is a series of comments made by prominent individuals stressing the necessity for executives, managers, supervisors, and employees to have a set of shared values and purposes if an organization is to be successful and achieve its objectives. To this end, many companies have developed mission statements and ethical conduct statements in order to provide a foundation for the type of corporate culture that is desired.

Figure 1-6 is an example of a values and beliefs statement that was developed by the top management of the medical center described in the opening "You Make the Call" section that began this chapter. As a new ER department supervisor, Charlotte Kelly can use this type of values and beliefs statement as a reference point for many of the decisions that will confront her. Supervisors are a major influence in determining the direction of the corporate culture within their departments. Supervisors play a significant role in informing, educating, and setting an example for ethical behavior. Although ethical behavior and

FIGURE 1-5   On leadership, shared values, and achievement.

The following are selected excerpts from fairly recent comments made by a number of prominent individuals concerning the necessity for executives, managers, supervisors, and employees to have a set of shared values and purposes if an organization is to be successful and achieve its objectives.

DAN R. BANNISTER, BOARD CHAIRMAN, DYNCORP

An important element of building trust is building ownership. I don't mean stock ownership, though we have that, too. We want people to be accountable for what the company is doing and where it's going. To do that, we have to make them part of our strategic planning team. Having a piece of the plan helps assure they will buy into it. So commitment goes along with it.

MORT FEINBERG, PH.D., CHAIRMAN OF BSF PSYCHOLOGICAL ASSOCIATES AND PROFESSOR EMERITUS, BARUCH COLLEGE, N.Y.

Let your people solve all the soft causes themselves, and bring only the hard causes to you for resolution. You should also talk to them, so they'll know the difference between a hard cause and a soft cause. What they can do themselves and what they need to bring to you. Eighty percent of the issues they can solve on their own.

FRANCES HESSELBEIN, FORMER CEO OF THE GIRL SCOUTS OF THE U.S.A.

A leader leads by example and from the front, with clear, consistent messages and values that are moral and a

sense of ethics that works full-time. Leaders acknowledge that people are their greatest asset. The really great leaders I know manage for a mission, innovation, and diversity.

THOMAS R. HORTON, FORMER SENIOR EXECUTIVE OF IBM AND FORMER CEO OF THE AMERICAN MANAGEMENT ASSOCIATION

The absolute basic building block is integrity. A lot of leaders don't have it. It's not a matter of degree. Either you have it or you don't. There is someone cutting a corner here or shading the truth there, and I get very nervous. It's not a matter of degrees. You have to have an absolute commitment to it.

ED RIDOLFI, VICE-PRESIDENT OF EXECUTIVE DEVELOPMENT FOR THE MCGRAW-HILL COMPANIES

Business is changing from a top-down, hierarchical model to a flatter, more collegial one that is also being driven by a huge social upheaval. Today's workforce won't tolerate others "telling" them what to do and keep their mouth shut. They want to share in the knowledge gathering and have an impact on decisions . . . The old managerial model focused on retaining control; being in charge. The new model involves being a coach and facilitation, empowering people, building relationships, and a heavy dose of sharing.

Source: Anthony Vlamis, *Smart Leadership* (New York: American Management Association, 1999), pp. 4, 20, 25, 32, and 56.

fair dealing have always been foundations for good management, it is clear that ethical conduct has become one of the most challenging issues confronting U.S. business. The daily news is filled with information regarding the misuse of business power and the contention that corrupt business practices are the primary way to make profits. In the future, as never before, it will be important that ethical behavior and fair dealing are at the forefront of good management practices, beginning at the supervisory level. The personal ethics that a supervisor holds are also an important guide for making decisions when fac-

Every Pine Village Community Medical Center employee is important. With mutual respect, trust, and open communication, we will work together to create an organization that consistently meets or exceeds the expectations of patients, visitors, physicians, employees, and other stakeholders.

Pine Village Community Medical Center is dedicated to providing consistently superior services to all of our customers. We believe in fostering an environment that encourages superior service and performance.

We believe that superior service and performance results from:

- A clear understanding of goals.
- Effective communication.
- Proper application of skills, knowledge, and abiltiy.
- Wise use of resources.
- High standards of conduct.
- A safe and aesthetically pleasing work environment.
- Shared involvement in attaining goals.

ing ethical problems in the workplace. Chapters 5 and 19 will further discuss the importance of ethical standards that can serve as guides for decision making.

Other Governmental and Societal Issues

Other emerging governmental and societal issues will continue to complicate the supervisory management position in the future. For example, numerous environmental concerns remain as serious long-term problems for business, government, and the general public. Energy availability and costs may be determined by international and domestic political and economic changes. These types of issues and societal pressures often become part of business planning and operations.

A list of federal legislation that affects the supervisor's job is found in the Appendix at the end of the book. In addition, state and local governments have laws and regulations that impact businesses. The effect of such legislation can be quite costly, and organizations may be required to change their methods of operation in order to comply.

Supervisors are influenced both directly and indirectly by such governmental requirements, and they must continue to stay abreast of any legislation that may influence their operations. Furthermore, supervisors must be sensitive to pressures exerted by special-interest groups. Consumer groups, in particular, have demanded better products and services from business, labor, and government. Environmentalists seek to influence business decisions that may have an adverse environmental impact. Some employees (especially parents of young children or employees who have elderly parents) will expect that their employers provide day-care facilities so that they can better combine their family and job responsibilities. It seems likely that numerous other permanent and temporary special-interest groups will continue to place community and political demands on firms in ways that will affect how supervisors will operate in the future.

All indications are that these pressures will remain intense. A utility company supervisor said recently, "I have to be more of a lawyer, cop, teacher, accountant, political scientist, and psychologist these days than a manager!" Although a bit overstated, this supervisor's comment reflects a realistic aspect of every supervisor's contemporary role.

EMPOWERMENT AND EMPLOYEE PARTICIPATION IN DECISION MAKING

Employees will continue to expect to have a greater voice in workplace decision making. Whether or not a labor union or employee association represents employees in an organization, many employees will want more from their jobs and will demand a voice in decisions that concern their employment. This does not have to be objectionable to a supervisor. In fact, once supervisors realize that their employees have something to contribute, they will welcome employee participation in decisions rather than fear it.

Empowerment
Giving employees the authority and responsibility to accomplish their and the organization's objectives.

Empowerment means giving employees the authority and responsibility to achieve objectives. Opportunities to make suggestions and participate in decisions affecting their jobs can and should be supported. However, some supervisors become worried when workers challenge what have traditionally been management rights, and they prefer to think that certain areas should be beyond employee challenge. Many quality circles and other participatory management approaches of the last decade failed, in part, because managers failed to listen to the suggestions of employees, did not act on those suggestions in a timely fashion, or felt threatened by those suggestions. Nevertheless, there will continue to be pressure from employees, labor unions, minorities, and other groups for more influence in decisions pertaining to the workplace.

Participative management
Allowing employees to influence and share in organizational decision making.

Many supervisors have become accustomed to the practice of **participative management,** which essentially means a willingness to permit employees to influence or share in managerial decisions. If supervisors learn to react to this in a positive way, it should improve their own and their company's performance.[24]

Although forecasts are always precarious, experienced supervisors will recognize that these trends have already begun. Supervisors must understand and plan for them. Empowerment and participative management will be discussed further in other chapters of the text.

4
Explain why supervisors must continually grow and develop as professionals.

SUPERVISION: A PROFESSIONAL PERSPECTIVE

For most supervisors, their primary responsibility is to manage their firm's most important resource—the human resource. It is the human resource upon which any organization ultimately depends. Managing people starts with selection and training to fill job openings, and it continues with ongoing development, motivation, and leadership and with preparing employees for promotion.

Thus, supervisors will have to become true professionals with a growing professional perspective. Supervisors will have to develop as innovators and idea people. They must look to the future with a professional awareness of the trends influencing human behavior and observe how these trends impact the management of people in a complex society.

In all of this there is an imperative to take the professional perspective, which recognizes the need for constant self-improvement and self-renewal. No amount of formal or informal education can ever be enough to fulfill a supervisor's personal program of self-improvement. Supervisors must recognize that they, too, can become obsolete unless they constantly take measures to update their own skills and knowledge through a program of continuous self-development.

Students as well as practicing managers need to understand that "as long as you live, keep learning to live." Peter Senge, author of *The Fifth Discipline*, provides further insight:

Real learning gets to the heart of what it means to be human. Through learning we recreate ourselves. Through learning we become able to do something we never were able to do. Through learning we extend our capacity to create, to be part of the generative process of life. There is within each of us a deep hunger for this type of learning.[25]

Stephen Covey, author of *The Seven Habits of Highly Effective People*, presented the following illustration:

Suppose you were to come upon someone in the woods working feverishly to saw down a tree.

"What are you doing?" you ask.

"Can't you see?" comes the impatient reply. "I'm sawing down the tree."

"You look exhausted!" you exclaim. "How long have you been at it?"

"Over five hours," he returns, "and I'm beat! This is hard work."

"Well, why don't you take a break for a few minutes and sharpen the saw?" you inquire. "I'm sure it would go a lot faster."

"I don't have time to sharpen the saw," the man said emphatically.

"I'm too busy sawing."[26]

Both newly appointed and experienced supervisors should begin each day by asking, "What can I do to sharpen my saw?" Covey suggests renewing the four dimensions of your nature—spiritual (value clarification and commitment, study and meditation), mental (reading, visualizing, planning, writing), social/emotional (service, empathy, synergy, intrinsic security), and physical (exercise, nutrition, stress management)—to improve your personal effectiveness.[27]

Supervisors who master the managerial concepts and skills discussed in this textbook should make considerable progress in terms of personal development, but just knowing concepts and approaches is not enough. They must constantly seek new ways to apply this knowledge in the challenging, complex, and dynamic situations they will encounter.

What Call Did You Make?

Every chapter in this book concludes with a section titled, "What Call Did You Make?" This section refers back to the case problem posed in the section titled "You Make the Call" at the beginning of each chapter. In this and other concluding sections, we will provide our analysis and recommendations, which you should compare with your own and then consider and discuss relevant areas of agreement and differences.

As Charlotte Kelly, your decision to accept the supervisory management position appears to be an opportunity and a considerable challenge. In order to make a successful transition from a team leader to a supervisor on the hospital's management team, you need first to ask yourself what additional information you will need in order to get off to a successful start. What are the strengths (SKAs) and the weaknesses of the employees you will be supervising? Your department will be comprised of diverse people with different needs and expectations. Your success, in part, will depend on how well you get these different people to work together effectively. Remember that your performance as a supervisor will depend primarily upon your gaining the acceptance and respect of your employees.

You may want to review the principles of scientific management discussed in this chapter. What are the tasks associated with each of the jobs in the ER department? Identify those employees who are capable of instructing you and others on the essential tasks associated with each job. You have a good understanding of how the department functioned under Amy Talmadge, so don't make the same mistakes she did.

One problem that can arise from promoting someone from outside the department is resentment. Some employees may feel that they possessed the skills or department-specific knowledge that qualified them for the position. These employees may hold a grudge against you. There even may be one or more employees who are distressed by Amy's dismissal; even the worst supervisors may have friends or allies in the department.

A major problem will be how the ER employees will adapt to this change. From your experience and classes, you have learned "what not to do" in supervising others. You need to remember the characteristics that made Pat Graham an effective supervisor. Also, remember what got you to this point, that is, the traits that Bob Murphy cited while offering you the job. Try to place yourself in positions every day to apply those skills.

As soon as possible, you need to establish guidelines and ground rules for the department. A meeting with Bob Murphy and other department heads should clarify their expectations for the ER department. You should ascertain what authority you will have. Over time, you should attempt to convey a positive vision for the department and develop sound objectives that can serve as benchmarks for accomplishment.

A common mistake made by some new supervisors is that they are too eager to please. New supervisors may try to show what an excellent choice they were for the position and neglect to listen or ask questions for fear that this would imply incompetence or uncertainty. You have a great deal of respect for Mr. Ray, the community college instructor. Perhaps you could call Mr. Ray and discuss situations with him that arise from time to time. Such an exchange will give you an unbiased sounding board and also a chance to ask questions about your new responsibilities and analyze problems you have experienced. Maintain open dialogue with your former boss, Pat Graham, and try to develop ongoing collaborative relationships and communications with your fellow supervisors/managers throughout the hospital.

You have much to learn and apply if you intend to become an effective supervisor. You will need to enhance and maintain your professional knowledge and skills. Plan for an ongoing personal program of continuing your education through readings, classes, seminars, meetings, and other such opportunities that will develop your professional perspectives and competence in your demanding new role as a supervisor.

SUMMARY

1

Supervisors are the first tier of management. They manage entry-level and other departmental employees. New ways of managing employees will be the supervisor's challenge. In the face of a contemporary mindset and an environment that is rapidly changing, the success of the supervisor will rest in the ability to balance the requirements for high work performance with the diverse needs of the workforce.

Supervisory management focuses primarily on the management of people. For many people, being a supervisor provides a variety of satisfying experiences. However, what one person sees as an opportunity and a reason for accepting the supervisory challenge, others see as a negative. Among these are the challenge of getting diverse people to work together, the increased responsibility that comes with climbing the management hierarchy, the unpredictable nature of the job, and the sense of accomplishment from doing a job well. Conversely, there are reasons why people avoid supervisory responsibility. Being a supervisor is a demanding position that often places the supervisor in the middle of organizational pressures and conflict. A supervisor must endeavor to reconcile the needs of the organization and the needs of employees, which often is an elusive target.

In addition, major environmental factors impact everything the organization does. These factors are not static; the whole word is changing rapidly, and some people do not want to deal with change.

2

There is no one universal school of management thought. The scientific management approach attempts to find the most efficient or "one best way." The manager's primary function is to plan the work; time and motion study and the other principles of industrial engineering are used to analyze the work to be performed. The functional approach assumes that there are a series of essential functions that all managers should perform. The human relations/behavioral science approach emphasizes that managers need to understand what causes employees to behave the way they do. This approach began with the Hawthorne studies at Western Electric Company. The quantitative/systems approach applies mathematical models to help solve organizational problems. An understanding of the various schools of management thought gives supervisors a foundation upon which to build their own supervisory philosophy.

3

Many factors and trends surrounding the workforce will have an impact on how most organizations operate. The workforce will grow at a somewhat faster rate than the overall population, and the age composition of the workforce will change drastically. Women and minorities will continue to enter the workforce in increasing numbers, and they will be utilized more fully than they have been in the past, including further advancement in supervisory and management positions. Substantial numbers of part-time employees and contract employees will be found in the workplace. The more diverse workforce will create numerous problems (e.g., multicultural and multilingual problems, family obligations versus job obligations). The workforce generally will consist of more college graduates, but millions of people will not be prepared educationally to qualify for many of the employment opportunities available.

Occupational and industry trends, changing technology and business conditions, and the competition from the global marketplace will be significant influences on supervisory management. Government laws and regulations will continue to have a major impact on the policies and activities of most organizations.

Supervisors will have to be sensitive to existing and expected employee trends. For example, more employees than ever before will expect their jobs to have greater personal meaning to them as individuals. It is likely that supervisors will have to be somewhat flexible in their approaches to managing. Employees will continue to expect a greater voice in workplace decision making. Employees will expect to be empowered.

The habits of highly effective people can be developed. Supervisors who want to be more effective will put themselves into situations in which they can practice those techniques. Finally, supervisors who aspire to become more effective leaders need to have a professional outlook and must recognize the necessity for a personal program of continuous self-development.

KEY TERMS

Supervisor (page 4)
Working supervisors (page 4)
Scientific management approach (page 7)
Functional approach (page 8)
Hawthorne effect (page 9)
Human relations movement/behavioral
  science approach (page 9)
Quantitative/systems approaches (page 9)
Diversity (page 10)
Flextime (page 13)
Job sharing (page 13)

Telecommuting (page 13)
Glass ceiling (page 15)
Glass walls (page 15)
Underemployment (page 16)
SKAs (page 16)
Competitive advantage (page 17)
Contingent workforce (page 19)
Two-tier wage systems (page 20)
Corporate culture (page 21)
Empowerment (page 24)
Participative management (page 24)

QUESTIONS FOR DISCUSSION

1. What are some of the advantages of being a supervisor? What are some of the disadvantages?
2. How would you respond to someone who suggests that the principles and functions of management apply to all organizations? Justify your response.
3. From the standpoint of the prospective supervisor, what is the significance of the following: Taylor's scientific management, Fayol's functions of management, the Hawthorne studies and behavioral science, quantitative/systems approaches?
4. Of those factors or trends projected to reshape the workplace, which will create the greatest challenge for supervisors? Why do you think so?
5. From your point of view, analyze how the shifting workforce values toward work and expectations will influence a supervisor's planning and functioning in the future.

6. Do you look forward to working in a more diverse workforce? Why or why not? What adjustments will you have to make?
7. Discuss the pros and cons of the part-time/temporary workforce. How has this further complicated the supervisor's job?
8. Define "corporate culture" and discuss how an organization's culture might affect its ability to compete more effectively in the marketplace.
9. Why is continuous self-development vital to the supervisory role?

SKILLS APPLICATIONS

Skills Application 1-1: The "Pluses and Minuses" of Supervision

1. Make arrangements to interview two to four supervisors/managers, preferably from different organizations or companies. These may be classmates if they already are practicing as supervisors. In your interview, pose the following questions:
   a. How did you become a supervisor, for example, were you promoted from a non-supervisory position, or did you come to it directly from your academic preparation, or in what way?
   b. What do you see as the primary satisfactions/rewards that are associated with being a supervisor or manager?
   c. What do you see as the downside (negative aspects) of being a supervisor or manager?
   d. What do you consider to be the primary differences in being a supervisor/manager as compared to being an employee/subordinate?
   Feel free to probe the responses given you by the supervisors/managers whom you interview to see whether they have any unique insights to offer.
2. After completing your interviews, compare the responses that you receive in your interviews with the concepts presented in this chapter, particularly those included in Figure 1-1, "The Pluses and Minuses of Supervision." To what degree were the interviewee responses similar/different? How do you account for the differences that may be present?
3. As a result of completing this application project, are your aspirations to become a supervisor/manager lesser or greater than before? Explain.

Skills Application 1-2: Identify Management Concerns

1. Review the "You Make the Call" section at the beginning of the chapter.
2. Make a complete list of the major concerns that face Charlotte Kelly as she begins her new assignment.
3. Prioritize the items on your list.
4. Compare your list with that of a classmate. Why are certain items similar? Why are certain items different?
5. Why is it important for new managers to make a list of the concerns they face in their assignment?

INTERNET ACTIVITY

Skills Application 1-3: Surfing the Net for Job Opportunities

Your career will be a series of beginnings and endings, of doors opening and closing, and of new and challenging experiences. What companies are you interested in? How are they structured? What is their culture? What are their needs? What kinds of skills, knowledge, abilities, and experience will be relevant to their needs?

1. Using the Internet, search for all the information you can find on various job openings. Figure 1-7 in this chapter's Appendix provides a partial listing of existing Web sites. Select a particular type of supervisory/managerial position that appeals to you.
2. Make a list of the attractive features of the job.
3. Make a list of the things you do exceptionally well.
4. Compare the lists compiled in Steps 2 and 3. What will you need to do to become better prepared for securing the job? Develop a plan.
5. Develop a list of questions that you would ask if you were selected for a job interview.

Skills Application 1-4: Developing Your Management Philosophy

INTERNET ACTIVITY

In this chapter you were introduced to the corporate vision and philosophy of Hewlett-Packard and the "HP Way." Visit the Hewlett-Packard Web site (**www.hewlett-packard.com**) and learn more about the values of this company.

1. Based on what you've learned about HP, how would you describe the company's management philosophy?
2. Draft your personal management philosophy. What values are most important to you? What values do you most want to communicate to those you will supervise?

APPENDIX: GETTING INTO SUPERVISION

Job hunting is never easy. For some people, opportunities appear when they least expect them. For example, at the outset of this chapter's "You Make the Call" segment, Charlotte Kelly was a nurse whose formal training and early work experiences were in that profession. Then her desire to raise her family dictated that she drop out of the workforce, but a family tragedy subsequently necessitated her return to full-time employment. The only thing she could find was an evening shift position in a hospital admitting department as a team leader. Although it was new to her, Charlotte began almost immediately to seize upon it as an opportunity. She "paid her dues" by attending college part-time and working toward an associate's degree in supervision and organizational leadership. Charlotte also learned about supervision from her supervisor Pat Graham, who was a valued mentor. Charlotte Kelly's talents and efforts were soon recognized by higher management, and she was promoted to a supervisory position.

Many individuals get their first supervisory position from a nonsupervisory job within the same organization. It may be in the same department or in another area. They may have formally applied for the position or had a manager recommend them. In either case, the organization made a conscious effort to promote from within.

If you are already employed while going to school, it can be tough to find the time to do an effective job search for a position outside your current firm. In addition, you will have the added burden of being discreet—many employers take a dim view of employees who are looking for employment elsewhere; their loyalty and commitment are questioned. Be discreet; do not make or receive job-search-related calls at work. Advise prospective employers to contact you at home or through the college placement office. Schedule interviews before or after work or on your days off.

A former student told one of the authors of this experience. She had sent her resume to a blind advertisement—neither the firm nor its address was listed. Her immediate supervisor informed her that he had received her resume and was wondering why she was unhappy with her current position. She had applied for a job similar to the one she currently had, but the advertisement listed broader responsibilities and sounded challenging. She was at a loss for words. She later left the organization—not for a better job but because she felt the supervisor never gave her a chance after that.

Where to Look for Information

Students in need of more detailed information, additional career opportunities, and salary information can refer to the latest *Occupational Outlook Handbook* published by the U.S. Department of Labor. The most recent *Planning Job Choices: A Guide to Career Planning, the Job Search, Graduate School, and Work-Related Education* published by the College Placement Council contains information on successful job search strategies, how to research companies, what employers really want from applicants, interviewing techniques, networking, and finding additional employer information. Check with your college placement office and review these publications prior to beginning your job search.

Many supervisors find that *networking* is a useful strategy. This means meeting and talking with personal and professional colleagues and friends to help you identify potential opportunities. Talk to people you know through school, church, family, or other activities to gather information and referrals. "I'm finishing my degree in June and am thinking about making a change. Your company has a reputation of being a good place to work. Do you know of any opportunities there?" Such an approach could be a good networking start.

A visit to the library or the Internet will turn up lots of information, such as annual reports, trade magazines, and newspaper articles, about the organization. This will give you a good picture of the company's financial position, management style, future, and the like. Increasingly, employers are listing jobs on-line and offer descriptions of their products and services on "home pages" posted on the World Wide Web (WWW). Figure 1-7 contains a partial listing of on-line services. You can also submit your resume to databases that employers consult for candidates.

The best way to get or keep a supervisory position is to make yourself more valuable; one way to do this is to volunteer in a meaningful activity.

FIGURE 1-7

Sources for on-line job searches.

This list of on-line sources is far from complete. There are always new bulletin boards, databases, and job search information on the Internet. Once you become familiar with the Internet job search process, you can access information quickly. If you need help with your Internet search, talk with the staff at the college or local public library. Enjoy the journey!

AARP Webplace (www.aarp.org/working_options) offers tips to assist with career transitions. Not surprisingly, AARP research indicates that 80 percent of the baby boomers expect to work, at least part-time, past the typical retirement age, many of them in different jobs and occupations. This site includes information on starting your own business, charting a career change, or reentering the job market. This site also links with thousands of job listings via the U.S. Department of Labor's America's Job Bank.

America's Job Bank (www.ajb.dni.us/) provides job market information for both employers and job seekers, and enables employers to register job openings.

American Recruitment (www.americanrecruitment.com/) provides job candidate and company information from the nation's leading producer of sales, retail and management career fairs.

Bureau of Labor Statistics (stats.bls.gov/) offers data and economic information including wage/salary surveys for various job classifications.

Career Mosaic (www.careermosaic.com/) uses key words to search the jobs offered in newsgroup listings. It links to Usenet newsgroups—on-line discussion groups dedicated, for the most part, to single topics. Tens of thousands of new job listings appear every day and old listings are deleted after seven days. *Fortune* and Career Mosaic combined to include a variety of career management tools. *Fortune Career Resource Centers* provides tips on job-hunting, resume writing, and salary information. *College Connection* allows you to view job opportunities and resources needed for entry-level positions.

Careers 2000 (www.resumepls.com/) allows job seekers to post their resumes and search the on-line database of job opportunities and allows employers to post their needs and search the database of resumes. This site also provides tips on interviewing and making a successful resume.

Hotjobs.Com (www.hotjobs.com/) receives thousands of hits each month from both job seekers and recruiters.

Monster.Com (www.monster.com) is one of the largest on-line recruiting sites. See also (www.executive.monster) for listings of top-level managerial positions.

Professional Associations List (www.yahoo.com/Business_and_Economy/Organizations/Professional/) lists professional organizations that you can join to network and gain access to their job placement services.

The Riley Guide (www.rileyguide.com) is a gateway to on-line job resources.

Make Yourself More Valuable

In general, we believe that the best way to get a supervisory position and/or to prosper in your current position is to find ways to make yourself more valuable. Always try to improve yourself. For example, if you are a student, make yourself available for internships and co-ops, or perhaps volunteer for some type of meaningful activity. Volunteer experiences in community groups can provide you with ideas and practical experiences, and you will become more comfortable working with and leading groups of diverse people. Get involved in one or more student organizations on your campus. Benefits gained by applying your expertise and utilizing opportunities to enhance communication and leadership skills are invaluable.

Remember, too, that continuing your educational preparation is an ongoing challenge. Finishing an academic degree is only a start; consider going further by enrolling in graduate study degree and non-degree programs that may enhance your technical/managerial/supervisory knowledge. Increasingly there are colleges and universities that offer on-line programs that can be taken at home via desktop computers.[28]

Referring once again to the opening "You Make the Call" segment, Charlotte Kelly was a nurse who had a career opportunity to accept a position as a supervisor with more responsibility and challenges. She had been working toward this through a combination of educational and job experiences. Like Kelly, becoming a supervisor and prospering in that role means matching your SKAs and aspirations with the opportunities available. Remember, when applying for any position and particularly for a supervisory one, discover the specific needs of the hiring organization and show how your SKAs can add value to the firm.

ENDNOTES

1. See Timothy D. Schellhardt, "Off the Ladder: Want to Be a Manager? Many People Say No, Calling Job Miserable," *The Wall Street Journal* (April 4, 1997), p. A1.

2. For a more recent discussion of managerial approaches, see Jon L. Pierce and John W. Newstrom, *The Manager's Bookshelf: A Mosaic of Contemporary Views* (New York: HarperCollins College Publishers, 1996). For a discussion of the problems of developing universal agreement on management approaches, see H. Koontz, "The Management Theory Jungle Revisited," *Academy of Management Review* (Volume 5, 1980), pp. 175–188. An overview of the evolution of management thought is provided in J. Baughman, *The History of American Management* (Englewood Cliffs, N.J.: Prentice-Hall, 1969); C. George, *The History of Management Thought* (Englewood Cliffs, N.J.: Prentice-Hall, 1972); and Allen C. Bluedorn, ed., "A Special Book Review Section on the Classics of Management," *Academy of Management Review* (Volume 11, April 1986).

    The principles of scientific management are described in Frederick W. Taylor, *Shop Management* (New York: Harper & Brothers, 1911); Frank G. Gilbreth and Lillian M. Gilbreth, *Applied Motion Study* (New York: Sturgis & Walton, 1917); and Edwin A. Locke, "The Ideas of Frederick W. Taylor: An Evaluation," *Academy of Management Review* (Volume 7, January 1982), pp. 22–23.

    See Henri Fayol, *General and Industrial Management,* trans. Constance Storrs (London: Pitman Publishing Corp., 1949), for the functional approach to describe and analyze management principles.

    Additional information on the human relations/behavioral science school of thought can be found in E. Mayo, *The Human Problems of Industrial Civilization* (New York: Macmillan, 1933); Fritz J. Roethlisberger and W. J. Dickson, *Management and the Worker* (Boston: Harvard University Press, 1939); A. Maslow, "A Theory of Human Motivation," *Psychological Review* (Volume 50, July 1943), pp. 370–396; D. McGregor, *The Human Side of Enterprise* (New York: McGraw-Hill, 1960); and J. A. Sonnenfeld, "Shedding Light on the Hawthorne Studies," *Journal of Occupational Behavior* (Volume 6, 1985), pp. 111–130.

For an overview of quantitative/systems approaches to management, see Andrew J. DuBrin and R. Duane Ireland, *Management and Organization* (2nd ed.; Cincinnati: South-Western Publishing Co., 1993), pp. 43–46.

3. Statistics and projections included in this and other sections are drawn from U.S. government publications: *Statistical Abstract of the United States, 1997* (Washington, D.C.: U.S. Government Printing Office); and "Population Projections of the United States by Age, Sex, Race, and Hispanic Origin: 1995–2050" (Population Division, U.S. Bureau of Census—Pop@Census.gov—or www.census.gov/ftp/pub).

4. Laura D'Andrea Tyson, "Open the Gates Wide to High-Skill Immigrants," *Business Week* (July 5, 1999), p. 16.

5. From Andrea Healey, "Figuring Out Generation X," *ACA News* (February 1998), pp. 10–15. Workforce classifications described in this article were from Ann S. Clurman and J. Walker Smith, *Rocking the Ages: The Yankelovich Report on Generational Marketing* (New York: Harper Business, 1997). See also Bruce Tulgan, "Managing Generation X," *HR Focus* (November 1995), pp. 22–23.

6. Carol Kleiman, "Superwoman Has Taken Off the Cape," *St. Louis Post-Dispatch* article reprinted from the *Chicago Tribune* (June 24, 1999), p. C8.

7. Winston Churchill as quoted in *My Early Life* (1930) Reprint. (New York: Charles Scribner's Sons, 1987), Ch. 9.

8. Maureen Minehan, "Future Focus," *HR Magazine* (1998 50th Anniversary Edition), pp. 86–87.

9. Del Jones, "What Glass Ceiling?" *USA Today* (July 20, 1999), p. 18.

10. "Women at Work: Executive Summary—A Special Report on the Status and Satisfaction of Working Women and Initiatives for Their Advancement," conducted by Fortune Marketing Research for Deloitte & Touche LLP (1995). A complete copy of the report is available by contacting Deloitte & Touche LLP.

11. Diane Stafford, "Minorities are Leaving Their Jobs Faster," article originally published in *The Kansas City Star* and reprinted in the *St. Louis Post-Dispatch* (June 7, 1999), p. BP4.

12. Marc Adams, "The Stream of Labor Slows to a Trickle," *HR Magazine* (October 1998), pp. 84–88.

13. Steve Bates, "Building Better Workers," *Nation's Business* (June 1998), pp. 18–27.

14. Hal Lancaster, "Saving Your Career When Your Position Has Been Outsourced," *The Wall Street Journal* (December 12, 1995), p. B1.

15. Don Clark, "Managing the Mountain: For Many People, Information is Proving to be More of a Burden Than a Resource," *The Wall Street Journal* (June 21, 1999), p. R4.

16. Adapted from "Conversations with Tom Peters," *Quality Digest* (November 1996), pp. 37–38. Peters' books *In Search of Excellence, Passion for Excellence, Thriving on Chaos,* and *Liberation Management* ranked at or near the top of *The New York Times* best-seller list. *The Pursuit of WOW!* is his most recent book.

17. Rebecca Blumenstein and Gabriella Stern, "Man of Many Parts: How a Tough Boss Managed to Salvage a Messy Unit at GM," *The Wall Street Journal* (June 3, 1996), pp. A1 and A8.

18. See Merrill Goozner, "Longtime Temporary Employees are Rebelling," reprint of article in *St. Louis Post-Dispatch* that originally was published in the *Chicago Tribune* (July 1, 1999), p. C7. Also see Aaron Bernstein, "A Leg Up for the Lowly Temp," *Business Week* (June 21, 1999), pp. 102–103.

19. From "Workweek," *The Wall Street Journal* (June 8, 1999), p. A1.

20. See Bill Leonard, "Employees Want More Quality Time with Families," *HR Magazine* (June 1999), p. 28.

21. "The New Workplace: An Interview With Robert B. Reich," interview conducted and article written by Maggie A. Coil, *ACA News* (May 1998), pp. 11–14. In 1998, the compensation for CEOs of major corporations in the United States was reported by the Department of Labor to be 419 times that of the average blue-collar worker. See Jennifer Reingold with Ronald Grover, "Executive Pay," *Business Week* (April 19, 1999), pp. 72–90. Also see Jerri Stroud, "Top Executives Continued to Rake It In: The Gap Between Executives and Workers Widens," *St. Louis Post-Dispatch* (July 18, 1999), p. E1.

22. Adapted from *Hewlett-Packard Statement of Corporate Objectives and Annual Reports.* Also see "Hewlett-Packard: Where Slower Growth Is Smarter Management," *Business Week* (July 9, 1975), pp. 50–58. The statement was first put in writing in 1957, has been modified occasionally since then, and has been a significant part of the "HP Way."

23. "Dave Packard: The Legacy Endures," *Hewlett-Packard 1996 Annual Report* (Palo Alto, Calif.: January 1997), pp. 6 and 7. Packard died March 26, 1996 at age 83.

24. A 1994 survey indicated that 75 percent of employers had incorporated some means of employee involvement to empower employees. For another twist to the employee involvement issue, see Mary E. Pivec and Howard Z. Robbins, "Employee Involvement Remains Controversial," *HR Magazine* (November 1996), pp. 145–150.

25. The statement "As long as you live, keep learning to live" is from Seneca as quoted in Burton E. Stevenson, *The Home Book of Quotations, Classical and Modern* (10th ed.; New York: Dodd, Mead, 1967), p. 1131. See Peter Senge, *The Fifth Discipline: The Art and Practice of the Learning Organization* (New York: Doubleday, 1990), p. 14. Also see Senge, et al., *The Fifth Discipline Fieldbook: Strategies and Tools for Building a Learning Organization* (New York: Doubleday, 1994).

26. Stephen R. Covey, *The Seven Habits of Highly Effective People: Restoring the Character Ethic* (New York: Simon & Schuster, 1989), p. 287. Also see Covey's *Principle-Centered Leadership: Strategies for Personal & Professional Effectiveness* (Bellevue: Simon & Schuster, 1992) and *First Things First: To Live, to Love, to Learn, to Leave a Legacy* (New York: Simon & Schuster, 1994).

27. Ibid., p. 288.

28. See Vicky Phillips, "Online Universities Teach Knowledge Beyond the Books," *HR Magazine* (July 1998), pp. 121–126; or Kathleen Morris, "Wiring the Ivory Tower: Will Online Courses Lower Standards?" *Business Week* (August 9, 1999), pp. 90–92.

Chapter 2

The Managerial Functions

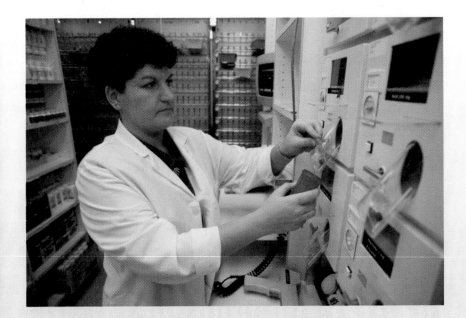

You Make the Call!

You are Carol Reeves, supervisor of Kincaid Pharmacy's State Street store. The pharmacist has responsibility for the pharmacy operations while you have total responsibility for the rest of the store. You report to Donald Kincaid, manager of operations for the 16-store chain. The firm's philosophy emphasizes, "Customer service is your number one job. Do whatever is necessary to exceed the needs of the customer!"

Kelly, one of your cashiers, is a single parent with one preschool-aged child. She has exhausted her vacation hours for the year and has no personal time left. On a day she is scheduled to work, her daughter develops a high temperature and seems very ill. Even though the sitter is willing to take her, she would prefer not to. Kelly knows that she needs the money to make ends meet and that she has no paid leave time. Fifteen minutes before store opening, Kelly calls the store.

KELLY: Carol, I'm not feeling well this morning. I think it might be that new strain of flu, and I'd hate to spread it to anyone else. I'll call you later in the day and let you know how I'm feeling, because I'm scheduled to work tomorrow also.

You know that it will be difficult to get coverage at that late hour and that the pharmacy's staffing is lean to begin with.

YOU: I'm sorry that you are not feeling well, Kelly. Take good care of yourself and get it under control. Please let me know as soon as possible regarding tomorrow.

KELLY: Thanks for your understanding. I really appreciate it.

You contemplate the work ahead. You call several employees, and none is available to fill in for Kelly until later in the day. You wonder how you will get through the day. What will you do to alleviate the situation?

You Make the Call!

THE PERSON IN THE MIDDLE

1
Summarize the difficulties supervisors face in fulfilling managerial roles.

The supervisory position is a difficult and demanding role. Supervisors are "people in the middle"—the principal link between higher-level managers and employees. A supervisor is a first-level manager, that is, a manager in charge of entry-level and other departmental employees. Every organization, whether a retail store, a manufacturing firm, a hospital, or a government agency, has someone who fills this role.

Throughout this textbook we use the terms *worker, employee,* and *subordinate* interchangeably to refer to individuals who report to supervisors or managers. An increasing number of companies are using the term *associate* or *team member* instead of *employee.* Regardless of the term used, employees may view their supervisor as the management of the organization; the supervisor is their primary contact with management. Employees expect a supervisor to be technically competent and to be a good leader who can show them how to get the job done.

But the supervisor also must be a competent subordinate to higher-level managers. In this role the supervisor must be a good follower. Moreover, the supervisor is expected to maintain satisfactory relationships with supervisors in other departments. Thus, a supervisor's relationship to other supervisors is that of a colleague who must cooperate and must coordinate his or her department's efforts with those of others in order to reach the overall goals of the organization.

In general, the position of any supervisor has two main requirements. First, the supervisor must have a good working knowledge of the jobs to be performed. Second—

and more significant—the supervisor must be able to manage, that is, run, the department. It is the managerial competence of a supervisor that usually determines the effectiveness of his or her performance.

MANAGERIAL SKILLS MAKE THE DIFFERENCE

2
Explain why effective supervisors should possess a variety of skills.

In most organizations there are some supervisors who appear to be under constant pressure and continuously do the same work their subordinates do. They are getting by, although they feel overburdened. These supervisors endure long hours, may be very devoted to their jobs, and are willing to do everything themselves. They want to be effective, although they seldom have enough time to actually supervise. Other supervisors appear to be on top of their jobs, and their departments function in a smooth and orderly manner. These supervisors find time to sit at their desks at least part of the day, and they are able to keep their paperwork up to date. What is the difference?

Of course, some supervisors are more capable than others, just as some mechanics are better than others. If we compare two maintenance supervisors who are equally good mechanics, have similar equipment under their care, and operate under approximately the same conditions, why might one be more effective than the other? The answer is that effective supervisors manage their departments in a manner that gets the job done through their people instead of doing the work themselves. The difference between a good supervisor and a poor one, assuming that their technical skills are similar, is the difference in their managerial skills.

The managerial aspects of the supervisor's position too often have been neglected in the selection and development of supervisors. Typically, people are selected for supervisory positions on the basis of their technical competence, their seniority or past performance, and their willingness to work hard. When appointed supervisors, they are expected to assume responsibilities of management, even though their previous job did not involve these skills. New supervisors must make a conscious effort to develop their managerial skills by learning from their own manager, through company training programs, and by any other avenues available to them.

To this end, we have grouped the managerial skills needed by supervisors into the following major classifications:

Technical skills
The ability to do the job.

Human relations skills
The ability to work with and through people.

Administrative skills
The ability to plan, organize, and coordinate activities.

Conceptual skills
The ability to obtain, interpret, and apply information.

Political skills
The ability to understand how things get done outside of formal channels.

1. **Technical skills:** the ability to perform the actual jobs within the supervisor's area of responsibility.
2. **Human relations skills:** the ability to work with and through people; includes the ability to motivate team members and openmindedness.
3. **Administrative skills:** the ability to plan, organize, and coordinate the activities of a work group.
4. **Conceptual skills:** the ability to obtain, interpret, and apply the information necessary to make sound decisions.
5. **Political skills:** the savvy to ascertain the hidden rules of the organizational game and to recognize the roles that various people play in getting things done outside of formal organizational channels.

Emotional intelligence skills

The ability to intelligently use your emotions.

6. **Emotional intelligence skills:** the "intelligent use of your emotions to help guide your behavior and thinking in ways that enhance your results. You can maximize your emotional intelligence by developing good communication skills, interpersonal expertise, and mentoring abilities."[1]

Chess master Bruce Pandolfini stresses that there are two basic forms of intelligence: the ability to read other people, and the ability to understand one's self.[2] The notion of knowing thyself is not a new concept. Unfortunately, it was not too many years ago that corporate America believed that you could take "the best mechanic" or "the best salesperson," give them the title of supervisor or manager, and success would automatically follow. Everyone has heard the horror stories—the supervisor who did his or her homework, did everything aboveboard, and called on the aforementioned skills, But somehow, something went wrong. They made an error in judgment—some said they lacked *common sense* (see this chapter's "Contemporary Issue" box for some thoughts on maturity).

Managerial Skills Can Be Learned and Developed

Many people believe that good managers, like good athletes, are born, not made. Much research has indicated that this belief is generally incorrect, even though it is true that people are born with different potential and that, to some degree, heredity does play a role in intelligence. An athlete who is not endowed with natural physical advantages is not likely to run 100 yards in record time. On the other hand, many individuals who are so-called "natural athletes" have not come close to that goal either.

Herb Kelleher, CEO of Southwest Airlines, is recognized nationwide for his managerial skills (see page 40).

Most superior athletes have developed their natural endowments into mature skills by practice, learning, effort, and experience. The same holds true for a good manager. The skills involved in managing are as learnable as the skills used in playing golf. It does take time, effort, and determination for a supervisor to develop managerial skills. Supervisors will make some mistakes, but people learn from mistakes as well as from successes. By applying the principles discussed in this textbook, the supervisor can develop the skills that make the supervisory job a challenging and satisfying career.

Simply talking about supervisory management is somewhat like Mark Twain's comment about the weather: "Everybody talks about it, but no one does anything about it." Therefore, throughout this textbook there are various activities designed to reinforce the concepts presented. There is no guarantee of supervisory success. Jack Nicklaus, one of the greatest golfers of all time, wrote *Golf My Way*. If you wanted to learn to play golf, we could give you a copy of the book to read, but we would also have to provide you with the proper tools (clubs) and a time to practice (learn from your mistakes and make corrections). The challenge for supervisors is to stay on the path of continuous improvement.

contemporary issue

Do You Have What It Takes?

Southwest Airlines, the only airline that has made money each year for the past twenty-some years, has been led by Herb Kelleher. The chairman, president, and CEO of Southwest Airlines doesn't have an MBA (he's a lawyer by trade) and didn't work his way up the corporate ladder. But he did create a corporate culture that inspired his employees to deliver top-notch service on the ground and in the air—Southwest has the best customer-complaint record in the industry and turns planes around in about half the industry average. The "nutty" style of management has earned Southwest the reputation of being a great place to work. If everyone knows Southwest's strategy, why is it different? In a recent interview, Kelleher stated the secret:

> *"You have to recognize that people are still most important. How you treat them determines how they treat people on the outside. We have people going around the company all the time doing other people's jobs, but not for cross-utilization. We just want everyone to understand what everybody else's problems are."[1]*

In short, Kelleher's answer seems like "common sense." But he says, "there is no magic formula. It's like building a giant mosaic—it takes thousands of little pieces." The glue that binds the pieces together comes with *maturity.* The following describe some thoughts on maturity:

- Maturity is many things. It is the ability to base a judgment on the big picture, the long haul. It means being able to resist the urge for immediate gratification and opt for a course of action that will pay off later.

- Maturity is perseverance. It is the ability to sweat out a project or a situation in spite of heavy opposition or discouraging setbacks and stick with it until it is finished.

- Maturity is the ability to control anger and settle differences without violence or destruction. The mature person can face unpleasantness, frustration, discomfort, and defeat without complaining. Mature people know they can't have everything their own way every time.

- Maturity is humility. It is being big enough to say, "I was wrong." And when he or she is right, the mature person need not experience the satisfaction of saying, "I told you so!"

- Maturity is the ability to live up to your responsibilities, and this means being dependable. It means keeping your word. Do you mean what you say—and do you say what you mean?

- Maturity is the ability to make a decision and stand by it. Immature people spend their lives exploring endless possibilities and then do nothing—paralysis by analysis. Action requires sticking your neck out.

- Maturity is the ability to harness your abilities and your energies and do more than is expected. The mature person sets stretch targets and strives diligently to attain them.

- Maturity is the art of living in peace with that which we cannot change, the courage to change that which should be changed, no matter what it takes, and the wisdom to know the difference.[2]

Sources: (1) Hal Lancaster, "Herb Kelleher Has One Main Strategy: Treat Employees Well," *The Wall Street Journal* (August 31, 1999), p. B1. Also see Eryn Brown, "America's Most Admired Companies," *Fortune* (March 1, 1999), pp. 68–73; Stephanie Gruner, "Have Fun, Make Money; How Herb Kelleher Parties Profitably at Southwest Airlines," *Inc.* (May 1998), p. 123; Ronald B. Lieber, "Why Employees Love These Companies," *Fortune* (January 12, 1998), p. 73; and Kevin Freiberg and Jackie Freiberg, *Nuts! Southwest Airlines' Crazy Recipe for Business and Personal Success* (Austin: TX: Bard Press, 1996). (2) Adapted from columnist Ann Landers, "Maturity is Many Things and It's Worth Repeating," *Green Bay Press–Gazette* (July 17, 1999), p. D-2.

Benefits from Better Supervisory Management

You may recall from Figure 1-1 in Chapter 1 that there are many benefits accruing to the effective supervisor. A supervisor has daily opportunities to apply managerial principles on the job. Proper application of the principles will contribute to a smoother-functioning department in which the work gets done on time and the workers contribute toward stated objectives more willingly and enthusiastically. Thus, the supervisor will be on top of the job instead of being consumed by it. Supervisors who manage well are able to make suggestions to higher-level managers and to other supervisors. Effective supervisors become aware of the needs and objectives of departments as well as the interrelationships between those departments and their own. They seek to work in closer harmony with colleagues who supervise other departments. Briefly, better supervisory management means doing a more effective job with much less stress and strain.

In addition to direct benefits, there are indirect benefits. The supervisor who manages well will become capable of handling larger and more complicated assignments, which could lead to more responsible and higher-paying positions within the managerial hierarchy. Managerial skills are applicable in any organization and at all managerial levels, regardless of where a supervisor's future career may lead.

FUNCTIONS OF MANAGEMENT

3
Define management and discuss how the primary managerial functions are interrelated.

Management
Getting objectives accomplished with and through people.

The term *management* has been defined in many ways. In general, **management** is the process of getting things accomplished with and through people by guiding and motivating their efforts toward common objectives.

In most endeavors, one person can accomplish relatively little. Therefore, individuals join forces with others to attain mutual goals. In a business, top-level managers are responsible for achieving the goals of the organization, but this requires the efforts of all subordinate managers and employees. Those who hold supervisory positions significantly influence the effectiveness with which people work together and utilize the resources available to attain stated goals. In short, the managerial role of a supervisor is to make sure that assigned tasks are accomplished with and through the help of employees. Thus, the better the supervisor manages, the better will be the departmental results.

The Managerial Functions Are the Same in All Managerial Positions

The managerial functions of a supervisory position are similar, whether they involve supervision of a production line, a sales force, a laboratory, or a small office. Moreover, the primary managerial functions are the same regardless of the level within the hierarchy of management. It does not matter whether one is a first-level supervisor, a middle-level manager, or part of top-level management. Nor does the type of organization matter. Managerial functions are the same whether the supervisor is working in a profit-making firm, a nonprofit organization, or a government office. Supervisors, as well as other managers, perform the same basic managerial functions in all organizations. In this textbook we classify these functions under the major categories of planning, organizing, staffing, leading, and controlling. The following description of these functions is general and brief since most of the book is devoted to discussing their application—particularly at the supervisory level.

Planning.   The initial managerial function—determining what should be done in the future—is called **planning.** It consists of setting goals, objectives, policies, procedures, and other plans needed to achieve the purposes of the organization. In planning, the manager chooses a course of action from various alternatives available. Planning is primarily conceptual in nature. It means thinking before acting, looking ahead and preparing for the future, laying out in advance the road to be followed, and thinking about what and how the job should be done. It includes collecting and sorting information from numerous sources and using it to make decisions. Not only does planning include deciding what, how, when, and by whom work is to be done, but it must also include the development of "what if" scenarios. A word of caution: Regardless of how well a supervisor like Carol Reeves ("You Make the Call") plans, crises will happen and supervisors need to anticipate them, considering what they will do if this or that happens.

Many supervisors find that they are constantly confronted with one crisis after another. The probable reason for this is that they neglect to plan; they do not look much beyond the day's events. It is every supervisor's responsibility to plan, and this cannot be delegated to someone else. Certain specialists, such as a budget officer, a production scheduler, or an engineer, may provide the supervisor with assistance in planning. But it is up to each supervisor, as the manager of a department, to make specific departmental plans that coincide with the general objectives established by higher-level management.

Planning is the managerial function that comes first, and, as the supervisor proceeds with other managerial functions, planning continues, previous plans are revised, and different alternatives are chosen as the need arises. This is particularly true as a supervisor evaluates the results of previous plans and adjusts future plans accordingly.

Organizing.   Once plans have been made, the organizing function primarily answers the question, "How will the work be divided and accomplished?" This means that the supervisor defines the various job duties and groups these activities into distinct areas, sections, units, or teams. The supervisor must specify the duties required, assign them, and, at the same time, provide subordinates with the authority needed to carry out their tasks. **Organizing** means arranging and distributing work among members of the work group to accomplish the organization's goals.

Staffing.   The managerial tasks of recruiting, selecting, orienting, and training employees may be grouped within the function called **staffing.** This function includes appraising the performance of employees, promoting employees where appropriate, and providing them with further opportunities for development. In addition, staffing includes devising an equitable compensation system and rates of pay. Some activities involved in the staffing function are handled by the human resources (or personnel) department in many companies. For example, the human resources department and top-level managers establish the compensation system. Supervisors do not perform this task. However, day-to-day responsibility for essential aspects of the staffing function remains with the supervisor.

Planning
Determining what should be done in the future.

Organizing
Arranging and distributing work among members of the work group to accomplish the organization's goals.

Staffing
The tasks of recruiting, selecting, orienting, training, appraising, and evaluating employees.

Leading means guiding the activities of employees toward accomplishing objectives. It is the day-to-day process around which all supervisory performance revolves.

Leading

The managerial function of guiding employees toward accomplishment of organizational objectives.

Leading.   **Leading** means guiding the activities of employees toward accomplishing objectives. The leading function of management involves guiding, teaching, and supervising subordinates. This includes developing the abilities of employees to their maximum potential by directing and coaching them effectively. It is not sufficient for a supervisor just to plan, organize, and have enough employees available. The supervisor must attempt to motivate them as they go about their work. Leading is the day-to-day process around which all supervisory performance revolves. Leading is also known as *directing, motivating,* or *influencing* since it plays a major role in employee morale, job satisfaction, productivity, and communication. It is through this function that the supervisor seeks to create a climate that is conducive to employee satisfaction and at the same time achieves the objectives of the department. Finding ways to satisfy the needs of a diverse employee workforce is a significant challenge. In fact, most of a supervisor's time normally is spent on this function since it is the function around which departmental performance revolves.

Controlling

Ensuring that actual performance is in line with intended performance and taking corrective action.

Controlling.   The managerial function of **controlling** involves ensuring that actual performance is in line with intended performance and taking corrective action as necessary. Here, too, the importance of planning as the first function of management should be obvious. It would not be possible for a supervisor to determine whether work was proceeding properly if there were no plans against which to check. If plans or standards are superficial or poorly conceived, the controlling function is limited. Thus, controlling means not only making sure that objectives are achieved, but also taking corrective action in case of failure to achieve planned objectives. It also means revising plans if circumstances require it.

The circular concept illustrates the close and continuous relationship between the management functions.

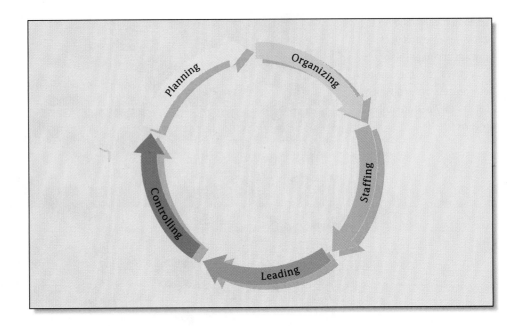

The Continuous Flow of Managerial Functions.   The five managerial functions can be viewed as a circular, continuous movement. If we view the managerial process as a circular flow consisting of the five functions (Figure 2-1), we can see that the functions flow into each other and that each affects the performance of the others. At times there is no clear line to mark where one function ends and the other begins. Also, it is not possible for a supervisor to set aside a certain amount of time for one or another function since the effort spent in each function will vary as conditions and circumstances change. But there is no doubt that planning must come first. Without plans, the supervisor cannot organize, staff, lead, or control.

Remember: All managers perform essentially the same managerial functions, regardless of the nature of the organization or their level in the hierarchy. The time and effort involved in each of these functions will vary depending on the rung of the management ladder the manager occupies, the type of tasks performed by subordinates, and the scope and urgency of the situation.

Discuss the important characteristics of the supervisor as team leader.

THE SUPERVISOR AS TEAM LEADER

Many firms have implemented a team-based organizational structure focused on customer satisfaction, productivity, profitability, and continuous improvement. It is not the intent of the authors to discuss the pros and cons of the team approach at this point. Teams are a means to an end—and that end is superior performance to what team members would achieve working as individuals.[3] Author, trainer, and consultant Fran Rees identified several reasons for the increasing use of teams:

- Given the complexity of jobs and information, it is nearly impossible for managers to make all the decisions. In many cases, the person closest to the job is the one who should decide.
- The focus on quality and customer satisfaction has riveted attention on the importance of each employee's work.
- The shift from a homogeneous to a diverse workforce requires managers to work effectively with multiple employee perspectives.
- There is a growing realization that an autocratic, coercive management style does not necessarily result in productive, loyal employees. The fact that people support what they help create is behind the team approach.
- People are demanding to have a strong voice in their own work lives, to have meaningful work, and to be treated with respect and dignity.[4]

Increasingly, workers from different areas or specializations are forced to work together to recommend things, make or do things, and run or manage things. Often, the term *leader* or *facilitator* refers to the manager or supervisor of the team. This term more closely defines the new function of the manager: that of teacher, coach, mentor, coordinator, and team leader.[5] The supervisor's role as team leader is illustrated in Figure 2-2 (see page 46). Work teams will be discussed again in Chapter 15.

One example of how well teams perform is illustrated in the movie *Apollo 13*. The five little words, "Houston, we have a problem," caused a diverse group of ground crew specialists at Mission Control—working against the clock, borrowing and fabricating resources, and working against the odds—to figure out a way to bring the astronauts home.

MANAGERS AND LEADERS: ARE THEY DIFFERENT?

5
Explain the difference between management and leadership.

In the years since the classic *Harvard Business Review* article, "Managers and Leaders: Are They Different?" much debate has abounded among scholars regarding the difference.[6] Not surprisingly, hundreds of articles and books have attempted to clear up the confusion. While some have contended that it is only a labeling or semantical difference, others have identified more substantive differences. For example, author Stephen Covey wrote, "Leadership is not management. Leadership deals with the top line—What are the things I want to accomplish? Leadership is doing the right things. In the words of both Peter Drucker and Warren Bennis, 'Management is efficiency in climbing the ladder of success; leadership determines whether the ladder is leaning against the right wall.' "[7] One of the most noted writers on leadership, Bennis has pointed out other differences between managers and leaders (see Figure 2-3 on page 47).

Harvard Professor John P. Kotter also draws a similar distinction between leadership and management. He contends that management involves keeping the current system operating through planning, budgeting, staffing, controlling, and problem solving while leadership is the development of vision and strategies, the alignment of relevant people behind those strategies, and the empowerment of people to make the vision happen. The authors of this text concur wholeheartedly with Kotter when he states:

FIGURE 2-2

The supervisor's multiple roles as team leader.

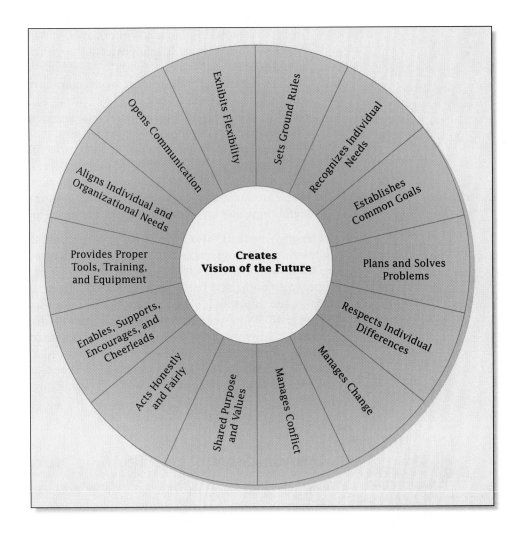

"*The point here is not that leadership is good and management is bad. They are simply different and serve different purposes. Strong management with no leadership tends to entrench an organization in a deadly bureaucracy. Strong leadership with no management risks chaos; the organization might walk off a cliff.*"[8]

If a person has the title of manager, does it necessarily follow that he or she will be a leader? Clearly the answer is no—title alone does not guarantee success. On the other hand, if a person has the title of team leader, does it mean that he or she will display the skills, knowledge, and abilities to excel in that position? Again, the answer is no. What does it take for an individual to be both a good manager and a good leader? Is it possible for individuals to learn to be both a good manager and a good leader? To that end, in subsequent chapters we clearly identify the necessary ingredients—the managerial skills necessary for success—and devote the bulk of Chapter 14 to a further discussion of leadership and change.

FIGURE 2-3

Who does what?

- The manager does things right; the leader does the right thing.
- The manager relies on control; the leader inspires trust.
- The manager focuses on systems and structures; the leader focuses on people.
- The manager administers; the leader innovates.
- The manager asks how and when; the leader asks what and why.
- The manager accepts the status quo; the leader challenges it!

Source: Adapted from Warren Bennis, *On Becoming a Leader* (Reading, MA: Addison-Wesley Publishing Company, paperback edition 1994), pp. 44–45.

6

Discuss the concept of authority as a requirement of any managerial position.

Authority

The legitimate right to direct and lead others.

MANAGERIAL AUTHORITY

Does the individual possess the authority to perform the managerial functions? If the answer is no, the individual cannot perform well as a manager (see Figure 2-4 on page 48). **Authority** is the legitimate or rightful power to lead others, the right to order and to act.[9] Managerial authority is not granted to an individual but rather to the position the individual holds at the time. When the individual leaves the job or is replaced, he or she ceases to have that authority. When a successor takes over the position, that person will then have the authority.

Having managerial authority means that the supervisor has the power and right to issue directives in order to accomplish the tasks that have been assigned to the department. This authority includes the power and right to reward and discipline, if necessary. If a subordinate performs well, then the supervisor has the power to give a raise or other reward to the subordinate, within company guidelines. If a worker refuses to carry out a directive, the supervisor's authority includes the power and right to take disciplinary action, even to the extent of discharging the subordinate. Of course this power, like all authority, has limitations. For example, a union contract and legal restrictions may require that certain conditions be fulfilled before a worker can be discharged. Also, upper-level managers establish guidelines for the size of raises supervisors may give employees based on performance.

Avoiding Reliance on Managerial Authority

Most successful supervisors know that to motivate workers to perform their required duties it usually is best not to rely on their formal managerial authority but to employ other approaches. Generally, it is better for a supervisor not to display power and formal authority, and in practice many supervisors prefer not even to speak about their authority. They prefer to speak of their responsibility, tasks, or duties instead of stating that they possess authority. Some supervisors consider it better to say that they have responsibility for certain activities, instead of saying that they have authority within that area. Using the words *responsibility, tasks,* and *duties* in this sense—although these certainly are not the same as authority—helps the supervisor to avoid showing the "club" of authority.

FIGURE 2-4

Performance of managerial functions and possession of authority are essential components of a managerial position.

In general, how you treat employees on the job and develop their sense of worth are more important to employees in the long run than salary.[10] Research shows that approaches that foster mutual trust and respect between supervisor and subordinate generally result in increased job satisfaction and higher productivity. We contend that employees are likely to perform better if they understand why the task needs to be done and have a voice in how to do it rather than simply being told to do it. Regardless of how a supervisor applies authority, the point to remember is that the supervisory position must have it. Without managerial authority, a supervisor cannot perform well as a manager.

Delegating Authority

Delegation

The process of entrusting duties and related authority to subordinates.

Included within positional managerial authority are the right and duty to delegate authority. **Delegation** of authority is the process by which the supervisor receives authority from a higher-level manager and, in turn, makes job assignments and entrusts related authority to subordinates. Just as the possession of authority is a required component of any managerial position, the process of delegating authority to lower levels within the hierarchy is required for an organization to have effective managers, supervisors, and employees. Chapters 8 and 14 discuss in detail the concepts of authority, responsibility, and the delegation of authority.

POWER—THE ABILITY TO INFLUENCE OTHERS

Among the most confused terms in management are *authority* and *power*. The effective supervisor must understand the difference between authority and power. Some behavioral scientists contend that a manager's power comes from two sources: position power and personal power.[11] **Position power** comes from the organizational position the person occupies. For example, the division manager has more position power than the first-line supervisor. **Personal power,** on the other hand, emanates from the relationship that the supervisor has with other people. A supervisor's personal power depends to a greater extent on the follower's perceptions of his or her knowledge, skill, and expertise.

Other theorists, such as French and Raven, purport that power arises from the following five sources:

Position power

Power derived from the formal rank a person holds in the chain of command.

Personal power

Power derived from a person's skill, knowledge, or ability and how others percieve them.

1. *Reward power:* A supervisor has reward power if he or she has the ability to grant rewards.
2. *Coercive power:* The supervisor who uses threats of punishment and discipline is using coercive power.
3. *Legitimate power:* Some supervisors gain compliance by relying on their position or rank, e.g., "I'm the boss, do it my way."
4. *Expert power:* Knowledge or valuable information gives a person expert power over those who need such information.
5. *Referent or charismatic power:* People are often influenced by others because of some tangible or intangible aspect of the other's personality.[12]

Effective supervisors need to understand the effect their power has on others. Research indicates that reward power, coercive power, and legitimate power often force employees to comply with directives but do not get their commitment to organizational objectives. Accordingly, supervisors who use expert power and referent power effectively have the greatest potential for achieving organizational goals.[13]

The acceptance theory of authority also has relevance to the application of power. For example, you can be an expert in computer applications, but if others do not need that knowledge, you will have very little influence over them. Therefore, two supervisors can hold the same title, occupy the same level in the hierarchy, and have equal authority yet have different degrees of power, depending on their abilities and how others perceive them.

COORDINATION

Management was generally defined as a process of getting things done through and with the help of people by directing their efforts toward common objectives. In a sense, all levels of management could be broadly visualized as involving the coordination of efforts of all the members and resources of an organization toward overall objectives. Some writers, therefore, have included the concept of coordination as a separate managerial function.

Coordination

The synchronization of employees' efforts and the organization's resources toward achieving goals.

Coordination is the orderly synchronization (or putting together) of efforts of the members and resources of an organization to accomplish the organization's objectives. Coordination is not a separate managerial function; it is an implicit, interrelated aspect of the five major managerial functions previously cited. That is, coordination is fostered whenever a manager performs any of the managerial functions of planning, organizing, staffing, leading, and controlling. In a sense, coordination can best be understood as being a direct result of good management rather than as a managerial function in itself. The ability to communicate clearly and concisely is essential for coordination.

Achieving coordination typically is more difficult at the executive level than at the supervisory level. The chief executive officer has to synchronize the use of resources and human efforts throughout the entire organization, that is, throughout numerous departments and levels. A supervisor of one department has the responsibility to achieve coordination primarily within the department. However, this, too, can be difficult to achieve, especially during periods of rapid change.

Cooperation As Related to Coordination

Cooperation

The willingness of individuals to work with and help one another.

Cooperation is individuals' willingness to work with and help each other. It primarily involves the attitudes of a group of people.

Coordination is more than the mere desire and willingness of participants. For example, consider a group of workers attempting to move a heavy object. They are sufficient in number, willing and eager to cooperate with each other, and trying their best to move the object. They are also fully aware of their common purpose. However, in all likelihood their efforts will be of little avail until one of them—the supervisor—gives the proper orders to apply the right amount of effort at the right place at the right time. Then they can move the object. It is possible that by sheer coincidence some cooperation could have brought about the desired result in this example, but no supervisor can afford to rely on such a coincidental occurrence. Although cooperation is helpful and the lack of it could impede progress, its presence alone will not necessarily get the job done. Efforts must be coordinated toward the common goal.

Attaining Coordination

Coordination is not easily attained, and the task of achieving coordination is becoming more complex. As an organization grows, coordinating the many activities of various departments becomes an increasingly complicated problem for higher-level managers. At the supervisory level, as the number and types of positions within a department increase, the need for coordination to obtain desired results similarly increases. On the other hand, organizational downsizing may force supervisors to be even more effective in coordination (see Chapter 8).

Complexities of human nature present additional problems of coordination. Many employees understandably are preoccupied with their own work because, in the final analysis, they are evaluated primarily on how they do their jobs. Therefore, they tend not to become involved in other areas, and often they are indifferent to the fact that their activities may affect other departments.

Networking

Individuals or groups linked together by a commitment to shared purpose.

Supervisors can achieve coordination by building networks focused on attaining common objectives. According to the dictionary, a *network* is a "fabric or structure of cords or wires that cross at regular intervals and are knotted or secured at the crossings." This visual image is helpful in conceiving of a network from a supervisor's perspective. A supervisor should think of a network as any number of individuals or groups linked together by a commitment to shared purpose and values. **Networking** is the process by which supervisors become connected with other individuals or groups to achieve particular goals. Simply stated, networking is people connecting with people, linking ideas, resources, and work effort. Carol Reeves, supervisor of Kincaid Pharmacy ("You Make the Call"), should develop networks with others, both inside and outside the pharmacy. Also, she must understand that the network runs on both sides of the street. When Carol has a need, she contacts another person in her network who might have a resource, and vice versa. Networking enables Carol to maintain a balance between autonomy on the one hand and dependence on the other. Networking facilitates the flow of ideas across organizational barriers and thereby eases the coordination effort.

Coordination as Part of the Managerial Functions. While performing the managerial functions, the supervisor should recognize that coordination is a desired result of effective management. Proper attention to coordination within each of the five managerial functions contributes to overall coordination.

The planning stage is an important time for fostering coordination since a supervisor must see to it that the various plans within the department are properly interrelated. For example, a supervisor may wish to discuss departmental job assignments with the employees who are to carry them out. In this way the employees have the op-

Joining a professional organization is one way for people with a common purpose to network.

portunity to express their opinions or objections, which need to be reconciled in advance. Furthermore, employees may be encouraged to make suggestions and to participate in discussing the merits of proposed plans and alternatives. If employees are involved in departmental planning at the initial stages, the supervisor's chances for achieving coordination usually will be improved.

The concern for coordination must be prevalent when a supervisor organizes. The purpose of establishing who is to do what, when, where, and how is to achieve coordination. For example, whenever a new job is to be done, a supervisor assigns it to the unit that has employees best suited to accomplish the work. Thus, whenever a supervisor groups activities and assigns subordinates to them, coordination should be uppermost in the supervisor's mind. Achieving coordination also should be of concern as a supervisor establishes authority relationships within the department and among employees. Clear statements as to specific duties and reporting relationships in the department will foster coordination and prevent duplication of efforts and confusion.

Similarly, coordination should be a high priority when a supervisor performs the staffing function. There must be the right number of workers possessing the proper skills in all of the positions to ensure the group's effective performance. The supervisor must see to it that employees have the abilities and job training they need to contribute to the coordination of their efforts.

When leading, the supervisor is significantly involved in coordination. The essence of giving instructions is to coordinate the activities of employees in such a manner that the overall objectives will be reached in the most efficient way possible. In addition, a supervisor must assess and reward the performance of employees to maintain a harmonious work group.

The supervisor is also concerned with coordination when performing the controlling function. By checking, monitoring, and observing, the supervisor makes certain that activities conform to established plans. If there are any discrepancies, the supervisor should take immediate action to reprioritize or reassign tasks and, in so doing, may achieve coordination at least from then on. The very nature of the controlling process contributes to coordination and keeps the organization moving toward its objectives.

Coordination with Other Departments.   Not only must supervisors be concerned with coordination within their own departments, but they also must coordinate the efforts of their departments with those of others. For example, a production department supervisor must meet with supervisors of scheduling, quality control, maintenance, and shipping to coordinate various activities. Similarly, an accounting supervisor typically meets with supervisors from production, sales, and shipping to coordinate cost accounting, inventory records, and billing. Achieving coordination is an essential component of the supervisory management position.

Cooperation and Coordination—Easier Said Than Done.   A group of employees becomes a team when its members possess shared values and a shared purpose. How well the objectives are achieved depends on the supervisor's coordination and team-building skills. The move toward increased employee participation, broader spans of control, and fewer managerial levels will result in a greater need for coordination skills. Meanwhile, many supervisors have higher aspirations; they eventually want to be promoted to positions of increased responsibility. Referring back to the opening "You Make the Call" section, you will notice that there is less opportunity as a person moves up in the organization. As Carol Reeves, one of the 16 store supervisors at Kincaid Pharmacy, you, in all likelihood, will be competing with the other 15 store supervisors for the position of operations manager. The challenge for the organization is to get people to cooperate and work together when in reality the structure of the organization may impede cooperation.

What Call Did You Make?

Kincaid Pharmacy places a high value on customer service, and as supervisor Carol Reeves, you must do whatever it takes to fulfill that expectation. Since none of the State Street store employees can come in on short notice, perhaps one of the other stores has someone who can fill in on his or her day off. Hopefully, as the supervisor, you have previously developed networks to help you with your current need. Your previous networking and cooperative efforts with the other store supervisors may pay off, and they will assist you in finding someone to provide coverage. Perhaps the human resources department can help you by recommending a temporary help service or other options. If they cannot help you, you should get back to the person who said he or she could come in later in the day.

In all likelihood, you will have to roll up your sleeves and fill in where needed. You have the technical skills, and periodically you will have to use them. You will need to communicate to the other employees that Kelly's absence will necessitate an extra effort on their part. Generally, the employees you ask to provide extra coverage are likely to perform better if they understand why the task needs to be done and have a voice in how to do it. Unfortunately, time is not on your side because the store opens in a few minutes.

Your coordination skills will be taxed. You might have to spread your existing staff to cover the work. Conflicts may arise, and your ability to perform the leading function will make the task less difficult. Can you prevent the problem from recurring? The answer is no, but you can learn from this experience and develop contingency plans for when it happens again.

A word of caution: Often employees who show up for work regularly are burdened when someone like Kelly does not show up on her scheduled work day. They will be asked to pick up the slack, and some may resent it. As the supervisor, you need to find ways to reward employees who give extra effort during a crisis.

SUMMARY

Supervisors are the "people in the middle." Employees see their supervisors as being management, but supervisors are subordinates to their own managers at higher levels. To supervisors of other departments, they are colleagues who must cooperate with each other. Supervisors must have good working knowledge of the jobs being performed in their department and the ability to manage.

The effective supervisor needs to possess technical, human relations, administrative, conceptual, and political skills. It is also critical that the supervisor be able to intelligently use his or her emotions. The supervisor must understand the technical aspects of the work being performed. While attempting to manage job performance, understanding employee needs is essential. The "people skills" help the supervisor to accomplish objectives with and through people. It is equally important for the supervisor to possess an understanding of the dynamics of the organization and to recognize organizational politics.

These skills are important to all levels of management. Most supervisors come to the job equipped with some of the skills. Supervisors have daily opportunities to apply managerial skills and must continually strive to develop those skills. Blending these skills with a dose of common sense and applying them with maturity will contribute to the accomplishment of organizational objectives and will allow the supervisor to stay on top of the job. Supervisors who effectively apply these skills will be able to contribute suggestions to higher-level managers and will be able to work in harmony with their colleagues. In short, the skilled supervisor will be a candidate for advancement and additional job responsibilities.

While there are numerous definitions of management, we have defined *management* as the process of getting things accomplished through people by guiding and motivating their efforts toward common objectives.

The five major managerial functions are planning, organizing, staffing, leading, and controlling. The functions are viewed as a continuous flow—that is, the functions flow into each other, and each affects the performance of the others.

Planning is the first function of management, and the performance of all other managerial functions depends on it. The five managerial functions are universal, regardless of the job environment, the activity involved, or a person's position in the management hierarchy. Typically, supervisors spend most of their time leading and controlling. A supervisor's planning will cover a shorter time and narrower focus than that of a top-level executive.

Some companies have redefined the role of the supervisor as team leader. While team leaders must possess certain skills as identified earlier in the chapter, it is important to remember that teams are usually formed for such purposes as improving customer service, productivity, or quality. As such, developing a work environment where team members have a shared purpose and common goals is essential. The supervisor as team leader is more of a coach who must be able to apply all of the characteristics presented in Figure 2-2. While not all have an equal impact on the success of the team, information giving and information gathering will allow team members to function most effectively. The team leader must want to be part of change.

Leadership and management go hand in hand. As one of the management functions identified in this text, leadership is concerned with establishing a vision, aligning people behind that vision, and empowering them to accomplish the intended results (doing the right thing) while management is getting things done. The distinction is more than a semantical one.

A supervisor must possess authority in order to perform well as a manager. Authority is the legitimate or rightful power to lead others. Authority is delegated from top-level managers through middle-level managers to supervisors, who in turn delegate to their employees. All supervisors must be delegated appropriate authority to manage their departments. Most supervisors, rather than relying primarily on formal managerial authority, prefer to use other approaches for enhancing employee performance.

7

Supervisors have power because of the position they occupy. Position power increases as a person advances up the organizational hierarchy. The supervisor derives personal power from his or her relationship with others. Subordinates' perceptions of the supervisor's skill, knowledge, and ability play an integral role in the supervisor's ability to influence them.

Theorists French and Raven identify five sources of power: reward, coercive, legitimate, expert, and referent or charismatic. Research indicates that supervisors who use expert power and referent power effectively have the greatest potential for achieving organizational goals. The power that a supervisor has is based, for the most part, on the willingness of the employee to accept it.

8

Coordination is the orderly synchronization of efforts of the members and resources of an organization toward the attainment of stated objectives. Cooperation—as distinguished from coordination—is the willingness of individuals to work with and help each other. While cooperation is helpful, it cannot itself get the job done. Efforts must also be coordinated. Both coordination and cooperation are attainable through good management practices.

KEY TERMS

Technical skills (page 38)
Human relations skills (page 38)
Administrative skills (page 38)
Conceptual skills (page 38)
Political skills (page 38)
Emotional intelligence (page 39)
Management (page 41)
Planning (page 42)
Organizing (page 42)
Staffing (page 42)

Leading (page 43)
Controlling (page 43)
Authority (page 47)
Delegation (page 48)
Position power (page 49)
Personal power (page 49)
Coordination (page 50)
Cooperation (page 50)
Networking (page 51)

QUESTIONS FOR DISCUSSION

1. Identify the major managerial skills needed by every supervisor. Why are these important? Are emotional skills more or less important than the other skills? Why or why not?
2. Does maturity come automatically as one grows older? Why or why not?
3. How would you respond to someone who says, "I really get along well with everyone. I think I would be a good manager."
4. Define each of the five managerial functions. Are these functions adequate to describe the complexities of a managerial position? Discuss.
5. It is often said that planning is the most important managerial function. Do you agree? Why or why not?
6. Do you agree with Stephen Covey, Warren Bennis, and John Kotter that there is a distinction between management and leadership? Why or why not? Why is the distinction important for one who desires to be a team leader?
7. Define authority and discuss its importance.
8. What is the difference between authority and power?
9. Define the concept of cooperation. How are coordination and cooperation interrelated?

SKILLS APPLICATIONS

Skills Application 2-1: Attributes of a Successful Manager

Think of the most successful manager you have ever known or heard about. Write a paragraph describing what that manager does to be described as successful. Compare your paragraph with that of a classmate. Are there skills, knowledge, or abilities common to both? Why do you think there are common items?

Skills Application 2-2: Self-Assessment of Supervisory Skills

1. From the following list select the six items that you believe are most critical to supervisory success. Give them a weight of 3.
2. Select the six items that are the least critical. Select only six items for either most critical or least critical. Give them a weight of 1.
3. Give all other items a weight of 2.
4. Rate your abilities on each of these items as follows:
   major strength = 3   minor strength = 2   minor weakness = 1   major weakness = 0
5. Multiply the weight of each item by your assessed strength.
6. Sum the strength ratings.

Item	Weight	× Rating	= Strength Rating
Ability to develop contingency plans	____	____	____
Technical competency	____	____	____
Follows direction from above	____	____	____
Ability to obtain needed information	____	____	____
Ability to make sound decisions	____	____	____
Leads by example	____	____	____
Ability to plan	____	____	____
Ability to get job done in most efficient manner	____	____	____
Ability to coordinate activities of others	____	____	____
Ability to get things done through others	____	____	____
Ability to delegate	____	____	____
Ability to empower employees	____	____	____
Ability to listen actively	____	____	____
Ability to work under pressure	____	____	____
Anticipates crises	____	____	____
Keeps up to date on work-related matters	____	____	____
Ability to give effective instructions	____	____	____
Accepts responsibility for the results of others	____	____	____
Uses praise for job well done	____	____	____
Ability to get diverse people to function as a team	____	____	____
Ability to establish priorities	____	____	____
Provides feedback on performance	____	____	____
Ability to train and develop employees	____	____	____
Provides employees with a vision	____	____	____
Ability to select employees with potential	____	____	____

Ability to evaluate employees fairly   ＿＿＿ ＿＿＿ ＿＿＿

Adept at disseminating information to others   ＿＿＿ ＿＿＿ ＿＿＿

Total Strength Rating   ＿＿＿

To derive your total supervisory strength rating, add the strength rating for each item. If your score is less than 116, you need to focus your attention on those critical items where improvement is most needed.

Skills Application 2-3: A Night at the Movies

In an era of endless restructuring, cutting off heads like Robespierre on a rampage is just average for many managers. They inflict pain by messing with your mind as well. Visit your local video store and get a copy of one of the following: (1) *On the Waterfront,* (2) *Norma Rae,* (3) *Working Girl,* (4) *Grapes of Wrath,* or (5) *Nine to Five.* After reviewing the movie, answer the following questions.

1. In what ways was the management style "ruthless?" In what ways was it effective?
2. To what extent did the manager(s) correctly use the various managerial functions (plan, organize, staff, lead, and control)?
3. What, if anything, did various managers do to guide and motivate the efforts of the subordinates toward common objectives?
4. Assume you are in a subordinate position, just below one of the primary managers in the movie. How did you feel about the way you were supervised? What would you have done about it? Why?
5. What did you learn about how to manage? About how not to manage?

Skills Application 2-4: Characteristics of a Good Leader

INTERNET ACTIVITY

1. The following sites focus on leadership development and resources. According to these groups, what competencies and skills characterize good leaders?
   - Hagberg Consulting Group (www.leadership-development.com/p-best.html)
   - Institute for Leadership Dynamics (www.leadership-dynamics.com)
2. Think of a manager you've known or worked for in the past. Based on the skills you just outlined, was this manager also a leader? Why or why not?
3. Based on what you've learned about the characteristics of a good leader, how would you assess yourself? What are your strengths and weaknesses as a leader?

ENDNOTES

1. Following on the works of others, Hendrie Weisinger identified four building blocks that help one to develop skills and abilities. They are the ability (1) to accurately perceive, appraise, and express emotion; (2) to access the ability or generate feelings on demand when they can facilitate understanding of yourself or another person; (3) to understand emotions and the knowledge that derives from them; and (4) to regulate emotions to promote emotional and intellectual growth. See Weisinger, *Emotional Intelligence at Work* (San Francisco: Jossey-Bass, 1998). Also see John D. Mayer and Peter Salovey, "Emotional Intelligence and the Construction of Regulation of Feelings," *Applied and Preventive Psychology* (4, 1995), pp. 197–208; Mayer, Salovey, and Caruso, *Emotional IQ Test: CD-ROM Version* (Needham: MA: Virtual Entertainment, 1997); and Steve Bates, "Your Emotional Skills Can Make or Break You," *Nation's Business* (April 1999), p. 17.

2. For additional information on Pandolfini's principles for making the right decision under pressure, see "All the Right Moves," *Fast Company* (May 1999), p. 34.

3. Glenn M. Parker, *Cross-Functional Teams: Working with Allies, Enemies, and Other Strangers* (San Francisco: Jossey-Bass, 1998). Also see John R. Katzenbach, "The Right Kind of Teamwork," *The Wall Street Journal* (November 9, 1992), p. A10. Support for the team concept comes from testimonials like those cited in Paulette Thomas, "Teams Rule According to U.S. Manufacturers," *The Wall Street Journal* (May 28, 1996), p. 1. You can contact the Center for the Study of Work Teams (workteam@unt.edu).

4. Fran Rees, *How To Lead Work Teams: Facilitation Skills* (San Diego: Pfeiffer & Company, 1991), pp. 1–2.

5. Michale Jaycox, "How to Get Nonbelievers to Participate in Teams," *Quality Progress* (March 1996), p. 49. Each year *IndustryWeek* magazine recognizes the outstanding manufacturing facilities in America. See the October 18, 1999 issue for a list of 1999 award-winning plants. The recipients all exhibited extensive employee involvement and empowerment programs, especially efforts to create and provide training for high-performance work teams.

6. See Abraham Zaleznik, "Managers and Leaders: Are They Different?" *Harvard Business Review* (May–June 1977), pp. 126–135 and "Letting Leaders Replace Corporate Managers," *Washington Post* (September 27, 1992), pp. 1–5. For a definitive description of managerial roles, see Henry Mintzberg, *The Nature of Managerial Work* (New York: Harper & Row, 1973); "Planning on the Left Side and Managing on the Right," *Harvard Business Review* (January–February 1994), pp. 107, 111; and Peter F. Drucker, *Management Challenges for the 21st Century* (New York, Harper-Business, 1999).

7. Stephen R. Covey, *The 7 Habits of Highly Effective People* (New York: Simon and Schuster, 1989), p. 101; and *Principle-Centered Leadership: Strategies for Personal & Professional Effectiveness* (Bellevue: S&S Trade, 1992).

8. Adapted from John P. Kotter, *John P. Kotter on What Leaders Really Do* (Boston: Harvard Business School Press, 1999). Also see Kotter's *A Force For Change: How Leadership Differs From Management* (New York: The Free Press, 1990) and *The Leadership Factor* (New York: The Free Press, 1988).

9. One of Fayol's 14 principles of management defined formal authority as the "right to give orders." Henri Fayol, *General and Industrial Management,* trans. Constance Storrs (London: Sir Isaac Pitman & Sons, 1949), pp. 19–43.

10. Raymond L. Hilgert, as quoted in Frank Shipper, "Ten Qualities of Great Managers," *The Wall Street Journal–National Business Employment Weekly* (May 19–25, 1996), pp. 15–16. For another perspective, see Carol Quintanilla, "As Jobs Go Begging, Bosses Toil Nights—and Improvise," *The Wall Street Journal* (March 31, 1997), pp. B1, B8. An analysis of *Business Week*'s top 25 managers found the key trait to be adaptability. See "The Best Managers: What It Takes," *Business Week* (January 10, 2000), pp. 60+.

11. Much has been written about power. For additional information on position power and personal power, see Amitai Etzioni, *A Comparative Analysis of Complex Organizations* (New York: The Free Press, 1961), pp. 4–6; and John P. Kotter, "Power, Dependence, and Effective Management," *Harvard Business Review* (July–August 1977), pp. 131–136.

12. John R. P. French and Bertram Raven, "The Bases of Social Power," in *Studies in Social Power,* ed. Dorwin Cartwright (Ann Arbor: University of Michigan Press, 1959), pp. 150–167. Also see A. J. Stanhelski, D. E. Frost, and M. E. Patch, "Uses of Socially Dependent Bases of Power: French and Raven's Theory Applied to Working Group Leadership," *Journal of Applied Social Psychology* (March 1989), pp. 283–297.

13. See Timothy R. Hinkin and Chester A. Schriesheim, "Relationships Between Subordinate Perceptions and Supervisor Influence Tactics and Attributed Bases of Supervisory Power," *Human Relations* (March 1990), pp. 221–237.

Chapter 3

Communication: The Vital Link in Supervisory Management

After studying this chapter, you will be able to:

1
Define communication and discuss its implications for effective supervisory management.

2
Discuss the major channels of communication available to the supervisor.

3
Explain the benefits of the various methods of communication.

4
Identify and discuss barriers to effective communication.

5
Describe ways to overcome the communication barriers.

Learning Objectives

You Make the Call!

You are Carl O'Connor, department supervisor of maintenance, grounds, and housekeeping at Community Hospital. Six months earlier, you were promoted from day-shift supervisor. As department supervisor, you practiced the technique of "management by wandering around" (MBWA). You can be expected to show up during any of the four shifts—days (7 A.M. to 3 P.M.), evenings (3 P.M. to 11 P.M.), mornings (11 P.M. to 7 A.M.), or weekends (7 A.M. to 7 P.M.; 7 P.M. to 7 A.M.). You believe that you are familiar with all employees and know their strengths and weaknesses. Your employees know that you are willing to help out when needed even though you prefer to let employees work through problems on their own. One of your first actions was to promote George Harris to the position of evening-shift team leader.

About a month ago, you heard through the grapevine that Thomas Smith, an employee on the evening shift, had threatened Harris during a verbal confrontation witnessed by several employees. When you discussed the incident with Harris, he apologized about the incident and said he had resolved the disagreement. Harris further explained that Smith appeared to be having some personal problems that were negatively affecting his work performance, and in the discussion about his performance, Smith became angry and raised his voice. Harris assured you that the problem had been resolved. Harris explained that he was extremely busy with his new supervisory responsibilities and therefore had not bothered you about the incident.

Less than two weeks later, you heard (again through the grapevine) that Smith had been overheard to say, "I'm going to shoot that SOB!" Another visit to Harris revealed that he thought the grapevine had blown the situation out of proportion. You became concerned and contemplated going to see the director of human resources to discuss the matter. You pondered what future actions you should take.

Shortly before midnight last Thursday, the ringing of the telephone woke you from a sound sleep. The call from the on-duty emergency room policeman informed you that George Harris had been shot in the employee parking lot and was pronounced dead at the scene.

A call from the sheriff's department dispatcher informed you that Thomas Smith had strolled into the county jail, admitted the crime, and turned himself in. Smith, a 25-year veteran of Community Hospital, had allegedly waited in the parking lot with a .22-caliber handgun. Police reported that Smith shot Harris three times, twice at close range and once—the final shot—when standing over Harris, who had fallen to the ground. Smith told police that Harris "was ruining his life and giving him a hard time."

Later, as you interviewed several employees, you realized that you didn't know the workers as well as you thought. Not only were both Harris and Smith separated from their wives, but most employees knew more about the situation than you did. They also knew that Harris and Smith had recently fought over a woman.

The local newspapers were filled with additional details. Smith's attorney announced that a set of mitigating circumstances should weigh in his client's favor when the case went to trial. Smith turned himself in almost immediately and had no criminal record. Even though Smith and Harris had been friends for many years, Smith accused Harris of being hostile toward him since becoming a supervisor. Smith further claimed that Harris was having a relationship with his wife. Smith said that Harris had flowers delivered to her on the day of the shooting

You are having trouble sleeping at night and wonder what you could have done to prevent this tragedy.[1]

You Make the Call!

NEED FOR EFFECTIVE COMMUNICATION

1

Define communication and discuss its implications for effective supervisory management.

Communication

The process of transmitting information and understanding.

Communication is the process of transmitting information and understanding from one person to another. Effective communication means that there is a successful transfer of information, meaning, and understanding from a sender to a receiver. In other words, communication is the process of imparting ideas and making oneself understood by others. While it is not necessary to have agreement, there must be a mutual understanding for the exchange of ideas to be successful.

Most supervisory activities involve interaction with others, and each interaction requires skillful handling of the information process. The ability to communicate effectively is a key to supervisory success. Communication is the process that links all managerial functions. There is no managerial function that a supervisor can fulfill without communicating. In managing their departments, supervisors must explain the arrangement of work. They must instruct employees, describe what is expected of them, and counsel them. Supervisors must also report to their managers, both orally and in writing, and discuss plans with other supervisors. All of these activities require communication.

Noted author Peter Senge encourages people to

look beyond their own organizational walls for ideas and support. Because no single organization has the resources to conduct all the necessary experiments on its own, managers seek avidly to learn about each others' attempts, results, and reflections. The people who develop and exchange this information are not merely talking about the learning organization; they use it as a springboard for experiments and initiatives. With each effort they make, they create a new facet of the overall image of what the learning organization can be.[2]

Senge feels that "if there is one single thing a learning organization does well, it is helping people embrace change. People in learning organizations react more quickly when their environment changes because they know how to anticipate changes that are going to occur (which is different than trying to predict the future), and how to create the kinds of changes they want."[3] Sharing information takes a concerted effort on the part of everyone.

There is a universal belief that an organization's effectiveness depends on good communication. Yet today more messages are being sent and received but we are communicating with each other more poorly than ever before. This chapter's first "Contemporary Issue" box illustrates why communication difficulties are persistent.

Effective Communication Requires a Two-Way Exchange

Communication was defined as a process of transmitting information and understanding from one person to another. The significant point is that communication always involves at least two people, a sender and a receiver. For example, a supervisor who is alone in a room and verbally states a set of instructions does not communicate because there are no receivers present. While the lack of communication is obvious in this case, it may not be so obvious to a supervisor who sends a letter. Once the letter has been mailed, the supervisor may believe that communication has taken place. However, this

contemporary issue

Are We Good Communicators?

POINT: WE ARE NOT PREPARED!

While most chief executive officers say that more than half of their daily work routine involves giving and receiving information, little in their education prepares them for the task. Their formal training is often limited to basic writing and speaking courses in college. For others in the organization, the level of training and skills is dismal."[1]

Richard Todd at the Federal Reserve Bank of Minneapolis states, "Good writing is one of the two key abilities I focus on when hiring; the other is the ability to read critically. I can train people to do almost anything, but I don't have time to teach this."[2] A senior manager at a Fortune 500 company adds, "I hire MBAs with five to ten years of work experience. These people are utterly incapable of expressing their research findings and recommendations on paper."[3]

A Roper Starch Survey found that 57 percent of students thought they had sufficient oral communications skills while only 9 percent of employers agreed.[4] The new millennium will mean different things to different people. It will require each of us to make a resolution for continuous self-improvement—to improve our communication skills!

- I will improve my information-giving skills.
- I will improve my persuasive skills.
- I will listen more and talk less.
- I will improve my writing skills.
- I will improve my critical reading skills.

Sources: (1) Paul A. Argenti, "Should Business Schools Teach Aristotle?" *Strategy & Business* (Third Quarter, 1998), p. 4. (2) Adapted from Anne Fisher, "Readers Speak Out on Illiterate MBAs . . . ," *Fortune* (March 1, 1999), p. 242. (3) ibid. (4) See a news release, "Workforce Preparedness," *Roper Starch* (April 19, 1999), reporting the results of a study commissioned by Junior Achievement with the support of Amway exploring what employers want in graduates and what skills students are developing.

supervisor has not really communicated until and unless the letter has been received and information and understanding have been transferred successfully to the receiver (see Figure 3-1).

It cannot be emphasized too strongly that effective communication includes both sending and receiving information. A listener may hear a speaker because the listener has ears, but the listener may not understand what the speaker means. Understanding is a personal matter between people. If the idea received has the same meaning as the one intended, then we can say that effective communication has taken place. But if the idea received by a listener or reader is not the one intended, then effective communication has not been accomplished. The sender has merely transmitted spoken or written words. This does not mean that the sender and receiver must agree on a particular message or issue; it is possible to communicate and yet not agree.

Effective Communication Means Better Supervision

Some supervisors are more effective as communicators than others. Usually these supervisors recognize that communication is vital, and they give it their major attention.

FIGURE 3-1 Communication does not take place unless information is transferred successfully.

Unfortunately, many supervisors simply assume that they know how to communicate, and they do not work at developing their communication skills. Yet a supervisor's effectiveness will depend greatly on the ability to transfer information or ideas to employees. The employees must understand the supervisor's instructions to achieve their objectives. Similarly, the supervisor must know how to receive information and understand the messages sent by employees, other supervisors, and higher-level managers. Fortunately, the skills of effective communication can be developed. By becoming a more effective communicator, a supervisor will also become a more effective manager.

CHANNELS OF THE COMMUNICATION NETWORK

2

Discuss the major channels of communication available to the supervisor.

In every organization the communication network has two primary and equally important channels: the formal, or official, channels of communication and the informal channels, usually called the *grapevine.* Both channels carry messages from one person or group to another in organizations, downward, upward, and horizontally.

Formal Channels

Formal communication channels are established primarily by the organizational structure. The vertical formal channels can be visualized by following the lines of authority from the top-level executive down through the organization to supervisors and lower-level employees.

Downward Communication.   The concept of a downward formal channel of communication suggests that someone at the top issues instructions or disseminates information that managers at the next level in the hierarchy pass on to their subordinates, and so on down the line. The downward direction is the channel most frequently used by higher-level managers for communication. Downward communication helps to tie different levels together and is important for coordination. It is used by managers to start action by subordinates and to communicate instructions, objectives, policies, procedures, and other information to them. Generally, downward communication is mostly of an informative and directive nature and requires action on the part of subordinates. Downward communication from a supervisor involves giving instructions, explaining information and procedures, training employees, and engaging in other types of activities designed to guide employees in performing their work.

Upward Communication.   Upward is an equally important direction of communication in the official network. Supervisors who have managerial authority accept an obligation to keep their superiors informed and to contribute their own ideas to management. Similarly, employees should feel free to convey their ideas to their supervisors and to report on activities related to their work. Managers and supervisors should encourage a free flow of upward communication.

Upward communication usually is of an informing and reporting nature, including questions, suggestions, and complaints. This is a vital means by which managers can determine whether proper actions are taking place and obtain valuable employee insights about problems facing a unit. For example, employees may report production results and also present ideas for increasing production in the future.

Frequently, no one knows the problems and possible solutions to those problems better than the employees who are doing the work.

contemporary issue

Management By Wandering Around (MBWA) Improves Communication

The most effective leaders, from Mohandas Gandhi to Sam Walton of Wal-Mart to GE's Jack Welch, have always led from the front line, where the action is. Today, any leader, at any level, who hopes for even limited success must likewise lead from the trenches. Getting out and about (commonly known as management by wandering around, or MBWA) deals with gathering the information necessary for decision making, with making a vision concrete, with engendering commitment and risk-taking, and with caring about people.[1]

D. Michael Abrashoff, commander of the USS Benfold—one of the Navy's most modern $1 billion warships,—sits down with new crew members and tries to learn something about them: Why did they join the Navy? What's their family situation like? What are their goals while they're in the Navy—and beyond? How can I help them chart a course through life? Our bottom line is combat readiness. Getting them to contribute in a meaningful way

to each life-or-death mission is a matter of knowing who they are and where they're coming from—and linking that knowledge to our purpose.[2]

Fujio Matarai, Canon's president and CEO, says, "We are moving from stand-alone machines to networked machines. We are transforming ourselves from a company that is known for high-quality image processing into a company that is known for high-quality digital network technology." What if some young engineer comes up with a nifty new idea for enhancing that technology? How does Matarai ensure he gets the information?

"It's easy," replies Matarai. "You just visit my page on the Internet. There's an e-mail link there, and the message will come straight to me. Communication and accessibility are crucial parts of our corporate culture. It's important for me to stay in touch with everyone."[3]

The technique of *probing*—asking the right questions and encouraging everyone to ask questions, listening to those affected by the problems, learning all the facts, and "walking the talk"—and acting on and incorporating suggestions as part of the process—can lead to a more productive organization.

Sources: (1) Management guru Tom Peters has strongly advised that managers need to become highly visible and do a better job of listening to subordinates. For additional information on MBWA, see Peters, *Thriving on Chaos* (New York: Alfred A. Knopf, 1988), pp. 423–440. (2) See Polly LaBarre, "The Agenda—Grassroots Leadership," *Fast Company* (April 1999), pp. 114+. (3) "Canon: Where Communication is King," *Working Women* (May 1999), p. S-4.

Supervisors should encourage upward communication among employees and give ample attention to the information transmitted. Supervisors must show that they want employee suggestions as well as the facts and then must evaluate them promptly. As this chapter's second "Contemporary Issue" box shows, no one often knows the problems—and possible solutions—better than the employees doing the work.[4] To tap into this important source of information, supervisors must convey a genuine desire to obtain and use the ideas suggested by employees. The key word is *probe:* ask questions such as "How can we improve . . . ?" "What can we do better?" "What if . . . ?" "What will make it work?" Effective supervisors will develop good rapport with their employees and other stakeholder groups—really listen to their ideas and suggestions—and act upon their suggestions. A supervisor with effective information-getting skills usually will win the respect and admiration of colleagues and employees.

Most supervisors will acknowledge that it is often easier for them to converse with subordinates than to speak with their own manager. This is particularly true if they have ever had to tell their manager that they did not meet a schedule or that they made a mistake. Nevertheless, it is a supervisory duty to advise the manager whenever there are significant developments and to do this as soon as possible, either before or after such events occur. It is quite embarrassing to a manager to learn important news elsewhere; this can be interpreted to mean that the supervisor is not on top of his or her responsibilities.

Higher-level managers need to have complete information because they retain overall responsibility for organizational performance. Of course, this does not mean that supervisors need to pass upward every bit of trivial information. Rather, it means that supervisors should mentally place themselves in their managers' position and consider what information their managers need to perform their own jobs properly.

A supervisor's upward communication should be sent on time and in a form that will enable the manager to take necessary action. The supervisor should assemble and check the facts before passing them on. This may be quite difficult at times. A natural inclination is to "soften" the information a bit so that things will not look quite as bad in the manager's eyes as they actually are. When difficulties arise, it is best to tell the manager what is really going on even if this means admitting mistakes. Higher-level managers depend on the supervisor for reliable upward communication, just as the supervisor depends on his or her employees for the upward flow of information.

Horizontal Communication.   There is a third direction of formal communication that is essential for the efficient functioning of an organization. This is lateral, or horizontal, communication, which is concerned mainly with communication between departments or people at the same levels but in charge of different functions. A free flow of horizontal communication is needed to coordinate functions among various departments.

Horizontal communication typically involves discussions and meetings to accomplish tasks that cross departmental lines. For example, a production manager may have to contact managers of the marketing and shipping departments to ascertain progress on a delivery schedule for a product. Or someone from the human resources department may have a meeting with a number of supervisors to discuss how a new medical leave policy is to be implemented at the departmental level. Still another example is the cashier who pages the stock clerk to inquire when a particular item will be available. Without effective horizontal communication, any organization would find it virtually impossible to coordinate specialized departmental efforts toward common goals.

Informal Channels—The Grapevine

Grapevine
The informal, unofficial communication channel.

Informal communication channels, commonly referred to as the **grapevine,** are a normal outgrowth of informal and casual groupings of people on the job, of their social interactions, and of their understandable desire to communicate with one another. Every organization has its grapevine. This is a perfectly natural activity since it fulfills the employees' desires to know the latest information and to socialize with other people. The grapevine offers members of an organization an outlet for their imaginations and an opportunity to express their apprehensions in the form of rumors.

Understanding the Grapevine.   The grapevine can offer considerable insight into what employees think and feel. An alert supervisor acknowledges the grapevine's presence and tries to take advantage of it whenever possible. The grapevine often carries factual information, but sometimes it carries half-truths, rumors, private interpretations, suspicions, and other bits of distorted or inaccurate information. Research indicates that many employees have more faith and confidence in the grapevine than in what their supervisors tell them.[5] In part, this reflects a natural human tendency to trust one's peers to a greater degree than one trusts people in authority, such as supervisors or parents.

The grapevine has no definite patterns or stable membership. Its workings cannot be predicted since the path followed today is not necessarily the same as yesterday. The vast majority of employees hear information through the grapevine but some do not pass it along. Any person within an organization may become active in the grapevine on occasion, although some individuals tend to be more active than others. They feel that their prestige is enhanced by providing the latest news, and they do not hesitate to spread and embellish upon the news. The rumors they pass on serve in part as a release for their emotions, providing an opportunity to remain anonymous and say what they please without the danger of being held accountable.

The grapevine sometimes helps clarify and supplement formal communications, and it often spreads information that could not be disseminated as well or as rapidly through official channels.

The Supervisor and the Grapevine.   The supervisor should accept the fact that it is not possible to eliminate the grapevine. It is unrealistic to expect that all rumors can be stamped out, and the grapevine is certain to flourish in every organization. To cope with it, supervisors should tune in to the grapevine and learn what it is saying. They should determine who its leaders are and who is likely to spread information.

Many rumors begin in the wishful-thinking stage of employee anticipation. If employees want something badly enough, they may start passing the word along to each other. For example, if secretaries want a raise, they may start the rumor that management will offer an across-the-board raise. Nobody knows for certain where or how it started, but the story spreads rapidly because everyone wants to believe it. Of course, morale will suffer when hopes are built up in anticipation of something that does not happen. If such a story is spreading and the supervisor realizes it will lead to disappointment, the supervisor should move quickly to refute it by presenting the facts. The best cure for rumors is to expose the true facts to all employees and to give a straight answer to all questions whenever possible.

Other frequent causes of rumors are uncertainty and fear. If business is slack and management is forced to lay off some employees, stories multiply quickly. During periods of insecurity and anxiety, the grapevine becomes more active than at other times. Often the rumors are far worse than what actually will happen. If the supervisor does not disclose the actual facts to the employees, they will make up their own "facts," which may be worse than reality. Thus, much of the fear caused by uncertainty can be eliminated or reduced if the truth of what will happen is disclosed. Continuing rumors and uncertainty may be more demoralizing than even the saddest facts presented openly.

Especially during periods of economic uncertainty, the grapevine carries bits of distorted information that flow quickly through the organization.

Rumors also arise out of dislike, anger, or distrust. Rumors spread through the grapevine can be about such topics as the company, working conditions, or the private or work life happenings of its members. Rumors, like idle gossip or storytelling, are used to break the everyday boredom of organizational life or, in some extreme cases, to personally harm someone. Every once in a while there is an employee who grows to hate the company, the supervisor, or a fellow employee. The employee fabricates a sensational story about the person. The following example illustrates the difficulty encountered in dealing with unfounded malicious rumors:

Former President Lyndon B. Johnson (LBJ) loved to tell a bawdy joke about a Texas politician trying to manipulate the media with an outrageous untruth. An old Texas congressman tells his press secretary, "I want you to plant a story in the newspapers saying my opponent had sexual relations with a barn yard animal!" And when the startled aide asks what they have for proof, the old coot snorts: "Proof hell! Just get him to deny it!"[6]

Rumors such as this start small but are quickly spread by a few others who rush to fan the flames. Others will be shocked to hear such an unfounded rumor but their trust and respect for the person may be eroded. Unfortunately, in this situation there is no effective means to repudiate the rumor and build credibility. If you mention the rumor without refuting it, some people may speculate that the rumor has some truth to it. Again, the best prescription is to state the facts openly and honestly. If the supervisor does not have all the necessary information available, he or she should frankly admit this and then try to find out what the situation actually is and report it to the employees. One of the best ways to stop a rumor is to expose its untruthfulness. The supervisor should bear in mind that the receptiveness of a group of employees to rumors is directly related to the quality of the supervisor's communications and leadership. If employees believe that their supervisor is concerned about them and will make every effort to keep them informed, they will tend to disregard rumors and look to the supervisor for proper answers to their questions.

As stated before, there is no way to eliminate the grapevine, even with the best efforts made through all formal channels of communication. The supervisor, therefore, should listen to the grapevine and develop skills in dealing with it. For example, an alert supervisor might know that certain events will cause undue anxiety. In this case, the supervisor should explain immediately why such events will take place. When emergencies occur, changes are introduced, and policies are modified, the supervisor should explain why and answer all employee questions as openly as possible. Otherwise employees will make up their own explanations and often these will be incorrect. There are situations, however, when the supervisor does not have the facts, either. Here the supervisor should seek out the appropriate higher-level manager to explain what is bothering the employees and to ask for specific instructions as to what information may be given, how much may be told, and when. Also, when something happens that might cause rumors, it is helpful for supervisors to meet with their most influential employees to give them the real story. Then the employees can spread the facts before anyone else can spread the rumors.[7]

METHODS OF COMMUNICATION

3
Explain the benefits of the various methods of communication.

The preceding section described the various communication flows or channels of communication. The effective supervisor must be concerned with not only the content of communication directed at others but also the context of communication. The following sections explore various methods for delivering a message.

Behavior Is Communication

Body language

All observable actions of either the sender or the receiver.

Supervisors should realize that their behavior as managers on the job is an important form of communication to their subordinates. **Body language** is the observable actions of either the sender or the receiver. The supervisor's body language communicates something to employees whether it is intended to do so or not. Gestures, a handshake, a shrug of the shoulder, a smile, even silence—all of these have meaning and may be interpreted differently by different people. For example, a supervisor's warm smile and posture slightly bent toward employees can send out positive signals to the employees. Conversely, a frown on a supervisor's face may communicate more than 10 minutes of oral discussion or a printed page.

A word of caution: Body language does not have universal meaning as illustrated in Figure 3-2 (see page 70). The message sent by different expressions or postures varies from situation to situation and particularly from culture to culture. Touching, as illustrated by the traditional "pat on the back," may be perceived differently by different people. Studies report that women distinguish between touching for the purpose of conveying warmth and friendship and touching to convey sexual attraction, while men

FIGURE 3-2 Olympic Games Staff working with international visitors were trained in what to say and how to gesture. The illustration shows several examples.

OK Sign
France: you're a zero; **Japan:** please give me coins; **Brazil:** an obscene gesture; **Mediterranean countries:** an obscene gesture

Thumbs Up
Australia: up yours; **Germany:** the number one; **Japan:** the number five; **Saudi Arabia:** I'm winning; **Ghana:** an insult; **Malaysia:** the thumb is used to point rather than the finger

Thumbs Down
Most countries: something is wrong or bad

Thumb and Forefinger
Most countries: money; **France:** something is perfect; **Mediterranean:** a vulgar gesture

Open Palm
Greece: an insult dating to ancient times; **West Africa:** you have five fathers, an insult akin to calling someone a bastard

Source: *Atlanta Committee for the Olympic Games* as presented by Sam Ward, "The Olympic Don'ts of Gestures," *USA Today* (Thursday, March 14, 1996), p. 7C.

may not.[8] A male supervisor must recognize that misinterpretation of his touching female employees may generate resentment or even charges of sexual harassment.

A supervisor's inaction is a way of communicating, just as unexplained action may communicate a meaning that was not intended. For example, a supervisor arranged to have some equipment removed from the production floor without telling the employees that the equipment was removed because it needed mechanical modifications. To the employees, who feared a threatened shutdown, this unexplained action communicated a message that the supervisor had no intention of sending.

Oral and Written Communication

Spoken and written words are the most widely used forms of communication in any organization. They also constitute a challenge to every supervisor who wishes to communicate effectively. Words can be tricky. Instructions that mean one thing to one employee

Body language often communicates more than words.

may have a different meaning to someone else. There is a story about a collection agency supervisor who told a new employee, "Get tough with Mr. Stump. His account is two months overdue." Upon checking an hour later, the supervisor found that the new employee had started foreclosure proceedings against Mr. Stump. Obviously, instructions like "get tough" can be interpreted in several different ways!

Since words are the essence of oral and written communication, supervisors should constantly try to improve their skills in speaking, listening, writing, and reading. A well-balanced communication system uses both written and oral media. Supervisors do not have as many occasions to use the written medium since a high proportion of supervisory communication takes place by word of mouth.

Oral communication generally is superior to written communication because it facilitates better understanding and takes less time. This is true both with telephone and face-to-face communication. Face-to-face discussion between a supervisor and employees is the principal method of two-way communication. Employees like to see and hear the supervisor in person, and no written communication can be as effective as an interpersonal discussion. In a face-to-face discussion, both employees and supervisors can draw meaning from body language as well as the oral message. Another reason for the greater effectiveness of oral communication is that most people can express themselves more easily and completely by voice than by a letter or memo.

Probably the greatest single advantage of oral communication is that it can provide an immediate opportunity for determining whether or not effective communication has been accomplished between the sender and receiver. Although the response may be only an expression on the receiver's face, the sender can judge how the receiver is reacting to what is being said. Oral communication enables the sender to find out immediately what the receiver hears and does not hear. Oral communication enables the receiver to ask questions immediately if the meaning is not clear, and the sender can clarify. The human voice can impart a message with meaning and clarity that pages of written words cannot convey. Body language and tone of voice help convey the message.

The principal problem with oral communication is that usually there is no permanent record of it and, over time, speakers' and listeners' memories will blur the meaning of what was conveyed. This is why many supervisors follow up certain meetings and discussions with some type of memorandum or document to have a written basis for recalling what was discussed.

To reiterate, a supervisor must always remember that effective communication takes place only when the meaning received by the listener is the same as that which the sender intended to send. Supervisors who are effective communicators know how to speak clearly and be aware of the listener. They are sensitive to the many barriers to effective communication that can distort communication lines. They know how to over-

Pictures, charts, cartoons, and symbols can be effective visual aids.

come these barriers, how to "clear the pipelines." Such supervisors recognize that a speaker and a listener are unique individuals who live in different worlds and that many factors can interfere with messages that pass between them.

A Picture Is Worth a Thousand Words

The power of visual media in conveying meaning to people should never be underestimated. Pictures, charts, cartoons, and symbols can be effective visual aids, and the supervisor should employ them where appropriate. They are particularly effective if used in connection with well-chosen words to complete a message. Businesses make extensive use of visual aids such as blueprints, charts, drafts, models, and posters to communicate information. Movies, videos, and comic strips demonstrate the power of visual media in communicating.

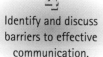

Identify and discuss barriers to effective communication.

BARRIERS TO EFFECTIVE COMMUNICATION

Human differences and organizational conditions can create obstacles that distort messages between people. These obstacles can be referred to as **noise.** Misunderstandings and conflicts can develop when communication breaks down. These breakdowns not only are costly in terms of money but also create dilemmas that hurt teamwork and morale. Many supervisory human relations problems are traceable to faulty communication since the way a supervisor communicates with subordinates constitutes the essence of their relationships.

Noise
Obstacles that distort messages between people.

Language and Vocabulary Differences

People vary greatly in their ability to convey meaning that others understand. For example, words in themselves can be confusing even though language is the principal vehicle people use to communicate with each other. Even in regions of the world with common languages, cultural differences, accents, dialects, and word meanings can be profound. People at different levels or in different departments sometimes seem to speak in different "languages" even though they are actually speaking English.[9] For example, an accounting department supervisor may use specialized words that may be meaningless when conversing with the computer technician. Similarly, if the information technologist uses "technobabble" when interfacing with the accounting department supervisor, the latter will probably be confused. This is the communication problem known as **jargon,** or the use of words that are peculiar to a person's particular background or specialty.

Jargon

The use of words that are peculiar to a particular occupation or specialty.

Another consideration relates to the different languages that may be spoken in a work environment. Some Hispanic Americans and native Mexicans may speak Spanish fluently but have difficulty with English. Or a native of Southeast Asia may speak Vietnamese but very little English. It has even been observed that some African-Americans have unique dialect variations of English (sometimes called Ebonics) and that they use certain words that are unfamiliar to most white people. Recently, an increasing number of immigrants from various Asian, Eastern European, Central American, and Latin American countries has led to a clamor from some that "English only" be spoken in the workplace.

Semantics

The multiple meaning of words.

Another communication problem lies in the multiple meanings of words, known as **semantics.** Words can mean different things to different people, particularly in the English language, which is one of the most difficult in the world. The way some words are used in sentences can cause people to interpret messages in a manner other than the way that was intended. *Roget's Thesaurus,* a dictionary of synonyms, identifies the numerous meanings that commonly used words can have. Where a word can have multiple meanings, the meaning intended must be clarified since listeners tend to interpret words based on their own perceptions, past experiences, and cultural backgrounds.

The question is not whether the employee ought to understand the words; it is whether the employee does understand. Therefore, supervisors should strive to use plain, direct words in brief, uncomplicated statements. If necessary, they should restate messages in several ways to clarify the proper (semantic) meaning or context that was intended.

Too Much Information—TMI[10]

In today's business world, employees and supervisors are inundated with hundreds of bits of information every day. Many of these informational messages are long and wordy, which can result in misunderstanding and lost productivity. Why can't people just "keep it short and simple?" Look at the typical written message—it is loaded with words that have little or no bearing on the intended purpose. Keeping it short and simple means getting a message down to as few words and sentences as possible. Consultant Gary Blake identified a group of words that can be trimmed for more thoughtful and effective writing:

- enclosed please find
- pursuant to your request
- thank you in advance for your cooperation
- contained herein
- please do not hesitate to contact me
- under separate cover[11]

Studies have indicated that supervisors spend between 70 and 90 percent of their time sending and receiving information. Noted author Tom Peters stated, "The market will demand that each employee be . . . turned into a business person. Yes, it means being empowered. It also means having all the organization's information at your fingertips—make that everyone's fingertips."[12]

The Internet and TMI.   With the advent of electronic forms of communication, it seems that employees should have all the information they need to do their jobs. On one hand, companies want employees to have access to the best and latest information and resources to do a better job. On the other hand, Internet use can become a time-consuming activity for some employees. Many small business owners have cited the possibility of lost productivity as the major reason for not letting employees use the Internet.[13] Just how are employees using the Internet? It is estimated that U.S. businesses lose 26 million man-hours a year to on-line game playing by employees, and 68 percent of companies have detected employees surfing sexually explicit Web sites.[14]

No one would disagree that an employee's ability to gather information is very valuable. But what information do they need to do their job? The data presented in Figure 3-3 illustrates the dimensions of too much information. The Internet has the potential to adversely affect productivity. Supervisors need to tell employees what is expected—what is and what isn't allowed. Effective supervisors (1) encourage everyone to ask questions and gather essential information, (2) keep their messages short and simple, and (3) avoid giving employees TMI.

Status and Position

The organization's structure, with its several levels in the managerial hierarchy, creates a number of status levels among members of the organization. **Status** refers to the attitudes that are held toward a position and its occupant by the members of the organization. There is a recognized status difference between an executive-level position and a supervisory-level position and between supervisors and employees. Differences in status and position become apparent as one level tries to communicate with another. For example, a supervisor who tries to convey enthusiasm to an employee about higher production and profits for the company may find that the employee is indifferent to these types of company goals. The employee may be primarily concerned with achieving higher personal wages and security. Thus, the supervisor and the employee may repre-

Status

Attitudes toward a person based on the position he or she occupies.

FIGURE 3-3

Too much information.

3,062	Number of U.S. newspapers and magazine articles published in the past two years that talk about information overload.
15,652	Number of Web sites discussing information overload.
40%	Percentage of workers who say their duties are interrupted more than six times an hour by intrusive communication.
40%	Percentage of workers who repeatedly receive messages that say the same thing.
190	Number of messages in all media sent and received daily by the average *Fortune 1000* office worker.
80%	Percentage of information that is filed but never used.
150	Hours that the average person spends looking for lost or misplaced information each year.
71%	Percentage of workers who say their main job is tracking down information.
1	Number of seconds it takes the WWW to expand by 17 pages.

Source: Adapted from extensive list presented in "Data, Data," *Inc.* (January 1999), p. 70.

sent different points of view merely by virtue of their positions in the company, and this may present a serious obstacle to understanding each other.

When employees listen to a message from the supervisor, several other factors become operative. They evaluate the supervisor's words in light of their own backgrounds and experiences. They also take into account the supervisor's personality and position. It is difficult for employees to separate a message from the feelings that they have about the supervisor who sends the message. Therefore, the employees may infer nonexistent motives in the message. For example, union members may be inclined to interpret a management statement in very uncomplimentary terms if they are convinced that management is trying to weaken the union.

Obstacles due to status and position also can distort the upward flow of communication when subordinates are anxious to impress management. Employees may screen information passed up the line; they may tell the supervisor only what they think the latter likes to hear and omit or soften the unpleasant details. This problem is known as **filtering.** By the same token, supervisors are also anxious to make a favorable impression when talking to managers in higher positions. They may fail to pass on important information to their managers because they believe that the information would reflect unfavorably on their own supervisory abilities.

Filtering

The process of omitting or softening unpleasant details.

Resistance to Change or New Ideas

Many people prefer things as they are, and they do not welcome changes in their working situation. If a message is intended to convey a change or new idea to employees—

something that will upset their work assignments, positions, or part of their daily routine—the natural inclination is for the employees to resist the message. It is normal for people to prefer that their existing environment remain the status quo. Consequently, a message that will change this equilibrium may be greeted with suspicion. The employees' receiving apparatus works just like a screen, rejecting new ideas if they conflict with a currently comfortable situation.

In the same fashion, most listeners are likely to receive that portion of a message which confirms their present beliefs and will tend to ignore whatever conflicts with those beliefs. Sometimes beliefs are so fixed that the listeners do not hear anything at all. Even if they hear a statement, they will either reject it as false or find a convenient way of twisting its meaning to fit their own perceptions.

Receivers usually hear what they wish to hear. If they are insecure or fearful in their positions, this barrier becomes even more difficult to overcome. Supervisors often are confronted with situations in which their employees do not fully attend to what is being said. Employees become so preoccupied with their own thoughts that they give attention to only those ideas they want to hear and select only those parts of the total message that they can accept. Bits of information that they do not like or that are irreconcilable to their biases are brushed aside, not heard at all, or easily explained away. Supervisors must be aware of these possibilities, particularly when a message intends to convey some change that may interfere with the normal routine or customary working environment.

Perceptual Barriers

Deborah Tannen's book, *That's Not What I Meant!*, shows that people have different conversational styles. When people from different parts of the country or the world or of different ethnic or class backgrounds talk to each other, it is very likely that their words will not be understood exactly as they were meant.[15] In the workplace, we all work with people who are different from us. The message is often misunderstood because we all see the world differently. Thus, perception is one of the major barriers to effective communication. Some barriers arise from deep-rooted personal feelings, prejudice, and physical conditions.

Stereotyping

The perception that all people in a certain group share common attitudes, values, and beliefs.

The perception that all people in a certain group share common attitudes, values, and beliefs is called **stereotyping.** Stereotyping influences how people respond to others. It becomes a barrier to effective communication as people are categorized into certain groups because of their gender, age, or race instead of being treated as unique individuals. Managers need to be aware of stereotyping because it can adversely affect communication.

In *You Just Don't Understand*, Tannen illustrates a common problem. In the workplace, if women's and men's styles of conversation are shown to be different, it is usually the women who are told to change. Tannen asks the reader to consider the following conversation that took place between a couple in their car:

The woman had asked, "Would you like to stop for a drink?" Her husband had answered truthfully, "No," and they hadn't stopped. He was later frustrated to learn that his wife was annoyed because she had wanted to stop for a drink. He wondered, "Why didn't she just say what she wanted?" "Why did she play games with me?" The wife was annoyed not because she had not gotten her way, but because her preference had not been considered. From her point of view, she had shown concern for her husband's wishes, but he had no concern for hers.

Tannen further comments that, "Both parties have different but equally valid points. In understanding what went wrong, the man must realize that when she asks what he would like, she is not asking an information question but rather starting a negotiation about what both would like. The woman must realize that when he answers 'yes' or 'no' he is not making a non-negotiable demand. Men and women must both make adjustments."[16] It is sad that neither party worked toward what is really important and targeted that with specific inquiries. Imagine how the conversation could have gone: "No, not really. But if you'd like to do that it would be ok with me." Being considerate of the other person and keeping an open mind will go a long way toward improving understanding. Finally, Tannen's illustration clearly indicates the importance of "saying what you mean and meaning what you say."

Insensitive Words and Poor Timing

Sometimes, one party or the other uses so-called "killer phrases" in a conversation. Comments such as "That's the stupidest idea I've ever heard!" "You do understand, don't you?" or "Do you really know what you're talking about?" can kill conversation. Often, the result is that the receiver of the "killer phrase" becomes silent and indifferent to the sender. Sometimes, the receiver takes offense and directs anger back to the sender. Insensitive, offensive language or impetuous responses can cause difficulty in understanding. It is not difficult to think of many workplace illustrations of these occurrences. Often, the conflict that results impedes the accomplishment of organizational goals.

Another barrier to effective communication is the timing factor. Employees come to the workplace with extra "baggage"—that is, they sometimes carry to work events that have happened off the job. From personal experience, you can understand why it is hard to pay attention to someone else when you are anticipating an upcoming test. You pretend to listen politely but you probably are not listening carefully. Under these circumstances your attentiveness and responsiveness to information will not be as the other party expected.

Since barriers to effective communication are numerous and diverse, supervisors should not assume that the messages they send will be received as they were intended. In fact, supervisors may want to assume that most of the messages they send are likely to be distorted. If supervisors operate from this premise, they more likely will do everything within their power to overcome these barriers and improve the chances for mutual understanding.

Many companies have installed "impersonal media"—e-mail, fax, Internet, PC-based video conferencing, and voice-mail systems. Such systems enable employees to have almost immediate contact with many more people. However, there is a downside. Rambling is an oft-cited complaint by those receiving voice-mail messages. Some callers forget their phone number or reason for ringing, wasting other people's valuable time as they babble and fumble through notes. Don't say your message so fast that it's like a blur. Remember to identify yourself clearly and concisely. Susan Bixler, who counsels business executives on social graces, emphasizes the basics of voice mail: "I have to tell them to be articulate, never to eat, drink, chew gum or suck on candy while they're leaving their messages."[17] Properly used, these electronic communication systems can help provide information in a timely manner.

Inability to Create Meaning

Communication begins when the sender encodes an idea or thought. For example, when a manager sets out to draft a response on a particular issue, he or she addresses several types of questions: (1) What *conclusion* have I formed about this issue? What *claim* do I want to make? (2) What *evidence,* or reasons, can I offer, in support of my claim? (3) What *data* can I provide to back it up?[18]

Decoding is the receiver's version of encoding. It is when the receiver puts the message into a form that he or she can interpret. In order to analyze the position of the manager on the issue, the employee must find and weight management's claim, evidence, and data. But the receiver of the message can ask more: Does the writer's choice of words influence the way I feel about this issue? Do I agree with management's basic premise (belief) or with the assumptions that underlie their position? Often the receiver's interpretation of a message will differ from what the sender intended. To examine argument analysis, study Candidate ZZZ's letter to the editor in the fictional town of Okay (Figure 3-4). Read the boxed comments as you go along.

5
Describe ways to overcome the communication barriers.

OVERCOMING BARRIERS TO EFFECTIVE COMMUNICATION

Most techniques for overcoming communication barriers are relatively easy and straightforward. Supervisors will recognize them as techniques that they use sometimes but not as frequently as they should. A supervisor once remarked, "Most of these are just common sense." The reply to this comment was simply, "Yes, but have you ever observed how uncommon common sense sometimes is?" The 1996 Olympic Games staff were urged to use common sense in their communications with others. Figure 3-5 (see page 80), for example, cites several common-sense guides. The lesson to be learned is that "if you do not know, find out—then follow up." In short, supervisors must take a proactive approach to ensure that communication is effective.

Preparation and Planning

A first major step toward becoming a better communicator is to avoid speaking or writing until the message to be communicated has been thought through to the point that it is clear in the sender's mind. Only if supervisors can express their ideas in an organized fashion can they hope for others to understand. Therefore, before communicat-

FIGURE 3-4   A letter to the editor.

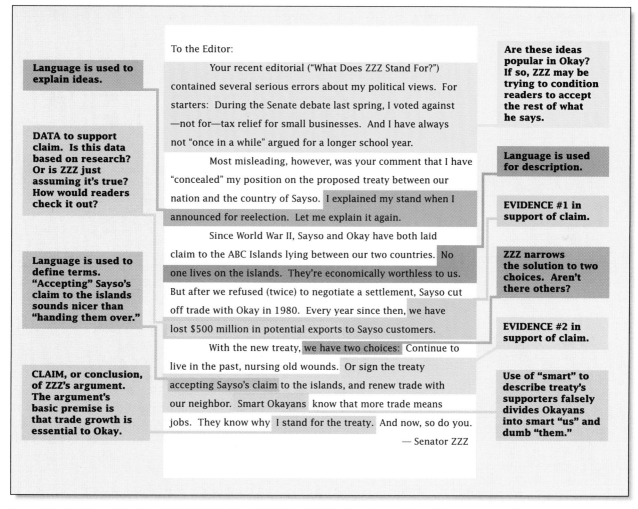

Source: Adapted with permission from *Critical Thinking About Critical Issues* (Williamsburg, VA: Learning Enrichment, Inc., © 1995), pp. 9–10.

ing, supervisors should know what they want and should plan the sequence of steps necessary to attain their objectives (see Figure 3-6 on page 81). Regardless of the method of communication—face-to-face; written; signs, posters, graphs, or charts; fax; or e-mail—supervisors need to consider many elements before sending the message.

For example, if supervisors want to make a job assignment, they should first analyze the job thoroughly so they are able to describe it properly. Additionally, the employee's ability to do the job depends on determining what information is important. Therefore, the supervisor needs to plan the method of communication—visual (the body language they present), vocal (the tone of voice they use), verbal (the words they choose), and emotional (the feelings they project).

FIGURE 3-5

Communication and common sense.

Most of the policies and procedures for the 1996 Olympic Games staff were not unusual; they were common sense. Among the guidelines offered were:

- Have a friendly, helpful attitude.
- Be sure to say "please," "thank you," and "you're welcome."
- Pointing with your fingers is considered offensive in several cultures. To indicate a direction or to point to a person or object, use your full hand, palm up.
- Try not to use slang expressions, like "you bet" or "what's up?" Some visitors will look up at the ceiling, trying to figure out what you're talking about.
- Remember to smile. However, even smiles don't translate the same way. The Japanese will smile when they're feeling anger or sadness.
- Enunciate clearly and be precise.
- If someone asks a question, *do not guess* at the answer. If you do not know for sure, say, "I'm not sure about that, but I will find out for you." *Then follow through.*
- If you do not know the right way to deal with a problem, *do not hesitate to ask questions* if something is unclear to you.
- There are times when you will need help completing a job or handling an assignment. *Ask for help when you need it.*

Source: *Olympic Games Staff Handbook: Your Guide to Making Every Moment Count During the Centennial Games* (Atlanta, 1996), pp. 29–32.)

If supervisors need to deliver bad news to their boss, they should study the problem until it is so clear in their minds that they will have little difficulty explaining it. They may want to turn themselves 180° and attempt to see the situation from the boss's point of view. The important points to be covered should be written down so that nothing is left out of the conversation. A point of caution: Don't take only gripes or problems to your boss without taking some suggestions on how to resolve the situation or prevent it from happening again. If a communication is to involve a disciplinary action, supervisors should have sufficiently investigated the case and compiled all relevant information before issuing a penalty. All of these illustrations clearly demonstrate that communication should not begin until supervisors know what they ought to say in relation to what they want achieved.

Using Feedback

Feedback

The receiver's verbal or nonverbal response to a message.

Among the methods available to improve communication, **feedback** is by far the most important. In communication, feedback is the receiver's verbal or nonverbal response to a message. Feedback can be used to determine whether or not the receiver understood the message and to get the receiver's reaction to it. To obtain feedback, the sender can initiate feedback by using questions, discussion, signals, or clues. Merely asking the receiver, "Do you understand?" and receiving a "yes" as an answer may not be enough

FIGURE 3-6

Steps to achieve your communication objective.

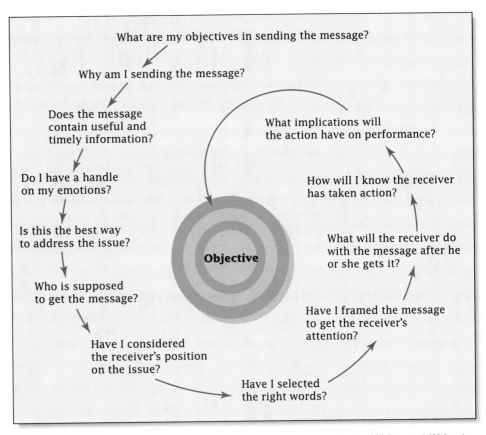

What are my objectives in sending the message?

Why am I sending the message?

Does the message contain useful and timely information?

Do I have a handle on my emotions?

Is this the best way to address the issue?

Who is supposed to get the message?

Have I considered the receiver's position on the issue?

Have I selected the right words?

Have I framed the message to get the receiver's attention?

What will the receiver do with the message after he or she gets it?

How will I know the receiver has taken action?

What implications will the action have on performance?

Objective

Source: Content for Figure 3-6 generated from ideas presented in the following: Curtis Sittenfeld, "How to WOW an Audience—Every Time," *Fast Company* (September 1999), pp. 86+; Carol Leonetti Dannhauser, "Shut Up and Listen," *Working Women* (May 1999), p. 41; Sean Morrison, "Keep It Simple," *Training* (January 1999), p. 152; Douglas Stone, Bruce Patten and Sheila Heen, *Difficult Conversations: How to Discuss What Matters Most* (New York: Viking, 1999); Paul A. Argenti, "Should Business Schools Teach Aristotle?" *Strategy & Business* (Third Quarter, 1998), pp. 4–6; and A. Blanton Godfrey, "Quality Management: Getting the Word Out," *Quality Digest* (June 1996), p. 7.

feedback. More information than this is usually required to make sure that a message was actually received as it was intended.

A simple way to do this is to observe the receiver and to judge that person's responses by nonverbal clues such as an expression of bewilderment or understanding, a raised eyebrow, a frown, or the direction or movement of eyes. Of course, this kind of feedback is possible only in face-to-face communication, and this is one of the major advantages of this form of communication.

Perhaps the best feedback technique to ensure that the sender's message is understood is for the sender to ask the receiver to "paraphrase" or "play back" the information just received. This is much more satisfactory than merely asking whether the instructions are clear. The process of restating in the receiver's own words rather than "parroting back verbatim" all or part of the sender's message shows that communication has taken place. If the receiver states the content of the message, then the sender will know what the receiver has heard and understood. At that time, the receiver may ask additional questions and request comments which the speaker can provide immediately.

The feedback technique is also applicable when a supervisor is on the receiving end of a message from an employee or a higher-level manager. To clear up possible misunderstandings, a supervisor can say, "Just to make sure I understand what you want, let me repeat in my own words that message you just gave me." An employee or a manager will appreciate this initiative to improve the accuracy of communication. A similar technique to paraphrasing is reflective feedback. This is used when the supervisor reflects the feelings (emotions) expressed by the sender. To illustrate, the supervisor might say, "You feel _____ because _____."

Feedback also can be helpful when written communication is involved. Before sending a written message, the supervisor can have someone else—perhaps a colleague—read the message for comprehension. Most writing can be improved. It may be necessary to develop several drafts of a written message and have various people provide feedback as to which draft is the most clearly stated and readily interpreted.

Similarly, after sending a memo, fax, letter, or e-mail message, it often is desirable to discuss the written correspondence over the telephone or face to face to make sure that the receiver understands it. When a supervisor receives a written message from someone else and there is any doubt about its meaning, the supervisor should contact the sender to discuss the message and clarify it as necessary.

Direct and Clear Language

Another sound approach to attaining effective communication is to use words that are understandable and as clear as possible. Supervisors should avoid long, technical, and complicated words. They should use language that the receivers will be able to understand without difficulty. Jargon or "shop talk" should be used only if the receiver is comfortable with it. The old "KISS" approach is usually a good motto to remember: "Keep It Short and Simple."

A Calm Atmosphere

Tension and anxiety were mentioned previously as being serious barriers to effective communication. If a supervisor tries to communicate with an employee who is visibly upset, chances for mutual understanding are minimal. It is much better to communicate when both parties are calm and not burdened by unusual tension or stress. One of the best ways for a supervisor to ensure the proper atmosphere for communicating or discussing a problem with an employee is to set an appointed time for a meeting in a quiet room. This usually enables both parties to prepare to discuss the problem in a calm and unhurried fashion. Similarly, if supervisors want to discuss something with their managers, they should arrange for an appointment at a time and place that is mutually conducive to having an uninterrupted discussion.

Taking Time and Effort to Listen

Another approach to overcoming barriers to communication is for both the sender and the receiver to take more time to listen, that is, to give the other person full opportunity to express what is on his or her mind. The supervisor who listens to what the employee is saying will learn more about the employee's values and attitudes toward the working environment. The supervisor should provide feedback by restating the employee's message from time to time and asking, "Is this what you mean?" A supervisor should always patiently listen to what the employee has to say. Intensive listening helps to reduce misunderstandings, and by listening the supervisor will be better able to respond in ways that are appropriate to the concerns of the employee.

One of the worst things supervisors can do is to sit with faked attention while their minds are on mental excursions. The supervisor can avoid this situation by politely stating, "Right now is not a convenient time for us to have this discussion. It needs my full attention, and if we can reschedule this meeting for 10:00 in the morning, you will have my undivided attention." Attentiveness to the speaker will go a long way toward building a climate of trust. Figure 3-7 contains some practical dos and don'ts for effective listening.

FIGURE 3-7

The dos and don'ts of effective listening.

DOS FOR LISTENING

1. Do adopt the attitude that you will always have something to learn.
2. Do take time to listen, give the speaker your full attention, and hear the speaker out.
3. Do withhold judgment until the speaker is finished. Strive to locate the main ideas of the message.
4. Do try to determine the work meanings within the context of the speaker's background. Listen for what is being implied as well as what is being said.
5. Do establish eye contact with the speaker. Read body language. Smile, nod, and give an encouraging sign when the speaker hesitates.
6. Do ask questions at appropriate times to be sure that you understand the speaker's message.
7. Do restate the speaker's idea at appropriate moments to make sure that you have it correctly.

DON'TS FOR LISTENING

1. Don't listen with only half an ear by "tuning out" the speaker and pretending that you are listening.
2. Don't unnecessarily interrupt the speaker or finish the speaker's statement because of impatience or wanting to respond immediately.
3. Don't fidget or doodle while listening. Don't let other distractions bother you and the speaker.
4. Don't confuse facts with opinions.
5. Don't show disapproval or insensitivity to the speaker's feelings.
6. Don't respond until the speaker has said what he or she wants to say.
7. Don't become defensive.

Listening is a very important part of the supervisor's job, whether in one-on-one conversations or in meetings. The ability to listen is critical to success as a supervisor. Therefore, supervisors should work to develop their listening skills every chance they get.

Repetition of Messages

It is often helpful to repeat a message several times, preferably using different words or different methods. For example, a new medical insurance claim process might be mentioned in a staff meeting, discussed in an article in the company newsletter, posted on the bulletin board, and maintained in a policy file available for employee use. The degree of repetition will depend largely on the content of the message and the experience and background of the employees or other people involved in the communication. However, the message should not be repeated so much that it gets ignored because it sounds too familiar or boring. In case of doubt, some repetition probably is safer than none.

Reinforcing Words with Action

To succeed as communicators, supervisors need to complement their words with appropriate and consistent actions. Supervisors communicate much by what they do, that is, by their actions; and as the cliché goes, actions speak louder than words (see Figure 3-8).

FIGURE 3-8

A supervisor communicates by actions as much as words.

OFFICE OPEN 9:00 to 5:00

SUPERVISOR

Therefore, one of the best ways to give meaning to messages is to act accordingly. If verbal announcements are backed up by action, the supervisor's credibility will be enhanced. However, if the supervisor says one thing but does another, sooner or later the employees will be influenced primarily by what the supervisor does.

What Call Did You Make?

Communication is a two-way street. It is easy to tell the other person what to do, but it takes real skill to listen to what the person is really saying. Skillful communication depends not only on what you say, but on how you say it and when you say it. It is very easy for supervisors to get so wrapped up in the pressures of their work that they do not effectively listen to what is being said.

This "You Make the Call" situation exemplifies the problems that occur when people hear what is said but do not understand the full meaning of the message. Clearly, it is "what was not being said" that was critical. The barriers to communication prevented understanding. George Harris failed to tell Carl O'Connor the unpleasant details of his personal problems and the altercation with Thomas Smith. Harris may not have wanted to share information that might reflect unfavorably on his abilities as team leader.

In a sense, everyone involved in this tragedy shares some culpability for the events that occurred. As Carl O'Connor, you need to assess the entire situation, recognizing and accepting that the situation occurred and that life goes on. Would you have felt less guilt if the incident occurred off company premises? Probably, but the point is that the incident happened and you can't turn the clock back. You need to learn from this experience and develop a work culture where all employees can speak their minds and you can count on everyone to be open and honest.

Most of the principles of effective communication were violated. It appears that you did not adequately take the time to gather information. You intended to discuss the grapevine concerns with the director of human resources but never got around to it. Setting priorities and dealing with potential crisis situations in a timely fashion is a requisite skill for effective supervision. Immediately upon hearing through the grapevine of the threats made by Smith, you needed to interview both employees—separately and together—and involve the human resources director. While it may not have been comfortable for you to do this or he may have felt that by interviewing Smith you would be diluting Harris's authority, it was the right thing to do. Sometimes managers, no matter how carefully they plan the message, say the wrong things. The ability to ask probing (information-getting) questions, regardless of their unpleasantness, will make you more effective as a supervisor.

Remember that your ability to do the job is dependent on information. The information was available and you failed to follow up. You must assume responsibility for improving your communication skills. Nothing is gained by finger-pointing or self-pity.

A thorough analysis of this "You Make the Call" situation requires more specific knowledge about preventing/dealing with workplace violence (Chapter 15) and strategies for resolving conflict (Chapter 17).

SUMMARY

1

Effective communication means that a successful transfer of information and understanding takes place between a sender and a receiver. The ability to communicate effectively is one of the most important qualities leading to supervisory success.

Communication is a two-way process. Communication is successful only if the receiver understands the message. The receiver need not agree with the message, just understand it as the sender intended.

2

Formal channels of communication operate downward, upward, and horizontally. These communication channels primarily serve to link people and departments in order to accomplish organizational objectives. Supervisors communicate downward to their employees. Equally important is the supervisor's duty to communicate upward to management and horizontally with supervisors in other departments. In addition to formal channels, every company has an informal channel, called the *grapevine.* The grapevine can carry rumors as well as facts. Supervisors should stay in touch with what is being transmitted on the grapevine and counteract rumors with facts where necessary.

3

Methods of communication range from oral, written, and visual to the unspoken body language. Spoken and written words are the most important means of communication. However, body language—a person's actions, gestures, posture, and so forth—also communicates, often in more powerful ways than words themselves. Oral communication is generally superior because it enables face-to-face interaction. Feedback is instantaneous. Written words and visuals are often preferred because of their permanency. Visual aids, such as pictures, charts, and videos, can be powerful tools in conveying meaning.

4

Human differences and organizational conditions can create obstacles, called *noise,* which distort messages between people. The use of jargon that the receiver does not understand can impede communication. Also, words have different meanings, so the sender must make sure that the receiver understood the intended meaning. However, TMI (too much information) is just as bad as giving employees too little information. Information overload has become a major problem in today's society.

People who have different status or position levels within an organization bring different points of view to an interaction, which can distort meaning. People may "filter out" unpleasant information in communications with their managers. Also, people's natural resistance to change can cause them to avoid "hearing" messages that upset the status quo or conflict with their own beliefs.

Individuals perceive the world from the context of their own backgrounds and prejudices. Perceptual barriers between sender and receiver, such as biases and stereotyping, can impede communication, as can conversation-killing phrases and poor timing.

Both sender and receiver share responsibility to ensure that information is successfully transferred. The inability of the receiver to properly analyze the content of the message causes misunderstanding. Misunderstanding may lead to suspicion and a lack of trust.

5

To overcome communication barriers, supervisors should adequately prepare what they wish to communicate. During face-to-face communication, the receiver's verbal and nonverbal responses, called *feedback,* can help the supervisor determine whether or not the receiver understood the message. Asking the receiver to restate the message is one feedback technique that helps verify understanding. For written communication, the supervisor can obtain feedback by asking a colleague to comment on the message before it is sent and by discussing it with receivers after it is sent to check understanding.

Using clear, direct language that the receiver can understand will facilitate communication. Also, both parties should agree on a time to talk when both parties will not be overly stressed and will have time to really listen to each other. Repeating the message in various words and formats can improve understanding, if not done to excess. Also, to be effective, words must be reinforced by consistent actions.

KEY TERMS

Communication (page 61)
Grapevine (page 66)
Body language (page 69)
Noise (page 72)
Jargon (page 73)

Semantics (page 73)
Status (page 74)
Filtering (page 75)
Stereotyping (page 76)
Feedback (page 80)

QUESTIONS FOR DISCUSSION

1. What is meant by effective communication? Why is mutual understanding at the heart of any definition of effective communication?
2. In the electronic age, how have changes in technology altered the ways that you communicate with other people on a day-to-day basis? What can the effective supervisor do to ensure that understanding takes place?
3. Why should the supervisor be able to use all the communication channels? Relate this to Carl O'Connor, the supervisor in the opening "You Make the Call." How can a supervisor facilitate good upward communication?
4. Discuss the techniques by which a supervisor can cope with the grapevine effectively.
5. How should management respond to a false rumor that is spreading through the organization?
6. Discuss the various methods of communication used in an organization. Why is the old cliché that actions speak louder than words applicable to the supervisory position?
7. Think of some good speakers you know. Make a list of the things they do that make them effective.
8. What types of communication barriers exist in a classroom setting? How can they be overcome?
9. In *Dirty Politics,* Kathleen H. Jamieson argues that "the first test of any political claim . . . [should be]: Is it factually accurate?"[18] The same is true of any management communication. Select any five statements from ZZZ's letter (Figure 3-4) that could be checked for accuracy. List the five statements and describe how each might be verified for accuracy.
10. What specific steps do you need to take to improve your listening skills?

SKILLS APPLICATIONS

Skills Application 3-1: Unpleasant Situations

1. Read the following situations.
   a. An employee is performing a task improperly and you show him or her how you want it done. The employee says: "I was doing this before you were born and I don't need your advice."

    b. An employee has suddenly developed a tardiness problem. When you confront him/her, he/she says: "My spouse is an alcoholic; I am worried about her/him. I have to get the kids breakfast and send them off to school before I can get here."

    c. One of your better employees has been caught in the organization's downsizing. As you hand him/her a "pink slip," he/she says: "I don't know what I'm going to do. I guess my kids will have to drop out of college and go to work."

2. For each situation, make a list of all the questions that you will ask to determine the meaning of the employee's message.

3. Decide on an appropriate response.

4. Pair up with a classmate. Decide which of you will play the supervisor and which will be the employee. (We suggest alternating roles for each situation so that both of you get an opportunity to play the supervisory role.) Pick up the action from where the situation leaves off.

5. Evaluate the interaction. Are you pleased with your follow-up to the situation? What did you do well? What could you have done more effectively?

Skills Application 3-2: Dealing With Difficult People—"Stretch"

1. Read the following statement from Alice, a project engineer at Supreme Electronics.

    "I work for a boss who had the uncanny ability to 'stretch' the truth. He would selectively remember things and use his selective memory to nullify agreements or change things. On a proposal we submitted to a customer, we spelled out that a particular key team member would be leaving the project after two weeks, and he altered it to make it look like he would be running the whole thing. Another time, he cited his ability to develop people as the reason why there was a high turnover rate in the department. In fact, most employees jump at a chance to transfer to other departments or to leave the organization. Not long ago, during a department meeting, he was talking about the importance of mental toughness. To illustrate the point, he told us about how he had played football at Cornell against Mike Ditka, among others. A coworker got a copy of the Cornell media guide, and nowhere in the All-Time Roster List was our boss's name. When the coworker confronted him, he said that we misunderstood. The guy is a compulsive liar. I'm locked into this job and can't afford to leave. I've repeatedly tried to transfer out of the department, but while he tells me to my face that 'he'll support my efforts for advancement,' I found out that he continually stonewalled my requests."

INTERNET ACTIVITY

2. Using the Internet, find information on how to deal with people that "stretch" the truth. Based on your findings, what suggestions would you make to Alice on how to deal with her boss?

3. OPTIONAL ACTIVITY: Review Brinkman & Kirschner's *Dealing With People You Can't Stand: How to Bring Out the Best in People at Their Worst* (McGraw-Hill, 1994) or visit their Web site (thericks.com). Write a one-page paper telling why you think the difficult people identified in the book are typical in organizations. Conclude the paper by writing how this skill application increased your working knowledge of coping with the behaviors of a difficult person.

Skills Application 3-3: Develop a "Bad News" Plan

The instructor will divide the class into groups of three or four students. Each group will complete the following project.

Assume that your group is Atlas Construction Company's project team responsible for a multidivision design-build project for St. Thomas Energy Company. Your company sold St. Thomas Energy Company, in part, on a guaranteed maximum price and finish date. The expected finish date is less than a month away and, due to circumstances beyond your control, the project will be at least two weeks late unless significant costs are incurred by your company to bring the project back in on time. For each day the project goes beyond the due date, Atlas must pay St. Thomas a $20,000 penalty.

1. Develop a plan for communicating the bad news to your immediate supervisor.
2. Develop a plan for communicating the bad news to the customer.
3. Critique and analyze the activity:
   a. In what ways did working as a team hinder the development of a communication plan? Help the development of a communication plan?
   b. In your opinion, why would it have been easier to develop a communication plan if the project was being completed seven days earlier than expected?
   c. Compare your responses with those of other groups. In what ways was your plan better? What would you do differently in the future?

INTERNET ACTIVITY

Skills Application 3-4: Cleaning Up Communication Clutter

Information overload is a key communication issue for today's supervisor. Review the following, or other Web sites dealing with TMI, then consider the questions that follow.

- www.cnn.com/TECH/9704/15/info.overload/index.html
- www.cnet.com/Content/Tv/Stories/Overload
- www.careerbuilder.com/wl_work_9905_overload.html
- www.cfopub.com/html/Articles/CFO/1998/98SEinfo.html

1. Based on your research, what are some of the primary effects of information overload? List at least five. Have you encountered any of these in your own life?
2. What are some key strategies for managing information overload? List at least five.
3. Based on what you've learned in these articles, evaluate your own e-mail practices. List five steps you can take to manage your e-mail input and output.

SKILL DEVELOPMENT VIDEO

SKILL DEVELOPMENT MODULE 3–1: COMMUNICATION

This video segment introduces Ken Foley, a production development supervisor with Carson Products, a manufacturing firm. J. C. Marko, a systems designer, has encountered problems and needs Ken's help.

Questions for Discussion: The Ineffective Version

1. Discuss how Ken did not use effective communication skills to efficiently run his department.
2. What barriers are present to hinder communication?
3. What specifically should Ken do to overcome the communication barriers?
4. Review Figure 3-7. What aspects of the Dos and Don'ts of Good Listening did Ken violate?

Questions for Discussion: The More Effective Version

1. Discuss how Ken used good communication skills to effectively run his department and solve problems.
2. What aspects of good listening did Ken exhibit (refer to Figure 3-7)?
3. What else could Ken Foley have done to be more effective?
4. How does this version reinforce the notion that good communication skills and good supervisory skills go hand in hand?

ENDNOTES

1. The opening "You Make the Call" section was a case originally prepared by Edwin C. Leonard, Jr. and Sherry Hockemeyer, *"Bang! Bang! Bang! You're Dead!"* and first appeared in *Annual Advances in Business Cases,* 1996 (New York: SCR and McGraw-Hill, Inc., 1996), pp. 17–27. Adapted with permission. While the issue of workplace violence is more fully explored in Chapter 15, perceptive students will readily identify that O'Connor did not heed the warning signs that trouble was brewing in his department. Second, if he had taken these warning signs seriously, he needed to know how to react to them. An article by Suzanne M. Crampton and John W. Hodge, "Training the Supervisor to Prevent Employee Workplace Violence," *The Journal of Property Management* (July/August 1996), pp. 14–16, discusses both of these issues.
2. Peter M. Senge, Art Kleiner, Charlotte Roberts, Richard B. Ross, and Bryan J. Smith, *The Fifth Discipline Handbook: Strategies and Tools for Building a Learning Organization* (New York: Doubleday, 1994), p. 6
3. Ibid., p. 11. Senge's latest fieldbook, *The Dance of Change: The Challenges of Sustaining Momentum in Learning Organizations* (New York: Doubleday, 1999) uses theory, case studies, and exercises to illustrate the importance of "open, honest, sincere, and genuine" communication in order to create change within an organization, foster real learning environments, and sustain a positive culture.
4. Tom Peters has strongly advised that managers need to become highly visible and do a better job of listening to subordinates. We could not agree more. For additional information on management by wandering around, see Tom Peters, *Thriving on Chaos* (New York: Alfred A. Knopf, 1988), pp. 423–440.
5. The grapevine cuts across the formal channels of communications. See Stanley J. Modic, "Grapevine Rated Most Believable," *Industry Week* (May 15, 1989), pp. 11 and 14; and Walter Kiechel III, "In Praise of Office Gossip," *Fortune* (August 19, 1985), pp. 253, 254, and 256. The classic article on the subject is Keith Davis's "Management Communication and the Grapevine," *Harvard Business Review* (September–October 1953), pp. 43–49.
6. Adapted from Martin Schram, "Media Devour 4th-Hand Gossip About Clinton," *Journal Gazette* (Fort Wayne, Indiana, July 7, 1996), p. 1C.
7. For further discussion of informal channels of communication and the grapevine, see Rudolph F. Verderber and Kathleen S. Verderber, *Inter-Act: Using Interpersonal Communication Skills* (Belmont, Calif.: Wadsworth Publishing Company, 1995); William W. Hull, "Beating the Grapevine to the Punch," *Supervision* (August 1994), pp. 17–19; "Stopping Those Nasty Rumors," *HRFocus* (November 1990), p. 22; J. Mishra, "Managing the Grapevine," *Public Personnel Management* (Summer 1990), pp. 213–228; Keith Davis, "The Care and Cultivation of the Corporate Grapevine," *Dun's Review* (July 1973), p. 47; and Curtis Sittenfield, "Good Ways to Deliver Bad News," *Fast Company* (April 1999), pp. 58+.
8. Brenda Major, "Gender Patterns in Touching Behavior," in Nancy M. Henley, ed., *Gender and Non-Verbal Behavior* (New York: Springer-Verlag, 1981).
9. Quality guru, Joseph Juran, used the simple explanation that managers needed to be bilingual—that is, they had to speak the language of both upper management and of the workforce. See A. Blanton Godfrey, "Speak the Right Language," *Quality Digest* (July 1998), p. 18. The English language is estimated to contain some 750,000 words, but the vocabulary of the average person is only 20,000 to 40,000 words. While English is generally recognized as the world's primary business language, not all employees will understand the common tongue. In one section of their new book, Rodin and Hartman observe that information technology people speak only technobabble because at most companies "they're herded into one isolated department." They argue that "the best IT professionals *live* with the

business units." Rob Rodin and Curtis Hartman, *Free, Perfect, and Now: Connecting to the Three Insatiable Customer Demands* (New York: Simon & Schuster, 1999).

10.   The term *TMI* was first brought to the author's attention in Rebecca Ganzel, "Editor's Notebook: Too Much Information," *Training* (February 1999), p. 6. Also, Michael Schrage, "Working in the Data Mines: Sixteen Tons of Information Overload," *Fortune* (August 2, 1999), p 244, provided impetus for this discussion.

11.   See Eric Krell, "Worthy Business Solutions You Can Use," *Business Finance* (December 1998), p. 8a. Gary Blake is president of the Communication Workshop and has developed a list of "The 25 Deadliest Phrases in Accounting and Insurance Writing."

12.   Thomas J. Peters, *Liberation Management* (New York: Knopf, 1992), p. 14.

13.   Respondents to the March 1997 Where I Stand poll in *Nation's Business.* Also see Tim McCollum, "Preventing a Productivity Drain," *Nation's Business* (March 1998), p. 56.

14.   Ibid. Also, "You've Got Junk," *Training* (June 1999), p. 18, reports that nearly one-third of all Internet e-mail poses a threat to corporate assets and worker productivity.

15.   See Deborah Tannen, *You Just Don't Understand: Women and Men in Conversation* (New York: William Morrow, 1990), pp. 13–15. Also see Tannen, *That's Not What I Meant! How Conversation Style Makes or Breaks Your Relations with Others* (New York: Morrow, 1986).

16.   Ibid.

17.   Nancy Keates, "After the Beep, Please Mind Your Manners," *The Wall Street Journal* (May 29, 1996), pp. B1, B5.

18.   *Critical Thinking About Critical Issues* (Williamsburg, VA: Learning Enrichment, Inc., 1995), p. 9.

Chapter 4

Learning Objectives

After studying this chapter, you will be able to:

1
Discuss reasons why people behave the way they do.

2
Compare various motivational theories and explain their importance for understanding employee behavior.

3
Compare the assumptions and applications of Theory X and Theory Y in supervision.

4
Discuss supervisory approaches for stimulating employee motivation—especially broadened job tasks, job redesign, and participative management.

Motivational Principles As Applied to Supervision

You Make the Call!

You are John Jackson, production supervisor for Amity Cable and Wire Products, located in Indiana. You supervise 28 assembly-line production workers. About a year ago, the Illinois facility was closed and six of the workers from that site were transferred into your group. Jim Collins, the plant manager, has been greatly concerned because production has remained constant but quality has varied greatly. The wire products produced by your group are used in the auto industry, and your prime customer, Ford Motor Company, has said that you must improve your quality or the work will go to other suppliers. You know that the loss of Ford as a customer would result in massive layoffs.

Several of the younger employees have you baffled. Sandy Hall and Tony Aquirre appear to speak for the group and are the informal leaders. They set the pace for the group but on occasion they have a tendency to loaf on the job. When they slow down, everyone else slows down, seeming to think it is the social hour. Sandy loves to tell stories, and when she does she has the attention of all employees. The trouble is that although their output quantity is better than most, on occasion their reject rate approaches an unacceptable 10 percent. A discussion with the two did not go the way you expected.

"You must be crazy," Tony said. "I've always wondered why you expect us to work so hard. We make the same money—and not much of it, at that! The way I figure it, why bust your tail? Chances are that it will only lead to a layoff."

Sandy added, "Yeah, like what happened over at Carter Products. They started a quality improvement program, and before long they didn't need as many employees. Look, I like what I'm doing, and it's important to me to do a good job. But that's all I want to do, no more, no less."

Tony said, "I've seen too many people—my dad, for example—sweat their whole life away, and what did it get them? My dad's plant closed several years ago and left him high and dry. Sandy's right. You know we'll keep up our end of production, but it's impossible to meet those quality standards Ford imposes. Only Superman could do it right all the time."

You know that you will have to do something and quickly. But what will you do?

You Make the Call

DETERMINANTS OF HUMAN BEHAVIOR

1

Discuss reasons why people behave the way they do.

In Chapter 2, we defined *management* as getting things accomplished with and through people by guiding and motivating their efforts toward common objectives. To manage effectively, as this definition suggests, supervisors must understand employee motivation and develop approaches that encourage employees to work to the full extent of their capabilities.

Human beings constitute a resource that is quite different from any other the supervisor is asked to manage. Our society places great value on the worth of human beings. Human beings have values, attitudes, needs, and expectations that significantly influence their behavior on the job. The feelings people have toward their supervisors, their job environment, their personal problems, and numerous other factors are often difficult to ascertain. Yet they have a tremendous impact on employee motivation and work performance.

What causes employees to behave the way they do? This question is difficult to answer because each individual is unique. The behavior of people as individuals and in groups at work is often rational, consistent, and predictable. However, at times, people's behavior may seem irrational, inconsistent, and unpredictable. When an employee's behavior is not consistent with the organization's expectations, problems arise for the supervisor. Behavior is influenced by many forces, making it difficult for the supervisor to formulate simple principles that apply to every situation.

The forces that stimulate human behavior come from within individuals and from their environment. To illustrate, think about why parents' behavior changes when they become grandparents. One answer might be that the parents are now older (perhaps more mature or experienced). They have received feedback on their earlier parenting efforts and have taken corrective action. Many grandparents have extra income to spend or more time to devote to grandparenting. As grandparents, their duties and responsibilities have changed. Also, they can always send the grandchildren home to the parents. All of these factors acting in combination may lead to a behavioral change.

Every day employees are confronting issues that were unheard of a decade or two ago. The typical employee spends more of his or her waking hours "going to, being at, and coming home from work." Yet with the explosion of two-income households, employees find less time to spend with aging parents and growing children, or on taking vacations and pursuing other leisure-time activities. Often, employees find themselves in intolerable or soured personal relationships. Many experienced managers speak about the person who was their star performer, but now they find it hard to say anything good about the person. Understanding "the baggage" that affects employee performance is critical to the supervisor's success in dealing with people.

Determinants of Personality[1]

Personality

The knowledge, attitudes, and attributes that combine to make up the unique human being.

Every individual is the product of many factors, and it is the unique combination of these factors that results in an individual human personality. **Personality** is the complex mix of knowledge, attitudes, and attributes that distinguish one person from all others.

Many people use the word *personality* to describe what they observe in another person. However, the real substance of human personality goes far beyond external behavior. The essence of an individual's personality includes his or her attitudes, values, and ways of interpreting the environment, as well as many internal and external influences that contribute to his or her behavior patterns. There are several major schools of personality study that can help us comprehend the complexity of human beings. We will first discuss the primary determinants of personality and then describe how some major theories relate these factors to employee motivation.

Physiological (Biological) Factors.   One major influence on human personality is a person's physiological (or biological) makeup. Such factors as sex, age, race, height, weight, and physique can affect how a person sees the world. Intelligence, which is at least partially inherited, is another. Most biological characteristics are apparent to others, and they may affect the way in which a person is perceived. For example, a person who is tall is sometimes considered to possess more leadership ability than a shorter person. One research study showed that tall male job applicants usually were offered higher starting salaries than were shorter male applicants. While physiological characteristics should not be the basis for evaluating an employee's capabilities, they do exert considerable influence on an individual's personality as well as define certain physical abilities and limitations.

Early Childhood Influences.   Many psychologists feel that the very early years of a person's life are crucial in an individual's development. The manner in which a child is trained, shown affection, and disciplined will have a lifelong influence. In their classic work, *The Managerial Woman,* Hennig and Jardim illustrated how early childhood influences were conducive to their personal and professional success:

For each, their "typical" mother provided a warm, caring and socially sanctioned feminine model . . . , while their fathers supported them and confirmed them in believing that these were not binding models of behavior but a matter of choice and option. . . .
    As little girls they were free to take part in activities usually reserved for little boys . . . their fathers confirmed their freedom to be more. . . .[2]

Parents who encourage autonomy, independence, exploration, and the ability to deal with risk while instilling a willingness to work with others provide the child with valuable lessons. Various biographies illustrate that an individual's ability to cope with problems and work in harmony with others may be determined partly through the influences to which that individual was subjected as a child.

Environmental (Situational) Factors.   Sociologists and social psychologists emphasize the immediate situation or environment as being the most important determinant of adult personality. Such factors as education, income, employment, home, and many other experiences that confront an individual throughout life will influence what that person is and eventually becomes.

Each day's experiences contribute to an individual's makeup. This is particularly true in terms of the immediate working environment. For example, the personality of the blue-collar worker performing routine, manual labor on an assembly line is affected by this type of work in a different manner than the personality of a professional white-collar worker who performs primarily mental work involving thought and judgment. Stating this another way, what a supervisor does in a work situation affects the personalities of the people being supervised.

Cultural (Societal) Values.   The broader culture also influences personality. In the United States, such values as competition, rewards for accomplishment, equal opportunities, and similar concepts are part of a democratic society. Individuals are educated, trained, and encouraged to think for themselves and to strive for the achievement of worthwhile goals. However, some cultural values are changing. For example, for many years the workforce in the United States was relatively homogeneous and the cultural values of the majority of workers tended to be similar. In recent decades, however, the workforce has become increasingly diversified, reflecting many different subcultures and subgroups. As the diversity of the workforce has increased, so has the effect of different cultural norms and values on the workplace. In particular, the values of certain ethnic, age, and other minority groups may be quite different from the values of the supervisor. By recognizing and respecting different cultural values, supervisors should become more adept in dealing effectively with people unlike themselves.

From their study of workplace issues, Priority International found some startling similarities—that people are working harder and longer to maintain their standard of living. The survey of management personnel from Australia, Belgium, Canada, Ireland, New Zealand, Portugal, Singapore, Spain, the United Kingdom, and the United States indicated that greater financial security, more exercise, and more family time were the three most important things that would make them happier.[3]

Recognizing Human Differences and Similarities

The many complexities of human personality have been discussed here only briefly because there are any number of factors that cause personality to adapt and change over time. Ideally, supervisors should get to know their employees so well that they can tailor their supervisory approaches to the uniqueness of each individual's personality. Realistically, however, it is impossible to understand all the unique characteristics of a person's personality.

Fortunately, behavioral studies have demonstrated that people tend to be more alike than different in their basic motivational needs and their reasons for behaving the way they do. Supervisors can implement managerial techniques that emphasize the similarities rather than the differences among people. This does not mean that unique differences in people should be overlooked. Supervisors can understand the unique needs and personality makeup of individual employees enough to adapt general approaches to individuals to some extent. But a consistent supervisory approach based on similarities rather than differences is a practical way to lead a group of employees toward achieving company goals.

UNDERSTANDING MOTIVATION AND HUMAN BEHAVIOR

2
Compare various motivational theories and explain their importance for understanding employee behavior.

Too often motivation is viewed as something that one person can give to or do for another. Supervisors sometimes talk in terms of giving a worker a "shot" of motivation or of having to "motivate their employees." However, motivating employees is not that easily accomplished since the concept of human motivation really refers to an inner drive or an impulse. Motivation cannot be poured down another's throat or injected intravenously! In the final analysis, it comes from within a person. **Motivation** is a willingness to exert effort toward achieving a goal stimulated by the effort's ability to fulfill an individual need. In other words, employees are more willing to do what the organization wants if they believe that doing so will result in a meaningful reward. The supervisor's challenge is to stimulate that willingness by making sure that achievement of organizational goals results in rewards that employees want. The rewards need not always be money; they can be anything employees value. For example, praise and recognition can be powerful motivators.

Motivation
A willingness to exert effort toward achieving a goal stimulated by the effort's ability to fulfill an individual need.

Because employee motivation is crucial to organizational success, it is a subject about which there has been much research. The theories presented in this chapter are fundamental, and much more has been written elsewhere. However, most theories emphasize the similarities rather than differences in the needs of human beings.

The Hierarchy of Needs (Maslow)

Most psychologists who study human behavior and personality generally are convinced that all behavior is caused, goal oriented, and motivated. Stating this another way, there is a reason for everything that a person does, assuming that the person is rational, sane, and not out of control (e.g., not under the influence of drugs or alcohol). People constantly are striving to attain something that has meaning to them in terms of their own particular needs and in relation to how they see themselves and the environment in which they live. Often we may not be aware of why we behave in a certain manner but we all have subconscious motives that govern the way we behave in different situations.

One of the most widely accepted theories of human behavior is that people are motivated to satisfy certain well-defined and more or less predictable needs. Psychologist Abraham H. Maslow formulated the concept of a **hierarchy** (or priority) **of needs.**[4] He maintained that these needs range from lower-level needs to higher-level needs in an ascending priority (see Figure 4-1). These needs actually overlap and are interrelated, and it may be preferable to consider them as existing along a continuum rather than as being separate and distinct from one another.

Maslow's theory of a hierarchy of human needs implies that people attempt to satisfy these needs in the order in which they are arranged in the hierarchy. Until the lowest-level or most basic needs are reasonably satisfied, a person will not be motivated strongly by the other levels. As one level of needs is satisfied to some extent, the individual focuses on the next level, which then becomes the stronger motivator of behavior. Maslow even suggested that once a lower level of needs was reasonably satisfied, it no longer would motivate behavior, at least in the short term.

Biological (Physiological) Needs.   At the first level are the **biological** (or physiological) **needs.** These are the needs that everyone has for food, shelter, rest, recreation, and

Hierarchy of needs

Maslow's theory of motivation, which suggests that employee needs are arranged in priority order such that lower-order needs must be satisfied before higher-order needs become motivating.

Biological needs

The basic physical needs, such as food, rest, shelter, and recreation.

FIGURE 4-1

Hierarchy of needs.

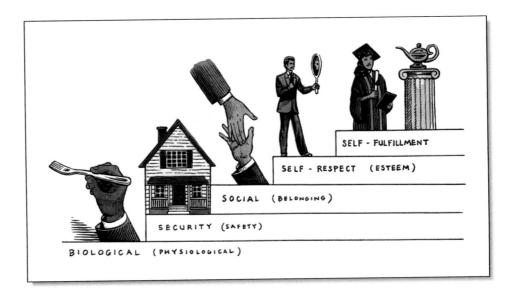

other physical necessities. Virtually every employee views work as being a means for taking care of these fundamental needs. The paycheck enables a person to purchase the necessities vital to survival as well as some of the comforts of life.

Security (Safety) Needs.
Once a person's physiological needs are reasonably satisfied, other needs become important. The **security** (or safety) **needs** include the need to protect ourselves against danger and to guard against the uncertainties of life. Most employees want some sense of security or control over their future. In order to satisfy such expectations, many employers offer a variety of supplementary benefits. For example, medical, retirement, hospitalization, disability, and life insurance plans are designed to protect employees against various uncertainties and their possible serious consequences. Wage and benefit packages are designed to satisfy employees' physiological and safety needs. By fulfilling these basic needs, organizations hope to attract and retain competent personnel.

Security needs

Desire for protection against danger and life's uncertainties.

Social (Belonging) Needs.
Some supervisors believe that good wages and ample benefits are sufficient to motivate employees. These supervisors do not understand the importance of the higher-level needs of human beings, beginning with social (or belonging) needs. **Social needs** are those that people have for attention, for being part of a group, for being accepted by their peers, and for love. Many studies have shown that group motivation can be a powerful influence on employee behavior at work in either a negative or a positive direction. For example, some employees may deliberately perform in a manner contrary to organizational goals in order to feel that they are an accepted part of an informal group. On the other hand, if informal group goals are in line with organizational goals, the group can influence individuals toward exceptional performance. Some employers provide off-the-job social and athletic opportunities for their employees as a means of helping them satisfy their social needs and to build loyalty to the organization as a whole.

Social needs

Desire for love and affection and affiliation with something worthwhile.

Self-Respect (Esteem) Needs.
Closely related to social needs are **self-respect** (or esteem or ego) **needs.** These are needs that everyone has for recognition, achievement, status, and a sense of accomplishment. Self-respect needs are very powerful because they relate to personal feelings of self-worth and importance. Supervisors should look for ways by which these internal needs may be satisfied, such as providing variety and challenge in work tasks and recognizing good performance. Something as simple as saying "good job" to someone can keep that person doing good work.

Self-respect needs

Desire for recognition, achievement, status, and a sense of accomplishment.

Self-Fulfillment Needs.
At the highest level of human needs are **self-fulfillment** (or self-realization) **needs**—the desire to use one's capabilities to the fullest. People want to be creative and to achieve within the limits of their capacities. Presumably, these highest-level needs are not satisfied until a person reaches his or her own full potential. As such, they persist throughout the person's life and probably can never be completely satisfied. Many jobs frustrate rather than fulfill this level of human needs. For example, many factory and office jobs are routine and monotonous, and workers must seek self-fulfillment in pursuits off the job and in family relationships. However, supervisors can

Self-fulfillment needs

Desire to use one's abilities to the fullest extent.

Some employers provide off-the-job social and athletic opportunities for their employees to help them satisfy their social needs and to build loyalty to the organization.

provide opportunities for self-fulfillment on the job by assigning tasks that challenge employees to use their abilities more fully.

Application of the Needs Theories to Supervisory Management

Supervisors can use the model of a hierarchy of human needs as a framework to visualize the kinds of needs that people have and to assess their relative importance in motivating individuals in the work group. The supervisor's problem is to make individual fulfillment a result of doing a good job. For example, if the supervisor senses that an employee's most influential motivator at the time is social needs, then the employee is most likely to do a good job if he or she is assigned to work with a group and the whole group is rewarded for doing the job well. If an employee seems to be seeking self-respect, then to influence this employee toward good performance the supervisor might provide visible signs of recognition, such as a trophy or praise in front of the employee's peers at a departmental meeting. The key for the supervisor is to recognize where each employee is in the hierarchy so that the supervisor can determine what needs are currently driving the employee.

As mentioned previously, many supervisors believe that motivation is something they do to get a response from their employees. However, the essence of motivation is what individuals feel and do in relation to their own particular needs. Ultimately, all motivation is self-motivation. Thus, a good supervisor structures the work situation and reward systems in such a manner that employees are motivated to perform well because good work performance leads to satisfaction of their particular needs. This chapter's first "Contemporary Issue" box illustrates the dual edge of need fulfillment. At the time of writing this text, it is evident that work has been at the center of the lives of Lora

contemporary issue

Lifetime Employees

FACT: Aging, by definition, means to grow older and more mature. Aging is a normal process; we are aging from the moment we are born.

FACT: In today's society, the word *aging* sometimes holds a negative connotation. Some employers fear that older workers lack the skills and willingness to learn new technologies and procedures; others think they no longer have the energy and motivation to compete in today's fast-paced and stressful work environment; still others believe that older workers will have significant health problems and thus be absent from work more frequently; and others are unwilling to pay older workers the salaries they deserve and prefer to hire younger, less experienced employees at lower rates.

FACT: Recent studies indicate that the single most common reason employees leave their place of employment is lack of praise and recognition. So why do they stay? Consider the cases of Lora Figgins and F. William Sunderman.

Figgins, who has worked for the Navy since shortly after the attack on Pearl Harbor, starts her day with a 1½-hour vanpool commute. She has almost 60 years of experience and didn't even consider quitting when her job with the Naval Air Systems Command moved from Crystal River to Patuxent River Naval Air Station in 1997. At work, she sits in an austere cubicle, with no photos or frills. As a contracts assistant, her job is to help draft and review contracts the Navy signs for aircraft, weapons, and parts. "I drafted about 10 million of them, it seems," she said.

Her supervisor describes Figgins, a GS-7, as one of his best employees. She is always finding something the negotiators overlooked. "She's just a wealth of information. She brings up some interesting points. She won't let people take shortcuts." The issue isn't about whether Figgins likes her job—as someone who lived through the Great Depression, she considers the notion daft. "I don't think about enjoying it, I just do it," she said.[1]

She refuses to retire, considering it a death sentence, and looks shocked at the mention of the word. She is filled with cautionary tales about the poor souls who retired in their fifties or sixties, only to quickly drop dead. "Retirement is a bad word," she said, "I've seen too many people, they're ready to retire the moment they start to work." What's the secret? "I don't know. I guess I'm made out of good stuff," she said.[2]

At age 100, Dr. Sunderman is a world-renowned physician, author, editor, photographer, and a lifelong violinist, still giving concerts on his rare Stradivari. He has been a professor at eight universities, and the chief of clinical pathology at the Centers for Disease Control and Prevention (CDC). He teamed with researchers on the Manhattan Project, and worked as a medical consultant with NASA. "I am convinced that one of the most important items of longevity is the maintenance of a daily work schedule," he says. Sunderman still works an eight-hour day, editing the *Annuals of Clinical and Laboratory Science* and organizing seminars, workshops, and scientific field trips for the Association of Clinical Scientists. Sunderman, recognized as America's Oldest Worker, says, "I have always taken to heart that profound statement of Voltaire: 'How infinitesimal is the importance of anything I can do, but how infinitely important it is that I should do it.' "[3]

Sources: Ideas for the facts adapted from "Myths and Realities of Aging," *Covenant Healthcare* (1998); and William J. Clinton, "National Older Workers Employment Week, 1999" (*A Proclamation from the White House,* March 11, 1999). (1) Adapted from Steve Vogel, "She Just Keeps Rolling Along," *Washington Post* (June 4, 1998), p. D-1. (2) Ibid. (3) Adapted from *Green Thumb Web Site* (Green Thumb, Inc., is America's oldest and largest provider of mature- and disadvantaged-worker training and employment). For information on other older workers recognized by Green Thumb, see their Web site at www.greenthumb.org.

Figgins and Dr. F. William Sunderman. Figgins and Sunderman are not unique, because many others have found work to be a source of comfort, security, and meaning. Their values combine both Edison's "There is no substitute for hard work . . ." and Emerson's "We put our love where we put our labor." For others, the continuous employment enjoyed by Lora Figgins may be a thing of the past. For them, work may be viewed as a means for satisfying their off-the-job needs.

It is normal for employees to expect good wages, generous benefit plans, and job security. The key to longer-term, positive motivation of employees resides in better satisfying their higher-level needs (social, self-respect, and self-fulfillment). Supervisors should recognize that just giving employees more money, better benefits, and better working conditions will not bring about excellent work performance. For many employees, these items may play a secondary role in day-to-day motivation.

But is money everything? For some time, employees have been saying it is not the only thing. According to a recent survey, one-third of the respondents place a positive work environment at the top of a list of factors for keeping employees satisfied.[5] A retail store manager recently said to one of the text's authors: "We have employees [for whom] time is just as important as money. A lot of working mothers need time off to spend with kids. Time is sometimes more valuable than money." The slogan "*Different strokes for different folks*" should be a part of every supervisor's management practice.

On the other hand, downsizing has become a fact of life. As downsizing continues, loyalty to the individual company may lessen. Managers who are asked to develop effective work teams may find it increasingly difficult as employees become less enthusiastic about "winning one for the gipper!" Further, the lack of trust and low job security may create a strong individual orientation that one must take charge of one's own future. Realistically, the notion that an employee should spend his or her lifetime in the same firm is no more. Kevin Becraft, director of human relations and resources at IBM, said it well when he said,

"It's lifetime employability. The key difference: shared responsibility. Employers have an obligation to provide opportunity for self-improvement; employees have to take charge of their own careers."[6]

Negative Employee Motivation and Frustration

Conditions that do not bring about the fulfillment of a person's needs will ultimately result in dissatisfaction and frustration. Thus, when their needs are not satisfied on the job, many employees resort to behavior patterns that are detrimental to their job performance and to the organization. A typical approach for frustrated employees is to resign themselves to just getting by on the job. This means that they simply go through the motions and put in time without trying to perform in other than an average or marginal manner. They look for personal satisfaction off the job and are content to do just enough to draw a paycheck.

Some employees constantly find things that distract them from doing the job, and at times they even try to beat the system. They often are absent or tardy, or they break the rules as a way of trying to get back at situations they find frustrating.

Still other employees who are dissatisfied adopt aggressive behavior, which ultimately may cause them to leave the job. Examples of aggressive behavior are poor attitudes, vandalism, theft, fighting, and temper outbursts. When the situation becomes intolerable, they quit or almost force their supervisors to fire them.

These types of reactions to job situations are undesirable and should be prevented. Costs of employee turnover, absenteeism, tardiness, poor performance, and other unsatisfactory conduct on the job can be extremely high to an organization. Rather than just accepting an employee's behavior, a supervisor should endeavor to relieve frustration by providing more opportunities for need fulfillment.

Motivation–Hygiene Theory

Motivation-hygiene theory

Herzberg's theory that factors in the work environment primarily influence the degree of job dissatisfaction, while intrinsic job content factors influence the amount of employee motivation.

Another theory of motivation is the **motivation-hygiene theory,** sometimes called the two-factor theory or the dual-factor theory, developed by Frederick Herzberg.[7] Herzberg's research has demonstrated that some factors in the work environment that traditionally were believed to motivate people actually serve primarily to reduce their dissatisfaction rather than motivate them positively.

Herzberg and others have conducted numerous studies in which people were asked to describe events that made them feel particularly good or bad about their jobs. Other questions were designed to determine the depth of their feelings, the duration for which these feelings persisted, and the types of situations that made employees feel motivated or frustrated. These studies were made of employees in various organizations and industries, including personnel at all levels and from different technical and job specialties. Interestingly, the general pattern of results was fairly consistent. It revealed a clear distinction between factors that tend to motivate employees (motivation factors) and those that, while expected by workers, are not likely to motivate them (hygiene factors).

Motivation factors

Elements intrinsic in the job that promote job performance.

Motivation Factors.   Herzberg identified the **motivation factors** as elements intrinsic in the job that promote job performance. Among the most frequently identified motivation factors are the following:

- Opportunity for growth and advancement
- Achievement or accomplishment
- Recognition for accomplishments
- Challenging or interesting work
- Responsibility for work

Stating this another way, job factors that tend to motivate people positively are primarily related to their higher-level needs and aspirations. These factors are all related to outcomes associated with the content of the job being performed. Opportunity for advancement, greater responsibility, recognition, growth, achievement, and interesting work are consistently identified as the major factors that make work motivating and meaningful. The absence of these factors can be frustrating and nonmotivating. These motivation factors are not easily measured, and they may be difficult to find in certain types of jobs.

Hygiene factors

Elements in the work environment that, if positive, reduce dissatisfaction but do not tend to motivate.

Hygiene Factors.   Also referred to as the "dissatisfiers," **hygiene factors** are elements in the work environment that, if positive, reduce dissatisfaction but do not tend to motivate. Herzberg identified the following hygiene factors:

- Working conditions
- Money, status, and security
- Interpersonal relationships
- Supervision
- Company policies and administration

The factors that employees complained about the most were conditions in the work environment: poor company policies and administrative practices, lack of good supervision in both a technical and a human relations sense, poor working conditions, and inadequate wages and benefits. Herzberg concluded that these job-context factors tend to dissatisfy rather than motivate. In recent years, the conflict between work demands and personal life has been identified as another hygiene factor. Where these factors are negative or inadequate, employees will be unhappy. However, where these factors are adequate or even excellent, they do not, by themselves, promote better job performance. This does not mean that hygiene factors are unimportant. They are very important but they serve primarily to maintain a reasonable level of job motivation, not to increase it.

Application of Herzberg's Theory to Supervision

Herzberg's theory suggests that, to obtain better performance, the supervisor should implement strategies that target the motivation factors—that is, those that contribute to the satisfaction of employees' social, self-respect, and self-fulfillment needs. One of the supervisor's strategies should be to "catch people doing something right" and "give them credit when credit is due." A note of caution: Praise and other forms of recognition must be highly individualized and genuinely deserved in order to be effective. A key

A bit of sincere, genuine praise goes a long way.

element in effective supervision is to give employees an opportunity to fulfill their needs as a result of good job performance.

The supervisor should not conclude from Herzberg's work that hygiene factors such as money, benefits, good working conditions, and the like are unimportant. These factors are extremely important, and organizations must strive continuously to be competitive in these areas. However, employees often take such factors for granted, especially when job opportunities are plentiful. Positive employee motivation is more related to people's higher-level needs.

Expectancy Theory

Expectancy theory

Theory of motivation that holds that employees will perform better if they believe such efforts will lead to desired rewards.

Another interesting and practical way of looking at employee motivation is provided by expectancy theory.[8] **Expectancy theory** is based on the worker's perception of the relationships among effort, performance, and reward. According to expectancy theory, workers will be motivated to work harder if they believe that their greater efforts will actually result in improved performance and that such improved performance will then lead to rewards they desire. The expectancy theory model is illustrated in Figure 4-2.

Expectancy theory is based on worker perceptions and on relationships referred to as *linkages*. Employee motivation is dependent on workers being able to perceive an effort–performance linkage as well as a performance–reward linkage. If an employee cannot recognize that such linkages clearly exist, he or she will not be highly motivated.

For example, if computer operators have not received adequate training, they will probably not be able to perceive a relationship between their effort and performance. Instead they will conclude that no matter how much effort they expend, there will be no significant improvement in their job performance. Similarly, if nurses' aides in a hospital perceive that their high-performing coworkers are not being rewarded any more than average or even substandard performers, they will not believe that there is a performance–reward relationship, so they will not be motivated toward good performance.

FIGURE 4-2

Expectancy theory.

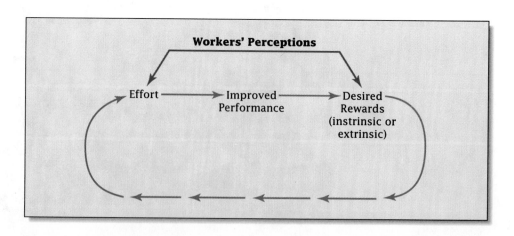

Supervisors may believe that their organization rewards high-quality work. However, such a belief may be based on management's perception of the reward system. Supervisors should try to verify whether the workers perceive the linkages. Supervisors and employees often do not view reward systems in the same way. For example, on his last day on the job, an assembly-line employee in a manufacturing plant participated in an exit interview. When the interviewer asked him why he was leaving, the worker said that he had become extremely frustrated waiting for work to come to his workstation. The worker said that he became fed up with coming to work every day knowing that no matter how hard he worked, it would not be visible on the production chart.

It does not matter how clearly supervisors view the linkages among effort, performance, and rewards. If the workers cannot see them, the linkages might just as well not be there. Supervisors should strive to show employees that increased effort will lead to improved work performance, which in turn will result in increased rewards. Rewards may be extrinsic, in the form of additional pay, or intrinsic, such as a sense of accomplishment or some type of praise or recognition. Probably the most important characteristic of a reward is that it is something the person desires.

A supervisor may have limited control over the rewards that are available. Union–management agreements and other pay and promotional systems typically are tied to seniority. Supervisors often complain that many employee wage increases are automatic with little relation to merit and job performance. Even in these types of situations, however, there are approaches available to supervisors that can yield motivational results.

Equity Theory

How many times have you heard the following: Ed, an employee, complains to anyone who will listen, "It's not fair! I've been here as long as Carl, we do the same job, but he gets paid more than I do." Ed's belief of inequity rests on the notion that his outcome/input ratio is lower than Carl's (see Figure 4-3 on page 106). Inputs include things such as seniority, experience, age, skill, ability, job knowledge, and effort. Ed's exasperated statement suggests that Ed and Carl have similar inputs: they have both held the same job for the same amount of time. Inequity exists because Carl evidently receives more outcomes (he is paid more) than Ed. Outcomes can include salary, working conditions, degree of employee involvement and decision making, opportunity for advancement and promotion, challenging assignments, pay and benefits, and assorted forms of recognition.

Equity theory

Explains how people strive for fairness in the workplace.

Based on the works of J. Stacy Adams, **equity theory** is a theory of motivation that explains how people strive for fairness in the workplace. Since the beginning of time, people have compared themselves to others. They compare their own input/outcome ratio to that of someone else, the *referent* or *comparison other*. If there is inequality when the ratios are compared, there is inequity. This inequity will be followed by a motivation to achieve equity, or fairness, by making the outcome/input ratios equal to each other.

Adams also stressed that what is important in determining motivation is the *relative* rather than the *absolute* level of outcomes a person receives and the inputs a person

FIGURE 4-3

It's not fair!—equity theory at work.

Ed's inputs are the same as Carl's; they both have the same job. Carl has higher outcomes than Ed because he gets paid more. This makes Carl's outcome/input ratio greater than Ed's, which creates a feeling of unfairness. Equity theory holds that Ed will be motivated to change the situation so that his and Carl's ratios are equal.

contributes.[9] In Figure 4-3, Ed compares himself to Carl—a person performing similar work in the same organization. It is important to realize that while Ed believes Carl is paid more, this may not actually be the case. However, inequity still exists because of what Ed believes, and Ed will still be motivated to achieve equity.

People can make a number of different kinds of comparisons with others in which to draw conclusions about fairness. We have seen that Ed compares himself with Carl, someone who has the same job. Ed might also be inclined to compare himself to individuals or groups of people in other departments within his organization, even if they do different work than Ed. Ed might compare himself against his own expectations, such as where he expected to be at this stage of his career. Ed could even compare himself with an individual or group in another organization. To illustrate, consider the following scenario where Ed uses a referent from another company.

Ed's next door neighbor, Carolyn, works at Donnelly Corp.—the Holland, Michigan, manufacturer of mirrors, windshields, and other precision glass products for the auto industry. Part of Carolyn's work satisfaction comes from Donnelly's governance system, called "equity structure," which operates as a republic. Her factory is organized into small teams, which set their own goals and have broad discretion in how they do their work. Each team chooses a representative to serve on the "equity committee"—a forum for the entire building. One person from the equity committee is chosen as their representative to the Donnelly Committee, whose members also include senior management. The Donnelly Committee's power is limited to matters that directly concern employees. It solicits ideas from employees, studies, and debates issues, and develops plans for running the plan in a way that is perceived to be fair.

To an interested audience of coworkers, Ed laments, "You should see how Donnelly listens to their employees and the input they have. No one listens to us. It's not fair!" In this case, Ed is comparing his work situation with his perceptions of the working environment in another organization. Needless to say, Ed is frustrated with his situation and prepares a poster like that found in Figure 4-4.

Types of Inequity.   There are two types of inequity in the work environment. The first is *negative* or *underpayment* inequity. Ed perceives that he and Carl have relatively equal inputs and perform the same work. Since Carl's outcomes are greater—he is paid more—Ed's outcome/input ratio is lower than Carl's. Ed believes this to be unfair. Equity theory purports that when there is substantial felt inequity, people will be motivated to correct the situation. Ed might attempt to maximize the amount of positive outcomes he receives. In this case, Ed will be motivated to correct the perceived inequity by contacting his boss and building a case for a pay raise, or he may search for other positive outcomes. If Ed is unable to increase his outcomes, then he may resort to lowering his inputs by putting forth less effort on the job, staying away at critical times, or by being physically present at work but psychologically tuned out (inattentive) to the goals of the department. While Ed could also increase his inputs by coming to work earlier,

FIGURE 4-4

A disgruntled employee's response.

How This Company Considers Your Input!

Put your ideas here.

One flush should do it!

staying later, or taking classes to add to his knowledge base, research shows that most employees will resist increasing their inputs when it requires substantial effort, or when there is a belief that the outcomes will not be proportional to the effort expended.

The other type of inequity is *positive* or *overpayment* inequity. Carl, for example, experiences positive inequity because his outcome to input ratio is higher than Ed's. To say that he enjoys the situation may be incorrect. It is doubtful that he will be motivated to correct the situation. It is not common to find an employee saying he or she is overpaid. Yet the employee may sense that the situation is not fair and realize that a similar situation could impact him or her at a later point. These feelings of discomfort may negatively impact performance. However, some individuals may be motivated (willing to put forth the effort) to maintain the overpayment inequity.

Supervisors and Equity Theory.   What are the implications of equity theory for supervisor? First, it provides another explanation for how perceptions and beliefs about what is fair influence job performance. Secondly, it acquaints managers with the potential disasters that can occur when rewards are not aligned with performance. Ed's constant whining about the unfair situation could have a negative effect on other employees. While some people like to distant themselves from the whiners (negativists), others will find solace in Ed's continuing claims of unfairness and jump on the bandwagon. The situation can get out of hand: divisive factions can develop that threaten organizational effectiveness. Effective supervisors must be constantly vigilant for signs of unfairness and immediately address employee concerns. Questions such as "*what is not fair?*" "*why is it not fair?*" "*what would it take to make it fair?*" and the like need to be asked. Additionally, the supervisor may give Ed information that will help him to better assess his own and Carl's outcomes/inputs. However, research indicates that rather than change perceptions about oneself, Ed is more apt to change his cognitions about Carl's outcomes/inputs or to change to another referent other.

Often, employees like Ed feel they have to go somewhere else because their organization does not appreciate their contributions. How many times have you heard someone say "I'm not happy with the way I was treated!" An understanding of equity theory and the other motivational theories is not enough. Supervisors must find out what employees want, need, and perceive as just and equitable rewards for their contributions.

3

Compare the assumptions and applications of Theory X and Theory Y in supervision.

COMPARING THEORY X AND THEORY Y

A continuous (and unresolved) question that often confronts supervisors is what general approach, or style, will best contribute to positive employee motivation. This age-old dilemma typically focuses on the degree to which supervisory approaches should be based on satisfying employees' lower-level and higher-level needs. This often becomes an issue of the degree to which supervisors should rely on their authority and position as compared with trying to utilize human relations practices that may provide greater opportunities for employee motivation.

Research concerning supervisory management styles is replete with many findings and some contradictions. Here we first review the contributions of Douglas McGregor.

McGregor's Theory X and Theory Y

In his book *The Human Side of Enterprise,* Douglas McGregor noted that individual supervisory approaches usually relate to each supervisor's perceptions concerning what people are all about. That is, each supervisor manages employees according to his or her own attitudes and ideas about people's needs and motivations. For purposes of comparison, McGregor stated that the extremes in attitudes among managers could be classified as Theory X and Theory Y.

The basic assumptions of Theory X and Theory Y as stated by McGregor are as follows:[10]

Theory X
Assumption that most employees dislike work, avoid responsibility, and must be coerced to do the job.

Theory Y
Assumption that most employees enjoy work, seek responsibility, and are capable of self-direction.

Theory X: the assumption that most employees dislike work, avoid responsibility, and must be coerced to work hard.

Theory Y: the assumption that most employees enjoy work, seek responsibility, and are capable of self-direction.

Supervisors who are Theory X oriented have a limited view of employees' capabilities and motivation. They feel that employees must be strictly controlled; closely supervised; and motivated on the basis of money, discipline, and authority. Theory X supervisors believe that the key to motivation is in the proper implementation of approaches designed to satisfy employees' lower-level needs.

Theory Y supervisors have a much higher opinion of employees' capabilities. They feel that if the proper approaches and conditions can be implemented, employees will exercise self-direction and self-control toward the accomplishment of worthwhile objectives. According to this view, management's objectives should fit into the scheme of each employee's particular set of needs. Therefore, Theory Y managers believe that the higher-level needs of employees are more important in terms of each employee's own personality and self-development.

The two approaches described by McGregor represent extremes in supervisory styles (as illustrated in Figure 4-5 on page 110). Realistically, most supervisors are somewhere between Theory X and Theory Y. Neither of these approaches is right or wrong in and of itself, for the appropriateness of a given approach will depend on the needs of the individuals involved and the demands of the situation. In practice, supervisors may on occasion take an approach that is contrary to their preferred one. For example, even the strongest Theory Y supervisor may revert to Theory X in a time of crisis, such as when the department is shorthanded, when there is an equipment failure, when a serious disciplinary problem has occurred, or when a few employees need firm direction.

Advantages and Limitations of Theory X.   Supervisors who adopt the Theory X style typically find that in the short term a job is accomplished faster. Since the questioning of orders is not encouraged, it may appear that the workers are competent and knowledgeable and that work groups are well organized, efficient, and disciplined.

A major disadvantage of the Theory X approach is that there is little opportunity for employee personal growth. Since supervision is close and constant, employees are unlikely to develop initiative and independence. Moreover, most workers resent Theory X supervision, and this may breed negative motivation. Traditionally, supervisors who

FIGURE 4-5   The two extremes of managerial approach are typified by the Theory X and Theory Y supervisors.

advocated the Theory X approach could get employees to do what they wanted by using the "carrot-and-stick" approach ("Do what I want you to do and you will be rewarded!"). Punishments were applied when the job was not done. This approach is still used by many. However, employees may rebel when confronted with the stick, and supervisors may not have sufficient rewards to get employees to subject themselves to this tight control.

Advantages and Limitations of Theory Y.   An overriding advantage of Theory Y supervision is that it promotes individual growth. Since workers are given opportunities to assume some responsibility on their own and are encouraged to contribute their ideas in accomplishing their tasks, it is possible for them to partially satisfy their higher-level needs on the job.

Although the Theory Y approach is often viewed as more desirable, it is not without some disadvantages. Theory Y can be time consuming in practice, especially in the short term. Since personal development is emphasized, supervisors must become instructors and coaches if they are to help their employees move toward the simultaneous attainment of organizational and personal goals. Some supervisors find the extreme application of Theory Y to be more idealistic than practical since some employees expect firm direction from their supervisors.

4

Discuss supervisory approaches for stimulating employee motivation—especially broadened job tasks, job redesign, and participative management.

SUPERVISORY APPROACHES FOR ATTAINING POSITIVE EMPLOYEE MOTIVATION

Having reviewed several prominent theories of employee motivation, the next question is how can these be applied in the most meaningful ways? There is no simple set of dos and don'ts that a supervisor can implement to achieve high motivation and excellent performance. Human beings are much too complex for that. Although supervisory skills can be learned and developed, no one formula will apply in all situations and with all people.

Broadening the Scope and Importance of Each Job

There are ways to give employees new tasks and new work experiences by which the basic nature of the job can be broadened in scope and importance. Variety and challenge can keep jobs from becoming monotonous and can fulfill employee needs.

Job rotation

The process of switching job tasks among employees in the work group.

Job Rotation.   Switching job tasks among employees in the work group on a scheduled basis is known as **job rotation.** This is a process that most supervisors can implement, and it often is accompanied by higher levels of job performance and increased employee interest. Job rotation not only helps to relieve employees' boredom, but also enhances their job knowledge. Although the different tasks may require the same skill level, learning different jobs prepares employees for promotion in the future. A major side benefit to the supervisor is that job rotation results in a more flexible workforce, which can be advantageous during periods of employee absence. Moreover, job rotation should mean that employees share both pleasant and unpopular tasks so work assignments are perceived as fair.

Job enlargement

Increasing the number of tasks an individual performs.

Job Enlargement.   Another motivational strategy is **job enlargement,** which means expanding an employee's job with a greater variety of tasks to perform. For example, tasks that previously were handled by several employees may be combined or consolidated within one or two enlarged jobs.

Some employees respond positively to job enlargement, and this is reflected in their performance and in increased job satisfaction. In one furniture factory, for example, a number of routine jobs were changed so that each job required five or six operations rather than just one constantly repeated operation. Employees were supportive of the change. Such comments as, "My job seems more important now" and "My work is less monotonous now" were common reactions.

There can be problems in implementing job enlargement. Union work rules and job jurisdictional lines may limit the supervisor's authority to change job assignments.

Attitudes toward the idea of job enlargement may also present significant difficulties. Some employees, for example, object to the idea of being given expanded duties because they are content with their present jobs and pay. Usually they will not object if at least a small increase in pay comes with the enlarged job.

Job enrichment

Job design that helps fulfill employees' higher-level needs by giving them more challenging tasks and more decision-making responsibility for their jobs.

Job Enrichment.   A motivational approach that is increasingly advocated is **job enrichment,** which means assigning more challenging tasks and giving employees more decision-making responsibility for their jobs. Job enrichment goes beyond job rotation and job enlargement in an effort to appeal to the higher-level needs of employees. To enrich jobs, the supervisor should assign everyone in a department a fair share of the challenging as well as the routine jobs and give employees more autonomy in accomplishing the tasks. Unfortunately, many supervisors prefer to assign the difficult, challenging jobs only to their best employees and the dull jobs to the weaker employees. This can be defeating in the long term. The supervisor should provide opportunities for all employees to find challenging and interesting work experiences within the realistic framework of the department's operations. Sometimes job enrichment can be accomplished by committee assignments, special problem-solving tasks, and other unusual job experiences that go beyond the routine performance of day-to-day work. In its most developed form, job enrichment may involve restructuring jobs in such a way that employees are given direct control and responsibility for what they do.

Supervisors may be uncomfortable with job enrichment at first. It may require them to relinquish some control and delegate some planning and decision making. But if job enrichment is practiced sincerely, subordinates usually assume an active role in making or participating in decisions about their jobs over time. The result can be bet-

Job enrichment can help reduce boredom and increase interest and knowledge for employees by giving employees more decision-making responsibility

ter decisions and a more satisfied and motivated workforce. For example, one supervisor enriched the jobs of machine operators by giving them a greater role in scheduling work and devising their own work rules for the group. The result was a schedule that better met their needs and rules that they were willing to follow since they helped create them.

In a sense, job enrichment involves the employees' assumption of some of the supervisor's everyday responsibilities. The supervisor remains accountable, however, for the satisfactory fulfillment of these obligations. Therein lies a major risk inherent in job enrichment; yet, despite the risk, many supervisors endorse job enrichment because it works.

Comparing the Approaches to Job Enhancement.   The differences among job enrichment, job enlargement, and job rotation are a matter of degree. Each is an attempt to diversify work and make it more meaningful to employees. Job enrichment adds a vertical dimension, or greater depth, to the task so that employees can satisfy their higher-level needs through their work. Job enlargement emphasizes the horizontal dimension of the task since it gives employees more duties. Job rotation moves an employee from one job to another on a periodic basis with the intent of reducing boredom and increasing employee interest and breadth of knowledge. These three job design strategies are similar in the sense that each attempts to increase employee performance by improving job satisfaction.

Job Redesign

It is generally believed that well-designed jobs lead to increased motivation, higher-quality performance, higher satisfaction, and lower absenteeism and turnover. These desirable outcomes occur when employees experience three critical psychological states:

1. They believe that they are doing something meaningful because their work is important to other people.
2. They feel personally responsible for how the work turns out.
3. They learn how well they performed their jobs.

Many job redesign programs are based on the model developed by Professors Hackman and Oldham (see Figure 4-6 on page 114). Their model says that the greater the experienced meaningfulness of work, responsibility for the work performed, and knowledge of the results, the more positive the work-related benefits will be. According to this model, any job can be described in terms of the following five core job dimensions:

1. *Skill variety:* the degree to which an employee has an opportunity to do various tasks and to use a number of different skills and abilities.
2. *Task identity:* the completion of a whole, identifiable piece of work.
3. *Task significance:* the degree to which the job impacts the lives or work of others.
4. *Autonomy:* the amount of independence, freedom, and discretion that an employee has in making decisions about the work to be done.
5. *Feedback:* the amount of information an employee receives on job performance.[11]

FIGURE 4-6

The job characteristics
model.

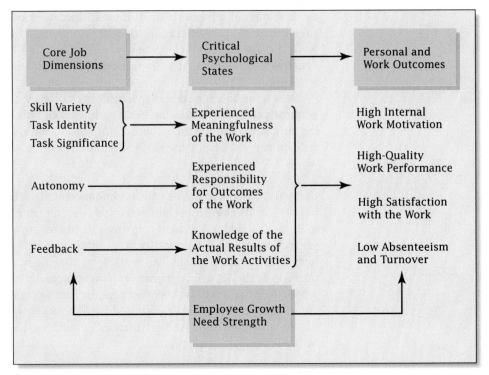

Source: J. Richard Hackman and Greg R. Oldham, *Work Redesign* (adapted from Figure 4.6), © 1980 by Addison-Wesley
Publishing Company, Inc. Reprinted by permission of Addison-Wesley Longman, Inc.

The instrument contained in Skills Application 4-2 can be used to evaluate your
own job to determine the extent to which each of these characteristics is present. With
this instrument it is possible to calculate a "motivating potential score" (MPS) for the
specific job. Low scores indicate that the individual will not experience high internal
motivation from the job. Such a job is a prime candidate for job redesign. Suppose that
close examination reveals that the task significance score is relatively low. The supervisor could, for example, assign workers in a word processing pool to specific departments
as opposed to letting the word processing pool serve the company as a whole. This approach could increase both skill variety and task significance scores, thereby increasing
the job's motivating potential.[12]

On the other hand, high scores indicate that the job is currently stimulating high
internal motivation. According to Hackman and Oldham's theory, internal motivation
occurs because the employee is "turned on to [his or her] work because of the positive
internal feelings that are generated by doing well, rather than being dependent on external factors (such as incentive pay, job security, or praise from the supervisor) for the
motivation to work effectively."[13]

Participative Management

In his best-selling book *A Great Place to Work,* Robert Levering postulates that the high morale of great workplaces consists of pride in what you do (the job itself), enjoying the people you're working with (the work group), and trusting the people you work for (management practices and economic rewards).[14] Levering has been tracking great employers since 1981 and in 1998 reported that the Dallas-headquartered Southwest Airlines received the coveted number one ranking. Why Southwest? According to comments received from enthusiastic employees: "Working here is truly an unbelievable experience. They treat you with respect, pay you well, and empower you. They use your ideas to solve problems. They encourage you to be yourself. I love going to work!!"[15]

But do the comments from the Southwest Airlines employees translate into better company performance? While it is not the intent of the authors to enter the "employee job satisfaction—company performance" debate, we would like to reaffirm our belief that "happy cows do give more milk." A Gallup poll of 55,000 workers found that four attitudes, taken together, correlate strongly with higher profits. These attitudes are as follows:

- Workers feel they are given the opportunity to do what they do best every day.
- Workers believe their opinions count.
- Workers sense their fellow workers are committed to quality.
- Workers make a direct connection between their work and the company's mission.[16]

To support our contention, consider Great Plains Software, a leading supplier of accounting software for small businesses. In addition to having been selected three times to *The 100 Best Companies to Work For* list, Great Plains is the first company to be recognized by Arthur Andersen with an award in two different categories—"Exceeding Customer Satisfaction" and "Motivating and Retaining Employees." See this chapter's second "Contemporary Issue" box.

As mentioned in Chapter 1 of this text, *empowerment* refers to giving employees the authority and responsibility to accomplish organizational objectives. (For another perspective, see Figure 4-7 on page 117.) Providing opportunities to make suggestions and participate in decisions affecting their jobs is one of the most effective ways to build a sense of employee pride, teamwork, and motivation. This supervisory approach, in which employees have an active role in decision making, has historically been referred to as *participative management.*

Delegation, to be discussed in greater detail in Chapter 14, is important to building positive motivation among employees. This does not mean turning over all decisions to employees, nor does it mean just making employees believe that they are participating in decisions. Rather, it means that the supervisor should earnestly seek employees' opinions whenever possible and be willing to be influenced by their suggestions and even by their criticisms. When employees feel that they are part of a team and that they can have an influence on the decisions that affect them, they are more likely to accept the decisions and seek new solutions to future problems.

However, if supervisors want employees to be increasingly responsible for business results, they must teach them how the business works. Noted author Ken Blanchard as-

contemporary issue

Company Profile: Great Plains Software, Inc.—Fargo, North Dakota

Founded in 1981, Great Plains is a leading provider of enterprise business management software that includes financial, distribution, manufacturing, human resource, consolidation and budgeting, and service management solutions. Selected as one of The 100 Best Companies to Work for in America, Great Plains employs nearly 900 people worldwide. The company's products and services automate essential business and financial management functions. Its products are sold and implemented by a unique network of independent partner organizations who share its commitment to lasting customer service.

"Customer service is a key component of each employee's performance measurement," says Dennis Erdle, vice president of global services, vertical markets. "Each employee is a shareholder (stock options are granted to each employee), and therefore has a genuine stake in the success of the company. We have a companywide bonus incentive plan that is very specific with respect to department goals, and they tie in with the overall company targets. Everyone knows how they can affect the achievement of these goals on a daily basis."

Customers have direct access to the company—from support to upper management. Executives—from supervisors to the CEO—call customers and partners regularly to make sure service and product expectations are being met. Employees also conduct on-site visits to ensure customer satisfaction.

In a knowledge-based business, retaining and motivating team members is essential to an organization's success," says Doug Burgum, Great Plains chairman and CEO. "Smart, happy, empowered employees provide the foundation for superior customer service, and that helps us deliver on our mission of improving the lives and business success of partners and customers." Great Plains has been able to tie individual and team performance to its company mission and shared values and has used the imagery of the "plains" region to articulate these strong performances.

Among the key employee-oriented practices are an automated performance management process; companywide bonus plan based on company profitability and growth; team-based recognition events [recognition occurs frequently and creatively, yet with emotion and sincerity]; annual recognition awards include Jesse James (Innovation), Heritage (Customer Service), Frontier (Learning), Harvest (Quality), and Pioneer (Lifetime Achievement), among others; and paid sabbaticals. Great Plains offers employee training in a variety of media including Great Plains University, which offers just-in-time training 24 hours a day.

The mission statement "To improve the life and business success of partners and customers," and core values are prominently displayed on red paper everywhere. "The culture of Great Plains can be described as 'casually intense,'" says Jodi Uecker-Rust, executive vice-president. "We foster a work hard/play hard environment where employees dress casually, create personal workspaces and have fun, but also strive to always exceed customer and partner expectations."

Sources: Adapted with permission of Arthur Andersen Enterprise Group, "Special Advertising Section," *Fortune* (March 1, 1999). Information verified by Kim Albrecht, public relations manager, Great Plains (September 20, 1999). Also see Robert Levering and Milton Moskowitz, "The 100 Best Companies to Work for in America" *Fortune* (January 12 1998); and "Far Out in Fargo," *Stanford Business* (June 1999).

serts that "management must start by sharing information about its financial performance, its market share, its profitability, its costs—everything managers use to make informed decisions. Sharing information that tells it like it really is creates a sense of ownership in employees."[17] Supervisors who practice participative management properly are aware of the importance of their information-giving and information-getting

Empowerment: another viewpoint.

Great damage is being done by overuse and misuse of the term *empowerment*. We are reaching a stage where the word means whatever a particular manager wants it to mean. Some of the examples quoted to show the importance of empowerment are laughable. To allow the counter hand at a burger bar to distribute additional sachets of sauce if the customer wants them is not empowerment, it's a modification to the standard. If the same counter hand were allowed to close down the burger bar for an hour because she believed the french fries were below standard, that would be empowerment. In some cultures, management's use of words "employee empowerment" can be a harbinger of fear. The employee's expectation is that they are going to have to take responsibility for everything that goes wrong.

Empowerment quite simply means granting supervisors or workers permission to give the customer priority over other issues in the operation. In practical terms, it relates to the resources, skill, time, and support to become leaders rather than controllers or mindless robots. The concept lies at the heart of managing with *common sense*.

Source: John MacDonald, *Calling a Halt to Mindless Change*, copyright © 1998. Reprinted by permission of AMACOM, a division of American Management Association International, New York, NY. All rights reserved. http://www.amanet.org

skills. They also know that it is vital to respond fully to subordinates' suggestions as soon as they have had sufficient time to consider them.

The major advantages of participative management are that decisions tend to be of higher quality and that employees are more willing to accept them. One disadvantage is that this approach can be time consuming. Also, participation makes it easier for employees to criticize, which some supervisors find threatening. On balance, however, participative management is widely recognized as an effective motivational strategy. Its advantages far outweigh its disadvantages.

Employee Suggestion Programs.   Organizations like Dana Corporation continue to actively solicit employee input. "We encourage and expect two ideas per person per month with 80 percent implementation," says company spokesperson, Gary Corrigan. He says some of the best ideas have been the simplest ones, such as the employee who started using a $1.29 bicycle mirror to inspect the underside of an axle, rather than having to turn the heavy piece over.[18] While some suggestion systems provide monetary rewards to employees for suggestions that are received and accepted, the monetary reward is only part of the employee's overall compensation. Employees like to have their suggestions heard and answered. To some employees, the fact that a suggestion has been implemented may mean more than the monetary reward.

Employee Involvement Programs.   During the past two decades, most organizations have adopted various forms of participatory management programs. These types of programs often are known by other labels, such as employee involvement programs, problem-solving teams, quality circles, semi-autonomous or self-directed work teams, and the like. Regardless of what they are called, they are based on the beliefs that employees want to contribute to the long-term success of the organization and that

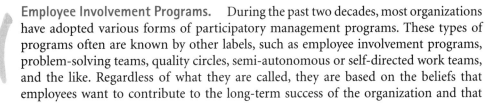

managers have a strong commitment to participatory management as a way of organizational life.

Supervising with a Management-by-Objectives Emphasis. Another well-known motivational approach that has been widely adopted is called "management by objectives" (MBO), or "management by results." Stated simply, **management by objectives** involves (1) having individual employees set or participate in setting their own performance targets within certain limits (rather than having the targets unilaterally set by supervisors or higher-level managers) and (2) having employees initially appraise themselves in the context of their own objectives. Some organizations have elaborate MBO systems that extend from top-level managers all the way down to entry-level employees.

Management by objectives (MBO)
Participative management system through which jointly set objectives are used for performance appraisal.

MBO will not work with everyone, and it is not a cure-all for supervisory problems. However, it does offer an approach by which the burden of certain aspects of planning and performance appraisal is placed on the employee rather than on the supervisor. This in itself should make it attractive to supervisors. Chapter 6 describes a step-by-step outline of the MBO process in greater detail.

What Call Did You Make?

Motivating employees is central to the challenge facing John Jackson. Currently, the goals of the employees are not consistent with organizational expectations.

As John Jackson, you must facilitate motivation by taking supportive actions. You will need to strive to understand your employees and their needs. Remember: Each employee is unique. Therefore, the next time you discuss productivity with Sandy and Tony, do it individually. You might learn more about their personal values, attitudes, needs, and expectations that way.

You will need to establish and clarify desired behavior patterns for the employees. Ask yourself these questions: What happens when employees do the job right? Are they being appropriately recognized for achievement? You will need to develop a reward system for reinforcing employee accomplishments. The reward system for performing the job well must be consistent with employees' individual needs. You should ascertain what they consider to be not fair about the work, the working conditions, the work environment, and the like. Review the section of the chapter on equity theory and ask questions.

Good communication is essential to your success. You must listen and observe to assess your employees' needs, and you must communicate your expectations. Quality is one of the most important accomplishments of an organization. Therefore, you must constantly stress its importance. You might consider allowing small groups of employees to interact directly with the major client, Ford, to fully appreciate the importance of doing the job right the first time. This would elevate the task significance aspect of their jobs. You might arrange to have a group of Ford employees visit your facility or allow your informal leaders to visit the Ford facility. This will enable your employees to understand how they can better meet the needs of the customer.

There are other strategies you might use to increase the meaningfulness of employees' jobs. The self-reporting questionnaire presented in Skills Application 4-

2 could be used to assess the motivating potential of these jobs. If scores are low, you can attempt to discover which of the core job characteristics is causing the problem. If the scores are high, you will need to look for other factors that are causing the dissatisfaction.

In addition, it may be appropriate to use management by objectives or one of the other employee participation programs cited in the chapter. However, if the comments by Sandy and Tony are reflective of the feelings of the majority, then you will have to deal with these feelings of inequity and frustration before you can begin an employee participation program. Discipline may be appropriate if performance does not improve. Ultimately, if quality does not improve substantially, Amity may lose its major customer, and many employees may lose their jobs.

SUMMARY

Every human being is unique. Behavior is influenced by many factors within both the individual and the environment. Personality is the complex mix of knowledge, attitudes, and attributes that distinguishes one person from another.

Prominent factors that interact to form the personality of each individual include physiological makeup, early childhood experiences, the immediate and continuing environment through life, and cultural values. The working environment is one of the almost unlimited number of influences that become part of an employee's personality.

Supervisors need to be sensitive to individual differences and similarities among human beings. A consistent supervisory approach based on similarities is a practical way to lead employees.

Motivation is a willingness to exert effort toward achieving a goal, stimulated by the effort's ability to fulfill an individual need. According to Maslow, needs in ascending order of importance are biological, security, social, self-respect, and self-fulfillment. When a lower-level need is fulfilled, higher-level needs emerge that influence one's motivation.

It is important for supervisors to recognize the different need levels. Supervisors can influence employee motivation in a positive way if they rely on supervisory approaches that promote higher-level need fulfillment. When employee needs are not satisfied on the job, job performance usually suffers. Some employees express their dissatisfaction through absenteeism; others may display aggressive and disruptive behavior; still others quit. The result is that the organization suffers from a decrease in production and a loss of quality.

Herzberg's motivation-hygiene research studies indicate that hygiene factors such as money, management policies, working conditions, and certain aspects of supervision must be adequate to maintain a reasonable level of motivation. Forces that stimulate good performance, called *motivation factors,* are intrinsic to the job—for example, the employees' needs for achievement, opportunity for advancement, challenging work, promotion, growth, and recognition. Effective supervisors implement strategies that target motivation factors to promote good job performance.

Expectancy theory suggests that employees will be motivated if they perceive links between their efforts and performance and between their performance and rewards. Supervisors must clarify such relationships for the workers or strive to develop them.

Equity theory of motivation explains how people strive for fairness based on an outcome/input ratio. Employees can compare themselves with many other people, even ones who do not work in their organization, to determine if perceived equity or inequity exists. Supervisors need to watch for felt inequity, know the possible effects, and address employee concerns.

The Theory X (authoritarian) supervisor believes primarily in authoritarian techniques, which relate to the lower-level human needs. The Theory Y supervisor prefers to build motivation by appealing to employees' higher-level needs.

The major approaches to job design include job rotation, job enlargement, and job enrichment. The job characteristics model has been used to guide job redesign efforts.

The advantages of participative management are that decisions tend to be of higher quality, and employees are more willing to accept decisions. Employee participation programs are widely used and varied in application. Delegation strategies, suggestion programs, quality circles, self-directed work teams, and management by objectives are approaches that emphasize employee involvement.

Getting people at all levels of the organization involved in objective setting and problem solving, rearranging duties and responsibilities, and creating ways to reward people for their accomplishments are the essence of the approaches to motivate employee performance. The supervisor must learn to implement different supervisory approaches as appropriate to different people and settings.

KEY TERMS

Personality (page 94)
Motivation (page 96)
Hierarchy of needs (Maslow) (page 97)
Biological needs (page 97)
Security needs (page 98)
Social needs (page 98)
Self-respect needs (page 98)
Self-fulfillment needs (page 98)
Motivation-hygiene theory (Herzberg)
    (page 102)
Motivation factors (page 102)

Hygiene factors (page 102)
Expectancy theory (page 104)
Equity theory (page 105)
Theory X (page 109)
Theory Y (page 109)
Job rotation (page 111)
Job enlargement (page 111)
Job enrichment (page 112)
Management by objectives (MBO)
    (page 118)

QUESTIONS FOR DISCUSSION

1. Why is human behavior a complex subject? How can determinants of personality be influenced or controlled by the supervisor?
2. From the aspect of practical application, what are the benefits of each of the motivational theories discussed in the chapter?
3. Lora Figgins' and F. William Sunderman's work lives may have left them exhausted and frustrated at times, but obviously they found meaning in their work (see this chapter's first "Contemporary Issue" box). What are some of the most likely factors that caused them to continue working? Are those factors important for you? Why or why not?
4. What are the basic elements of Theory X and Theory Y? Can you think of any reasons why Theory Y would not be appropriate for every supervisor?
5. What are the benefits of job rotation? Why might an employee resist job rotation?

6. Why might an employee not respond positively to the supervisor's efforts to enrich his or her job?
7. How might the concepts of the job characteristics model be used to increase the internal motivation of Sandy and Tony in the "You Make the Call" section?
8. How confident are you that Great Plains' (see this chapter's second "Contemporary Issue" box) style of management will continue in the future? After reading about Great Plains and Southwest Airlines, what recommendations would you have for your employer? For your future employer?
9. What does the term *empowerment* mean to you? How will your definition change the role of the supervisor?
10. What should a supervisor do to solicit employee input?

SKILLS APPLICATION

Skills Application 4-1: Satisfying Attributes of the Job

1. Working independently, rank the following 12 items in the order of their importance to you. In the left-hand column place the number 1 next to the most important item, the number 2 next to the second most important, and so on through item 12.
2. When everyone has completed the task, your instructor will aggregate the rankings of all individuals. Enter the aggregate ranking in the right-hand column.
3. Compare your individual rankings with those of the entire class. How do you explain the differences?
4. Why did perceptions differ among class members? What factors account for these differences?

What Do People Want From Their Jobs?

____   Freedom to do my job   ____

____   Supervisors and coworkers that care about me as a person   ____

____   A work environment where others listen and act upon my ideas and suggestions ____

____   Opportunity to learn new skills   ____

____   The material and equipment to do the job right the first time   ____

____   Good compensation and benefits   ____

____   Opportunity to make work-related decisions   ____

____   Job security   ____

____   Praise and recognition for a job well done   ____

____   Interesting and challenging work   ____

____   Opportunity to use a variety of skills   ____

____   Knowing what is expected of me   ____

Skills Application 4-2: Job Diagnostic Survey

Hackman and Oldham developed a self-report instrument for managers to use in diagnosing their work environment. The first step in calculating the "motivating potential score" (MPS) of your job is to complete the following questionnaire.

1. Use the scales below to indicate whether each statement is an accurate or inadequate description of your present or most recent job. After completing the instrument, use the scoring key to compute a total score for each of the core job characteristics.

   5 = Very descriptive   2 = Mostly nondescriptive
   4 = Mostly descriptive   1 = Very nondescriptive
   3 = Somewhat descriptive

   _____ 1. I have almost complete responsibility for deciding how and when the work is to be done.

   _____ 2. I have a chance to do a number of different tasks, using a wide variety of different skills and talents.

   _____ 3. I do a complete task from start to finish. The results of my efforts are clearly visible and identifiable.

   _____ 4. What I do affects the well-being of other people in very important ways.

   _____ 5. My manager provides me with constant feedback about how I am doing.

   _____ 6. The work itself provides me with information about how well I am doing.

   _____ 7. I make insignificant contributions to the final product or service.

   _____ 8. I get to use a number of complex skills on this job.

   _____ 9. I have very little freedom in deciding how the work is to be done.

   _____ 10. Just doing the work provides me with opportunities to figure out how well I am doing.

   _____ 11. The job is quite simple and repetitive.

   _____ 12. My supervisors or coworkers rarely give me feedback on how well I am doing the job.

   _____ 13. What I do is of little consequence to anyone else.

   _____ 14. My job involves doing a number of different tasks.

   _____ 15. Supervisors let us know how well they think we are doing.

   _____ 16. My job is arranged so that I do not have a chance to do an entire piece of work from beginning to end.

   _____ 17. My job does not allow me an opportunity to use discretion or participate in decision making.

   _____ 18. The demands of my job are highly routine and predictable.

   _____ 19. My job provides few clues about whether I'm performing adequately.

   _____ 20. My job is not very important to the company's survival.

   _____ 21. My job gives me considerable freedom in doing the work.

   _____ 22. My job provides me with the chance to finish completely any work I start.

   _____ 23. Many people are affected by the job I do.

2. Scoring Key:
   Skill variety (SV) (items #2, 8, 11*, 14, 18*) = ___ /5 = ___
   Task identity (TI) (items #3, 7*, 16*, 22) = ___ /4 = ___
   Task significance (TS) (items #4, 13*, 20*, 23) = ___ /4 = ___
   Autonomy (AU) (items #1, 9*, 17*, 21) = ___ /4 = ___
   Feedback (FB) (items #5, 6, 10, 12*, 15, 19*) = ___ /6 = ___

(Note: For the items with asterisks, subtract your score from 6.)

Total the numbers for each characteristic and divide by the number of items to get an average score.

3. Now you are ready to calculate the MPS by using the following formula:

$$\text{Motivating Potential Score (MPS)} = \frac{SV + TI + TS}{3} \times AU \times FB$$

MPS scores range from 1 to 125.

4. You can compare your job characteristics with those of a fellow classmate or with norms that your instructor has. Is the MPS of your job high, average, or low?
5. What could be done to increase the motivating potential of your job?

Source: J. Richard Hackman and Greg R. Oldham, *Work Redesign* (adapted from pp. 80, 81, 90, and 303–306) © 1980 by Addison-Wesley Publishing Company, Inc. Reprinted by permission of Addison-Wesley Longman, Inc.

Skills Application 4-3: Motivating Different People

The 450-person workforce at Omni Computer Works, Inc., breaks out into several distinctive classifications. The following stereotypes describe the employees.

"Whiners"—a handful of employees whose behavior typifies that of Sandy Hall and Tony Aquirre (see this chapter's "You Make the Call").

"GenXers"—that group of employees often described in the media as the disenchanted, disenfranchised Americans now in their mid-20s to mid-30s. They comprise about 33 percent of Omni's workforce.

"Generation Yers"—the teens of today. This group, clustered in entry-level, routine jobs, represents about 5 percent of Omni's workforce.

"Baby Boomers"—the group born between 1946 and 1963 that makes up 30 percent of Omni's employee base.

"Gray Hairs"—employees 55+ years of age. They represent 10 percent of Omni's workforce.

"Techies" or *"Geeks"*—the group that cuts across a wide age range but is identified separately. This highly skilled group creates great software and the hardware to run it. They think logically and if you ask them a question, they will give you a precisely truthful answer. The demand for this group is very high. At least ten positions at Omni are currently vacant.

INTERNET ACTIVITY

1. Using the Internet or a search vehicle such as ABInform, review the contents of recent articles written about the groups identified above.
   a. Make a list of the adjectives that describe the typical person in each group.
   b. Identify and rank order the needs that drive the typical person. How would you explain the similarities and differences among the groups? Would you expect there to be differences within each group? Why or why not?
   c. Identify from this chapter or your outside reading sources a list of what you believe to be the most important motivational application concepts that a supervisor should apply in order to motivate the typical employee in each group to peak performance.
2. Your instructor will divide you into small groups that represent a cross-section of the class. Each small group will be assigned one of the employee classifications and is to discuss the following questions/statements as they relate to their assigned classification. The instructor may have each group present their analysis to the entire class.

a. "Money is the prime motivator of people."
b. "Time off is the primary motivator of people"
c. "Freedom to do the job is the primary motivator."
d. "Different strokes for different folks is the only way to motivate people"

3. Write a paragraph identifying what you learned from this skill application.

Skills Application 4-4: Motivation and Success

INTERNET ACTIVITY

Visit the *Fortune* magazine Web site (www.fortune.com), click on Company Lists, and view a listing of the 100 Best Companies to Work For. View the top ten companies from the list.

1. In the company profiles you view, what key factors have contributed to their success? Compile a list of the benefits and perks you find.

2. Which of these benefits and perks are most motivational to you? On the Company Lists page, click on Rank the 100 By Your Own Criteria. Rank your criteria, select your state, and see which companies rank at the top of your list. Compare your list with that of another classmate.

SKILL DEVELOPMENT VIDEO

SKILL DEVELOPMENT MODULE 4–1: MOTIVATION

This video segment features Ken Foley, production development supervisor at Carson Products.

Questions for Discussion: The Ineffective Version

1. It is obvious that motivation theories are not entirely clear to Ken Foley as he dealt with Jennifer Swanson, Alice Temprance, and J. C. Marko. List specific illustrations to support the observation.
2. Discuss what Foley can do to improve communication between the employees and himself.
3. What can Foley do to effectively motivate his employees to work extra hours and finish the project?

Questions for Discussion: The More Effective Version

1. Discuss how Ken Foley motivated his employees to continuously improve.
2. Discuss how Ken could broaden the scope and importance of each job.
3. What can Ken do to be more effective?

ENDNOTES

1. Many companies rely in part on personality assessment programs to evaluate employees. One of the more widely recognized approaches to the identification of individual differences is the Myers-Briggs Type Indicators. If your college has available the Myers-Briggs test, use it to identify your basic personality type. You can also use it to identify those personality types that do not complement your style.
2. Margaret Henning and Anne Jardim, *The Managerial Woman* (New York: Anchor Press/Doubleday, 1977), p. 82. The social grouping of children at an early age can have lifelong psychological consequences, see Hara Estroff Marano, "The Friendliness Factor," *Working Mother* (November 1998),

pp. 42ff. Additional research supports the contention that early influence was important in leadership development, see Sandra J. Hartman and Jeff O. Harris, "The Role of Parental Influence in Leadership," *Journal of Social Psychology* (April 1992), pp. 153–167. For additional information on personality development, see J. M. George, "The Role of Personality in Organizational Life: Issues and Evidence," Journal of Management (Volume 18, 1992), pp. 185–213; R. D. Arvey, T. J. Bouchard, N. L. Segal, and L. M. Abraham, "Job Satisfaction: Environmental and Genetic Components," *Journal of Applied Psychology* (Volume 74, 1989), pp. 187–192; and R. C. Carson, "Personality," *Annual Review of Psychology* (Volume 40, 1989), pp. 227–248.

3. Priority Management Systems, Inc., *The Values Gap: An International Survey of Time and Value Conflicts in the 1990s Workplace* (Vancouver, Canada, 1996), p. 2.

4. See Abraham H. Maslow, *Motivation and Personality* (2d ed.; New York: Harper & Row, 1970), Chapter 4. Also see Ron Zemke, "Maslow for a New Millennium," *Training* (December 1998), pp. 54–58.

5. See "Executives Note Worker Emphasis on Positive Work Environment," *Quality Digest* (July/August 1999), pp. 14–15. Also see Donna Finn, "Redesign Work: What Do Employees Want?" *Inc.* (June 1999), pp. 75ff for a comparison with previous studies. See Jeffrey L. Seglin, "The Happiest Workers in the World," *Inc. Special Issue: The State of Small Business* (May 21, 1996), pp. 62–74; Timothy Aeppel, "Full Time, Part Time, Temp—All See the Job in a Different Light," *The Wall Street Journal* (February 28, 1997), pp. B1, B6; Linda Morris, "What Makes People Tick?" *Training & Development* (July 1995), pp. 58–62; and Kenneth Kovach, "What Motivates Employees? Workers and Supervisors Give Different Answers," *Business Horizons* (September/October 1987), pp. 58–65.

6. Special Report, "Rethinking Work," *Business Week* (October 17, 1994), pp. 74–87.

7. The complete dual-factor theory is well explained in Frederick Herzberg, Bernard Mausner, and Barbara Bloch Snyderman, *The Motivation to Work* (2d ed.; New York: John Wiley & Sons, 1967); and in Herzberg's classic article, "One More Time: How Do You Motivate Your Employees?" *Harvard Business Review* (Volume 46, January–February 1968), pp. 53–62.

8. For a discussion of expectancy theory, see Victor H. Vroom, *Work and Motivation* (New York: John Wiley & Sons, 1964); and Terrence R. Mitchell, "Expectancy Models of Job Satisfaction, Occupational Preference, and Effort: A Theoretical, Methodological, and Empirical Appraisal," *Psychological Bulletin* (Volume 81, 1974), pp. 1053–1077.

9. J. Stacy Adams, "Toward an Understanding of Inequity," *Journal of Abnormal and Social Psychology* (No. 67, 1963), pp. 422–436. Also see Jerald Greenberg and Claire L. McCarty, "Comparable Worth: A Matter of Justice," in Gerald R. Farris and Kendrith M. Rowland, eds., *Research in Personnel and Human Resource Management* (Greenwich: CT: JAI Press, 1990), pp. 265–303; Greenberg, "Cognitive Reevaluation of Outcomes in Response to Underpayment Inequity," *Academy of Management Journal* (March 1989), pp. 174–184; R. T. Mowday, "Equity Theory Predictions of Behavior in Organizations," in R. M. Steers and L. W. Porter, eds., *Motivation and Work Behavior* (New York: McGraw-Hill, 1987), pp. 89–110; and Robert P. Vecchio, "Predicting Worker Performance in Inequitable Setting," *Academy of Management Review* (January 1982), pp. 103–110.

10. Douglas McGregor, *The Human Side of Enterprise* (New York: McGraw-Hill, 1960), pp. 45–57.

11. J. Richard Hackman, Greg R. Oldham, Robert Janson, and Kenneth Purdy, "A New Strategy for Job Enrichment," *California Management Review* (Summer 1975), pp. 51–71; J. R. Hackman and G. R. Oldham, "Development of the Job Diagnostic Survey," *Journal of Applied Psychology* (Volume 60, 1975), pp. 159–170; J. R. Hackman and G. R. Oldham, *Work Redesign* (Reading, Mass.: Addison-Wesley, 1980); and Carol T. Kulik, Greg R. Oldham, and Paul H. Langner, "Measurement of Job Characteristics: Comparison of the Original and the Revised Job Diagnostic Survey," *Journal of Applied Psychology* (August 1988), pp. 462–466.

12. Hackman, Oldham, Jenson, and Purdy, p. 58.

13. Ibid.

14. Robert Levering, *A Great Place to Work* (New York; Random House, 1988).

15. Robert Levering and Milton Moskowitz, "The 100 Best Companies to Work for in America," *Fortune* (January 12, 1998), pp. 84ff.

16. Linda Grant, "Happy Workers, High Return," *Fortune* (January 12, 1998), p. 81. Also see Jeffrey Pfeffer, *The Human Equation: Building Profits by Putting People First* (Boston: Harvard Business School Press, 1998); Marcus Buckingham and Curt Coffman, *First, Break All the Rules: What the World's Greatest Managers Do Differently* (New York: Simon & Schuster, 1999); and Douglas K. Smith, *Make Success*

Measurable (New York: John Wiley & Sons, 1999). For a different viewpoint, see Glenn Bassett, "The Case Against Job Satisfaction," *Business Horizons* (May/June 1994), pp. 61–68.

17. Ken Blanchard, "Empowerment Is the Key," *Quality Digest* (April 1996), p. 23. Also see Ken Blanchard, Alan Randolph, and John Carlos, *Empowerment Takes More Than a Minute* (San Francisco: Berrett-Koehler, 1996); and Ken Blanchard, John P. Carlos, and Alan Randolph, *The Three Keys to Empowerment: Release the Power Within People for Astonishing Results and Make Success Measurable! A Mindbook-Workbook for Setting Goals and Taking Action* (San Francisco: Berrett-Koehler, 1999).

18. Gary Corrigan as quoted in "If We Might Make a Suggestion," *Training* (July 1999), pp. 20–21. The oldest documented system of formal employee involvement is Eastman Kodak's employee suggestion program, established in 1898. The Employee Involvement Association (EIA) annually reports suggestion system information. Contact EIA, Fairfax, VA 22030; (703) 303-1010 or visit their Web site (www.eia.com). Also see Jeff Washburn's Web site (www.weakleycounty.com/employeeinvolvement) for illustrations of research done on employee involvement concepts.

Chapter 5

Solving Problems: Decision Making and the Supervisor

After studying this chapter, you will be able to:

1
Explain the importance of problem-solving and decision-making skills.

2
Describe the types of decisions made in organizations.

3
Describe and apply the basic steps of the decision-making process.

4
Explain why a supervisor should not make hasty decisions.

Learning Objectives

You Make the Call!

You are Tina Leeming, supervisor of the shipping department of Zeltins Corporation. You and other company supervisors have been given strict instructions that all authorization for overtime had to come from your boss, the plant manager. In previous years, department supervisors possessed the authority to have employees work overtime at time-and-a-half rates whenever they considered it absolutely necessary. The supervisors generally had not taken advantage of this privilege. However, when a recent fiscal report showed a decline in profits and a substantial increase in labor costs, the company president issued a directive stating that all overtime had to be approved by the plant manager. In the absence of a plant manager, the president's authorization was needed.

You have been experiencing a significantly increased workload. Further, due to employee absences, the shipping department is several days late in sending out a number of important orders. You know that these orders might be canceled by the customers if they are not shipped before the week is over. Since you were convinced that overtime work would help alleviate this situation, you tried to contact the plant manager. However, the plant manager was out of town at a convention and could not be reached. You also had heard that some time ago a similar problem had occurred in the maintenance department, and that the supervisor in charge had authorized overtime without the necessary permission of the plant manager. Although the maintenance department supervisor claimed that waiting for the plant manager's return the next day would have made the repair job much more difficult and costly, he was severely disciplined for his unauthorized action.

You are confused about what to do. If you authorize overtime, you might be stepping beyond your area of authority. If you do not, some of the orders will not be shipped in time and they likely will be canceled. You inquired about contacting the president of the company, but you were told that the president also was out of town. It is now mid-afternoon on Thursday, and you must decide what to do.

You Make the Call!

1

Explain the importance of problem-solving and decision-making skills.

THE IMPORTANCE OF DECISION-MAKING SKILLS TO SUPERVISORS

All human activities involve decision making. Everyone has problems at home, at work, and in social groups for which decisions must be made. Thus, decision making is a normal human requirement that begins in childhood and continues throughout life.

In work settings, when asked to define their major responsibilities, many supervisors respond that "solving problems" and "making decisions" are the most important components of what they do on a daily basis and throughout their ongoing supervisory management tasks. **Decision making** is the process of defining problems and choosing a course of action from among alternatives. The term *decision making* often is used together with the term *problem solving*, since many supervisory decisions focus on solving problems that have occurred or are anticipated. However, the term *problem solving* should not be construed as being limited only to making decisions about problem areas. Problem solving also includes making decisions about realistic opportunities that are present or available if planned for appropriately. Therefore, throughout the discussion to follow in this chapter, we will use these terms interchangeably.

Decision-making

Defining problems and choosing a course of action from among alternatives.

While decision making is an integral part of all managerial functions, it is particularly at the core of the planning function of management. However, we have placed this chapter on decision making in Part One of the text because the principles to be discussed here are applicable when supervisors carry out all of their managerial functions and duties.

Many of the problems that confront supervisors in their daily activities are recurring and familiar; for these problems, most supervisors have developed routine answers. But when supervisors are confronted with new and unfamiliar problems, many find it difficult to decide on a course of action.

Managers and supervisors at all levels are constantly required to find solutions to problems that are caused by changing situations and unusual circumstances. Regardless of their managerial level, they should use a similar, logical, and systematic process of decision making. Although decisions made at the executive level usually are of a wider scope and magnitude than decisions made at the supervisory level, the decision-making process should be fundamentally the same throughout the entire management hierarchy.

Of course, once a decision has been made, effective action is necessary. A good decision that no one implements is of little value. However, in this chapter we are not concerned with the problem of getting effective action. Here, we discuss the process that should lead to the "best" decision or solution before action is taken.

A decision maker often is depicted as an executive bent over some papers, with pen in hand, contemplating whether or not to sign on the dotted line. Or the image may be that of a manager in a meeting, raising an arm to vote a certain way. Both of these images have one thing in common: they portray decision makers as people at the moment of choice, ready to choose an alternative that leads them from the crossroads. Often, a supervisor would like to know in which direction to go, but has not given a lot of thought to the end result (see Figure 5-1 on page 130). Supervisors need to understand that information gathering, analysis, and other processes precede the final moment of selecting one alternative over the others.

Decision making is an important skill for supervisors. It is a skill that can be developed—just as the skills involved in playing golf are developed—by learning the steps, practicing, and exerting effort. By doing this, supervisors can learn how to make more thoughtful decisions and improve the quality of their decisions.

At the same time, supervisors should ensure that their employees learn to make their own decisions more effectively. A supervisor cannot make all the decisions necessary to run a department. Many daily decisions in a department are made by the employees who do the work. For example, what materials to use, how a job is to be done, when it is to be done, and how to achieve coordination with other departments are decisions that employees often have to make without their supervisor. As evidenced by this chapter's "Contemporary Issue" box, many companies are giving employees a more active role in workplace decision making.[1] Therefore, training subordinates in the process of making decisions should be a high priority for all supervisors.

2

Describe the types of decisions made in organizations.

TYPES OF DECISIONS

Management decision-making theorists often classify managerial decisions as being either programmed or nonprogrammed, with many decisions falling somewhere between these two extremes.[2]

To make a decision, you must first know the result you want to accomplish.

Programmed decisions

Solutions to repetitive and routine problems provided by existing policies, procedures, rules, and so on.

Programmed decisions are solutions to problems that are repetitive, well structured, and routine. The term *programmed* is descriptive in the same sense that it is used in computer programming; there is a specific procedure, or program, that can be applied to the problem at hand. Many daily problems that confront supervisors are not difficult to solve because a more or less "pat" answer is available. These problems usually are routine or repetitive, and fixed answers, methods, procedures, rules, and the like exist. Supervisors can delegate these kinds of decisions to subordinates and be confident that the decisions will be made in an acceptable and timely manner.

Nonprogrammed decisions

Solutions to unique problems that require judgment, intuition, and creativity.

Nonprogrammed decisions occur when supervisors are confronted with new or unusual problems for which they must use their intelligent, adaptive problem-solving behavior. Such problems may be rare, unstructured, or unique, and they are typically one-time occurrences. There are no pat answers or guidelines for decision making in these situations. Nonprogrammed decisions tend to be more important, demanding, and strategic than programmed decisions. In nonprogrammed decision making, supervisors are called on to use good judgment, intuition, and creativity in attempting to solve problems. In these situations they should apply a decision-making process by which they can approach the problems in a consistent and logical, but adaptable, manner.[3] The remainder of this chapter will refer primarily to nonprogrammed decision making.

contemporary issue

Employee Decision Making in the Workplace Can Work, If Management Works at It

Many management authorities believe that in the workplace of the 21st century, decision making will be pushed further and further down the organizational ladder. To this end, many companies are turning to "empowered employee teams" by which knowledgeable and skilled employees from various departments are teamed in company projects and delegated considerable authority to make project decisions. Major companies such as Motorola, General Electric, and Whirlpool have discovered that empowering employees to make many decisions, instead of relying on traditional managerial decision-making processes, can result in increased productivity, profitability, and customer and employee satisfaction. At the same time, however, these companies have learned that in order for employee workplace decision making to be successful, it requires extensive training, communication, proper timing, and management flexibility if the employee decision making is to be a real presence and not just a facade where there is more form than substance.[1]

A rather dramatic example of employee decision making is that of the Algoma Steel Company in Canada, where workers own approximately one-third of the company and share control with managers. This developed out of a bankruptcy restructuring in the early 1990s. Many business decisions in this firm are discussed and decided by a steering committee of eight Algoma managers and eight union employees who meet on a weekly basis. Major decisions are made in a joint decision-making process involving all aspects of company operations.[2]

In a large-scale study of suppliers of the automotive industry in the United States and Canada, including both unionized and non-unionized operating units, Professors Gretchen Spreitzer and Aneil Mishra concluded that involving lower-echelon employees in decision making requires a certain amount of risk and trust on the part of higher-level managers. Based upon their research data, they concluded that employee involvement in decision making was most successful where managers had a high degree of trust in subordinates to make decisions in the best interests of the organization. Additionally, the successful employers were willing to provide considerable performance information to the employees regarding the results of various decisions that were made, and they were willing to reward employees economically when the performance of the organization improved or became superior. Apparently, managers who are willing to do these types of things will find that they indeed can give up a certain amount of control to employees without fear of losing control of the direction of the firm.[3]

Sources: (1) Mary Ann Hellinghausen and Jim Myers, "Empowered Employees: A New Team Concept," *Industrial Management* (September/October 1998), pp. 21–23. (2) Craig Stedman, "Worker's Rule On Business Changes," *Computer World* (October 5, 1998), pp. 41–42. (3) Gretchen M. Spreitzer and Aneil K. Mishra, "Giving Up Control Without Losing Control: Trust and Its Substitute Effects on Managers Involving Employees in Decision Making," *Group and Organization Management* (June 1999), pp. 155–187.

3

Describe and apply the basic steps of the decision-making process.

Decision-making process

A systematic, step-by-step process to aid in choosing the "best" alternative.

THE DECISION-MAKING PROCESS

In making nonprogrammed managerial decisions, supervisors should follow the steps of the **decision-making process** (see Figure 5-2 on page 132). First, they must define the problem. Second, they must analyze the problem using available information. Third, they need to establish decision criteria—factors that will be used to evaluate the alternatives. Fourth, after thorough analysis, they should develop alternative solutions. After these steps have been taken, the supervisor should carefully evaluate the alternatives and

FIGURE 5-2

The effective supervisor follows the steps of the decision-making process.

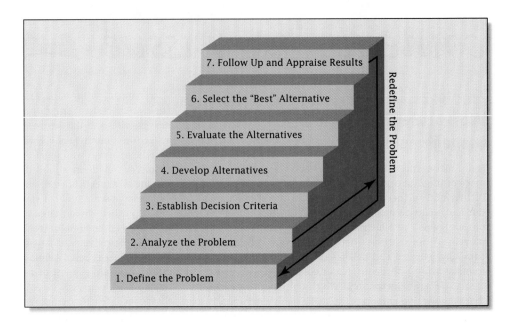

select the solution that appears to be the "best" or most feasible under the circumstances. The concluding step in this process is follow-up and appraisal of the consequences of the decision.

Step 1: Define the Problem

Before seeking answers, the supervisor first should identify what the real problem is. Nothing is as useless as the right answer to the wrong question. Defining the problem is not an easy task. What appears to be the problem might be merely a symptom that shows on the surface. It usually is necessary to delve deeper to locate the real problem and define it.

Consider the following scenario. Tom Engle, an office supervisor, believes that a problem of conflicting personalities exists within the department. Two employees, Diana and Stuart, are continually bickering and cannot get along together. Because of this lack of cooperation, the job is not being done in a timely manner. Engle needs to develop a clear, accurate problem statement. The problem statement should be brief, specific, and easily understood by others. A good problem statement should address the following key questions:

- What is the problem?
- How do you know there is a problem?
- Where has the problem occurred?
- When has it occurred?
- Who is involved in or affected by the problem?

FIGURE 5-3

Example of a problem
statement.

> The bickering between the employees detracts from the completion of work assignments. Last Monday and Tuesday, assigned customer callbacks were not completed. Customers, other department employees, and the shipping department are all affected.

Expressing a problem through a problem statement can help the supervisor understand it. A careful review of answers to the key questions can lead to a problem statement, as shown as Figure 5-3, which reveals that the major problem is that the work is not getting done in a timely manner. When checking into this situation, the supervisor should focus on why the work is not getting done.

Defining a problem often can become a time-consuming task, but it is time well spent. A supervisor should not go any further in the decision-making process until the problem relevant to the situation has been specifically determined. Remember, a problem exists when there is a difference between the way things are and the way they should be. The effective supervisor will use problem solving not only to take corrective action but also as a means to make improvements in the organization.

Step 2: Analyze the Problem: Gather Facts and Information

After the problem—not just the symptoms—has been defined, the next step is to analyze the problem. The supervisor begins by assembling facts and other pertinent information. This is sometimes viewed as being the first step in decision making, but until the real problem has been defined, the supervisor does not know what information is needed. Only after gaining a clear understanding of the problem can the supervisor decide how important certain data are and what additional information to seek.

Tom Engle, the office supervisor in the Step 1 scenario, needs to find out why the work is not getting done. When he gathers information, he finds out that he never clearly outlined the expectations for each employee—where their duties begin and where they end. What appeared on the surface to be a problem of personality conflict was actually a problem caused by the supervisor. The chances are good that once the activities and responsibilities of the two employees are clarified, the friction will end. Engle needs to monitor the situation closely to ensure that the work is being completed on time.

Being only human, a supervisor will find that personal opinion is likely to creep into decision making. This is particularly true when employees are involved in the problem. For example, if a problem involves an employee who performs well, the supervisor may be inclined to show this person greater consideration than would be accorded a poor performer. Therefore, the supervisor should try to be as objective as possible in gathering and examining information.

Sometimes the supervisor does not know how far to go in searching for additional facts. A good practice is to observe reasonable time and cost limitations. This means gathering all the information that can be obtained without undue delay and without excessive costs.

In the process of analysis the supervisor should try to think of intangible factors that play a significant role. Some intangible factors are reputation, morale, discipline, and personal biases. It is difficult to be specific about these factors; nevertheless, they should be considered in the analysis of a problem. As a general rule, written and objective information is more reliable than opinions and hearsay.

Another way of depicting Steps 1 and 2 of the decision-making process is the so-called **fishbone technique,** also referred to as the **cause-and-effect diagram.** This approach has the problem solver not only identify the various factors that have brought about the problem at hand but also consider the potential interrelatedness of causes of the problem. A set of guidelines and a depiction of this process are provided in the Appendix to this chapter (see pages 148–149).

Fishbone technique (cause-and-effect diagram)
Cause-and-effect approach to consider potential interrelatedness of problem causes in decision making.

Step 3: Establish Decision Criteria

Decision criteria are standards or measures to use in evaluating alternatives; they typically are statements of what the supervisor wants to accomplish with the decision. Such criteria can also be used to determine how well the implementation phase of the process is going—that is, whether the decision is doing what it was intended to do. To illustrate, suppose that Tom Engle's initial actions do not remedy the situation. It will be appropriate to establish decision criteria. Figure 5-4 provides examples of the decision criteria that can be used for evaluating other courses of action.

Decision criteria
Standards or measures to use in evaluating alternatives.

Once the decision criteria are established, the supervisor must determine which criteria are absolutely necessary and their order of priority. Because it is likely that no solution alternative will meet all the criteria, the supervisor needs to know which criteria are most important so that alternatives can be judged by how many of the important criteria they meet. The supervisor may want to consult with upper-level managers, peers, or employees to assist in prioritizing the criteria.

Step 4: Develop Alternatives

After the supervisor has defined and analyzed the problem and established decision criteria, the next step is to develop various alternative solutions. The supervisor should

FIGURE 5-4

Examples of decision criteria.

The solution
- should result in the work assignments being completed on time.
- should incur no financial cost to implement.
- must not impede quality of service to the customer.
- should not put any employee's job in jeopardy.
- should allow us to differentiate our product or service in the marketplace.
- should not have a negative impact on other employees.
- must alleviate the problem within one week.

consider as many possible solutions as can reasonably be developed. By formulating many alternatives, the supervisor is less apt to overlook the best course of action. Stating this another way, *a decision will only be as good as the best alternative that has been developed.*

Almost all problem situations have a number of alternatives, not just "either this or that." The choices may not always be obvious, but supervisors must search for them. If they do not do this, they are likely to fall into the "either/or" kind of thinking. It is not enough for supervisors just to decide from among alternatives that employees have suggested, because there may be other alternatives to consider. Thus, supervisors must stretch their minds to develop additional alternatives, even in the most discouraging situations. None of the alternatives might be desirable, but at least the supervisor can choose the one that is least undesirable.

Suppose that an office supervisor has been directed to make a 20 percent reduction in employment because the firm is experiencing financial problems. After careful study, the supervisor develops the following feasible alternatives:

1. Lay off employees who have the least seniority, regardless of their jobs or performance, until the overall 20 percent reduction is reached.
2. Lay off employees who have the lowest performance ratings until the overall 20 percent reduction is reached.
3. Analyze department duties and decide which jobs are essential. Keep the employees who are best qualified to perform those jobs.
4. Without laying off anyone, develop a schedule of reduced work hours for every employee that would be equivalent to a 20 percent reduction.
5. Develop proactive alternatives to increase the firm's revenues so that no employee has to be laid off.

While alternative 5 is most attractive, it is not realistic, given the current economic situation. Although none of the other alternatives may be an ideal solution to this unpleasant problem, at least the office supervisor has considered several alternatives before making a decision. Unfortunately, these are "no-win" situations, but the illustration does portray the realities of organizational life.

Brainstorming and Creative Problem Solving. When enough time is available, a supervisor should get together with a group of other supervisors or employees to brainstorm solution alternatives to a perplexing problem. **Brainstorming** is a free flow of ideas within a group, with judgment suspended, in order to come up with as many alternatives as possible. Using this technique, the supervisor presents the problem and the participants offer as many alternative solutions as they can develop in the time available. It is understood that any idea is acceptable at this point—even those that may at first appear to be wild or unusual. Evaluation of ideas is suspended so that participants can give free rein to their creativity.

Alex Osborn, an authority on creativity and the brainstorming approach, has suggested the following four major guidelines for effective brainstorming:

1. Defer all judgment of ideas. During the brainstorming period, allow no criticism by anyone in the group. It is natural for people to suppress new ideas both con-

Brainstorming
A free flow of ideas within a group, while suspending judgment, aimed at developing many alternative solutions to a problem.

Using the brainstorming technique, the supervisor presents the problem and the participants offer as many alternative solutions as they can in the time available.

sciously and unconsciously, and this tendency must be avoided. Even if an idea seems impractical and useless at first, it should not be rejected by quick initial judgments because such rejection could inhibit the free flow of more ideas.

2. Seek quantity of ideas. Idea fluency is the key to creative problem solving, and fluency means quantity. The premise here is that the greater the number of ideas, the greater the likelihood that some of them will be viable solutions.

3. Encourage "free wheeling." Being creative calls for a free-flowing mental process in which all ideas, no matter how extreme, are welcome. Even the wildest idea may, on further analysis, have some usefulness.

4. "Hitchhike" on existing ideas. Combining, adding to, and rearranging ideas often can produce new approaches that are superior to the original ideas. When creative thought processes slow or stop, review some of the ideas already produced and attempt to hitchhike on them with additions or revisions.[4]

The preceding guidelines are applicable for brainstorming both on an individual or group basis. When it involves a fairly large group of people, an unstructured brainstorming session can become rather long, tedious, and unproductive because many of the ideas are simply not feasible and because conflicts may develop within the group due to individual biases. For this reason, the so-called **nominal group technique (NGT),** which provides a means to enable group members to generate ideas in a more efficient process, is advocated. Typically, it first involves having individual members of the group develop and write down their own list of ideas and alternatives to solve the problem at hand. Then there is a sharing of ideas among group members with ensuing discussion, evaluation, and refinements. The group's final choice(s) may be made by a series of confidential votes in which the list of ideas is narrowed until a consensus is attained.[5]

Nominal group technique (NGT)

A group brainstorming and decision-making process by which individual members first identify alternative solutions privately and then share, evaluate, and decide on them as a group.

Creative approaches and brainstorming meetings are particularly adaptable to non-programmed decisions, especially if the problem is new, important, or strategic in dimension. Even the supervisor who takes time to mentally brainstorm a problem alone is likely to develop more alternatives for solving the problem than one who does not brainstorm.[6]

Ethical Considerations. Both in the development and the evaluation of alternatives, a supervisor should consider only those that are lawful and acceptable within the organization's ethical guidelines. In recent years, many firms have become concerned that their managers, supervisors, and employees make ethical decisions because they recognize that, in the long term, good ethics is good business. Consequently, many firms have developed handbooks, policies, and official statements that specify the ethical standards and practices expected.[7] Ethical policy statements and other behavioral/ethical standards will also be discussed in Chapter 19.

The following list of guidelines or **ethical "tests"** for decision making is not comprehensive, but these considerations are relevant in addressing the ethical aspects of most problem situations.

> *Legal-compliance test:* Laws, regulations, and policies are to be followed, not broken or ignored. The rationale and explanation that "everybody's doing it" and "everybody's getting away with it" are poor excuses if you get caught violating a law, policy, or regulation. If in doubt, ask someone who knows the law or regulation for proper guidance. However, compliance should be only a starting point in most ethical decision making.
>
> *Public-knowledge test:* What would be the consequences if the outcome of a particular alternative decision became known to the public, one's family, the media, or a government agency?
>
> *Long-term-consequences test:* What would be the long-term versus short-term outcomes? Weigh these against each other.
>
> *Examine-your-motives test:* Do the motives for a proposed decision benefit the company and others? Or are they primarily selfish in nature and designed to harm or destroy other people and their interests?
>
> *Inner-voice test:* This is the test of conscience and moral values that have been instilled in most of us since childhood. If something inside you says that the choice being contemplated is or may be wrong, it usually is. It is prudent then to look for a different and better alternative.

It cannot be stressed enough that if a supervisor believes that a particular alternative is questionable or might not be acceptable within the firm's ethical policies, the supervisor should consult with his or her manager or with a staff specialist who is knowledgeable in the area for guidance in how to proceed. Figure 5-5 (see page 138) is an example of guidelines for ethical decision making developed by a major corporation for all of its managers, supervisors, and employees. This firm—like many others—has an ethics "hot line" that individuals can call to seek assistance when confronted with ethical dilemmas.

Ethical "tests"

Considerations or guidelines to be addressed in developing and evaluating ethical aspects of decision alternatives.

FIGURE 5-5

Example of a company's guidelines for ethical decision making.

Ethical Decision Making

It is not always easy to determine the ethical or "right" thing to do in a particular business or work situation. Sometimes, because of the highly complex rules and regulations that govern the way we do business, a decision is not clear cut.

A decision or situation could be difficult when the ethical issue includes

A close call: These situations involve the careful balancing of different and, yet valid, interests. Sometimes the correct decision is just not clear.

A new problem: These situations usually involve facts that have not yet been specifically addressed by the policies or procedures of the company.

Multiple considerations: The decision in these situations requires the input of so many different people that the decision process becomes very inefficient.

Personal cost: The right and fair thing to do is clear, but the decision maker bears so much cost in lost time or personal sacrifice that the decision is difficult.

By reviewing the following outline, each of us can, at the very least, ensure that we have applied a process that is designed to call to mind sound principles of ethical decision making. Unless we apply such a process honestly and consistently, we run the risk of failing to provide our customers, whether internal or external, with the quality of products and services they deserve.

ANALYSIS

- *What are the facts?*
- *Who is responsible to act?*
- *What or whose interests are involved?*
- *What are the consequences of the action?*
- *What is fair treatment in this situation?*

SOLUTION DEVELOPMENT

- *What solutions are available to me?*
- *Have I considered all of the creative solutions that might permit me to reduce the amount of harm, to maximize the benefits, to acknowledge more interests, or to be fair to more individuals?*

Step 5: Evaluate the Alternatives

The ultimate purpose of decision making is to choose the specific course of action that will provide the greatest number of wanted and the smallest number of unwanted consequences. After developing alternatives, supervisors can mentally test each of them by imagining that each has already been put into effect. They should try to foresee the probable desirable and undesirable consequences of each alternative. By thinking the alternatives through and appraising their consequences, supervisors will be in a position to compare the desirability of the various choices.

The usual way to begin is to eliminate alternatives that do not meet the supervisor's previously established decision criteria and ethical standards. The supervisor should evaluate how many of the most important criteria each remaining alternative meets. The final choice is the one that satisfies or meets the most criteria at the highest priority levels. More often than not, there is no clear choice.

Nonprogrammed decisions usually require the decision maker to choose a course of action without complete information about the situation. Because of this uncertainty, the chosen alternative may not yield the intended results. Thus, there is risk involved. Some supervisors will consider the degree of risk and uncertainty involved in each course of action. There is no such thing as a riskless decision; one alternative may simply involve less risk than the others.[8]

The issue of time may make one alternative preferable, particularly if there is a difference between how much time is available and how much time is required to carry out one alternative in comparison with another. The supervisor should consider the facilities, tools, and other resources that are available. It is also critically important to judge different alternatives in terms of economy of effort and resources. In other words, which action will give the greatest benefits and results for the least cost and effort?

In cases in which one alternative clearly appears to provide a greater number of desirable consequences and fewer unwanted consequences than any other alternative, the decision is fairly easy. However, the "best" alternative is not always so obvious. At times, two or more alternatives may seem equally desirable. Here the choice may become a matter of personal preference. It is also possible that the supervisor may feel that no single alternative is significantly stronger than any other. In this case, it might be possible to combine the positive aspects of the better alternatives into a composite solution.

Sometimes none of the alternatives is satisfactory; all of them have too many undesirable effects, or none will bring about the desired results. In such a case, the supervisor should begin to think of new alternative solutions or perhaps even start all over again by attempting to redefine the problem.

Moreover, a situation might arise in which the undesirable consequences of all the alternatives appear to be so overwhelmingly unfavorable that the supervisor feels that the "best" available solution is to take no action at all. However, this may be self-deceiving, since taking no action will not solve the problem. Taking no action is as much a decision as is taking a specific action, even though the supervisor may believe that an unpleasant choice has been avoided. The supervisor should visualize the consequences that are likely to result from taking no action. Only if the consequences of taking no action are the most desirable should it be selected as the appropriate course.

Step 6: Select the "Best" Alternative

Optimizing
Selecting the "best" alternative.

Satisficing
Selecting the alternative that minimally meets the decision criteria.

Selecting the alternative that seems to be the "best" is known as **optimizing.** However, sometimes the supervisor makes a **satisficing** decision—selecting an alternative that minimally meets the decision criteria. A famous management theorist, Herbert Simon, once likened the difference to the comparison between finding a needle in a haystack (satisficing) and finding the biggest, sharpest needle in the haystack (optimizing).[9] Nevertheless, after developing and evaluating alternatives, the supervisor needs to make a choice.

A manager rarely makes a decision that pleases everyone.

Among the most prominent bases for choosing the "best" alternative are experience, intuition, advice from others, experimentation, and statistical and quantitative decision making. Regardless of the process used, a supervisor will rarely make a decision that is equally pleasing to everyone.

Experience. In making a selection from among various alternatives, the supervisor should be guided by experience. Chances are that certain situations will recur, and the old saying that "experience is the best teacher" does apply to a certain extent. A supervisor often can decide wisely based on personal experience or the experience of some other manager. Knowledge gained from experience is a helpful guide, and its importance should not be underestimated. On the other hand, it is dangerous to follow experience blindly.

When looking to experience as a basis for choosing among alternatives, the supervisor should examine the situation and the conditions that prevailed at the time of the earlier decision. It may be that conditions still are nearly identical to those that prevailed on the previous occasion and that the decision should be similar to the one made then. More often than not, however, conditions have changed considerably and the underlying assumptions are no longer the same. Therefore, the new decision probably should not be identical to the earlier one.

Experience can be helpful in the event that the supervisor is called on to substantiate his or her reasons for making a particular decision. In part this may be a defensive approach, but there is no excuse for following experience in and of itself. Experience must always be viewed with the future in mind. The underlying circumstances of the past, the present, and the future must be considered realistically if experience is to be of assistance in selecting from among alternatives.

Intuition. Supervisors admit that at times they base their decisions on intuition. Some supervisors even appear to have an unusual ability to solve problems satisfactorily by subjective means.[10] However, a deeper search usually will disclose that the so-called "intuition" on which the supervisor appeared to have based a decision was really experience or knowledge that had been stored in the supervisor's memory. By recalling similar situations that occurred in the past, supervisors may better reach a decision even though they label it as "having a hunch."

Intuition may be particularly helpful in situations in which other alternatives have been tried previously with poor results. If the risks are not too great, a supervisor may choose a new alternative because of an intuitive feeling that a fresh approach might bring positive results. Even if the hunch does not work out well, the supervisor has tried something different. The supervisor will remember this as part of his or her experience and can draw upon it in reaching future decisions.

Advice from Others. Although a supervisor cannot shift personal responsibility for making decisions in the department, the burden of decision making often can be eased by seeking the advice of others. The ideas and suggestions of employees, other supervisors, staff experts, technical authorities, and the supervisor's own manager can be of great help in weighing facts and information. Seeking advice does not mean avoiding a decision, since the supervisor still must decide whether or not to accept the advice of others.

Many believe that two heads are better than one and that input from others will improve the decision process. The following four guidelines can help the supervisor decide whether groups should be included in the decision-making process:

1. If additional information would increase the quality of the decision, involve those who can provide that information.
2. If acceptance of the decision is critical, involve those whose acceptance is important.
3. If people's skills can be developed through participation, involve those who need the development opportunity.
4. If the situation is not life threatening and does not require immediate action, involve others in the process.[11]

Generally, the varied perspectives and experiences of others will add to the decision-making process.

Two heads can be better than one in the decision-making process.

Experimentation. In the scientific world where many conclusions are based on tests in laboratories, experimentation is essential and accepted. In supervision, however, experimentation to see what happens often is too costly in terms of people, time, and material. Nevertheless, there are some instances in which a limited amount of testing and experimenting is advisable. For example, a supervisor may find it worthwhile to try several different locations for a new copy machine in the department to see which location employees prefer and which is most convenient for the work flow. There are also some instances in which a certain amount of testing is advisable in order to provide employees with an opportunity to try out new ideas or approaches, perhaps of their own design. While experimentation may be valid from a motivational standpoint, it can be a slow and relatively expensive method of reaching a decision.

Quantitative Decision Making. Numerous techniques and models of quantitative decision making have received much attention in management literature and practice. Included among these techniques are linear programming, operations research, and probability and simulation models. These tend to be sophisticated statistical and mathematical approaches, often used in connection with computers.[12] They require the decision maker to quantify most of the information that is relevant to a particular decision. For many supervisors, these quantitative decision-making techniques are rather remote, yet many large firms have management decision support systems that assist supervisors in making nonprogrammed decisions. One desirable feature of quantitative decision making is the ability of the user to perform "what if" scenarios—the simulation of a business situation over and over again using different data in each case for selected decision areas.

With the increasing use of desktop computers and networks, many firms are able to develop programs and information storage and retrieval systems that supervisors can use relatively easily for certain types of decisions, especially when historical and statistical databases are involved. For some types of problems, supervisors may be able to seek the help of mathematicians, engineers, statisticians, systems analysts, and computer specialists who can bring their tools to bear on relevant problems. This can be an involved and costly procedure, however, and decisions like those facing Tina Leeming in the "You Make the Call" section that began this chapter usually cannot be made from statistical or quantitative models.

Step 7: Follow Up and Appraise the Results

After a decision has been made, specific actions are necessary to carry it out. Follow-up and appraisal of the outcome of a decision are actually part of the process of decision making.

Follow-up and appraisal of a decision can take many forms, depending on the nature of the decision, timing, costs, standards expected, personnel, and other factors. For example, a minor production scheduling decision could easily be evaluated on the basis of a short written report or perhaps even by the supervisor's observation or a discussion with employees. However, a major decision involving the installation of complex new equipment will require close and time-consuming follow-up by the supervisor, technical employees, and higher-level managers. This type of decision usually requires the supervisor to prepare numerous detailed written reports of equipment performance under varying conditions, which are compared closely with plans or expected standards for the equipment.

Quantitative decision-making techniques are sophisticated statistical and mathematical approaches usually involving computers.

The important point to recognize is that the task of decision making is not complete without some form of follow-up and appraisal of the actions taken. If the supervisor has established decision criteria or specific objectives that the decision should accomplish, it will be easier to evaluate the effects of the decision. If the consequences have turned out well, the supervisor can feel reasonably confident that the decision was sound.

If the follow-up and appraisal indicate that something has gone wrong or that the results have not been as anticipated, then the supervisor's decision-making process must begin all over again. This may even mean going back over each of the various steps of the decision-making process in detail. The supervisor's definition and analysis of the problem and the development of alternatives may have to be completely revised in view of new circumstances surrounding the problem. In other words, when follow-up and appraisal indicate that the problem has not been resolved satisfactorily, the supervisor will find it advisable to treat the situation as a brand new problem and go through the decision-making process from a completely fresh perspective.

TIME IMPACTS THE DECISION-MAKING PROCESS

Explain why a supervisor should not make hasty decisions.

In some situations, supervisors may feel they do not have enough time to go through the decision-making process outlined here. Frequently, a manager, a coworker, or an employee approaches the supervisor, says "Here's the problem," and looks to the supervisor for an immediate answer. However, supervisors cannot afford to make a decision without considering the steps outlined here. Most problems do not require an immediate answer.

Often when an employee brings up a problem, the supervisor should ask questions such as the following:

1. How extensive is the problem? Does it need an immediate response?
2. Who else is affected by the problem? Should they be involved in this discussion?
3. Have you (the employee) thought through the problem, and do you have an idea of what the end result should be?
4. What do you recommend? Why?

This approach is a form of participative supervision and can help to develop the employee's analytical skills. The supervisor can then better think through the problem, apply the decision-making steps, and make a decision.

Many supervisors get themselves into trouble by making hasty decisions without following all of the steps outlined in the decision-making process. A word of caution here: during any stage of the process, if supervisors tell other people that they "will get back to them," the supervisors should state a specific time. If a supervisor fails to make a decision or give feedback to the other people by the specified time, he or she may incur a serious breach of trust.

What Call Did You Make?

As Tina Leeming, you are in a difficult situation that requires a decision on your part. You are under strict orders not to work overtime without authorization from higher management, which you have not been able to obtain. You are convinced that unless your employees work overtime, certain orders will not be shipped on time and may be canceled, probably to the detriment of Zeltins Corporation.

Certainly, top management is at fault for its failure to clarify the overtime directive. There is no specified alternative method for supervisory decision making when top managers are not present. It is a strict directive that was bound to cause difficulties. However, Tina

Leeming and other supervisors should have raised questions about this before such situations happened. They are also to blame for just leaving the directive as a "policy" that had an unclear application. Situations like the one described in this case can be prevented if supervisors and managers discuss policies and directives in meetings in order to resolve ambiguities or possible conflicts. Asking the question "what if" in regard to applications of a policy or directive can often bring about clarification that will avoid these types of situations.

But at this point, as Tina Leeming, you are "on your own" and you must decide what to do. If you believe that your primary responsibility is to meet the important goal of customer satisfaction, then you will authorize the overtime in order to fulfill this objective, and you will take your chances of being disciplined accordingly.

However, if you believe that the important short-term objective of the company is to reduce the cost of wages, even at the expense of losing customers, then you should not go beyond your authority by approving the overtime. That is to say, if you believe that your first obligation is to comply with a management directive while at the same time being on the safe side with regard to your authority, you will not work any overtime and you will hope that the adverse consequences will not be too great.

Before you decide what to do, review the steps of the decision-making model described in this chapter. In particular, consider what other alternatives might be feasible that could enable you to "harmonize" what appears to be a "no-win" situation. There are a number of alternatives that might be suggested here, such as shifting some delivery priorities, contacting affected customers, borrowing some workers from other departments, etc. At times like this, supervisory decision making requires a certain amount of thoughtful problem solving, perhaps using some of the principles of creative problem solving discussed in this chapter.

SUMMARY

All supervisory activities involve problem solving and decision making. Supervisors must find solutions for problems that are caused by changing situations and unusual circumstances. Decision making based on careful study of information and analysis of the various courses of action available is still the most generally approved avenue of selection from among alternatives. Decision making is a choice between two or more alternatives, and the decisions made by supervisors significantly affect departmental results.

Decision making is a skill that can be learned. Organizations are giving employees a more active role in decision making today than they did in the past. A decision made today often sets a precedent for decisions made tomorrow.

Supervisors confront many decision situations that can vary from the programmed type at one extreme to the nonprogrammed type at the other. Decisions for routine, repetitive-type problems are usually made easier by the use of policies, procedures, standard practices, and the like. However, nonprogrammable decisions are usually one-time, unusual, or unique problems that require sound judgment and systematic thinking.

Better decisions are more likely to occur when supervisors follow the steps of the decision-making process. These are as follows:

a. Define the problem.
b. Gather facts and information and analyze the problem.
c. Establish decision criteria.
d. Develop a sufficient number of alternatives.
e. Evaluate alternatives by using the decision criteria or by thinking of them as if they had already been placed into action and considering their consequences.
f. Select the alternative that has the greatest number of wanted and least number of unwanted consequences.
g. Implement, follow up, and appraise the results.

It may be necessary to take corrective action if the decision is not achieving the desired objective.

The supervisor should develop a problem statement that answers the questions of what, how, where, when, and who. Proper problem definition clarifies the difference between the way things are and the way they should be.

After defining the problem, the supervisor must gather information. Decision criteria, which are measures or standards of what the supervisor wants to accomplish with the decision, should be specified. In developing alternatives, supervisors can use brainstorming and creative thinking techniques.

Only alternatives that are lawful, and ethical within the organization's guidelines, should be considered. In the process of evaluation and choice, a supervisor can be aided by ethical guidelines, personal experience, intuition, advice from others, experimentation, and quantitative methods.

Once the decision has been made, specific actions are necessary to carry it out. Follow-up and appraisal are essential.

Supervisors run the risk of getting themselves into trouble unless they follow the steps of the decision-making process. The process is time consuming. Most problems do not require an immediate answer. It is often valuable to allow subordinates to assist in the decision-making process. They may see the problem from a different perspective, and they may have information that bears on the problem.

KEY TERMS

Decision making (page 128)
Programmed decisions (page 130)
Nonprogrammed decisions (page 130)
Decision-making process (page 131)
Fishbone technique (cause-and-effect diagram) (page 134)

Decision criteria (page 134)
Brainstorming (page 135)
Nominal group technique (NGT) (page 136)
Ethical "tests" (page 137)
Optimizing (page 139)
Satisficing (page 139)

QUESTIONS FOR DISCUSSION

1. Think of a major decision you have made in your life. For example, why did you decide to go to college? Why did you decide on the college you selected? Why did you decide on your major? Explain how you applied the decision-making steps identified in this chapter. What factors should you have considered to make a better choice?
2. Define decision making. Does the decision-making process vary depending on where a manager or supervisor is located in the managerial hierarchy? Discuss.

3. Distinguish between programmed and nonprogrammed types of decisions. Enhance your answer by identifying a significant decision and an insignificant decision for each type.
4. Why should supervisors write a problem statement to assist them in defining the problem?
5. Review the steps of the decision-making process in their proper sequence. What pitfalls should the supervisor avoid at each step?
6. Identify the major elements of the brainstorming approach.
7. Describe a situation in which you would prefer to solve the problem in a group rather than by yourself. Why? What are the advantages of each approach? The limitations?
8. Define and discuss the factors that a supervisor should consider in developing and evaluating alternatives in the decision-making process. To what degree should ethical issues be a consideration? Discuss the five ethical "tests" in this process.
9. Discuss how a decision to take no action concerning a problem can be a valid approach.
10. When deciding on a course of action, do you tend to rely more on past experiences or on the need to be creative? Cite an illustration to support your answer.

SKILLS APPLICATIONS

Skills Application 5-1: Identifying Supervisory Problems

1. Interview at least three people in supervisory positions. Ask them to identify (a) a major problem they have in doing their job and (b) a major problem facing their organization.
2. Compare the problems identified by the supervisors. Did the supervisors state the problems in a way that makes them understandable to others? How serious are the problems? Can the problems be solved by the supervisors, or do they need the assistance of others to solve them?
3. In your opinion, would the supervisors be better off solving the problems themselves or eliciting the input of others? Why?

Skills Application 5-2: Mastering the Registration Process

The notion of continuous improvement assumes that every process can be improved. Think back to the registration process at your college. Were you able to complete the registration process with a minimum of effort, or was the process cumbersome and inefficient?

1. Break into groups of seven or more people. Each student should consider the registration process from one of the following perspectives:
   a. The registrar (responsibility for scheduling classes and rooms).
   b. The business office (responsibility for collecting fees).
   c. The dean of students.
   d. The president of the college.
   e. The bookstore manager.
   f. A faculty member (responsibility for teaching a variety of courses at various times).
   g. Student (one or more).
2. As a group, formulate a clear problem statement for the problem.
3. Make a list of the information you feel you will need in order to solve the problem. Where will you get the information?
4. List the decision criteria that any solution must meet.
5. Brainstorm alternative solutions.

6. Suppose the college president says that the registrar has the responsibility for making the final decision. If the registrar solves the problem from his or her own perspective, does that person run the risk of creating greater problems for others? Explain.

Skills Application 5-3: An Exercise in Brainstorming

A long-term customer tells you that your competitor can provide the same service that you offer but at a significantly lower price. The customer wants to know whether you can meet or beat the price. You have the authority to reduce prices, but not to the extent the customer implies. The competitor's price is less than your breakeven point. You promise to give the matter some thought, check with others, and get back with an answer tomorrow afternoon.

1. Working alone, take a few minutes to make a list of at least three reasons the customer may have for wanting a price reduction.
2. Get together with three other people and brainstorm as many options as you can, other than cutting price, that might meet the customer's needs.
3. Analyze the brainstorming activity. Did the process take more time than working alone? Did the process enable you to see a variety of options? Did the group generate several options that you would not have thought of?
4. What did you conclude from this exercise about the benefits and limitations of brainstorming?

INTERNET
ACTIVITY

Skills Application 5-4: Creative Problem Solving

Learn more about brainstorming and creative problem solving at The Creativity Site (**www.mindbloom.com**), or visit other sites dealing with creativity and decision making. What suggestions do you find here that you might implement as a supervisor in your decision-making process? Create a list of five creativity-generating ideas.

SKILL
DEVELOPMENT
VIDEO

SKILL DEVELOPMENT MODULE 5-1: DECISION MAKING

This video segment shows McElvey Department Store's operations supervisor, Janet Ferrell, as she tries to prepare for the biggest sale of the year.

Questions for Discussion: The Ineffective Version

1. What does Janet Ferrell do well?
2. Discuss what Janet Ferrell should do to be a more effective supervisor.
3. After observing the video, list as many situations as you can that require a decision.
4. Decide which problem confronting Janet Ferrell is most urgent. Following the steps in the decision-making process identified in Figure 5-2, solve the problem.

Questions for Discussion: The More Effective Version

1. Discuss how Janet Ferrell used the decision-making process to solve the store's problem.
2. What could Janet Ferrell have done to become an even more effective supervisor?
3. Explain why supervisors often involve subordinates in the decision process.
4. Would Janet Ferrell be more effective if she delegated the decisions to others? Why or why not?

APPENDIX: THE FISHBONE PROCESS

The *fishbone technique,* or *cause-and-effect diagram,* is a process primarily associated with Steps 1 and 2 of the decision-making model presented in this chapter. It facilitates analytical understanding by providing a visual depiction of a problem and its probable causes. An advantage of this approach is that it helps individuals to see the problem on one sheet of paper and to perceive significant relationships between major causes of the problem. Figure 5-6 is an example of a completed fishbone-type diagram.

Guidelines for Using the Fishbone Process

1. Once the problem is defined, print the problem on the head of the fish. Starting the diagram with the problem reminds all involved that the goal is to solve the problem.
2. The supervisor, independently or with the assistance of a problem-solving team, should identify the causes of the problem. This can be done by asking, "What are the factors that cause the problem?" The diagram should be limited to a number of major causes, usually classified as people, machines or equipment, materials, methods and procedures, company policies, and management style. Alternatively, the latter three causes might be classified broadly as working conditions. The causes are attached to the fins of the fish.
3. The supervisor or problem-solving team usually will want additional information; therefore, contributors to the various causes must be identified. Asking the right questions to uncover the contributing causes is an essential requirement of the process. Once they are identified, print them on the horizontal lines connecting them to the appropriate cause. A person's brain works by association; grouping together the contributors to a specific

| FIGURE 5-6 | Example of fishbone (cause-and-effect) diagram.

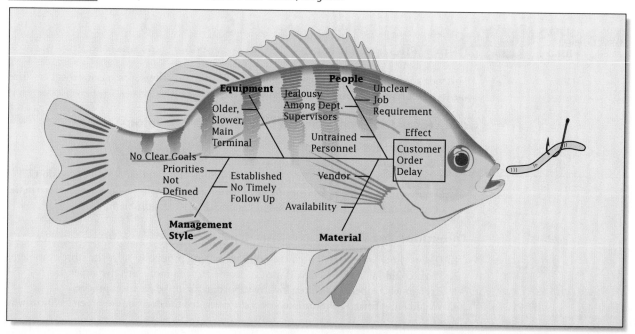

cause reflects the associative nature of the information. The diagram doesn't have to be perfect as long as everyone understands what it represents.

4. After the information has been entered on the diagram, the major causes of the problem can be isolated and circled on the diagram.

Solving the Problem: The "3 by 5" Technique

After the problem has been defined, contributors to the causes investigated and verified, and decision criteria established, alternative solutions can be developed. Instead of or in addition to a brainstorming approach, the supervisor may elect to use the "3 by 5" technique. Assume that an employee survey has revealed a substantial number of employee complaints regarding inadequate maintenance assistance. The process is as follows:

a. The supervisor writes the goal on the board for all to see; for example, "How can we reduce the number of employee complaints regarding maintenance without adversely affecting quality or costs?"

b. The supervisor gives each team member a stack of 3 by 5 cards. Each person is to write down as many alternatives as he or she can in the next five minutes. Only one idea per person may be written anonymously on a 3 by 5 card.

c. The team is divided into subgroups of three to five persons each. The 3 by 5 cards are randomly distributed to each subgroup.

d. Each subgroup is charged with identifying the preferred alternatives and then expanding on them.

e. The subgroup presents its recommendations to the overall group or team.

f. The group then evaluates which alternatives are most relevant to solving the problem and how to implement them.

As the alternatives are implemented, contributors to the causes should be reduced substantially or eliminated.

The fishbone technique has gained acceptance as many organizations have embraced quality circle and TQM concepts and have encouraged teams of employees to become more involved in the problem-solving process. The use of a diagram helps employees to understand how problem causes relate to each other. Harold R. McAlindon, a leader in innovative management and author of *A Pocket Course in Creative Thinking* (Parlay International, 1993), has stated that the art of drawing or sketching "can stimulate your thinking and may lead to other ideas." Also see The Mescon Group, Inc., *Techniques for Problem Solving: Participant's Guide* (Cincinnati: Thomson Executive Press, 1995), pp. 28–30; and C. Carl Pegels, *Total Quality Management: A Survey of Its Important Aspects* (Cincinnati: Boyd & Fraser Publishing Company/ITP, 1995), pp. 97–106.

ENDNOTES

1. In addition to the sources listed with the "Contemporary Issue" box, see Jane E. Henry, "Lessons From Team Leaders," *Quality Progress* (March 1998), pp. 57–59; Ben Nagler, "Recasting Employees Into Teams," *Workforce* (January 1998), pp. 101–106; or David Smith, "Whirlpool's New Human Resources Model: Tapping the Power of Employee Decision Making," *Employment Relations Today* (Spring 1995), pp. 41–46.

2. See Harold Koontz and Heinz Weirich, *Management* (9th ed.; New York: McGraw-Hill, 1988), p. 143; or James A. F. Stoner and R. Edward Freeman, *Management* (5th ed.; Upper Saddle River, N.J.: Prentice-Hall, 1992), pp. 251–252.

3. See Andrew J. DuBrin and R. Duane Ireland, *Management and Organization* (2nd ed.; Cincinnati: South-Western Publishing Co., 1993), pp. 90–100; or John R. Schermerhorn, Jr., *Management* (6th ed.; New York: John Wiley & Sons, 1999), pp. 59–64. For a detailed study concerning effectiveness of the decision-making process, see James W. Dean, Jr., and Mark P. Sharfman, "Does Decision Process Matter? A Study of Strategic Decision-Making Effectiveness," *Academy of Management Journal* (April 1996), pp. 368–396.

4. For more information on brainstorming and creative problem solving, see Alex F. Osborn (with Alex Faickney), *Applied Imagination* (3rd rev. ed.; Buffalo: Creative Education Foundation, 1993). Also see Alan G. Robinson and Sam Stern, *Corporate Creativity: How Innovation and Improvement Actually Happen* (San Francisco: Berrett-Koehler Publishers, 1997); or Floyd Hurt, "A Problem Briefing," *Successful Meetings* (February 1990), p. 128.

5. For an expanded discussion on NGT, see David H. Holt, *Management: Principles and Practices* (3d ed.; Upper Saddle River, N.J.: Prentice-Hall, 1993), pp. 139–141. Still another group-type of brainstorming approach that has gained some acceptance in recent years is called *storyboarding*. Originally attributed to Walt Disney and his organization in developing animated cartoons, storyboarding can be especially helpful in generating alternatives and choosing among them. Depending on the nature of the problem, it may be appropriate to use a neutral party to manage the team process when alternatives, ideas, and other information are listed on index cards and arranged on "storyboards." For information concerning storyboarding, see James M. Higgins, "Story Board Your Way to Success," *Training and Development* (June 1995), pp. 13–17; or "Putting the Bang Back in Your TQM Program," *Journal for Quality and Participation* (October/November 1995), pp. 40–45.

6. See Charles W. Prather and Lisa K. Gundry, *Blueprints for Innovation: How Creative Processes Can Make You and Your Company More Competitive* (New York: American Management Association, 1995); Oren Harari, "Turn Your Organization into a Hotbed of Ideas," *Management Review* (December 1995), pp. 37–39; Ralph D. Stacey, *Complexity and Creativity in Organizations* (San Francisco: Berrett-Koehler Publishers, 1996).

7. For excellent discussions on both the theory and practice of sound business ethics, see Richard T. De-George, *Business Ethics* (4th ed.; Upper Saddle River, N.J.: Prentice-Hall, 1995); O. C. Farrell and John Fraedrich, *Business Ethics: Ethical Decision Making and Cases* (3rd ed.; Boston: Houghton Mifflin Company, 1997); Laura Pincus Hartman, *Perspectives in Business Ethics* (Chicago: Irwin/McGraw-Hill, 1997); Marianne M. Jennings, *Business Ethics: Case Studies and Selected Readings* (3rd ed.; Cincinnati: West Educational Publishing Company, 1999).

8. Some management theorists distinguish between the terms *risk* and *uncertainty* in decision making. According to Stephen Robbins, *risk* involves conditions in which the decision maker can estimate the likelihood of certain alternatives occurring, usually based on historical data or other information that enables the decision maker to assign probabilities to each proposed alternative. *Uncertainty* involves a condition in which the decision maker has no reasonable probability estimates available and can only "guesstimate" the likelihood of various alternatives or outcomes. See Stephen P. Robbins, *Managing Today* (Upper Saddle River, N.J.: Prentice-Hall, 1997), pp. 64–65.

9. See J. G. March and H. A. Simon, *Organizations* (New York: John Wiley & Sons, 1958), pp. 10–12.

10. See Russ Holloman, "The Light and Dark Sides of Decision Making," *Supervisory Management* (December 1989), pp. 33–34.

11. The guidelines were adapted from Robert Kreitner and Angelo Kinicki, *Organizational Behavior* (3d ed.; Homewood, Ill.: Richard D. Irwin, 1995), pp. 312–313.

12. For a general overview of several quantitative approaches to decision making, see Andrew J. DuBrin and R. Duane Ireland, *Management and Organization* (2d ed.; Cincinnati: South-Western Publishing Co., 1993), pp. 436–442; Ricky W. Griffin, *Management* (5th ed.; Boston: Houghton-Mifflin, 1996), pp. 702–721. For a comprehensive discussion of problem-solving and decision making which includes a number of applied quantitative models and examples, see William J. Altier, *The Thinking Manager's Toolbox: Effective Processes for Problem Solving and Decision Making* (New York: Oxford University Press, 1999).

Case

1–1

THE OPPORTUNITY OF A LIFETIME?

Randy Harber, a 36-year-old construction crew chief, is employed by one of the largest mechanical contractors in the country. His employer operates in 44 states and 14 foreign countries. Randy and his spouse, Eileen, have two children, Kelly, aged seven, and Jason, aged three. Eileen is a registered nurse and works part time in a family practice office. Randy began his career in the construction field by entering the apprenticeship program immediately upon completion of high school. He served as an officer in the local union and became a crew chief three years ago. His technical skills rank among the best. During the past two years, he has taken evening courses at the local community college to enhance his supervisory skills and to improve his chances of becoming a field superintendent. However, the construction industry has experienced no real growth, and opportunities for advancement are slim. During the past winter, Randy and others suffered reduced work weeks and had their use of the company truck severely restricted.

Randy Harber had been called to meet with Kevin Cook, vice president of field operations, in Cook's office. The following conversation took place:

KEVIN: Randy, you know that our revenues are down about 25 percent from last year.

RANDY: Yes. (Thinking to himself, "Here it comes; I'm going to get laid off.")

KEVIN: We've been trying to expand our base of operations and as such have bid on contracts all over the world. I think we have the opportunity of a lifetime and you figure to be one of our key players. The United Methodist Church is collaborating in a joint venture in Liberia to build a hospital on the outskirts of Monrovia, the capital city. They have a medical missionary program there and this hospital is a $23 million project. The general contractor will be out of Milan, Italy, and we got the mechanical portion of the contract.

RANDY: That's great! We can use the work.

KEVIN: This project will give us a strategic advantage in the European-African corridor. Top management has talked it over and we would like for you to be our field superintendent on this project. Not only is this a great opportunity for us but it will give you invaluable experience. In addition, your salary will almost double. All of the people on this project will be our very best. You'll be leaving in three weeks and we'd expect you to be on-site for 14 months. What do you think?

RANDY: Geez, that sounds fascinating. How soon do you need an answer?

KEVIN: Go home, think it over, talk to Eileen, and let's get back together tomorrow afternoon about three.

Questions for Discussion

1. Evaluate the offer made to Randy Harber. Do you agree that this is the opportunity of a lifetime? Why or why not?
2. What factors should Harber consider, and how should Harber evaluate his career options?
3. What should Harber do? Consider alternatives.
4. If you were Randy Harber, what would you do?

Case

1-2

THE SOCIALIZING TEAM LEADER

Terry Miles was promoted to a team leader position in Metro Insurance Company's Operations Division. She was chosen for the position by the manager of operations, Ronnie Callahan, who felt Miles was the "ideal" candidate for the position. Miles had been hired five years earlier as a general purpose employee. Metro cross-trained all new employees so they were capable in a variety of functions. Two other employees had been in the division for at least 10 years but they had consistently expressed their dislike for any leadership responsibilities. In addition, Miles's job performance ratings were very good, her attendance was near perfect, and she seemed to be well liked by her colleagues and others who knew her well.

When Callahan told Miles that she was to become team leader of the word processing department, she asked him how she should handle the problem that her fellow employees now would be her "subordinates." Callahan told her not be concerned about this and that her former associates would soon accept the transition. Callahan also told Miles that the company would send her to a supervisory management training program sponsored by a local college just as soon as time became available.

After several months, however, Callahan was getting the impression that Miles was not making the adjustment to her new position. Callahan was particularly concerned that he had observed Miles socializing with her employees during lunch breaks, coffee breaks, and the like. Callahan had received reports that Miles often socialized with several of her employees after work, including going on double-dates and parties arranged by these employees.

Furthermore, Callahan had received a number of reports from managers and team leaders of other departments that the work performed by the word processing department was not being performed as efficiently as it should be. Several managers in the company told Callahan that the word processing department employees spent too much time away from their work on longer than normal breaks, lunch periods, and the like. One manager even told Callahan, "Since Miles became team leader, there is little discipline in the department, and it's just a big social group that reluctantly does a little work."

After reviewing various productivity reports, Callahan realized that Miles had not made a good adjustment to supervising employees in her department. He wondered how much of this was attributable to her lack of experience as a team leader and worried that her former colleagues might be taking advantage of her. At the same time, Callahan was concerned that Miles perhaps did not have the desire to disassociate herself from socializing and being a "buddy" to her employees. Callahan wondered what his next step should be.

Questions for Discussion

1. Evaluate the decision to promote Terry Miles to team leader. Discuss the problems in promoting anyone to team leader or supervisor over his or her former fellow employees.
2. Besides sending Miles to a supervisory training program, what other actions could Callahan and Miles have taken to prepare Miles for the transition to the team leader role?
3. Why is it dangerous for a team leader or supervisor to socialize with direct-report employees? Why does this leave a team leader or supervisor open to criticism, as exemplified in this case?
4. At the end of the case, what should Ronnie Callahan do? Consider alternatives that may be open.

Case

1-3

FEAR OF BEING PASSED ON THE CORPORATE LADDER

Mark Wells was the evening shift (3 P.M. to 11 P.M.) warehouse supervisor for a large west coast grocery store chain. Over the past twelve years, Mark had worked his way up from being a laborer to a supervisor despite not having any formal education beyond high school. The 35-year-old Wells was married with two school-aged children, and he had been wanting to move to the day shift (7 A.M. to 3 P.M.) so he could spend more time with his family.

Two days ago, Mark's boss, John Swanson, told him that the current day-shift supervisor was retiring at the end of the month, and that Mark was first in line for the job. This would be a lateral move, that is, there would be no change in title and no pay increase. Actually, Mark would take a $20 per week reduction because the evening shift salary included a premium shift differential. Nevertheless, Mark Wells was very interested, because he saw it as his only near-term opportunity to move to the day shift.

Mark's assistant (or leadman) on the evening shift was Sam Melton, an energetic and intelligent young man in his mid-twenties who had been with the company for three years. Sam had been attending a local community college, and he recently completed a two-year management certification program. Mark felt somewhat intimidated by Sam's credentials, his easy-going personality, his exceptional communication skills, and his ability to get work crews to go the extra step. On several occasions, Sam was able to get work crews to complete difficult projects that Mark could not accomplish. Mark knew that if he took the day shift position, Sam likely would be promoted to evening shift supervisor. Then Sam would be able to demonstrate to upper management his superior supervisory skills. Since opportunities for advancement beyond the supervisory position were limited, Mark was concerned that his "rival" employee, Sam, would soon pass him by on the corporate ladder. Thus, Mark "forever" would be trapped in a first-tier supervisory position with little hope for future advancement.

Questions for Discussion

1. What factors account for Mark Wells' apprehensions in this situation?
2. What should Mark do if the day shift supervisory position is offered to him? Why?
3. Is it realistic for supervisors such as Mark Wells to expect that younger, former subordinates will not pass them on the corporate ladder? Why?
4. What specifically could Mark Wells do to increase the value of his services and potential, for example, the skills, knowledge, and abilities (SKAs) he brings to work each day?

Case
1–4

COPING WITH THE NEW MANAGER

Cindy Smith was a supervisory training facilitator at Blan Automotive's plant in Marion, Kentucky. The Marion plant made composite plastics components for the automotive industry. Plastic components were more durable and resisted dents and scratches better than ones made with steel. The nonunionized Blan facility employed about 450 personnel. Eight years ago, Smith began as a second-shift entry-level worker in the modeling section. After a series of advancements, she was promoted to production supervisor and then to training facilitator, and she had been performing this function for about sixteen months. New employees were assigned to Smith's section for orientation and training, usually lasting a week or more. Depending on the company's needs, employees then were reassigned to a specific production department. In recent months, however, the high turnover rate—25 percent of new hires quit within six weeks of hire—coupled with requirements to produce a variety of high-quality products for individual customer specifications had led to a deterioration of morale.

Traditionally, the average car buyer waited 36 to 45 days from the time a custom order was placed at a dealership until the customer could drive the vehicle off the lot. However, during the last decade some manufacturers had cut the time to build a car—

from the moment the customer places an order at the dealership to the time the vehicle rolls off the assembly line—to five days, and not more than five days for travel was allotted from the plant to the dealership. Reducing the time to build a car to customer specifications including color, engine type, and other options, had been an ongoing effort. As a supplier to the automotive industry, additional quality and production pressures were placed on Blan's Marion facility.

About one year previously, Operations Manager George Patterson was replaced by Don May. Even though the Marion plant often had missed delivery deadlines, and labor costs as a percentage of product costs were escalating, Patterson had been content with the status of the plant. Patterson had the reputation of expecting department managers to correct problems after they occurred, and "crisis management" was the prevalent style. Don May, a former military officer, was expected to turn the place around. Under May's direction, the culture of the plant seemed to change overnight. May immediately announced to all supervisors that he was not willing to accept the high rate of product rejects. May practiced management by wandering around (MBWA), and he met and talked with supervisors, group leaders, and facilitators one-on-one. Further, he met with small groups of employees and listened to their concerns. Initially, May was positively received, but this soon deteriorated.

Shortly after assuming the position of Operations Manager, Don May informed all managers and supervisors that they were being placed on a salary and bonus system. He told them that their hard work was appreciated and would be rewarded. Yet, because of costly rework production delays and overtime for hourly employees, the bonus system did not yield any tangible benefits. Among the supervisory complaints: "You told us the new system would result in greater compensation, and it hasn't. We're making less than before. We'd be better off financially if we were hourly production workers!"

Most supervisors now were working six days a week, ten to twelve hours a day. Employees and machinery were being stretched to the limit. Several supervisors had quit during the last month, and some took less-demanding plant jobs. Surviving supervisors often worked "double duty" in overseeing several production departments. On any given day, 10 to 20 percent of employee production positions could be vacant. Cindy Smith and her only remaining employee (five were assigned to fill in for vacant supervisory positions and one was placed in the quality department) were directed by Don May to cut the normal one-week training time to a half day. The most recent customer quality audit was a disaster. There were rumors that some work would be transferred to other Blan plants or even to competitors.

To Cindy Smith, it was like someone had turned a switch. Any supervisor who spoke out and didn't agree with Don May "fell from grace." May put pressure on all who questioned what he was doing, so that most supervisors were afraid to speak up. To Smith, supervisors appeared to be "mindless robots going through the motions." Smith's crowning blow came at a choir rehearsal in her church Wednesday night. Amy Swanson, a fellow choir member and a front office secretary to Don May, told Smith, "Mr. May told me that when he was meeting with and interviewing our supervisors, he was actually getting the scoop on everyone. He took names and tucked them away. I even heard him tell Bill Arnold, Blan's president, that he'd get rid of all malcontents."

Cindy Smith felt betrayed.

Questions for Discussion

1. How would you evaluate Cindy Smith's situation in terms of job satisfaction?
2. Compare and contrast the management styles of George Patterson and Don May.
3. What should Cindy Smith do? Why?
4. Have you ever experienced a situation like the one described in this case? If so, how did you handle those problems?
5. (Optional) The Web site www.myboss.com has become a gathering place for disgruntled employees. Every Monday a new batch of stories and one-liners are posted to be read and "rated." The best ones go into the site's "Hall of Fame." Using the Internet, find at least two sources that provide examples of how employees view managers who use their authority to an extreme. Write a one-page paper explaining what you learned from this experience.

INTERNET ACTIVITY

Case

1–5

SUPERVISORY HUMOR

Don Wilmes, supervisor of customer service at Software-n-More, was articulate and possessed a dry sense of humor. He could be counted on for occasional practical jokes, and he was not discriminating in his selection of targets.

Software-n-More was a major computer software, supplies, and services firm. The company had recently experienced some tough financial times. As a result, there had been layoffs of employees, several supervisors, and one middle-level manager. This restructuring had resulted in a consolidation of positions. The surviving supervisors were assigned additional employees and duties. Virtually everyone felt stressed from seeing colleagues depart and having more to do in the same amount of time.

Wilmes decided that he would write a humorous news item to try to boost morale. He wrote and posted on several employee bulletin boards a one-page memorandum titled "The Chopping Block." A few excerpts follow:

QUESTION: Rich, what is your reaction to the loss of your beloved supervisor, Karen Kates?

RESPONSE: Ding Dong, the Witch is Gone!!

QUESTION: Jackie, how do you like taking on the responsibilities of the parts department while continuing to supervise the testing lab?

RESPONSE: My boss, Dave Kohenski, gave me a half-hour pep talk, and I was up to speed and on top of things at the end of the morning.

QUESTION: Employees, how do you feel about our fearless leader's new motto, "Do More with Less!"?

RESPONSE: We feel that our president, Bob Swan, can teach us the true meaning of this motto, since he has lived it since birth.

Wilmes also printed copies of this memorandum and put it on virtually everyone's desk. One copy somehow made it to the executive suite. It was the talk of the company, and everyone was laughing—that is, everyone but the company president, Bob Swan.

Swan contacted Jean Mane, director of human resources, and asked her to arrange a meeting with Don Wilmes and his boss, Bernie Collins. Swan told Mane that he was deeply concerned over the offensive remarks in the bulletin. He stressed that this type of so-called humor was not acceptable. If carried to extremes, it could result in lawsuits by individuals who felt they were being ridiculed or defamed.

Later that day Don Wilmes was summoned to Jean Mane's office. Bernie Collins already was present when Wilmes arrived. Mane said, "Don, your behavior was unprofessional and inappropriate." He replied, "It was just a joke. Company management needs to lighten up. Everyone is so uptight here that my little memo will be forgotten quickly." Mane replied, "Don, this is serious. You didn't exercise good supervisory judgment. Other supervisors and employees have been fired for less than this." However, Bernie Collins told Jean Mane that if Wilmes was disciplined, it would alienate all of the other supervisors. He felt that the humor was "a bit sarcastic, but everyone is saying the same things in private."

When the meeting ended, Jean Manes pondered what her recommendation to Bob Swan should be.

Questions for Discussion

1. Was Don Wilmes's memorandum just a bit of humor to improve morale, or was it a serious breach of a supervisor's responsibilities? Discuss.
2. Evaluate the general positions as stated by each individual in this case. Which of these do you find the most and which the least credible?
3. If you were Jean Manes, what would you recommend, and why?

Case

1-6

THE PICNIC CONVERSATION

The annual picnic of Mendoza Company was well attended as usual. It was a well-planned, day-long family affair for all the employees of the firm, giving them an opportunity to have an informal get-together. At the picnic, Charlene Knox, one of the supervisors, had a long chat with her boss, Jim Cross, the general manager. They spoke about many things, including some work problems. Cross put great emphasis on the need for cutting costs and a general "belt-tightening." He told Knox that he had already received a number of written suggestions and plans from some of the other supervisors. He highly praised their efforts as appropriate and helpful.

Three weeks after the picnic, Charlene Knox received a memo from her boss asking her why her "report in reference to cost-cutting had not yet arrived." At first she wondered what Jim Cross was referring to, and then she remembered their talk at the picnic. She realized that was the only time Cross had discussed with her the need to cut costs! Knox pondered what her response should be.

Questions for Discussion

1. Is it appropriate for a supervisor to give a directive to a subordinate in a social, off-the-job setting? Why or why not?
2. Was Charlene Knox at fault for not having understood what her boss told her at the picnic conversation? Was Jim Cross at fault? Were both managers at fault?
3. What should Knox do?

Case

1-7

ROMANCE ON THE ASSEMBLY LINE

Louise Nance had been working on the assembly line of Jackson Manufacturing Company for about six months. During recent weeks, her supervisor, Ben Miller, noticed that her production had gone down to such an extent that she could not keep up with the pace, and she had caused serious delays. When Miller called this to her attention, Nance told him about the difficulties she was having at home. Her husband had recently left her without any explanation. Miller replied that her personal affairs were of no interest to him and that he was concerned only with her work. He warned her that unless her production improved she would be separated from the company.

A few days thereafter, Ben Miller was promoted to a higher-level management position. His place was filled by Jack Armstrong, who had recently joined the company. Armstrong immediately took a liking to Louise Nance and started dating her. Although she told him about her marital difficulties, he kept seeing her. When she remarked to him one day that her car needed some repairs, he offered to see whether he could fix it for her.

On the following Saturday, Nance's estranged husband appeared and found Armstrong repairing her car, which was parked on the street in front of her apartment. The two men got into a fight on the street, and police were called to separate them. The local newspapers carried a short report about the incident, mentioning the fact that Nance and Armstrong were employed at Jackson Manufacturing Company.

A few days later, Jack Armstrong was called into the office of Kay McCaslin, the human resources director, who had read the newspaper reports. McCaslin advised Armstrong to stop seeing Louise Nance or he might be fired. McCaslin reminded Armstrong that informal company policy discouraged close fraternization between supervisors and employees, since this tended to weaken a supervisor's authority in dealing with employees. Moreover, publicity of this sort would undoubtedly hurt the company's image in the community. Armstrong replied that this was none of the company's business and that he could spend his time away from the plant any way he chose. He stated that a threat of discharge was totally improper, since his private life was his own and not subject to company regulations. Furthermore, Nance's work record had improved under his supervision, and it was now about the same as the records of most of the other people on the line. Armstrong left McCaslin's office with the comment that he would continue to date Louise Nance, since they were very much in love.

Kay McCaslin wondered whether she should drop the matter or discuss it with higher-level management—including Ben Miller, who now was Jack Armstrong's superior.

Questions for Discussion

1. Is the informal company policy that discourages close fraternization between supervisors and employees sound? Why or why not?
2. What alternatives are open to Kay McCaslin, the human resources director? What should she do?
3. Should Jack Armstrong's own supervisor, Ben Miller, be called into the situation?
4. If you were Jack Armstrong, what would you do?
5. If you were Louise Nance, what would you do?

Case

1-8

TO ACCEPT OR NOT TO ACCEPT?

Dave Harris was a newly hired information services (IS) supervisor for Cedarville Wholesale Supply and Distribution Center (CWSADC). He joined the firm three months ago after a 10-year stint with Washington Insurance's office of information services. As contrasted with the publicly owned Washington Insurance, CWASDC was a family-owned, $30 million enterprise. The owner of the firm had instituted a number of personnel policies including a "no gift-gratuity" policy. Although the owner had issued the "no gift-gratuity" policy to all employees, it was well known throughout the organization that, over the past year, the owner had received gifts, tickets, vacation trips, and other perks from vendors, customers, government officials, and the like.

Stewart Clark, the operations vice-president, had asked Dave Harris to join him in a vendor-sponsored golf outing to be held at a prestigious country club. Harris liked the game of golf, had played on his college team, and had won several men's amateur golf tournaments. He decided to participate in the golf event, believing this to be acceptable under the company's policy.

However, at the dinner following the golf festivities, the vendor had a door-prize giveaway. Stewart Clark was announced as the winner of a four-day golf trip to Hilton Head Island, South Carolina. The final name drawn was Dave Harris, and he was summoned to come forward and accept a new 35-inch television set. As Harris walked to the award stand, he contemplated his alternatives.

Questions for Discussion

1. What is the purpose of a "no gift-gratuity" policy?
2. What should Dave Harris do? If you were Dave Harris, would you accept the TV set? (Suggestion: Refer to the five "ethical tests" that are included in Chapter 5 as guidelines for making ethical decisions).
3. What, if anything, should Dave Harris do in regard to Stewart Clark's acceptance of the golf-trip gift?

Case
1–9

THE TROUBLED TECHNICIAN

As part of its main office, Centaur Electric Company has a development engineering department. This department's work consists of control and revision of old products and design of new products.

The chief development engineer and head of the department is Vincent Gabris. Assigned to Gabris are three development engineers and their technicians. In general, the development engineers do all the creative and design engineering work. The technicians work closely with the engineers in mechanical and electrical testing, physical layouts, equipment and product plans, and on various other tasks as assigned.

The engineers schedule the work of the technicians and are responsible for their training and performance. The engineers, however, do not determine the technicians' rate of pay. Development engineers are salaried, while technicians are paid hourly wages. In scheduling the workload of a technician, an engineer is responsible for the number of hours per day that the technician will work. However, Vincent Gabris often assigns projects to technicians; he is supposed to notify the development engineers when a technician is assigned to a different project or job.

The educational level of the engineers and the technicians differs by an average of about four years. Typically, development engineers have graduate degrees; none of the technicians has more than one year of college.

John Turner, a technician, has been working at Centaur for two years. He had no previous experience in this type of position. Turner had attended a local school of engineering for two semesters, dropped out, and gone to work as a factory laborer. On the basis of high scores on the firm's mechanical aptitude and intelligence tests, Turner was hired by Centaur for a technician's job. His training at Centaur was internal and informal. Turner, age 28, is married and has two children, and his wife is expecting another. Barbara Kurton, an engineer, is Turner's current supervisor. Kurton considers Turner to be conscientious, task oriented, and a perfectionist in his work. She also believes that he tries to learn from his work experiences.

However, in recent months Kurton has detected a serious drop-off in Turner's output. He seemed to wander about the work area, doing little and complaining that he had too many bosses. It had been a particularly trying month, with considerable overtime work, so Kurton thought little about it. But when the problem persisted the next month, Kurton started to investigate. She talked with Turner and learned that he felt that too many people were making too many demands on him—often all at the same time. He said that he had tried to please everyone but that there wasn't enough time to work for all. This frustration was the cause of his lowered output. Kurton immediately set to work to alleviate the demands on Turner by asking everyone to channel all work requests for him through her. This, she felt, would give Turner the impression, at least, that he had a lighter workload, because she could assign priorities to the work given. It also could actually stabilize Turner's workload and ease the tension.

After this system was put into effect, Turner's workload did level out considerably, but his output nevertheless dwindled steadily. It eventually reached the point where Kurton felt that discharging Turner was justified. Hoping to avert this, she had several long talks with him. From these talks came the revelation that Turner was thousands of dollars in short-term debt. This included what he owed on his mobile home and car. A problem with his car had triggered the conflict. When Turner had tried to sell the car, he found that he owed more on it than it was worth. With a new baby on the way, he was continually worried about the future and his money troubles. Kurton also learned that Turner had little understanding of financial matters or budgets.

Kurton pondered what she could do to help motivate this employee to return to his previous productive self, or whether she should simply solve the problem by discharging him. She also wondered whether she should take the problem to her own boss, Vincent Gabris.

Questions for Discussion

1. Should a supervisor become involved in the personal problems of an employee?
2. Should Barbara Kurton try to work with John Turner to straighten out his personal life? Is Turner worth extra effort on the part of his supervisor?
3. Should Turner be discharged because his work has not been up to standard? How would such a discharge affect the other employees in the department? How would the other workers be affected if Kurton kept Turner despite his low productivity?
4. If you were Barbara Kurton, what would you do?

Case

1–10

ABUSIVE RUMORS

John Jacobs was supervisor for the electronics department of Appliances Galore, a chain of large superstores specializing in appliance sales to both retail and commercial customers. The company had a reputation for extensive involvement in community activities. In fact, the company strongly promoted family values and had sponsored a variety of family-oriented activities throughout the years. In addition, the company provided financial and other incentives to employees who volunteered their time in not-for-profit and other service activities.

Andy George, manager of marketing operations, just confided in Jacobs that he had heard "through the grapevine" that Steve Shepard's wife and two children showed up last night at the local women and children's shelter. George also indicated that Shepard's wife was reported to have been badly bruised and that this was not the first time they had sought refuge.

Steve Shepard was one of Jacob's outstanding salespersons. Last year Shepard won the company's award for the most sales. George suggested to Jacobs that he should investigate the matter and make a recommendation about what the company should do.

Questions for Discussion

1. If Steve Shepard's job performance was not affected by his personal life, should the company become involved in any way? Discuss.
2. If Steve Shepard's alleged actions off the job became public knowledge and reflected on the image and reputation of Appliances Galore, should the company take any actions?
3. What would you recommend that Jacobs and George do? Consider alternatives.

Case

1–11

A JOB MADE JUST FOR ME

Malcolm Peters couldn't believe his ears. He was sitting in a classroom at Old Ivy University for his morning class with Professor Cary Ramond. On this day, however, an invited guest and young alumnus, Donnie Sanchez, was speaking to the class. Sanchez was holding forth about how his experiences as a student had prepared him for the "real world." Sanchez first recalled that about a year earlier, he had been sitting where the students were sitting and wondering what the future would hold. As Malcolm Peters listened intently, he heard echoes of some of Professor Ramond's recent lectures. Peters thought to himself, "Can it be that my professor actually knows what he is talking about?" Donnie Sanchez continued:

Where do you want to go tomorrow was the question Professor Ramond posed to our class each term. Every semester, he preached that we needed career self-reliance or at least a career self-direction. It was the question facing each of us as we planned our sprint into the full-time job market. Throughout the nineties, the U.S. economy had surged but then peaked with the dawn of the millenium. Jobs were in plentiful supply for the "techies" and those willing to work for basic entry-level wages. I played on the college baseball team and in summer leagues, so a co-op program or internship was out of the question. I felt I had pretty good interpersonal skills, persistence, and a high energy level, but no experience. The college placement officer told me that I would probably have trouble finding meaningful work. After posting my resume on the Web and reviewing many Internet databases, I found that restaurants, computer companies, and engineering firms were hiring at a brisk pace. Even though I love to eat, the restaurant field was not appealing, and I lacked technical and computer courses and experience to apply for a computer or engineering firm job. As a native of Puerto Rico, I had braved the cold midwest winters to play college sports and pursue a basic liberal arts degree. Midway through my sophomore year, I heard some of my teammates extolling the virtues of Professor Cary Ramond. After enrolling in his "Principles of Management" class, I changed my major to general management.

I don't want to embarrass Professor Ramond in front of his students, but I can honestly say that he was my best teacher. He played the role of brain surgeon; he asked thought-provoking questions and demanded a lot from us. He extracted my best efforts and output, even after a strenuous day of practice. Professor Ramond required us to read What Color is Your Parachute? A Practical Manual for Job-Hunters and Career-Changers. *I decided to follow the advice offered by the author, Richard Boles, and contacted Tom Mercer, a supervisor at a local electronics firm, Luxor. Luxor employs about 280 people and manufactures and assembles electronic components for the telecommunications industry. I had the opportunity to shadow Tom Mercer as part of my senior class project in Professor Ramond's "Management of Technological Change" course. Mercer's project team was changing some of Luxor's methods and processes. I learned a lot about the process of change and gained a mentor and friend in the experience. Toward the end of my last senior semester, I really just wanted to touch base with Tom Mercer and ask him one simple question: Do you know of any jobs in general management? I got the surprise of my life when he told me to come to Luxor that afternoon and meet with him and Philip Lynn, the plant manager. I was hired on the spot. I guess having a recommendation from Professor Ramond didn't hurt!*

Even though the work is somewhat technical, I was hired. They put me through a series of tests to prove that I was a self-starter and a team player. Mr. Lynn says that he hires for attitude over aptitude. He claims that technical stuff is teachable, but that initiative and ethics aren't. The plant is organized on a self-directed work team approach. Teams elect their own leaders to oversee quality, training, scheduling, and communication with other teams. The goals are created by Mr. Lynn and his staff after in-depth consultation with all teams. The plant follows simple ground rules, such as commit yourself to respect all team members, communicate openly and honestly, continually look for ways to improve on what we do well, and do the right job the right way the first time. The sales staff, customers, engineers, and assemblers constantly "noodle ideas around," and there are no status symbols or an attitude of "us" versus "them." There are no sacred cows in the company. Many procedures are written down, but any employee can propose changes to any procedure, subject to approval by those whose work it affects. When we change processes or methods, an employee logs onto the network to make it a part of the record—the law of the plant. There is plenty of feedback on performance. Team leaders share the good and the bad. Each day begins with a recap of the previous day's performance. Every employee knows the destination of every product they touch. Each employee puts his or her signature on the part. In conclusion, let me say that I have been in an intensive apprenticeship with experienced employees as my guides. Tom Mercer serves as my mentor, and we meet each day to discuss my progress. I have visited customers to understand how they use our products. The company has a bonus system based upon individual performance, team performance, and ideas generated. Last year the bonus averaged in excess of 20 percent of regular pay. Even though I have only limited authority, I'm getting an education for a lifetime and getting paid to learn. It doesn't get any better!

Malcolm Peters reflected on Donnie Sanchez's remarks, "Is he making this up, or are there really companies like Luxor, and how in the world could I be as lucky as this guy in finding a great job?"

Questions for Discussion

1. Do you think Donnie Sanchez was "making this up" or exaggerating on his experiences? Why or why not?
2. Evaluate why Sanchez is excited about his job and future.
3. Evaluate the "techniques" Donnie Sanchez used which led to his obtaining the job at Luxor. Do you think that Malcolm Peters could use the same "techniques" for finding a great job? Discuss.
4. Would you like to work at Luxor? Why, or why not? What would be your concept of a "great job to launch a great career?"

Planning

Essentials of Planning

You Make the Call!

You are Joan McCarthy, supervisor of the "hottest" new project design group within an original equipment manufacturing company employing over 15,000 people. You have ten years experience with the company working at several locations, the last seven with the company's engineering facility. Your strengths for the company are your communication and leadership skills. "Give me a direction and authority, and I will be able to get it done!" has always been your motto. Although you were viewed by some as not being technically competent enough for your last job, you were always able to compensate with the human skills you had developed. Accompanying your appointment as supervisor of the new group, you were selected as one of the "Top 100 Employees" in the company for this year.

The new project design group (or team) developed from your interactions with your coworker Bryan Barton, your manager Lyle Hasaka, and a consulting firm. The new group was to have one supervisor and six employees. You were instrumental in gaining support from senior management for the program. Bryan Barton worked with several functional areas through all the internal systems to implement the new project team processes.

When it came time to launch the group, you were the obvious choice for supervisor. Bryan Barton filled the first reporting position. Others were selected as they could be found. Only the best from the available workforce was taken for the project team. It was a whole new world of responsibility. This was the first time that you had served in a supervisory position, and you looked forward to the opportunity.

The outline for operations was to rely on the expertise of the team to gather the data, make decisions, and direct the flow of changes within the new ordering and design systems. Your role would be to provide guidance where necessary and provide the "big picture" perspective. You decided to delegate many of the supervisory functions to Bryan Barton. Thus, Barton would be able to expedite various supervisory tasks quickly, for example, training new employees in the computer and telephone systems. Carefully designed metrics were developed to evaluate product change decisions. Existing team members handled the training of new employees, and responsibilities were to be shared by team members and handed back and forth. You were thus generally free for travel and meetings with customers at their locations, which you did often. You always made sure to keep in contact with the team while away.

Problems began to arise only a few months after the launch of the group. A sense of dissatisfaction was growing from team members who had been on the team from the outset. Two of the team members usually ended up doing more work than the rest of the group combined. A number of unforeseen changes had caused a great deal of extra work for the team. Updates typically were not completed until the last possible moment. The newest employee, Lois Hunter, who had been hired from outside the company, still had not come up to speed and could not really contribute. Bryan Barton claimed that he was unable to help Hunter until some basic orientation and training could be given to her by other team members.

Team morale really began to decline when you brought in some changes that had been requested by a vice president. The team had been struggling to use the decision metrics already laid out, and now they were going to have to use some data and procedures that clearly violated the team's previous operating rules. The vice president's ideas were not totally bad, but members of the team argued that they should be allowed to refuse what the VP was trying to mandate.

You know that the team has made some strides over the first few months, but there is a clear need for action on your part to improve the functioning of the team.

You Make the Call!

MANAGEMENT FUNCTIONS BEGIN WITH PLANNING

There is some disagreement among management scholars and practitioners concerning the number and designation of managerial functions. However, there is general consensus that the first and probably most crucial managerial function is planning.

Planning means deciding in advance what is to be done in the future. It includes analyzing the situation, forecasting future events, establishing objectives, setting priorities, and deciding what actions are necessary to achieve those objectives. Planning logically precedes all other managerial functions since every manager must project a framework and a course of action for the future before attempting to achieve desired results. For example, how can a supervisor organize the operations of a department without having a plan in mind? How can a supervisor effectively staff and lead employees without knowing which avenues to follow? How can a supervisor possibly control the activities of employees without having standards and objectives for comparison? Thus, all other managerial functions depend on planning.

Planning is a managerial function that every supervisor must perform every day. It should not be a process used only occasionally or when the supervisor is not too engrossed in daily chores. By planning, the supervisor realistically anticipates future problems and opportunities, analyzes them, anticipates the probable effects of various alternatives, and decides on the course of action that should lead to the most desirable results. Of course, plans alone do not bring about desired results. But without good planning, activities would become random, producing confusion and inefficiency.

Strategic planning

The process of establishing goals and making decisions that will enable an organization to achieve its long- and short-term objectives.

THE STRATEGIC-PLANNING PROCESS

Turbulent and rapid changes in economic conditions and technology, coupled with increasing domestic and international competition, have forced organizations to do a more thorough and systematic job of planning. As the first function of management, planning must start at the top level of management and permeate throughout all levels of the organization. For the organization as a whole, this means that top management must develop an outlook and plans for the future that will guide the organization as a whole. We will refer to this overall process as **strategic planning,** which essentially means establishing goals and making decisions that will enable an organization to achieve its long- and short-term objectives.

For many years, noted management scholar Peter Drucker has stressed that every organization must think through its reasons for being and constantly ask the question, "What is our business?" Only by asking this question can a firm set goals and objectives, develop strategies, and make decisions that will lead to future success. Drucker emphasizes that this has to be done by that part of the organization that can see the entire business and balance all of the objectives and needs of today against the needs of tomorrow and allocate resources to key results.[1]

CEO Linda Yates and Director Peter Skarzynski of Strategos, a global strategy innovation firm, have echoed Drucker's assertions with their own emphasis upon innovation as being the guiding necessity for all companies in the future. They write:

Getting to the future first . . . requires companies and their leaders to be courageous and far-sighted. The company that wins the race to the future is driven by innovation. Not an innovation, but a conscious, built-in, continuous process of innovation that keeps a company on a pathbreaking streak. Innovation must become, like the quality revolution of 20 years ago, the right and responsibility of every individual in a company, not the pet project of the executive suite. Companies that eat and breathe innovation never suffer from prosperity-induced slumbers. They are not predicting the future; they are inventing it.[2]

In most organizations, top-level managers are primarily responsible for developing and executing the strategic or long-term plans. However, once the strategic goals and plans have been identified, middle managers and supervisors must be involved in

contemporary issue

Keep Strategic Planning Focused, Flexible, and Understandable

Strategic planning certainly is one of the major tools advocated by major corporations and management analysts. A recent study indicated that 89 percent of international managers use strategic planning to drive success through their organizations.[1] Strategic planning should be thought of as a process of determining what an organization is trying to accomplish. It includes developing a shared vision of the organization's future and then attempting to determine ways to make the vision occur. Both large and small businesses that utilize strategic planning tend to outperform their counterparts who do not use strategic planning.[2]

However, numerous questions have risen concerning the viability of strategic planning in the face of major technological and other changes in the marketplace. Strategic plans can quickly become outdated unless there is a constant updating and review. In particular, the market-driven focus of high-performing companies means that the market often will be more crucial in shaping business strategies. This requires constant monitoring of

strategic plans, and making new plans and actions to maintain market leadership.[3]

Many critics of strategic planning claim that too much of it is just verbage and rhetoric, and that it often is too high-sounding and not clearly communicated to those who would use it. One analyst, John Mariotti, stresses that a good strategic plan does not have to be voluminous; more important is its clarity and focus. According to Mariotti, strategic plans should be concise and written in understandable language that can easily be adjusted where appropriate. He advocates that the key questions any continuing strategic plan should answer are (1) What business are you in? (2) What is the competitive situation? (3) What is your strategy? (4) How are you going to do that? (5) What are the critical assumptions? and (6) What are the critical unresolved issues?[4] In this regard, according to a study by the Hackett Group, the average company spends up to nine months annually on strategic and tactical planning and reporting and forecasting. Yet this study also showed that the top-performing companies typically condensed their planning processes to a period of less than four months.[5] The message seems to be clear: keep strategic planning focused, understandable, and also flexible.

Sources: (1) Gay Gooderham, "Debunking the Myths of Strategic Planning," *CMA Magazine* (May 1998), pp. 24–26. (2) Bryan W. Barry, "A Beginner's Guide to Strategic Planning," *Futurist* (April 1998), pp. 33–36. (3) David W. Cravens, Gordon Greenley, Nigel F. Piercy, and Stanley F. Slater, "Mapping the Path to Market Leadership," *Marketing Management* (Fall 1998), pp. 28–39. (4) John Mariotti, "Failing to Plan is Fatal," *Industry Week* (July 6, 1998), p. 66. (5) "Planning Processes Overlong and Inefficient," *Internal Auditor* (December 1998), p. 13–14.

the planning activities throughout the organization.[3] They must plan their work units' policies and activities toward achieving the organization's overall goals. A supervisor, like Joan McCarthy in the "You Make the Call" section at the outset of this chapter, likely will become involved in developing and carrying out certain overall strategic plans for her corporation. McCarthy perhaps will not be part of strategic capital budget decisions; but she certainly will become involved in planning issues related directly to the operations of the project design group that contribute to carrying out the mission of the firm.

As this chapter's "Contemporary Issue" box makes clear, strategic planning does not have to be a burdensome, voluminous undertaking. In this regard, strategic planning principles are just as applicable to small business operations as they are to major corporations. The lack of strategic planning often is a serious obstacle for small business owners. The benefits of strategic management in giving direction to the organization as a whole are just as important to small business. Regardless of the size or nature of the organization, managers need to be involved in strategy formulation because their participation in the strategic-planning process is essential to gaining commitment for the chosen directions and strategies.[4]

Mission Statements and Visioning

Mission statement
A statement of the organization's basic philosophy, purpose, and reason for being.

Effective strategic planning usually begins with the development of a **mission statement** that reflects the philosophy and purpose of the organization as defined by its top leadership. An organization's mission usually is understood to be the purpose or reason for the organization's existence. Figure 6-1 (see page 171) is an example of a mission statement used by a major supermarket chain; this statement is displayed in every store and office of the firm.

Mission statements can become mere window dressing and little more than public relations "fluff" unless such statements really reflect the values and core behaviors that are to be manifested throughout an organization. The entire management team is responsible for providing the leadership that results in setting the patterns for employees' treatment of each other, customers, and suppliers. In so doing, the mission statement can provide a springboard or basis for assessing the company's performance and results.[5]

Visioning
Management's view of what the company should become that reflects the firm's core values, priorities, and goals.

The concept of visioning goes beyond that of a mission statement. **Visioning** is the process of developing a mental image of what the firm or organization could become; it seeks to define what it is that distinguishes the organization and what will make it better. The vision then can become the foundation for all of a firm's activities.

There is, of course, some overlap in the nature of vision statements and mission statements. Figure 6-2 is an example of a major corporation's vision statement that was sent to all of its employees. Notice that it is entitled "Our Values," and that there is some similarity with a number of the items included in the mission statement shown in Figure 6-1.

Visioning and vision statements should not be mere "advertising slogans" that primarily laud the organization and its accomplishments. Rather, visioning should reflect the firm's core values, priorities, and goals that can be translated into concrete plans and actions in the future.[6]

FIGURE 6-1   Corporate mission statement of a major supermarket chain.

Mission Statement

NATURE OF BUSINESS

We are committed to excellence as an innovative retailer of quality foods, drugs, consumable products, and services. We focus on providing value through quality, variety, service, competitive pricing, and friendliness.

CUSTOMERS

Customers are our most important asset and must receive our total effort toward their satisfaction.

FINANCIAL OBJECTIVES

We must achieve profits above the industry average to maintain leadership and provide for future growth.

ASSOCIATES

We will employ and promote only competent people of high integrity with a strong work ethic. We are committed to having a diversified work force.

BUSINESS CLIMATE

We will conduct our business by treating all customers, associates, suppliers, and the communities we serve with honesty, fairness, and respect.

FIGURE 6-2   Example of a corporate vision statement.

Our Values

In all our relationships we will demonstrate our steadfast commitment to:

LEADERSHIP

We will be a world-class leader in every aspect of our business—in developing our team leadership skills at every level; in our management performance; in the way we design, build, and support our products; and in our financial results.

INTEGRITY

We will always take the high road by practicing the highest ethical standards and by honoring our commitments. We will take personal responsibility for our actions and treat everyone fairly and with trust and respect.

QUALITY

We will strive for continuous quality improvement in all that we do, so that we will rank among the world's premier industrial firms in customer, employee, and community satisfaction.

CUSTOMER SATISFACTION

Satisfied customers are essential to our success. We will achieve total customer satisfaction by understanding what the customer wants and delivering it flawlessly.

PEOPLE WORKING TOGETHER

We recognize our strength and our competitive advantage is—and always will be—people. We will continually learn, and share ideas and knowledge. We will encourage cooperative efforts at every level and across all activities in our company.

A DIVERSE AND INVOLVED TEAM

We value the skills, strengths, and perspectives of our diverse team. We will foster a participatory workplace that enables people to get involved in making decisions about their work that advance our common business objectives.

GOOD CORPORATE CITIZENSHIP

We will provide a safe workplace and protect the environment. We will promote the health and well-being of our people and their families. We will work with our communities by volunteering and financially supporting education and other worthy causes.

ENHANCING SHAREHOLDER VALUE

Our business must produce a profit, and we must generate superior returns on the assets entrusted to us by our shareholders. We will ensure our success by satisfying our customers and increasing shareholder value.

As mentioned previously, visioning should not be thought of as being the sole responsibility of top management. In fact, effective supervisors can use the process of visioning to guide their particular part of the organization. For example, in the "You Make the Call" section at the beginning of this chapter, supervisor Joan McCarthy not only is responsible for improving her project group's current operations, but she also should strive for continuous improvement that will shape the direction of the group and its services for years to come. McCarthy can involve her staff in the visioning process by soliciting ideas from them, as well as from others in the organization who are affected by and use the group's services. Widespread participation in the visioning process is crucial to future attainment of the vision.

3

Describe the supervisor's role in organizational planning.

ALL MANAGERIAL LEVELS PERFORM THE PLANNING FUNCTION

Planning is the responsibility of every manager, whether chairperson of the board, president, division manager, or supervisor of a department. However, the magnitude of a manager's plans will depend on the level at which they are carried out. Planning at the top level is more far-reaching than it is at the supervisory level. The top-level executive is concerned with overall operations of the enterprise and long-range planning for new facilities and equipment, new products and services, new markets, and major investments. At the supervisory level, the scope is narrower and more detailed. The supervisor usually is concerned with day-to-day plans for accomplishing departmental tasks—for example, meeting production quotas for a particular day.

Although planning always involves looking to the future, an evaluation of what has happened in the past should be part of managerial planning. Every manager can learn to plan more effectively for the future by evaluating earlier plans and trying to benefit from past successes and failures.

In formulating plans, a supervisor may find that certain aspects of planning call for specialized help—such as, for implementing employment policies, computer and accounting procedures, or technical know-how. In such areas, the supervisor should consult with specialists within the organization to help carry out the required planning responsibilities. For example, a human resources staff specialist can offer useful advice concerning policies involving employees. A supervisor should utilize all of the available help within the organization to accomplish thorough and specific planning. This includes consulting with employees for their suggestions on how to proceed in certain situations. Employees like to be consulted, and their advice may help the supervisor develop day-to-day plans for running the department. In smaller firms, expertise may not be readily available, so the supervisor may want to draw on personal contacts outside the firm. In the final analysis, however, it is each supervisor's personal responsibility to plan.

PLANNING PERIODS

For how long a period should a manager plan? Usually a distinction is made between long-range and short-range planning. The definitions of long-range and short-range planning will depend on the manager's level in the organizational hierarchy, the type of enterprise, and the kind of industry in which the organization is operating. Most managers define short-term planning as that which covers a period of less than one year. Long-term planning goes beyond a year and may involve a span of three, five, or ten or more years. In some firms, planning for one to five years is known as intermediate planning. Figure 6-3 shows how the planning process might flow in a manufacturing firm from top-level management down through the supervisory level. Note how planning becomes more short range and detailed as it progresses down the organization chart.

Strategic plans

Long-range overall plans developed by top management.

Although terminology is quite varied, some organizations identify or distinguish their planning time horizons as being "strategic," "tactical," or "operational" in nature. **Strategic plans** are developed by top or executive management and stem from the vi-

---

FIGURE 6-3   The planning flow.

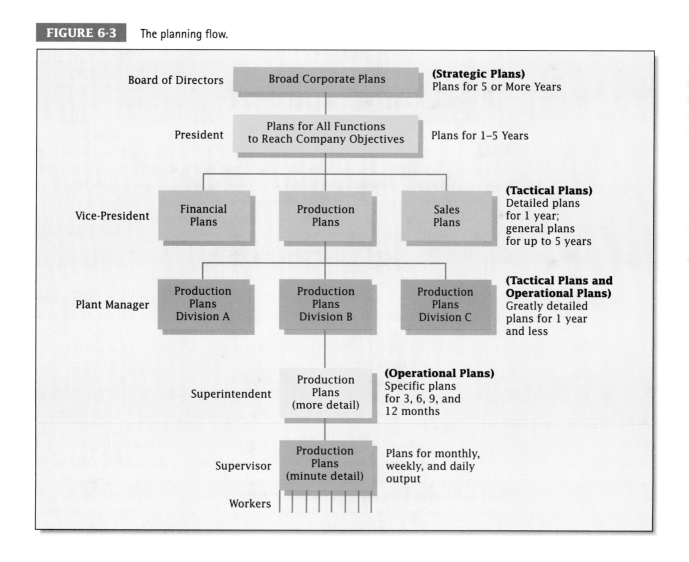

sion and mission of the firm; typically, strategic goals may be stated with five-year (or more) targets and/or indefinite "enduring" trends.

Tactical plans are usually developed by middle and staff managers who identify annual objectives—or objectives for several years' duration sometimes called *medium range* or *intermediate*—in regard to performance targets and other measures. **Operational plans** are usually the responsibility of first-line managers, supervisors, and department heads who develop short-term objectives of a year or less to cover specific areas of activities and accountability.[7] Of course, there is considerable overlap in the time horizons of strategic plans, tactical plans, and operational plans (see Figure 6-3). Irrespective of terminology, they must be supportive of each other at all management levels. As previously stated and for purposes of brevity in the discussion to follow, we will simply refer to "long-range" and "short-term" planning with the arbitrary dividing line between them being a year.

Tactical plans
Annual or intermediate-range plans developed by middle managers and staff specialists.

Operational plans
Short-range plans of supervisors to cover specific areas and activities of accountability.

Supervisory Roles in Long- and Short-Term Planning

Supervisors occasionally are involved in long-range planning. As the need arises, middle-level managers may discuss with supervisors the part they are to play in planning for the future. For example, a company may be considering a major restructuring, or an introduction of new technology may be contemplated due to competition and other developments. Supervisors might be asked to project the long-term trends of their particular activity, especially if it seems apparent that the activity will be affected by increasing mechanization, automation, robotics, or downsizing. Supervisors may be asked to submit suggestions about long-range plans, and they will have to stay informed and be ready to adapt as these plans are implemented. This may require supervisors to develop longer-range plans for their own departments, which could indicate that (a) there is a need to reassign or retrain some employees; (b) people with new skills must be hired; or (c) new techniques are necessary due to changing market or competitive conditions. Thus, from time to time every supervisor will participate in long-range planning.

For the most part, however, supervisors give most of their attention to short-range planning. This means that a supervisor must take time to think through the nature and amount of work that is assigned to the department. Many supervisors prefer to do this at the end of a day or at the end of a week when they can evaluate what has been accomplished in order to formulate plans for the immediate future. This is the very least amount of planning that every supervisor must do.

Short-range plans made by a supervisor should be integrated and coordinated with the long-range plans of higher-level management. Supervisors who are well informed about an organization's long-range plans are in a better position to integrate their short-range plans with the overall plans. All too often there is a gap between the knowledge of top-level managers and what middle- and supervisory-level managers are told about future plans. This often is justified by the claim that certain plans are confidential and cannot be divulged. However, effective top-level managers know that lower-level managers and supervisors need to know as much as possible about company plans in order to plan their groups' activities effectively.

Most of the time, a supervisor will plan for several months, one month, a week, or perhaps just one day or one shift. Very short-range planning is involved, for example, in scheduling a production line or departmental employees in a retail store. There are some activities for which the supervisor can plan for several months in advance, as, for example, in planning preventive maintenance.

Top-level, long-range plans should be communicated and fully explained to lower-level managers and supervisors as soon as possible so that they will be in a better position to formulate plans for their departments. By the same token, each supervisor should bear in mind that employees will be affected by the plans. Whenever possible, a supervisor should explain to employees in advance what is being planned for the department. The employees can contribute helpful ideas and begin preparing themselves for new skills they will need. At the very least, well-informed employees will appreciate the fact that they have been kept informed and that they do not have to look to the grapevine for information about their future.

EFFECTIVE PLANNING IS REQUIRED FOR SUCCESSFUL MANAGEMENT

4

Identify the benefits of planning.

Planning promotes efficiency and reduces waste and costs. Through thorough planning, haphazard approaches can be minimized and duplication avoided. The minimum time for completion of activities can be planned and scheduled, and facilities can be used to optimum advantage. Even in a small department or small firm, the total investment in physical and human resources may be substantial. Only by planning will the supervisor be able to utilize resources, both human and physical, to their fullest potential. It is not an overstatement to assert that effective planning is an absolute requirement for a supervisor to be a successful manager. Planning establishes objectives, standards, and targets that can serve as incentives for performance, measurement, and control. Planning primarily is a mental process that enables the supervisor to anticipate in advance what must be done and also how to adjust to changing circumstances and shifting priorities.

PLANNING FOR QUALITY IMPROVEMENT AND KNOWLEDGE MANAGEMENT

5

Explain the role of planning in quality improvement and knowledge management.

Total quality management (TQM)

An organizational approach involving all employees in the effort to satisfy customers by continual improvement of goods and services.

In recent decades, successful firms have shown an emerging commitment to quality. Many firms have turned to total quality management (TQM) and continuous improvement. In manufacturing firms, quality traditionally meant inspecting the product at the end of the production process. Today, the notion of **total quality management** means that the total organization is committed to quality—everyone is responsible for doing the job right the first time. TQM means a total effort toward meeting customer needs and satisfaction by planning for quality, preventing defects, correcting defects, and continuously building increased quality into goods and services as far as economically and competitively feasible.[8]

Knowledge management
Systematic storage, retrieval, dissemination, and sharing of information.

Although not as widely known as TQM, many firms have been involved in planning and carrying out short- and long-term strategies for more effective **knowledge management.** The "knowledge explosion" has been driven by computer technology, and it requires more systematic storage, retrieval, dissemination, and sharing of information in ways that are conducive to producing desired results. Knowledge management has been defined as

(a) Adding actionable value to information by capturing, filtering, synthesizing, summarizing, storing, retrieving, and disseminating tangible and intangible knowledge; (b) Developing customized profiles of knowledge so individuals can get at the kind of information they need when they need it; (3) Creating an interactive learning environment where people transfer and share what they know and apply it to create new knowledge.[9]

To this end, many firms have planned and implemented a variety of approaches, processes, and techniques which, according to a recent survey, have improved customer and employee satisfaction levels, and contributed to product or service innovations.[10] Some of these approaches have been within, or similar to, other quality management efforts.

Benchmarking
The process of identifying and improving on the practices of the leaders.

The increased emphasis on achieving higher product and service quality has led many firms to follow guidelines or criteria developed by others. The process of identifying and improving on the best practices of the leaders in the industry or related fields is called **benchmarking.** Some executives even advocate benchmarking using "best in the world" comparisons.[11] All of us have used benchmarking. When we evaluate the performance of our favorite sports team, we look to see how well it is doing in comparison with the team on top. We analyze the attributes of the players of the top team, the coaching styles, and so forth and conclude that our team could be just as good—if not better—if the owners/managers would make the necessary changes and copy the successful practices of the leaders of the top team.

The essence of benchmarking is to be as good as or better than the best in the field. The steps in the benchmarking process are as follows:

1. Determine what to benchmark, for example, a particular process or procedure, quality, costs, customer service, employee development, or compensation.
2. Identify comparable organizations both within and outside the industry.
3. Collect comparative performance data.
4. Identify performance gaps.
5. Determine the causes of the differences.
6. Ascertain the management practices of the "best."

ISO 9000
A rigorous series of manufacturing quality standards created by the International Organization for Standardization.

Once these steps are completed, management can develop plans that will strive for meeting or beating "best in the industry"—or even "best in the world"—standards.

Baldrige Quality Award
U.S. Department of Commerce award to outstanding firms that exemplify world-class business quality standards.

In recent years, many firms have given serious attention to ways of achieving quality improvements. Adherence to the quality standards established by **ISO 9000** and the **Baldrige Quality Award** are two options available to firms that wish to compare themselves to the best. ISO 9000 is a series of quality management and assurance standards that were originally developed for the manufacturing sector, although they can also be applied to service organizations.[12] ISO 9000 was created in 1987 by the International

The Malcolm Baldrige Quality Award was established to recognize firms that exemplify world-class business quality as well as satisfy the needs of their customers.

Organization for Standardization of Geneva, Switzerland. ISO has nudged firms into creating more interchangeable parts by establishing a rigorous quality standard that focuses on the firm's overall plan for quality management—structure, responsibilities, processes, and resources. Firms that want to compete internationally will have to produce products and services that conform to quality standards that only the "best" will be able to meet. Also in 1987, the U.S. Department of Commerce established the Malcolm Baldrige National Quality Award to recognize firms that exemplify world-class business quality as well as satisfy the needs of their customers. Many more firms than those that apply for the Baldrige National Quality Award subject themselves to the rigorous analysis of the effectiveness of their integration of customers' quality requirements into their business plans. Figure 6-4 (see page 178) lists seven examination categories for the Baldrige Award.[13]

Interestingly, as total quality management efforts have spread rapidly throughout business, government, and other organizations, some authorities believe that these major awards no longer are needed. That is to say, the criteria inherent in these awards have become widely accepted standards for corporate concerns and processes, and they are well established to emphasize excellence in business practices and performance.[14] But others still maintain that awards programs such as the Baldrige and ISO 9000 provide a structure and a set of well-defined targets that help to keep quality efforts focused and on course.[15]

In Chapter 15, we will discuss how TQM and other organized participative management programs can be integral in developing effective work teams and improving morale. In the remainder of this chapter, we will focus primarily on how the planning function of management plays an essential role not only in product and service quality, but also in setting direction for all other aspects of the firm.

FIGURE 6-4

Malcolm Baldrige National
Quality Award criteria.

1. **Leadership:** the success of top-level managers in creating a vision for quality and building quality values into the way the firm operates.
2. **Information and analysis:** the effectiveness of the firm's collection and analysis of information for quality improvement and planning.
3. **Strategic quality planning:** the effectiveness of the firm's integration of customers' quality needs into its business plan.
4. **Human resources utilization:** the success of the firm's efforts to realize its workforce's full potential for quality.
5. **Quality assurance of products and services:** the effectiveness of the firm's systems for assuring quality control of all its operations and for integrating quality control with continuous quality improvement.
6. **Quality results:** the firm's improvements in quality and demonstration of excellence in quality on quantitative measures.
7. **Customer satisfaction:** the effectiveness of the firm's systems to determine customers' requirements and its demonstrated success in meeting them.

ORGANIZATIONAL GOALS AND OBJECTIVES

Discuss the need for well-defined organizational goals and objectives, particularly as they relate to the supervisor.

A major first step in planning is to develop a general statement of goals and objectives that will identify the overall purposes and results toward which all plans and activities are directed. Setting overall goals is a function of top-level management, which must define and communicate to all managers the primary purposes for which the business is organized. These overall goals usually reflect upper-level managers' vision for the firm concerning the production and distribution of products or services, obligations to the customer, being a good employer and responsible corporate citizen, profit as a just reward for taking risks, research and development, and legal and ethical obligations. Figure 6-5 is an example of a company's statement of its corporate goals and objectives, which sometimes may be called a mission statement (see Figure 6-1).

While some firms make a distinction between the terms *goals* and *objectives,* we will use these terms interchangeably. Some firms define a *goal* as any long-term target—that is, one that will take more than a year to achieve—and an *objective* as a short-term target—that is, one that will take less than a year to achieve. Other firms define these terms to mean exactly the opposite.

The goals formulated for an organization as a whole become the general framework for operations and lead to the formulation of more specific objectives for divisional and departmental managers and supervisors. Each division or department in turn must clearly set forth its own objectives as guidelines for operations. These objectives must be within the general framework of the overall goals, and they must contribute to the achievement of the organization's overall purposes. Sometimes these objectives are established on a contingency basis—that is, some may be dependent or contingent on the availability of certain resources or reflect changing priorities.

Objectives usually are stated in terms of what is to be accomplished and when. A department's "what by when" statements are generally more specific than the broadly

FIGURE 6-5

Statement of corporate
goals and objectives.

XYZ CORPORATION

XYZ Corporation's existence is dependent on having the respect and support of four groups—its customers, employees, shareholders, and the public, which includes the citizens of each country in which we do business. For us to have a satisfactory future, we must continuously earn the support, respect, and approval of all four groups. This requires that XYZ:

For customers	Be committed to total customer satisfaction and continuous quality improvements.
For employees	Offer stability of employment, fairness in promotion, and opportunity for individual growth.
For shareholders	Offer both security of principal and competitive return through a combination of increased value of stock and dividends.
For the public	Conduct all of its business affairs not only in a legal manner but in a morally acceptable manner. XYZ must be a good neighbor.

XYZ's long-term corporate objectives and its interim goals must meet all of the obligations imposed by each of the four groups.

Corporate Objectives

1. To achieve continuing long-term growth in earnings and a record of financial stability that attracts to XYZ the capital—equity and debt—required to support its growth.

2. To concentrate our efforts in business and product areas in which XYZ can realistically expect to achieve a leadership position and in which leadership will be rewarded.

3. To offer our products and services wherever in the world XYZ's operations can be consistent with its management principles and corporate benefits.

4. To have a working environment in which each individual is treated with fairness that encourages and rewards excellence and stimulates maximum growth of the individual.

5. To anticipate the needs of the future sufficiently well to develop the human talent necessary to remain and be a leader.

6. To be a responsible corporate citizen.

stated objectives of the organization. While the higher-level goal may be "to provide quality maintenance services for the entire organization," the maintenance supervisor's objective might be "to reduce machine downtime by 12 percent by year end." While the supervisory level objectives are more specific than the broadly stated objectives of an organization, they are consistent with and give direction to departmental efforts toward organizational objectives.

Whenever possible, objectives should be stated in measurable or verifiable terms, such as "to reduce overtime by 5 percent during the month"; "to increase output per employee hour by 10 percent during the next quarter"; "to achieve a 10 percent increase in employee suggestions during the next year"; and so on. This enables a supervisor to evaluate performance against specific targets. This approach is an essential part of management by objectives programs, which have been implemented by many organizations as a system for planning and attaining results.

MANAGEMENT BY OBJECTIVES—A SYSTEM FOR PARTICIPATIVE MANAGEMENT

7

Explain management by objectives (MBO) and describe how it is applied.

Management by objectives (MBO)

A process in which the supervisor and employee jointly set the employee's objectives, and the employee receives rewards based on the achievement of those objectives.

Management by objectives (MBO) is a management approach in which managers, supervisors, and employees jointly set objectives against which performance is later evaluated. It is a management system—that is, a total approach to management—that involves participative management. Management by objectives requires full commitment to the objectives of the organization, which must start with top-level management and permeate throughout all levels. MBO is also referred to as *managing by results* or *managing for performance*. Some surveys have indicated that MBO or MBO-type systems are utilized in 80 percent or more of the top firms in the United States.[16]

As depicted in Figure 6-6, an effective MBO system has four major elements. The determination of specific, measurable and verifiable objectives is the foundation. The other elements are the inputs, or the resources, necessary for goal accomplishment; the activities and processes that must be carried out to accomplish the goal; and the results, which are evaluated against the objectives. While MBO emphasizes results rather than the techniques used to achieve them, an effective system of MBO must be constructed in such a way that all of the aforementioned elements are integrated and support each other.

FIGURE 6-6

Elements of the management by objectives approach.

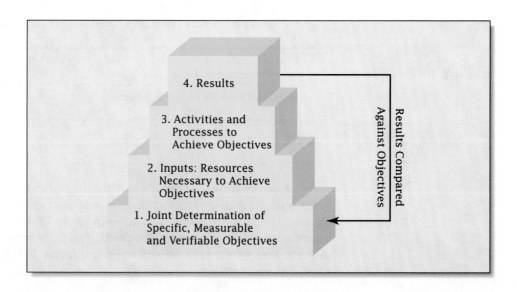

4. Results

3. Activities and Processes to Achieve Objectives

2. Inputs: Resources Necessary to Achieve Objectives

1. Joint Determination of Specific, Measurable and Verifiable Objectives

Results Compared Against Objectives

Why Use Management by Objectives?

There are numerous reasons why many firms have adopted the management by objectives approach. The following are among the most important. First, MBO is results oriented. It requires thorough planning, organization, controls, communication, and dedication on the part of an organization. Properly implemented, MBO influences motivation and encourages commitment to results among all employees. It provides a sound means for appraising individuals' performance by its emphasis on objective criteria rather than vague personality characteristics. In addition, it provides a more rational basis for sharing the rewards of an organization, particularly compensation and promotion based on merit.

James L. Pate, Chairman and CEO of Pennzoil—Quaker State Company, has described the "game plan" for his corporation as an MBO-type system involving four major elements:

- Setting individual goals and targets that are clear, quantifiable, and achievable.
- Communicating and recommunicating the plan and vision throughout the organization.
- Holding everyone accountable.
- Rewarding people who perform above expectations.

Mr. Pate contends that organizational success requires "relentless focus, strong commitment, and great enthusiasm throughout the organization," which his MBO-type "game plan" can make a reality.[17]

A Step-by-Step Model

Any management by objectives system must be developed to meet the unique purposes and character of the organization. There is no such thing as a "pure" model that fits all situations and all places. The following, however, is a suggested step-by-step model that would apply in most organizational situations.

Step 1. Top-level managers identify the major goals of the organization for the coming period. Usually this is done at about the same time the annual budget is prepared. Top-level managers determine the broad objectives for the coming period in such areas as sales, production levels, costs, profitability, employee development, and the like. Although corporate objectives may be broad, the more specifically they are stated, the better they can be communicated throughout the organization. Top-level managers develop these goals in consultation with managers at the next level of management. When finalized, there should be a consensus that the goals are challenging yet realistic and attainable within the established timeframe.

Step 2. The next step, which in some respects must be done in conjunction with Step 1, is for all managers, supervisors, and employees to review their job descriptions to be sure they understand their responsibilities and authority. A thorough review of the organizational structure will help to reveal gray areas where overlapping responsibilities need to be clarified.

Step 3. The crucial third step is for all employees to develop their own specific objectives in relation to the broader organizational and departmental objectives. Each individual prepares a list of objectives—typically about six or so—that cover major results expected within their areas of responsibility. Objectives must be stated in terms that are measurable and verifiable, that is, with a number, ratio, due date, or some other specific criterion of accomplishment. It is important for employees to develop not only routine objectives for their normal areas of responsibility but also objectives that involve some elements of creativity and personal growth.

Step 4. A meeting must be arranged between each individual and his or her supervisor to discuss the employee's list of objectives. The final list of objectives should be negotiated to attain mutual agreement between supervisor and employee. Both parties should strive to agree on objectives that are challenging but realistic and attainable. Priorities must be established where appropriate.

Although it does not always happen, research results have shown that employees often stipulate more challenging objectives than their supervisors initially thought they were capable of attaining. Once the list of objectives is finalized, both the supervisor and the employee sign a copy, and this becomes the primary document on which the employee's performance will be judged.

Step 5. Employees and their supervisors periodically review progress toward accomplishment of the agreed-upon objectives. Some authorities suggest a quarterly review during which objectives are compared with progress. During such reviews, objectives may be adjusted upward or downward as deemed appropriate.

Step 6. The next step is to compare results against objectives at the end of the period, usually a year. Performance appraisal and the appraisal meeting are discussed in greater depth in Chapter 13. A good approach is to have each individual do a self-evaluation of performance in terms of the objectives that were to be accomplished. Here, too, some employees will be more critical of their performance than are their supervisors.

The supervisor and employee then meet to discuss the employee's performance. They discuss such questions as the following: What was the employee's overall "batting average"? Were objectives accomplished (or not accomplished) due to the employee's performance or because of circumstances beyond anyone's control? What does the comparison of performance with objectives indicate about the employee's strengths and weaknesses? It is important to build on each individual's strengths and seek ways to improve areas of weakness. Step 6 in reality starts the cycle all over again, since setting the next period's objectives will flow logically from the analysis of the results achieved in the previous period.

Most MBO experts believe that salary adjustments should not be a part of the discussion described in Step 6. Of course, those who have performed well expect to be rewarded generously, while those who fail to meet most of their objectives should receive little or no reward. Thus, it is desirable to discuss salary several weeks after the discussion concerning performance results. Done properly, salary adjustments should reinforce the MBO program as a management system designed to reward most favorably those who have contributed the most.

MBO Facilitates Better Planning and Coordination of Efforts

The foregoing was a brief outline of the format of management by objectives. There are other considerations that any management team should be aware of before deciding whether or not to adopt an MBO program. It should not be looked upon as a panacea that will cure all management problems. However, some aspects of MBO already exist in most organizations of any appreciable size. Most managers, for example, have plans that revolve around production goals, sales targets, profit goals, cost containment, budgets, and the like. With or without MBO, effective higher-level managers recognize the importance of delegating authority along with responsibility to managers, supervisors, and employees if goals and objectives are to be achieved. The advantage of a formal MBO system is that it ties together many plans, establishes priorities, and coordinates activities that otherwise might be overlooked or handled loosely in the press of business operations. A sound MBO program encourages the contributions and commitment of people toward common goals and objectives.

STANDING PLANS

Identify the major types of standing plans and explain how these are helpful in supervisory decision making.

Standing plans
Policies, procedures, methods, and rules that can be applied to recurring situations.

After setting major goals and objectives, all levels of management participate in the design and execution of additional plans for attaining desired objectives. In general, such plans can be broadly classified as (a) standing or repeat-use plans, which can be used over and over as the need arises, and (b) single-use plans, which focus on a single purpose or specific undertaking.

Many of a supervisor's day-to-day activities and decisions are guided by the use of so-called **standing plans,** or repeat-use plans. Although terminology varies, these types of plans typically are known as policies, procedures, methods, and rules. All of these should be designed to reinforce one another and should be directed toward the achievement of both organizational and work unit objectives. Top-level managers formulate companywide standing plans, and supervisors formulate the necessary subsidiary standing plans for their work units.

Policies

Policy
A standing plan that serves as a guide to thinking when making decisions.

A **policy** is a general guide to thinking when making decisions. Corporate policies are usually statements that channel the thinking of managers and supervisors in specified directions and define the limits within which they must stay as they make decisions.

Effective policies promote consistency of decision making throughout an enterprise. Once policies are set, managers find it easier to delegate authority since the decisions a subordinate supervisor makes will be guided by the boundaries of the policies. Policies enable the supervisors to arrive at about the same decisions their managers would make or, at least, to be within acceptable parameters. While policies should be considered as guides for thinking, they do permit supervisors to use their own judgment in making decisions as long as their decisions fall within the parameters of the policy.

For example, most companies have policies covering vacations with pay; Figure 6-7 is a typical example. Depending on length of service with the company, an employee is

Vacations

The following is a schedule of vacation time earned by you and paid for by the company:

1 full year	1 full week
2 through 6 years	2 full weeks
7 through 11 years	3 full weeks
12 years and over	4 full weeks

Vacation time is pro-rated as follows:

FIRST YEAR

3 months work earns 10 hours vacation pay
6 months work earns 20 hours vacation pay
9 months work earns 30 hours vacation pay
12 months work earns 40 hours vacation pay

SECOND YEAR

3 months work earns 20 hours vacation pay
6 months work earns 40 hours vacation pay
9 months work earns 60 hours vacation pay
12 months work earns 80 hours vacation pay

ALL VACATIONS MUST BE APPROVED IN ADVANCE BY YOUR SUPERVISOR AND THE HUMAN RESOURCES MANAGER.

Employees have options concerning earned vacation time and pay (subject to supervisory approval):

1. Can take money and work.
2. Can take money and time.

If any employee elects to receive money and work, the time off is forfeited.

entitled to one week, two weeks, three weeks, or more of vacation. All the supervisor has to do is ascertain an employee's years of service with the company in order to determine the length of that employee's vacation. However, the supervisor may have to develop a workable plan within the department concerning when each employee may take a vacation. The supervisor is likely to decide that the employee with the most seniority has first choice, the employee with the next highest seniority has second choice, and so on down the line. The supervisor may also limit the number of employees who can be on vacation at one time. In other words, the supervisor develops a departmental policy within the framework of the broader company policy. The supervisor's approval role is specifically included in the Figure 6-7 policy statement.

Origin of Policies. Major companywide policies are originated by top-level managers since policymaking is one of their important responsibilities. Top-level managers must develop and establish overall policies that guide the thinking of subordinate managers so that organizational objectives can be achieved. Broad policies become the guides for specific policies developed within divisions and departments. Departmental policies established by supervisors must complement and coincide with the broader policies of the organization. In this regard, a firm's policy manuals should not become too excessive in concept, design, and detail. One corporate executive expressed his disdain for "bloated policy manuals" by replacing a multi-volume manual at his company with two pages of "clear yet flexible guidelines." In his view, this "turned" his supervisors into decision makers who knew their responsibilities and acted accordingly.[18]

Smaller firms tend to have fewer policies. On the one hand, the absence of policies gives the supervisor greater flexibility in dealing with situations as they occur. For example, many small firms do not have policies for drug or alcohol use; they prefer to handle problems on an individual basis if and when such problems occur. The absence of policies, on the other hand, may cause inconsistent supervisory practice and lead to charges of unfairness or discrimination. Information concerning the kinds of policies and practices that exist in an area—especially those involving employee matters—usually is available through surveys conducted by employer associations. Such survey data can be helpful if a firm's management desires to make comparisons and perhaps adjust its policies and practices to align more closely with those in place among the majority of area employers.[19]

In addition to policies formulated by top-level managers, some policies are imposed on an organization by external forces such as government, labor unions, trade groups, accrediting associations, and the like. The word "imposed" indicates compliance with an outside force that cannot be avoided. For example, in order to be accredited, schools, universities, hospitals, and other institutions must comply with regulations issued by the appropriate accrediting agency. Government regulations concerning minimum wages, pay for overtime work, and hiring of people without regard to race, age, and gender automatically become part of an organization's policies. Any policy imposed on the organization in such a manner is known as an *externally imposed policy,* and everyone in the organization must comply with it.

Written Policy Statements Promote Consistency. Since policies are guides to decision making, they should be clearly stated and communicated to those in the organization who are affected by them. Although there is no guarantee that policies always will be completely followed or understood, they are more likely to be followed consistently if they are written. Few organizations have all of their policies in written form, and some have few or no written policies, either because they simply never get around to writing them down or because they would rather not state their policies publicly. However, the benefits derived from well-stated written policies usually outweigh the disadvantages. The process of writing policies requires managers to think through the issues more thoroughly and consistently. Supervisors and employees can refer to a written policy as often as they wish. The wording of a written policy cannot be changed by word of mouth; when there is doubt or disagreement, the written policy can be consulted. Additionally, written policies are available to supervisors and employees who are new in the organization so that they can quickly acquaint themselves with the policies. Every policy should be reviewed periodically and revised or discarded if conditions or circumstances warrant it.

Supervisory (Departmental) Policies.   Supervisors seldom have to issue policies. If a department is extremely large or geographically dispersed, or if several subunits exist within the department, the supervisor may find it appropriate to write departmental policies. But for the most part, instead of writing policies the supervisor will be called on to apply existing policies in making decisions. That is, most of the time it is the supervisor's role to interpret, apply, and explain the meaning of policies. Since supervisors will be guided by policies in many daily decisions, they must understand the policies and learn how to interpret and apply them.

A supervisor may occasionally experience a situation for which no policy exists or seems applicable. For example, suppose a group of employees asks the supervisor for permission to visit the end user of their product in order to better understand how the product is used. To make an appropriate decision in this matter, the supervisor should be guided by a policy so that the decision will be in accord with other decisions regarding time away from work. If, upon investigation, the supervisor finds that higher-level management has never issued a formal policy to cover such a request, the supervisor needs guidance and should ask his or her manager to issue a policy—a guide for thinking—to be applied in this case as well as in the future so that there is consistency not only within the supervisor's particular department but also across the organization. After consulting with other supervisors who may have a stake in the issue, the supervisor may want to draft a suggested policy and present it to the manager. In large firms, it is not likely that many such instances will happen, since top-level management usually has covered the major areas where policies are needed. However, in small firms where fewer policies exist, supervisors will have to use good judgment in determining when to make decisions themselves and when they should consult their managers.

Procedures

Procedure

A standing plan that defines the sequence of activities to be performed to achieve objectives.

Procedures, like policies, are standing plans for achieving objectives. They are derived from policies but are more specific. Procedures essentially are guides to action, not guides to thinking. They define a chronological sequence of actions that will carry out the terms and objectives of a policy. They promote consistency by listing the steps to be taken and the sequence to be followed. Procedures at times are combined with or incorporated within policy statements. Figure 6-8 is an example of a firm's combined policy and procedure statement concerning educational tuition reimbursement.

Another and very common example is a company policy that requires supervisors to use the human resources department in the preliminary steps of hiring. This policy may contain several guidelines designed to meet nondiscriminatory hiring goals. To carry out this policy, management develops a procedure governing the selection process. For example, the procedures to be followed by a supervisor who wants to hire a word processor might include filling out a requisition form, specifying the job requirements, interviewing and testing potential candidates, and other such actions. Thus, the procedure lists in more detail exactly what a supervisor must do or not do in order to comply with the company's hiring policies. All supervisors must follow the same procedure.

At the department level, the supervisor often must develop procedures to determine how work is to be done. If a supervisor were fortunate and had only highly skilled

Topic: Tuition Reimbursement

It is the Company's intention to substantially support employees in pursuing training and
education that will enhance the development of additional job-related skills and knowledge.

REQUIRED ATTENDANCE

A supervisor may require a subordinate to attend seminars, conferences, or classes or
enroll for specific courses. All fees and related expenses shall be paid for by the Company. Authorization and approval for reimbursement will be handled through normal disbursement procedures.

VOLUNTARY ATTENDANCE

1. All full-time employees, upon securing the necessary approval, may receive tuition reimbursement as follows:
   a. The Company will pay 100% of the tuition fee for courses that are reasonably job related and/or are necessary to the attainment of a job-related degree.
   b. The courses of study must be taken at an accredited institution.
2. Tuition will be paid as provided:
   a. The employee must submit in advance of attending classes a tuition reimbursement request form that identifies the school, course(s) to be taken, reason for taking the course(s) (for a degree), amount of tuition, starting and completion dates of course(s).
   b. The request requires the written approval of both the employee's supervisor and a vice president or above.
   c. Evidence of a passing grade (C or better, or completion of course(s) if no grade is given).
   d. The individual is in the employ of the Company upon completion of the course(s).
3. The Company will not:
   a. Pay tuition in advance.
   b. Grant time off to attend classes or do research.
   c. Reimburse for books, travel expenses, meals, etc.

employees to lead, he or she could depend on the employees to a great extent to select
efficient paths of performance. But this is not common, and most employees look to the
supervisor for instructions on how to proceed.

One advantage of preparing a procedure is that it requires an analysis of work to be
done. Another advantage is that once a procedure is established, it promotes greater uniformity of action, reduces the need for much routine decision making, and encourages
a predictable outcome. Procedures also provide the supervisor with a standard for appraising work done by employees. In order to realize these advantages, a supervisor
should devote considerable time and effort to devising departmental procedures to
cover as many phases of operations as practical, such as work operations and work flow,
scheduling, and personnel assignments.

Methods

Method

A standing plan that details exactly how a single operation is to be performed.

A **method** is also a standing plan for action but it is even more detailed than a procedure. Whereas a procedure shows a series of steps to be taken, a method is concerned with a single operation—one particular step. It indicates exactly how that step is to be performed. For example, a departmental procedure may specify the chronological routing of work in the assembly of various components of a product. At each subassembly point, there should be a stated method for the work to be performed at each step in the total process.

For most jobs, there is usually a "best method," that is, the most efficient way for the job to be performed given existing technology and circumstances. Again, if a supervisor can rely on skilled workers, the workers might know the best method without having to be told. However, for the most part, the supervisor or someone in management must design the most efficient method for getting the job done. Much time should be spent in devising methods since proper methods have all the advantages of procedures cited previously. In devising methods, the supervisor may utilize the know-how of a methods engineer or a motion-and-time-study specialist if such individuals are available in the organization. These are specialists who have been trained in industrial engineering techniques to study jobs systematically with the objective of making them more efficient. Where such specialists are not available, the supervisor's experience and input from experienced employees actually doing the work should be sufficient to design work methods that are appropriate for the department.

In some activities, a supervisor need not be overly concerned with devising procedures and methods because employees already have been trained in standard methods or standard procedures. For example, journeyman machinists are exposed to many years of education and training during which great emphasis is placed on proper procedures and methods of performing certain tasks. Similarly, in the supervision of a department in which highly skilled or professional employees work, the supervisor's main concern is to ensure that generally approved procedures and methods are carried out in professionally accepted ways. However, most supervisors have employees who are not well trained and for whom procedures and methods must be established.

Rules

Rule

A directive that must be applied and enforced wherever applicable.

A rule is different from a policy, procedure, or method, although it is also a standing plan that has been devised in order to attain objectives. A rule is not the same as a policy because it does not provide a guide to thinking, nor does it leave discretion to the parties involved. A rule is related to a procedure insofar as it is a guide to action and states what must or must not be done. However, it is not a procedure because it does not provide for a time sequence or set of steps. A **rule** is a directive that must be applied and enforced wherever applicable. When a rule is a specific guide for the behavior of employees in a department, the supervisor must follow it wherever it applies without deviating from it. For example, "No possession or consumption of alcoholic beverages on company premises" is commonly on the list of organizational rules. It means exactly what it says, and there are to be no exceptions.

Example of a rule from which there should be no deviation.

There are occasions when supervisors have to devise their own rules or see to it that the rules defined by higher-level managers are obeyed. For example, rules concerning employee meal periods usually specify a certain amount of time that employees may be away from their jobs for meals. Usually these rules are developed by higher-level managers, but often a supervisor will have to formulate departmental rules concerning the actual scheduling of meal periods. Regardless of who develops the rules, it is each supervisor's duty to apply and enforce all rules uniformly as they relate to each area of responsibility.

SINGLE-USE PLANS

Discuss the principal types of single-use plans in which supervisors play an important role.

As discussed in the preceding sections, policies, procedures, methods, and rules are known as repeat-use, or standing, plans because they are followed each time a given situation is encountered. Unless they are changed or modified, repeat-use plans are used again and again. In contrast to repeat-use plans are plans that are no longer needed or are "used up" once the objective is accomplished or the time period of applicability is over. These are known as **single-use plans.** Single-use plans include budgets, programs, and projects. Major budgets, programs, and projects are usually the concern of higher-level managers, but supervisors also play a role in developing and implementing single-use plans at the departmental level.

Single-use plans

Plans developed to accomplish a specific objective or to cover only a designated time period.

Budgets

Budget

A plan that expresses anticipated results in numerical—usually financial—terms for a stated period of time.

Although budgets are generally part of the managerial controlling function, a budget is first and foremost a plan. A **budget** is a plan that expresses anticipated results in numerical terms, such as dollars and cents, employee hours, sales figures, or units to be produced. It serves as a plan for a stated period of time, usually one year. All budgets eventually are translated into monetary terms, and an overall financial budget is developed for the entire firm. After the stated period is over, the budget expires. It has served its usefulness and is no longer valid. This is why a budget is a single-use plan.

As a statement of expected results, a budget is associated with control. However, the preparation of a budget is planning, and this again is part of every manager's responsibilities. Since a budget is expressed in numerical terms, it has the advantage of being specific rather than general. There is a considerable difference between just making general forecasts and attaching numerical values to specific plans. The figures that the supervisor finds in a budget are actual plans, which become standards to be achieved.

The Supervisor's Role in Budgeting.   Since supervisors have to function under a budget, they should have a part in its preparation. Supervisors should participate in what commonly is called *grass roots budgeting*. What this means is that supervisors should have the opportunity either to propose detailed budgets for their departments or at least to participate in discussions with higher-level managers before final departmental budgets are established. Supervisors will have to substantiate their budget proposals in discussions with their managers and possibly with the financial manager when the final budgets are being set.

Supervisors usually are more committed to budgets if they have had a role in formulating them. Even though supervisors are usually closest to the real needs of the department, this does not mean that the requests of the supervisor should always prevail. No budget should ever be accepted without careful analysis by both the supervisor and higher-level managers to be sure it is appropriate and accurate. Differences between budget needs and estimates should be discussed and resolved carefully.

There are numerous types of budgets in which supervisors can play a part. For example, supervisors may design budgets in which they plan the work hours to be used for jobs within their departments. Supervisors also may prepare budgets for materials and supplies, wages, utility expenses, and other departmental expenditures.

Budget Review.   Most organizations have interim monthly or quarterly reviews when the budget is compared to actual results. This is why a budget is also a control device. If necessary, the budget is revised to adjust to current results and revised forecasts. This topic is discussed further in Chapter 18.

Supervisors should carefully study and analyze significant variations from the budget to determine where and why plans went wrong, what and where adjustments need to be made, and what the revised budget should reflect, including new factors and any changes in the department. When an annual budget is about to expire, it becomes a guide for preparing the next year's budget. Thus, the planning process continues from one budget period to the next in a closely related pattern.

Program

A major single-use plan for a large undertaking related to accomplishing the organization's goals and objectives.

Programs and Projects

A **program** is a single-use set of plans for a specific major undertaking related to the organization's overall goals and objectives. A major program may have its own policies,

Expansion programs usually involve plans for the architectural design, new equipment or technology, financing, recruitment of employees, and publicity, all of which are part of the overall program.

Project
A single-use plan for accomplishing a specific nonrecurring activity.

procedures, and budgets. The program may take several years to accomplish. Examples of major programs are the expansion of a manufacturing plant or office and the addition of new facilities in a hospital. Such expansion programs usually involve plans for the architectural design, new equipment or technology, financing, recruitment of employees, and publicity, all of which are part of the overall program. Once the expansion program is completed, its plans will not be used again. Thus, a program is a single-use plan.

Supervisors are typically more involved in planning projects. While a **project** may be part of an overall program, it is an undertaking that can be planned and fulfilled as a distinct entity, usually within a relatively short period of time. For example, the preparation of a publicity brochure by the public relations department to acquaint the public with new facilities as part of a hospital expansion program would be called a project. Arranging the necessary construction financing for the building expansion would be another project. Although connected with a major program, these projects can be handled separately by individuals designated to implement them.

An example of a project at the supervisory level is the design of a new inventory control system by a warehouse supervisor. Another example is a research project conducted by a marketing department supervisor to determine the effectiveness of a series of television commercials. Projects such as these are a constant part of the ongoing activities at the departmental level. The ability to plan and carry out projects is another component of every supervisor's managerial effectiveness.

PLANNING TOOLS

While it is not our intent to go into great detail regarding techniques for developing procedures and methods, effective supervisors should become familiar with them since they are readily adaptable to most organizations. The following are some planning tools that supervisors can use.

Planning Inventory

Maintaining large inventories of component parts and finished goods is costly. It requires warehouse space that must be rented or bought, heated, and lit. It also requires workers to store and keep track of the materials. To reduce the costs of maintaining large inventories, many firms use inventory control techniques to better plan the inflow of materials needed for production.

A **just-in-time (JIT) inventory control system,** also called **kanban,** is a system for scheduling raw materials and components needed in the production process to arrive at the firm precisely when they are needed. This avoids having to keep large amounts of these items in stock. JIT requires close coordination between the firm and its suppliers. For the system to work, suppliers must be willing and able to supply parts on short notice and in small batches. Also, the firm must keep suppliers well informed about its projected needs for their products, so that suppliers can plan their production efficiently.[20]

Scheduling and Project Planning

Much supervisory time is spent planning various projects. Supervisors need to consider what needs to be accomplished, the necessary activities, the order in which they are to be done, who is to do each, and when they are to be completed. This process of planning activities and their sequence is called **scheduling.** Two well-known project planning tools are Gantt charts and PERT.

Gantt Charts. A **Gantt chart** is a graphic scheduling technique that shows the relationship between work planned and necessary completion dates.[21] Figure 6-9 depicts a simplified Gantt chart developed by a student for completing the college admission process. The student needs to decide what activities must be done to get admitted, the order in which they must be done, and the time that must be allocated to each activity. The project is broken down into separate major activities, and these are listed on the vertical axis. The timeframe is indicated on the horizontal axis. The bar shows the duration and sequence of each activity. Each bar is shaded to indicate the actual progress. Thus, it is possible to assess progress at a glance. A review of Figure 6-9 shows that everything has been accomplished to date except getting teachers to write letters of recommendation, which is one month behind schedule. Given this information, the student needs to make a special effort to catch up and ensure that no further delays occur. Unless corrective action is taken, admission to college will be delayed.

Gantt charts are helpful in projects in which the activities are somewhat independent of each other. However, if a large project such as a complex quality improvement program needs to be planned, PERT is more likely to be applicable.

Just-in-time (JIT) inventory control system

A system for scheduling materials to arrive precisely when they are needed in the production process.

Kanban

Another name for a just-in-time inventory control system.

Scheduling

The process of developing a detailed list of activities, their sequence, and the required resources.

Gantt chart

A graphic scheduling technique that shows the activity to be scheduled on the vertical axis and necessary completion dates on the horizontal axis.

FIGURE 6-9   Example of a Gantt chart.

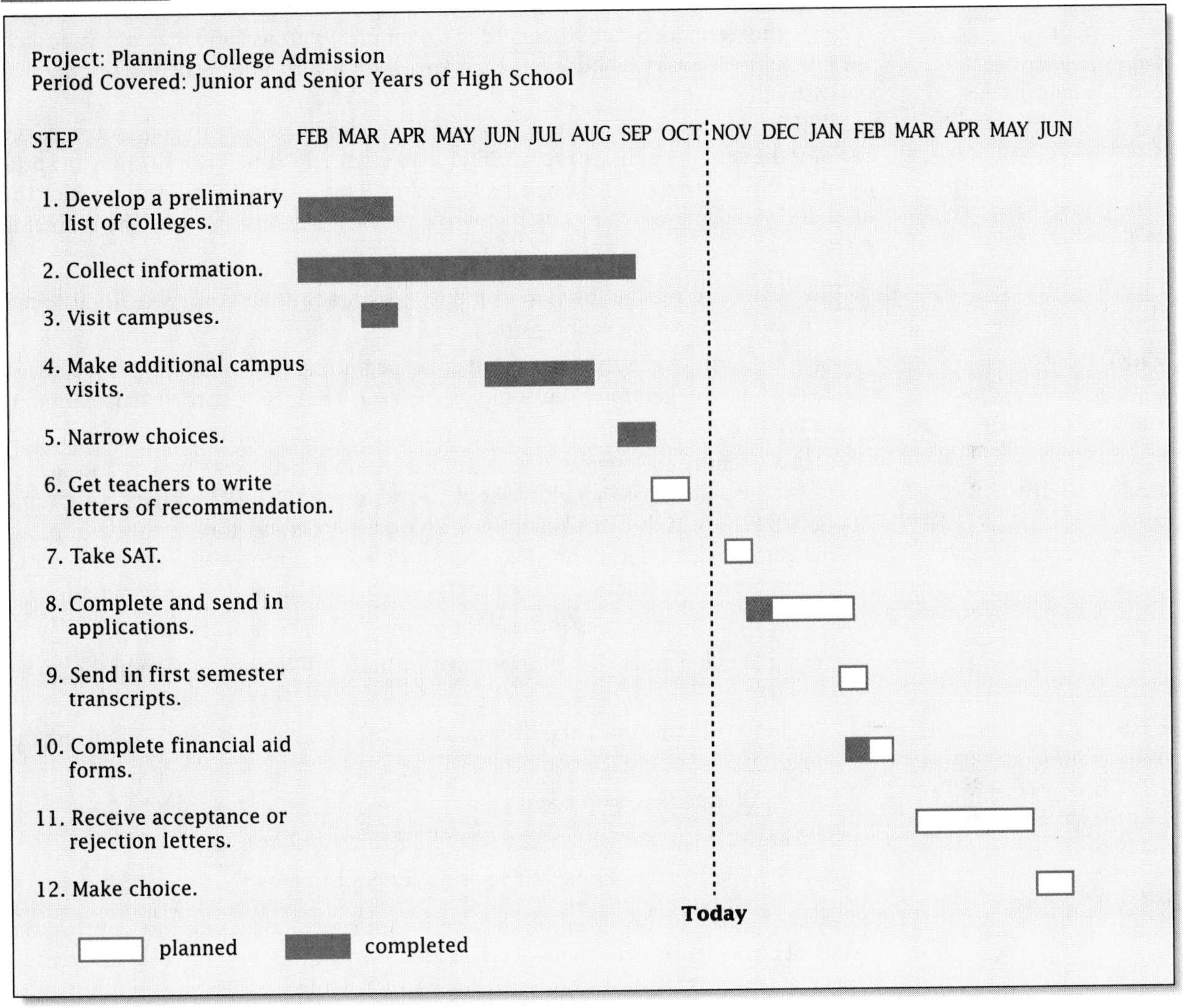

Project: Planning College Admission
Period Covered: Junior and Senior Years of High School

STEP	FEB MAR APR MAY JUN JUL AUG SEP OCT NOV DEC JAN FEB MAR APR MAY JUN

1. Develop a preliminary list of colleges.
2. Collect information.
3. Visit campuses.
4. Make additional campus visits.
5. Narrow choices.
6. Get teachers to write letters of recommendation.
7. Take SAT.
8. Complete and send in applications.
9. Send in first semester transcripts.
10. Complete financial aid forms.
11. Receive acceptance or rejection letters.
12. Make choice.

Today

☐ planned   ▮ completed

PERT

A flowchart for managing large programs and projects showing the necessary activities with estimates of the time needed to complete each activity and the sequential relationship among them.

PERT event

The beginning and/or ending of an activity.

PERT activity

A specific task to be accomplished.

Critical path

The path of activities in the PERT network that will take the longest time to complete.

Program Evaluation and Review Technique (PERT). Successfully used in many major production and construction undertakings, **PERT** is a flowchart-like diagram showing the sequence of activities needed to complete a project and the time associated with each. PERT goes beyond Gantt charts by clarifying the interrelatedness of the various activities.

PERT helps a supervisor think strategically. A clear statement of goals serves as the basis for the entire planning process. PERT begins with the supervisor defining the project not only in terms of the desired goal but also all the intermediate ones on which the ultimate goal depends. The construction of a PERT network includes the following steps:

Step 1: Determine the goal. For example, a firm may want to improve its customer service by improving delivery times.

Step 2: Clarify events. A **PERT event** is the beginning and/or ending of an activity. Receiving an order from a customer is an event. Thus, events are a particular point in time.

Step 3: Identify all activities that must be accomplished for the project and the sequence in which these activities should be performed. A **PERT activity** is a specific task to be accomplished. Contacting the customer, demonstrating how your product can provide a solution to a specific problem, and motivating the customer to action are activities. Activities require a certain amount of time to complete.

Step 4: Determine time estimates for the completion of each activity.

Step 5: Develop a network diagram that includes all the information in the previous steps.

Step 6: Identify the **critical path,** which is the sequence of activities requiring the longest period of time to complete.

Step 7: Allocate necessary resources.

Step 8: Record actual activity time and compare with estimates.

Step 9: Make necessary schedule revisions or adjustments.[22]

Suppose that the organization decides to implement a program to improve the quality of customer service. The supervisor identifies the PERT events, lists all activities that must be accomplished, and determines which activity must precede others. The data are then presented on a flowchart or network, which is a visual portrayal of the sequence and interrelationships among all the activities necessary for achieving improved customer service. A simple PERT network is shown in Figure 6-10. In the PERT network, events are represented by circles. Activities to be accomplished are represented by an arrow. Figure 6-10 illustrates that after "Complete quality audit" (Event A) has happened, certain activities represented by an arrow must be performed before "Implement quality improvement program" (Event G), represented by another circle, can happen. In developing the network, the supervisor provides realistic estimates of how much time it will take to complete certain stages of the work and what the costs will be.

Each event-activity path to the ultimate goal is analyzed to determine which path will require the most time. This path is termed "critical" and is represented by thick arrows in Figure 6-10. Any delay in the activities on this path will also delay the project's completion. The total time to complete the project can be determined by adding the individual time units on the critical path. The project in Figure 6-10 will take 45 time units to complete.

The idea of a "critical path" is a very important concept. It can help the supervisor decide where and when to put forth extra effort, additional employees, or other resources to avoid delaying the entire project. The supervisor may be able to shorten the 45 total time units in Figure 6-10 by allocating additional resources to tasks on this path or making corrective adjustments. For example, if the amount of time required to benchmark could be shortened by 3 units, the project could be completed in less time.

PERT is a helpful planning tool because it requires systematic thinking and planning for large, nonroutine projects. The development of PERT networks by hand is time consuming. However, the use of Gantt charts and PERT is likely to increase because of the proliferation of commercially available computer software packages that can assist supervisors in planning, decision making, and controlling. Effective supervisors will become familiar with the various planning tools and apply them as the situation warrants.

FIGURE 6-10

Example of a PERT network for quality improvement.

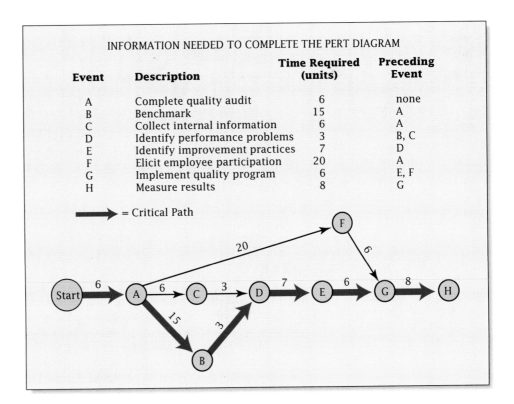

INFORMATION NEEDED TO COMPLETE THE PERT DIAGRAM

Event	Description	Time Required (units)	Preceding Event
A	Complete quality audit	6	none
B	Benchmark	15	A
C	Collect internal information	6	A
D	Identify performance problems	3	B, C
E	Identify improvement practices	7	D
F	Elicit employee participation	20	A
G	Implement quality program	6	E, F
H	Measure results	8	G

→ = Critical Path

What Call Did You Make?

As Joan McCarthy, you have a situation that needs some careful planning and decision making if the functioning of the project design group is to improve and live up to its promising potential. In retrospect, it appears that far too little attention was devoted to planning for a number of important aspects of the project design group's ongoing operations and relationships, even though there had been detailed planning for some of the technical processes.

As Joan McCarthy, you must realistically address the group's concerns and win their consensus and support. Employee involvement usually is the key to any system of total quality management and continuous improvement. Ask your employees to help you create a vision for the group, defining their responsibilities and objectives. Ask them questions such as the following: What does the company expect of this group now and within three to five years? What essential services will we be expected to provide? What will management be willing to pay for our services? Answers to questions such as these will help guide your continuous improvement efforts. Some immediate plans to make will be those within the team, such as how to provide new employees with orientation and training. Role statements should be developed that reflect each employee's skills and abilities; these statements should be revised to reflect the actual procedures and systems followed in practice.

Planning also means to look at the policies, procedures, and methods currently in place. Are they needed? Should some be refined or discarded? For example, how should requests/demands from higher management (such as the vice president) be handled, especially if these are burdensome and not feasible?

You may also want to determine whether or not planning devices such as Gantt charts, PERT, and the like could be implemented to improve your team's project scheduling. Perhaps some type of MBO approach could be implemented to more specifically define each team member's specific targets and accomplishments and relate them to a performance-based compensation system. These techniques are discussed in this chapter.

Finally, as Joan McCarthy, you may need to reevaluate your management style. Have you created resentment by letting the team more or less supervise itself? Although you wanted to "empower" your team, do they evaluate you as being a hands-off, noninvolved supervisor who prefers traveling and visiting customers rather than managing? As you rethink your situation, remember that whatever continuous improvement plans you and your group develop, they must complement the vision and strategic plans of the entire corporation.

SUMMARY

Planning is the managerial function that determines what is to be done in the future. It includes analyzing the situation, forecasting future events, establishing objectives, setting priorities, and deciding what actions are necessary to achieve objectives. It is a function of every manager from the top-level executive to the supervisor. Without planning there is no direction to the activities of the organization.

Strategic planning involves making decisions that will enable the organization to achieve its short- and long-term objectives. It may involve developing a mission statement that identifies the philosophy and purpose of the enterprise. Visioning goes beyond this; visioning is the process of developing a mental image of what the organization could become. Top-level management defines and articulates its vision so that everyone in the enterprise knows where the organization intends to be at some future time. Visioning thus can serve as a focus for the establishment of goals and objectives. The organization develops plans based on the vision.

While top-level managers are responsible for the development and execution of the overall strategic plan, supervisors direct their work unit plans toward achieving parts of it. Effective supervisors create a mental image of what their department could become. Plans are developed that complement this vision. The vision, when shared with employees, gives greater meaning to their work.

Planning is the responsibility of every manager. Often, the supervisor needs to consult with others to develop plans that are consistent with those of upper-level management. Supervisors devote most of their attention to short-term (operational) planning. The supervisor's short-term plans should be integrated and coordinated with the longer-term plans (strategic and tactical) of upper-level management. Supervisors need to communicate to employees in a timely fashion what is being planned.

Planning facilitates use of human and physical resources to their fullest potential. Planning how best to utilize the material, capital, and human resources of the firm is essential. The time and human resources needed to complete a particular activity can be utilized more effectively. Planning promotes efficiency.

Not surprisingly, various quality improvement concepts relate directly to planning. Total quality management (TQM) means planning for quality, preventing defects, correcting defects, and continuously improving quality and customer satisfaction. Knowledge management, which involves systematic planned approaches to store and disseminate information, increasingly has become an important part of many organizational efforts to improve customer and employee services and satisfaction.

Benchmarking—the process of identifying and improving on the best practices of others—precedes the development of plans. Organizations that want to be as good as or better than the "best in the world" strive to attain the quality standards established in ISO 9000 or the Malcolm Baldrige National Quality Award. Baldrige award criteria show that planning for effective human resources by utilizing and integrating the customer's needs into the business plan are major elements of the examination categories. Plans must be developed for establishing, maintaining, and increasing product and service quality. Quality improvement doesn't just happen; it has to be planned.

Setting objectives is the first step in planning. Although the overall goals and objectives are determined by top-level management, supervisors formulate departmental objectives, which must be consistent with efforts to achieve organizational goals and objectives. Objectives should state what should be done and when.

A management by objectives (MBO) approach relies upon participative setting of objectives and using those objectives as the primary basis for assessing performance. The development of specific, measurable and verifiable objectives serves as the foundation for determining the necessary resources, the activities that must be carried out, and the results that are to be worked toward. MBO ties together planning, establishes priorities, and provides coordination of effort. MBO-type approaches—which may be designated by other names—usually involve objectives being agreed upon by employees and their supervisor. Periodic reviews are conducted to make sure that progress is being made. At the end of the appraisal period, results are evaluated against objectives, and rewards are based on this evaluation. Objectives for the next period are then set, and the process begins again.

8

In order to attain objectives, standing plans must be devised. Top-level managers typically develop companywide policies, procedures, methods, and rules, and each supervisor formulates the necessary subsidiary standing plans for his or her work unit.

Policies are guides to thinking for decision making, and many of them originate with higher-level management. The supervisor's primary concern with policies is one of interpreting, applying, and staying within them when making decisions for the department. Policies are more likely to be followed consistently if they are written.

Procedures, like policies, are standing plans for achieving objectives. They specify a sequence of actions that will guide employees toward objectives. The supervisor often develops procedures to determine how work is to be done. The advantages of procedures are that they require analysis of what needs to be done, promote uniformity of action, and provide a means of appraising the work of employees.

In addition, the supervisor will be called on to design and follow methods and rules, which essentially are guides for action. They are more detailed than procedures. A rule is a directive that must be applied and enforced wherever applicable.

9

Supervisors should participate in establishing budgets, which are single-use plans expressed in numerical terms. A budget serves as a control device that enables the supervisor to compare results achieved during the budget period against the budget plan. Supervisors at times play a role in organizational programs and projects, which are single-use plans designed to accomplish specific undertakings on a one-time basis.

10

To reduce inventory costs and better plan for materials, just-in-time inventory control systems attempt to ensure that materials and components will arrive when they are needed. Gantt charts and PERT networks are graphic tools to aid supervisors in planning, organizing, and controlling operations. Gantt charts require supervisors to identify activities, determine their sequence, and specify the time spent on each activity. A visual check shows the progress of various activities. If the project is behind schedule, supervisors must develop plans for getting it back on schedule.

Program evaluation and review technique (PERT) is especially applicable for scheduling and sequencing large, complex projects. PERT aids in planning because it forces the supervisor to estimate the time the project will take to complete. The development of PERT networks can be time consuming. Computer software packages are available to assist in the development of PERT networks.

KEY TERMS

QUESTIONS FOR DISCUSSION

1. Define planning. Why is planning primarily a mental activity rather than a "doing" type of function?
2. What is the importance of an organization's vision? Why should the vision that top-level managers have for the organization be shared with all employees? Why do mission statements sometimes sound very similar to corporate vision statements?
3. Discuss how supervisors may have occasion to become involved in visioning and in developing strategic plans.
4. Distinguish between long-range planning and short-range planning. Relate these to the planning periods for top-level managers as compared with the planning periods for first-line supervisors. Why is there considerable overlap in the designations of strategic, tactical, and operational plans?
5. Define total quality management (TQM), knowledge management, and benchmarking. List guidelines a supervisor could follow to develop a system of continuous improvement or total quality management (TQM).
6. Why should a first-line supervisor understand the organization's objectives? Why is this knowledge important to planning?
7. Discuss the step-by-step model for management by objectives presented in the text. Explain why each step is crucial if MBO is to be implemented successfully.
8. Define and distinguish between each of the following:
    a. Policy
    b. Procedure
    c. Method
    d. Rule
9. If you were a supervisor in a small firm that had few policies and you believed that several employees were using illegal drugs, how would you go about developing a plan to handle the situation? Why would it be desirable to have the policy in written form?
10. Discuss the supervisor's role in the budgeting process and in planning of programs and projects.
11. Why do firms need to implement systems such as just-in-time inventory systems? Explain the application of planning tools such as a Gantt chart and PERT.

SKILLS APPLICATIONS

Skills Application 6-1: Planning Comparisons

1. Interview two or more supervisors from different areas (e.g., manufacturing, banking, health care, retail, etc.). Ask them the following questions:

    a. To what extent do you use planning in your daily work?

    b. What advantages do you gain from planning?

    c. What problems do you have in fulfilling your plans?

    d. What practical tips can you give me as a prospective supervisor that would enable me to do a better job of planning?

2. Compare the responses of the supervisors. What items are similar? Dissimilar?
3. Compare your tips for better planning with those of other students.
4. Make a composite list of tips. Which of those do you currently use in your planning process? Which should you add to your toolbox of skills?

Skills Application 6-2: Need for a Vision

Someone once said, "Nothing is more exciting than venturing into the unknown. There is a need to plan effectively to reach the unknown."

1. Close your eyes for a few seconds. Visualize what you would like to be doing five years from today.
2. Write a paragraph describing your vision. Assume that this vision is a goal that you want to attain, so conclude by writing specific objectives ("what" by "when") and statements (e.g., "Five years from today, I will . . .").
3. Briefly list the interim events that must be attained to reach your five-year vision.
4. Develop a timetable for achieving the things that will lead you to your vision.
5. Describe how you will periodically check your progress toward your objectives, making necessary corrections and adjustments.

Skills Application 6-3: PERT Application

Think of a group project, either real or hypothetical, that you must complete by the end of the term. The project must require the involvement of several other people.

1. Working backward from the end result (the due date), lay out the various activities required to complete the project.
2. Now estimate the amount of time required to complete each activity.
3. Follow the steps given in the chapter to draw a PERT diagram. Be sure to identify the critical path.
4. What difficulties did you have in developing your PERT diagram?
5. Summarize in a few words what you learned by using this planning tool.

Skills Application 6-4: The Role of Quality in Strategic Planning

The following organizations emphasize quality. Visit their sites to learn more about the Malcolm Baldrige Award, Baldrige Award winners, and best practices in quality. Then answer the following questions.

INTERNET ACTIVITY

- American Society for Quality (www.asq.org)
- The Enterprise Organization (www.theenterprise.org)
- American Productivity & Quality Center (www.apqc.org)

1. As you review the criteria for the Baldrige award, the profiles of award winners, and other best practices, what elements emerge as most critical in the pursuit of quality?

2. How has an emphasis on quality affected planning in these companies, and what have been the results?

3. As a supervisor, how can you support your organization's commitment to quality? Make a list of six key priorities for a supervisor who wants to promote quality.

ENDNOTES

1. See Peter F. Drucker, *Management: Tasks, Responsibilities, and Practices* (New York: Harper & Row, 1974), p. 611. Also see Drucker, *The Practice of Management* (New York: Harper Brothers, 1954), pp. 62–65, 126–129; Drucker, "Plan Now for the Future," *Modern Office Technology* (March 1993), pp. 8–9; and Peter F. Drucker as quoted in the article by Mike Johnson, "Drucker Speaks His Mind," *Management Review* (October 1995), pp. 11–14.

2. Linda Yates and Peter Skarzynski, "How Do Companies Get to the Future FIRST?" *Management Review* (January 1999), p. 17.

3. There are numerous books and articles on the subject of strategic management. For example, see Thomas L. Wheelen and J. David Hunger, *Strategic Management* (5th ed.; Reading, Mass.: Addison-Wesley, 1995); Robert A. Pitts and David Lei, *Strategic Management: Building and Sustaining Competitive Advantage* (St. Paul, Minn.: West Publishing Co., 1996); Terrence Fernsler, "Strategic Planning in 150 Pages or Less," *Non-profit World* (November/December 1998), p. 51; Robert Rothberg, "Managing Strategic Innovation and Change," *Journal of Product Innovation Management* (January 1999), pp. 111–112; Timothy C. Hoerr, "Strategic Planning: The Seven Foundations of High Performing Organizations," *Agency Sales Magazine* (January 1999), pp. 27–28; Bill Merrick, "How to Avoid These Seven Strategic Planning Pitfalls," *Credit Union Magazine* (February 1999), p. 45; and Lin Grensing-Paphal, "Taking Your Seat at the Table," *HR Magazine* (March 1999), pp. 90–94.

4. See Richard W. Oliver, *Seven Imperatives for Winning in the New World of Business* (New York: McGraw-Hill, 1999); or Ian Mitroff, *Smart Thinking for Crazy Times: The Art of Solving the Right Problems* (San Francisco: Berrett-Koehler Publishers, 1998).

5. From E. Thomas Behr, "Acting From the Center," *Management Review* (March 1998), pp. 51–55.

6. See James B. Lucas, "Anatomy of a Vision Statement," *Management Review* (February 1998), pp. 22–26. Also see Gail Dutton, "Wanted: A Practical Visionary," *Management Review* (March 1998), pp. 33–36.

7. For expanded discussions on planning time horizons, see John R. Schermerhorn, Jr., *Management* (6th ed.; New York: John Wiley & Sons, 1999), pp. 140–142; or Stephen P. Robbins, *Managing Today!* (Upper Saddle River, N.J.: Prentice-Hall, 1997), pp. 130–132.

8. For additional information on TQM and continuous improvement, see W. J. Duncan and J. G. Van Matre, "The Gospel According to Deming; Is It Really New?" *Business Horizons* (July–August 1990), pp. 3–9; Vincent K. Omachonu and Joel E. Ross, *Principles of Total Quality* (Delray Beach, Fla.: St. Lucie Press, 1994); James L. Truesdell, *Total Quality Management: Reports from the Front Lines* (St. Louis, Mo.: Smith Collins Company, 1994); Richard M. Hodgetts, *Implementing TQM in Small and Medium-Sized Organizations: A Step-by-Step Guide* (New York: AMACOM division of American Management Association, 1996; and Sheila M. Puffer and Daniel J. McCarthy, "A Framework for Leadership in a TQM Context," *Journal of Quality Management* (Vol. 1, No. 1, 1996), pp. 109–130.

9. From Louisa Wah, "Behind the Buzz: Knowledge Management Has Become a Red-Hot Buzzword in Management Circles," *Management Review* (April 1999), pp. 17–26. Also see, "Do You Know What You Know? New Study Reveals Top Knowledge Management Strategies," *Business Wire* (January 24, 2000). To view the full Executive Summary of this study, visit www.benchmarkingreports.com/knowledgemanagement/.

10. Wah, "Behind the Buzz."

11. Stratford Sherman, "Are You as Good as the Best in the World?" *Fortune* (December 13, 1993), p. 95. For an example of a major benchmarking study involving international comparisons of human resource (HR) departments and functions, see *Benchmarking HR: UK Benchmarking Survey Report*, prepared and published by Coopers and Lybrand International, 1996.

12. *ISO 9000: Handbook of Quality Standards and Compliance* (Waterford, Conn.: Bureau of Business

Practice, 1992). Also see Frank Voehl, Peter Jackson, and David Ashton, *ISO 9000: An Implementation Guide for Small to Mid-Sized Businesses* (Delray Beach, Fla.: St. Lucie Press, 1994).

ISO 9000 is about quality *assurance,* not quality *control.* Kemper Registrar Services, a division of Kemper Risk Management Services, is one of several companies which help clients gain the benefits of ISO 9000 registration. Information is available by calling 1-800-555-2928. Also see C. W. Russo, "10 Rules for Successful ISO Registration," *Quality Digest* (May 1996), pp. 28–31; and Scott M. Paton, Alen Karolyi, and Dirk Dusharme, "ISO 9000 Registrar Directory and Consultants Guide," *Quality Digest* (May 1996), pp. 33–44.

13. From *Application Guidelines: Malcolm Baldrige National Quality Award* (Washington, D.C.: United States Department of Commerce, 1993).

14. H. James Harrington, "The Malcolm Baldrige National Quality Award: Is It Friend or Foe?" *Quality Digest* (April 2000), p. 20.

15. Truesdell, *Total Quality Management,* p. 15.

16. For additional information on MBO, see George S. Odiorne, "MBO Means Having a Goal and a Plan—Not Just a Goal," *Manage* (Volume 44, Number 1, September 1992), pp. 8–11; Robert Rodgers and John E. Hunter, "Impact of Management by Objectives on Organizational Productivity," *Human Resource Management* (Volume 76, April 1991), pp. 322–336; Ronald Starcher, "Mismatched Management Techniques," *Quality Progress* (Volume 25, Number 12, December 1992), pp. 49–52; and David Halpern and Stephen Osofsky, "A Dissenting View of MBO," *Public Personnel Management* (Volume 19, Fall 1990), pp. 59–62.

17. James L. Pate, "Game Plan for a New Company," *Management Review* (June 1999), p. 13.

18. Jerre L. Stead (Chairman and CEO, Ingram Micro, Inc., Santa Ana, California), "Whose Decision Is It, Anyway?" *Management Review* (January 1999), p. 13.

19. For example, the AAIM Management Association in St. Louis, Missouri, periodically conducts a "Personnel Practices Survey," which covers a wide range of personnel policies and practices covering pay, benefits, working conditions, employment, and employee relations. Its 1997–1998 survey covered 212 company respondents, many of whom were small businesses.

20. For information on just-in-time inventory systems and kanban, see Lloyd S. Morris, "Management Heads into the Next Decade," *Security Management* (Volume 36, Number 12, December 1992), pp. 20–21; Caron H. St. John and Kirk C. Heriot, "Small Suppliers and JIT Purchasing," *International Journal of Purchasing & Materials Management* (Volume 29, Number 1, Winter 1993), pp. 11–16; Paul H. Zipkin, "Does Manufacturing Need a JIT Revolution?" *Harvard Business Review* (Volume 69, January–February 1991), pp. 40–50; Satish Mehra and Anthony Inman, "Determining the Critical Elements of Just-In-Time Implementation," *Decision Sciences* (Volume 23, Number 1, January–February 1992), pp. 160–173. For a contrary opinion on JIT, see R. Anthony Inman and Larry D. Brandon, "An Undesirable Effect of JIT," *Production and Inventory Management Journal* (Volume 33, Number 1, First Quarter 1992), pp. 55–58; or Gene H. Johnson and James D. Stice, "Not Quite Just in Time Inventories," *National Public Accountant* (Volume 38, Number 3, March 1993), pp. 26–29.

21. For additional information concerning Gantt charts, see Andrew J. DuBrin and R. Duane Ireland, *Management and Organization* (2d ed.; Cincinnati: South-Western Publishing Co., 1993), p. 34; or James A. F. Stoner and R. Edward Freeman, *Management* (5th ed.; Englewood Cliffs, N.J.: Prentice-Hall, 1992), pp. 288–289.

22. For additional information on PERT networks, see Li-Chih Wang and Wilbert E. Wilhelm, "A PERT-Based Paradigm for Modeling Assembly Operations," *IIE Transactions* (Volume 25, Number 2, March 1993), pp. 88–103; DuBrin and Ireland, *Management and Organization,* pp. 415–418; and Stoner and Freeman, *Management,* pp. 289–291.

Chapter 7

Supervisory Planning and Managing Time and Stress

After studying this chapter, you will be able to:

1
Discuss forecasting at the supervisory level.

2
Describe some tactical strategies for gaining acceptance of plans.

3
Summarize major areas of supervisory planning for the effective and safe use of material and human resources.

4
Discuss the importance of time management, especially in reducing stress, and suggest techniques for supervisors to plan better use of their time.

Learning Objectives

You Make the Call!

The rumors about the company's economic problems are at an all-time high. You are Phil Moore, a salaried maintenance supervisor for Paul's Home Center, a locally owned general merchandise store. Paul's Home Center has faced great competition since Wal-Mart, the nation's largest retailer, opened a store two miles down the road about three years ago.

You are 50 years old, married, with five children aged 9 to 18. Shortly after graduating from high school you were drafted into the Army and spent a tour of duty in Vietnam. Your military experience honed both your maintenance skills and your leadership skills. You returned home to marry your childhood sweetheart and have worked at the same job for the past 16 years. You are a working supervisor, and until three months ago you had four employees under your direction. When one of the younger employees quit to follow his spouse to another position out of state, Sally Paul, the sole owner of the store, decided not to allow you to fill the position.

You reflect on the events of the past several weeks: "This is not a dream or a newspaper story about someone else in another part of the country. This is happening here to us. I have to ask my people to do more, and I have been putting in 10- and 12-hour days to get the work done. The past two weeks have been unreal. The temperature set record highs almost every day, and the humidity hovered near 100 percent. Sally Paul has decided to face Wal-Mart head on. She purchased an adjacent building, added more parking space, lowered prices, and embarked on a customer service campaign that has employees bending over backward to give personal attention and greater service to customers."

You have been busy supervising the renovation of the adjacent building and the construction of the new parking lot. The past weekend should have been wonderful. Labor Day had always been a chance to put all the worries aside and relax at the in-laws' lakeside cottage. Historically, the store had always closed at 1:00 P.M. on Saturday, and old-man Paul would turn over in his grave if he could see all the changes. Basically, the store is now open from 9:00 A.M. to 9:00 P.M. Monday through Saturday and from noon to 6:00 P.M. on Sundays. The additional hours have led to increased stress for all members of your department. You have not spent a day away from the business in over two months.

You know very well that you are shorthanded and that if things do not improve your remaining employees will leave. Surely something can be done to improve the situation. What can you do?

You Make the Call!

1

Discuss forecasting at the supervisory level.

SUPERVISORY FORECASTING

The survival and success of any organization depend in large measure on its managers' skills in forecasting and preparing for the future. Planning, as discussed in Chapter 6, means establishing objectives based on the current situation and forecasts of the future and determining the actions necessary to achieve objectives. Thus, managers must make certain assumptions about the future even if it is fraught with uncertainties.

Top-level executives must forecast the future in a more general and far-reaching manner than the supervisor. To identify potential growth opportunities or threats to the organization's success, top-level managers must make predictions about the competitive and general economic climate in which the organization will operate during future years. Demographic changes, resource availability and costs, and many other social, political, financial, and economic problems that influence business operations must be anticipated in the strategic-planning process. Because of the unpredictable nature of many aspects of the business environment, some authorities advocate **scenario-based forecasting.**

Scenario-based forecasting

Developing a range of alternative forecasts that could impact a firm's future.

This approach calls for creatively developing a range of possible future scenarios or potential outcomes in the environment—including very extreme types of circumstances—that could impact the firm.[1] However, our concern in this chapter is with planning at the supervisory level, where day-to-day planning is less likely to involve such global and complicated dimensions.

Although they overlap to a certain degree, some distinction exists between planning and forecasting. **Forecasts** are an attempt to predict the future, but they do not spell out what actions to take. Forecasts are more like "building stones" on which plans are to be based. This means a supervisor has to look into the future and make forecasts in order to establish sound, realistic plans for the department.

Forecasts

Predictions of future events upon which plans are based.

Supervisory Concerns in Forecasting

Supervisors are responsible for forecasting future events that may affect departmental operations. In particular, supervisors should be familiar with recent developments in technology in their fields and be able to estimate how new technology might help their departments operate more efficiently. Supervisors can keep current by attending trade association meetings and exhibits and by reading journals and other appropriate literature. To some extent, supervisors can seek assistance from suppliers who are making new equipment that could be used in the department. Because technology is progressing so rapidly, a department's functions may be significantly different in a very short period of time. They may be reduced or simplified, or they may grow, become more sophisticated, and take on greater prominence. The supervisor's technological projections should include some ideas about what types of equipment will be used in the department in both the short term and the long term and how such equipment will influence production, work flow, space allocations, material requirements, and other related factors.

The supervisor must also be prepared to forecast the number and types of employees who will be needed in the department. The supervisor may foresee a need for better, differently educated, or more highly skilled employees, or for employees who possess skills not previously required in the department or in the organization. Conversely, the supervisor might foresee that due to a projected increase in mechanization or computer assistance, fewer or less-skilled employees will be needed to perform departmental jobs.

Conceivably, it might appear to the supervisor that the department will diminish in importance or become obsolete due to new discoveries or new methods. Although this is not a pleasant thought, if it is looming on the horizon, it is better for the supervisor to recognize it early than to be confronted with such an event without being prepared for it. If obsolescence is threatening, the supervisor should inform higher-level management accordingly. Managers usually are willing to find a new position for any supervisor who is so farsighted since such a person is recognized as being too valuable to lose. The supervisor can be just as capable of supervising another department, perhaps one that did not exist previously. In other words, farsighted supervisors who have the courage to suggest that their departments might eventually be eliminated are likely to survive and prosper themselves.

Supervisors should exchange forecasts, consult and check with each other, and share available information.

Only by making forecasts for the future will supervisors be able to clarify in their own minds the directions in which their departments must proceed. By forecasting, supervisors are in a position to formulate definite plans for implementation when and if the forecasted events occur.

Forecasting Means Readiness for Change

All forecasts contain certain assumptions, approximations, and estimates. At best, forecasting is an art, not an exact science.[2] Forecasting accuracy, however, increases with supervisory experience. As time goes on, making estimates about the future becomes a normal activity. Supervisors should exchange forecasts, consult and check with each other, and share information whenever it is available. By doing so, a supervisor becomes more accurate in forecasting. Even if some of the anticipated events do not occur exactly as anticipated, it still is better to have forecast them than to risk being confronted with unanticipated major changes and their consequences.

Having made needed forecasts, supervisors usually are in a better position to ready their departments to incorporate changes as they are needed. Although this may sound like a formidable task, all that really is required is to be alert to possible changes and trends. It is not uncommon for supervisors to review their years of work and, with hindsight, lament that they did not take seriously certain trends that had been visible earlier. If supervisors constantly estimate and anticipate the future, they will be more ready to implement necessary changes when those events do occur.

2

Describe some tactical strategies for gaining acceptance of plans.

SUPERVISORY PLANNING: TACTICAL STRATEGIES

Before making specific plans for the future, supervisors should consider a number of tactical strategies that may be crucial to a future plan. Planning cannot be done in a vacuum, nor can plans be implemented in a vacuum. Plans will have an impact on others, and they will elicit reactions from other supervisors, employees, the manager, and top-level management. Furthermore, implementation is critical to the success of a plan. A well-implemented average plan may be superior to a poorly implemented excellent plan. Therefore, effective planning should take into account certain tactical strategies that can help make a plan successful.

A supervisor should choose the strategies best suited for the problem. A few of the most commonly employed strategies will be suggested here, although they may not always be applicable. The application of these approaches will depend on the specific objective, the people involved, the urgency of the situation, the means available, and a number of other factors. By thinking through the strategy that is most appropriate for a particular plan, a supervisor will be in a much better position to make a plan become a reality and to minimize negative reactions.

Timing Alternatives

Timing is a critical factor in all planning. Thus, a supervisor may choose the "strike while the iron is hot" planning strategy. This strategy advocates prompt action when the situation and time for action are advantageous. For example, this strategy might be employed when a supervisor finds that many orders in the department have been delayed and a number of customers have complained because their orders have fallen behind schedule. The supervisor might then ask for more employees, more equipment, or other resources that are necessary for the department over the long term.

On the other hand, the supervisor may decide to invoke the "time is a great healer" approach. This is not an endorsement of procrastination. However, it is often advisable to move slowly in a difficult situation because some things take care of themselves after a short while. This is also referred to as the "wait and see" strategy, which suggests that it may be better to move a bit more cautiously than to propose a major change under duress or in a crisis. For example, the introduction of a new computerized customer checkout and billing system in a retail store may bring some initial problems and complaints from customers and employees. However, most retail managers have found that with careful planning, ample communication, patience, and time, most of the initial complaints are mitigated. People eventually become accustomed to and accept the computerized system as an improvement in service.

Target Dates and Deadlines

The amount of time allotted for planning sets a constraint on a supervisor. Using the "do the best you can in the time available" strategy, a supervisor may ask the manager to impose some time limits. Without any time limitation, a supervisor may either give a plan little attention or waste much time in search of a "perfect" plan. Either extreme is undesirable. Given a time constraint of two days, for example, a supervisor will have to develop a plan that is the most feasible within the time limitations. The practicality of this approach is illustrated by the response one supervisor gave her manager, who asked whether the plan she submitted for a work layout renovation was the best possible one. She replied, "No, it is not. But it is the best recommendation I could make given the time available to me." Deadlines help motivate supervisors to accomplish the planning task.

Responses to Organizational Change

When plans involve major organizational changes, the supervisor may choose the strategy of the "mass concentrated offensive." This strategy advocates quick, radical, or complete action in order to make an immediate, favorable showing. For example, an office supervisor might believe that office performance could be improved significantly by consolidating all word processing and other support services in a centralized location. To accomplish this plan, the supervisor might decide to make the change all at once in order to overcome potential opposition and to accomplish the objectives quickly.

On the other hand, the supervisor might prefer to use a different strategy, known as "get a foot in the door." This tactic advocates that it may be better to institute only a part of the planned change at the beginning, especially if it is of such magnitude that its total acceptance is doubtful. In choosing this strategy, the office supervisor might consolidate only part of the word processing and other services at a centralized location on a trial basis to see how it works out before changing the entire office procedure.

Gaining Reciprocity

Sometimes a plan might advocate changes that could come about more easily if supervisors of other departments participate in formulating and implementing the plan. A supervisor might find it advisable to have allies promote the change by seeking strength in unity. For example, if a supervisor hopes to gain a budget increase for new departmental furniture, it may be expedient to have other supervisors join in making similar requests to higher-level management. This strategy is "you scratch my back and I will scratch yours." This tactic of reciprocity is well known in political circles and in the activities of sales representatives and purchasing agents. It simply means returning a favor for a favor. Reciprocity also is helpful in building more cooperative relationships among supervisors in carrying out other day-to-day obligations.

SUPERVISORY PLANNING FOR USE OF RESOURCES

3

Summarize major areas of supervisory planning for the effective and safe use of material and human resources.

Because supervisors are especially concerned with day-to-day planning, they must plan for the "best" utilization of all the resources at their disposal. These include both physical and human resources.

Efficient Use of Space

Supervisors must always plan for the allocation and utilization of space. This means that they should determine whether too much or too little space is assigned to the department and whether the space is used efficiently. In most organizations, demands for space typically far exceed the office or plant space available. Therefore, ongoing planning by supervisors for the efficient use of space should be a high priority.

Some firms have a facilities manager or industrial engineering section that can assist the supervisor in space allocation. For most supervisors, however, this responsibility is their own.

When planning for use of space, a floor layout chart can be drawn and analyzed to determine whether there is sufficient space for the work to be performed and whether the space allocated has been laid out appropriately. If the chart indicates a need for additional space, the supervisor should include with the request a thorough analysis of how the current space is being allocated. Chances are that the supervisor has to compete with other departments that also would like to have more room. Unless the supervisor has planned thoroughly, the request for additional space has little chance of being granted. Even if the request is denied, the plans the supervisor assembled will not have been prepared in vain. They will alert the supervisor to some of the conditions under which employees are working and where improvements might be feasible.

Utilization of Other Major Physical Resources

At the same time, supervisors must plan for efficient utilization of their departments' other major physical resources, such as tools, machinery, computers, and various types of equipment and furniture. Usually, all of these represent a substantial investment. Where these items are poorly maintained or are not efficient for the jobs to be done, this will not only cause operating problems but also adversely affect employees' morale. A supervisor does not always have the most desirable or advanced equipment to work with; but the available equipment, when adapted and properly maintained, usually is sufficient to do the job. Therefore, before requesting new equipment, supervisors should first determine whether employees are using available tools and equipment properly. Many times when employees complain about poor equipment, investigation reveals that the equipment is being operated incorrectly. Thus, supervisors should periodically observe the employees using the equipment and ask them whether the equipment serves their purposes or needs improvement.

It is also the responsibility of the supervisor to work closely with the maintenance department in planning for periodic maintenance of tools, equipment, machinery, and the like. Poorly maintained equipment may be blamed on the maintenance department in some cases, but the supervisor must share in the blame if he or she has not planned or scheduled needed maintenance with that department. The maintenance group can do only as good a job as other departments allow them to do.

On occasion, the supervisor may decide that some equipment needs to be replaced. In making this request, the supervisor should also develop a plan to dispose of inefficient equipment and submit this plan to higher-level management. To determine when a change of a major physical resource should take place, supervisors should review trade journals, listen to what salespeople have to say about new products, read literature circulated by distributors and associations, and generally keep up with developments in the field. A stronger argument can be advanced to higher-level managers if the supervisor has thoroughly studied the alternatives available and is prepared to make a recommendation based on several bids and models. Facts are more likely than emotional arguments to persuade higher-level managers to decide in favor of the supervisor's position.

Even though a supervisor has recommended a change that is supported with well-documented reasons, higher-level managers may turn it down on the basis that it is not economically feasible at present. Although disappointed, the supervisor should support the decision and live with it. However, the supervisor should not hesitate to point out at any appropriate time the potential shortcomings in productivity, morale, and so on by failing to replace the equipment in question.

In the long term, a supervisor's plans for replacement or purchase of equipment probably will be accepted in some form. However, even when such requests are denied, the supervisor will be recognized as being on top of the job by planning for better utilization of physical resources in the department.

Properly maintained equipment can minimize breakdowns.

Improvement in Work Procedures and Methods

Supervisors often are so close to the job that they may not recognize when prevailing work procedures and methods need updating. Therefore, a supervisor should periodically try to look at departmental operations as a stranger coming into the department for the first time might view them. By looking at each operation from a detached point of view, the supervisor can determine answers to questions such as the following: Is each operation really necessary? What is the reason for each operation? Can one operation be combined with another? Are the steps performed in the best sequence? Are there any avoidable delays? Is there unnecessary waste?

Improvement generally means any change in the way the department currently is doing something that will lead to an increase in productivity, lowered costs, or improvement in the quality of a product or service. Improvement in work procedures, methods, and processes usually makes the job of the supervisor easier. Besides personally looking for ways to improve operations, the supervisor should solicit ideas from employees. Employees usually know their jobs better than anyone else in the organization. Alternatively, the supervisor may be able to enlist the help of a specialist, such as an industrial engineer or a systems analyst, if this type of person is available within the organization.

When studying areas for improvement, a supervisor should concentrate on situations in which large numbers of employees are assigned, costs per unit are unacceptably high, or scrap figures, waste, or injury reports appear out of line. A good reason for concentrating on such areas is that it will be less difficult for the supervisor to convince both employees and higher-level managers that recommended changes will bring about considerable improvement, savings, or other benefits.

Organizations need to become more proactive in meeting the pressures of increasing competition. Therefore, every supervisor should consider the benefits of a methods improvement program, perhaps in conjunction with a firm's employee suggestion system if one is in place.[3] At all times, a supervisor should urge employees to look for better ways to do the job.

At times the supervisor can apply work sampling techniques to cut costs, save time, and increase employee efficiency. Broadly stated, **work sampling** involves inspecting a small amount of typical work from an entire job to determine areas for improvement. Generally, work sampling techniques are the tools of the industrial engineer.[4] However, in smaller firms supervisors usually perform this role themselves. Although work sampling is a useful tool, every effort should be expended to ensure that the sample is typical of the whole it is intended to represent.

Work sampling

Inspecting a sample of work from an entire job to determine areas for improvement.

Use and Security of Materials, Supplies, Merchandise, and Data

Another supervisory responsibility is to plan for the appropriate use, conservation, and security of materials, supplies, and merchandise. In most departments substantial quantities of materials and supplies are used and maintained in inventory. Even if each single item represents only a small value, the items add up to sizable dollar amounts in the total budget. Many employees do not realize the magnitude of the money tied up in materials and supplies, and sometimes they are careless in using these items. The supervisor should remind employees that economical use of all resources ultimately is to their own advantage; whatever is wasted cannot be used to raise wages or improve working conditions.

A major problem in recent years has been loss and theft of materials, supplies, merchandise, and other company property, sometimes carried out by employees themselves. Statistically, such losses to U.S. businesses have been estimated to be in the billions of dollars annually. Some experts claim that the United States has the highest rate of employee theft and dishonesty in the world. To prevent such losses, supervisors must make sure that adequate security precautions are taken to discourage individuals from theft and to make it difficult for items to be lost or stolen. For example, many supplies can be kept locked up, with someone assigned the responsibility for distributing them as needed. If the firm has its own security force, the supervisor should meet with security personnel to plan and implement security devices and procedures that are suited to the department. In retail establishments, this may mean removing the opportunity for theft and training employees to pay attention to customers' bags, clothing, carts, boxes, and so forth. Increased attention can often deter a theft or a fraudulent return or exchange. A supervisor may even request such assistance from local police or a private security agency.[5]

In recent years, another major concern of many firms has been the theft of data and information, mostly associated with computer break-ins and related thefts. A late-1990s survey of major corporations, government agencies, and universities revealed that 88 percent of the respondents had been victims of computer crimes of both serious and minor consequences.[6] As a result of these and other potential problems, many firms have instituted plans and programs for protection of their information systems. Supervisors may become quite involved in working with information technology specialists to plan for limiting access to certain data, and in the protection of important hardware and software.

A supervisor's plans for utilization and security of materials, supplies, merchandise, and data cannot eliminate all waste and loss. However, such planning usually will reduce waste and loss, and promote a more efficient and conscientious workplace atmosphere among employees.

Safe Work Environment

Most managers and supervisors recognize that a safe work environment is one of their major responsibilities, since this is essential for the welfare and productivity of employees. Safety data have long indicated that employees themselves cause accidents more often than do faulty tools and equipment, due to carelessness, poor attitudes, inadequate training, and many other reasons. Yet the supervisor shares a major responsibility, both ethically and legally, to do everything possible to see that the safest possible work environment is maintained. Of course, there are some job categories that by their very nature are more hazardous than others. For example, supervisors in mining, construction, and heavy manufacturing face major challenges in working to reduce the potential for serious injuries and fatalities. By contrast, supervisors in the generally comfortable surroundings of an office usually do not have to worry about major injuries. Nevertheless, the potential for accidents exists in any situation if employees are not fully trained and reminded to follow safe work habits.

Although there has been some reduction in the number of reported workplace accidents and injuries, the U.S. Bureau of Labor Statistics figures for the 1990s still show

The supervisor has an ethical and legal responsibility to provide the safest possible working environment for employees.

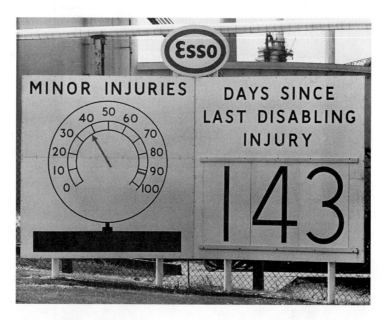

a disturbing picture. Annually, approximately 6,000 U.S. workers die from traumatic workplace accidents and 6 million workers experience workplace injuries and illnesses. An estimated 35 million workdays are lost each year.[7] This is despite the fact that there are major laws and safety regulations in place which most employers and employees recognize as being in their mutual self-interest.

Observance of OSHA and Other Safety Regulations. Both before and since the passage of the Occupational Safety and Health Act of 1970 (OSHA), supervisors have been expected to devote major attention to reducing and preventing injuries and accidents on the job. OSHA has had a significant impact on the scope and administration of safety programs in many organizations. It has expanded the responsibility of the supervisor in planning for and bringing about a safer job environment.

The Occupational Safety and Health Act is a very complicated law.[8] The federal agency called the Occupational Safety and Health Administration enforces the Act's regulations in about half of the states in the United States. The other states have their own agencies through which state or state-appointed officials enforce the law's rules and regulations. Supervisors should have a general understanding of all safety requirements associated with the law as it affects departmental operations. Larger firms usually will have someone in management—typically in human resources, safety, industrial engineering, or risk management—who is familiar with the technical requirements of OSHA, as well as any other laws, court rulings, and industry-mandated safety regulations that must be observed. Regardless of the size of the firm, supervisors must plan to meet with managers, as well as with employees, union leaders, and even with government officials if necessary, to do everything possible to maintain compliance with all safety regulations.

On-site visitations of a firm's premises by an OSHA inspector usually involve supervisors of the departments or areas being inspected. OSHA inspections mostly occur when there is a serious workplace accident or fatality, or when an employee lodges a complaint about safety conditions. Additionally, OSHA inspectors conduct random inspections as a check on a firm's compliance with the law. Since an OSHA inspection can bring about fines and penalties for violations that are discovered, it is essential that the firm have an established plan for handling and dealing with such inspections. Much of the OSHA inspection process will be the major responsibility of a firm's designated safety officer, human resources director, or plant manager. Supervisors, however, play important roles in safety inspections of their work areas, and therefore they should plan and prepare in advance for eventualities that might be associated with an OSHA site inspection. Figure 7-1 (see page 214) is a listing of some important aspects of supervisory responsibilities that are applicable before, during, and after an OSHA inspection. Of course, there are numerous OSHA legal and other considerations that may or may not involve supervisors, and which most likely will be handled by legal counsel and top management.

Safety Committees. If not already in place, supervisors should endeavor to establish and participate in safety committees. Many unionized firms have safety committees that are jointly sponsored by both management and the union(s). The purpose of a safety committee is to assist the supervisor in developing safer work areas and enforcing safety

FIGURE 7-1

Supervisory responsibilities for dealing with an OSHA inspection.

Some Supervisory Responsibilities for Dealing with an OSHA Inspection

BEFORE AN INSPECTION

- Display the official OSHA poster where notices to employees are usually posted.
- Determine which OSHA standards and regulations apply to your work site. Make sure that all required written programs and documents are up to date.
- Conduct a survey of your work site to find and correct possible safety or health violations.

DURING AN INSPECTION

- Refer the inspector immediately upon arrival to your designated safety officer.
- Have an opening conference with the inspector and establish the focus and scope of the planned walk-around inspection.
- To the extent possible, correct immediately any violation identified by the inspector.
- Take notes on problem areas indicated by the inspector, along with the applicable standards and suggested abatement procedures.

AFTER AN INSPECTION

- Review all topics of concern identified by the inspector, and make appropriate changes.
- If you are issued one or more citations by OSHA, post each citation in the affected area, and wherever safety notices are normally posted.

Source: Excerpted from a list of suggestions or "tips" compiled by Edwin G. Foulke, an attorney who was former chairman of the Occupational Safety and Health Review Commission. These were included in an article by Steve Bates, "When OSHA Calls," *Nation's Business* (September 1998), pp. 14–22.

regulations. The supervisor and safety committee can plan for periodic meetings and projects to communicate to employees the importance of safe work habits and attitudes.

Labor unions have been quite vocal in asserting their concerns that safe work environments and safe work practices are monitored closely. Joint union-management safety committees invariably involve supervisors, and usually there is a more concerted effort to reduce accidents and injuries. For example, a multi-union/multi-employer "Labor-Management Health and Safety Committee" was established for major construction projects in the city of Boston. As a result of ongoing site walk-throughs, safety committee representatives identified and corrected various problems such as improper use of personal protective equipment; unsafe stairways, ladders and aerial lifts; and improper illumination, electrical installation, and fire safety. To reinforce workers' awareness of proper safety practices and use of safety gear, supervisors and workers hold weekly "toolbox" safety meetings where they discuss such subjects as storing tools and equipment to avoid tripping accidents, proper lifting techniques, and the necessity for protective safety gear. As a result of these efforts, the rate of lost-time injuries on projects was cut by more than half between 1994 and 1998.[9]

Safety Problems and Safety Programs. Many jobs require employees to repeat the same hand or arm motions for extended periods of time. For example, employees who must use computer keyboards or who do repetitive body motions for hours at a time, day in and day out, may develop carpal tunnel syndrome (CTS). According to statistics compiled by the Department of Labor, *repetitive motion injuries* called **cumulative-trauma disorders** brought on by workplace ergonomic hazards have grown enormously. Ergonomic problems now rank as the single largest cause of serious workplace injuries. Another computer-related malady is computer vision syndrome (CVS). An estimated 10 million workers visit optometrists annually reporting vision-related symptoms such as headaches, eyestrain, and focus problems.[10]

Back pain injuries remain as one of the perennial workplace safety problems. In a major survey of 30,000 American workers, it was determined that almost 70 percent of the workdays lost due to back pain were because of work-related injuries. Other researchers discovered that job stress and low control over one's work requirements were highly associated with lower-back injuries.[11]

Obviously, such injuries can cost a businesses huge economic losses in health-care costs, downtime, and reduce quality and productivity. A safety committee can be helpful in finding ways to redesign employee workstations, for example, by changing the tilt or height of the keyboard, providing rests for the wrist, adjusting lighting arrangements, or finding other tasks to provide relief from the repetitive duties and job strains.

The supervisor's constant attention to safety is mandatory if a safe work environment is to be maintained. The large majority of reported accidents on the job are caused primarily by human failure (see Figure 7-2). This means that the supervisor must em-

Cumulative-trauma disorder

Workplace injury caused by repetitive motions usually of the hand or arm.

FIGURE 7-2

Inattention is a common cause of accidents.

phasize safe work habits in daily instructions to employees and make sure that all equipment in the department is used properly and has ample protective devices. The supervisor should plan meetings throughout the year to emphasize safety themes. Supervisors will find that employees and higher-level managers usually are willing to assist in developing a strong safety program.

A commonly held half-truth is that a safety program is the responsibility of the safety department or safety engineers. However, without the full support of supervisors and diligent supervisory observance of employee work practices in every department, almost any safety program will be unsuccessful. Safety planning and safety in practice are everyone's responsibility. One major corporation has summarized this well in a safety motto that is the cornerstone of its safety program efforts and which is posted prominently at all of its building locations: "No job is so important and no service is so urgent that we cannot take time to perform our job safely."

Employee Work Schedules

To plan effective work schedules for employees, supervisors should operate from the premise that most employees are willing to turn in a fair day's work. Supervisors should not expect all employees to work continuously at top speed. Rather, they should establish a work schedule based on an estimate of what constitutes a fair (rather than a maximum) output. Allowances must be made for fatigue, unavoidable delays, personal needs, and a certain amount of unproductive time during the workday. Some supervisors may be able to plan employee time with the help of a specialist such as a motion-and-time analyst. Even without such help, most supervisors have a good idea as to what they can expect, and they are capable of planning reasonable performance requirements that their employees will accept as fair. Such estimates are based on normal rather than abnormal conditions. In this regard, it may not be advisable for a supervisor to schedule a department to operate at 100 percent capacity because this would not leave any room for emergencies or changes in priorities and deadlines. Some flexibility is invariably needed to operate; thus, only short periods of 100 percent capacity should be scheduled. Also, several rest periods usually are a regular part of employee work scheduling.

Overtime and Absences.   On occasion, supervisors find it necessary to plan for overtime, although overtime should be considered primarily as an exception or as an emergency measure. As a general rule, supervisors should anticipate a reduction of between 5 and 10 percent in productivity from employees when they work overtime. If a supervisor finds that excessive overtime is required regularly, then alternative methods of doing the work should be found or additional employees should be scheduled or hired.

Supervisors must also plan for employee absences. Of course, a supervisor cannot plan for every instance when an employee will be absent because of sickness, injury, or personal problems.[12] However, the supervisor can plan for holidays, vacations, temporary layoffs, turnover, and other types of leaves or predictable absenteeism. Planning for anticipated absences will ensure the smooth functioning of the department.

In recent years, a growing number of firms have established so-called *group emergency time pools*. These are time-sharing plans by which employees can donate some of their vacation days to a company pooled account, and an employee who is on an extended sickness or disability leave can draw upon this account to receive needed income while off work. This type of arrangement is usually cost-effective for the employer, and it is a morale and team builder for the employees.[13] However, it can add some complications to a supervisor's tasks of vacation scheduling.

Alternative Work Schedules. Many organizations have adopted a variety of work schedules for their employees, such as flextime, part-time work, job sharing, telecommuting and other work-at-home arrangements, and unconventional hours. So-called alternative work schedule plans are quite diverse. In some organizations, employees are scheduled or may have the option to choose a four-day workweek—usually a four-day, 10-hour-per-day arrangement. The most common form of alternative work scheduling, however, is flextime, in which employees can choose—within certain limits—the hours they would like to work. Usually this involves permitting certain employees to select different starting and ending times within a five-day workweek. Alternative work arrangements are becoming more common, particularly in situations in which an employee's work is not closely interdependent or interrelated with that of other employees or departments.[14] Figure 7-3 is an example of a statement from an insurance company

FIGURE 7-3

Company policy concerning flexible work scheduling.

Work Week

Your normal workweek is 38 hours and 45 minutes—7 hours and 45 minutes per day, Monday through Friday.

The normal work day begins at 8:15 A.M. and ends at 5:00 P.M. However under our "flextime" program, you may be given the choice, when possible, of working one of the following schedules:

7:00 A.M.–3:45 P.M.
7:15 A.M.–4:00 P.M.
7:30 A.M.–4:15 P.M.
7:45 A.M.–4:30 P.M.
8:00 A.M.–4:45 P.M.
8:15 A.M.–5:00 P.M.
8:30 A.M.–5:15 P.M.
8:45 A.M.–5:30 P.M.
9:00 A.M.–5:45 P.M.

We think you will like having the opportunity of choosing a work schedule that best suits your personal needs. Your supervisor will tell you which options are available in your department.

Many of our employees are required by law to have their work time recorded on time cards. If you are in this category, your supervisor keeps a weekly record showing time lost during the week and any overtime that was worked. You and the supervisor will review and sign the time card at the end of each week to show that both of you agree with the information recorded.

employee manual regarding flexible working schedules and the role the supervisor plays in administering the schedule.

Supervisors have found that alternative work schedules create problems in maintaining coverage of all workstations or job positions, and that it may be difficult to exercise supervisory control at certain times of the workday. Nevertheless, supervisors who must cope with alternative work schedules learn to adapt within their departments and in their relations with other departments. In some situations, supervisors may be in charge of different work groups on different days and at different times of the day as a result of flexible work scheduling. This, in turn, requires that supervisors on different shifts and in different departments coordinate their activities to achieve overall organizational effectiveness.

Telecommuting and other work-at-home arrangements present a number of different problems for supervisors. In general, time scheduling is not that important, since the work-at-home employees tend to make their own work schedules. However, supervisors need to plan well in advance and communicate with these employees concerning such items as project work to be completed, deadlines, budget constraints, productivity expectations, and customer requirements. Some firms are making special efforts for training supervisors in how to manage teleworkers and other work-at-home employees.[15]

In general, most studies of alternative work schedule plans have concluded that employees generally appreciate the opportunity to select their work schedule preference. Further, flexible work schedules usually are associated with improvements in absenteeism rates, tardiness rates, retention, morale, and productivity.[16]

Part-Time and Temporary Employment. The use of part-time employees is increasing. Retailers, service establishments, and health-care centers, in particular, often have large numbers of part-time workers. Scheduling part-time employees requires considerable advance planning to match the needs of the department or business operation with the hours that the part-time people will be available. Part-time work arrangements must be developed and monitored if they are to be advantageous to both employees and management. Some part-time employees are content to work limited schedules. Other part-time employees, however, are anxious to work as many hours as possible, and they also are hopeful of obtaining full-time employment. Supervisors must be careful in planning work schedules so that part-time workers' special interests and needs are accommodated, while at the same time not creating scheduling problems with full-time employees and departmental work requirements.

Another complicating factor for supervisors in work scheduling is the growing phenomenon of temporary employment. Temporary employees (or "temps") are persons who hold jobs that are temporary in nature or jobs that are not expected to continue. For the most part, temporary employees fall into two basic categories. The first are those employees who are hired by an agency, and who then are "farmed out" for short-term work assignments with various employers. Companies typically contact the agency to obtain individuals who have certain skills, and the contracting company pays a specified rate to the agency for each employee who performs the services. A supervisor who uses these types of temporary employees must schedule them in conjunction with the temporary help agency. The second type of temporary employee is referred to as an *interim employee*. An interim employee is hired directly by a firm for a specific need or project, and the hiring is done with the clear understanding that there is no guarantee for future employment when the need for the individual or the project is over. Typically, the interim employee is paid a wage or salary with limited or no benefits.

Although the use of temporary employees is frequently justified to meet short-term staffing needs and as a cost-saving measure, there are associated problems that supervisors must be prepared to deal with. Among these are a lack of commitment to the firm, especially as the project or interim period of employment nears completion. Temporary employees often leave a job prematurely for other opportunities; they take knowledge and training with them that can be demoralizing to permanent employees; and they can leave the company in a difficult situation.[17] For the most part, supervisors should endeavor to give "temps" job assignments that they are capable of doing productively and without disrupting the regular workforce. Temporary employees should not be treated by the supervisor as "second-class citizens." They should be viewed as employees who are in the department to contribute to the successful attainment of the department's objectives and should be treated accordingly. At times, temporary employees can show by their performance that they are worthy of consideration for being hired into full-time positions; therefore, the temporary work situation can serve as a trial period that enables a supervisor to determine whether the "temp" should be offered full-time status.[18]

Full Utilization of Human Resources

Our perspective throughout this book is that employees usually are a firm's most important resource. Planning for their full utilization always should be uppermost in every supervisor's mind. Full utilization of the workforce means getting employees to contribute to their fullest capabilities. This requires plans for recruiting, selecting, and training employees; searching for better ways to group activities; training employees in proper and safe use of the materials associated with their jobs; supervising employees with an understanding of the complexities of human needs and motivation; communicating effectively with employees; appraising their performance; giving recognition; promoting the deserving; adequately compensating and rewarding them; and, if need be, taking just and fair disciplinary actions. All of these are ongoing aspects of a supervisor's plans for the full utilization of human resources.

Planning for the full utilization of employees is at the core of effective supervision. It is mentioned here again only briefly since most chapters of this text are concerned in some way with this overall primary objective of supervisory management.

Discuss the importance of time management, especially in reducing stress, and suggest techniques for supervisors to plan better use of their time.

TIME AND STRESS MANAGEMENT

To this point, we have emphasized the need for thorough planning for optimum use of physical and human resources. Another important resource that affects all other resources is the supervisor's own time. The old saying that "time is money" applies with equal relevance to both the supervisor's and the employees' time. A supervisor's time is

There is no substitute for daily preparation.

a major resource that must be expended carefully. Many supervisors are like Phil Moore in the "You Make the Call" section at the outset of this chapter. With all of the job demands, they feel that they can never take care of all the matters that need attention. The days and weeks are too short; they would like to "buy" additional time somewhere. However, the supply of time is inflexible, and it cannot be renewed or stored. If supervisors want "more time," they can find it only by better use of what they already have—which is the same for everybody.

Most supervisors would welcome even a modest increase in their effectiveness. Given the many pressures on them, supervisors who have a system for managing their time are far more likely to be effective than those who approach each day haphazardly. Although some supervisors insist that they need more time, what they really need is better use of the time they already have. As a starting point, this means preparing each day for the day at hand.

Some supervisors put in extremely long days, but they are not on top of their jobs. Similarly, there are dedicated supervisors who may equate long hours with devotion and effectiveness. Many times just the reverse is true. Such supervisors need to examine what effort is put into the hours worked and with what results, rather than looking only at the number of hours they have worked as a sign of their dedication. The key is to gain control over the workday rather than to be controlled by it. Time management, too, starts with careful planning.[19]

Managing Time Means Reducing Stress

Throughout the 1990s, stress-related claims under workers' compensation programs and insurance systems have been on an extraordinary upward spiral. Problems of stress on the job have become a recognized part of the business environment. Some of this has been blamed upon factors such as downsizing, workplace violence, technology, diversity issues, and the like. These areas have been (or will be) discussed at various places throughout the text, and they often are outside the supervisor's realm of control. Many causes of stress, however, are job-related, and they have become still another area of supervisory concern.

What exactly is meant by the term *stress* can be somewhat misunderstood. **Stress** has been defined as "a person's nonspecific bodily reactions to demands and conditions that he or she encounters."[20] Stress also has been defined as "an adaptive response, moderated by individual differences, that is a consequence of any action, situation, or event, that places special demands on a person."[21] These definitions reflect the notion that stress is a reaction to a situation or situations, and the individual responses can be quite varied, including being either positive or negative. In general, responses to symptoms

Stress

A person's nonspecific bodily reactions to demands and conditions that he or she encounters.

of stress tend to be viewed in a negative way, such as fatigue, headaches, irritability, and tension. Levels of stress have been tied to lower productivity, increased accidents, higher absenteeism, and alcohol and drug abuse. Thus, stress tends to be looked upon as being undesirable, but it is well documented that a certain amount of stress can be an incentive that motivates individuals toward accomplishment and achievement.

External stressors

Causes of stress that arise from outside the individual, such as job pressures, responsibilities, and work itself.

External stressors are causes of stress that come from outside the person, such as pressures of the job, family, and environmental conditions. Employees often assert that they are "stressed out" because of work overloads, poor supervisors, lack of recognition, and a host of practices that frequently reflect relationships with supervisors. By its very nature, the supervisory position itself is pressure prone, since supervisors are burdened by many demands from managers, employees, and fellow supervisors. Interpersonal conflicts with others on the job often are more difficult to cope with than pressures of difficult tasks and deadlines. At the same time, supervisors and employees have to deal with their own internal stressors. **Internal stressors** have been defined as pressures that people put on themselves for a variety of reasons, such as being ambitious, diligent, competitive, and aggressive. Supervisors may compound their problems of external stress by having personal stressors of an internal nature, especially in their desire to accomplish and satisfy others in the organization.

Internal stressors

Pressures that people put on themselves, such as feeling a need to be outstanding in everything.

Stress and Personal Characteristics. While it is beyond the scope of this book to give broad coverage to the topic of stress, it is interesting to note that many psychologists and consultants agree that individuals who handle stress well seem to share some common personal characteristics. Among these are that they have a good social support system, meaning a network of family and friends to relate to for understanding and fun; they take time out to relax, to meditate, or to pray; and they are physically fit.[22] Certainly many supervisors do not have all of these personal characteristics. Therefore stress is a real problem to them that must be managed along with everything else.

Managing Stress Means Managing Time. Many articles and seminars attempt to teach people ways of coping with pressures that may induce stress. Among the recommended stress-control techniques are exercise, meditation, bio-feedback training, and progressive relaxation. But it is also widely recognized that many of the suggested remedies for stress management relate primarily to better time management, or as one author has succinctly stated, "Managing stress means managing time. The two are so intertwined that controlling one can only help the other."[23] Supervisors who constantly complain that they "do not have enough time" to do all the things that must be done, and that they therefore are under severe stress, should understand that much of what is attributed to stress can be directly related to their ability (or lack thereof) to manage their time. The importance of managing time to reduce stressful conditions by following better time management practices and procedures cannot be overstated. Supervisors who learn to prioritize their duties and tasks and who in turn accomplish more of what they really need to get done will find that their professional and personal lives are more satisfactory and rewarding. Virtually by any definition, better time management means increased accomplishment and reduced stress and frustration.[24]

Classifying Duties with a Time-Use Chart

A first step toward better time management is for supervisors to analyze how they currently use time. A time-use chart, or time inventory, is an excellent tool to help supervisors examine how and where they currently are spending their time. Then they can begin to attack pockets of inefficiency.

Prior to constructing such a chart, supervisors should identify their primary job duties and daily activities and classify them as (a) routine duties, (b) regular duties, (c) special duties, or (d) innovative duties. They may wish to add another classification to cover time spent handling emergencies, although it is difficult to predict an emergency and the time needed to correct a crisis situation.

Routine duties are minor tasks that are done daily but make a limited contribution to the objectives of the department. Such work includes answering the telephone, reviewing the mail, chatting informally with others, cleaning up, and the like. Some of these tasks can be assigned to subordinates. **Regular duties** constitute the supervisory work most directly related to accomplishing the objectives of the department. Regular duties primarily involve the day-to-day activities that a supervisor must do personally and that are the essential components of the supervisor's responsibilities. Examples of these are giving directives, checking performance, writing reports, counseling employees, updating job descriptions, training new employees, and reviewing departmental operating procedures. **Special duties** consist of meetings, committee work, and special projects that are not directly related to core tasks of the department. **Innovative duties** are creative-thinking and improvement-oriented activities—for example, looking at new or improved work methods or finding better ways to communicate with employees.

Supervisors who are effective at managing their time do find time for innovative duties. Indeed, it is the innovative supervisor who usually stands out and is most often noticed by higher-level managers. This, of course, should not imply that a supervisor ought to work on innovative duties to the neglect of other duties. The amount of supervisory time spent on various duties will vary. Supervisors themselves must judge what are the appropriate proportions for their particular situations. One thing is clear, however: if a supervisor does not plan carefully, routine and special duties have a way of crowding out the time needed for regular and innovative duties.

A time-use chart is a useful technique for gathering information about how a supervisor is currently spending time. The supervisor can start by constructing a time-use chart similar to the one shown in Figure 7-4. Duties should be classified as routine, regular, special, or innovative. Then the supervisor should decide what amount of time should be allocated to duties under each category and correspondingly set goals for each day. Once these steps are taken, the supervisor should keep an ongoing record of the time that actually was spent on various duties. After a week or two of recording daily how time is actually spent, the supervisor should bring together the time-use charts and total the amount of time spent in each of the categories. These totals should be compared with the original estimates or goals. The supervisor is then in a position to evaluate his or her use of time. With rare exceptions, the supervisor will be in for some surprises!

Routine duties
Minor tasks, done daily, that make a minor contribution to achievement of objectives.

Regular duties
The essential components of a supervisor's job, such as giving directives and checking performance.

Special duties
Tasks not directly related to the core tasks of the department, such as meetings and committee work.

Innovative duties
Creative activities aimed at finding a better way to do something.

FIGURE 7-4   Time-use chart.

GOALS FOR THE DAY	ESTIMATED TIME (IN HOURS AND FRACTIONS OF HOURS)	PERCENTAGE (CALCULATE)
Routine		
Regular		
Special		
Innovative		

ACTUAL TIME USE	ROUTINE	REGULAR	SPECIAL	INNOVATIVE
		(Record the time spent in hours and fractions of hours)		
6:00–7:00				
7:01–8:00				
8:01–9:00				
9:01–10:00				
10:01–11:00				
11:01–12:00				
12:01–1:00				
1:01–2:00				
2:01–3:00				
3:01–4:00				
4:01–5:00				
5:01–6:00				
Totals				
Calculated Percentages				

Evaluation of Effectiveness

By analyzing the actual times versus the goals or estimates, the supervisor can determine whether appropriate amounts of time are being spent on various duties. For example, are some regular duties not getting done because too much time is devoted to routine duties or special projects? Could some tasks be eliminated altogether? Is there sufficient time for innovative work and planning? Answers to these and similar questions give the supervisor a better feel for what she or he ought to be working on, rather than simply tackling the problems that happen to come up first or seem most pleasant to work on at the moment.

Overcoming Time Wasters by Setting Priorities

Invariably, supervisors discover time wasters that have hampered their ability to work on important things in their department. Such time wasters as random activities, too much time on the telephone, too much time visiting or being visited, procrastination, unnecessary meetings, and lack of delegation may be revealed by a time inventory. The discovery and recognition of time wasters represent only one step. The supervisor must begin immediately to attack these old habits and build desirable ones.

Supervisors often have a "do-it-myself" mentality that causes them to do many tasks that could be handled by others, especially their own employees. The result is that supervisors spend valuable time on what has been called "scut work," meaning low-level tasks and trivial problems that others should be handling.[25] It is true that many supervisory problems appear continuously, often without an apparent sequence of priority. Therefore, supervisors must discipline themselves to decide between matters that they must handle personally and those that can be assigned to someone else. For every task delegated—particularly routine duties—a supervisor gains time for more important matters such as regular and innovative duties. Doing this may be worthwhile even if the supervisor has to spend extra time training an employee in a particular task. The su-

After the supervisor identifies time wasters, he or she must work to attack bad habits and replace them with desirable ones.

pervisor then should plan the remaining available time so that it is allocated properly among the duties that he or she alone must perform. These duties must be classified according to which are the most and the least urgent.

The "Pareto Principle," named after a famous 19th-century Italian economist, holds that many people, because they fail to set priorities, spend most of their time on minor, unimportant tasks. It has been estimated that some supervisors spend 80 percent of their time on duties that contribute to only 20 percent of the total job results. A supervisor who does not establish a priority of duties is inclined to pay equal attention to all matters at hand. This type of supervisor tends to handle each problem in the order it happens, and consequently, the most important matters may not receive the attention they deserve. When priorities are established, time is planned so that the most important things have sufficient space on the schedule. However, supervisors should leave some flexibility in their schedules because not every event that occurs can be anticipated. Emergencies and changing priorities do occur, and supervisors must attend to them. Flexibility permits supervisors to take care of unanticipated problems without significantly disrupting their schedule of priorities. There are numerous practical ideas for better time management that various practitioners and authorities have suggested. This chapter's "Contemporary Issue" box includes a selection of approaches, or "tips," that could have application for most supervisors.

Tools of Time Management

Effective time utilization requires mental discipline. This means that supervisors should assign priorities to duties and stop trying to do everything brought to their attention. Once such a mental attitude is fixed, they can better use a number of common tools as aids in managing their time.

Supervisors should use a pocket or desk calendar to note activities that need major attention, such as appointments, meetings, reports, and discussions. By scheduling such activities as far in advance as practicable and noting them on their calendars, supervisors are less likely to overlook them.

Another tool for effective time utilization is the weekly planning sheet (or, if preferred, a monthly planning sheet). Typically, a planning sheet for a week is prepared at the end of the previous week. The planning sheet shows the days of the week divided into mornings and afternoons and lists the items to be accomplished (see Figure 7-5 on page 227). At a glance the supervisor can check what is planned for each morning and afternoon. As each task is accomplished, it is circled. Tasks that have been delayed must be rescheduled for another time. Tasks that are planned but not accomplished during the week remain uncircled and should be rescheduled for the following week. This record indicates how much of the original plan was carried out, and it provides information concerning how the supervisor's time was spent.

Still another technique that many supervisors find helpful is the "to-do" list, which can be used in conjunction with a desk calendar or weekly planning sheet. This is essentially an ongoing listing of things to do—both major and minor—to which a supervisor can refer as each day progresses. As an item is accomplished, it is crossed off the list. The supervisor must prioritize all items on the list and schedule and perform

contemporary issue

Practical Approaches as Guidelines for Better Time Management

Most time management experts generally agree on the fundamental or basic techniques necessary to gain better control of one's time and reduce stress. Increasingly, however, many executives and analysts are offering their own unique experiences and suggestions that they have found helpful in their busy workday and personal lives. The following is a sample of practical or so-called "nontraditional" approaches for time management as gleaned from a survey of recent time management articles.

PROCRASTINATION REMEDIES. According to analyst Dennis Snedden, the major causes of procrastination are indecisiveness, and difficult and unpleasant tasks. His suggestions: (a) Overcome indecisiveness by habitual and continuous planning. (b) Break down difficult tasks into small and doable components until the first step becomes apparent. (c) Do unpleasant tasks first by placing the unpleasant tasks in the center of your work area to do immediately or the first thing tomorrow.[1]

THE TWO-HOUR RULE. Rick Duris offers the "two-hour rule" as follows: If you have been working on a problem for more than two hours, tell someone about it. If a competent technician cannot solve the problem in two hours or at least suggest a solution, then the technician is overlooking something. The simple act of explaining the problem to someone else usually creates a new mindset that leads to a solution.[2]

THE EIGHTY/TWENTY PRINCIPLE. Consultant Richard Koch claims that 80 percent of achievement comes from 20 percent of the time spent. He advocates following the "eighty/twenty principle" in two ways. As a consultant, he observed that 80 percent of profits came from working closely with 20 percent of the major clients. Secondly, 80 percent of the results would flow from concentrating on 20 percent of the most important issues.[3]

THE PROSPECTING CLOCK. Bill Bishop advocates several time improvement practices for scheduling meetings with clients or customers. First of all, he stresses setting more breakfast or lunch appointments wherever possible. Appointments late in the day usually are time wasters, since as the day wears on decisions grow smaller, slower, and fewer, and typically are postponed to another day. Secondly, schedule appointments earlier in the week rather than later in the week. As a week grinds on, people tend to run out of patience and money. The same general idea also holds true for weeks of the month.[4]

There is no doubt that the general principles of time management can be helpful, but there is a lot to be said for utilizing tips and practical approaches that come from experienced people. Using time wisely means planning and reallocating hours you spend on the job so that you can leverage yourself for greater effectiveness and prosperity.[5]

Sources: (1) Dennis Snedden, "Cure-alls for Proscrastination," *Association Management* (March 1998), p. 81. (2) Rick Duris, "Be Sure to Invoke the Two-Hour Rule," *Automatic I.D. News* (November 1998), p. 70. (3) Richard Koch, "Portrait of the Consultant as a Young Man," *Across the Board* (November/December 1998), p. 46. (4) Bill Bishop, "Secrets of Prospecting Time Management," *Financial Services Advisor* (January/February 1999), pp. 17–18. (5) Tom Metcalf, "Manage Your Life," *Life Association News* (January 1999), pp. 12–14.

important tasks before attending to the minor items. Many supervisors find that the best time to review and reprioritize their to-do lists is at the beginning of the workday or at the end of the day before they leave.

There are other tools that supervisors can implement to accomplish better time management. Regardless of what they decide to use, however, it is their responsibility to plan and manage their time for each day and week and to have a system for recording tasks that were planned and those that were accomplished.

FIGURE 7-5   The weekly planning sheet.

SUNDAY 9/21	MONDAY 9/22	TUESDAY 9/23	WEDNESDAY 9/24	THURSDAY 9/25	FRIDAY 9/26	SATURDAY 9/27
A.M.	A.M. 7:30 Staff Mtg. Monthly safety committee meeting	A.M. Discuss with human resources director interpretation of changes in policy	A.M. Talk to engineering about preventive maintenance plan	A.M. Turn in scrap report 11AM Staff Mtg.	A.M. Attend management seminar	A.M.
P.M.	P.M. Discuss direct labor cost figures with comptroller	P.M. Work on next year's departmental budget	P.M.	P.M. Check absentee, turnover, and accident rates	P.M. Meeting with Union Grievance Committee to discuss unresolved grievances	P.M.

Time for Creative and Innovative Thinking

Every supervisor needs to have some time for creative and innovative thinking. Although a manager's evaluation of a supervisor will depend primarily on how effectively the department functions, the manager also will recognize the supervisor for innovative changes, new ideas, and progressive suggestions. Unless supervisors allocate time for thinking about constructive improvements, they will find themselves bogged down with routine work and putting out fires.

One approach that supervisors can take in this regard is to develop a list of improvement projects or innovative ideas and write them on a special desk pad or wall chart. This list becomes a constant visual reminder of items that the supervisor would like to accomplish when time becomes available. When there are lulls in a day, or during slack periods, the supervisor can decide which of the innovative items on the list to tackle. Interestingly, the mere thought of having such a list can be a major incentive to attempt an improvement project that otherwise might not be attempted. When the improvement project is done, it is a good feeling to cross the item off the list and mark it as accomplished.

What Call Did You Make?

Some people work better under pressure, but a continuous diet of long hours with no end in sight is too much. Not only is Phil Moore feeling the stress, but it appears that his staff also is feeling it, particularly since the firm is understaffed. Unfortunately, this situation may be fairly typical with the current trends toward downsizing organizations and not filling positions when employees leave.

As Phil Moore, you do not appear to have time for creative or innovative thinking about how to handle the current situation. Nevertheless, you must "make time." For yourself and other members of the department, you need to prepare a time-use chart for a few days. "Know thyself," said Socrates. Evaluate how you are using the time you have. Perhaps you might want to seek anonymous assessments from others and com-

pare their perceptions with your own. Analysis of the time-use charts should tell you whether your time allotments are going where they will do the most good. Most likely you will find that you are not spending your time as wisely as you think. Many working supervisors tend to pay attention to all the little details instead of delegating them.

Depending on the analysis of the time-use chart, you may want to prepare a written list illustrating how the department's productivity is suffering and potentially affecting the entire organization. You could review the list with your staff before you present it to Sally Paul. You should also be prepared to propose solutions. If the current situation is unacceptable and you want to see a change soon, you will have to be assertive.

While Ms. Paul might allow you to add staff, you need to use the techniques presented in this chapter to help you make more efficient use of your employees' time and your own.

SUMMARY

1

Planning means establishing objectives based on the current situation and forecasts of the future, and determining the actions needed to achieve the objectives. Top-level managers forecast the future in a more general and far-reaching manner. Supervisory forecasting is an effort to predict future events that may affect departmental operations. Thus, supervisors need to be alert to possible changes and trends.

Forecasts serve as "building stones" on which plans are based. Supervisors who realistically try to anticipate certain events will be in a better position to prepare for them. Supervisors need to be alert for new technologies that will enable their departments to operate more efficiently. Supervisors must also project human resource needs and forecast the skills employees will need in the future.

Forecasting helps supervisors anticipate possible changes and their consequences. Supervisors should share information with others. They also need to be concerned with the effects their forecasts may have on their employees and other members of the organization. In so doing, they will be prepared to incorporate needed changes.

In making plans, supervisors should consider strategies that can be helpful in gaining acceptance of the plans by employees, higher-level managers, and/or other supervisors. The application of the strategy will depend on the specific objectives, the people involved, the urgency of the situation, the means available, and a number of other factors. The strategies include the following:

a. Choosing the best timing for proposing the plan, which may mean either taking prompt action when the situation and time for action are advantageous, or moving slowly and cautiously in difficult situations or when major changes are contemplated.

b. Establishing deadlines so that employees are motivated to complete the task within the preestablished time limit.

c. Making a major change all at once to reduce potential resistance to change and accomplish objectives quickly; alternatively, instituting only part of the planned change to see how it works out.

d. Involving other supervisors in the introduction of change.

While there is no one best strategy, supervisors should choose a strategy that is most likely to result in successful implementation of their plans.

Supervisory planning typically focuses on short-term operational matters. This requires that supervisors plan for efficient utilization of the department's space and major physical resources. Such planning may include close coordination with the maintenance department and/or other staff.

Planning for improvement in work procedures and methods means looking for more efficient ways to achieve objectives. Encouraging employees to look for a better way to do the job and periodic work sampling may result in substantial savings for the organization.

A major problem has been loss and theft of materials, supplies, merchandise, data, and other company property. Supervisors must ensure that adequate security precautions are taken to discourage individuals from misusing or stealing items.

Supervisors should have a general understanding of all safety requirements. Safety committees and safety programs are helpful in planning for and bringing about a safe work environment.

Planning work schedules for employees includes establishing reasonable performance requirements and anticipating overtime requirements and absences from the workplace. Many organizations are experimenting with various types of alternative, part-time, and temporary work schedules. Planning for the full utilization of employees is at the core of professional supervision.

Time is one of the supervisor's most valuable resources. Everybody has the same amount of it, so time is not the problem, but how we use it is. Therefore, supervisors must plan and manage their own time if they are to be effective. Supervisors are members of high-stress groups. Better time management means reduced stress.

Supervisors need to analyze and plan their schedules so as to maximize their time on regular and innovative duties and, by delegating and setting priorities, minimize the time they spend on routine and other low-priority tasks.

Since supervisors never seem to have enough time to do all the things that must be done, they must screen their time-use charts to identify the time wasters that "steal" time from them. Some of the basic tools are pocket calendars, weekly or monthly planning sheets, and to-do lists. Establishing priorities, developing a plan, and working the plan are essential to better use of time.

KEY TERMS

Scenario-based forecasting (page 204)
Forecasts (page 205)
Work sampling (page 211)
Cumulative-trauma disorder (page 215)
Stress (page 220)
External stressors (page 221)

Internal stressors (page 221)
Routine duties (page 222)
Regular duties (page 222)
Special duties (page 222)
Innovative duties (page 222)

QUESTIONS FOR DISCUSSION

1. Identify and discuss the most important factors a supervisor should consider in making departmental forecasts.
2. Evaluate the following statement: "Plan your work—work your plan!"
3. Evaluate each of the tactical strategies that can be used in a supervisor's planning function. Then identify guidelines a supervisor should use in choosing which strategy (or combination of strategies) to use in planning.
4. Discuss the supervisor's planning responsibilities for space and other major physical resources and for work procedures and methods.
5. Why has safety planning received more supervisory emphasis in recent years? Outline several steps supervisors can take to plan for a safer work environment.
6. What techniques should a supervisor use to plan for better security of space, materials, supplies, data, and merchandise?
7. Discuss the major considerations supervisors should keep in mind when planning employee work schedules. Discuss the pros and cons of flexible, part-time, and temporary employee scheduling.
8. Analyze the following statement: "Planning for the full utilization of employees is at the core of effective supervision."
9. Discuss each of the following types of supervisory duties in connection with a time-use chart:
   a. Routine duties
   b. Regular duties
   c. Special duties
   d. Innovative duties
10. "Managing stress means managing time." Discuss the meaning of this statement. Can all stress be reduced by better time management? Why or why not?
11. List and explain what a supervisor (like Phil Moore in the "You Make the Call" section) can do to maximize the efforts of his or her employees. Discuss general and specific approaches supervisors can use to plan their own time more effectively.

SKILLS APPLICATIONS

Skills Application 7-1: Getting Control Over Time

1. Ask several supervisors to identify factors that they personally regard as time wasters. From the lists of time wasters, ask each supervisor to identify the one that has the most adverse impact.
2. Ask the supervisors what they would do to minimize the impact of the time wasters.

3. Compare your list with the time wasters discussed in this chapter. To what degree do they coincide or differ? How do you account for the differences?

Skills Application 7-2: Developing a Personal Time Budget

1. Take one hour on Sunday evening as your personal weekly planning period. Develop a time plan for the forthcoming week. List all of the regular tasks that need to be done and estimate the time required for each.
2. Keep a time-use chart for the week, listing all activities and the time spent on each. Compare your time plan with the chart. How well did you plan? Identify the activities (time wasters) that impeded your schedule.
3. Indicate what time management techniques you plan to use in the future.

Skills Application 7-3: Flextime Analysis

You have been given a special assignment by your supervisor. Your charge is to investigate the advantages and disadvantages of flexible work scheduling. Your report is due in one day, so you must do the best you can in the time available.

INTERNET
ACTIVITY

1. Three things you would like to do are as follows:
   a. Visit the local library—or use the Internet—and run a data search to find at least three current articles on the scope of flexible scheduling.
   b. Develop a list of questions you would ask representatives of a firm about their use of flexible scheduling.
   c. Identify a local firm that uses flexible scheduling and interview the human resources manager or staff support person, a supervisor, and an employee using your previously prepared questions.
2. Prepare a list of the other things you might do to complete the project. Estimate the time required for each activity. Are all of the tasks doable within your time limits?
3. Prioritize your activities. If you cannot do everything in the time allotted, which tasks would you focus on first?
4. How did the time limits reinforce the notion that a supervisor's time is a major resource that must be managed carefully?

Skills Application 7-4: Safety First

Search the resources at OSHA's Web site (www.osha.gov), or other workplace safety sites, to learn more about workplace ergonomics.

INTERNET
ACTIVITY

1. Find three examples of successful ergonomics programs. What results did these companies see? What made these companies successful?
2. What components are most important in an ergonomics program?
3. As a supervisor, how can you recognize ergonomics hazards in your workplace?

SKILL
DEVELOPMENT
VIDEO

SKILL DEVELOPMENT MODULE 7–1: PLANNING AND TIME MANAGEMENT

This video segment focuses on Janet Ferrell, store operations supervisor for McElvey Department Store, and her planning and time management skills.

Questions for Discussion: The Ineffective Version

1. Identify what Janet Ferrell does well.
2. Discuss Janet Ferrell's planning and time management techniques.
3. What specific tips for overcoming time wasters does Janet Ferrell violate?
4. What additional planning and/or time management techniques should Janet Ferrell utilize to be more effective?

Questions for Discussion: The More Effective Version

1. Discuss Janet Ferrell's planning and time management techniques.
2. What else can Janet Ferrell do to be a more effective supervisor?
3. Explain the statement, "The quality of Janet Ferrell's planning is largely determined by the quality of her employees."
4. Explain the adage, "Effective planning by Janet Ferrell does not create emergencies for her subordinates."

ENDNOTES

1. See Charles M. Perrottet, "Scenarios for the Future," *Management Review* (January 1996), pp. 43–46.
2. For an expanded discussion on forecasting techniques, see Ricky W. Griffin, *Management* (5th ed.; Boston: Houghton-Mifflin Company, 1996), pp. 702–708. For a detailed discussion of human resource forecasting, see Vido Gulbinas Scarpello, James Ledvinka, and Thomas J. Bergmann, *Human Resource Management: Environment and Functions* (2d ed.; Cincinnati: South-Western Publishing Company, 1995), pp. 206–213.
3. See Kate Walter, "Employee Ideas Make Money," *HRMagazine* (April 1996), pp. 36–39.
4. For information on work sampling techniques, see Lawrence L. Lapin, *Statistics for Modern Business Decisions* (6th ed.; Fort Worth, Texas: Dryden Press, 1993), pp. 344–345; or Lee J. Krajewski and Larry P. Ritzman, *Operations Management; Strategy and Tactics* (3d ed.; Reading Mass.: Addison-Wesley, 1993), pp. 268–271.
5. For information and suggestions concerning various types of security and loss prevention efforts, see Jill A. Fraser, "Prevent Employee Theft," *Inc.* (February 1993), p. 39; Joseph T. Wells, "Internal Fraud and the Credit Business," *Credit World* (January–February 1993), pp. 36–38; Bruce Gathart, "Loss Prevention: Minimizing Risk, Maximizing Deterrents," *Discount Merchandiser* (January 1993), pp. 58–59; and James G. Vigneau, "To Catch a Thief . . . and Other Workplace Investigations," *HRMagazine* (January 1995), pp. 90–95.
6. Jenny C. McCune, "How Safe is Your Data?" *Management Review* (October 1998), pp. 17–21.
7. Wayne F. Cascio, *Managing Human Resources* (5th ed.; Boston: McGraw-Hill, 1998), pp. 566–567.
8. For expanded discussions concerning OSHA and other aspects of safety management, see David A. DeCenzo and Stephen P. Robbins, *Human Resource Management* (6th ed.; New York: John Wiley & Sons, 1999), pp. 418–448; Arthur Sherman, George Bohlander, and Scott Snell, *Managing Human Resources* (11th ed.; Cincinnati: South-Western Publishing Co., 1998), pp. 464–505.
9. From Mike Hall, "Health and Safety on the Job: The Union Difference," *America@Work* (AFL-CIO, March 1999), pp. 10–14.
10. These statistics, other aspects of CTS and CVS, and various approaches to dealing with some of these problems were included in the following: Colleen M. O'Neill, "Courts Turn a Blind Eye to Ergonomic Injuries," *AFL-CIO News* (April 1, 1996), p. 7; and "Work Week," *The Wall Street Journal* (April 9, 1996), p. A1. In early 1999, the U.S. Occupational Safety and Health Administration (OSHA) released a draft "Ergonomics Standard" that would require an employer with one recordable musculoskeletal disorder, such as carpal tunnel syndrome, a back injury, or even swelling, to set up a comprehensive ergonomics program. The major new rules would extend OSHA's enforcement focus beyond manufacturing to

cover financial services and other white-collar office environments, retail establishments, and other service-related industry sectors. At the time of writing of this text, it was not clear whether or not this type of standard would go into effect in the year 2000 as proposed by OSHA. See Gregory R. Watchman, "Federal OSHA Issues Broad Ergonomics Standard," *Legal Report* (July/August, 1999), pp. 4–6.

11. Reuters News Service, "Most Worker Back Woes Begin on the Job," *USA Today* (July 1, 1999), p. 10D.

12. Studies of absenteeism rates are not always consistent. The Bureau of National Affairs, Inc., reported that employee absenteeism during 1993–1995 in the United States was slightly under 2 percent of scheduled workdays. See "Business Bulletin," *The Wall Street Journal* (April 11, 1996), p. A1. Another study, however, which surveyed a cross-section of employees, indicated that the average employee missed about 11 days a year. See "Who Misses Work and Why," *Human Resources Forum* (April 1996), p. 2.

13. See Carla Shore, "Time Share: Emergency Time Pools Can Be a Cost-Effective Way to Give Workers Paid Time Off," *HR Magazine* (December 1998), pp. 104–108.

14. In a mid-1990s survey involving companies of all sizes and industries in the United States and Canada, flextime was reported as being used by 30 percent of the responding firms. See R. Wayne Mondy and Robert M. Noe, *Human Resource Management* (6th ed.; Upper Saddle River, N.J.: Prentice-Hall, Inc., 1996), p. 410. However, another survey also conducted in the mid-90s of 1,000 American employers found that 67 percent of the respondents offered "some kind of flexible scheduling." See John M. Ivancevich, *Human Resource Management* (7th ed.; Boston: McGraw-Hill, 1998), p. 488.

15. From Lin Grensing-Pophal, "Training Supervisors to Manage Teleworkers," *HR Magazine* (January 1999), pp. 67–72.

16. For example, see Sue Shellenbarger, "More Companies Experiment with Workers' Schedules," *The Wall Street Journal* (January 13, 1994), pp. B1 and B6; and D. Keith Denton, "Using Flextime to Create a Competitive Workplace," *Industrial Management* (January–February 1993), pp. 29–31.

17. See Douglas McLeod, "Risks From Hiring Temps May Have Long-Term Effects," *Business Insurance* (April 28, 1997), p. 30; Linda Stockman Vines, "Make Long-Term Temporary Employees Part of the Team," *HRMagazine* (April 1997), pp. 65–70; or Michael Mandel, "Nonstandard Jobs: A New Look," *Business Week* (September 15, 1997), p. 28.

18. For more in-depth analysis concerning temporary employment, see Raymond L. Hilgert, "Understanding and Managing Temporary Employees: Observations and Insights from a Case Study," paper presented at the meetings of the Business/Society/Government Division of the Midwest Business Administration Association (MBAA) (March 1998).

19. For expanded discussions on time management, particularly for supervisors, see R. Alex Mackenzie, *The Time Trap: The New Version of the 20 Year Classic on Time Management* (New York: AMACOM division of American Management Association, 1990); "Developing a Time Budget: How to Live with Tight Deadlines," *Supervisory Management* (November 1995), p. 7; William Keenan, Jr., "Time Management Made Simple," *Sales and Marketing Management* (September 1995), pp. 34–36; Christina Maccherone, "The Secrets of Managing Yourself," *Office Systems* (January 1998), p. 16; Steve Kaye and Irene Kim, "Time Management," *Chemical Engineering* (February 1998), pp. 137–129; Linda R. Dominguez, "Putting an End to Putting it Off," *HRMagazine* (February 1999), pp. 124–129.

20. See R. Wayne Mondy and Robert M. Noe, *Human Resource Management* (6th ed.; Englewood Cliffs, N.J.: Prentice-Hall, 1996), p. 444.

21. See John M. Ivancevich and M. T. Matteson, *Organizational Behavior and Management* (4th ed.; Burr Ridge, Ill.: Richard D. Irwin, 1996), p. 649.

22. From Lyric Wallwork Winik, "Let Go of Stress," *Parade Magazine* (July 11, 1999), pp. 4–6. Also see Michele Himmelberg, "Release Stress Before it Overwhelms You," *St. Louis Post-Dispatch* (August 9, 1999), p. BP22.

23. From Randall S. Schuler, "Managing Stress Means Managing Time," *Personnel Journal* (December 1979), pp. 22–25.

For expanded discussions concerning stress and coping with stress, the following are recommended: John Marks, "Time Out," *U.S. News & World Report* (December 1995), pp. 85–96; Susie Carlton, "Getaways from Stress," *Working Woman* (January 1996), pp. 70–74; Catherine Green, "Dealing with the Stress of Change," *People Management* (November 30, 1995), p. 40; and Suzanne M. Crampton, John W. Hodge, and Jitendra M. Mishra, "Stress and Stress Management," *SAM Advanced Management Journal* (Summer 1995), pp. 10–18.

24. For a detailed discussion and analysis of stress and stress management, see Richard S. DeFrank and John M. Ivancevich, "Stress on the Job: An Executive Update," *Academy of Management Executive* (August 1998), pp. 55–66. For an overview of corporate work/life programs designed in part to reduce work-related stresses, see Barbara Parus, "Survey Links Work/Life Programs to Employee Performance," *ACA News* (June 1, 1999), pp. 14–18. For a report of a study concerning work-related stress that particularly impacts fathers, see "Study Names Conditions that Cause Fathers Stress," *Wisconsin State Journal* (July 18, 1999), p. 8B.

A publication from CDC's National Institute for Occupational Safety and Health (NIOSH) suggests practical approaches that can be taken by employers and employees to prevent workplace stress. *Stress . . . At Work,* DHHS (NIOSH) Publication No. 99-101, offers a three-step process for preventing stress problems by identifying stress factors in the workplace, designing and implementing solutions, and evaluating the outcome. Copies are available by calling the NIOSH toll-free information number, 1-800-35-NIOSH (1-800-356-4674). For information on NIOSH research on work stress and other health and safety issues, call the information number or visit the NIOSH home page at www.cdc.gov/niosh.

25. See Louisa Wah, "The Dear Cost of Scut Work," *Management Review* (June 1999), pp. 27–31. Also see "Prioritize to Combat Stress," *Management Today* (December 1998), p. 83.

THE MICRO-MANAGER

Ann Wilson is 23 years old and a recent college graduate. She received her bachelor's degree in business with a major in human resource management. After graduation, Wilson had no success finding employment in her field of study. She eventually took a sales position with a computer firm and worked part-time as a server at a local restaurant called Caruso's American Cuisine. Actually, she liked her restaurant job better than her sales job, because she felt that the owner respected her and listened to her opinions. While the restaurant business was not exactly where she thought she would end up in life, she decided to accept a full-time position as day-shift supervisor at the restaurant, because it paid well and she felt it was a good opportunity for her to develop her managerial skills.

Several months ago, the owner of the restaurant, Joe Caruso, came to the conclusion that he needed someone to be general manager. Caruso owned several other enterprises, and he usually could be at the restaurant for only a few hours each day. To fill this position, Caruso recruited a local food company sales representative who had serviced the restaurant. Peter Morton, the sales representative, previously had been an assistant manager of a corporate-run steak house in the area. Joe Caruso thought that since Peter Morton already had some managerial experience in the restaurant business, he would be a good candidate. Peter Morton jumped at the opportunity to be general manager, and he accepted the position. His arrival at Caruso's American Cuisine Restaurant was announced in a brief meeting with all of the employees.

Ann Wilson initially felt that having a general manager was a good idea. Too often, she had to make supervisory decisions without having any clear guidance about what to do. She thought that a general manager would make her supervisory position easier. However, she was sadly disappointed in what quickly transpired.

When Peter Morton took over, he set out to change just about everything that previously existed. At an employee meeting, he stated that everyone should follow his lead without question. He made numerous rules, and he posted these rules along with memos that defined in detail other rules and regulations within a new employee handbook that everyone was given. Morton also caused Wilson problems by frequently assigning work directly to the servers and kitchen crews. At times, he reversed Wilson's directives, and, for the most part, he would not inform her about what he had done. Additionally, Morton occasionally made decisions which appeared to contradict some of the rules that he had created for everyone else. In Wilson's mind, Peter Morton was a "micro-manager," and a very poor one at that.

Ann Wilson was thoroughly frustrated. She contemplated having a meeting with Joe Caruso, the owner, but she feared that Peter Morton would retaliate if she did so. Further, Caruso might resent being accused of making a less-than-intelligent decision in hiring Morton for the general manager position. Even with her college major in human resource management, Wilson did not know what to do. She believed that the restaurant was doing about the same level of business as previously. However, she also felt that both customers and employees would be "deserting" the restaurant in droves if the situation created by Peter Morton was not corrected.

Questions for Discussion

1. Evaluate Peter Morton as a new manager. Why do you suppose he acted as he did?
2. If you had been Peter Morton, how would you have gone about planning for managing the restaurant?
3. If Ann Wilson reports the situation to Joe Caruso, what should he do?
4. If Peter Morton becomes aware of Ann Wilson's concerns, what should she do? Do you think he would retaliate against Wilson?
5. Evaluate Ann Wilson's position, and consider her options. If you were her, what would you do?

Case

2-2

A SHORTAGE OF POLICIES

Montclair Manufacturing Company produces a wide array of electronic gauges and employs about 250 people. Chuck Adams, the factory superintendent, was eating his lunch in the company cafeteria with Bill Whitaker and Gerry Parker, two supervisors on the assembly line; Mary Stoebeck, the purchasing agent; and Werner Koff, one of the district sales managers. Their conversation centered around a common complaint, namely, that the company had few written policies or guidelines and that this lack caused them unnecessary discomfort when they had to make decisions. Adams deplored the fact that some employees ate their lunches at the workbench, and he felt that there should be a policy forbidding this practice. Whitaker and Parker mentioned the need for a policy on granting employees leaves of absence. Stoebeck stated that she needed a clear policy specifying how to obtain bids from prospective suppliers. Koff was concerned that top-level management had not bothered to issue a policy regarding whether salespeople should wear informal sportswear or conventional business attire when making calls. In addition to these specific concerns, there were numerous other complaints that reflected a feeling of dissatisfaction among the company's managers.

The group concluded that the best way to attack this problem would be to confront the president of the company, Jay Montclair, with their questions and ask him to define policies in these and other areas. While they were deliberating this, May Murphy, the assistant to the president, joined them at lunch and listened to much of the conversation. Murphy asked, "Are these really matters for the president to decide, or should you as supervisors be making these types of decisions for your own departments?"

Questions for Discussion

1. Analyze each of the individual problem situations mentioned in the case. For which areas should policies have come from top-level management, and for which areas should policies have been made by departmental supervisors?
2. Is there an appropriate dividing line between policies to be made by top-level management and policies that must be made at the departmental level? Discuss.
3. Should the group of supervisors confront the president of the company with a request for more clearly defined policies? What strategies might be suggested for the supervisors to bring their concerns to the company president?

Case
2-3

INTERPRETING FUNERAL-LEAVE POLICY

Joan Sutherland supervised a unit of 15 nurses who worked on the evening shift at a large hospital located in a midwestern city. She had recently been promoted to the position of supervisor after having worked as a registered nurse in another unit in the hospital for three years.

One day Sutherland received a telephone call from one of her employees, a licensed practical nurse named Betty Sherman who had been employed at the hospital for about four years. It was obvious from Sherman's voice that she was upset; she had difficulty in speaking without crying. She said, "My Aunt Frances passed away last night. She was my foster mother who helped raise me for several years during my teens, after my parents separated and my mother remarried. I will need several days off in order to attend the funeral. Aunt Frances lived about 50 miles away from here, and the rest of the family will be gathering there this afternoon."

Joan Sutherland replied, "I'm terribly sorry that you had this death in your family. Let me check the policy manual to see what you are entitled to." Quickly, she opened the policy manual to the section marked "Death in Family." The section read as follows:

In the event of death in your immediate family (spouse, child, parent, brother, sister, father-in-law, mother-in-law), if you are a permanent employee, you will be granted an excused absence with pay of up to $3\frac{1}{2}$ successive days following the death.

Joan Sutherland said, "I'm not sure whether this policy provides time off for the death of a foster parent. I'll call the human resources department to see whether they have a ruling. Let me call you right back." With that she dialed the human resources department office, but she was informed by a secretary that the director of human resources would be out of town until the following week. The secretary did not know whether the hospital provided for funeral-leave benefits to employees who lost a foster parent.

As Joan Sutherland hung up the telephone, she wondered what she should say to Betty Sherman.

Questions for Discussion

1. Should the policy of the hospital be interpreted to include an employee's foster mother as part of the immediate family? Discuss.
2. What should Joan Sutherland do? Consider various alternatives that are open to her.
3. What are the precedent implications of this case?

Case

2-4

CONFLICT WITH THE NEPOTISM POLICY

Tim Simon was a proficient programmer/analyst who had worked for Global Investment Corporation for about two years. Among a group of eight programmers/analysts who worked for Henry Dillon, supervisor of the information systems department, Simon was the most requested and well-respected programmer/analyst in the company. Simon had a very quiet demeanor; yet some controversy was associated with him.

The controversy concerned his relationship with Candace Franklin, the human resources department administrative assistant. They had begun dating about a year after Simon joined the company. Franklin was a vibrant and lively person who was very friendly and talkative with everyone. Franklin had been with the company for about four years; she was hired as a clerk and was promoted to HR administrative assistant reporting to Delores Thomas, the human resources manager. Franklin had been very open and frank in discussing her romantic involvement with Simon. Simon, however, kept rather quiet about his relationship with Franklin.

Simon tried to maintain a professional relationship with everyone, including Franklin, while on company premises. However, off the job—besides dating—Franklin and Simon were very social with other employees in the information systems department and with other employees in the company. It was common for employee groups to have parties, gatherings, and even exchange baby-sitting roles for each others' families. At such employee gatherings, Franklin was known to talk about all types of company information, including who had received promotions, pay increases, and other human resource matters. Simon was uncomfortable about this, but he normally kept quiet when Franklin was sharing information of this nature with other employees.

Without any prior warning, Tim Simon suddenly announced his resignation to his boss, Henry Dillon. Everyone was astonished at this since he was an excellent programmer/analyst and popular with everyone both personally and professionally. Simon stated that he had resigned to accept another position, although his real reason was that he and Candace Franklin were soon to be married. Simon did not want to endanger either his position or Franklin's position in the company because of marriage since they both believed that one or the other would be forced to leave the company because of the company's nepotism policy. Simon felt that it would be better for him to leave voluntarily and on his own terms.

About a month later, Tim Simon and Candace Franklin were married in a private family ceremony. This came as a surprise to most of the people at the company since Franklin had not told anyone about her wedding plans. About three months after Simon and Franklin were married, Henry Dillon was still distressed that he could not find an appropriate replacement for Tim Simon. Dillon decided to telephone Tim Simon, and Simon confided to Dillon that he was not happy with his new position at a bank. Dillon asked Simon whether he would be interested in returning to Global Investment Corporation. Tim Simon responded that he might be interested in returning to his former position, but he did not think this was possible based on what he knew about the company's nepotism policy.

Shortly after having his conversation with Tim Simon, Henry Dillon decided to talk with Delores Thomas, human resources manager, about the nepotism policy and how it would apply in this situation. Dillon and Thomas reviewed the company policy as stated in the employee handbook. The relevant portions of this policy follow:

A member of an employee's immediate family will not be considered for employment by Global Investment Corporation. "Immediate family" includes: the employee's spouse, brother, sister, parents, children, step-children, father-in-law, mother-in-law, sister-in-law, brother-in-law, daughter-in-law, son-in-law, and any other member of the employee's household.

Employees who marry or who become members of the same household may continue employment as long as there is not:

- *A direct or indirect supervisor/subordinate relationship between such employees; or*
- *An actual conflict of interest or the appearance of a conflict of interest.*

Should one of the above situations occur, management will attempt to find a suitable position within the company to which one of the affected employees may transfer. If accommodations of this nature are not feasible, the employees will be permitted to determine which one will resign. Employees who resign under these circumstances shall remain for up to 120 days while they search for new employment.

After reviewing the policy and discussing a number of its provisions, Henry Dillon said to Delores Thomas, "I really would like to rehire Tim Simon. He was the best programmer/analyst that I ever had, and it was a major loss when he left the company. We need him back. Can I rehire him, or would this be a violation of company policy?"

Questions for Discussion

1. What actions, if any, could Henry Dillon and/or Delores Thomas have taken during early phases of the relationship between Tim Simon and Candace Franklin?
2. Why was Candace Franklin's position in the human resources department a complicating factor in the relationship that she had with Tim Simon and other employees? Discuss.
3. Would it be appropriate for Global Investment Corporation to rehire Tim Simon after he was married to Candace Franklin and previously had resigned? Discuss.

INTERNET ACTIVITY

4. (*Optional*) The practice of showing favoritism to relatives in employment matters, usually referred to as *nepotism,* can lead to a potential conflict of interest and charges of discrimination. Using the Internet, find relevant sources of information to determine whether corporate antinepotism rules are fair or unfair. Note: At the time of text publication, there were numerous sources available by entering the key words of "nepotism" or "anti-nepotism," for example, *http://www.fairmeasures.com* addressed the legal risks of antinepotism policies.

   After completing your search, write a short paper in which you:

   a. Make a list of the reasons why a company should have a nepotism policy.
   b. Make a list of the reasons why a company should not have a nepotism policy.
   c. Analyze and discuss the following statement: "Global Investment Corporation has the right and responsibility to restrict employment opportunities for family members and close friends of employees."

Case

2–5

THE SNOW DAY STIR

It was mid-February in a midwestern city when a major snowstorm was predicted for the following day. The forecast was for 8 to 12 inches of snow. Weather conditions normally weren't a concern for Wiess Products Company. However, in this situation management distributed a memorandum informing plant employees that if the plant was to be closed due to heavy snow, such a closing would be announced on local radio stations at 6:00 A.M.

On the morning of February 14 snow was falling, but it had only accumulated 1 to 2 inches by 6:00 A.M., and the plant wasn't closed. Virtually all the first-shift employees made it to work, and the snow continued to fall. At approximately 1:30 P.M., two hours before the end of the shift, the snow was still falling, and it had accumulated to 8 inches. After consulting with the company president, the director of human resources, Dick Smear, announced that the plant was closing. The first-shift employees were sent home, and second-shift employees were contacted by telephone about the closing. Radio announcements to the same effect were broadcast by several local stations at 2:00 P.M.

On the following day, again after consulting with the company president, Dick Smear announced that all plant employees would receive eight hours' pay for February 14. Wiess was a nonunion plant, and there was no formal policy for this type of event since this was the first such occurrence. Because all supervisors were salaried, they, too, would be paid as usual, even though the second-shift supervisors had stayed home on February 14. In Smear's announcement, he said that the company felt that employees should not suffer a loss of income for circumstances beyond their control.

The announcement that all employees would receive eight hours' pay for February 14 created a stir on the shop floor. It was around 3:30 P.M. when the shifts were in the process of changing. The first-shift employees were loudly complaining that it wasn't fair that they had to work for six hours, and that second-shift employees didn't have to work at all but still received eight hours' pay. This stir escalated when Carla Peters, a first-shift operator, and David Carpenter, a second-shift operator, started debating the fairness of the issue. A heated argument ensued among them and several other employees.

A first-shift supervisor, Doug Beck, and a second-shift supervisor, Marta Tropp, heard the argument and went to the floor to check out the situation. When they found out what the argument was about, Beck told Tropp that he agreed with Carla Peters. Beck said that it was "grossly unfair" that first-shift employees and supervisors who worked and had to contend with traveling in the snow were not treated any differently from the second-shift workers who had stayed comfortably at home. The conversation was going nowhere, so Beck and Tropp told the employees to "cool off" and that they would go see Dick Smear to review the matter further. Peters and Carpenter responded that the employees felt that the matter had been handled poorly and that the company managers should have consulted with the employees and supervisors before making such a decision.

Questions for Discussion

1. Do you agree with the company managers' decision in this situation? Why or why not? If you disagree, what would you have done differently?
2. Should the managers have consulted with any of the employees or supervisors before making the decision to pay everyone for the snow day? Discuss.
3. If you were Dick Smear, what would you recommend to the company president, and why?

Case

2-6

ETHICAL EXPENSE REPORTING

Ron Bush was supervisor of a merchandise sales department at the headquarters of a major retail store chain operation. He had been hired several years previously, and he currently was pursuing an MBA degree on a part-time basis. His salary had been adjusted upward because of his good performance at the firm, and he was participating in the company profit-sharing plan.

Bush was planning a business trip to Washington, D.C., that was to occur in about two months. In a conversation with another merchandise sales department supervisor, Kristy Whitcomb, he mentioned his forthcoming trip. Whitcomb proceeded to tell him that she had just returned from a business trip to Florida on which she had taken her husband along with her. Whitcomb said that they stayed an extra weekend and "really painted the town red on Saturday night." She confided to Bush that she put the entire weekend through as part of her expense report.

Bush pointed out to Whitcomb that the employee policy handbook stated that only "business-related expenses" were supposed to be reimbursed by the company. Whitcomb responded that she figured that all of her expenses including entertainment were part of a business trip. She rationalized that the plane fare did not cost the company any more by not leaving until Sunday, and she had been working very hard. Why shouldn't the company pay for her husband to stay with her and have a good time relaxing? Besides, she had been working long hours and had been out of town frequently; she was due some additional "rest and recreation." Whitcomb also told Bush that her manager did not reject any of the expenses that she had turned in, so it must have been all right; otherwise her manager would not have approved it.

A week or so after their discussion, there was a company reorganization. Kristy Whitcomb was promoted to a position of division marketing manager. With the departmental changes, Ron Bush now was a supervisor reporting directly to Whitcomb. Nothing more had been said about the conversation that they had regarding business expenses.

Several weeks later, Ron Bush went on his business trip, and he decided to invite his wife along for the weekend. Bush's wife had always wanted to go to Washington, D.C., and it was close to their wedding anniversary date. Bush rented a car and enjoyed the weekend entertaining his wife and seeing the sights. He saved all of their travel and other expenses and entertainment receipts. As he was relaxing on the flight home, Bush wondered whether he should submit all of the expenses that he had incurred on his trip to Washington, D.C.

Questions for Discussion

1. What are some of the ethical issues facing Ron Bush in this situation?
2. Enumerate and evaluate some of the alternatives that are open to Ron Bush.
3. Using the ethical "tests" identified in Chapter 5 as guidelines, what choice or choices should Ron Bush make in this situation?

Case

2-7

BREAK TIME IS MY TIME

Hi-Fi Tool & Die (HFTD) was a year-old division of Great Audio Dynamite (GAD), the market leader in compact disc replication machines. Being a young company, HFTD had not yet completed its own employee handbook, so in an effort to proceed with daily operations, HFTD had implemented GAD's employee handbook on an interim basis.

HFTD operated in a rural county on the outskirts of a major city. During its start-up year, GAD promoted some of the firm's best younger personnel into managerial roles at HFTD, and the remainder of the organization was staffed by HFTD's managers. Hiring quality workers to meet production demands became a formidable task as neighboring area companies had excellent wages and benefits to offer. In an effort to attract good workers to the company, HFTD advertised and promoted the advantages of a nonunion work environment and its generous packages of wages, benefits, and flexible work hours. When this failed to increase the pool of potential candidates, HFTD began to hire almost any applicant that walked through the door. This did not seem to pose major problems, since HFTD implemented GAD's well-established employee training programs to bring new employees "up to speed" as soon as possible.

During the hiring process, close relatives, including siblings and spouses, were hired due to the competitive circumstances. Informal suggestions to hire relatives were the norm at company lunches and social settings outside of business hours. Sid and Nancy Hendrix were both employed by HFTD. Nancy was hired as a draftsperson based on a previous job experience, while Sid was offered an interview and subsequently a job following a chance meeting with Tim Armstrong, production supervisor, at a local restaurant.

Both Sid and Nancy Hendrix were model employees. Sid was hired to work on the production floor operating industrial machines. He had completed his operator and teamwork training at a local college, and he graduated from the program at the top of his class. HFTD management saw Sid as being "highly promotable" and assigned him as a team leader on the first-shift production crew. Nancy worked in the office area of the company. Located just steps from the production floor, Nancy's job involved completing production drawings for use in the shop. Like Sid, Nancy also had taken coursework at the local community college and had received high marks in all of her pursuits. Based on her performance, HFTD was considering Nancy for a possible supervisory position next fall.

However, Tim Armstrong, Sid's supervisor, was not at all happy at what he frequently had observed. Tim Armstrong noticed that during production floor break periods, Sid Hendrix usually made his way into the office to spend his 15-minute break allotments with Nancy. Since Nancy worked within the office, she was not given a formal break period, but she could take breaks as needed. Sid and Nancy Hendrix usually spent this time together discussing family matters, and they did not interfere with the work operations of other employees.

Since Sid Hendrix had recently been promoted to crew leader, Tim Armstrong felt that production floor break time should be used by Sid to establish and improve relationships important to his production team. From his own experiences, Tim had found that break periods were an opportune time to get closer with his people on an informal level and to open lines of communication for work-related activities.

After explaining his point of view to Sid Hendrix on several occasions, Tim Armstrong became discouraged when Sid refused to change his ways. Sid stood firm in his response that, "Break time is my time!" Sid also went so far as to say, "If you don't like it, fire me!" Tim Armstrong contemplated the situation at hand and was struggling with how to resolve the issue with Sid. Tim considered whether he should consult with his boss (the plant manager) or with GAD's human resources director before taking any further action. Tim also wondered about how Nancy's supervisor, Angie Gilbert, felt about this situation.

Questions for Discussion

1. Evaluate Tim Armstrong's situation with Sid Hendrix. Do you agree that Tim should try to enforce his "break time is for team building" concept?
2. Should Tim Armstrong consult with anyone prior to resolving this issue? If so, whom?
3. What factors should Tim Armstrong consider when making his decision?
4. If you were Tim Armstrong, what would you do?

Case

2-8

GO HOME, BOB

Maria Martinez was a supervisor in a claims processing department of a state welfare agency. Martinez supervised 12 employees who worked on various aspects of processing and accounting for payments of dependent benefit claims.

One day Martinez received a report from several of her employees that Bob Turner, a clerk in the department, had a severe cold and cough and was disturbing other employees in the department. The employees told Martinez that Turner's "wheezing and coughing" were annoying and that they feared catching his cold. Subsequently, Martinez approached Turner and suggested that he go home and get some rest to improve his condition. Turner replied, "I'm not ill; I've got a little cough, but that's all." At this point Martinez stated, "Bob, I think you should go home because other employees are complaining about your condition." Turner replied, "You can't make me go home. I'm not ill. Besides, I've used up all my allowed sick leave days for this year, and you'll probably discipline me for being off again if I go home today." Martinez replied, "Are you telling me, Bob, that you won't go home like I've told you to do?" Turner responded, "If you try to force me out of here, I'll go to human resources and the agency's executive director about this because it just wouldn't be right for you to send me home! You're always complaining about people being off from work, and here I'm at work and you're making a big issue over a little cough." Martinez pondered what she should say and do next.

Questions for Discussion

1. What options are open to Maria Martinez if Bob Turner continues to refuse to go home as requested?
2. Evaluate Bob Turner's reasons for not going home. Which are most persuasive? Least persuasive?
3. If Turner is disciplined in this case—either for insubordination or for excessive sick days—and he complains to the human resources department or higher-level management, how should higher-level management or the human resources department respond to such a complaint? Discuss.

Case

2–9

THE BUSY MANAGER

Paul Jackson, president of Laclede Manufacturing Company, arrived at his desk and found a stack of papers on it, although he remembered that he had cleared everything away before he left at eight o'clock the pervious night. He asked his secretary what these papers contained. She informed him that they had arrived in the mail late yesterday afternoon and that they were requisitions and letters for authorization from the Texas plant. Since she had read them, he asked her to tell him briefly what each request contained. He thought he could save time by doing this. The discussion went as follows:

SECRETARY: Request for approval for the purchase of five acres of land adjoining the Ft. Worth plant amounting to $215,000, as discussed while you were in Ft. Worth the last time.

JACKSON: Okay, I'll sign it.

SECRETARY: Request for approval to purchase an additional computer and printer for word processing, $4,500.

JACKSON: I know nothing about this. Please inquire why it is needed and who is supposed to get it.

SECRETARY: Requisition for a new sign at the entrance of the plant costing $990.

JACKSON: Okay, I'll sign it.

SECRETARY: Request for approval to place an ad amounting to $200 as a contribution to the local Police Circus.

JACKSON: Why not! I'll approve.

SECRETARY: Requisition to contribute $1,000 to the company's bowling league expenses.

JACKSON: Absolutely not. Get some more information on this.

SECRETARY: This needs your approval, also. Some of the offices need painting, and the contractor's estimate is $3,200. (Jackson didn't answer, but put his signature on this paper.)

SECRETARY: Request for approval of the purchase of stationery and factory work tickets, totaling $855. (Again, Jackson signed the paper without comment.)

On and on it went. After more than an hour, Paul Jackson was finished with these requisitions, and all the other incoming mail from the morning was placed on his desk. As he started to read, he received numerous telephone calls. He was informed that five people were waiting in the anteroom to discuss some matters with him. While he was still reading the mail, his secretary informed him that the plant superintendent had an important problem on the factory floor and asked that he come to the plant at once. Jackson immediately left his desk and returned after half an hour, wondering to himself why the superintendent could not have solved the problem on his own. All day things were piled up regardless of how many decisions he made and how many problems he solved.

On his way home late in the afternoon, Paul Jackson asked himself, "Why do I seem to be so terribly busy and yet, when the day is over, I don't know where all the hours have gone? The day passes all too quickly, and too little is accomplished. And there are so many people who think that being the president of a company is a soft job."

Questions for Discussion

1. What is the major problem in this case? Why?
2. What would you recommend to Paul Jackson to help him manage personal time? Discuss.
3. How can a subordinate (e.g., the secretary or a supervisor) help his or her manager manage time more effectively?

Organizing

Concepts of Organizing

You Make the Call!

You are Alice Austin, supervisor of the information services department of Gatewood Community College. You supervise about 15 word processors and administrative service employees. You report directly to the dean of administration, who in turn reports to the president of the college. However, your department is located in a different classroom building since you provide services for faculty as well as for other administrative, operations, and maintenance departments.

Several problems facing you have grown in recent months. Although all work orders and requests are supposed to come directly through you, faculty members, supervisors, administrators, and others are taking their work requests directly to individual employees in the department. The dean of administration and the college president or their secretaries have bypassed you on occasion by making direct work requests or demanding expedited services from selected employees. Several employees have told you that these requests or demands were impossible to meet, or that they required shifting other job requests or priorities that you had established. The matter came to a head this morn-ing. While you were temporarily out of the office, two faculty members from the psychology department came into your office and gave instructions to two employees to have a major report typed by the next day. When your employees protested, the faculty members became vocal and angry and criticized them in front of other employees in the department. Hearing this report, you know that you will have to do something to remedy these problems.

What should you do?

You Make the Call!

1
Identify the organizing function of management.

ORGANIZING AS AN ESSENTIAL MANAGERIAL FUNCTION

As one of the five major functions of management, the organizing function requires that every manager be concerned with building, developing, and maintaining working relationships that will help achieve the organization's objectives. Although organizations may have a variety of objectives and may operate in many kinds of environments, the fundamental principles of organizing are universal.

A manager's organizing function consists of designing a structure—that is, grouping activities and assigning them to specific work units (e.g., departments, teams). Organizing includes establishment of formal authority and responsibility relationships among the various activities and departments. In order to make such a structure possible, management must delegate authority throughout the organization and establish and clarify authority relationships among the departments. We will use the term **organization** to refer to any type of group structured by management to carry out designated functions and accomplish certain objectives.

Management should design the structure and establish authority relationships based on sound principles and organizational concepts, such as delegation of authority, unity of command, span of supervision, division of work, departmentation, and line and staff authority.

Organizing the overall activities of the enterprise is the responsibility of the chief executive. However, eventually it becomes the responsibility of supervisors to organize their departments. Therefore, supervisors must understand what it means to organize. Although the range and magnitude of problems associated with the organizing function are broader at higher managerial levels than for supervisors, the principles to be applied are the same.

Organization
Group structured by management to carry out designated functions and accomplish certain objectives.

Organizations Are People

Throughout this chapter's discussions on the concepts and principles of organizing, never forget that people are the substance and essence of any organization, irrespective of how the enterprise is structured. Managers and supervisors may become so preoccupied with developing and monitoring the formal structure that they neglect the far more important aspects of relationships with and among their people. For example, a major survey of a large cross-section of employees revealed that 70 percent of the "core workers" said they were committed to the success of their firms, but only about half of them felt that their organizations really cared about their job satisfaction. Significantly, too, these workers claimed that their sense of loyalty to their firms had been threatened by their dissatisfaction with the many organizational changes they had experienced.[1]

It is not an oversimplification to state that organizational success is more likely to happen if employees truly are given top-priority attention by their managers and supervisors.[2] Our focus in this chapter will be on building sound organizational structures which can provide building blocks and foundations that support the mutual goals of effective work performance and high job satisfaction. Following good and accepted organizational principles does not ensure organizational success, but it usually means preventing many problems and irritations that otherwise would occur.

2

Explain the unity of command principle and its applications.

UNITY OF COMMAND AND AUTHORITY RELATIONSHIPS

Unity of command principle

Principle that holds that each employee should report directly to only one supervisor.

The chief executive groups the activities of the organization into divisions, departments, services, teams, or units and assigns duties accordingly. Upper-level management places managers and supervisors in charge of divisions and departments and defines their authority relationships. Supervisors must know exactly who their managers and their subordinates are. To arrange authority relationships in this fashion, management normally follows the **unity of command principle,** which holds that each employee should report directly to only one immediate supervisor, that is, there is only one person to whom the employee is directly accountable. Formal communications and delegation of authority normally flow upward and downward through the chain of command, although there are exceptions such as the use of functional authority and matrix organizational structure, which are discussed later in this chapter. Similarly, the use of task forces, project groups, and committees to handle certain types of assignments may blur the unity of command concept. Committees and problem-solving groups are discussed in later chapters.

Since Biblical times, at least, it has been recognized that it is difficult, if not impossible, to serve two masters. Having more than one supervisor usually leads to unsatisfactory performance by the employee due to confusion of authority. When the principle of unity of command is violated, conflicts or confusion usually result. Therefore, a supervisor should make certain that—unless there is a valid reason for an exception to be made—only one supervisor gives directives to an employee.

3
Define the span of management principle and the factors that influence its application.

Span of management principle
There is an upper limit to the number of subordinates that a supervisor can manage effectively.

THE SPAN OF MANAGEMENT PRINCIPLE

The establishment of departments and the creation of several managerial levels are not ends in themselves; actually, they are the source of numerous difficulties. Departments are expensive because they must be staffed by supervisors and employees. Moreover, as more departments and levels are created, communication and coordination problems arise. Therefore, there must be valid reasons for creating levels and departments. The reasons are associated with the **span of management principle,** which holds that there is an upper limit to the number of employees a supervisor can effectively manage. Often this principle is called "span of supervision," "span of authority," or "span of control" (see Figure 8-1).

Because no one can manage an unlimited number of people, top-level managers must organize divisions and departments as separate operating units and place middle-level managers and supervisors in charge. Top-level managers then delegate authority to the middle-level managers, who redelegate authority to supervisors, who in turn supervise the employees. If a manager could supervise 100 or more employees effectively, each of the 100 would report directly to that manager and their different activities would not have to be grouped into departments. Of course, such a wide span of management is not practical.

The principle that a manager can effectively supervise a limited number of employees is as old as recorded history.[3] However, it is not possible to state a definite figure as to how many subordinates a manager should have. It is only correct to say that there is some upper limit to this number. In many industrial concerns, the top-level executive will have from three to eight subordinate managers. But the span of management usually increases the farther down a person is within the managerial hierarchy. It is not unusual to find a span of management of from 15 to 25 employees at the first level of supervision.

FIGURE 8-1

A manager can effectively supervise only a certain number of employees.

contemporary issue

Is Bigness Badness?

There appears to be no end to the longstanding debate about what size of a firm or organization is optimal. The managerial principle of *span of control* suggests that there is an upper limit to the number of persons and functions that a manager can effectively manage. Does such a principle extend to the question of the size of an organization itself?

Tom Brown, a contributing editor of *Across the Board,* a journal published by the Conference Board, has concluded from his review of literature that the answer to the above question is an authoritative "maybe so, maybe not." Brown points out that there are those who assert that mega-size corporations by their very nature are inefficient, and that a merger or acquisition of one mega-size corporation with another mega-size firm raises even more serious problems of effective management due to corporate bloat. Some organizational theorists and practitioners even claim that the optimal size of a firm is somewhere in the range of only 150 to 400 personnel.

However, the "bigness is badness" premise is probably an oversimplification. Brown notes that the evidence seems to show that managerial strategies and approaches are far more important than the mere size of a firm itself. If management learns to "reach out and connect" the tens of thousands of people working within a mega-corporation, there may be no maximum size that inhibits an organization from being effective. Mitchell Marks, an organizational psychologist and consultant who has spent 15 years studying scores of mergers and acquisitions, has concluded that there is no optimal size for an organization. More importantly, Marks advocates a managerial strategy and approach for managers at any level who want to bring "hugeness down to size." Among his recommended strategies to management are: sell people throughout the organization on the need for a large organization to compete in the marketplace; define and establish priorities for each unit and division in the structure; clearly specify to each individual what that person's role will be to help the corporation succeed; and communicate thoroughly at all levels by whatever means, particularly by listening as much as talking.

Whether or not managers in the 21st century will seriously address the issue of corporate size and what to do about it probably will remain an open question.

Source: Adapted from Tom Brown, "How Big Is Too Big?: Are Corporations Growing So Large That They Are Becoming Unmanageable?" *Across the Board* (July/August 1999), pp. 15–20.

Although there is no direct corollary organizational principle regarding actual sizes of organizations themselves, there long has been a question concerning the link between organizational size and organizational performance. The economic "law of diminishing returns" has been applied to suggest that organizational efficiency can be impacted by size considerations. However, the "optimal size" for a firm has never been defined, and the search for such a concept remains elusive. This chapter's "Contemporary Issue" box addresses the nature of the organizational size debate and some important related considerations.

Factors Influencing the Span of Management

The number of employees that one person can supervise effectively depends on a number of factors, such as the abilities of the supervisor, the types and amounts of staff assistance available, the employees' capabilities, the location of employees, the kinds of activities performed, and the degree of objective performance standards in place.

Supervisory Competence. Among the most significant factors that influence the span of management are the training, experience, and know-how that the supervisor possesses—in other words, the supervisor's competence. Some supervisors are capable of handling more employees than others. Some are better acquainted with good management principles, have had more experience, and are better managers overall. For example, what a supervisor does during the time available is of major importance. The supervisor who must make individual decisions on every departmental problem takes more time than does the supervisor who has established policies, procedures, and rules that simplify decision making on routine problems. Comprehensive planning can reduce the number of decisions the supervisor has to make and hence increase the potential span of management. Thus, the number of employees a supervisor can supervise effectively depends to some degree on the supervisor's managerial capabilities.

Specialized Staff Assistance. Another factor on which the span of management depends is the availability of help from specialists within the organization. If numerous staff experts are available to provide specialized advice and service, then the span of management can be wider. For example, when a human resources department assists supervisors in recruiting, selecting, and training employees, supervisors have more time available for their departments. If supervisors themselves are obligated to do all or most of these activities, then they cannot devote that portion of time to otherwise managing their departments. Therefore, the amount and quality of staff assistance available influence the span of management.

Employee Abilities. How broad a span a supervisor can handle also depends on the abilities and knowledge of employees in the department. The greater the employees' capacities for self-direction, the broader the feasible span. Here, of course, the employees' training and experience are important. For example, the span of management could be greater with fully qualified mechanics than with inexperienced mechanics. However, the factor of employee competence may be offset to some degree by the location of the employees and by the nature of the activities being performed.

Location of Employees. The location and proximity of employees to a supervisor can be a factor in influencing the span of management. When departmental employees are all located in close proximity to each other and to the supervisor—such as being in the same office or same part of a building—a supervisor generally can supervise more employees because observation and communication are relatively easy. However, if the employees are widely dispersed—such as being located in different stores, or working in their homes, or working as separate outdoor crews throughout a metropolitan area—this may limit the span of management somewhat because of probable communication and coordination difficulties. Problems associated with managing telecommuting employees and others involved in work-at-home and other alternative work scheduling arrangements were previously discussed in Chapter 7.[4]

When employees are located close to each other and the supervisor, the supervisor can easily observe and communicate with them.

Nature and Complexity of Activities. The amount, nature, complexity, and predictability of activities influence the span of management. The simpler, routine, and more uniform the work activities, the greater the number of people one supervisor can manage. If the tasks are repetitive, the span may be as broad as 25 or more employees. If the activities are varied or interdependent, or if errors would have serious consequences, the span may be as small as 3 to 5. In departments engaged in relatively unpredictable activities—for example, nurses in an intensive care unit in a hospital—the span will tend to be narrow. In departments concerned with fairly stable activities—such as an assembly line or a word processing center—the span can be broader.

Objective Performance Standards. Still another factor influencing the span of management is whether a department has ample objective standards for guiding and measuring employee performance. If each employee knows exactly what standards are expected—for example, a certain number of sales units each week, or the production of a specific amount each day—the supervisor will not need to have frequent discussions with employees about performance. Thus, good standards support a broader span of management.

Weighing the Factors

As stated previously, there is no set number of employees that a supervisor can manage effectively. The principle of span of management indicates only that an upper limit exists. In most situations there must be a weighing (or balancing) of the factors just discussed to arrive at an appropriate span of management for each supervisor. Such weighing of factors for the most part is the responsibility of higher-level management, although supervisors often will be asked to express their opinions concerning what they believe is an appropriate span of management for their departments.

How Managerial Levels and Span of Management Are Related

If a higher-level manager concludes that the span of management for a certain activity or department is too broad, he or she may decide to divide the span into two or three groups and place someone in charge of each group. By narrowing the span to a smaller number of employees, the manager creates another organizational level because a supervisor or "lead person" has to be placed over each of the smaller groups. A **lead person,** sometimes called a "working supervisor," usually is not considered to be part of management, especially in unionized firms. Nevertheless, these individuals perform most of the managerial functions, although their authority is somewhat limited, particularly in evaluation and discipline of employees.

Lead person

Employee placed in charge of other employees who performs limited managerial functions but is not considered part of management.

Other things being equal, the narrower the span of management becomes, the more managerial levels have to be introduced into organizational design. Stating this another way, organizational structures will tend to be taller when spans of management are narrower, and structures will tend to be flatter when spans of management are wider, especially at the supervisory level. Of course, this is only a generalization that may vary because of other organizational considerations. Adding or reducing levels of management may or may not be desirable. For example, adding levels can be costly and complicate communication and decision making. On the other hand, reducing levels may widen the spans of management to the extent that supervisors become overburdened and cannot maintain adequate control of employees and activities of the department. Thus, there is a trade-off between the width of the span and the number of levels. The managerial problem is: which is best—a broad span with few levels, or a narrower span with more levels? (see Figure 8-2 on page 256). This is an important question that often confronts higher management. A first-line supervisor normally does not directly confront this question, but supervisors should understand how it influences the design and structure of their organizations.

Organizational Changes from Restructuring. In recent decades, many firms have undergone major downsizing and restructuring changes. There have been numerous reports about the wholesale reductions of middle management and supervisory positions. However, assertions that there has been a total demise of middle management and supervision have been exaggerated. According to a number of studies, the number of managers per one hundred employees has declined only slightly in the last decade. For example, according to data from major corporations compiled by the Equal Employment Opportunity Commission, in the mid-1990s there were 11.17 managers per one hundred employees as compared with 11.83 at the outset of the decade. Thus, although it is true that thousands of middle managers and supervisors lost their jobs and many organizations were flattened, nevertheless major opportunities for line managers and

| FIGURE 8-2 | How span of management and organizational levels are related. |

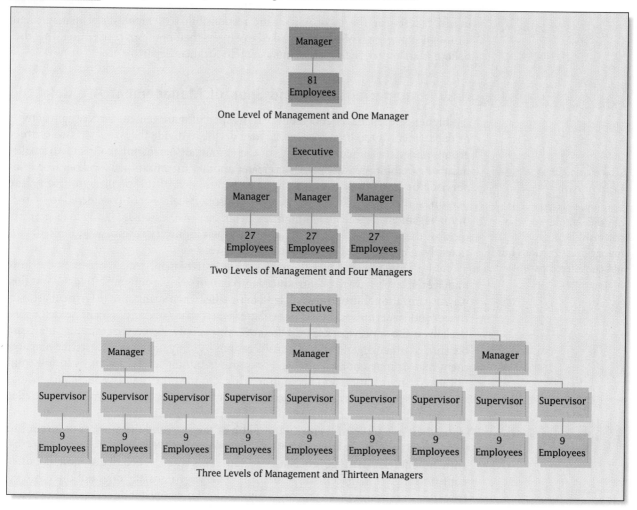

professional staff managers opened because of changes in technology, operations, and marketing opportunities.[5] It would appear that the overall impact of organizational restructuring on middle managers and supervisors perhaps has been more on where they are placed rather than on their numbers per se. The impact of organizational downsizing is discussed in more detail later in this chapter.

Describe departmentation and alternative approaches for grouping activities and assigning work.

DEPARTMENTATION

Organizational structure is largely influenced by the principle of **division of work** or **specialization.** This principle holds that jobs can be divided into smaller components and specialized tasks to achieve greater efficiency and output. Technological advances

Division of work (specialization)

Dividing work into smaller components and specialized tasks to improve efficiency and output.

Departmentation

The process of grouping activities and people into distinct organizational units.

Department

An organizational unit for which a supervisor has responsibility and authority.

and increasing complexity make it very difficult for employees to keep up with everything about their work or specialty. Dividing the work into smaller tasks allows employees to specialize in narrower areas within their fields. Employees can then master these smaller tasks and produce more efficiently. For example, as cars become more complex and diverse, it becomes more difficult for a mechanic to know how to fix everything on every type of car. Thus, specialty repair shops such as muffler shops, oil-change services, and foreign car specialists have sprung up. Even within shops that do many types of repairs, mechanics often specialize in certain repairs. By specializing, employees can become expert enough in their areas to produce efficiently.

Departmentation is the process of grouping activities and people into distinct organizational units, usually known as departments. A **department** is a designated set of activities and people over which a manager or supervisor has responsibility and authority. Terminology used by organizations is quite varied. A department in one may be called a division, an office, a service, a unit, or some other term, in another. Most organizations have departments of some sort, since division of work and specialization contribute to efficiency and better results.

Approaches to Departmentation

Whereas major departments of an organization are established by top-level managers, supervisors primarily are concerned with activities within their own areas. Nevertheless, from time to time supervisors will be confronted with the need to departmentalize within their areas, and they should be familiar with the alternatives available for grouping activities. These are the same options available to top-level managers when they define the major departments. Departmentation is usually done according to function, products or services, territory, customer, process and equipment, or time.

Functional Departmentation. The most widely used form of departmentation is to group activities by function—the jobs to be done. Consistent with the idea of specialization and division of work, activities that are alike or similar are placed together in one department and under a single chain of command. For example, word processing, data-entry, and duplicating services may be grouped together into a clerical department or information processing center; sales and promotional activities into a marketing department; manufacturing assembly work into a production department; inspection and monitoring activities into a quality control department; and so on. As an enterprise undertakes additional activities, these new activities—for the most part—are simply added to the already existing departments.

Functional departmentation is a method that has been and still is successful in most organizations. It makes sense since it is a natural and logical way of arranging activities. Grouping departments along functional lines takes advantage of occupational specialization by placing together jobs and tasks that are performed by people with the same kinds of training, experience, equipment, and facilities. Each supervisor is responsible primarily for an area of operation upon which his or her energy and expertise can be concentrated. Functional departmentation also facilitates coordination since a supervisor is in charge of one major area of activity. It is easier to achieve coordination this way than to have the same functions performed in different departments under different supervisors.

In recent years, many companies have utilized extensive cross-training and multi-skilling of employees in order to develop more flexibility in operations. A **flexible workforce** is one that has employees trained to handle a variety of skills needed to perform multiple tasks in production, customer-service departments, or processes. This is in contrast to the more traditional functional arrangement where each worker is responsible for only one job, or where each worker performs narrowly defined tasks in the operation. Although developing a flexible workforce can be costly and time consuming, the advantages can be well worth the effort. Supervisors can more easily delegate work to employees who better understand the total departmental functions, and the employees also can assume additional responsibilities and tasks in a more collaborative fashion aimed at getting the departmental work done.[6]

Flexible workforce
Employees are trained in a variety of skills to perform multiple tasks.

Product or Service Departmentation. Many companies utilize product or service departmentation. To departmentalize on a product basis means to establish each major product (or group of closely related products) in a product line as a relatively independent unit within the overall framework of the enterprise. For example, a food products company may choose to divide its operations into a frozen food department, a dairy products department, a produce department, and the like. Product departmentation can also be a useful guide for grouping activities in service businesses. For example, most banks have separate departments for commercial loans, installment loans, savings accounts, and checking accounts. Many home maintenance firms have separate departments for carpentry, heating, and air-conditioning services.

Geographic (Territorial, Locational) Departmentation. Another way to departmentalize is by geographical considerations. This approach to departmentation is important for organizations with physically dispersed activities. Large-scale enterprises often have divisions by territories, states, and cities. Increasingly, many companies also have international divisions. Where units of an organization are physically dispersed or where functions are to be performed in different locations—even different buildings—geographic departmentation may be desirable. Locational considerations may be significant even if all activities are performed in one building but on different floors. An advantage of territorial departmentation is that decision-making authority can be placed close to where the work is being done.

Customer Departmentation. Many organizations find it advisable to group activities based on customer considerations. The paramount concern here is to service the differing needs and characteristics of different customers. For example, a university that offers evening programs in addition to day programs attempts to comply with the requests and special needs of part-time and full-time students. Companies may have special departments to handle the particular requirements of wholesale and retail customers. Major department stores may attempt to reach different segments of the buying public, such as customers for a "bargain basement" or lower-priced division at

Some companies use time departmentalization, thereby grouping work according to the time it is to be performed. Common time departmentalizations are day, afternoon, and night shifts.

the one extreme and an exclusive high-priced fashion division at the other extreme. Most hospitals have separate units for outpatient services.

The importance of maintaining close customer relationships in today's competitive climate is well recognized by most organizations. Supervisors often are the key representatives in the effort to build strong interpersonal relationships with customers. Coordinated efforts to communicate and build trust with customers has been referred to as **relationship management** (**RM**).[7] This type of effort may be spearheaded by the marketing/sales department, but supervisors from other departments with customer linkages are usually expected to be part of whatever processes are appropriate and helpful to build customer goodwill and loyalty.

Relationship management

Coordinated efforts to communicate and build trust with customers.

Process and Equipment Departmentation. Activities also can be grouped according to the process involved or equipment used. Since a certain amount of training and expertise are required to handle complicated processes and operate complex equipment, activities that involve the use of specialized equipment may be grouped into a separate department. This form of departmentation often is similar to functional departmentation. For example, in a machine shop department, specialized equipment is used but only certain functions are performed; function and equipment become closely allied. A data processing department utilizing a mainframe computer may serve the processing requirements of a number of operations and departmental needs throughout an organization.

Time Departmentation. Another way to departmentalize is to group activities according to the period of time during which work is performed. Many organizations are engaged in round-the-clock operations and departmentalize on the basis of time by having work shifts. Activities are departmentalized by time (day, afternoon, night shift), although the work operations of all the shifts for the most part may be the same. Here, too, there may be an overlap in the departmentation process. Where time is a partial basis for departmentation, it is likely that other factors will be involved. For example, a maintenance division—based on function and services—may be further departmentalized by shifts, such as the maintenance night shift. Shift departmentation can create organizational questions of how self-contained each shift should be and what relationships should exist between regular day-shift supervisors and the off-shift supervisors.

Shift work also can contribute to numerous other employee problems and concerns, including personal safety, sleep deprivation, child care, and work/family conflicts. Night-shift workers often perceive that they are viewed as "second-class citizens" who have limited access to the training and development opportunities afforded to day-shift personnel. Supervisors of all shifts need to be cognizant of and sensitive to these types of shift workers' concerns. It may be possible for supervisors to coordinate certain types of scheduling rotation, training opportunities, and other efforts (perhaps with the assistance of the human resources department) designed to raise and maintain shift worker morale and job performance to acceptable levels.[8]

Mixed Departmentation. In order to achieve an effective structure, a supervisor may have to apply several types of departmentation at the same time. This is referred to as "mixed" departmentation. For example, there may be an inventory control clerk (functional) on the third floor (geographic) during the night shift (time). In practice, many organizations have a composite departmental structure involving functional departmentation, geographic departmentation, and other forms. All of these alternatives may be available to supervisors to facilitate the grouping of activities in their departments (see Figure 8-3).

There are some departments in which additional subgroupings are not needed. However, supervisors of departments of considerable size may find it necessary to divide various jobs and skills into different groups under a lead person or foreman, who in turn will report to the supervisor. Whatever structure is chosen, the purpose of departmentation is not to have a beautiful, well-drawn organization chart. The purpose is to have a sound structure that will best achieve the objectives of the department and the entire organization.

Work Assignments and Organizational Stability

The problem of how and to whom to assign work confronts a supervisor much more frequently than does the problem of how to organize departments. This problem always involves differences of opinion. Nevertheless, the assignment of work should be justifiable and explainable on the basis of good management, rather than on personal likes and dislikes or hunch and intuition. The supervisor is subject to pressures from different directions. Some employees are willing and want to assume more work, while others believe that they should not be burdened with additional duties. One of the supervisor's most important responsibilities is to assign work so that everybody has a fair share and all employees do their parts equitably and satisfactorily (see Figure 8-4 on page 262).

FIGURE 8-3 Example of mixed departmentation.

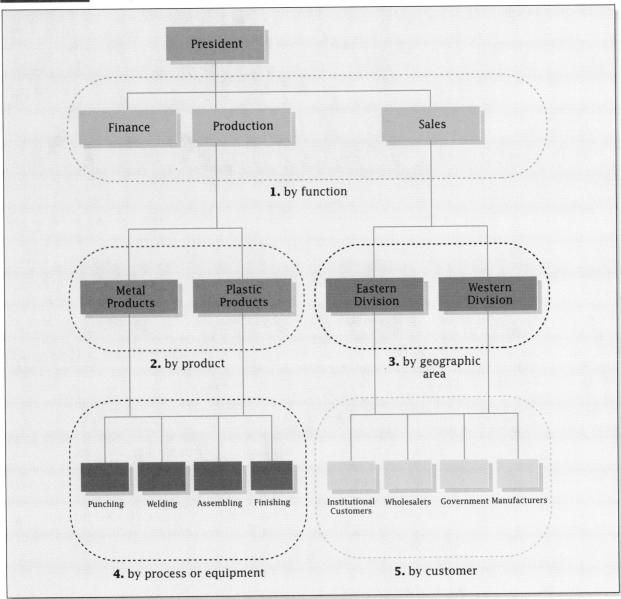

As emphasized previously, a supervisor's task of assigning departmental work will be less difficult if the supervisor consistently utilizes the strengths and experience of all employees. However, supervisors often are inclined to assign heavier and more difficult tasks to the capable employees who are most experienced. Over the long term it is advantageous to train and develop the less experienced employees so that they, too, can

The assignment of work should be made on an equitable basis, but at times supervisors may rely too much on certain people.

Principle of organizational stability

Principle that holds that no organization should become overly dependent on one or several key "indispensable" individuals.

perform the difficult jobs. If supervisors rely too much on one person or a few people, a department will be weakened if the top performers are absent, are promoted, or leave the enterprise. The **principle of organizational stability** advocates that no organization should become overly dependent on one or several key "indispensable" individuals whose absence or departure would seriously disrupt the organization. Organizations need a sufficient number of employees who have been trained well and have flexible skills. One way to develop such flexibility is to assign certain employees to different jobs within the department on a temporary basis, for example, during vacation periods or employee absences. In this way there will usually be someone available to take over any job if the need arises.

At times, it may be necessary for a supervisor to hire temporary employees in order to meet workload demands for a project or specific needs. As discussed in Chapter 7, the use of temporary employees can be helpful if they are given work assignments that they are capable of filling and which do not cause disruptions or disagreements with the regular employees. Some temporary employees may prove themselves to be so competent that the supervisor will want to hire them for permanent positions if openings become available.[9]

5

Explain the importance of authority to supervisory management.

AUTHORITY IN SUPERVISION

Once management establishes departments, it must then establish and clarify relationships among and within the departments. In Chapter 2, we briefly defined managerial authority and the process of delegation. Here we will expand upon those concepts, which will serve as a basis for discussing how management establishes authority and responsibility relationships in organizational structures.

Understanding Managerial Authority and Its Delegation

Managerial authority

The legitimate right to direct and lead others.

Delegation of authority

The process of assigning duties and related authority to subordinates.

Managerial authority is the legitimate or rightful power to direct and lead others, the right to order and to act. It is the formal, positional right by which a manager can require subordinates to do or not to do a certain thing that the manager deems necessary to achieve objectives. Included within positional managerial authority are the right and duty to delegate authority.

Delegation of authority is the process by which the supervisor receives authority from a higher-level manager and, in turn, makes job assignments and entrusts related authority to subordinates. Just as the possession of authority is a required component of any managerial position, the process of delegating authority to lower levels within the hierarchy is required for an organization to have effective managers, supervisors, and employees.

In training personnel, the military employs two major principles embodied in the following statements:

- In order to learn how to give an order, you must first learn how to take an order.
- If you give people a job to do, give them the authority they need to carry out their responsibilities.

These statements are as relevant to a civilian supervisor as they are to a military person. They focus on the importance of delegating authority along with responsibility. Delegation of authority means entrusting job duties and related authority to subordinates so that they can perform within prescribed limits.

Origin of Formal Authority.

In most organizational structures, supervisors have been delegated formal authority directly by an immediate superior. The supervisor receives authority, for example, from a middle-level manager who in turn receives authority from a higher-level manager, who in turn traces authority directly back to the chief executive. In a small company such as a bicycle shop, there are fewer management layers but the principle is the same. The store owner grants authority to the department supervisors who pass on to the sales clerks and repair specialists the authority they need to do their jobs. This is the traditional, or formal, way of looking at the origin of authority, which arises from the recognition of private property rights. It has been said humorously that this is a version of the "Golden Rule"—that is, "Those who have the gold make the rules!"

In most major for-profit corporations, the ultimate managerial authority usually resides in a board of directors that has been selected or elected to represent the ownership interests of the stockholders. Corporate boards primarily decide on major strategy and policy matters, and they delegate to executive managers the responsibility and authority for running the corporation.[10] Similarly, for many not-for-profit organizations, such as governmental entities, religious and educational institutions, and hospitals, top formal authority usually resides in boards of directors who in turn appoint or elect executives and administrators to manage the resources of the organization.

The Acceptance Theory of Authority. Most supervisors will not rely solely on formal authority in day-to-day relations with employees, as the following story illustrates. An argument occurred between a supervisor and a worker concerning a directive. When the argument intensified, the supervisor finally shouted, "Jack, unless you do what I tell you, you're fired!" Jack, in the same heated manner, replied, "You can't fire me . . . I quit!" Jack walked off the job because he chose to lose his job rather than accept the supervisor's authority. His remark, "You can't fire me . . . I quit," illustrates why a supervisor should be concerned about other strategies and not depend solely on the sheer weight of formal authority.

Acceptance theory of authority
Theory that holds that the manager only possesses authority when the employee accepts it.

The **acceptance theory of authority** states that a manager does not possess real authority until and unless the subordinate accepts it. For example, a supervisor may instruct an employee to carry out a certain work assignment. The employee has several alternatives from which to choose. Although such a response is not likely, the employee can refuse to obey, thereby rejecting the supervisor's authority and becoming exposed to possible disciplinary action. Alternatively, the employee may only grudgingly accept the supervisor's direction and carry out the assignment in a mediocre fashion. Or the employee may accept the order and carry it out with varying degrees of performance and enthusiasm. For example, the employee may go well beyond the requirements of the supervisor and do far more than was expected. Thus, the degree to which the employee accepts the supervisor's authority—or the amount of "upward authority" granted the supervisor—is an important part of the employee's choice of alternatives. The acceptance theory states that unless employees accept managerial authority, the supervisor actually does not possess such authority. Of course, employees sometimes have little choice between accepting authority and not accepting it; the other alternative they obviously have is to leave the job. Since this is not a desirable choice, there is merit in considering authority as something that must be accepted by the employees if exercise of authority is to bring about the desired results.

Some employees willingly accept direction from the supervisor.

Briefly stated, then, the origin of authority can be considered from two viewpoints: (a) the formal way of looking at authority as something that originates with ownership rights—formally handed from the top all the way down to the lowest-level employee; and (b) the consideration of authority as something that subordinates confer on a supervisor by the degree of willingness with which they accept or respond to the supervisor's direction.

Limitations to Authority. Numerous limitations to authority usually exist—explicit and implicit, external and internal, political, legal, ethical, moral, social, and economic. Such considerations place limitations on the exercise of authority. For example, many organizations have adopted policies of nondiscrimination in employment, in part because they recognize that these policies are socially and ethically desirable, but also because they are required to do so by law. An organization's articles of incorporation may limit the authority of the chief executive, and the bylaws may present further restrictions. Many laws and contracts clearly limit the authority of managers. For example, wage and hour laws require employers to pay certain minimum wages and overtime rates and restrict the use of child labor. Union contracts limit a manager's freedom to take various actions, for example, in disciplining employees. In addition, every manager is subject to the specific limitations stemming from the assignment of duties and delegation of authority.

Generally, the scope of authority is more limited the farther one descends in the management hierarchy. Usually, the lower the level at which supervisors are located in the management hierarchy, the more restrictions are placed on their authority. First-line supervisors, for example, usually find that there are definite limits placed on their authority to utilize resources and to make certain types of managerial decisions. A supervisor should not resent this since it is a natural part of the process of delegating authority in any organization.

LINE AND STAFF AUTHORITY RELATIONSHIPS AND ORGANIZATIONAL STRUCTURES

ⓖ
Explain the meaning of line and staff authority and how these influence organizational structures and supervisory relationships.

Organization chart
Graphic portrayal of a company's authority and responsibility relationships.

In planning their organizational structures, many firms develop organization charts for all or parts of their operations. An **organization chart** is a means of graphically portraying organizational authority and responsibility relationships. An organization chart primarily depicts managerial and supervisory positions as rectangular boxes. (See Figures 8-5, 8-6, and 8-7.) Some organization charts use lines, circles, or other artistic designs to depict organizational positions or categories of employees.

Line and Staff As Authority Relationships

In many organizations it is common to speak of the sales staff, the human resources staff, the nursing staff, the administrative staff, and other staff designations. In such a context, the word *staff* is used to identify groups of people or departments who are engaged primarily in one activity or several related activities or jobs. However, in most books and other writings about formal organizational structure, the meaning of the word *staff* is quite different. In this text—consistent with other management literature—the terms *line, staff,* and *functional* represent different types of authority relationships within an organization.

Much has been written and said about line and staff, and few aspects of management have evoked as much debate as these concepts. Yet many of the difficulties and frictions encountered by today's supervisors are due to line and staff problems. Misconceptions and lack of understanding of what constitutes line and staff can be the source of confrontation, personality conflicts, disunity, duplication of effort, waste, and lost efficiency.

All supervisors should know whether they are part of the organization in a line or a staff capacity and what these words imply in terms of their positions and in relation to other departments. Supervisors should consult their job descriptions or organizational manuals. If necessary, they should ask higher-level managers for clarification, because it is top-level management that confers line or staff authority on a department.

In the previous section, we referred to managerial authority as an essential component of the managerial job, and we defined it as the legitimate managerial right to direct the activities of subordinates. Technically this is line authority. Here we will add to and further clarify the meaning of authority.

Line-Type Organizational Structure

Line authority

The right to direct others and to require them to conform to decisions, policies, rules, and objectives.

Line-type organizational structure

A structure that consists entirely of line authority arrangements with a direct chain of authority relationships.

In every organization there is a vertical, direct line of authority that can be traced from the chief executive to the departmental employee level. **Line authority** (also referred to as "scalar authority") provides the right to direct others and require them to conform to decisions, policies, rules, and objectives. Line authority establishes who can direct whom throughout the organization. A primary purpose of line authority is to make the organization work smoothly.

Some organizations consist entirely of line authority arrangements (see Figure 8-5). Usually these organizations are fairly small, both in operations and in number of employees. A **line-type organizational structure** enables managers to know exactly to whom they can give directives and whose orders they have to carry out. Throughout, there is unity of command, which can be traced in a direct line (or chain) of authority relationships. With a line-type organizational structure, decisions can usually be made and carried out more quickly as compared to other structures. It is particularly appropriate for small organizations, such as sole proprietorships.

Many small companies essentially are line-type organizations, built around one or several key people who also may own the firm. These owner/managers usually are quite versatile, and they make most of the decisions necessary to carry out business operations. When they need special assistance, they often go outside the firm to request assistance or pay consultants or others for services. Many small companies are built around such key individuals, who must have knowledge in a wide range of business areas. These types of enterprises can be successful as long as the business remains relatively small and operations focus on a limited range of activities. As a small business grows, it can outgrow its owner/manager's expertise. Then more specialists are hired into the company to fill gaps in the owner/manager's knowledge.

Line-and-Staff-Type Organizational Structure

Staff authority

The right to provide counsel, advice, support, and service in a person's areas of expertise.

With organizational growth, activities tend to become more specialized and complicated. Managers cannot be expected to direct subordinates adequately and expertly in all phases of operations without some assistance. Line managers, in order to perform their managerial functions, need the assistance of specialists who have been granted staff authority. **Staff authority** is the right and duty to provide counsel, advice, support, and service in regard to policies, procedures, technical issues, and problems within a person's areas of expertise. Certain specialists are granted staff authority because of their posi-

FIGURE 8-5

Line-type organizational
structure.

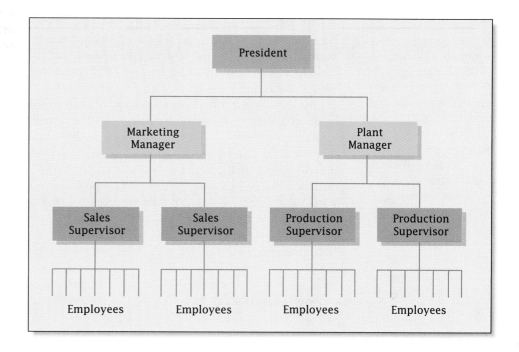

tion or specialized knowledge. People who hold staff positions do not issue orders or directives except within their own staff departments. Rather, staff people assist other members of the organization whenever the need arises for specialized help. For example, human resources specialists often screen applicants for line managers and recommend only the most qualified candidates for line managers to interview. While the human resources managers can direct the work of employees within their own department (line authority), they can only advise managers in other departments in human resources matters (staff authority). Staff authority is not inferior to line authority; it is just different. The objectives of staff groups ultimately are the same as those of the line departments, namely, the achievement of overall organizational objectives.

Staff supervisors primarily provide guidance, counsel, advice, and service in their specialty to those who request it. Typically they also have the responsibility to see that certain policies and procedures are being carried out by line departments. However, staff supervisors do not have the direct authority to order line people to conform to policies and procedures; they can only persuade, counsel, and advise. Line supervisors can accept the staff person's advice, alter it, or reject it; but since the staff person is usually the expert in the field, line supervisors mostly accept and even welcome the advice of the staff person.

It does not matter whether a particular department is a line or staff department. Supervisors are line managers with direct authority over the employees in their departments, regardless of whether their departments serve the organization in a staff or line capacity. For example, human resources managers can tell their direct reports to put a job ad in the paper. However, they can only advise line managers about how to conduct interviews.

Line department

Department whose responsibilities are directly related to making, selling, or distributing the company's product or service.

Staff department

Specialized department responsible for supporting line departments and providing specialized advice and services.

Line-and-staff-type organizational structure

Structure that combines line and staff departments.

Human resources management (HRM)

Organizational philosophies, policies, and practices that strive for the effective use of employees.

As previously defined, *line* and *staff* refer to different types of authority. In practice, however, these terms also refer to departmental responsibilities within an organizational structure. In this context, **line departments** are those directly involved in making, selling, or distributing the company's product or service. **Staff departments** are specialized departments that support the line departments. Most organizations of appreciable size use a **line-and-staff-type organizational structure,** which is a combination of these two types of departments. For example, certain departments, such as human resources (personnel), legal, or accounting, usually are classified as staff since they mainly support other departments. This is illustrated by Figure 8-6, which shows the controller and director of human resources as staff. These staff relationships are illustrated with dashed lines. However, these positions and departments are not always staff. As stated before, line and staff are characteristics of authority relationships and not necessarily of functions. Nor does a person's title indicate line or staff. For example, in manufacturing organizations it is common to find a vice president of production, a vice president of sales, a vice president of human resources, and so on. Merely looking at an organization chart is not sufficient to identify staff relationships, because most positions on a chart are shown only as small rectangular boxes with solid lines showing line relationships.

Supervisory Relationships with the Human Resources Department

In a broad sense, **human resources management (HRM)** is the philosophy, policies, procedures, and practices related to the management of people within an organization. To perform the activities necessary to accomplish its goals, every organization must have

---

FIGURE 8-6   Line-and-staff-type organizational structure.

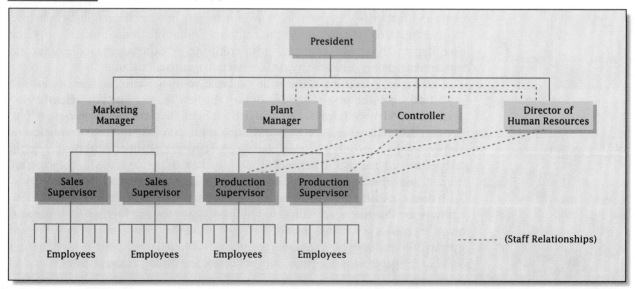

the necessary human resources and use them effectively. To facilitate this, many firms have a human resources department with a director of human resources and other staff personnel.

In most organizations the director of human resources and the human resources department operate in a staff capacity. The **human resources department**—which may be called the "personnel department," the "industrial relations division," the "employee relations section," or some other name—usually exists to provide advice and service to all departments concerning employment matters, such as recruiting, screening, and testing applicants; maintaining personnel records; providing for wage and salary administration; advising line managers on problems of discipline and required fair employment practices; and providing other services and assistance. If line supervisors have difficult employee problems, the human resources department is available for assistance. Staff persons in the human resources department are qualified to furnish advice and current information since this is their expertise and specialty.

Not every organization has a human resources department. Very small firms, for example, usually do not need or cannot afford to have specialized staff personnel. In these firms, supervisors, in consultation with their managers, may carry out certain employment-related tasks. Or the firm may designate someone to be responsible for hiring and recordkeeping duties who generally shares these responsibilities with other managerial personnel. However, when an organization grows, at some point top-level managers will likely hire a human resources director and staff specialists to assist in carrying out the HRM function. For most organizations, the role and size of the typical human resources department have expanded considerably in recent decades. Because of expanded needs, many organizations have found it cost effective to contract out, or "outsource," some of the human resources activities. Concerned over the costs associated with HRM matters, certain firms are finding other firms to do part of the work they used to do.[11]

HRM's Evolving Role. Particularly in large organizations, many human resources departments have evolved into becoming **strategic business partners** within corporate management. This means that human resources staff are much more involved in planning and decision making along with line managers concerning meeting business needs, customer relationships, and bottom-line results. Some analysts believe that human resources departments may themselves be transformed by this type of emphasis, although it still will be necessary for human resources departments to see to it that needed staff services are provided in some manner.[12]

The demanding nature and growing number of human resources management issues certainly have enhanced the human resources function's role and image. According to a large-scale national survey conducted by a major accounting/consulting firm, human resources departments are now generally accorded "equal status' with line operations; about three-quarters of the respondents indicated that their human resources department's effectiveness was assessed primarily by its "overall contribution to the bottom line."[13]

Achieving the Proper Balance. Regardless of whether or not a human resources department is expected to be a "strategic business partner" within a firm, the day-to-

Human resources department

Staff department which provides advice and service to other departments on human resources matters.

Strategic business partners

Staff personnel collaborate with line managers to continuously improve overall organizational performance.

day usefulness and effectiveness of a human resources department primarily depends on its ability to develop close working relationships with line managers and supervisors. The quality of these line/staff relationships, in turn, depends on how clearly top-level managers have defined the scope of activities and authority of the human resources department.

Most organizations have tried to achieve a proper balance of influence and authority between line supervisors and human resources staff. Line supervisors and human resources staff must work together because their activities are interdependent. Their primary roles and areas of authority should not shift substantially. The human resources department should focus primarily on advising and assisting line supervisors who need help in certain areas. Line supervisors should take full advantage of the human resources department's expert assistance while supervising their own departments within the framework of the organization's personnel policies and procedures and any union contract that may exist. As a first step in this direction, supervisors should have a major role in defining employee qualifications and describing job requirements for their own departments.

Human resources staff managers usually prefer to offer suggestions to line supervisors, who in turn must decide whether to accept, alter, or reject those suggestions or recommendations. If a line supervisor feels that a suggestion of the human resources manager is not feasible, the supervisor will make his or her own decision. For the most part, line supervisors will accept the recommendations of human resources staff people because the staff individuals are experts on problems in their areas. Thus, staff authority—whether it is exercised by human resources staff or by individuals in other staff departments—typically is derived from the staff's knowledge and expertise in dealing with specialized areas and related problems. Staff people "sell" their ideas based on the authority derived from their positions and expertise but they cannot force compliance. If a recommendation of a staff person is carried out, it is carried out as a line directive under the name and responsibility of the line supervisor, not that of the staff person. Various types of examples of human resources staff relationships with supervisors will be presented in later chapters of this text.

THE ROLE OF FUNCTIONAL AUTHORITY

7

Describe how functional authority may be granted to specialized staff for certain purposes.

Generally, in a line-and-staff organization, staff managers provide counsel and advice to line managers but do not have the right to give them direct orders. This arrangement maintains the principle of unity of command. However, there are exceptions to this generalization. For example, if an organizational policy requires a supervisor to consult with a staff person before making a certain type of decision, this is known as following the **principle of compulsory staff advice** (or **compulsory staff service**). The supervisor still may accept or reject the staff person's advice unless functional authority is granted to the staff person.

Functional authority (or "functional staff authority") is a special right given by higher-level management to certain staff people to direct other members of the organization about certain matters within the staff person's specialized field. For example,

Principle of compulsory staff advice (service)

Situation in which supervisors are required by policy to consult with specialized staff before making certain types of decisions.

Functional authority

The right granted to specialized staff people to give directives concerning certain matters within their expertise.

assume that a company president wants to be sure that the grievance procedures in the labor agreement are interpreted uniformly. Therefore, the president decides to confer sole authority to the labor relations director for the final settlement of grievances—a function that otherwise might belong to line managers. The labor relations director is part of the human resources department, which is a staff department. By giving sole authority for the final adjustment of grievances to the labor relations director, the company president confers authority for this function on someone who ordinarily would not hold this authority. Now the labor relations director has this authority, and it no longer belongs to the line supervisors.

Another example of functional authority is the common case in which a human resources department is given full authority to maintain legal compliance with wage and hour laws, equal employment opportunity laws, and the like. The decisions of line supervisors in these matters must conform to the stipulations of the human resources department. (In many situations, the human resources department itself may rely on advice it receives from the company's legal department or from an outside attorney.)

Because functional authority may be an extension of staff authority conferred upon certain staff specialists, in practice it may be difficult to clearly distinguish between these in some situations. In general, however, the use of functional authority violates the principle of unity of command since it introduces a second source of authority for certain decisions. Yet in numerous situations, functional authority is advantageous because it facilitates a more effective use of staff specialists. It is up to top-level management to weigh the advantages and disadvantages of granting functional authority to staff specialists before conferring it.

Discuss applications of matrix-type organizational structure.

Matrix-type organizational structure

A hybrid structure in which regular functional departments co-exist with project teams made up of people from different departments.

THE MATRIX-TYPE ORGANIZATIONAL STRUCTURE

In many organizations the need to coordinate activities across department lines has contributed to the development of the **matrix-type organizational structure.** The matrix form of organization is also called "project structure," "product management structure," or "grid," among other designations. The matrix arrangement is superimposed on the line-staff organization. It adds horizontal dimensions to the normal vertical (top-down) orientation of the organizational structure. It is a hybrid arrangement in which both regular (functional) line and staff departments co-exist with project teams or group assignments across departmental lines.

Many high-tech firms employ project (matrix) structures in order to focus special talents from different departments on specific projects for certain periods. Project structure enables managers to undertake several projects simultaneously, some of which may be of relatively short duration. Each project is assigned to a project manager who manages the project from inception to completion. Employees from different functional departments are assigned to work on each project as needed, either part time or full time.

Although the complexity of matrix structure varies, a basic matrix form might resemble the chart shown in Figure 8-7 (see page 272). This chart illustrates how some managers have been given responsibility for specific projects within the firm, while de-

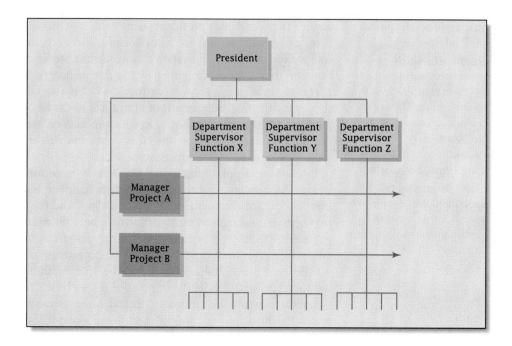

partmental supervisors primarily have the responsibility for supervising employees within their regular departments.

The type of arrangement shown in Figure 8-7 might apply to an engineering or architectural firm. The project managers (A and B) are responsible for coordinating activities on their designated projects. However, the project managers must work closely with the departmental supervisors of functions X, Y, and Z. The employees who work in these departments report directly (functionally) to the departmental supervisors, but their services are utilized under the authority and responsibility of the project managers to whom they are assigned for varying periods of time.

There are several problems associated with the matrix-type organizational structure. The most frequent problem is the question of direct accountability. Like functional authority, the matrix structure violates the principle of unity of command since departmental employees are accountable to a departmental supervisor and project managers (see Figure 8-8). Other problems involve priorities of scheduling for individual employees who are assigned to work on several projects. These problems can be avoided, or at least minimized, by proper planning and clarification of authority relationships by the top-level manager prior to the start of a project.

Despite such problems, the matrix structure is widely used because organizations find it advantageous. The success of a matrix arrangement depends primarily on the willingness of both the project managers and the departmental supervisors and their employees to coordinate various activities and responsibilities in working toward completion of each project. Such coordination is vital in the scheduling of work, and it is imperative in the performance appraisal of employees. Employees must recognize that

FIGURE 8-8

A disadvantage of the matrix-type organization is that it violates the principle of unity of command.

they remain directly accountable to their departmental supervisor, who will rely to a great extent on the project managers' evaluations of the employees' work when he or she conducts the performance appraisals and salary reviews. These are discussed at length in Chapter 13.

Define downsizing (restructuring) and its implications for organizational principles.

Downsizing (restructuring, right-sizing)

Large-scale reduction and elimination of jobs in a company that usually results in reduction of middle-level managers, removal of organizational levels, and a widened span of management for remaining supervisors.

ORGANIZATIONAL PRINCIPLES IN AN ERA OF ORGANIZATIONAL DOWNSIZING

Among the most publicized aspects of corporate business during recent years has been the large-scale reduction and permanent elimination of thousands of job positions in many major companies. This has been accomplished by plant and office closings, sales of divisions, extensive employee layoffs, attrition and early retirements, and the like. As a result, many companies have eliminated large segments of their workforce; this has been referred to as **downsizing, restructuring,** or **right-sizing.** Typically, management downsizes to reduce costs, streamline operations, and become more efficient and competitive. A major organizational impact is a reduction in the number of middle-level managers and the removal of a layer or more of organizational levels. The span of management is usually widened for first-line supervisors and other managers who survive the downsizing. Many supervisors are stretched by being required to add unfamiliar departments or functions to their previous departmental operation.[14]

Some middle-level management and staff positions have been eliminated because information technology has made it possible for higher-level managers to acquire data and information quickly and to keep in close touch with operations. As a result, remaining supervisors and employees usually have to become more widely knowledgeable about numerous aspects of operations than they were in the past. Noted management scholar Peter Drucker contends that the knowledge/information explosion requires restructured organizations to depend upon the remaining employees throughout the firm for decision making, rather than upon traditional "command-and-control structures."[15]

Studies of the pros and cons of downsizing have revealed a mixed pattern of results. The forecasted economic returns often are not realized as expected, and the impact on organizational morale and productivity often is negative or detrimental to efficiency efforts. However, the firms that have downsized most effectively appear to be those that have planned for it systematically and have tried to harmonize (insofar as possible) the previous organizational structures and operations with the newer realities in a way that is compatible and acceptable to those who remain. Usually this means an early involvement of human resources department staff specialists in planning to smooth the downsizing process. Workforce planning, training, and skills assessment, and widespread communication of what will happen throughout the organization, are typical areas that require the human resources department's skills and major participation.[16] Additionally, ideas about authority and the use of authority must be reshaped to give supervisors and employees greater decision-making responsibility.[17] Even with a lessening of organizational structure, most individuals still need to have clear lines of accountability for their performance to be evaluated. This, in turn, is vital if reward systems are to be meaningful and motivational.[18]

Some organizational theorists predict that downsizing will continue indefinitely, and that in some firms there will be a "radical restructuring." This could result in organizational structures and practices that conflict with time-honored organizational principles. The concept of **re-engineering** has been offered (and tried by some firms) whereby firms restructure more on the basis of processes (e.g., meeting customer orders and requirements) than on the basis of departments or functions (e.g., sales and production). Such an approach requires supervisors and employees to directly focus on customer needs and services rather than on their own functions and specialties. Focusing on the customer may enhance a firm's efforts to be more efficient and competitive in the marketplace, but it also can mean a blurring of line and staff functions and roles. Some authorities have suggested that re-engineering will require an emergence of "process managers" who will manage key processes and whose broadened responsibilities will cut across line and staff functions and levels of an organization.[19] A number of major corporations already have restructured parts of their organizations along customer–process dimensions. If carried out throughout a firm, this could create what has been referred to as the **horizontal corporation** in which organizational structures would become quite flattened and managerial authority relationships would be minimal.[20]

Perhaps the most extreme forecast about the corporate organization of the future has been called the **virtual corporation.** Companies presumably could join together as temporary partners or networks and share skills, employees, and access to each other's markets to exploit various types of opportunities. A virtual corporation would have no organizational chart or hierarchy, and it could be considered as the "ultimate" project-type organization. At the end of the collaboration in a project or market opportunity, the various partners would separate and have no continuing permanent relationship. Of course, a virtual corporation would require member companies to have networks with

Re-engineering

Concept of restructuring a firm on the basis of processes and customer needs and services, rather than by departments and functions.

Horizontal corporation

Where a firm is restructured by customer process and organizational structure is very flattened.

Virtual corporation

Where companies link together on a temporary basis to take advantage of marketplace opportunities.

other firms with whom they share a high level of trust and collaboration. Even with this, a concern would be that individual firms might lose control over their own operations. Although a number of companies have moved in this direction in certain types of joint ventures, at this writing the virtual corporation is far more a theory than a reality.[21]

Whether or not radical restructurings will become commonplace in the future is speculative. Moreover, it is not clear that re-engineering differs significantly from what many firms try to concentrate on with or without downsizing. What does seem likely, however, is that the application of organizational principles will always be part of the supervisory position, and that any types of organizational change will require that supervisors understand how to apply and adapt certain organizational principles to their situations.[22] Applying organizational principles at the supervisory level is the primary focus of Chapter 9.

What Call Did You Make?

As Alice Austin in the chapter-opening vignette, you should review and apply the basic organizational principles that were discussed in this chapter. Probably the most important is to take steps to restore the unity of command principle in your department. All direct work requests must be communicated through you, and you must not be bypassed if you are going to retain work control. It may be that your span of supervision is too wide. Perhaps you need to identify one or two lead persons who can serve in your absence in order to have a proper chain of command.

Although there are several approaches that you can take, you probably should first discuss this with your manager, the dean of administration, in order to get support to rectify the situation. You need to review the organizational structure and to clarify the various types of line and staff authority that impact your position. After doing this, then all parties who use your services need to be informed again of the proper workflow procedures. Further, you need to instruct your employees that they are to accept no direct work requests unless they have your approval to do so, or the approval of a lead person if you decide to appoint such an individual.

You also must remind your employees that their jobs require a customer point of view as well as just carrying out work requests. You should solicit their ideas concerning how departmental procedures and organizational structure can be improved.

SUMMARY

The organizing function of management is to design a structural framework, that is, to group and assign activities to specific work areas so as to achieve the desired objectives. Organizing includes establishing authority relationships among managers, supervisors, and departments.

An organization normally should adhere to the principle of unity of command. This principle maintains that everyone be directly accountable to only one supervisor and that formal communications should normally flow through the chain of command.

In assigning the number of employees reporting to one supervisor, the principle of span of management should be observed. Also known as the span of supervision or span of control, this principle recognizes that there is an upper limit to the number of individuals a supervisor can manage effectively. The actual span of management is determined by factors such as the competence of the supervisor, the previous training and experience of employees, their work locations, and the amount and nature of work to be performed. Other things being equal, the smaller the span of management, the more levels of management will be needed; the broader the span of management, the fewer levels will be required.

Departmentation is the process of grouping activities and people into distinct organizational units. The most widely used basis of departmentation is to group activities according to functions. Other bases include departmentalizing along geographic lines, by product or service, by customer, by process and equipment, or by time. Rather than designing new departments, supervisors most often will be faced with the task of assigning activities and employees within an existing department to achieve efficiency and stability.

A supervisor must possess authority in order to perform as a manager. Managerial authority is the legitimate or rightful power to direct and lead others. Authority is delegated from top-level managers through mid-level managers to supervisors, who in turn delegate to their employees. All supervisors must be delegated appropriate authority to manage their departments. Generally, supervisors must first learn how to take an order before they can learn how to give an order. Supervisors assign job duties and authority to employees so they can perform within prescribed limits. In essence, delegation of authority means empowering employees to make decisions.

The acceptance theory of authority suggests that supervisors have authority only if and when their subordinates accept it. In reality, an employee's choice between accepting or not accepting a supervisor's authority may be the choice between staying in the job or quitting. But the degree of acceptance will affect the quality and quantity of the employee's work and the enthusiasm with which the employee performs the job.

Supervisors are attached to an organization in either a line or a staff capacity. Within their own departments, supervisors are line managers with line authority to direct their employees. If a person is in a staff authority position, his or her normal role is to furnish counsel, guidance, advice, and service in a specialized field.

A line-type organizational structure has only line authority relationships in a direct chain-of-command arrangement. This is commonplace in very small firms. As organizations increase in size, they usually adopt a line-and-staff-type structure. This enables the use of staff people whose specialized knowledge and skills support line managers and others throughout the organization. In a line-and-staff structure, a line supervisor usually has the discretion to accept or reject the staff's advice. The human resources department is typically a staff department whose services and advice are generally utilized by line supervisors.

When higher-level management grants functional authority to a specialized staff person, this person has the right to issue directives about certain matters within his or her expertise. When a staff person has been granted functional authority over a specialized area, line supervisors are not free to reject the advice or directives that this person may give.

A matrix (project)-type organizational structure places certain managers in charge of project teams whose members are drawn from different departments. At the same time, line supervisors manage the employees in regular departments. This structure facilitates more efficient use of employees on multiple projects without disrupting the regular departmental arrangements. However, a matrix structure may create problems of priority scheduling and accountability of employees both to a departmental supervisor and project managers.

9

Downsizing usually involves the elimination of job positions and a level (or levels) of management. Supervisors who survive a downsizing have to adapt organizational principles to the changes that have occurred. This usually includes a widened span of management and the need to provide more latitude to employees in sharing in decision making.

KEY TERMS

Organization (page 249)
Unity of command principle (page 250)
Span of management principle (page 251)
Lead person (page 255)
Division of work (specialization)
    (page 257)
Departmentation (page 257)
Department (page 257)
Flexible workforce (page 258)
Relationship management (page 259)
Principle of organizational stability
    (page 262)
Managerial authority (page 263)
Delegation of authority (page 263)
Acceptance theory of authority (page 264)
Organization chart (page 265)
Line authority (page 266)
Line-type organizational structure (page
    266)
Staff authority (page 266)

Line department (page 268)
Staff department (page 268)
Line-and-staff-type organizational
    structure (page 268)
Human resources management (HRM)
    (page 268)
Human resources department (page 269)
Strategic business partners (page 269)
Principle of compulsory staff advice
    (service) (page 271)
Functional authority (page 271)
Matrix-type organizational structure (page
    271)
Downsizing (restructuring, right-sizing)
    (page 273)
Re-engineering (page 274)
Horizontal corporation (page 274)
Virtual corporation (page 274)

QUESTIONS FOR DISCUSSION

1. Define the organizing function.
2. What is meant by unity of command? Is this principle realistic in today's large, complex organizations?
3. Define the span of management principle. What are some of the major factors that influence a supervisor's span of management?
4. Explain the trade-off between the number of levels of management and the span of management. How does this problem typically affect a first-line supervisor?
5. Define departmentation. Why is the functional approach the most widely adopted approach to departmentation? Discuss other approaches to departmentation and how these often overlap.
6. How does fair assignment of work activities involve both quantity and quality of work? Why is this important for the stability of a department's operation?

7. Define managerial authority. Discuss the following issues related to the concept of authority:
   a. Delegation of authority
   b. The origin of formal authority
   c. The acceptance theory of authority
   d. Limits to a supervisor's authority

8. Define line authority and staff authority. What is the difference between a line-type organization and a line-and-staff-type organization?

9. Discuss the functions of staff personnel. Does the relationship between a line supervisor and a staff person (from whom the line supervisor seeks advice or counsel) violate the concept of unity of command? Why or why not?

10. Identify the departments in organizations that are most likely to function in a staff capacity. Can you tell from looking at an organizational chart or from a person's title whether that individual is line or staff? Why or why not?

11. Discuss the nature of supervisory relationships with staff personnel in a human resources department. Why do line supervisors usually rely upon the advice and services provided by human resources staff?

12. Discuss the concept of functional authority. Give several examples of how organizations have used this concept. Does the use of functional authority (or functional staff authority) violate the principle of unity of command? Discuss.

13. Does the matrix organization violate the unity of command principle? Discuss. What are the advantages of the matrix structure?

14. What is meant by downsizing (restructuring)? Is it likely that organizational principles will be rendered obsolete by future downsizing and radical restructuring efforts? Discuss.

SKILLS APPLICATIONS

Skills Application 8-1: Organizational Principles and Concepts

1. Identify from this chapter what you believe to be the most important concepts concerning the organizing function of management that a supervisor should understand.

2. After you have developed your list, try it out with someone who is a supervisor to determine how many of the concepts that person is familiar with.

3. If the supervisor is not familiar with the majority of the concepts on your list, does this mean that he or she is not effective? Why or why not?

Skills Application 8-2: Organization Chart Analysis

Review the following organization chart for an insurance company and answer the questions that follow.

1. Identify the departmentation options that appear in the chart.

2. How would the chart change if the level immediately below the home office were changed to a product/service form of departmentation?

3. What would be some reasons for having only the regional offices report to the home office?

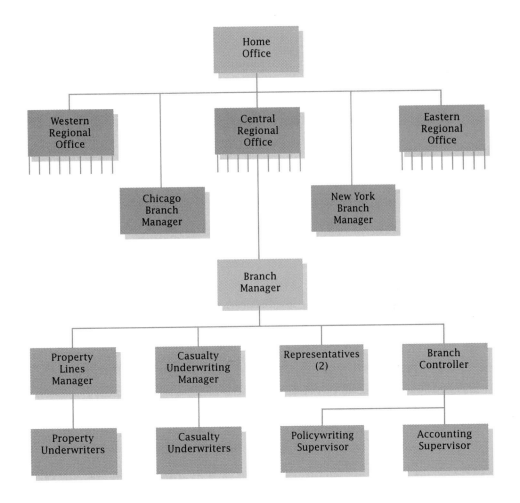

Skills Application 8-3: Organizing a Company

Following is a list of job titles for an organization as well as the number of people in each position. From this information, construct an organization chart. You may eliminate or change job titles but do not reduce the number of people working for the company.

The company produces and sells a variety of freeze-dried products throughout the United States and Canada. Sales have been growing at about 5 percent a year, slightly above the inflation rate. As a result of the slow growth, projections reveal no new job openings except for replacements.

Job Title	Number of Employees	Job Title	Number of Employees
Production Worker	60	Vice President—Human Resources	1
Production Supervisor	6	Salesperson	100
Production Manager	1	Area Sales Manager	8
Vice President—Production	1	District Sales Manager	8
Bookkeeper	6	Regional Sales Manager	6
Accountant	3	Vice President—Marketing	1
Accounting Supervisor	6	President	1
Accounting Manager	2	Staff Specialist	6
Comptroller	1	Chemists	3
Vice President—Finance	1	Technicians	6
Clerk	4	Research & Development Supervisor	2
Payroll Coordinator	2	Vice President—Research & Development	1
Compensation Manager	1		
Benefits Specialist	1		
Personnel Manager	1		

Secondary Assignment: After developing your organization chart, define the departments and their relationships that you believe could most likely be downsized (restructured). Explain what you would propose to do and why.

Skills Application 8-4: A Lesson from the Movies

Visit your local video store and rent a copy of *Gung Ho*. This 1986 movie starring Michael Keaton and Gedde Watanabe illustrates the conflict that occurs when different types of organizational structures and leadership styles come into play. After viewing the movie, answer the following questions.

1. Identify some of the cultural and attitudinal differences between the Japanese managers and American workers.
2. Why didn't the organizational structure envisioned by the Japanese managers work as well as intended?
3. What were the key ingredients that finally contributed to getting the workers to pull together and achieve the goals set for them?
4. What did you learn from this film about the organizing function as related to the people themselves within the organization?

INTERNET ACTIVITY

Skills Application 8-5: Restructuring and Its Effects

The media constantly report illustrations of corporate America's downsizing and restructuring efforts. Using the Internet, find a recent example of a corporation's reported downsizing/restructuring. (For example, in early 2000 Coca-Cola announced its intention to significantly reduce its worldwide workforce. Visit Coca-Cola's home page for additional information on this restructuring.) Write a report answering the following questions.

1. What are the corporation's objectives in general?
2. What was the purpose of the restructuring?
3. How will the effectiveness of the restructuring be measured?
4. What has been the impact of the restructuring on the managers? On employees? On customers? On shareholders?
5. Will the corporate culture change as a result of the restructuring?
6. Do you expect the organization to become more or less decentralized and participative? Why?

INTERNET ACTIVITY

Skills Application 8-6: Managing Virtually

Many of today's supervisors will be asked to manage virtual employees or workgroups. Gil Gordon Associates' Web site (www.gilgordon.com) specifically addresses the topics of telecommuting and working in a virtual environment for both managers and employees. After using this or other sites, find information regarding telecommuting and working in a virtual environment. Then answer the following questions.

1. As a supervisor, what specific management issues will you have to address?
2. What specific concerns might a supervisor have about managing telecommuters? As a supervisor, how can you address these concerns?

ENDNOTES

1. Elizabeth J. Hawk and Garrett J. Sheridan, "The Right Staff: Are Your Core Workers Happy?" *Management Review* (June 1999), pp. 43–48.
2. See Jeffrey Pfeffer and John F. Veiga, "Putting People First for Organizational Success," *Academy of Management Executive* (May 1999), pp. 37–48. This article was adapted from the book by Jeffrey Pfeffer, *The Human Equation: Building Profits by Putting People First* (Boston: Harvard Business School Press, 1998).
3. See Exodus, Chapter 18, in the Bible for the story of Moses and Jethro. Jethro has been referred to as the "world's first management and organization consultant."
4. Greater numbers of employees are working from their homes, automobiles, hotel rooms, and the like. Offices are becoming more open with fewer walls and more temporary partitions. These arrangements usually save money for firms but numerous human problems can be associated with their existence. See Lina S. Kadaba, "Taking 'Place' Out of Workplace," *St. Louis Post Dispatch* (August 28, 1995), p. 40; Barbara Ettorre, "When the Walls Come Tumbling Down," *Management Review* (November 1995), pp. 33–37; Sandra E. O'Connell, "The Virtual Workplace Moves at Warp Speed," *HRMagazine* (March 1996), pp. 50–57; and Joan Hamilton, with Stephen Baker and Bill Vlasic, "The New Workplace," *Business Week* (April 29, 1996), pp. 107–117.
5. See Alex Markels, "Restructuring Alters Middle-Manager Role But Leaves It Robust," *The Wall Street Journal* (September 25, 1995), pp. A1–A6.
6. See Glenn L. Dalton, "The Collective Stretch: Is Workforce Flexibility Delivering the Goods?" *Management Review* (December 1998), pp. 54–59.
7. See James P. Masciarelli, "Are You Managing Your Relationships?" *Management Review* (April 1998), pp. 41–45.
8. See Carla Joinson, "Don't Forget Your Shift Workers," *HRMagazine* (February 1999), pp. 81–84.

9. See Kent Blake, "She's Just a Temporary," *HRMagazine* (August 1998), pp. 45–51.

10. See Ram Charan, *Boards at Work: How Corporate Boards Create Competitive Advantage* (San Francisco: Jossey-Bass, 1998).

11. According to a survey conducted by the Society for Human Resource Management (SHRM) and the Bureau of National Affairs, Inc. (BNA), the budgeted median cost per employee for HRM activities and programs in 1998 was $1,053, an increase of about 6 percent from the previous year. The median "HR Staff Ratio," defined as the number of human resources staff members for every 100 employees served by the human resources department, was 1.0 in 1998; this was similar to other recent years. However, this ratio fluctuated widely depending on the size and nature of the firm. See "SHRM-BNA Survey No. 63: Human Resources Activities, Budgets, and Staffs—1997/98," *Bulletin to Management* (Washington, D.C.: Bureau of National Affairs, Inc., June 18, 1998).

The outsourcing of human resources management functions has created a growth industry of *professional employer organizations (PEOs)*. PEOs are subcontractors who assume numerous human resources management responsibilities, primarily for firms of from 10 to 500 employees. Depending on the nature of the contractual agreement, the PEO typically will handle payroll, taxes, benefits, insurance, and regulatory compliance with federal, state, and local laws. Some PEOs also provide recruitment, selection, and job-training services. There are an estimated 2,000 PEO firms in the United States. Their clients have both white-collar and blue-collar, nonunionized and unionized employees; however, clients tend to be more white-collar and nonunion. Fee charges are negotiable; 3 to 4 percent of a client's payroll costs is a typical fee arrangement. See William Flannery, "PEOs Change the Face of Human Resources," *St. Louis Post-Dispatch* (August 24, 1999), p. C6.

12. See Carla Joinson, "Changing Shapes: As Organizations Evolve, HR's Form Follows its Functions," *HRMagazine* (March 1999), pp. 41–48.

13. "HR Department Gaining Respect," *HRMagazine* (February 1999), p. 30.

14. See Wayne F. Cascio, "Downsizing: What Do We Know? What Have We Learned?" *Academy of Management Executive* (February 1993), pp. 95–104; or Alex Markels and Matt Murray, "Call it Dumbsizing: Why Some Companies Regret Cost-Cutting," *The Wall Street Journal* (May 14, 1996), pp. A1 and A6.

15. Peter F. Drucker as cited by Jennifer Reingold, "The Power of Cosmic Thinking," *Business Week* (June 7, 1999), p. 17.

16. Sherry Kuczynski, "Help! I Shrunk the Company," *HRMagazine* (June 1999), pp. 40–45.

17. See K. S. Cameron, S. J. Freemand, and A. K. Mishra, "Best Practices in White Collar Downsizing: Managing Contradictions," *Academy of Management Executive* (August 1991), pp. 57–73; and Susan Sonnesyn Brooks, "Managing a Horizontal Revolution," *HRMagazine* (June 1995), pp. 52–58.

18. See Sandra O'Neal, "Reengineering and Compensation: An Interview with Michael Hammer," *ACA Journal* (Spring 1996), pp. 6–11.

19. See "Management's New Gurus," *Business Week* (August 31, 1992), pp. 44–47 and 50–52; and Robert B. Blaha, "Forget Functions, Manage Processes," *HRMagazine* (June 1993), pp. 109–110.

20. See John A. Byrne, "The Horizontal Corporation," *Business Week* (December 20, 1993), pp. 76–81; and Frank Ostroff, *The Horizontal Corporation: What the Organization of the Future Actually Looks Like and How it Delivers Value to Customers* (New York: Oxford University Press, 1999).

21. See "The Virtual Corporation," *Business Week* (February 8, 1993), pp. 98–99 and 100–103; and Roger Nagel as quoted in *Challenges* (Published by the Council on Competitiveness, June 1993), p. 4.

22. For a detailed look at the organization charts and other organizational aspects of more than 400 major U.S. corporations, the *Organization Chart Collection, 1999–2000 Edition,* published by The Conference Board, Inc., is recommended. Charts can be ordered individually and/or in any numbers as requested. For ordering and other information, access the Web site at www.conference-board.org. For a comprehensive view of likely trends that will impact organizational structures and practices, see Maureen Minehan, "SHRM—Futurist Task Force," *HRMagazine* published by the Society for Human Resource Management (1998 50th Anniversary Issue), pp. 77–84.

Chapter 9

Supervisory Organizing at the Departmental Level

You Make the Call!

You are David Simms, store manager of a local restaurant that is part of a nationwide chain of popular family restaurants. According to company policy, all supervisors and managers are to be promoted from within the corporation. You know of a few situations where stores went outside for qualified persons, but this practice is generally frowned upon by top management. This is due to the fact that management believes in promoting their own and giving them goals to shoot for. You always have prided yourself on the fact that you have dedicated yourself to this policy. You have seen quite a few of your own employees attain supervisory positions, and several have received their own stores. You also are proud of your own abilities as a store manager. The store you manage has a reputation for being profitable, stable, and relatively problem-free. Your employees and supervisors get along quite well, and employee turnover is the lowest in the area. However, during the past week you have been faced with a perplexing problem.

June Teevers, your weeknight supervisor, has just notified you that in two weeks her husband is being promoted and transferred across the country. Teevers apologized for the short notice, and she explained that she and her husband had no choice but to accept this "once-in-a-lifetime" offer. Therefore, Teevers will be supervising her last shift in about a week. You never foresaw this happening, and you have done little to prepare for such an occurrence.

In the past couple of days you have tried to find someone who could fill her position, but you have reached only "dead ends." You contacted your regional manager and explained your situation. She informed you that there was not a store in the area that could spare a supervisor or supervisory trainee. The labor market is very tight right now, and you expected such an answer. The only other option you can think of is to promote an employee named Margo James, who is a great server and who has helped you out on a couple of occasions when supervisors were sick or on vacations. However, you have heard through the employee grapevine that although she is liked as a server, Margo was thoroughly disliked as a temporary supervisor. her fellow employees complained that she was belligerent, a "control freak," and extremely autocratic whenever she was a temporary supervisor. You don't think promoting Margo would be a prudent choice, but you also know that you are supposed to promote from within, so you have a difficult set of decisions to make.

As David Simms, what options do you have open to you? Is there any way that you can promote Margo James and maintain employee morale and stability? How can you prevent encountering such a problem in the future?

You Make the Call!

Identify the supervisor's role in organizing for employee empowerment.

SUPERVISORY ORGANIZING FOR EMPLOYEE EMPOWERMENT

Proponents of organizational downsizing and restructuring (discussed in the previous chapter) typically have also advocated the adoption and application of employee empowerment. Empowerment, as identified in a number of places in this text, essentially means delegating sufficient authority to employees along with broadened responsibility to make decisions and to become involved contributors in the accomplishment of organizational objectives. Organizations that fully practice employee empowerment have been called "high-involvement" workplaces; such firms make a conscious effort to delegate as much as possible to employees at lower levels, allowing them to participate in or make decisions that affect their jobs. Empowerment also means a sharing of resources and information with supervisors, employees, or work teams that previously would have been retained by middle- or top-level managers. In essence, empowerment means that participative management is a commitment throughout the organization.[1] The goal of employee empowerment, of course, is the better achievement of organizational and economic objectives that will be accompanied with an appropriate sharing of compensation and other rewards throughout all levels of the firm.[2]

Self-directed (self-managed) work teams

When employee groups are given wide latitude and considerable authority to make many of their own job-related decisions.

To empower employees, effective supervisors structure their departments so that they can delegate more to them and take advantage of their ideas and experience. Employees and associates who are actually doing the jobs can contribute excellent ideas about how to solve problems concerning their work and related matters. Involving them can result in better decisions, and since most people like to have a voice in decisions that affect them, participation can result in more satisfaction and motivation. When employee groups are given wide latitude and considerable authority to make many job-related decisions, empowerment is associated with the creation or emergence of **self-directed (self-managed) work teams.**[3] One study indicated that approximately 80 percent of *Fortune 500* organizations had about half of their employees on work teams of some dimension. Self-directed work teams (abbreviated as SDWTs) typically received extensive training in setting targets and defining processes, and they even participated in hiring and disciplinary decisions. Supervisors were described as being more involved in monitoring results than managing methods.[4] We will discuss SDWTs and workplace teams in further detail in Chapter 15.

Most departmental supervisors are not involved in major decisions concerning the design of the overall organizational structure of their firms. Supervisors primarily are involved in decisions about the structure of their own departments. To understand concepts of organizing at the departmental level, we need first to review the importance of delegating and decentralizing authority and the occasional need for recentralizing.

DELEGATION, DECENTRALIZATION, AND RECENTRALIZATION

2

Explain the importance of delegating and decentralizing authority and identify when recentralizing is appropriate.

In Chapter 8, we advocated that a supervisor's strategy for getting work done should be based on the delegation of authority commensurate with responsibility. An organization does not really exist without delegation of authority. It is not a question of whether to delegate, but rather how much and in what forms authority should be delegated to subordinates at different levels. The extent to which authority is delegated determines the degree of organizational **decentralization.** When authority has been widely delegated downward and throughout levels of a firm, the firm has decentralized its decision-making authority. Decentralization, therefore, is an essential component of supervisory and employee empowerment.

Decentralization

When decision-making authority is widely delegated downward and throughout organizational levels.

If decentralization (empowerment) is to be effective, a sincere desire and effort to delegate must permeate the entire management team. Top-level managers must believe in delegation. Yet even though top-level managers may intend it, the desired degree of decentralization may not be achieved. Somewhere along the line there may be an authority "hoarder" who refuses to delegate further. Some supervisors are afraid or unwilling to delegate because they fear they may lose control of their departments.

In this regard, there appears to be a continuing debate among scholars and practitioners concerning the current status and application of concepts of decentralization and empowerment. Some proponents view traditional organizational structure as being out of date. They claim that hierarchy, reporting relationships, and accountability should be replaced by a "boundaryless organization" that is "barrier-free." Minimal structure should permeate the entire organization so that everyone focuses on common goals and objectives. Old hierarchies presumably would be replaced by self-managed work teams in organizational environments built upon self-responsibility and trust.[5] However, some observers believe that "the more things change, the more they stay the same." Tom Peters, prominent consultant and author of *In Search of Excellence,* claims that most decentralization and empowerment approaches are more form than substance. According to Peters, "The average decentralized corporation is not decentralized. It is a sham, a sick joke." Peters asserts that most managers do not really understand the meaning of decentralization, and they are not willing to change their authoritative approaches, despite the many problems that today's organizations face.[6]

Achieving the Desired Decentralization

There are several ways to achieve the desired degree of decentralization. Some organizations make great efforts to indoctrinate their entire management team in the philosophy of decentralization and empowerment. Managers are made to understand that by

By delegating authority, managers do not lose status or absolve themselves of responsibility.

delegating authority they neither lose status nor absolve themselves of their responsibilities. One way to accomplish decentralization is to organize so that each manager has a fairly large number of subordinate supervisors. By stretching the span of management, the manager has little choice but to delegate.

Another means that some organizations use is to establish a policy that managers cannot be promoted if they have not developed subordinates who can take over their positions. This policy provides an incentive to delegate and develop junior supervisors to assume additional responsibilities.

Increasingly, compensation systems for managers, supervisors, and employees are being linked to performance measures that involve recognition of how well objectives are met through the collaborative (e.g., team) efforts of personnel throughout the organization. These compensation systems usually encourage the practice of decentralization (empowerment) because everyone can identify their own self-interests as being tied both to their performance and the overall results of the firm.[7]

When Recentralization Is Appropriate

From time to time, top-level management will take a look at a firm's organizational structure—checking, questioning, and appraising whether it is sound. There may be a need for changes due to technological advances, changes in the environment, changes in the enterprise itself, and other reasons. Reorganization may be needed to overcome perceived shortcomings. Consequently, management may decide to realign, "tighten up," or recentralize. Management may feel that it has lost control over certain activities, perhaps because established controls were not effective. **Recentralization** is the process of reducing or revoking delegated authority in connection with realigning functions or responsibilities. For example, in recent years, as companies decentralized their sales, service, and other operating divisions, many of them centralized their budgetary and financial departments in order to have better financial control over the operations that otherwise were decentralized. A periodic review of the amount of delegated authority is both advisable and necessary in any organization. This also applies to any authority that the supervisor has delegated to employees.

Whenever recentralization takes place, there are apt to be tensions and resistance among members of the organization whose authority is lessened. Feelings of discouragement, mistrust, suspicion, and insecurity will be common. To ease these feelings, higher-level managers should explain thoroughly to subordinate managers the reasons for recentralization. Similarly, if a supervisor decides to revoke certain authority that has been delegated to an employee, the supervisor should discuss the reasons for this decision with the employee, as well as with others who are affected. For example, a housekeeping supervisor of a local motel might decide that employees who previously had wide latitude to determine the order of their tasks now must follow a written daily work schedule to meet the changing priorities of the motel manager. The supervisor may be able to lessen the resulting resentment by discussing the reasons for the change and encouraging the employees to suggest ways to improve the work scheduling process. Generally, recentralization is a difficult process. Appropriate and prudent decentralization of authority in the first place is the best way to avoid the need to recentralize.

Recentralization

Reducing or revoking delegated authority when realigning functions or responsibilities.

Describe why and how to develop a supervisory understudy (assistant).

DELEGATING BY DEVELOPING UNDERSTUDIES

In this chapter's opening "You Make the Call" segment, store manager David Simms finds himself in a serious organizational predicament because he does not have anyone trained and available to replace one of his shift supervisors who is leaving the firm on very short notice. The problem facing Simms is somewhat analogous to that of a supervisor who must be absent from the department for a valid reason and who is in a quandary about needing someone to take charge while he or she is away.

This chapter's focus has been upon the importance of a supervisor's delegation of authority as a means of building organizational structure and teamwork within the department. If the supervisor is away or removed from the scene and operations go on in a productive and orderly fashion, this usually means that the supervisor has selected and developed an understudy to whom authority and responsibility can be entrusted.

Why Have an Understudy?

In many situations the number of employees within a supervisor's department will be rather small, and the supervisor may wonder whether it is really necessary to delegate authority to any employees. Regardless of the size of the department, however, every supervisor needs someone who can assist and even be able to run the department if the supervisor is not present. For purposes of brevity, we will define this person as an **understudy.** Terminology varies in many organizations; for example, an understudy may be called an *assistant,* a *lead person, working supervisor,* or some other appropriate title. Regardless of the designation, every department should have someone who can take over when the supervisor has to be away from the job for sickness, meetings, vacations, or other reasons. As mentioned before, a supervisor personally may miss a promotion if no one is capable of taking over the department. Sooner or later, every supervisor needs an understudy.

There are several advantages that supervisors will discover if they decide to select, train, and develop understudies. Training understudies usually forces supervisors to formulate a much clearer view of their own duties, departmental operations, and ways to arrange jobs more efficiently. The supervisor will usually discover more effective ways of delegating throughout the department. Further, if the supervisor has two or three equally good employees as potential candidates in the department, it may be desirable to train all of them. This provides the supervisor with even more backup leadership. It also gives the supervisor more information and greater opportunities to observe potential understudies in action before making a definite selection.

Selecting an Understudy

The first step in developing an understudy is to select the right person for the position. For discussion purposes, we will assume that the supervisor is not restricted in choosing an understudy, as might be the case in a unionized firm with seniority criteria. Further, in the following sections, we mainly will consider the selection and development of a single understudy. In general, the same process would apply if the supervisor de-

Understudy

Someone who can assist the supervisor and is able to run the department in the supervisor's absence.

Every supervisor needs an understudy.

cides to select two or more individuals to receive this type of training and development (for example, if the size of the department should warrant a number of assistants).

A supervisor usually knows which employees are the most capable. Thus, the individual selected preferably should be someone to whom other employees turn in case of questions—a person who is regarded by fellow workers as a leader. He or she should be recognized as one who knows how to do the job, handles problems as they arise, avoids arguments, and is respected by other employees. A potential understudy should have demonstrated good judgment in carrying out assignments and in approaching, analyzing, and solving problems. This person should be interested in developing himself or herself for a better position. Without ambition to advance, even the best training will not achieve the desired results. Also, this employee must have shown dependability and a willingness to accept responsibility. Even though he or she has not had the opportunity to display all of these qualities, whatever latent attributes exist usually will be discovered during the training and development process.

Developing the Understudy

Although the word *training* frequently is used to denote the educational process for a supervisory understudy, it is not an altogether fitting term. Rather, it should essentially be a process of developing or "bringing along" an employee—an experience of *self-development* on the understudy's part. Understudies must indicate their eagerness to develop themselves and have the initiative to be self-starters. Bringing understudies to the point where they can assume considerable authority may be a slow and tedious process, but it is worth the effort.

Since no two people are alike, no exact procedures or time schedules can be outlined that will work in every case. However, there are some common steps in the development process that seem to work well in most situations. Gradually, supervisors should bring understudies in on the detailed workings of their departments. For example, supervisors should share departmental reports and explain where, when, and how information is provided. They should inform understudies why such reports are necessary and what is done with them. They should introduce the understudies to other supervisors, staff members, and personnel with whom they must associate and have them contact these people as time goes on. It is advisable to permit understudies to attend supervisory meetings after they have had a chance to learn general aspects of the supervisory job. Supervisors should discuss with them how the work of each department is related to that of other departments. As daily problems arise, supervisors should encourage understudies to try to solve some problems on their own. As understudies develop their own solutions, supervisors will have a chance to see how they analyze situations and approach decision making. Supervisors can teach the understudies the steps of decision making, pointing out guidelines to follow and pitfalls to avoid (such as the concepts presented in Chapter 5).

Over time, supervisors should give their understudies responsibility for some activities, in other words, delegate more duties and commensurate authority to them. This relationship requires an atmosphere of confidence and trust, with the supervisor recognized by the understudy as a *coach* and *mentor*. In an eagerness to develop understudies as rapidly as possible, supervisors should not overload them or pass on problems that are beyond their capabilities; it may take some time for understudies to be able to handle complex problems. Moreover, supervisors must be aware that sooner or later the understudies will expect some tangible rewards to compensate for the additional duties.

This process may take much effort and many supervisory hours. It could happen that about the time the understudy can be of major help, he or she may be transferred to another job outside of the supervisor's department or be promoted. This can be discouraging for the moment, but the supervisor can be confident that higher-level managers will appreciate the supervisor's efforts and success in the development of a competent assistant. Further, having a part in the development or advancement of an employee is one of the most satisfying personal feelings that a supervisor can experience.

Encouraging the Reluctant Understudy

The development of an understudy and delegation of authority involve a two-sided relationship. Although the supervisor may be willing to delegate authority, a subordinate

Although the supervisor may be ready and willing to delegate authority, an employee may be reluctant to accept it.

may be reluctant to accept it. Some employees are unsure of themselves and feel that they may not be able to tackle the job. Or they fear having additional responsibilities that may add to the burden of their daily work. Some employees do not want to move up since they are reluctant to leave the security of their peer group—for example, if they are part of a labor union or have several friends in their work group. Merely telling someone to have more self-confidence, or "pull yourself together," will have little effect. However, the supervisor can contribute to a potential understudy's self-confidence by gradually coaching and training the person to undertake additional and more difficult assignments. Employees who have a high sense of responsibility often underrate themselves. Yet these may be the very employees who will develop into excellent understudies if they are encouraged and assisted to accept the challenge.

To delegate effectively, the supervisor should develop both a professional and personal relationship with the understudy. This often will be a growing and shifting relationship that becomes more meaningful with the passage of time. At some point, the understudy should be able to take over the complete supervision of the department. When that happens, the supervisor truly will have organized a department that will carry on even if he or she should leave the position. Of course, with increased responsibilities should come positive incentives for supervisory assistants, such as pay increases, appropriate titles, recognized status within the organization, and other tangible or intangible rewards.

PLANNING THE "IDEAL" DEPARTMENTAL STRUCTURE

4
Identify why a supervisor should plan for an "ideal" departmental structure and work toward this objective.

Although some supervisors will have an opportunity to structure a totally new department, most supervisors are placed in charge of existing departments. In either case, supervisors should think of an *ideal departmental structure*—a structure that the supervisor believes can best achieve the department's objectives. It is not essential that a supervisor's plans for the department appear beautiful on paper or that the organization chart look symmetrical and well balanced. Nor should an "ideal" structure be thought of as being in the distant future. Rather, it should be a goal or standard by which the supervisor can assess the present organizational arrangement and which should serve as a guide for rearrangements and for long-range plans for the department.

The supervisor should plan the departmental structure on the basis of sound organizational principles, not around personalities. If the organization is planned primarily to accommodate current or available individuals, existing shortcomings probably will be perpetuated. If a department is structured around one or a few persons, serious problems can occur when key employees are promoted or leave.[8] But if departmental organization is planned on the basis of the necessary activities and functions to be performed, then qualified people can be sought to fill the positions. For example, if a supervisor relies heavily on one or two key employees who are "Jacks of all trades," then the department will be disrupted if one or both of these employees leave. Conversely, if a number of weak employees do not carry their share of the load, the supervisor may assign too many employees to certain activities to compensate for poorly performing individuals. Therefore, a structure should be designed that will best serve the objectives of the department; then the available employees can be matched with the tasks to be performed.

This is easier said than done. It frequently happens, particularly in smaller departments, that available employees do not fit well in the planned "ideal" structure. In most situations the supervisor will be placed in charge of an existing department without having had the chance to decide its structure or to choose the employees. In these circumstances the supervisor can gradually adjust to the capacities of the available employees. Then, as time goes on, the supervisor can make personnel and other changes that will move the department toward the supervisor's concept of an "ideal" structure. In all of this, of course, the supervisor's primary focus still should be placed upon finding, placing, and motivating the best people that are available, which this chapter's "Contemporary Issue" box emphasizes as being more important than just structural concerns.

ORGANIZATIONAL TOOLS AND THEIR APPLICATION

5

Define and discuss organizational tools that are useful in supervisory organizing efforts.

Some managers, supervisors, and employees do not understand how their positions and responsibilities fit in with the positions and responsibilities of other employees. Organization charts and manuals, job descriptions, and job specifications can reduce the confusion. These tools clarify the organization's structure and assist supervisors in understanding their positions and the relationships between various departments throughout the enterprise. The obligation to prepare a firm's overall organization chart and manual rests with top-level management. However, supervisors will usually develop these tools for their departments and also keep them up to date.

Departmental Organization Charts

As discussed in Chapter 8, organizational charts graphically portray authority and responsibility relationships. By utilizing boxes or some other depictions, these are usually interconnected to show the grouping of activities that make up a department, division, or section. Each box normally represents one position category, although several or more employees may be included in a position category. For example, Figure 9-1 (see page 294) shows a position called "Day Nurses." This is one position, although there may be many day nurses. By studying the vertical relationships between the categories depicted, anyone can readily determine who reports to whom. Although different types of organization charts are used, the vast majority are constructed vertically and show levels of organization arranged in some type of pyramid fashion.

A supervisor will gain a number of advantages from establishing and maintaining an organization chart of the department. It requires, first of all, a careful study and analysis of the departmental structure. Preparing the chart might reveal duplication of efforts or inconsistencies in certain functions or activities. A chart might enable the supervisor to spot where dual-reporting relationships exist (that is, where one employee is reporting to two supervisors) or where there are overlapping positions. The chart may also suggest whether the span of management is too wide or too narrow.

contemporary issue

Concentrate on People, Not Structure

Although the need for a sound organizational structure long has been recognized as a cornerstone for effective management, it is apparent from considerable research and observation that organizational structure is becoming less of a necessary requisite than previously thought. This was expressed in separate and somewhat different presentations by two authoritative speakers at the 1999 convention of the Society for Human Resource Management (SHRM). Jim Collins, a former university professor and coauthor of the book *Built to Last: Successful Habits of Visionary Companies,* asserted, "People are *not* your most important asset; the *right* people are." According to Collins, many firms too often fill open positions within an organizational structure with mediocre individuals. This may fill a slot, but only by staffing with the very best people and putting them to work on addressing opportunities (rather than just solving problems) can a firm really become a great one. Collins claims that it is more important for companies to focus on "getting the right people on the bus," rather than just trying to decide where the organizational bus is heading.[1]

Speaking at the same SHRM convention, Professor Karen Stephenson, a professor of management at UCLA and a cultural anthropologist who has studied organizations, claimed that most senior managers are more concerned and knowledgeable about management hierarchies and authority than they are with the actual human networks that make an organization function. She further noted that organizational hierarchies are easy to identify. However, informal networks of people that really drive a firm are primarily based on trusting relationships. People in these relationships are scattered among various levels of authority and structure. Stephenson noted that both hierarchies and networks can successfully co-exist within an organization, although too often the effect of authority and hierarchy is "to crush a network" rather than to unleash potential for making the organization more effective and rewarding to its participants.[2]

Although their topics were somewhat separate and distinct, it appears that their messages were similar in meaning for management; namely, concentrate on people rather than on structural concerns if you want to make your organization a more effective one.

Sources: (1) Excerpted from Robert W. Thompson, "Focus Should Be on Right People," *HR News* (August 1999), pp. 4 and 6. (2) Robert W. Thompson, "Informal Networks Play Important Workplace Role," *HR News* (August 1999), pp. 2 and 5.

Organization charts are a convenient way to acquaint new employees with the structure of the department and the entire enterprise. Most employees want to know where they stand and where their supervisor stands relative to higher-level managers. Of course, there are limitations to charts, especially if they are not kept up to date. All changes should be recorded promptly since failure to do so makes the chart as outdated and useless as last week's newspaper. Also note that organization charts show formal authority and responsibility relationships; they do not reflect the informal organization, which we discuss later in this chapter.

Organization Manuals

The organization manual is another helpful tool because it provides in comprehensive written form the decisions about a company's organizational structure. Not every com-

FIGURE 9-1

Organization chart for nursing services department of a hospital.

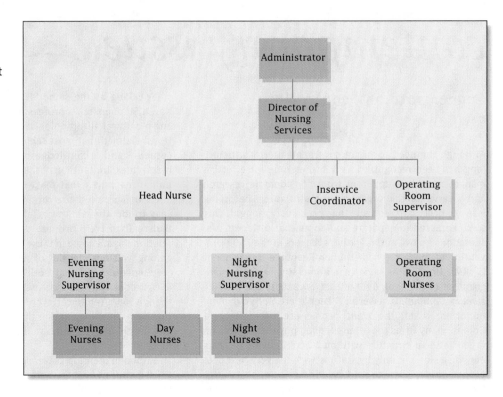

pany has an organization manual, but most firms of appreciable size do. They may be identified by any number of designations, including terminology unique to the firm. By whatever designation, typically the **organization manual** defines and describes the scope of authority and responsibilities of managerial and supervisory positions and the formal channels for obtaining information, assistance, or certain decision-making authority. The manual usually specifies the responsibilities of supervisory positions and how each position is related to other positions within the organization. The manual may outline functions of each department and explain how relationships within the organization contribute to accomplishing the objectives. The manual may also contain major policies and procedures, particularly those relating to personnel. Every supervisor should be thoroughly familiar with the contents of the organization manual, especially with those sections that most affect their own department.

Job Descriptions and Job Specifications

Job descriptions often are included in an organization manual or can be obtained from the human resources department. A **job description,** sometimes called a "position description," identifies the principal elements, duties, and scope of authority and responsibility involved in a job. Some job descriptions are brief; others are lengthy. Job

Organization manual

Written description of the authority and responsibilities of managerial and supervisory positions as well as formal channels, major objectives, and policies and procedures.

Job description

Written description of the principal duties and responsibilities of a job.

descriptions often are based on information obtained from employees who actually perform the jobs and from their supervisors.

Some firms include certain expectations—such as the availability to work evenings or to travel—as part of the job descriptions. Some even indicate specific productivity or quality performance standards that must be attained after a training period.[9]

For supervisory and managerial positions, many firms prefer to use the term *position guide* in identifying the duties, responsibilities, and results expected for supervisors and managers.

In practice, there is some overlap in the use of the terms *job description* and *job specification*. Generally speaking, a job description describes the major duties of a position, whereas a **job specification** refers to the skills, capacities, and qualities—personal qualifications—that are necessary to perform the job adequately. Many organization manuals include the job specification as part of each job description. Figure 9-2 (see page 296) is an example of a combined job description and specification. Note that the requirements to fill the job are called "placement criteria" on this form.[10]

If a department does not have job descriptions and job specifications for existing jobs, or if new jobs are to be created, the supervisor should see to it that they are developed and written up. If help is needed, the supervisor should ask the human resources department, which usually has the necessary experience and know-how to facilitate this task. We will discuss this more in Chapter 12.

Job specification

Written description of the personal qualifications necessary to perform a job adequately.

INFORMAL ORGANIZATION

6

Discuss the impact of the informal organization, informal group leaders, and how supervisors should deal with them.

Informal organization

Informal groupings of people, apart from the formal organizational structure, that satisfy members' social and other needs.

Every enterprise is affected by a social subsystem known as the **informal organization** (sometimes referred to as the "invisible organization"). The informal organization reflects the spontaneous efforts of individuals and groups to influence the conditions of their environment. Whenever people work together, social relationships and informal work groups inevitably will come into being. Informal organization develops when people are in frequent contact with each other, although their relationships are not necessarily a part of formal organizational arrangements. Their contacts may be a part of or incidental to their jobs, or they may primarily stem from the desire to be accepted as a member of a group.

At the heart of informal organization are people and their relationships, whereas the formal organization primarily represents the organization's structure and the flow of authority. Supervisors can create and rescind formal organizations that they have designed; they cannot eliminate an informal organization since they did not establish it.

Informal groups come into existence in order to satisfy needs and desires of their members that the formal organization does not satisfy. Informal organization particularly satisfies the members' social needs by providing recognition, close personal contacts, status, companionship, and other aspects of emotional satisfaction. Groups also offer other benefits to their members, such as protection, security, and support. They further provide convenient access to the informal communications network or grapevine (discussed in Chapter 3). The grapevine provides a channel of communication and facilitates satisfaction of the members' desires to know what is going on. In-

Job description and specification for insurance company senior terminal operator.

JOB TITLE	JOB CODE	POSITION STATUS	
Senior Terminal Operator	0408	_____ Exempt	XX Nonexempt

ORGANIZATIONAL UNIT		LOCATION	
Administration	XX Home Office		XX Region

SUMMARY STATEMENT (A brief statement of the purpose of this position)

Performs routine and nonroutine input functions on computer terminal under moderate supervision. Provides clerical support as directed by supervisor. In certain regional offices, individual works under an activity standard.

RESPONSIBLE TO: Administration Manager/Supervisor

POSITION DUTIES AND RESPONSIBILITIES (Listed in order of importance to performance in this position. Developed from Job Analysis Questionnaire completed September 15.)

WEIGHT		DUTIES/RESPONSIBILITIES
60%	1.	Key input to system according to established procedures, meeting established time constraints. Review all displays to verify accuracy of input.
10%	2.	Assemble material received daily; prioritize material to establish the day's work flow. Review material for accurate completion and send back to source if unable to ascertain correct information. When appropriate, maintain activity records according to established procedures.
10%	3.	Perform necessary clerical tasks as directed by supervisor if system is not functioning; notify supervisor of system problems.
10%	4.	May analyze information to determine whether original material is incomplete and may obtain information from original material for input directly into the system, without prior review by established resources.
5%	5.	Produce various reports according to an established routine and time constraints.
5%	6.	Render clerical support to unit staff as directed by supervisor.
100%		

** IMPORTANT **

The above-listed duties and responsibilities are not totally inclusive, but are intended to represent the principal elements of this position.

PLACEMENT CRITERIA (Minimum educational, skill and/or experience requirements as of September 15.)

1. Keyboarding skills and familiarity with computer operations.
2. Knowledge of general clerical functions as normally acquired through a high school education and/or related experience.
3. Knowledge and general understanding of the basics of the line of insurance for which individual is to be responsible, as normally acquired through one (1) year of work experience.
4. Ability to prioritize work flow and organize diverse material.
5. Ability to perform effectively according to an established quota and/or production system with moderate supervision and within established time limits and ongoing deadlines.

WORKING CONDITIONS: Normal office environment. Incumbent will be seated at a computer terminal for the majority of the work day.

EXCEPTIONS TO THE ABOVE HIRING CRITERIA must be approved in writing by Home Office Human Resources.

formal organization also influences the behavior of individuals within the group. For example, an informal group may exert pressure on individuals to conform to certain standards of performance agreed upon by the majority of the group. This phenomenon may occur in any department or at any level in the organization.[11]

The Informal Organization and the Supervisor

At times the informal organization may make the job of the supervisor either easier or more difficult. Because of their mutual interdependence, the attitudes, behavior, and customs of informal work groups affect the formal organization. Every organization operates in part through informal work groups, which can exert either a constructive or a negative force on the operations and accomplishments of a department.

Numerous research studies have demonstrated that informal groups can influence employees to either strive for high work performance targets or restrict production; either cooperate with supervisors or make life miserable for them, even to the point of having them removed. Supervisors must be aware that informal groups can be very strong and can even shape the behavior of employees to an extent that interferes with supervision. So-called "organizational negativity" has become a major area of concern in many firms during recent decades.[12] Negative attitudes that lead to negative behavior patterns often are traceable to work groups that influence individual members to conform to the group's norms of conduct. Thus, pressures from informal groups can frustrate the supervisor in getting the results that higher-level managers expect the supervisor to achieve.

Informal work groups can have a constructive or negative influence on the operations and accomplishments of a department.

To influence the informal organization to play a positive role, the supervisor first must accept and understand it. The supervisor should group employees so that those most likely to comprise harmonious teams will be working together on the same assignments. Moreover, the supervisor should avoid activities that would unnecessarily disrupt those informal groups whose interests and behavior patterns support the department's overall objectives. Conversely, if an informal group is influencing employees in a negative direction to the extent that there is a serious threat to the department's functioning, a supervisor may have to take action, such as redistributing work assignments or adjusting work schedules.

Supervising and Informal Work Group Leaders

Most informal work groups develop their own leadership. An informal leader may be chosen by the group or may just assume the reins of leadership by being a spokesperson for the group.[13] Work group leaders play significant roles in both the formal and informal organizations; without their cooperation, the supervisor may have difficulty controlling the performance of the department. A sensitive supervisor, therefore, will make every effort to gain the cooperation and goodwill of informal leaders of different groups and will solicit their cooperation in furthering departmental objectives. If properly approached, an informal leader can be helpful to the supervisor, especially as a channel of communication. An informal leader may even be a viable candidate for the supervisor's understudy if that person would accept such a position. However, it is questionable whether this person can still function as an informal leader once he or she has been designated as an understudy.

Instead of viewing informal leaders as "ringleaders," supervisors should consider them as employees who have influence and who are "in the know," and then try to work with them. For example, in an effort to build good relationships with informal leaders, a supervisor periodically may provide information to them before anyone else or ask their advice on certain problems. However, the supervisor must be careful to avoid having informal leaders lose status within their groups because the leaders' close association with the supervisor certainly is being observed and could be interpreted negatively by employees. Similarly, the supervisor should not extend unwarranted favors to informal leaders as this could undermine their leadership roles. Rather, the supervisor should look for subtle approaches to have informal groups and their leaders dovetail their special interests with the department's activities. We will discuss this and other aspects of work groups in Chapter 15.

What Call Did You Make?

As David Simms, you first must analyze the problem and base your decisions on facts and available information. Review the concepts of problem solving and decision making presented in Chapter 5. Then, beyond the facts and information you now have, contact local employment and temporary help agencies to determine the availability and cost of external candidates to fill the position. You might explore your network of personal contacts as well. You also should find out if supervisors hired from outside the company in the past have been successful, and how the managers who hired them were evaluated. This information will be useful if you decide to go against the grain of company policy to promote from within.

As David Simms, you should not rely solely on the grapevine for assessing supervisory potential. Review the performance evaluations of all your employees to assess their skills and potential. The feedback from the grapevine about Margo James as a temporary supervisor probably should not be ignored. It might be possible to promote Margo and still maintain employee morale, since Margo is an excellent server and she has had some experience with the supervisory position. However, her performance in the past suggests that she may be deficient in supervisory and human relations skills required to maintain performance, morale, and stability at desired levels. If you promote Margo James, you will need to spend long hours to train her extensively on the skills and behaviors necessary for an effective supervisor. She must learn that the things she does to be a successful server are different from the things she will need to do as a supervisor. However, if you conclude that good employee morale and stability are your top objectives, promoting Margo James at this time is questionable. She probably is not yet qualified to be a permanent supervisor, although recognize that this usually is the case for any promotion-from-within decision of an employee into a supervisory position.

You might decide to hire a temporary supervisor until someone from within is trained and qualified to take the job. If you find a temporary supervisor through an agency or an employment service, you should closely monitor how the temporary person performs and not rule out the possibility of keeping that person if he or she is successful. Document your decision-making process and communicate it to your boss as something to consider for other locations.

Probably the most important lesson for you to learn from this experience is how to prevent this type of situation from happening again. As discussed throughout this chapter, it is important to have an established plan for filling various positions long before the need actually occurs. Your problem arose because no qualified supervisory candidates were ready to step in when June Teevers resigned. You now should give much attention to developing selected employees by giving them opportunities to learn and practice supervisory skills. Rotating certain servers to be temporary supervisors when there is a need to cover absences and vacation periods could enable them to learn supervisory management skills. This can provide you with a number of candidates for which you have a basis to evaluate their supervisory potential. Then the next time a supervisor leaves the company, you should be ready to fill the position internally with a qualified person.

SUMMARY

1. Empowerment means a companywide commitment to delegating authority and responsibility to employees at lower levels so that they can participate in decision making. To empower employees, supervisors should structure their departments to allow more employee participation. Employees actually doing the job can then help solve problems that affect their jobs. This can result in better decisions and more satisfied employees.

2. Delegation and decentralization of authority are vital if empowerment is to be a reality and there is to be a broad sharing of decision making throughout the enterprise. Decentralization is not achieved easily because some managers and supervisors are unwilling to delegate. At times, recentralization of authority is appropriate due to organizational realignment or the necessity to tighten up certain operations.

3. At the departmental level, supervisory delegation can be fostered through the selection, training, and development of understudies. Unless the supervisor develops someone to be an understudy and grants authority to this person, the department may be hampered seriously if the supervisor is absent for extended periods.

4. In designing the organizational framework of a department, the supervisor should conceptualize an "ideal" arrangement based on the assumption that all required and qualified employees would be available. Since seldom are there people available with all of the exact qualifications desired, employees who are available must be fitted into the structure. Over time, the supervisor should make the changes and adjustments needed to move the department toward its "ideal" structure.

5

6

A departmental organization chart shows a graphic picture of authority and responsibility relationships. Organization manuals contain statements of objectives, policies, and procedures; identify the authority and responsibilities of managerial and supervisory positions; and describe formal channels for obtaining information, assistance, or certain decision-making authority. The manual also may contain job descriptions, which identify major elements of a job position, and job specifications, which identify personal requirements to qualify for or perform a job position.

The informal organization interacts with, yet is apart from, the formal organization structure. It can have either a constructive or a negative influence on departmental work performance. In order to make positive use of the informal organization, supervisors should become familiar with the workings of the informal groups and their leaders and determine how to enlist their cooperation to promote accomplishment of departmental objectives.

KEY TERMS

Self-directed (self-managed) work teams (page 285)
Decentralization (page 285)
Recentralization (page 287)
Understudy (page 288)

Organization manual (page 294)
Job description (page 294)
Job specification (page 295)
Informal organization (page 295)

QUESTIONS FOR DISCUSSION

1. Define "empowerment" and "self-directed work teams." Why should supervisors empower their employees?
2. Why are delegation of authority and decentralization highly interrelated concepts? Is it proper to say that delegation of authority is necessary in order to have an organization? Discuss.
3. Why does top-level management sometimes resort to recentralization? Will a supervisor have occasions to revoke authority (i.e., recentralize)? Discuss.
4. What are the major issues involved in the selection and development of an understudy at the supervisory level?
5. Why do some employees resist opportunities to accept an understudy assignment? What can the supervisor do to encourage capable employees to seek advancement within the organization?
6. Discuss the issues involved in the question of whether a supervisor should organize on an "ideal" basis or on a "real" basis.
7. Define and discuss the application of the following organizational tools at the supervisory level:
   a. organization charts
   b. organization manuals
   c. job descriptions
   d. job specifications
8. What is meant by informal organization? How does the informal organization affect the formal organization? Discuss approaches by which the supervisor can foster cooperation with informal groups and their leaders.

SKILLS APPLICATIONS

Skills Application 9-1: Departmental Organization Chart Development

To complete this project, refer to Figure 9-1, which shows an organization chart for a hospital department. Recognize that Figure 9-1 was simplified for demonstration purposes.

Develop a departmental organization chart for a department of a firm, or for any enterprise for which you can obtain the required information and assistance. If you are currently employed, ask your supervisor for permission and help in this project.

Use rectangular boxes to show either an organizational unit or a position. Place the title of each position in the box. The title should be descriptive and show the function (e.g., sales-manager). Vertical lines of authority should enter at the top center of a box and leave at the bottom center. An exception to this might be where there is a supervisory assistant and a horizontal relationship is involved. Vertical and horizontal solid lines should show the flow of line authority. Dotted or broken lines should show the flow of functional authority, if this is needed.

Keep the chart as simple as possible. Include comments to explain any special aspects.

Skills Application 9-2: The Informal Work Group

Using your current or most recent job, answer the following questions.
1. What informal groups exist, and why do they exist?
2. What pressures, if any, do they exert or can they exert on the supervisor?
3. Do the informal groups affect job performance at any time? If so, how and why? Who are the informal group leaders, and how do they influence job performance?
4. If you are the supervisor, what can you do to influence the groups in a desired direction?

Skills Application 9-3: Supervisory Organizing Applications

1. Identify from this chapter a list of what you believe to be the most important principles/concepts that a supervisor should apply at the departmental level in order to supervise effectively.
2. Next, think of the best and worst supervisors you have known or worked for. To what degree did they practice or not practice each of the items on your list?

Skills Application 9-4: Mentoring

INTERNET ACTIVITY

When you select an understudy, you initiate a mentoring relationship. To learn more about mentoring, access the Mentor Teacher Handbook at http://apollo.gse.uci.edu, or other sites that discuss mentoring.

1. According to your findings and your own experience, what characterizes an effective mentor? Think of someone who has been a mentor in your life. Which of these characteristics did they exhibit?
2. What are the stages in the development of a mentor?
3. Describe two different approaches to mentoring.
4. Would you be a good mentor? Complete the "Should I Become a Mentor" checklist to find out.

ENDNOTES

1. For expanded discussions concerning employee empowerment as related to organizational changes, see Florence M. Stone and Randi T. Sachs, *The High Value Manager: Developing the Core Competencies Your Organization Demands* (New York: AMACOM Division of American Management Association, 1995); or James R. Emshoff, "How to Increase Employee Loyalty While You Downsize," *Business Horizons* (March/April 1994), pp. 49–57. For an excellent discussion of techniques for keeping empowered work teams on the right track, see Donna Deeprose, *Recharge Your Team: Keep Them Going and Going,* (New York: American Management Association, 1998).

2. See Charlotte Roberts as interviewed by Thomas B. Wilson, "Linking Incentives and Organization Strategy," *ACA News* (March 1998), pp. 17–19.

3. See Darrel Ray and Howard Bronstein, *Teaming Up: Making the Transition To a Self-Directed, Team-Based Organization* (New York: McGraw Hill, 1995).

4. Carla Joinson, "Teams at Work: Getting the Best From Teams Requires Work on the Teams Themselves," *HRMagazine* (May 1999), pp. 30–35.

5. See Gregory G. Dees, Abdul M. A. Rasheed, Kevin J. McLaughlin, and Richard L. Priem, "The New Corporate Architecture," *The Academy of Management Executive* (August 1995), pp. 7–18; or Ken Blanchard, John P. Carlos, and Alan Randolph, *Empowerment Takes More Than A Minute* (San Francisco: Berrett-Koehler Publishers, 1996).

6. Tom Peters as quoted in, "Ever in Search of a New Take on Excellence," *Business Week* (August 3, 1992), p. 52.

7. See Edward G. Vogeley and Louise J. Schaefer, "Link Employee Pay to Competencies and Objectives," *HRMagazine* (October 1995), pp. 75–81. These and other compensation considerations will be discussed in Chapter 13.

8. This type of problem is inherent in the "principle of organizational stability" discussed in Chapter 8, which advocates that no organization should become overly dependent upon the talents/abilities of a single individual or a few individuals, that is, no one should be indispensable to the continuity of the enterprise.

9. See J. E. Osborne, "Job Descriptions Do More Than Describe Duties," *Supervisory Management* (February 1992), p. 8; or Danny G. Langdon and Kathleen S. Whiteside, "Redefining Jobs and Work in Organizations," *HRMagazine* (May 1996), pp. 97–101.

10. As mentioned in Chapter 1, these personal qualities are sometimes referred to as SKAs—skills, knowledge, and abilities.

11. See Michael R. Carrell, Daniel F. Jennings, and Christina Heavrin, *Fundamentals of Organizational Behavior* (Upper Saddle River, N.J.: Prentice-Hall, Inc., 1997), pp. 342–345; or David A. DeCenzo, *Human Relations* (Upper Saddle River, N.J.: Prentice-Hall, Inc., 1997), pp. 201–207.

12. Gary S. Topchik, "Attacking the Negativity Virus," *Management Review* (September 1998), pp. 61–64.

13. In Chapter 11, we will discuss supervisory relationships with the departmental union shop steward where a labor organization represents employees in a firm. Some of the same types of supervisory considerations should apply to a union shop steward as to an informal work group leader.

Managing Meetings

Learning Objectives

You Make the Call!

You are Martha Landram, a district supervisor for eleven retail outlets of Good n' Tastee Pizza in a metropolitan area. Each store is headed by a manager. In turn, each store manager has several assistants. All stores offer eat-in, carry-out, and delivery. The staffing level and the hours of operation vary depending on store size, sales volume, and location. The store managers report directly to you.

You used to schedule weekly meetings with your store managers and sometimes with their assistants. The Tuesday 9:00 A.M. meetings usually were held in your district office. The meetings primarily were held to present information about marketing promotions, deal with customer problems, and discuss other issues of mutual interest. However, these meetings were difficult to schedule because of pressing business, vacations, absences, and other activities. At times only a few store managers would show up for the scheduled meeting. This caused difficulties in trying to inform those who were not present concerning what had been discussed and decided. Also, you received complaints from your supervisors that some meetings had been a waste of time, including travel time. Responding to their complaints, you agreed to install an intranet system between the district office and the stores whereby you could send messages and information to all stores.

The Internet-like computer network was expected to facilitate communication, collaboration, and information management within Good n' Tastee. The consulting firm that sold Good n' Tastee the system elaborated on the efficiencies. It would help to manage documents and information, connect people to the Internet, and facilitate group application such as e-mail, sales and cost analysis, employee scheduling, inventory management, and ordering raw materials. Consultant Rudy Michaels said, "It's a way for people to quickly share and access information in a paperless way." Each store would receive the same information at the same time, and store managers could read the messages when they had time to do so.

The intranet system has been in operation for about six months. Although it has been useful in sending out information, you sense something is missing in the process. You rarely get feedback from the store managers concerning information you have disseminated. In several instances, store managers claimed they had not received a message. Moreover, it appears that the store managers are not using the system to exchange information among themselves. Yesterday, Sam Cook, manager of the Maplecrest Store, complained that he has "fallen from grace"—he never sees you or the other store managers to share experiences and to discuss and decide certain problems that you would like them to handle. In particular, he mentioned the development of a recruitment and retention plan to handle the companywide staffing shortage. What should you do?

You Make the Call!

1

Explain why meetings, committees, and being able to lead meetings are important components of supervision even in an age of electronic communications.

THE NEED FOR MEETINGS AND COMMITTEES IN AN ELECTRONIC AGE

Electronic mail, facsimile transmission, voice mail, teleconferencing—these and other high-tech communication channels have become commonplace in many organizations. Messages flow continuously upward, downward, and sideways through most organizations to the degree that individuals often complain about information overload.

Further, as more employees work in locations such as their homes, automobiles, and other temporary workplaces—sometimes referred to as *virtual offices*—various types of electronic meetings have become the norm rather than the exception. An

contemporary issue

You Have Till Noon To Get Your Team's Collective Input!

Technology may be the most critical attendee at this morning's meeting. It lets meeting agendas wait till the last minute, and attendees can actively participate even if they are halfway around the world. Deloitte & Touche had scheduled a meeting for its top executives in Scottsdale, Arizona. The problem was, one executive was in Japan. His participation was needed. His advice was necessary, and he needed to know what was happening as it happened.

International Conference Resort's media director, Martin Dempsey, had the answers in minutes. Bring the missing executive face to face with his peers through a videoconference. "We have all the equipment on-site, so it was just a matter of the executive finding a location that has all the equipment. They're all over the world now so it wasn't a problem," says Dempsey. "Then we just made the connection and the man was seen live on the 43-inch flat-plate display. It's as simple as using a television remote."

Companies like Deloitte & Touche are using just-in-time meetings and on-line training meetings. Videoconferencing and other collaborative technology can help meeting planners make meetings better. But it is not something that most of us have had much experience using. "Using a meeting facility with an in-house audiovisual department increases your comfort zone," says Deloitte's meeting planner Debi Losey. "But it's often a challenge to get all the technology needed on the other end," Losey continues. "For example, our executive in Japan had to make arrangements and pull components from a couple of sources to get hooked up. This was difficult considering the time zone change and the short notice. Ideally, you want at least one person available (on both ends) every second in case something goes wrong. We would prefer not to use videoconferencing on a daily basis, but it does give us the best alternative to a face-to-face meeting."

Technology alone will not ensure a successful meeting. Planners need to be educated on the benefits and traps of meeting technology. Nevertheless, from pre-planning to post-meeting follow-up, electronic technology is the wave of the future.

Source: Adapted from "Meetings Matter: Meeting Insights from International Conference Resorts," Special Advertising Section, *Training* (Summer 1999), pp. 1–8. Additional information gleaned from telephone interview with Debi Losey (October 22, 1999).

Electronic meeting

Group meeting via electronic transmissions in which participants are not physically together in one location.

electronic meeting, which includes certain forms of teleconferencing, is one in which participants do not come physically together in one location on a face-to-face basis but communicate electronically. One of the most advanced forms of electronic meetings uses a computer system known as *group decision support software* (GDSS). This system enables individuals at various locations to discuss and decide issues without actually getting together in one location. Participants can input information and opinions in an anonymous way, and they also can vote on an anonymous basis when this is applicable.[1]

Other types of electronic communications such as e-mail, voice mail, and the like have enabled swift and more efficient communication in many situations. Critics claim that these forms of electronic communications do not allow for the full and open discussion possible in the dynamics of a face-to-face setting. This chapter's "Contemporary Issue" box illustrates how electronic technology can be applied.

The Supervisor's Role in Calling and Leading Meetings

There can be little doubt that the flow of electronic messages will continue to be an important part of most organizations' information systems. Yet with all of this flow of information, gaps and misunderstandings still occur, which often harm interpersonal relationships and job performance. As Martha Landram, the supervisor in this chapter's "You Make the Call" segment, has discovered, electronic message systems are not the complete answer to effective supervision of employees and others. More is needed in order to ensure the full flow of communication and understanding in ways that are necessary for people to carry out their jobs.

Complex organizational structures, job specialization, matrix projects and other work teams, and increased complexity of operations require—even more now than previously—that all organizational efforts be coordinated properly. To achieve this, there still is no substitute for bringing together the people who are responsible for dealing with the problems at hand. In other words, it still is necessary to call meetings or form committees. Without meetings and committees it would be impossible for most organizations to operate. Of course, there are other ways to supply information that people need to perform their jobs and to receive their ideas and opinions. However, holding a meeting is often the most effective way to achieve these objectives. This particularly is true at the departmental level. Supervisors frequently need to meet with their employees, work teams, other supervisors and associates, and higher-level managers in order to discuss, plan, and decide on issues and what actions are to be carried out.

We have placed this chapter under the organizing function of management because committees and meetings are an integral part of organizational life. For the most part, they are not shown on organization charts or identified in organization manuals, and many are temporary. Since meetings and committees are a vital part of the organizational network of any firm, all of the concepts and principles discussed in Chapter 3 on communication can be applied to committee and meeting situations. Further, certain aspects of the decision-making process presented in Chapter 5 are applicable to many group meetings.

TYPES OF MEETINGS

2

Identify the major types of meetings, their purposes and benefits, and their limitations.

Most meetings may be described as being either informational, discussional, or decisional in nature. In the **informational meeting,** the group leader does most of the talking, and the purpose of the meeting is to present information and facts. For example, a supervisor may call a meeting to announce a new job-scheduling system as a substitute for posting a notice or speaking to each employee separately. Such a meeting enables everyone in the department to be notified at the same time. It also provides employees with a chance to ask questions about the meaning and consequences of the announcement.

Informational meeting

People gathered together to hear the group leader present information.

In a **discussional meeting,** the group leader encourages the participation of group members in order to secure their ideas and opinions. For example, instead of asking employees individually for their suggestions on how to solve a problem, the supervisor could call a meeting for the same purpose. A number of suggestions may be offered and

Discussional meeting

People gathered together to participate in a discussion with the group leader by offering their opinions, suggestions, or recommendations.

Decisional meeting

People gathered together to make decisions on a particular problem or task for which the group has been granted some decision-making authority.

discussed in the meeting. Typically, the implementation of an idea that was suggested and discussed will receive more employee support since the employees have participated in the solution.

A **decisional meeting** takes place when a discussional group has been delegated some authority to make decisions on a particular problem or task. Just as a supervisor can delegate authority to an individual employee to make a decision, a supervisor can call a meeting and delegate authority to a group. For example, if a group of grocery store clerks are concerned about the allocation of overtime and they ask the supervisor to make a decision, the supervisor might prefer that the employees themselves find a solution. The supervisor therefore empowers the clerks to decide for themselves how overtime will be allotted. If the majority of the group make a decision, the solution probably will be more acceptable to the employees. Even if the group's solution is not the very best, it may be better for the supervisor to have an adequate solution that is implemented by the group than to impose a supervisory decision that they resist.

A supervisor may not be concerned with the detailed solution of a problem as long as the solution remains within certain limits. Such limits must be clearly stated when the problem is submitted to a group for a decision. For example, if the group is to decide on the allocation of overtime, the number of hours available must be stated. Also, the supervisor may need to point out that no one should work for more than a certain number of hours a day, and so forth. When feasible, it is desirable to let the group decide for themselves what should be done within stated guidelines.

Benefits from Meetings

A group of individuals exchanging information, opinions, and experiences usually will develop a better solution to a problem than could any one person who thinks through a problem alone. People bring to a meeting a range of experiences, backgrounds, and

Electronic meetings are extremely beneficial when people from two or more geographical locations must meet face-to-face.

abilities that rarely would be available if the same subject had been assigned to one person alone. Many problems are so complicated that one person could not possibly have all the knowledge, background, and experience needed to arrive at proper solutions. An open interchange of ideas can stimulate and clarify thinking. Solutions or recommendations that a group reaches will tend to be better than those that any single member of the group would have selected.

Group deliberation also can promote cooperation. Suggestions from members of a group are likely to be carried out more willingly than suggestions that come from only one person. When people have participated in the formulation of a plan, they tend to be more motivated toward its implementation than if they have not been consulted. It matters less how much they have actually contributed to the plan so long as they were part of the meeting. Thus, group meetings are advantageous in promoting cooperation and motivation.

Meetings can also be an opportunity for employees to demonstrate their creativity and problem-solving ability and perhaps get noticed as candidates for promotion. Also, if meetings are conducted in an atmosphere of mutual respect, members will feel responsible for achieving a successful outcome.

Limitations of Meetings

Despite its benefits, the meeting device often is abused. A common complaint of supervisors is that there are too many meetings in their organizations. Another complaint is that many meetings are too time consuming. This complaint usually surfaces when each person at a meeting wants to have a major say and uses up a great amount of time to convince the others of his or her particular point of view. Meetings can also waste time if the agenda is not clearly focused on the problem at hand, the group leader or the members are not well prepared, or the leader allows the group to wander off the subject.

Another shortcoming of meetings is the concept of divided responsibility. When a matter is assigned to a group for deliberation, responsibility does not weigh as heavily on the individual members as it does if the matter is assigned to one person. The problem becomes everybody's responsibility, which really means it is nobody's responsibility. Although the group leader technically is responsible for the action or inaction of the group, this person can hardly be held accountable for the group's decision. Similarly, it is difficult to criticize the group as a whole or its individual members if each member can hide behind the responsibility of the total group. This thinning out of responsibility is natural, and there is no way to avoid it when a problem is referred to a committee for a decision.

Groupthink

Phenomenon that occurs in meetings when members do not express dissenting views in order to avoid conflict rather than realistically appraise alternatives.

Still another possible shortcoming is the phenomenon of **groupthink.** This occurs when the group's desire for consensus becomes paramount over its desire to reach the best possible decision. Deliberations become dominated by efforts to avoid conflict within the group, and therefore individuals do not express dissenting views that might be helpful in realistically appraising alternative choices of action.[2]

The supervisory problem is to weigh the many advantages emanating from group deliberation against the shortcomings of holding a meeting. Fortunately, the advantages usually exceed the disadvantages. If group members are carefully selected and if meetings are led and managed well, most meetings will become a vital, contributing part of any organization.

COMMITTEES: TYPES, COMPOSITION, AND SIZE

We will use the term **committee** to identify a group of people drawn together to solve a problem or complete a task. We will use this term to include other designations, such as *commission, team, task force, board,* and the like. Supervisors should be familiar with the workings of meetings and committees because they are frequently members. Moreover, supervisors themselves often conduct meetings; thus, they need to develop their ability to lead a meeting.[3] Members of a committee typically have other full-time jobs, and their committee work is an additional duty or corollary assignment.

Permanent (Standing) Committees

A **permanent (standing) committee** usually has an official, even permanent, place in an organization. Its members are appointed by someone in higher-level management— or they are elected or nominated in some fashion—to deal with certain recurring issues or problems. Members of a standing committee are expected to serve either for a stated period of time or indefinitely. Usually they are drawn from various departments and represent supervisors, employees, and specialist personnel. Some common examples of permanent standing committees are a plant's safety committee, a university's affirmative-action monitoring committee, an employees' credit union committee, and the like.

Temporary (Ad Hoc) Committees

A **temporary (ad hoc) committee** is a group that meets only for a certain time period and usually for a limited, specific purpose. When the work of the temporary committee is finished, the group usually is disbanded. Ad hoc committees can discuss almost any type of organizational issue that is not already assigned to a permanent committee. Many of the group meetings that supervisors conduct within their own departments and with other departmental supervisors are of an ad hoc nature.

Membership and Size of a Committee

The membership (or composition) of a committee is important to its success. For far-reaching issues, the committee should bring together representatives from each group affected by the committee's decisions. If specialists from different departments are to be brought together, affected groups should have adequate representation in order to have balanced group deliberation. This allows the interests of departmental personnel to be heard and considered (see Figure 10-1 on page 310). Although this consideration is important, the supervisor who is appointing the committee should not carry it to extremes. It is more important to have capable members serve on a committee than to have representatives from every group that may be affected. Committees with decision-

---

3

Discuss the major types of committees and suggest guidelines for determining the composition and size of a committee.

Committee

Group of people drawn together to solve a problem or complete a task.

Permanent (standing) committee

Group that meets on a more or less permanent basis to deal with recurring issues or problems.

Temporary (ad hoc) committee

Group that meets only for a limited time and for a specific purpose.

making responsibility should be composed of people who bring knowledge and experience related to the issue. Individuals selected should be able to express and support their opinions, but they also should be open to other points of view. It is advisable that they be independent of each other (i.e., not in a direct authority-reporting relationship).

There is no optimal committee size. Some authorities have suggested that twelve members is near the upper limit for effectiveness. In any event, a committee should be large enough to provide for ample sources of information and thorough group deliberation. However, it should not be so large that it will be unwieldy. If the nature of the subject requires a very large committee, then subcommittees may be needed. For example, a large managerial committee formed to discuss a major program consisting of manufacturing and marketing a new product probably would find it advantageous to divide into subcommittees. The subcommittees meet separately to consider detailed aspects of the program, such as design, production, advertising, and distribution. After the subcommittees have deliberated, the committee meets as a whole to hear reports from each subcommittee and then proceeds accordingly.

4

Identify the major factors contributing to effective meetings, especially the chairperson's leadership role.

LEADING EFFECTIVE PROBLEM–SOLVING MEETINGS

Meetings should be called only when necessary. If a matter can be handled by e-mail, a telephone call, or personal discussion, there is no need to call a meeting. But if a supervisor decides that a meeting is necessary, then the topic should be communicated to the meeting participants, and the participants' role should be clarified. It must be clear whether the meeting is to serve an informational, discussional, or decisional purpose. If the supervisor is forming a temporary committee, members should be selected appropriately, and their numbers should be reasonable. However, as previously mentioned, more important than the number of committee members are their qualifications and their willingness to tackle the problems at hand.

Most meetings—especially at the supervisory level—are of a problem-solving nature. These typically are discussional and/or decisional meetings in which a team or work group is asked to grapple with problems and may or may not have delegated authority to implement solutions. In this regard, when a problem is assigned to a committee to make a decision and carry it out, the committee has been given line authority. However, if the charge to the committee is only to deliberate, debate, advise, and make recommendations, then the committee acts in a staff role. For example, the specific meeting objectives stated for a work team might be stated as follows:

1. To improve safety at our plant, each team will recommend plans that can be implemented within one week for under $100.
2. To improve morale in the department, team members will generate at least 20 ways to build team spirit during the next 30 days.
3. To conduct more effective meetings, each participant will evaluate our most recent meeting and make suggestions for improvement.

For a meeting involving problem solving to be successful, the goals should be reasonable and achievable. Generally, the goals of the meeting should be (a) to come up with the best feasible solution to the problem, (b) to do this with unanimity or a majority consensus, and (c) to accomplish this in a short period of time.

The Chairperson and Teamwork

Chairperson
Group leader who is responsible for guiding a meeting toward completion of its stated objectives.

The success of any meeting depends largely on the group leader's skills in guiding the meeting toward completion of its stated objectives. We will refer to this individual as a **chairperson,** although designations are quite diverse.[4] A chairperson may be elected or appointed, formally or informally. In many situations supervisors serve as chairpersons, especially in meetings held with their own employees.

A chairperson should recognize that participants bring to a meeting unique points of view and behavior patterns. It is human nature for participants to think first of how a topic, issue, or proposal will affect them, their jobs, their departments, and their own work environments. These thoughts can easily lead to friction.[5] The chairperson should approach the members in such a way as to fuse individual viewpoints to promote teamwork.

A frequent observation about meetings is that the problems on the table are not as difficult to deal with as the people around the table. Individuals at a meeting often react to each other more than they do to issues or ideas. For example, whatever Sam Jones suggests might be rejected because he talks too much. Tania Smith might oppose whatever the group is for. Gloria Sanchez might keep her mouth shut most of the time. The chairperson's patience and skill can reduce such difficulties so that participants eventually start concentrating on the issues and not just on the individuals around the table. For a meeting to be successful, the chairperson should encourage participants to set aside personalities and outside allegiances and to work as a team to arrive at a workable solution. When confronted with people like Sam, Tania, and Gloria, a supervisor should strive to preserve a collegial environment in which all participants recognize the value of each individual and commit to a common goal. An unpleasant part of the chairperson's job is dealing with difficult personalities and/or nonteam players. He or she should seek to eliminate or minimize the problem behavior. Prior to the next meeting, the chairperson could talk with each of the individuals and point out the specific behavior that will not be tolerated and ask for commitment from each person to work together in order to accomplish the task. It is important that the self-esteem of the participant causing the problem be maintained. Thus, the chairperson should address the issue head on and in private.

A chairperson must be adept at keeping the meeting focused. Many of the more successful work teams have adopted ground rules for their meetings. Suggested ground rules might include the items listed in Figure 10-2. While this list is far from comprehensive, effective meeting management requires that supervisors develop ground rules and lay out their expectations.

FIGURE 10-2
Suggested ground rules for meetings.

- Everyone will be candid and specific.
- Everyone will have a say.
- Everyone will stop what they are doing and listen carefully to other team members' comments.
- Every team member must support his or her opinion with facts.
- No one will be allowed to interrupt another—we will hear each other out.
- We are a TEAM and working together everyone will achieve more.

Conducting Meetings: The Role of the Chairperson

The role of a chairperson is a demanding one. As stated before, the goal of a problem-solving meeting is to develop a good solution with as much unanimity as can be gained in a short period of time. However, the quality of a group's decision may depend in part on the amount of time spent. A hasty meeting may not produce the most desirable solution. On the other hand, meetings should have a time limit. If a meeting drags on too long, participants become bored and frustrated. It is the chairperson's role to offer members a chance to participate fully and to voice suggestions and opinions. The chairperson may have to persuade a minority to go along with the decision of the majority. On other occasions the chairperson will have to persuade the majority to make concessions to the minority. This takes time, and it may result in a compromise that does not necessarily represent the optimum solution but is at least an acceptable one.

FIGURE 10-3

The autocratic chairperson does not want members to participate in the discussion.

Variations in the chairperson's role can run anywhere from one extreme of being autocratic and very directive (Figure 10-3) to the other extreme of being very democratic. At times, a normally democratic chairperson may have to control a meeting more tightly; at other times only the loosest control is needed. For example, if the purpose of the meeting is to gather as many creative ideas as possible for a new advertising campaign, then the chairperson should foster a loose, freewheeling atmosphere to promote creative thinking. However, if the purpose of the meeting is to make a final decision for an imminent deadline, the chairperson should focus the participants' thinking more tightly on a few feasible alternatives. Regardless of the approach used, the chairperson is ultimately responsible for the effectiveness of the meeting. Figure 10-4 (see page 314) provides a useful list of questions to consider.

The Agenda. A useful technique for keeping a meeting from wandering off into a time-consuming discussion of irrelevant matters is a well-prepared agenda. Before the meeting, the chairperson should outline the overall meeting plan with an agenda. Topics to be discussed should be listed in sequence, and there should be a tentative time limit for the meeting. The chairperson may even have in mind a general timetable for discussing each item on the agenda, although this should be for planning guidance only and not be strictly enforced in the meeting. The actual agenda should be distributed in ample time for participants to prepare themselves for the meeting, and it may identify individuals responsible for making presentations. The chairperson should emphasize that the meeting will begin promptly at the time indicated on the agenda. Figure 10-5 (see page 315) is an example of an agenda that contains most of these desired criteria.

FIGURE 10-4

Questions to consider when planning a meeting.

WHAT is the purpose (goal) of the meeting?
WHAT are the opportunities, threats, conflicts, problems, concerns, issues, or topics that should be considered?
WHAT information needs to be disseminated prior to the meeting?
WHAT information needs to be gathered prior to the meeting?
WHAT advance preparation on the part of the participant is needed?
WHAT work must be completed prior to the meeting?
WHAT additional resources will be needed to accomplish the purpose?
WHAT are the ground rules for conducting the meeting?

WHO are the people that are involved with the concerns, issues, or topics?
WHO needs to do advance work or make decisions regarding the agenda?
WHO should be invited because they can provide information needed for problem solving or discussion on the issue?
WHO will develop and distribute the agenda?
WHO are the people that need to attend?
WHO will facilitate the meeting?
WHO will be assigned as the scribe?

HOW much time do we need to allot to each topic?
HOW should the meeting room be arranged?
HOW do we strive to find consensus and areas of agreement?
HOW do we stay focused on the subject(s)?

WHEN and WHERE should the meeting be scheduled?
WHEN should the meeting end?
WHEN and HOW should the meeting be evaluated?
WHEN and WHAT follow-up is needed to the meeting (for example, distribute a summary of the meeting and the actions to be taken)?

Although an agenda outlines the meeting plan, it must not be so rigid that there is no means for adjusting it. The chairperson should plan and apply the agenda with a degree of flexibility so that if a particular subject requires more attention than originally anticipated, time allocated to other topics can be adjusted. Although staying close to an agenda will help reduce irrelevant discussion, the chairperson must not be too quick to cut off discussion. What seems trivial to the chairperson may be important to some of the participants. In fact, some irrelevant discussion actually may contribute to a more relaxed atmosphere and relieve tension.

Since the chairperson's role is to keep the meeting moving toward its goals, he or she should pause periodically during the meeting to consult the agenda and remind the group what has been accomplished and what remains to be discussed. Astute leaders learn to sense when the opportune time has arrived to summarize one point and move on to the next item on the agenda. If experience tells them that their meetings have a tendency to run overtime, it might be advisable to schedule them shortly before the lunch break or just before quitting time. This tends to speed up meetings since no one wants a meeting to cut into personal time.

FIGURE 10-5

Example of an agenda for a meeting of supervisors in a firm's accounting services division.

October 1, 20 – —

MEMORANDUM

TO: Department Supervisors, Accounting Services Division
FROM: Helen Stages, Controller
RE: Monthly Staff Meeting

Our next meeting is scheduled for *Wednesday, October 11,* in the conference room (Room 122). We will convene promptly at 3 P.M. and adjourn no later than 4:45 P.M. The agenda is as follows:

1. Review of meeting action summary from September 13 meeting. Follow-up on these items to be completed with progress reports from responsible person(s).
2. Review of recent implementation of new internal control procedure for payroll tax determinations.
3. Proposal for revised policy for follow-up on delinquent accounts (draft proposal previously sent via e-mail on 9/25—Tom Barrett).
4. Discussion concerning supervisory requests for additional office space.
5. Such other business as may arise.

If you cannot attend this meeting, please notify me by Friday, October 6.

Meeting Structure. If participants are well motivated, formality may be minimal or unnecessary. Normally, however, meetings need some structure and leadership from the chairperson, who is responsible for keeping the meeting moving with orderly discussion directed toward an efficient conclusion. Sensitive judgment on the chairperson's part is required to maintain an appropriate balance of formal structure with the necessary amount of informality that encourages active participation by all members.

Some organizations deliberately avoid having supervisors and managers chair meetings when their subordinates are participants so as to encourage an atmosphere conducive to open discussion. If this is to be the case, whoever is selected to chair the meeting should be chosen for his or her ability to manage the meeting and not because of other considerations.

Many work teams have experimented with the concept of a *meeting facilitator.* Generally, the leader of the group or the supervisor does not conduct the meeting. This role falls to the facilitator—this function often is rotated among team members. This approach allows the supervisor, for example, to observe, listen, and ask probing questions of team members. In addition, team members gain experience in a leadership position. A downside of this approach is that all team members must be adept at meeting management. Further, the *scribe* (note taker) responsibility is rotated among team members.

Encouraging Full Participation. After a few introductory remarks and social pleasantries, the chairperson should make an initial statement of the matter(s) to be discussed. All members should be encouraged to participate in the discussion and to bring out information that is important to them. There are usually some participants who talk too much and others who do not talk enough. One of the chairperson's most important roles is to encourage the latter to speak up and to keep those who talk too much from doing so. This does not mean that all members of a meeting must participate equally. There will be some who know more about a given subject than others, and some will have stronger feelings about an issue than others. The chairperson should strive to stimulate as much overall participation as possible.

The chairperson's general approach is of crucial importance. Initially everyone's contribution should be accepted without judgment, and everyone should feel free to participate. The chairperson may have to ask controversial questions in order to get discussion and participation started. This is sometimes done by asking provocative, open-ended questions that ask who, what, why, where, and when. Questions that can be answered with a simple "yes" or "no" should be avoided.

As you remember from our discussion of communication (Chapter 3), the supervisor is responsible for *giving* and *getting* information. To get information or to open discussion on a particular topic, the supervisor might want to ask the "W" questions—what, where, why, when, and who, before getting to the how. For example, the chairperson could use questions to get and keep the discussion going such as "What is the relationship between quality and machine set-up times?" "Hank, what would be your suggestion?" "Where did the problem occur?" "Why is that important to you?" "When will we have the new machine on-line?" "Who might have the experience to handle such an assignment?" "Who would like to comment on Wally's question?" "How can we exceed the customer's expectations?"

Another technique is to start at one side of the conference table and ask each member in turn to express his or her thoughts on the problem. Although this approach forces everyone to participate, it discourages spontaneous participation and allows the rest of the group to sit back and wait until called on. This approach may also cause some individuals to take a stand on an issue before they are mentally prepared to do so.

A chairperson may be so anxious to have everyone say something that there is considerable aimless discussion just for discussion's sake. The chairperson should observe facial expressions for clues as to whether someone has an idea but is reluctant to speak up. This is particularly important when talkative members of the group dominate the meeting while other participants struggle to contribute their comments. There are several techniques the chairperson can use to cope with the member who talks too much. After the talkative member has had sufficient opportunity to express opinions, the chairperson can conveniently overlook that person, calling on other participants to speak. Or the chairperson may ask the talkative member to please keep any additional remarks brief so that others may contribute. Most of the time, however, other members of the meeting will find subtle ways of "censoring" those who have too much to say.

If a meeting is made up of a large number of participants, it may be advisable to divide it into smaller groups. Each of the small subgroups reports back to the overall meeting after a specified period of time. This is similar to the subcommittee approach mentioned previously, and it encourages those who hesitate to say anything in a larger group to be more comfortable and willing to offer their opinions.

It is important for the meeting leader to maintain balance between content and process functions. Questions that the meeting leader/facilitator can ask himself/herself to help maintain the balance are:

- Are all participants involved in the discussion?
- Are participants listening to the discussion?
- Are comments being heard and paraphrased?
- Is everyone bringing the issues and concerns to the table or is there a reluctance to discuss delicate issues?
- Are sensitive and/or critical issues being thoroughly explored?
- Are alternative solutions being generated?
- Are employees piggy-backing on the ideas of others?
- Are decisions being made?
- Is the discussion performance-focused rather than people-focused?

The Chairperson's Personal Opinions. A chairperson generally should strive to assist meeting participants in reaching their own decisions by encouraging them to offer and consider different ideas and alternatives. If the chairperson expresses too many personal views, participants may hesitate to disagree. This is especially true if the leader is the manager or part of top-level management. Yet there are occasions when it would be unwise and unrealistic for the chairperson not to express any views. He or she may possess relevant facts or opinions, and the value of the group's deliberations would be lessened without these contributions.

On the whole, therefore, a leader should express opinions but at the same time must clearly state that those opinions are open to constructive criticisms and suggestions from the group. Silence on the part of a chairperson, especially when he or she is the manager or the highest-ranking member of the group, may be interpreted to mean that the chairperson cannot make decisions or does not want to do so for fear of assuming

To open discussion on a particular topic, the supervisor should use the "W" questions.

responsibility. Thus, the chairperson must use good judgment in determining when and to what extent personal opinions are relevant or needed.

Guiding the Group to a Decision.

After a problem is identified and generally understood by members of the group, and the relevant facts have been presented, discussed, and evaluated, the next appropriate step for the group is to suggest alternative solutions for the problem. From this point, the chairperson should guide the group through the remaining steps of the decision-making process as outlined in Chapter 5.

A chairperson should always realize that the "best" solution will only be as good as the "best" alternative considered. Accordingly, the chairperson should strive to make certain that no realistic solution is overlooked, and participants should be urged to propose as many alternatives as they can develop. The next step is to evaluate alternative solutions and to discuss the advantages and disadvantages of each proposal. Discussion eventually will narrow to several alternatives on which general agreement can be reached. It then may be advisable to eliminate all other alternatives by unanimous consent. Those alternatives that remain should be evaluated thoroughly in order to arrive at a solution.

The chairperson may have to play the role of a mediator by proposing an overall solution that would be acceptable to most members of the group, possibly even convincing some members that their opinions are not as persuasive as others. Preferably, the final solution will be a synthesis of the desirable outcomes of the few remaining alternatives. By a process of integration, the most important points are incorporated into the most desirable solution. The chairperson also has the sensitive job of helping those holding minority viewpoints to accept the group's decision. It is easier to achieve this if the final decision can incorporate something of each person's ideas so that everyone has contributed. Of course, this can be a long and tedious process, and a compromise may not result in the strongest solution.

The chairperson may be confronted by a group that is hostile to virtually every proposal. In such a situation, it is necessary to find out what is bothering the group, to bring their opposition into the open, and to discuss it frankly and objectively. When confronted with a new idea, participants often concentrate on the objectionable features rather than on the desirable results that may be gained. Objections thus have to be clarified and discussed. If open discussion does not reduce the real and unwarranted fears and objections, it may be appropriate to adjourn the meeting and try again at a later time.

Taking a Vote.

A chairperson must decide whether or not to take a vote. Although voting is a democratic way to make decisions, at times it actually accentuates differences among members of a group. Once individuals publicly commit themselves to a position, it becomes difficult for them to change positions. If they are members of the losing minority, they may not carry out the majority decision with enthusiasm. Therefore, whenever possible, it is better not to take an early formal vote but to work toward unanimous or near-unanimous agreement.

A major disadvantage of working toward total agreement is that such a process can take a long time, and unanimity may cause serious delay. Also, for the price of unanimity, the solution may be reduced to a common denominator that is not as ingenious, bold, or imaginative as it would have been otherwise. Whether the chairperson should seek unanimity in a solution or not depends on the situation and the magnitude of the problem.

The skilled chairperson usually can sense the feeling of the meeting. A remark such as, "It seems to me that the consensus of the group is that 'such and such' is our solution," may be appropriate. This type of summary statement can avoid a formal vote. If this is not possible, a vote should be taken in order to reach a decision. In a small group, a show of hands or secret written ballot is adequate. For large group meetings, the observance of normal voting procedures can save time and keep the meeting from becoming unwieldy. The form of the voting procedure may be less important than whether the participants understand the issue involved, believe that a fair hearing has been held in the meeting, and are ready to vote.

Importance of Follow-Up. As a general rule, the chairperson should appoint someone (the scribe or secretary) to record and summarize what happened during the meeting. Subsequently, the chairperson should see to it that the written summary, called the meeting action summary (or minutes), is provided to every participant. The summary should also be distributed to all other personnel who have a need to know what took place or are essential in accomplishing the necessary action. See Figure 10-6 for an example of a *meeting action summary*. In short, the meeting action summary lists the actions to be taken by the group, fixes accountability (who will do what by when), and becomes a record for follow-up and feedback.

FIGURE 10-6

Meeting action summary.

Meeting date: _____	Facilitator: _____		Scribe: _____
Start time: _____	End time: _____	Length: _____	
Action to be taken	Person responsible	Deadline	Completion date
1.			
2.			
3.			
Next meeting: _____		Start time: _____	Location: _____
Issues to be addressed:			
1.			
2.			
3.			
List of attendees on the back side.			

The chairperson may have the scribe orally summarize the action decided upon prior to adjournment of the meeting, so that all participants have a chance to review what took place. The written summary serves as a permanent record or a guideline for future situations involving similar issues. If some matters are left undecided, the summary can provide a review of the alternatives that were discussed and help to crystallize the thinking of the participants. For permanent standing committees such as the organization's safety committee, it will be advisable to use the summary as the opportunity to announce to others when the group will next meet to take up unresolved problems or to consider new issues.

MANAGING MEETINGS WITH THE BOSS

Describe how supervisors can better manage meetings with their own managers.

Still another supervisory responsibility is communicating "up the organization." For example, the supervisor may want to report at his/her manager's staff meeting about the most recent department/team meeting. Supervisors should communicate not only the issues and items that impact their department but also should pass along positive comments about their team members and other members of the organization who have contributed in a positive manner.

Throughout this text, we focus on how to manage subordinates, teams, projects, and the processes within the organization. As discussed in Chapter 3, all managers should develop a climate that encourages a free flow of upward communication. However, in reality, the responsibility for upward communication typically falls on the shoulders of the supervisor. Increasingly, in an era of intense global competition replete with organizational mergers and restructurings, supervisors have the responsibility to keep upper management informed and manage the relationship with their immediate supervisor in a positive manner. Supervisors also must be prepared to contribute suggestions, ideas, and opinions in a timely basis.

How many times have you heard someone say, "treat others the way you want to be treated?" The same holds true for the supervisor's relationship with upper management. Most communications upward are meetings between the supervisor and his or her manager. Generally, the supervisor should be building a bond between himself/herself and the boss. Informational meetings, discussional meetings, decisional meetings, and simply sharing time with the boss all affect organizational performance. The fact is that each meeting impacts the boss's perception of the supervisor and vice versa. Obviously, how the supervisor *manages up* is of vital importance to his or her career. The following list provides insight on how the supervisor can more effectively manage meetings with the boss:

1. *Respect the boss's time.* Remember that "every boss has a boss" and as such has demands placed on his or her time that you aren't aware of. Many bosses advocate an open door policy, so be careful and don't burden your boss with trivial issues or issues you can handle yourself. Choose a time when the boss is not busy and can give you and the issue undivided attention. A good approach might be, "I need about 5 minutes of your time to discuss. . . . What would be a convenient time?" If the boss

says, "two o'clock" then be a few minutes early. It may sound basic, but think of the impression you make if you're late.

2. *Check your motives.* Is a meeting the best way to address the issue or problem and achieve your purposes? If the answer is no, the meeting may not be worth having at this time.

3. *Plan your agenda.* Have a few notes on the important points or issues in front of you to make sure you cover what you want in the meeting with the boss. Don't wing it! Successfully managing up begins with preparation and planning. When planning the agenda, remember the *KISS* technique—<u>k</u>eep <u>i</u>t <u>s</u>hort and <u>s</u>imple.

4. *Don't go to the boss "naked."* An effective manager encourages subordinates to develop alternatives, solutions, or suggestions to problems. No one wants a problem or issue dumped on them. You should start with a review of the situation, and end with your suggestions. You want to leave the boss with the feeling that you are on top of things.

5. *Commit to the truth.* In the *Fifth Discipline,* noted author Peter Senge calls honesty a commitment to the truth which he argues is necessary for the discipline of personal mastery.[6] We could not agree more. A meaningful relationship is built on mutual trust and respect. Explain your position on the issues objectively, using facts, figures, and examples.

6. *Advertise success.* Make certain that upper management knows the successes of your work group and others that you rely upon for success. The supervisor who in a meeting tries to claim all the credit will lose the respect of others and be known as a "glory hound."

7. *Learn to say no.* Upper managers often impose unrealistic workloads or deadlines. There may be tremendous pressure from above to "buy in." Don't overcommit your team to "mission impossible." The supervisor who doesn't learn to say "no" will lose respect from subordinates and end up looking bad in the eyes of the boss.

8. *Don't filter information from your boss.* Don't tell the boss only what he or she wants to hear. Supervisors sometimes fail to pass along information because it might reflect unfavorably on themselves.

9. *Anticipate problems.* If there is a situation where you might need the boss's help, do not hesitate to ask for it in a timely fashion. The best time to get the help you need is at the beginning. A common error supervisors make is to wait until they are buried under by the project or job assignment, or when failure is imminent before they ask for help.

10. *Don't be a whiner.* As mentioned above, it is essential to apprise the boss of problems, but don't be a constant complainer or whiner. The supervisor who only approaches the boss to grumble about things becomes marked as part of the problem, not part of the solution.

11. *Don't put the boss on the defensive.* Often, supervisors become upset or angry. They barge into the boss's office and attack by demanding, pointing fingers, or venting their anger. These behaviors and words are seen as aggressive—an attack on the boss. Many people lack the ability to cope with attacks on them and attack back with great vigor. The meeting becomes a war zone rather than one where a favor-

able work environment is created. The latter focuses on understanding the issues from the viewpoint of the other and striving to reach agreement and develop follow-up steps. Attack the problem, not the person!

12. *Make a resolution.* I want to treat my boss as though I am the most dedicated and competent employee, ready to make a difference. For example, I will put into practice a plan for effectively managing up.[7]

What Call Did You Make?

As Martha Landram, you have discovered that the intranet system is not a substitute for holding a meeting. The system allows Martha to send information and have a record of its receipt. But as you recall from Chapter 3, just because the message is sent does not ensure understanding. Holding a meeting in which communication flows in all directions on a face-to-face basis between participants is a more vital way for communicating and understanding information. Meetings enable discussion, debate, and decisions that can build commitment among those who participate.

You probably should decide to reinstate scheduled meetings of your store managers on some predetermined basis. For example, you might decide that there

will a regular meeting held on the first Tuesday of each month at 9:00 A.M. You may want to vary the meeting site among the stores rather than always have them come to your office. You must impress upon your store managers that this will be a priority claim on their time and they are expected to attend. Then it will be important that you master the skills for conducting meetings as described in this chapter. A desirable part of your strategy would be to have the store managers participate in suggesting meeting agenda items. Know in advance your purpose for the meeting and then be sure to follow through promptly to make the most of your meeting time. The topic regarding the development of a companywide recruitment and retention strategy might be a good place to start. You must take the time to make the meetings more productive and relevant to the needs of the store managers.

SUMMARY

1

Supervisors are involved in meetings and committees either as members, organizers, or chairpersons. Meetings usually are called to disseminate information or to discuss or solve problems. There is no real substitute for bringing together the people who are responsible for dealing with a problem.

2

Informational meetings are primarily for the purpose of presenting information and facts by the group leader. In discussional meetings, participants offer opinions and suggestions. In a decisional meeting, the group has been delegated some authority to make decisions on a problem or task.

Group deliberations often produce more satisfactory and acceptable conclusions than those that might be reached by an individual. Major complaints about meetings are that there are too many of them, they are time consuming, and they divide responsibility.

The function of standing committees is to deal with recurring problems or issues. Temporary (ad hoc) committees usually are appointed to serve for a limited time and for a specific task.

In selecting the membership of a committee, groups most affected by the committee's decisions should be represented. Members should be people who bring knowledge and experience related to the issue. They should be willing to present their views, but also be open to other ideas. The size of a committee should be large enough to permit thorough deliberations, but not so large as to make it cumbersome.

The success of any meeting depends largely on effective leadership. For discussional and decisional meetings, the chairperson's task is to obtain an optimal solution in a minimal amount of time with the greatest amount of unanimity. The chairperson constantly is faced with the problem of how directive or democratic to be. The chairperson should strive for full group participation that has just enough structure to arrive at an effective and efficient conclusion.

Most people are not comfortable managing up. In today's fast-paced business world, it is essential that supervisors keep higher management abreast of the developments in their work areas. The tips for managing up contained in this chapter blend practical application with common sense. The supervisor that effectively manages meetings with higher management will gain credibility, and likely lead to the accomplishment of organizational objectives.

KEY TERMS

Electronic meeting (page 305)
Informational meeting (page 306)
Discussional meeting (page 307)
Decisional meeting (page 307)
Groupthink (page 308)

Committee (page 309)
Permanent (standing) committee (page 309)
Temporary (ad hoc) committee (page 309)
Chairperson (page 311)

QUESTIONS FOR DISCUSSION

1. Why are face-to-face meetings preferable even with all of the electronic messaging available?
2. Think about the "best" meeting you have been a part of, either as the chairperson or as a participant. What behaviors or activities occurred in that meeting that were particularly effective?
3. Discuss the distinctions between (a) an informational meeting, (b) a discussional meeting, and (c) a decisional meeting. Are these distinctions always clear? Why or why not?
4. Discuss and evaluate the benefits and limitations of a group discussion of problems requiring a departmental decision. Why is the lack of fixed responsibility both an advantage and disadvantage of referring problems to a group?
5. Is the complaint that "there are too many meetings and they take up too much time" valid? How should meetings be viewed by the supervisor in relationship to his or her managerial role?

6. What are some of the major factors to be considered in deciding on the composition of a committee? Is there an "optimal size" committee? Discuss.

7. Gail's boss expected a miracle from her project team. With the help and cooperation of another team, the project was completed on time and under budget. She is concerned that upper management will fail to recognize the efforts of the other team. How can Gail ensure that the efforts of her team and the other team will be adequately recognized?

8. Why is the ability to hold, lead, and participate in meetings an important skill for a supervisor to develop? What steps can supervisors take to ensure that meetings they participate in or chair will be successful?

9. What are the ingredients for successful meeting management? If a supervisor fails to consider one or more of the ingredients will disaster occur? Why or why not?

10. Read the following statements:
    a. "There's not much good to be said for meetings."
    b. "To get the most out of meetings, don't go!"
    c. 'The role of the meeting leader is to get everyone involved."
    d. "Meetings can be a tool for developing employee skills."
    e. "It is management's absolute responsibility to hold a minimum of one staff meeting per week."
    What are the merits of each statement? What are the drawbacks?

11. Why is it advisable for a supervisor to learn how to manage meetings with his or her boss?

SKILLS APPLICATIONS

Skills Application 10-1: Rate a Meeting

1. Rate a meeting you attended recently, applying the following rating scale to each statement.
   Strongly Agree = 4   Agree = 3   Disagree = 2   Strongly Disagree = 1

Scoring

_____	1. The agenda was prepared and distributed beforehand.
_____	2. All participants knew the purpose of the meeting.
_____	3. All participants were prepared.
_____	4. The meeting started on time.
_____	5. During the meeting, all members participated.
_____	6. I really felt like I was part of the meeting.
_____	7. Participants openly communicated disagreements with others' viewpoints and with the chairperson.
_____	8. The chairperson encouraged participation from all members.
_____	9. I benefited from participation in the meeting.
_____	10. The chairperson kept the discussion focused and on target.
_____	11. The chairperson ensured that all participants agreed on the issues discussed and the action to be taken.
_____	12. The meeting ended on time.
_____	TOTAL (Add your scores)

2. Compare your total with the following:

42–48	Meeting was very effective and very important to you.
30–41	Meeting was generally effective and your participation was useful.
18–29	Meeting was marginally effective and a source of some frustration for you.
12–17	Meeting was rather ineffective and your participation created stress for you.

3. What could have been done to make the meeting more effective?

Skills Application 10-2: Planning a Quality Improvement

Assume that you are the general manager of a steel fabricating facility. At the insistence of your major customer, you have scheduled a one-day quality improvement workshop for the key personnel of the facility. You have identified 30 potential participants from 8 different functional areas. The workshop will take place one week from this coming Saturday. The agenda has not yet been determined except that it is to focus on strategies for meeting or exceeding the increased quality needs of the major customer. You ponder whether a planning committee should help you develop the agenda.

1. Why would a planning committee be beneficial to you? What might be its drawbacks?
2. Assuming you were to form a planning committee, what factors would you consider to determine the membership composition?
3. Working in a group of three to five students, develop an agenda for the workshop. Then outline how you would conduct the meeting. Compare and contrast your recommendations with those of other student groups. Is there anything your group failed to consider? If so, what caused you to overlook certain items?

Skills Application 10-3: Handling a Difficult Person

Sterling Medical Center has utilized self-directed work teams for several years. The self-directed approach was designed to allow all team members more involvement and responsibility in department decision making. As leader of the maintenance and engineering team, you have tried to focus on the development of each team member so that they can more effectively perform their job functions and the team can become a high-performance team. As team leader, you have constantly stated that solutions to problems no longer come "from the top," but must be generated by team members. Further, you have repeatedly told team members that their ideas on how to improve work processes, quality, safety, and working conditions are listened to and considered important. The team has a formal meeting every Thursday morning. Your analysis of the most recent meeting disclosed that two members had become difficult.

Claude, an electrician with 20+ years of seniority, usually "sits on his hands" and never participates in the discussion. You recently overheard two employees express their disgust with Claude—*the clam*. At the other extreme is Harry, a mechanical engineer/MBA, who tries to dominate every discussion. Whenever there is a lull in the discussion, Harry takes it upon himself to fill in. Yesterday, several employees approached you to express displeasure with Harry's "holier than thou—I know everything" attitude. One said, "When he peers over his horn-rimmed glasses and gives me that stern look, I'd like to reach across the table and "pop" him one."

1. Have you ever known anyone like Claude—*the clam*—or Harry—*the wise owl*? How did you deal with them?

INTERNET ACTIVITY

2. Using the Internet or other reference sources, find information that will help you deal more effectively with Claude. What skills will you use to get Claude into the team spirit?

3. Using the Internet or other reference sources, find information that will help you deal more effectively with Harry. Given that Harry is an essential member of your team, how do you get him to be appreciative of the inputs of others? Without directly telling him to "shut up," what should you do to calm his enthusiasm without destroying his will to contribute?

4. What have you learned about how to reconcile the conflicting behaviors of team members in a meeting?

Skills Application 10-4: Facilitating Meetings

INTERNET ACTIVITY

When you call a meeting, you'll most often be in the role of facilitator. Visit www.thefacilitator.com or other sites dealing with the subject of managing meetings to find some practical tips on facilitating meetings.

1. From your search, create a list of at least five helpful tips for facilitating meetings (different from those suggested in this chapter).

2. Share your results with the class.

SKILL DEVELOPMENT VIDEO

SKILLS DEVELOPMENT MODULE 10-1: MEETING MANAGEMENT AND FACILITATION

In this video segment the staff at McElvey Department Store gather for a meeting called by their supervisor, Janet Ferrell.

Questions for Discussion: The Ineffective Version

1. Discuss the reasons that Janet Ferrell's meeting never got off the ground.

2. Evaluate Janet Ferrell's effectiveness in running a meeting (see "Questions to consider when planning a meeting," Figure 10-4).

3. If you were Janet Ferrell, explain what you would do to conduct a more effective meeting.

4. Explain the results of poor meeting leadership.

Questions for Discussion: The More Effective Version

1. Discuss how Janet Ferrell handled the meeting with her staff.

2. What could Janet Ferrell have done to be even more effective?

3. Evaluate the statement, "Conducting the meeting is easy if everyone understands its purpose."

4. In your opinion, would Janet Ferrell be more effective in gathering information and understanding the true feelings of her staff if she allowed Denny Mercer, the operations assistant, to facilitate the meeting while she sat on the sidelines?

ENDNOTES

1. Microsoft Office 2000 enables teams of workers to work as one using an intranet (www.microsoft.com/office/2000). For an interesting discussion of electronic meetings, see Michael Finley, "Welcome to the

Electronic Meeting," *Training* (July 1991), pp. 28–32; and Michael Schrage, "Robert's Electronic Rules of Order," *The Wall Street Journal* (November 29, 1993), p. A12. For a discussion of meeting management tips, see Eric Matson, "The Seven Sins of Deadly Meetings," *Fast Company* (April 1999), p. 122; "Learning Some Ways to Make Meetings Slightly Less Awful," *The Wall Street Journal* (May 16, 1998), p. B1; and Michael Schrage, "Meetings Don't Have to Be Dull," *The Wall Street Journal* (April 26, 1996), p. A22.

2. See Virginia Johnson, "The Groupthink Trap," *Successful Meetings* (September 1992), pp. 145–146.

3. For comprehensive sources on leading meetings, see Julie Baker, "Under the Gun: How to Plan Short-Term Meetings Without Losing Your Mind—or Breaking Your Budget," *Successful Meetings* (January 1996), pp. 36–42; Milo Frank, in Julie Rubenstein, ed., *How to Have a Successful Meeting in Half the Time* (New York: Pocket Books, 1990); Clyde W. Burleson, *Effective Meetings: The Complete Guide* (New York: John Wiley & Sons, 1990); Arthur H. Bell, *Mastering the Meeting Maze* (Reading, MA: Addison-Wesley, 1990).

4. The term *chairperson,* or more simply *chair,* has been used in recent years to avoid gender implications inherent in the term *chairman.* Some work teams use the term *meeting facilitator* in lieu of the term *chair.* Regardless of the term used, the responsibilities are the same.

5. See Gina Imperato, "You Have to Start Meeting Like This," *Fast Company* (April 1999), pp. 204+; Cathy Olofson, "Meeting I Never Miss: Start the Day with Coffee and Scrum," *Fast Company* (February 1999), p. 60; Carl Sherman, "Deal with It: Muzzling Motormouths," *Working Women* (September 1998), p. 80; Larry Tuck, "Meeting Madness," *Presentations* (May 1995), pp. 20–28; and Catherine Petrini and Rebecca Thomas, "Meetings, Stressful Meetings," *Training & Development* (October 1995), p. 11.

6. Peter M. Senge, *The Fifth Discipline* (New York: Currency/Doubleday, 1980), pp. 159–161.

7. The ideas and suggestions contained in the list were inspired by material contained in Meryl Natchez's Web site, "Managing Up: The Overlooked Element in Successful Management," (www.techprose.com/managing_up.html); Mike Lynch and Harvey Lifton's *Training Clips: 150 Reproducible Handouts, Discussion Starters and Job Aids* (Amherst, MA: HRD Press, 1998), p. 16; and Douglas Stone, Bruce Patton, and Sheila Heen's, *Difficult Conversations: How to Discuss What Matters Most* (New York: Viking, 1999). Also see Anna Muoio, "Boss Management," *Fast Company* (April 1999), pp. 91+; Bruce Tulgan, "Work This Way: Maximize Your Internship by Managing Your Boss," *Rainmaker Thinking, Inc.,* 15th ed., (December 1998) (www.rainmakerthinking.com); and Deborah A. Brophy, "Managing Your Boss," (www.accessjobs.org/boss.html). For a most interesting approach to managing the relationship with your boss, see Sue Shellenbarger, "The Care and Feeding (And the Avoiding) of Horrible Bosses," *The Wall Street Journal* (October 20, 1999), p. B1.

Chapter 11

After studying this chapter, you will be able to:

1

Explain why and how labor unions continue to affect organizations and the supervisory position.

2

Identify aspects of good management that are likely to deter a union organizer's appeal.

3

Outline procedures for supervisors to follow if confronted with a union-organizing effort.

4

Discuss the importance of good union–management relationships and the supervisor's key role in maintaining them.

5

Discuss the limited but important role of the supervisor in negotiating the labor agreement.

6

Discuss the major role of the supervisor in the interpretation and application of the labor agreement at the departmental level.

7

Describe the nature and importance of a good relationship between a supervisor and the union shop steward.

Learning Objectives

The Labor Union and the Supervisor

You Make the Call!

You are Leslie Brown, supervisor of housekeeping services at Benevolent General Hospital, a 300-bed hospital. You are responsible for the overall housekeeping services. You have several assistants (working supervisors) who report to you. There are about 80 full- and part-time employees in your department.

In recent weeks, rumors have been circulating about a major organizational campaign being undertaken by the Service Workers Union. There have been union organizers reported at several of the hospitals in the city, but you have not noticed any union organizers at your own hospital. This morning, however, Tom Mayes, one of your best employees who has worked for you for seven years, comes into your office. This is what he says:

"Leslie, I need your advice. Several of my co-workers have cornered me on three occasions, trying to get me to sign union authorization cards. They're trying to organize all of the housekeeping employees into a union bargaining unit. They are saying we're being treated unfairly, both in wages and benefits, and we need a union to get a fair shake. They really are putting the pressure on me and others to sign. They even have been going after me and others while we're trying to get our work done in the hospital. Maybe we do need a union here. I really don't know whom to believe. I know the names of most of the individuals who want the union here in the hospital. Perhaps you could talk to them to see if you can resolve some of their complaints. What should I do in the meantime?"

You know that you must respond to Tom. What should you say and do?

You Make the Call!

1

Explain why and how labor unions continue to affect organizations and the supervisory position.

Labor union (labor organization)

Legally recognized organization that represents employees and negotiates and administers a labor agreement with an employer.

Labor agreement (union contract)

Negotiated document between union and employer that covers terms and conditions of employment for the represented employees.

LABOR UNIONS ARE STILL PART OF SUPERVISORY ORGANIZATIONAL CONCERNS

Although the strength and influence of labor unions have declined considerably in recent years, labor unions nevertheless continue to be a major organizational consideration for supervisors. As of 2000, over 16 million employees, or about 14 percent of the U.S. labor force, were represented by labor unions and other employee associations and organizations. There are some technical distinctions in their designations, but we will use the terms **labor union** and **labor organization** interchangeably to describe any legally recognized organization that exists for the purpose of representing a group or "bargaining unit" of employees and that negotiates and administers a labor agreement with an employer. A **labor agreement,** also called a **union contract,** is the negotiated document between the union and the employer that covers terms and conditions of employment for the represented employees.

Historically, labor unions most often were identified with blue-collar employees. In recent years labor organizations have made gains in obtaining representational rights for white-collar employees such as office workers, salespeople, nurses, teachers, and even engineers. Many government employees, who generally do not have a legal right to strike and whose bargaining rights are somewhat different, have achieved the right to form and join labor organizations. In fact, the public sector of the workforce in the United States has been one of the few growing segments of the labor movement. An estimated 40 percent of public-sector workers belong to a union or association that represents them collectively.

Although many unions have lost members and the percentage of workers in labor organizations has declined significantly over the past two decades, unions remain an important element of the workforce that supervisors should know about and be prepared to deal with appropriately. This is especially true where employees are represented by a labor union and supervisors must abide by the requirements of a labor agreement.

The Labor Relations Framework

Most unionized employees are members of local unions that are affiliated with national and international labor organizations. In the United States, the American Federation of Labor-Congress of Industrial Organizations (AFL-CIO) is the dominant federation of national and international unions. As the major federation of organized labor, it continues to play a significant role in political, legislative, and other areas, even though many of its unions have undergone significant changes and mergers. The AFL-CIO provides assistance to its member unions with programs to represent employee interests and in ongoing efforts to organize workers who currently are not in labor unions.

As the new century begins, organized labor has embarked upon an aggressive strategy and campaign to rebuild its ranks and influence. The AFL-CIO has committed millions of dollars to hire, train, and send out hundreds of new organizers. Other millions will be spent in a "grassroots" political campaign to take labor's agenda to workers and voters everywhere. Targeted efforts will be made to register voters and to support the nomination and election of political candidates at all levels who are sympathetic and supportive of labor's objectives.

Whether or not organized labor will be able to capitalize on workers' discontent and get more people to join labor unions is an open question. Organized labor may be at a crossroads which could determine its future place of influence in the 21st century. If their efforts fail, organized labor may find itself facing a further decline in membership and having even less influence in the overall economy and in determining what happens in the workplace concerning the typical worker.[1]

Historically, most labor unions adopted an adversarial posture toward employers in order to obtain economic and other gains through collective bargaining. In recent years, the adversarial approach has been tempered with more cooperative efforts in many companies. In particular, some unions have supported programs where workers are given increased participation in workplace decision making aimed at improving output and quality, which presumably enhances their job and income security.[2] However, the longstanding adversarial climate between management and organized labor is still widespread, as this chapter's "Contemporary Issue" box illustrates.

Labor Relations Laws and the Supervisor. For the most part, unionized employees have divided or dual loyalties concerning their unions and their employers which a supervisor must understand and accept, especially in regard to labor relations laws. Of course, it is beyond the scope of this text to cover the history of labor relations or to discuss at length the federal and state labor laws that govern union–management relations.[3] Suffice it to say that most employees in the private sector of the U.S. workforce

contemporary issue

Is There a "War" Against the Right to Unionize?

There have been numerous pronouncements and suggestions that the traditional adversarial relationship between management and labor has tempered in recent decades. Although it is true that strikes and labor walkouts have decreased significantly, there does not appear to be any real change in the level of resistance and hostility that management typically displays toward labor unions. At least, this is the opinion of top officers of the American Federation of Labor-Congress of Industrial Organizations (AFL-CIO) as asserted in their recent statements included within the Federation's official publication.

AFL-CIO Secretary-Treasurer Richard Trumka, speaking to a major labor rally, stated: "It's a war against workers who had no idea—like most of America doesn't—that intimidation and interference by employers is such standard practice in today's workplaces that the freedom to form a union doesn't really exist at all."[1] Trumka was referring to AFL-CIO statistics which claimed that:

- When workers try to exercise their right to join a union, 80 percent of employers force them to attend mandatory, closed-door meetings where bosses and consultants attack the union and attempt to scare employees.
- Employers fire workers who are active in union campaigns; workers were actually fired in 31 percent of union elections.

- 80 percent of employers hire outside consultants to run anti-union campaigns when workers try to join a union.[2]

AFL-CIO President John Sweeney claimed that corporate greed was a primary factor in the continuing and escalating resentment of workers—both unionized and nonunionized—toward corporate managements. Sweeney stated: "When I talk to workers around the country, I hear again and again that they know their success is tied to that of their employers. But those employers don't seem to realize their fortunes are tied closely to ours. Corporate greed has helped make our wage and wealth gap the widest of any industrialized nation in the world. Our movement is directly challenging corporate greed in its many ugly forms. We're doing it because working families deserve a fairer share of the wealth we help create. But we're also doing it to force corporate America to ask itself some tough questions about the self-defeating consequences of unbridled greed . . . When you pay your CEO 419 times what you pay other workers, thumb your nose at the notion of loyalty, and treat employees as distant second-bests, how long can you expect them to give you their best?"[3]

Union-organizing efforts are expected to increase significantly during the next five years. There is little reason to believe that the alleged "war against workers" will end in the foreseeable future.

Sources: (1) Richard Trumka as quoted in Mike Hall, "Seven Days in June," *America@Work* (August 1999), p. 14. (2) *Ibid.*, p. 13. (3) John J. Sweeney, "Challenging Corporate Greed," *America@Work* (May 1999), p. 7.

have legal rights to join or not to join labor unions under provisions of the National Labor Relations Act as amended. Federal government workers have their collective bargaining rights established under the Civil Service Reform Act. Rights of other public-sector workers generally are covered by various state and local government legislation. Labor law is very complicated, and it addresses many areas of concern such as which employees are and are not covered, protected rights, unfair labor practices, and a host of requirements concerning collective bargaining. Because of the many legal and other ramifications, most firms find it desirable to have human resources staff specialists handle many or most of the labor relations matters, typically with the assistance and advice of legal counsel.

A supervisor must understand that unionized employees have divided or dual loyalties concerning their unions and their employers.

Since much of this will not directly concern a typical supervisor, this chapter will discuss only some of the most important organizational considerations, obligations, and rights of supervisors who are confronted with (a) employee attempts to unionize and (b) union activities in a firm whose employees are already represented by a union. This chapter's discussion will represent a composite of considerations that generally are valid irrespective of the nature of the work setting and will not delve into technical details of labor laws. In Chapter 17 we will address specific aspects of handling grievances under a labor–management grievance procedure in a unionized firm.

In the discussion to follow, it should be noted that under our labor relations laws, those supervisors who are not part of management—such as working supervisors, understudies (see Chapter 9), and lead persons—may join the same labor union as their fellow employees. But most supervisors who are part of management do not have the legal right to join and be represented by labor unions. Regardless, as management's first-line representatives, supervisors play a major role in determining whether or not the employees will turn to a labor union in an effort to improve wages and other conditions of employment.

UNDERSTANDING EMPLOYEE EFFORTS TO UNIONIZE

2

Identify aspects of good management that are likely to deter a union organizer's appeal.

A major union official once made the following comment to one of the authors of this text: "Labor unions don't just happen; they're caused. And it's the management, not the unions, that causes them!" This labor official was quite candid about his opinion that labor unions were a direct response to failures of management to respond to employee needs. Further, he implied that the sentiments of workers are usually determined more by the conditions existing in their work situations than by a union organizer's campaign. Many studies of employee and labor relations have verified the opinion of this union official. These studies recognize that good management and supervision, particularly as exemplified by positive human relations approaches, are usually the most important determinants in preventing the unionization of a work group.

Numerous aspects of good management that contribute to "union avoidance" or a climate that deters unionizing efforts have been discussed previously throughout this text. Factors rooted in good employee relations make it more difficult for a union organizer's appeal to succeed. These factors include the following:

1. Wages and benefits that are good and reasonably comparable to those offered by other companies.[4]
2. Personal facilities for employees that are generally satisfactory or improving.
3. A stable employment pattern (that is, no severe ups and downs in hiring and layoffs of large numbers of employees).
4. Supervisors who communicate well with their employees and treat them with dignity and respect.
5. Employees who have been well trained and see opportunities for advancement to higher-paying or upgraded positions. This is especially important for employees in low-level jobs who do not like to feel that they will be in "dead-end" positions forever.
6. Supervisors who demonstrate a participative approach to management that encourages employees to share in making decisions about their jobs.[5]
7. Employees who feel that they are treated fairly by being given an opportunity to resolve their complaints through a complaint procedure.[6]

For the most part, the economic conditions surrounding wages, benefits, and employment patterns are not within a supervisor's direct control. However, the supervisor has a significant role in most of the other factors that may cause employees either to join or not join a labor union.

It does happen that some employees turn to a labor union even though their employer has worked diligently to develop and implement policies and procedures consistent with those listed. Employees may join a labor union primarily to achieve economic objectives such as higher wages and greater benefits. Or they may join to satisfy objectives of a psychological or sociological nature. For example, some employees feel that membership in a labor union provides them with greater security and better control over their jobs through a seniority system. Other employees feel that it is important for a union to be present in processing grievances and complaints in order to get a fairer settlement of their disputes. Still others find a greater sense of identity when they are part of a labor union. Further, attitudes of unionized employees and their leaders often are based upon past failed initiatives and broken promises from management. They often view management with suspicion, believing that if management considers something good for the company, it must be bad for them.[7] Supervisors who encounter these types of attitudes—which sometimes are shared by nonunionized personnel—usually find it difficult to build trust among the workers that their legitimate concerns and complaints will be addressed.

There are many reasons why
employees join unions.

Union Security Arrangements

Union shop

A labor agreement
provision in which
employees are required to
join the union as a
condition of employment,
usually after 30 days.

When a labor union gains representational rights, or if a union already is in place, employees may have to join it as a requirement under a **union shop** provision of the labor agreement. A union shop provision in a labor agreement requires an employee to join the union as a condition of employment after a certain period of time, usually 30 days. Even though such employees initially are required to join the union through the union shop provision, eventually most of them become loyal to the union because they believe that they can achieve more collectively than they would individually.

The union shop is sometimes referred to as a "closed shop," but these are not identical terms. A *closed shop* is illegal under federal labor law; such an arrangement requires an individual to be a union member in order to obtain a job. There are other union security arrangements besides the union shop that are permitted by federal labor law but which may be unlawful in some states. For example, the *agency shop* is one in which an employee does not have to join the union in order to keep a job, but the employee is required to pay a fee or dues equivalent to the union, which must represent the employee within the bargaining unit.

As of 2000, 21 states (mostly located in the southern part of the United States) had so-called "right-to-work" laws that prohibit the union shop and other types of union security arrangements. Also, labor organizations representing employees within the federal government and much of the public sector generally are not permitted to have a union shop. Nevertheless, in firms and organizations that are unionized but which do not have a union shop, all or most of the employees may belong to the union because they want to be part of the overall, combined group effort of promoting employees' rights and interests.

3

Outline procedures for supervisors to follow if confronted with a union-organizing effort.

UNION-ORGANIZING EFFORTS AND THE SUPERVISOR

Union-organizing efforts can take place both outside and within a firm. In recent years, some unions have tried rather sophisticated approaches in their efforts to contact workers and persuade them to vote for a union to represent them. For example, a number of unions are utilizing the Internet and e-mail in order to inform employees about their rights and advantages of unionization.[8] However, most union-organizing efforts still occur on a person-to-person basis, usually on or near the premises of the firm. [9]

If a supervisor notices that union-organizing activities are taking place among employees, the supervisor should report what he or she observes to higher-level managers or to the human resources department. This must be done so that the company's response to the union-organizing efforts can be planned. In the meantime, the supervisor should be very careful not to violate—by either actions or statements—the labor laws governing union-organizing activities. Since these labor laws are quite complicated, many companies hire a consultant or attorney to advise higher-level managers and supervisory personnel about what they should and should not do under these circumstances.[10]

The following guidelines, although not comprehensive, are recommended for supervisors during a union-organizing period:

1. Supervisors should not question employees either publicly or privately about union-organizing activities in the department or elsewhere in the company. Doing this—even merely out of curiosity—can violate labor laws, which provide employees the right to choose a union to represent them without interference or discrimination by the employer.
2. Supervisors should not make any threats or promises related to the possibility of unionization. Any statement that can be construed as a threat (for example, loss of job or loss of privileges if the union succeeds) or a promise (for example, some favor or benefit to the employee if the union fails) is a violation of federal labor law.
3. Supervisors should respond in a neutral manner when employees ask for their opinions on the subject of unionization.
4. Supervisors have the right to prohibit union-organizing activities in work areas if these take place during work hours and interfere with normal work operations. Supervisors may also prohibit outside union organizers from coming into the department to distribute union bulletins and information. However, employees who support the union have the right to distribute these materials to other employees during lunch and break periods so long as this does not interfere with work operations. If in doubt about what can be done to control union-organizing activities within the department, supervisors should first consult higher-level managers or the human resources department.
5. Supervisors should not look at union authorization cards that employees may have signed. This, too, is considered illegal interference with the employees' rights to organize.
6. Supervisors should continue to do the best supervisory management job possible.

A union-organizing campaign often results in a representational election conducted by the National Labor Relations Board (NLRB) or some other government agency. If the majority of the employees vote for the union, the union becomes the exclusive bargaining representative for these employees. If the union loses the representational election, this means only that the employees will not have a union for the immediate future—perhaps for a minimum of one year. Many companies have found that employees, after having rejected a union in previous elections, later vote it in. The transition from a nonunion to a unionized workplace can be a trying period of change for all concerned. With the passage of time, most supervisors eventually accept the place and role of the union and learn to adjust their supervisory roles accordingly.

Discuss the importance of good union–management relationships and the supervisor's key role in maintaining them.

THE SUPERVISOR'S INVOLVEMENT IN UNION–MANAGEMENT RELATIONSHIPS

Labor unions are a permanent part of our free-enterprise economy. A union, just like any other institution, has the potential for either advancing or interfering with the common efforts of an organization. Thus, it is in management's self-interest to develop a union-management climate that is conducive to constructive relationships. However, there are no simple formulas for fostering such a climate overnight. It takes patience, sensitivity, and hard work for all managers in an organization to show in their day-to-day relationships that the union is accepted as the official and responsible bargaining representative for the employees.

In any mutual efforts to maintain a constructive relationship between management and the union, often the most important link is the supervisor. It is the supervisor's daily relationships with employees and union representatives that make the labor agreement a living document for better or for worse. This is why it is essential that supervisors be well informed in the fundamentals of collective bargaining and be knowl-

Employers may hire an attorney or consultant to help the human resources staff and management develop a plan for collective bargaining.

edgeable about the labor agreement. For the most part, the supervisor's involvement in union–management relations consists of two phases: (1) a limited role in negotiating the labor agreement and (2) a major role in applying the terms of the agreement on a day-to-day basis.

<table>
<tr><td>

5

Discuss the limited but important role of the supervisor in negotiating the labor agreement.

</td></tr>
</table>

The Supervisor's Limited Role in Labor Agreement Negotiations

Labor agreement negotiations, also called *collective bargaining,* are the process of discussion and compromise among representatives from labor and management leading to an agreement governing wages, hours, and working conditions for union employees.[11] Negotiations often involve meetings between the parties extending over months. On occasion, a union may threaten or call a work stoppage in an attempt to pressure the employer to agree to certain proposals or make concessions. Because collective bargaining can be complicated, an employer may hire an attorney or consultant to work with human resources department staff and management to develop and carry out its negotiating strategy.

Labor negotiations in a previously nonunionized company may be a stressful experience for employees, supervisors, and higher-level managers. Usually emotions run high, and the grapevine is active with rumors and speculation. Because of this climate, negotiations between management and union representatives are often held away from the company premises, perhaps at a lawyer's office or a conference room in a hotel. If a committee of union employees is participating in the negotiations, a line of communication with the other employees will be established. Supervisors usually are excluded from this line of communication, although higher-level managers may keep them informed.

Most labor agreements cover a period of two, three, or more years. As time goes on and new agreements are negotiated, the supervisor's role becomes an increasingly important one. Most supervisors do not sit at the negotiating table but it is desirable for higher-level managers to consult with them about (a) how provisions of the existing agreement have worked out and (b) what changes they would like to see in the next agreement. This exchange of information between higher-level managers and supervisors is essential prior to negotiations, and at times it even may be needed as negotiations proceed.

Supervisors should have some influence on negotiations because they bear a major responsibility for carrying out provisions of the agreement in the day-to-day operations of their departments. Many issues discussed during contract negotiations stem from relationships that the supervisors have experienced with their employees. For example, problems concerning work assignments between job classifications, work-shift schedules, seniority rights, working conditions, and transfer and promotion of employees can become important issues for negotiation. Therefore, it is to the supervisors' as well as the firm's advantage that provisions in the agreement be written in such a way that supervisors have as much flexibility as possible in running their departments.

To supply relevant information, supervisors should be keenly aware of what has been going on in their departments. Their views will be considered more credible if they

Labor agreement negotiations

The process of discussion and compromise among representatives from labor and management leading to an agreement governing wages, hours, and working conditions for union employees.

have facts available to substantiate their observations. As will be emphasized in Chapter 19, this underscores the importance of keeping ample records of prior grievances, productivity, and disciplinary problems. Supervisors should discuss with higher-level managers and the human resources department problems that management should consider in developing an overall bargaining strategy. Thus, even though the primary responsibility of negotiating a labor agreement rests with higher-level managers, supervisors should be prepared to provide relevant input to the negotiations. Supervisors must be willing to express their opinions and substantiate them with documents and examples so that management's representatives can negotiate desirable changes in the agreement at the bargaining table.

6

Discuss the major role of the supervisor in the interpretation and application of the labor agreement at the departmental level.

The Supervisor's Major Role in Applying the Labor Agreement

The labor agreement that has been agreed on by representatives of management and the union becomes the document under which both parties will operate during the life of the agreement. Although no two labor agreements are exactly alike, most agreements cover wages, benefits, working conditions, hours of work, overtime, holidays, vacations, leaves of absence, seniority, grievance procedures, and numerous other matters.

A labor agreement outlines union–management relationships. In essence, it is a policy manual that provides rules, procedures, and guidelines—as well as limitations—for both management and the union. To make it a positive instrument for fostering constructive relationships, the agreement must be applied with appropriate and intelligent supervisory decisions. The best written labor agreement will be of little value if it is poorly applied by the supervisor.

Compliance with the Labor Agreement.   Wherever it applies, supervisors are obliged to manage their departments within the framework of the labor agreement. This means that supervisors should know the provisions of the agreement and also how to interpret them. One way to accomplish this is for higher-level managers or the human resources department to hold meetings with supervisors to brief them on the contents of the agreement and to answer questions about any provisions that they do not understand. Copies of the contract and clarifications of various provisions should be furnished to the supervisors so that they know what they can and cannot do while managing their departments (see Figure 11-1).

Supervisors should recognize that a labor agreement has been negotiated, agreed upon, and signed by both management and union representatives. Even if a provision in the agreement causes a supervisor problems, the supervisor should not try to circumvent the contract in the hope of doing the firm a favor. For example, assume that a provision specifies that work assignments must be made primarily on the basis of seniority. Although this provision may limit the supervisor in assigning the most qualified workers to certain jobs, the supervisor should comply with it or be prepared to face probable conflict with the union. If a labor agreement provision is clear and specific, the supervisor should not attempt to ignore what it requires. If supervisors do not under-

The supervisor must know the provisions of the labor agreement and how to interpret them.

stand certain provisions, they should ask someone in higher-level management or the human resources department to explain before they attempt to apply the provisions that are in question.

Adjustments for the Union. A labor agreement does not fundamentally change a supervisor's position as a manager. Supervisors still must accomplish their objectives by planning, organizing, staffing, leading, and controlling. Supervisors retain the right to require employees to comply with instructions and to get the jobs done in their departments. The major adjustment required when a union is present is that supervisors must perform their managerial duties within the framework of the labor agreement. For example, a labor agreement may spell out some limitations to the supervisor's authority, especially in areas of disciplinary action, job transfers, and assignments. Or the labor agreement may specify procedures concerning the seniority rights of employees with regard to shift assignments, holidays, and vacations. Supervisors may not like these provisions. However, they must manage within them and learn to minimize the effects of contractually imposed requirements or restrictions by making sound decisions and relying on their own managerial abilities. Figure 11-2 (see page 340) shows selected provisions from a labor agreement that cover various areas where seniority considerations must be followed.

FIGURE 11-2

Example of labor agreement seniority provisions.

ARTICLE IV
SENIORITY

SECTION 1. The purpose of seniority is to provide a declared policy of right of preference in regard to layoff and recall and promotion and transfer. Length of service for seniority purposes shall be determined to start from the original hiring date at the Company plant, except as interrupted for reasons set forth in Section 5 of this Article.

SECTION 2. Seniority shall be plantwide with respect to the entire bargaining unit.

SECTION 3. In cases of layoff or recall, seniority shall govern, provided the employee is capable (with incidental training not to exceed 40 hours) of performing the job to which he or she may be transferred by reason of the layoff of an employee with less seniority.

The Company agrees that in the event that layoffs—other than disciplinary layoffs or temporary emergency shutdowns—are deemed necessary, the employees affected will be notified as far in advance as practicable, in no cases less than two (2) days.

SECTION 4. Transfers and promotions within the bargaining unit shall be made on the basis of seniority provided the employee is qualified and able to do the job. Requests for transfers will be honored only after an employee has completed a probationary period. An employee shall be considered a probationary employee during his or her first three (3) months, and the Company shall have the right to discharge an employee in such status and no grievance shall arise therefrom.

In no case shall the Company be under obligation to promote, transfer, or assign work because of preferred seniority status to an employee who is not capable (with incidental training not to exceed 40 hours) of doing the job.

SECTION 5. An employee shall cease to have seniority and be on the seniority list if the employee:

A. Quits.
B. Is discharged for just cause.
C. Is absent three (3) days without notifying the Company, except as the employee furnishes an explanation in writing satisfactory to the Company.
D. Fails to return to work within two (2) days upon completion of a vacation, leave of absence, or recall from layoff notice, except as the employee furnishes an explanation in writing satisfactory to the Company.

If an employee whose seniority has been broken by any of the causes mentioned above is again hired, he or she shall begin as a new employee for seniority purposes.

As members of management, supervisors have the right and duty to make decisions. A labor agreement does not take away that right. However, it does give the union a right to challenge a supervisor's decision that the union believes to be a violation of the labor agreement. For example, virtually all labor agreements specify that management has the right to discipline and discharge for "just" (or "proper") cause (see Figure 11-2). Thus, taking disciplinary action remains a managerial responsibility and right, but it must meet the just-cause standard. Since a challenge from the union may occur, the supervisor should have a sound case before taking disciplinary action. If a supervisor believes that disciplinary action is called for when an employee breaks a rule, the supervisor should examine thoroughly all aspects of the problem, take the required preliminary steps, and think through the appropriateness of any action. In other words, unless there is a contractual requirement to the contrary, the supervisor normally will carry out the disciplinary action independently of union involvement. However, some labor agreements require that a supervisor notify a union representative prior to imposing discipline or that a union representative be present when the disciplinary action is administered. In Chapter 19, we will discuss in detail the handling of disciplinary matters in both union and nonunion work environments.

Supervisory Decision Making and the Labor Agreement. In practice, the supervisor may amplify provisions of the labor agreement by decisions that interpret and apply them to specific situations. In so doing, the supervisor might establish precedents that arbitrators consider when deciding grievances.

Grievance

A formal complaint presented by the union to management that alleges a violation of the labor agreement.

Arbitrator

Person selected by the union and management to render a final and binding decision concerning a grievance.

A **grievance** is a complaint that has been formally presented by the union to management and that alleges a violation of the labor agreement. Most labor agreements specify several steps as part of a grievance procedure before a grievance goes to arbitration. An **arbitrator** is someone who is selected by the union and management to render a final and binding decision concerning a grievance when the union and management are unable to settle the grievance themselves. Procedures for arbitrating grievances are included in most labor agreements. Figure 17-3 in Chapter 17 is an example of a typical grievance-arbitration provision in a labor agreement.

It would be impossible for management and the union to negotiate an agreement that specified how to solve every possible situation that could occur in union–management relations. Therefore, the supervisor's judgment becomes paramount in applying the agreement to actual situations. Since the supervisor is part of management, an error in the supervisor's decisions becomes management's error. By interpretation and application, a supervisor's decisions may take on dimensions that go well beyond the department and perhaps be long lasting in impact. A decision may set a precedent that could become binding on both management and the union in the future. Supervisors should bear in mind that unions often base their claims on precedents, and arbitrators often base their decisions on previous decisions made by both sides.

A labor agreement usually contains provisions that specify how certain situations should be handled. Examples are provisions associated with work schedules, distribution of overtime, transfers, promotions or demotions, and other recurring matters. Usually the labor agreement identifies certain limits or procedures for handling these types of issues. For example, many agreements have provisions that require the supervisor to consider both seniority and ability in decisions that involve promotion, transfer, and layoff (see Figure 11-2). In these situations the supervisor's personal appraisal of the abilities of the involved employees becomes vitally important. Often the opinion of the union will be at odds with the opinion of a supervisor concerning certain contractual meanings. A supervisor should not be afraid to risk the possibility that the union will file a grievance so long as the supervisor believes that he or she understands the provisions and is complying with them.

Labor agreements also contain broadly stated clauses, such as those associated with the assignment of work between various job classifications, nondiscrimination, management rights, and disciplinary or discharge actions for just cause. In these areas supervisors often encounter difficulty in applying a general statement in the agreement when the situation requires a specific interpretation. If the supervisor has doubts about the meaning of a broadly stated provision, he or she should first consult higher-level managers or the human resources department. Even though the supervisor may be well versed in the content of the labor agreement, problems can develop that necessitate an interpretation beyond the supervisory level.

Maintaining Employees' Compliance with the Labor Agreement. It is also the supervisor's duty to take action whenever employees do not comply with provisions of the labor agreement. Employees may interpret lack of action to mean that the provisions are unimportant or not to be enforced. For example, if a contractual provision specifies that employees are entitled to a 15-minute rest period at designated times during a work shift, the supervisor should see to it that the employees take a 15-minute rest period— no more and no less—during the designated times. Supervisors should make certain that employees observe the provisions of the labor agreement just as supervisors themselves must operate within the agreement. Inaction on the supervisor's part could set a precedent or be interpreted to mean that the provision has been set aside.

THE SHOP STEWARD AND THE SUPERVISOR

7
Describe the nature and importance of a good relationship between a supervisor and the union shop steward.

Shop steward
Employee elected or appointed to represent employees at the departmental level, particularly in grievance processing.

Union business representative
Paid official of the local or national union who may be involved in grievance processing.

Supervisors probably will have most of their union contacts with the union shop steward. A **shop steward,** also called a "shop committeeman" or "shop committeewoman," usually is a full-time employee who is elected or appointed to represent the employees at the departmental level, particularly in processing of their grievances. Supervisors may also have to discuss certain issues and grievances with a **union business representative** or "business agent." This person is a paid, full-time official of the local or national union. Some shop stewards prefer to have the business agent present when discussing union-related problems with the supervisor.

For the most part, a shop steward is recognized by fellow employees to be their official spokesperson to management and for the union. This can be a difficult position since the shop steward must serve two masters. As an employee, the shop steward is expected to perform satisfactory work for the employer by following rules. As a union representative, the shop steward has responsibilities to other employees and to the union. The supervisor must understand this dual role of the shop steward because a good relationship with the shop steward can create an effective link between the supervisor and the employees.

The Shop Steward's Rights and Duties

Unless the labor agreement contains special provisions pertaining to the shop steward's position, the shop steward is subject to the same standards and regulations for work performance and conduct as every other employee of the department. The labor agreement may specify how much company time the shop steward can devote to union matters, such as meetings or discussions with members, collection of dues, and grievance handling. The labor agreement may also grant the shop steward the right to take time off to attend union conventions and handle other union matters.

A major responsibility of the shop steward is to process complaints and grievances on behalf of employees. The shop steward will communicate these to the supervisor, who then must work with the shop steward to resolve them. Labor agreements usually outline procedures for handling complaints and grievances, and the shop steward and the supervisor are obligated to follow those prescribed steps. We will discuss the handling of complaints and grievances in detail in Chapter 17.

Supervisory Relations with the Shop Steward

According to a late 1990s survey of staff human resources managers, a large majority of managers believe that labor unions do not adequately represent the interests of their members.[12] This survey result possibly reflected some anti-union biases and also some unpleasant situations managers had experienced with certain union leaders. By the same token, most supervisors in unionized firms typically have quite ambivalent attitudes about union shop stewards based upon their past relationships with a number of stewards. Some shop stewards are unassuming; others are overbearing. Some are helpful and courteous; others are aggressive and militant. Some take advantage of their position to do as little work as possible; others perform an excellent day's work in addition to their union duties. In other words, the day-to-day behavior of the shop steward depends considerably on his or her individual personality and approach.

At times the supervisor may feel that the shop steward processes petty grievances in order to harass management. This may happen because the shop steward has a political assignment and may feel it necessary to assure workers that the union is working on their behalf. However, an experienced shop steward knows that normally there are enough valid grievances to be settled that it is not necessary to submit shallow complaints that rightfully will be turned down by the supervisor.

Supervisors should bear in mind that the shop steward, as the official union representative, learns quickly what the employees are thinking and what is being communicated through the grapevine. Moreover, the national or local union will likely train the shop steward to be informed about the content of the labor agreement, management's prerogatives, and employee rights. The local union will expect the shop steward to submit grievances in such a way that they can be carried to a successful conclusion. Before submitting a grievance, the shop steward will ascertain which provisions of the labor agreement allegedly have been violated, whether the company acted unfairly, or whether the employee's health or safety was jeopardized. Once a grievance has been formally submitted, the shop steward will try to win it. In most grievance matters the union is "on the offensive" and the supervisor must be prepared to respond. If the shop steward challenges a supervisor's decision or action, the supervisor must be ready to justify what he or she did or otherwise develop a remedy and resolve the grievance.

Since shop stewards are necessarily interested in satisfying the union members, their behavior may at times antagonize supervisors. It may even become difficult for supervisors to keep a sense of humor or to hold their tempers. A supervisor may not care to discuss certain matters with the shop steward because, on a day-to-day basis, the shop steward is an employee in the department. But a shop steward is also the designated representative of union members and should be treated as an "equal" by a supervisor in matters pertaining to the union. If a sound relationship is developed, the shop steward will keep the supervisor alert and literally force the supervisor to be a better manager![13]

What Call Did You Make?

As Leslie Brown, your best response at this point is to tell Tom Mayes that you really don't know how to advise him until after you have checked out his questions with the human resources director and your own manager. Under no circumstances should you ask Tom or anyone else to provide you with the names of the employees who are involved in the union-organizing efforts or who favor the union. Doing this would be a probable violation of labor law. After adjourning your meeting with Tom, you should immediately report your conversation to the human resources director and your

manager and ask for guidance. They most likely will counsel you along the lines of the concepts and principles presented in this chapter. In particular, you should continue to treat all employees fairly, have them participate in some departmental decisions, and be willing to listen to and act on their legitimate complaints. You should not question, threaten, or interfere with your employees' efforts to organize. However, you should inform all of them that union-organizing efforts cannot take place in hospital working areas during regular work times. Hospital management may or may not decide to conduct a counter-campaign. If management decides to do so, you will receive additional instructions about what and what not to do and say.

SUMMARY

1

About one in seven employees in the United States is represented by a labor union. Unions continue in their efforts to organize, especially among white-collar and public-sector employees. Supervisors need to know how to respond to employee efforts to unionize and how to manage if departmental employees are represented by a union.

2

Good management practices can help deter a labor union from gaining representational rights. Employees may turn to a labor union for representation if they see the union as a vehicle for satisfying certain needs, including economic gains and fair treatment of their concerns. If management addresses employees' needs, then employees are less likely to feel the need for a union to promote their interests.

3

Confronted with a union-organizing campaign, the supervisor should report the campaign to higher-level managers or the human resources department. The supervisor must not interfere with or threaten employees or promise any benefits in an effort to influence their choice of whether or not to join the union. The supervisor does have the right to prohibit activities that directly interfere with job performance during working hours and in work areas.

4

5

6

7

Labor unions are a part of our economic system, and they can either advance or interfere with the objectives of an organization. Thus, good union–management relations are essential to the success of a unionized firm. The supervisor is the key to good relations since he or she applies the labor agreement in day-to-day contact with employees.

Most supervisors do not participate in labor agreement negotiations. Yet many demands that a union presents during negotiations stem from issues that supervisors have encountered with the union and departmental employees. Therefore, supervisors should make their opinions and suggestions known to higher-level managers so that management can attempt to negotiate needed changes in the labor agreement.

The supervisor's major role in union–management relations lies in the day-to-day interpretation and application of the labor agreement. Although a labor agreement does not in itself change a supervisor's job as a manager, it does give a union the right to challenge supervisory decisions. The supervisor still must carry out managerial duties within the terms of the labor agreement. It is to the supervisor's advantage to seek advice from higher-level managers or the human resources department in interpreting certain clauses of the agreement. The supervisor's actions can set precedents that bind management and the union in the future.

Supervisors have most of their union contacts with the union shop steward who represents employees at the departmental level. The shop steward is an employee as well as a union spokesperson for processing employee grievances. The shop steward should be treated as an "equal" by the supervisor in matters relating to the labor agreement. If a proper relationship is developed, a shop steward primarily will challenge only those actions of the supervisor that seem to be unfair or in violation of the agreement. In effect, this will force the supervisor to do a better job of managing the department.

KEY TERMS

Labor union (labor organization) (page 329)
Labor agreement (union contract) (page 329)
Union shop (page 334)
Labor agreement negotiations (page 337)

Grievance (page 341)
Arbitrator (page 341)
Shop steward (page 342)
Union business representative (page 342)

QUESTIONS FOR DISCUSSION

1. What is the magnitude of labor union and employee representation in the United States? Although labor unions have declined in membership in recent years, why should they still be a major organizational consideration for supervisors?
2. What are some of the principal reasons why employees join labor unions?
3. What are some of the major factors that typically are crucial in preventing the formation of a labor union? Over which of these does a supervisor have the most direct control?
4. Discuss the proper role of the supervisor regarding union-organizing activities. Why should a supervisor generally be neutral in responding to employees' questions about the union-organizing effort?
5. Evaluate the following statement: "The best guideline a supervisor can follow during a union-organizing campaign is to continue to do the best management job possible."
6. What is the supervisor's role in labor agreement negotiations? What input should a supervisor have in the negotiating process? Why?

7. Discuss why the supervisor should not attempt to ignore the labor agreement or circumvent it even if it seems like the smart thing to do.

8. Why should supervisors consult higher-level managers or the human resources department when they need interpretation of a clause in the labor agreement?

9. Evaluate the following statement: "A labor agreement does not fundamentally change a supervisor's position as a manager." Relate this question to the "You Make the Call" situation of Leslie Brown. If the union succeeds in organizing the hospital employees, how would Leslie Brown's supervisory position be affected by unionization?

10. How does a labor agreement complicate a supervisor's job?

11. Why does a supervisor retain the right to take action whenever employees do not comply with provisions of the labor agreement?

12. Discuss the role of the shop steward within a department. Why is this person in a key position of influence?

13. Why should the shop steward be treated as an "equal" by the supervisor in matters relating to the union?

SKILLS APPLICATIONS

Skills Application 11-1: Attitudes About Labor Unions

1. The following are statements about labor unions. Respond to each statement, applying the following rating scale.

Strongly Disagree	Disagree	Undecided	Agree	Strongly Agree
1	2	3	4	5

Scoring

_____ 1. Unions are necessary to protect employees from job favoritism and discrimination.

_____ 2. Job seniority is the fairest way to reward employees for their services.

_____ 3. Unions are needed to ensure that workers are paid good wages and receive adequate benefits.

_____ 4. Without a labor union, employees have little chance to have their complaints handled fairly.

_____ 5. Every employee who benefits from the union should be required to join and support the union (i.e., a union shop).

_____ 6. Most employees join a labor union because they want to join and they agree with the union's objectives.

_____ 7. The best form of employee job participation occurs when a union can negotiate a labor agreement with an employer to cover terms and conditions of employment.

_____ 8. Stronger unions and wider representation of employees by unions are needed in order to counter corporate greed and management's indifference toward workers.

_____ TOTAL

2. Add your scores and compare your total with the following:

8–19	You generally do not agree with or approve of labor unions.
20–27	You have mixed attitudes about labor unions.
28–40	You generally support unions and their objectives.

Do you agree with the results? Why or why not?

Optional: Compare your scores with those of another student (or students). Can you explain any differences in perceptions?

Skills Application 11-2: Management and Union Views in a Unionized Work Location

1. Supervisors and managers often differ in their viewpoints concerning what a labor union does for its members. Visit a plant or office that is unionized. Interview a supervisor, manager, or director of human resources using the first set of questions. Then interview a shop steward or union member using the second set of questions. (Interview several managers and union people if permission to do so is granted.)

   a. *Management Questions*

   (1) How would you describe overall relations between the union and management in this company?

   (2) In general, what things would you say the union members like most here? Least?

   (3) What in your opinion should be improved in the union–management relationship?

   (4) What would you do differently if the union did not exist?

   b. *Union Questions*

   (1) How would you describe the overall relations between your union and management in this company?

   (2) In general, what things would you say your members like most here, and what things do they like least?

   (3) What in your opinion most needs to be improved in the union–management relationship?

   (4) If the union did not exist, what do you think management would do differently?

2. a. What similarities and differences between the responses to each question were the most significant? Most surprising?

   b. Were any of your prior viewpoints about labor unions changed or influenced as a result of these interviews?

Skills Application 11-3: The Supervisor and the Shop Steward

1. From the principles and concepts presented in this chapter—and from your own observations and experiences, if applicable—make a list of what you consider to be the most desirable qualities and approaches that a supervisor should have in order to have a good working relationship with a union shop steward.

2. Discuss your list with a supervisor who has dealt with—or who currently is dealing with—a union shop steward.

   a. To what degree did the supervisor agree with your list?

   b. What additions and/or changes to the list did the supervisor suggest?

   c. How might the personal characteristics of the union shop steward influence how the supervisor would deal with this person?

Skills Application 11-4: The AFL-CIO

Visit the official AFL-CIO web site (www.aflcio.org) to learn more about the issues and concerns for today's labor unions.

1. Based on topics featured on this site, what are some of the primary concerns for today's workers according to the AFL-CIO? What is the union's role in addressing these concerns?
2. According to the AFL-CIO, what are some of the benefits of union membership?
3. Who is joining unions and why? View highlights from the AFL-CIO's publication, "Work In Progress."

ENDNOTES

1. See Bruce B. Auster and Warren Cohen, "Rallying the Rank and File," *U.S. News and World Report* (April 1, 1996), pp. 26–28; and G. Pascal Zachary, "Chief AFL-CIO Organizer to Try Civil Rights Tactics," *The Wall Street Journal* (February 8, 1996), pp. B1 and B10.

2. See Bill Leonard, "The New Face of Organized Labor," *HRMagazine* (July 1999), pp. 55–63.

3. For comprehensive information concerning U.S. labor relations laws, processes, and issues, the following texts are recommended: Terry L. Leap, *Collective Bargaining and Labor Relations* (2d ed.; Englewood Cliffs, N.J.: Prentice-Hall, 1995); E. Edward Herman, *Collective Bargaining and Labor Relations* (Upper Saddle River, N.J.: Prentice-Hall, Inc., 1998); Michael Ballot, *Labor–Management Relations in a Changing Environment* (2d ed.; New York: John Wiley & Sons, 1996).

4. According to a 1997 study reported by U.S. Department of Labor, Bureau of Labor Statistics, full-time unionized employees in the U.S. earned median weekly wages of $640 as compared to $478 for nonunion workers. When the cost of provided benefits was added to this, the difference was even greater. See Sherwood Ross, "Unions Altering Dues-Collecting," *Newsday* (New York: copyright by Reuters News Service, July 26, 1999), p. C02.

5. In a major 1995 study of 2,400 workers, approximately 63 percent said that they would like to have more influence in workplace decisions involving areas such as production, training, equipment, and working conditions. By about a 2 to 1 majority, the workers indicated a preference for "nonunion participation" (or "nonunion representation"). At the same time, however, the majority of surveyed workers indicated that they wanted workplace organizations that were "employee-selected" and that had some real "power" in being able to influence managerial decisions that affected workers. See "Workers Want Non-Union Participation," *Issues in HR* (January/February 1995), pp. 1–2.

6. In Chapter 17 we will discuss complaint procedures and alternative dispute resolution for employees in nonunionized firms.

7. See Glenn Dalton, "The Glass Wall: Shattering the Myth that Alternative Rewards Won't Work With Unions," *Compensation and Benefits Review* (American Management Association, November/December 1998), pp. 38–45.

8. See Mary Bardman, "Unions Go High-Tech," *HRMagazine* (May 1999), p. 160. Also see Laureen Lazarovici, "Virtual Organizing: Putting Your Union on the Web," *America @Work* (AFL-CIO, September 1999), pp. 8–11.

9. See Laureen Lazarovici, "Organizing—Union Member to Member," *America@ Work* (AFL-CIO, March 1999), p. 20. Also see James B. Parks, "Blueprint for Organizing," *America@Work* (AFL-CIO), June 1999), pp. 8–11.

10. For more detailed, technical information concerning guidelines to be followed during a union-representational campaign, see Michael R. Carrell and Christina Heavrin, *Labor Relations and Collective Bargaining* (5th ed.; Upper Saddle River, N.J.: Prentice-Hall, Inc., 1998), pp. 114–175; or Arthur A. Sloane and Fred Witney, *Labor Relations* (9th ed.; Upper Saddle River, N.J.: Prentice-Hall, Inc., 1997), pp. 98–137.

11. The following are recommended for overviews of negotiations and applications of a labor–management agreement: Raymond L. Hilgert, *Labor Agreement Negotiations* (5th ed.; Houston, Texas: Dame Publications, Inc., 1998); Arnold M. Zack and Richard J. Bloch, *The Labor Agreement in Negotiation and*

Arbitration (2d ed.; Washington, D.C.: Bureau of National Affairs, Inc., 1996); Roy J. Lewicki, David M. Saunders, and John W. Minton, *Essentials of Negotiation* (Burr Ridge, Ill.: Richard D. Irwin, 1997); Marlin M. Volz and Edward P. Goggin, eds. *How Arbitration Works* (5th ed.; Washington, D.C.: Bureau of National Affairs, Inc., 1997); Raymond L. Hilgert, *Cases in Collective Bargaining and Industrial Relations* (9th ed.; Burr Ridge, Ill.: Irwin/McGraw-Hill, 1999).

12. See "HR Pulse: Employee Unions' Poll Results," *HRMagazine* (November 1998), p. 21.

13. Some authorities believe that the time has arrived for union–management relationships to become far more cooperative than adversarial in nature. A comprehensive book that advocates such an approach—including the important roles played by supervisors—is Warner P. Woodworth and Christopher B. Meek, *Creating Labor–Management Partnerships* (Reading, Mass.: Addison-Wesley, 1994).

Case

3-1

THE CUSTOMER'S SON

Jack Wilder was a principal buyer for Amber Hardware Stores, a large hardware company in Metro City. In this capacity he was an important customer of the Faulkner Metal Co. Annually, Wilder bought hundreds of thousands of dollars worth of metal garden furniture from Faulkner, representing about 20 percent of Faulkner's sales volume. When Sarah Freund, sales manager of Faulkner, was making a call on Wilder, Wilder asked her to check with Faulkner's president to see whether she could find a job for Wilder's son Mark, who had dropped out of college and wanted to find work in industry. Freund assured Wilder that she would do her best and would let him know soon.

After a brief discussion and after considering the importance of the account, Harry Faulkner, the company president, agreed to have Mark Wilder come to his office for an interview. Mark was hired and was given the position of assistant to Phil Sullivan, Faulkner's plant superintendent. Sullivan had been apprised of the customer connection, but he was not given any choice in the decision to hire and place Mark Wilder. Mark's job duties essentially consisted of doing the things Phil Sullivan chose to delegate to him; that is, he had a personal assistant position.

Initially, Sullivan was impressed with Mark's willingness to learn, astuteness, and efforts. After a number of weeks, Sullivan told Harry Faulkner "how well young Wilder is coming along." This information was reported to Jack Wilder the next time Sarah Freund, the sales manager, called on him. All went smoothly for a few months, and the orders from Amber Hardware Stores increased at a growing rate. There was no way to judge whether this increase was due to the good news about Mark, to a business upturn, or whether it constituted preferential treatment.

However, after about six months of work, Mark Wilder's job performance took a turn for the worse. His initial enthusiasm seemed to decrease, his attitude left much to be desired, and he seemed to care less and less about how he was doing his job. Phil Sullivan had a friendly talk with Mark. During this conversation, Mark told Sullivan, "I can always work in my old man's firm if this job doesn't work out. But I can't predict how he'll feel about it and what he'll do if you guys decide to get rid of me." After this meeting with Mark Wilder, Phil Sullivan pondered what he should do next.

Questions for Discussion

1. Was it a prudent decision on the part of Faulkner management to hire Mark Wilder in the first place? Was the assignment of Mark Wilder to a personal assistant position for Phil Sullivan a particularly sensitive one in this type of situation?

2. Should Sullivan inform Jack Wilder that Mark Wilder's recent job performance has been lacking? Why or why not?
3. What should Phil Sullivan and/or Harry Faulkner do?
4. What are the ethical and business implications of this case?

Case

3-2

THE INTERFERING ADMINISTRATIVE ASSISTANT

Christine Moreno is vice president of manufacturing at Coyle Chemical Company. She has direct line authority over Ed McCane, plant superintendent; Charles Evans, chief engineer; Diane Purcell, purchasing and supplies supervisor; Ron Weaver, supervisor of maintenance; and Carol Shiften, supervisor of the shipping department.

Two years ago, Moreno hired Bernice Billings as a secretary. Billings was diligent, capable, and efficient. She quickly won the admiration and confidence of her boss. Moreno felt fortunate to have such a capable secretary, since Billings willingly assumed numerous duties that allowed Moreno to devote more time to her broad responsibility over the five departments. Moreno therefore changed Billings's job title to "administrative assistant" and increased her salary. After receiving this elevation in status, Billings began to do even more than she had previously. For example, at times Moreno's supervisors received written instructions in the form of memos that clearly originated with Billings, but came to them with Moreno's initials. Billings also took it upon herself from time to time to give oral directives to the supervisors. For example, several times she went to the plant superintendent, Ed McCane, and gave him instructions concerning plant scheduling problems. At times she went directly to the production floor and asked employees to rush orders along or made other requests of this sort without seeing McCane first. She often told maintenance employees to do various projects, which, she said, "Ms. Moreno would like you to do." Similar occurrences took place in the shipping department, where she frequently left instructions for special treatment of some customers' orders.

In most of these situations, Moreno was not aware that Billings had taken it upon herself to communicate directly with subordinates to solve problems that had come to her attention. Some individuals grumbled that these directives should have come from either Moreno or the appropriate departmental supervisor. In most cases, however, everyone concerned realized that Billings had the best interests of the firm in mind, and they normally complied with her requests.

However, as time went on, the supervisors began to feel that Billings was interfering more than she was helping. In several instances some of the employees on the production floor did not check with Ed McCane but went directly to Billings for instructions. Similar incidents took place in other departments. One day, over a cup of coffee, Ed McCane, Carol Shiften, and Ron Weaver angrily poured out their concerns to each other. At the outset, they had looked upon Billings favorably, but now they considered her to be a disruptive factor who was undermining their supervisory positions.

Questions for Discussion

1. Why would Bernice Billings take it upon herself to communicate directly with supervisors and employees to solve plant problems? Is this procedure to be admired or condemned? Discuss.
2. Why did various plant personnel comply with Billings's requests and orders, even though they were not sure that these had come from Moreno? Can informal authority be just as powerful as direct line authority?
3. What should the supervisors do? What alternatives are open to them?

Case

3-3

THE LOYAL, HARD-WORKING SUPERVISOR

Gary Roderick, controller of Rollings Manufacturing Company, was concerned about one of his supervisors, Walter Grant, who supervised the accounting and payroll department. Grant had started with the company over 25 years ago. He began as a one-person accounting department, and he now had ten employees in his department. He was known as a loyal and hard-working supervisor, but one who preferred to do as many things as possible himself instead of delegating duties to his employees.

In recent years, numerous complaints about the accounting and payroll department became more frequent and serious. Other company supervisors complained that Grant's department was "bogged down." Delays in getting up-to-date figures were increasing, and there also were numerous errors in payroll checks and other vital accounting information. Just last week, a major computer programming mistake attributed to Grant caused a week's delay and brought widespread complaints about payroll checks that had been computed in error.

Several department employees had spoken with Roderick privately about Grant. Although they liked him personally, they were concerned that Grant was "behind the times," and that he did not listen to their suggestions and ideas for improvement. Roderick acknowledged that most of the problems in the department centered on Grant. Roderick previously had urged Grant to assign more duties to employees and to delegate authority to them. Roderick also tried to impress upon Grant the need for new procedures and the importance of listening to ideas from employees. Until now, Grant had not gotten the message, and he had done nothing to change. In the meantime, things in the accounting and payroll department were getting worse.

Roderick was reluctant to fire Grant, because Grant was 60 years old and a close personal friend. There also were legal considerations about possible age discrimination that the director of human resources had mentioned to Roderick when he talked to her about perhaps removing Grant from his supervisory position. Roderick knew he had to do something, and the sooner the better.

Questions for Discussion

1. Why does the status of Walter Grant in this case pose a particularly difficult set of problems to his boss, Gary Roderick?
2. Does the firm have any duty or obligation to Walter Grant in view of his many years of dedicated service? Discuss.
3. Consider the alternatives open to Gary Roderick. For example, would it be advisable for Roderick to require Walter Grant to select and develop an understudy? Why or why not?
4. If you were Gary Roderick, what would you do, and why?

Case

3–4

A ROSE HAS ITS THORNS

Steve Hatter is general manager at Fritz & Toland Garden and Retail Centers. Fritz & Toland is a third generation, family-owned major retail company. As a previous member of the sales department, Steve Hatter had worked for about eight years under Sandra Johnson, the sales department's supervisor. At the time of Johnson's retirement two years ago, Hatter was promoted to general manager by Rose Bates, the firm's majority owner and president. For the thirteen years that Sandra Johnson had managed the sales department, there had been little employee turnover and few major problems within the department.

After Johnson's retirement, Emily Vargas was hired by Rose Bates from another local firm to become sales department supervisor. Unfortunately, Vargas' two-year tenure in the position had been marked by much higher employee turnover, and the sales department was finding it difficult to maintain a stable and trained sales force. To fill in, staff members from other departments frequently were pulled from their jobs to cover sales requirements as needed.

Steve Hatter's responsibilities as general manager allowed him to work closely with department supervisors and staff. Supervisors and staff had been sharing their frustrations over the sales department's situation with Hatter and each other. The supervisors and staff from the other departments complained that projects were not being completed with timeliness or efficiency because of being pulled into sales so often. Sales department personnel complained about being overworked and having to deal with negative attitudes from other employees when needing help.

Because these issues had become a continuing topic for informal complaints and the grapevine, Steve Hatter began talking with members of the sales department to try and understand why these problems existed, and why apparently nothing was being done to improve the situation. Through several revealing interviews, Hatter discovered that much of the department turnover was attributed directly to Emily Vargas. There were complaints that Vargas did not abide by agreements that had been made by Sandra Johnson with employees at the time of their hiring. Employee complaints lodged with Vargas were only ignored by her, and resolutions were rarely attained. During exit interviews conducted by Vargas, departing employees told Vargas that she was the main reason they were leaving, but this was never reported to Rose Bates. Vargas would report to Bates that the turnover was attributed to insignificant problems, or external reasons for leaving. As a result, employees throughout the organization were discouraged by higher management's failure to respond to the problems in the sales department.

Miles Swanson, design department supervisor, and Allyson Wang, the out-of-store operations supervisor, told Steve Hatter that several months ago they shared their opinions of the sales department's situation with Rose Bates. Bates' response to Swanson and Wang was quite defensive. Bates told them that, "Emily Vargas is the right person for that position," and that they (Swanson and Wang) had become "too critical and inflexible" after their many years (about two decades) of working for the company. Bates had recently stated to Hatter that she considered Vargas to be dependable, a hard worker, able with customers, a good organizer, and possessing valuable years of experience in retail sales. According to Bates, the shortage of employees in the sales department was because of the tight labor market, and "People just don't want to work anymore." Steve Hatter knew that he had to do something soon, and that it could be a formidable task to confront the situation.

Questions for Discussion

1. Why would Rose Bates' opinions about Emily Vargas be so different from those of Vargas' employees and opinions of other departmental personnel?
2. Since Steve Hatter is aware of Bates' previous responses to criticism of Vargas, does this place him in an untenable position if he should decide that Vargas should be replaced? Discuss.
3. What alternatives are open to Steve Hatter?
4. If you were Steve Hatter, what would you do and why?

Case

3-5

A COMPLICATED STATE OF AFFAIRS

Tina Thomas, age 30, is a supervisory manager of the claims department at the corporate headquarters of Compton Mutual Insurance Company. She has been with the company for three years, and has risen through the ranks to the management level. Thomas now has responsibility for four sections, each of which has a team leader. She is proud of her position and the advancement she has achieved. Thomas is well liked and respected by both fellow supervisors and her employees.

When Thomas was promoted several months previously, she inherited Laura Becker as her secretary. Becker had been with the company for about six years; she was a proficient secretary and very knowledgeable about the company. When Becker began at the company, there were only 25 personnel in the corporate offices. This has grown to some 50 managers and other personnel.

Thomas and Becker have been casual acquaintances since high school. When Thomas started at Compton Mutual Insurance Company in another part of the firm, she and Becker began taking lunch together. Thus began a casual social relationship which grew over Thomas's three years with the company. Occasional evening movies and dinner were shared as the friendship developed. Both always remained very professional at work, and they did not let their friendship interfere with responsibilities at work.

One day at lunch, several months after Thomas's promotion to her current position, Becker revealed her secret. Laura Becker acknowledged that she had been having an affair for the last three years with the CEO of the company, Ron Appleton. Rumors had floated throughout the company, but Thomas had never believed the rumors due to the respect she had for Becker and the CEO of the company. The news shocked Thomas. She felt hurt inside because she had liked working for the CEO and she did not want to believe that he was partaking in a clandestine affair while being married and the father of two small children. Thomas also was appalled that Becker was involved in such an affair because Becker had usually talked about "dos" and "don'ts" of proper behavior. Tina Thomas did not want to abandon her friend who now was also her secretary. Further, Thomas believed that Becker was somewhat of a "victim" since she had been recently divorced from a sour marriage when the affair began. She was also 10 years younger than the 40-year-old CEO.

Tina Thomas did not know how to handle this situation. She wondered who else might know about the affair. She was concerned that her friendship with Laura Becker could damage her career. In addition, Becker's work performance had not been the best. She often seemed to be preoccupied and busy with personal calls to and from her "boyfriend." Little did Thomas know that the so-called "boyfriend" at the time was the CEO of the company, her boss Ron Appleton.

A month after Thomas was told about the affair, it ended. Laura Becker told Thomas that Ron Appleton, the CEO, "broke it off." Becker was extremely upset, and her work performance became even more of a problem. Due to the nature of the affair, Ron Appleton—through use of company funds—paid Becker several thousand dollars to prevent a sexual harassment suit. Her silence was supposed to be a part of the deal. Laura Becker told Tina Thomas the details of the breakup situation and the payoff. Other employees also suspected something about the affair and its outcome.

It was July, and Tina Thomas was soon to be married. Before these events came to light, Thomas would have asked Laura Becker to be part of her wedding. Thomas now feared that her reputation and position in the company could be in jeopardy, and she even had doubts about inviting Becker to the wedding. Thomas also had concerns about inviting the CEO, Ron Appleton. In the past, everyone had invited the CEO to their weddings. Tina Thomas frequently had worked with Appleton, and she felt obligated to invite him to her wedding. But this could result in a possible sticky situation!

Concerned about what to do, Tina Thomas considered whether she should seek advice from the firm's director of human resources or simply make a decision on her own.

Questions For Discussion

1. Should Tina Thomas have continued her friendship and association with Laura Becker after she learned about the affair between Becker and the CEO of the firm?
2. Should Thomas have consulted with the director of human resources after Becker confided in her about the affair?
3. How should Tina Thomas have handled Laura Becker's work performance after Becker claimed that the CEO, her "boyfriend," was the cause?
4. If you were in Thomas's position, would you still consider having Becker in your wedding? Why or why not?
5. If you were Thomas, would you invite Becker and the CEO to your wedding? Why or why not?

Case

3-6

TRICK OR TREAT?

The customer relations department of a midwestern utility employed about 100 people whose primary function was to answer customer telephone complaints, problems, and inquiries. The department did not have face-to-face contact with the customers. It was open 24 hours a day, every day. During peak hours, 65 to 70 employees worked in the department.

One October 30, the day before Halloween, a group of 12 day-shift female employees decided to dress up as "ladies of the evening" for Halloween. None of the employees consulted her supervisor or the department manager. The next day—Halloween—the group appeared in full dress, including ribbons, extra makeup, and leather miniskirts. When several of the supervisors and the department manager noticed the women, they gave no indication of a negative response. In fact, two of the supervisors laughed at the group's attire and commended them on their originality. Most of the group's coworkers thought that the attire was humorous, although a few employees said that the costumes were "a bit much!"

Approximately an hour after the women had reported for work, one of the supervisors, Sheila Brookings, went into the department manager's office. Brookings was visibly upset. She said that she was outraged at the costumes, and she demanded that the employees be sent home for the day without pay. Brookings commented that in all her

15 years as a supervisor, "I've never been so offended as I am today!" She continued angrily, "This is a business, not a place for partying. Further, I find their dress to be personally offensive to me and my religious values!"

The department manager, Brenda Crampton, knew that this would be one of the busiest days of the year in the department and that she could not afford to send 15 to 20 percent of the staff home and still give proper, prompt service to customers. Crampton also considered the fact that none of the women in the group had had a serious disciplinary problem. Crampton pondered what, if any, action should be taken against the employees and how to respond to Brookings. Crampton knew that if she suspended or disciplined the employees, many of the office employees would become extremely upset. Crampton feared that she might find the total office disrupted if she took disciplinary action. At the same time, she also felt that she had to be sensitive in responding to Brookings's complaint.

Questions for Discussion

1. Was management's position compromised since no action was taken when the women reported to work? Discuss.
2. Did Sheila Brookings overreact, or was she justified in complaining to Crampton?
3. Should the women be sent home and/or disciplined? What alternatives are open to Brenda Crampton?
4. What might be done in the future to support employee activities on the job without violating certain individuals' personal values?

Case

3-7

UNWANTED HELP

Eureka Medical Center is a large hospital in a southern city. The purchasing department consists of six buyers, two clerical employees, and one supervisor. It is responsible for all hospital supplies.

Pat House is the newest buyer in the department. Included in her responsibilities are purchasing and inventory monitoring of vouchers, syringes, needles, and IV solutions that the hospital uses on a daily basis. The hospital's material requirements planning system (MRP) generates weekly reports for Pat House and the other buyers. These reports identify items that need to be reordered. House was instructed by a fellow buyer to review this report at the beginning of each week, and place the necessary orders before the end of the week.

John Davies had been promoted about six months previously from buyer to supervisor of the purchasing department. One of his first decisions had been to hire Pat House as his replacement. Davies had worked as a buyer for almost 10 years, and he knew the system inside and out. As supervisor, he reviewed the MRP reports of all the buyers each week to ensure that his buyers would stay on top of the hospital's needs. Shortages in certain supplies could be life threatening.

It was a Wednesday several months after Pat House had been hired. While reviewing the MRP reports, Davies noticed that certain necessary supplies for which House was responsible had not been ordered. Since Davies was very familiar with the needed supplies and the corresponding suppliers, he decided to place some orders to expedite them and also to convey to House that he was willing to help her when she was busy.

On Friday of that week, when House started placing orders that the MRP report had called for, her suppliers questioned her. They asked her if she really needed to double the amount that she usually ordered, since earlier in the week John Davies had placed orders for similar amounts. House was infuriated that Davies had placed orders with her suppliers without informing her. When she confronted Davies about it, he apologized and said he was only trying to help. Davies explained that he thought she had been extremely busy and wanted to reduce her workload.

House thought the problem had been resolved. But as time progressed, Davies continued placing some of her orders, although he always informed her of what he had done. She didn't say anything about this to any of the other buyers, because she was afraid of what they might think. House grew more distressed, because she didn't know how to tell her supervisor to let her do her job without causing hard feelings. House became increasingly concerned that Davies didn't have any confidence in her abilities and that he was unwilling to tell her what he wanted done differently. Her six-month performance appraisal was scheduled for the next week. She wasn't comfortable with her situation, and she worried that her days with the hospital might be numbered. House pondered whether she should quit now, or first see the director of human resources or Davies' boss (the hospital's associate administrator) to discuss what she should do.

Questions for Discussion

1. Should a supervisor do the work of an employee to assist the employee or reduce the workload? Discuss.
2. Why would John Davies continue to do some of Pat House's job duties?
3. Why do employees (such as Pat House) often resent it when a supervisor performs some of their job duties, even if this is well intentioned?
4. If you were Pat House, what would you do? Consider alternatives.

Case

3-8

SANDERS SUPERMARKETS STORE #32: WHY HAVE ANOTHER MEETING?

Sanders Supermarkets operates over 50 stores in a major metropolitan area. In an attempt to improve its market share, the company embarked on a new program in regard to the merchandising and pricing of meat products. A companywide meeting of all district managers and store supervisors was held.

At the meeting the company president stressed the important points of the new meat program, one of which was that each store supervisor should have a store meeting to explain the program to all the store's employees.

On a follow-up later that same week, Dick Barton, district manager, went into Store #32 to evaluate the progress of the program. Dan Rolan was its store supervisor. The following dialogue took place:

DISTRICT MANAGER: Dan, I just walked the store and talked with your bakery, deli, and meat department heads. It seems that there wasn't a store meeting here this week. Why not?

STORE SUPERVISOR: I didn't think we needed to have another meeting. I did talk to every one of my department heads about the new meat program, if that's what you're referring to.

DISTRICT MANAGER: That's exactly what I was referring to. You know that you were told by the president to have a meeting in the store. Also, you received a bulletin from the sales department explaining the new program, didn't you? And at the bottom of the first page, it said, "Have a store meeting."

STORE SUPERVISOR: Dick, do you expect me to have a store meeting every time the sales department writes that on a bulletin? If so, then I'll probably be having a store meeting every other day. When will I find time to manage this store? Besides, how long should such a meeting take? I've never had any training or instructions about holding meetings. Most of the meetings I have with my employees in the store seem to accomplish very little other than to waste my time and theirs.

DISTRICT MANAGER: Oh, come now, Dan, it doesn't take any special training to hold meetings. And what are you saying? Do you really mean that "Have a store meeting" appears on quite a few company bulletins?

STORE SUPERVISOR: Absolutely, and not only that, Dick. What about all the company mail I receive daily that I have to read? Usually in the middle of the page it says "All Stores Except—." Do you realize just how much store mail comes in every day? And the bad part is that most company bulletins either don't apply to my store or are so redundant that they put me to sleep.

DISTRICT MANAGER: Okay, Dan, but why didn't you complain about this before if it's a problem?

STORE SUPERVISOR: Frankly, I didn't think it would make any difference if I did complain. There are too many people in our organization who think that communication means just writing memos and having more meetings, even if they're not needed.

DISTRICT MANAGER: Well, at any rate, I want you to have a store meeting on the meat program right away. I don't want my boss complaining to me that one of my stores didn't follow through on instructions.

STORE SUPERVISOR: Okay, I'll have the meeting, but I think it will be a waste of time. My employees already are well informed on this program.

DISTRICT MANAGER: Dan, I understand your feelings, but we all have to follow orders. It seems to me that our discussion today has highlighted several problems. Think about them, and when I see you again in a few days perhaps we can discuss what we can do to attack them.

Questions for Discussion

1. Identify the problems of meetings and other communication issues that are apparent in this case.

2. If a store supervisor is to receive training or instructions about holding meetings, how could this best be accomplished?

3. Outline a number of suggestions for improving communications among all parties in this organizational setting. Would you recommend that some type of electronic meeting (see the "You Make the Call" segment in Chapter 10) be utilized for certain types of meetings?

INTERNET ACTIVITY

4. (*Optional*) Using the Internet, secure information on the "Dilbert Principle." The Dilbert Zone Web site is www.dilbert.com and Scott Adams's current and archived strips can be found at www.unitedmedia.com/comics/dilbert.

   After completing your search, write a short paper in which you:

   a. Report at least one illustration where Catbert, the "Evil Director of Human Resources," shows how not to conduct a meeting.

   b. Report at least one strip that depicts an instance of "management malpractice" (mismanagement).

   c. Assess the "Dilbert Principle" illustrations you found with the problems at Sanders Supermarkets.

   d. Compare your findings with those of another student or students (if possible).

Case
3-9

CAN THE COMPANY AVOID UNIONIZATION?

The family-owned Royal Furniture Company manufactures and assembles office furniture in a small community in a southern state. It employs about 100 people and is operated by the principal owner, Oliver Thomas. The relationship between management and the workers has been very good in a rather paternalistic way. Wages are competitive, and the employees have numerous extra benefits, which management provided whenever the need arose. For example, wages were advanced if an employee needed money for an emergency; court fines were paid by the company if the employee did not have the funds to do so; and when a worker could not meet a monthly installment obligation, the company usually would advance the amount needed. Several times, union organizers had approached the factory employees to organize them, but each time the union was unsuccessful in getting enough support.

However, in recent years the company has been experiencing more difficult economic times. Wages have not kept pace with inflation, and the company was becoming less generous in giving employees various benefits. Employees were becoming more and more dissatisfied, and a union organizer was again observed passing out union literature outside the plant.

Thomas had stated publicly on several occasions to his supervisors and some employees that, if a union were to win an election, he would either sell the company or close the plant. He did not want to go through union negotiations, and he did not want his managerial prerogatives diminished.

One of the company's office supervisors, Harriet Toole, recently took a human resources management course at a local community college, where she studied labor unions and union-organizing campaigns. She became concerned that Thomas's approach to the situation at Royal Furniture Company could lead to unionization of the plant and that he might even be violating the law. Toole wondered what she should do.

Questions for Discussion

1. Is a paternalistic management approach a desirable one? Can it work in a small company to a better degree than in a large company? Discuss.
2. Why would Thomas vow to sell his company or close his plant if the union organized his workers? Is this a threat, or just rhetoric designed to discourage unionization? Discuss.
3. How could Harriet Toole influence Oliver Thomas to develop a program of positive employee relations that might improve the situation at Royal Furniture Company? Discuss alternatives open to her.
4. Why would Oliver Thomas be well advised to seek the advice of an attorney or consultant who is an expert in union–management matters?

Case

3-10

WHAT IS "REASONABLE TIME" FOR THE SHOP STEWARD?

Sandra Whitworth supervises a group of 20 employees in the communication services division of a major state university. All employees in this division are represented by a local chapter of the Public Employees Office and Professional Union.

One day Whitworth called Eleanor Kane into her office. Kane was a technical specialist who served as union shop steward. "Elly," said Whitworth, "it's time that we had a showdown about the amount of time you've been spending on union matters in this office. For the last two weeks you've averaged over 2 hours each day away from your job, allegedly to handle union grievances. This is entirely too much. I won't tolerate this anymore!"

"What do you mean, too much?" responded Kane. "The union contract says I'm allowed a reasonable time to handle union grievances, and it does not specify an upper time limit. I take only the time necessary to do my job as union steward. And lately there's been a flock of complaints and grievances which have come to my attention."

"I don't care about your union affairs," replied Whitworth. "You've got a job to do, and being away from your job this much time is unreasonable by any standards. From now on, if you're gone more than one hour each day on union matters, I'm going to dock your pay accordingly."

"Sandra," snapped Kane, "if you do that, I'll file a grievance right away and will fight you all the way to arbitration if necessary. You haven't got a leg to stand on, and you know it. Go see Larry Niland, your director of human resources. He'll tell you the same thing. In the meantime, I'm going to report this harassment to our union business agent at the local union office!" With that, she left Whitworth's office.

Whitworth pondered what her next move, if any, should be. She also reviewed Article 3, Section 1, of the current labor agreement, which in part stated the following:

A Union shop steward shall be permitted reasonable time to investigate, present, and process grievances on the Employer's property without loss of time or pay during regular working hours, provided that the steward obtains permission from his or her supervisor prior to such absence from assigned duties. Such time spent in handling grievances during the steward's regular working hours shall be considered working hours in computing daily or weekly overtime if within the regular schedule of the steward.

Questions for Discussion

1. Whose responsibility is it to determine what is meant by the word "reasonable" in Article 3, Section 1 of the labor agreement? Does this have to be negotiated with the union in more specific terms? Discuss.

2. Should Sandra Whitworth attempt to handle this problem on her own, or should she refer it to Larry Niland, the director of human resources? Why?

3. Outline a series of recommendations for Whitworth and/or Niland in order to reach a satisfactory resolution of the problem.

Case

3-11

DIFFERENT HOURS AND RULES FOR UNION AND NONUNION EMPLOYEES

Oscar Pratt, superintendent of the unionized warehouse department of Ashley Department Stores, was discussing a serious problem with Harmon Ashley, president of the company. According to Pratt, his foremen and the union were complaining about the different treatment of union employees from nonunion employees. For example, only union warehouse workers were docked 15 minutes' pay for 5 minutes of tardiness, while nonunion employees were seen walking in and out of the company buildings at all times. Pratt said, "Apparently the nonunion employees can arrive at any time they care to, and they don't have to comply with regular hours like the unionized warehouse workers do!"

The unionized warehouse workers also told Pratt that nonunion employees could be found in the company cafeteria at all hours of the day and were apparently not restricted to certain regular times or to 15-minute coffee breaks as were the warehouse workers. Pratt pointed out to Ashley that he had handled several formal grievances over this issue and expected even more complaints after the labor agreement expired in about a year.

Pratt urged Ashley to take steps to correct the situation so that working hours and regulations would be more uniform for both union and nonunion employees. Pratt believed that Ashley should have a serious discussion with Gail Massen, the sales manager, and Eric Engel, the general manager, to bring about the desired results.

Ashley was sympathetic to Pratt's concerns. Ashley was known to believe in running a "tight" operation. As president, he reported to his desk before seven in the morning and remained until after the official quitting hour. He rarely took a coffee break himself. As he pondered what steps to take, his first reaction was to call Massen and Engel into his office and simply tell them that he wanted the nonunion employees also to put in a regular eight-hour day, to report to work on time, and to limit their break periods. But, on second thought, he realized that this would not always be possible. He was aware of the special problems of salespeople, who often had to work irregular hours to handle peak customer periods in the stores. Some sales representatives might return home late the night before from a business meeting or from entertaining a customer. Similarly, other nonunion personnel such as those in the office, advertising, and purchasing departments, including supervisors, were known to prefer some flexibility in their work schedules. They claimed that this flexibility was necessary in relation to their duties and that it contributed to good work performance and morale.

Harmon Ashley left a telephone message with Marcia Bush, the director of human resources, to come and discuss the situation with him.

Questions for Discussion

1. Should the same policies and rules be in place and enforced for all categories of employees? Why or why not?
2. What should Harmon Ashley, president of the company, do in this situation?
3. What should Marcia Bush, director of human resources, advise Ashley to do?
4. What would be your reaction if you were: (a) Oscar Pratt, the warehouse superintendent, (b) Eric Engel, the general manager, or (c) Gail Massen, the sales manager?

Case

3-12

MISTAKEN OVERTIME WORK

Central Container Company manufactures various types of metal container products on a three-shift basis. One of the maintenance employees, Art Glenn, reported for work at 11:00 P.M. on a Friday night shift through an error on his part. He had not been scheduled to work and he had not been called in, although a small crew was scheduled to work this shift.

At about midnight, Glenn's regular supervisor, Gerry Fresno, entered the plant on a trouble call and questioned Glenn regarding his presence in the plant. After some discussion, both realized that Glenn had reported in error.

However, Fresno told Glenn that he could finish the shift. Glenn worked eight hours. This was Glenn's sixth consecutive day of work, and by union contract as well as by law, Glenn was to be paid at a rate of time and one half for this shift.

The next day, however, another maintenance employee, Willie Flanders, filed a grievance because Glenn had worked a sixth day, although Glenn was junior to Flanders in seniority. Flanders claimed equal pay for the time Glenn worked (eight hours at time and one half, i.e., 12 hours of pay). Flanders and his union steward claimed that in accordance with a well-established practice at the company, overtime had to be offered first to employees in accordance with their seniority and their ability to perform the work.

Several days later, at a grievance meeting held in Fresno's office, Ann Marshall, the union business representative, argued that if Fresno had sent Glenn home after he found him working, no grievance would have been filed. However, since the past practice had been and still was to let the most senior employees work overtime, the union should be upheld in this case, and Flanders should be paid for all time at the appropriate rate that the junior employee (Glenn) was paid.

Fresno responded that the company should not be required to pay 12 hours of pay to another employee. Out of consideration for the employee who reported by mistake, Fresno had allowed Glenn to work the full shift instead of sending him home with one hour's pay. The claim of the union was unjust and inequitable. No union employee, neither Flanders nor anyone else, suffered any loss of work or income because Fresno had acted in a considerate manner. If Glenn had not erroneously reported for work, no one would have worked in that job. Fresno claimed that his decision to allow Glenn to continue to work after he was discovered in the plant should be commended and not criticized.

Ann Marshall ended the meeting with this comment, "If that's your decision, we'll have to pursue this case further, even to arbitration if necessary. You goofed on this one, and you ought to recognize it right now!"

After Marshall left his office, Gerry Fresno decided that he had better take up the grievance with his manager and the director of human resources.

Questions for Discussion

1. If Art Glenn had worked the entire Friday evening shift in error without having met his supervisor, would Glenn have been entitled to payment for the unscheduled work on his part? Why or why not?

2. Should Willie Flanders be entitled to overtime pay under the practice of offering overtime to employees in accordance with their seniority and ability? Why or why not?

3. Evaluate Gerry Fresno's statement that the claim of the union was unjust and inequitable. Evaluate his contention that no union employee, including Flanders, had suffered any loss of work or income because he had acted in a considerate manner.

4. Should the company grant the union grievance and pay Flanders, or should the company deny the grievance and go to arbitration, if necessary?

Staffing

Chapter 12

The Supervisor and Employee Recruitment, Selection, Orientation, and Training

You Make the Call!

You are Tom Garrett, vice president of human resources for Sanders Supermarkets, Inc., which has 23 stores located in the St. Louis area. Carrie Webster was hired a little over a year ago for an accounting position in the central office. The knowledge and skills required for the job indicated that the employee should have at least three years of job-related experience, preferably in the supermarket/retail industry, and a college degree in accounting. A review of Carrie's most recent performance appraisal showed that she is a satisfactory employee.

On Sanders' employee appraisal form, a satisfactory rating indicates that the employee's overall performance is good and that he or she is fully competent.

Bill Barton, the manager of Store # 11, has just informed you that Sam Zehner, an eight-year veteran of Sanders who was eliminated from consideration for that position because he did not possess the required degree, had confronted him and asked some very pointed questions. He stated that Carrie was currently enrolled in one of his undergraduate accounting courses. Sam asked, "How could she have met the degree requirements when she's taking the same course I am?" Zehner contends that she is going to school at night to get the degree she claimed to have had to get the job.

You review the job file and see that the competition for the job was keen. Stacie Stephens, the accounting department manager, interviewed six candidates—four outsiders plus one other internal candidate besides Sam Zehner. The post-interview evaluation forms indicate that the two internal applicants were eliminated from consideration for the position because they did not possess the required degree. Further, under educational attainment, Carrie Webster cited a B.S. in Business Administration, concentration in accounting, from Old Ivy University. However, on both the application form and on the résumé, she did not mention a specific completion date.

Before she was offered employment, Jane Bradley, one of your key assistants, verified her past employment record and found it to be very good. Apparently no one had checked her educational background. Upon further investigation, you discover that Carrie Webster does not have a college degree and barely has enough credits to qualify as a senior. She is currently enrolled in two courses and her degree completion is at least 18 months away.

You know that if Carrie is dismissed, it will take several months before a replacement can perform at Carrie's level. What should you do to rectify the situation?

You Make the Call!

1
Discuss the staffing function and describe the roles of the human resources staff and supervisors.

THE STAFFING FUNCTION AND THE HUMAN RESOURCES DEPARTMENT

The management of human resources is the supervisor's most important activity, and it begins with staffing. As defined in Chapter 2, staffing is the recruitment, selection, placement, orientation, and training of employees. These activities are part of every supervisor's responsibilities, although in large organizations staff specialists provide help and support. The supervisory staffing function also includes evaluation of employee performance and input into how employees are to be rewarded based on their performance.

As discussed in Chapter 8, the supervisor's relationship with the human resources department is vitally important. Not every organization has a human resources (personnel) department. In very small firms, supervisors, in consultation with their managers, carry out staffing tasks. Increasingly, organizations are finding other firms to do some of the human resource functions they used to do.

Historically, companies held the upper hand in the hiring process, but with the recent unemployment rate at very low levels, the tables have turned. It is not uncommon to find companies delaying new store openings or tabling expansion plans because qualified workers are not readily available. Many employers have resorted to temporary services or recruiting firms to help fill the void during the current labor crunch. Desperate to fill vacant positions, several organizations have resorted to innovative methods for solving staffing needs (see the "Contemporary Issue" box in this chapter).

Balancing Authority

Regardless of its official name, the usefulness and effectiveness of any human resources department depends on its ability to develop close working relationships with managers. The quality of these line–staff relationships, in turn, depends on how clearly top-level managers have defined the scope of activities and authority of the human resources department.[1]

Human Resources Staff Advice and Supervisory Decisions

Because employee problems arise continually, supervisors often consult with human resources department staff for assistance, information, and advice. At times, without even realizing it, supervisors may concede much of their authority and responsibility to that department unnecessarily. Whenever a member of the human resources staff has expertise and knowledge directly related to a decision, supervisors are well advised to follow that person's advice and recommendations.

Some supervisors readily welcome the human resources staff's willingness to make certain decisions for them so that they will not have to solve difficult employee problems in their own departments. These supervisors reason that their own departmental tasks are more important than dealing with issues that the human resources staff can handle just as well or better than they can. Other supervisors may accept the staff's decision based on the premise that if the decision later proves to be wrong, they can say, "It wasn't my choice; human resources made the decision—not me!" For them it is a relief to rely on the staff's advice and consider it a decision. By so doing, these supervisors defer to the human resources department in the hope they will not be held accountable for the outcome of the decision. However, even when supervisors follow the human resources staff's advice, they are still accountable for the outcomes of their decisions.

Although it is easy to understand why some supervisors are reluctant to reject a human resources staff person's advice, they should recognize that the staff person may see only a part of the entire picture. The director of human resources is not responsible for the performance of a supervisor's department. Usually there are many unique factors that are better understood by each departmental supervisor than by anyone else.

2

Explain how the supervisor prepares to fill job openings and why job descriptions and job specifications are critical to this task.

PREPARING TO FILL STAFFING NEEDS

The staffing function is an ongoing process for the supervisor; it is not something that is done only when a department is first established. It is more realistic to think of staffing

contemporary issue

Innovative Recruiting Tactics

When confronted with a question—"Which of the following will best protect your company from competitive threats in the next three years?"—chief financial officers responded:

- A focus on hiring the best people (25%)
- Strong company leadership (25%)
- Having up-to-date technology (23%)
- The ability to develop and implement new ideas quickly (17%)[1]

The last few years have been referred to as an employee's paradise—more job openings than applicants. What are companies doing to cope with the tight labor market?

PROVIDENT BANK OF MARYLAND—There is a skilled customer service representative in the waitress who served you lunch. Provident gives employees referral cards to give to talented service providers in any industry. The cards compliment people on their customer service skills and advertise that the bank is actively seeking such employees. Staffers who refer new hires receive $150 to $350, depending on the positions filled. Human resources director Jeanne Uphouse says that since introducing the program in 1997, Provident has hired more than half the applicants attracted by the referral card. In addition, employees on the lookout for recruits have become more mindful of what constitutes good service.[2]

SIGNAL CORPORATION OF FAIRFAX, VIRGINIA—One recent ad in the *Washington Post* featured a messy-faced CEO Roger Mody shortly after taking part in a company pie-eating contest, with the tag line, "And you should see us on casual day."[3] The use of humor in ads and locating them in different parts of the newspaper has generated better response than placing them in the traditional help wanted section.

MIRAGE RESORTS OF LAS VEGAS—Mirage had to reinvent the recruitment process to hire 9,600 workers for Bellagio, a huge new luxury hotel that opened in October 1998. Mirage ran a newspaper ad stating it was hiring and offered a toll-free number that operated from 8 A.M. to 8 P.M. Callers made an appointment to come in and fill out an application. Prospective employees were greeted promptly and courteously escorted to a computer station. Mirage had broken down the generic job application into 165 basic questions that appeared on the applicants' computer screen. Assistance was provided those that needed help with the point and click process. Then every department had someone who searched the database looking for people with backgrounds the department was looking for. Candidates were called in for interviews. A total of 180 management personnel had been specially trained as interviewers. Mirage checked for criminal records and looked into job, school, and credit histories of 18,000 candidates. The 11,600 finalists also took a drug test. The appraisal results were fed into a database and offers made. Mirage spent $1 million on a computerized process that let it screen 75,000 applicants in 12 weeks. It spent ten weeks interviewing 26,000 applicants. Vice president Arte Nathan said, "More important was what the process revealed about the applicants. If people didn't show up for their appointments, we figured they'd be no-shows at work, too."[4]

GENERAL ELECTRIC OF FAIRFIELD, CT—The company has more than 2,000 job openings listed on its Web page at www.gecareers.com. "We post the majority of our job openings at the site, whether they are entry-level or mid-career positions," says Steve Poole, GE's manager of recruiting and staffing services. The Internet offers a fast, easy way to reach a broad audience of job-seekers," says Doreen Collins, manager of staffing and quality initiatives in Fairfield, Connecticut, "and we can get a job posting out any time, any day." "By recruiting online," adds Poole, "GE finds people who may not live in the city where the job is but would relocate for the right opportunity." Of the 15,000 resumes GE receives monthly, roughly half are submitted online.[5]

Sources: (1) Responses from a survey developed by Robert Half International from a stratified random sample of companies with more than 20 employees as reported in "Hiring Smart Is the Best Line of Defense," *Quality Digest* (June 1999), p. 17. Also visit www.rhii.com for more information. (2) Geanne Rosenburg, "Playing Your Cards Right," *Working Women* (June 1998), p. 42. (3) "How to Hire," *Inc.* (October 1998), pp. 36+; and Roger Mody, "The People Chase," *Inc.* (May 1998), pp. 125+. (4) Eileen P. Gunn, "How Mirage Resorts Sifted 75,000 Applicants to Hire 9,600 in 24 Weeks," *Fortune* (October 12, 1998), p. 195. (5) Sarah Fister, "Online Recruiting: Good, Fast and Cheap," *Training* (May 1999), p. 26.

in the typical situation in which a supervisor is placed in charge of an existing department. Although it has a nucleus of employees, changes in the department's makeup take place due to employee separations from the workforce, changes in operations, growth, or other reasons. Since supervisors depend on employees for results, they must make certain that there are enough well-trained employees available to fill all positions.

Determining the Need for Employees

A continuous aspect of the supervisory staffing function is that of determining the department's need for employees, both in number and job positions. Supervisors should become familiar with departmental jobs and functions and consult the organization chart or manual if one is available. For example, the supervisor of a maintenance department may have direct reports who are painters, electricians, and carpenters, each with different skills. The supervisor should study each of these job categories to determine how many positions are needed to get the work done and how employees should work together. The supervisor may have to compromise by adjusting a preferred arrangement to existing realities or by combining several positions into one if there is not enough work for one employee to perform a single function. By carefully studying the organization of the department, the supervisor can reasonably determine how many employees and what skills are needed to accomplish the various work assignments.

Developing Job Descriptions and Job Specifications

After determining the number of positions and types of skills needed, the supervisor's next step is to match the jobs available with individuals to perform them. This usually is done with the aid of *job descriptions* (as discussed in Chapter 9), which indicate the duties and responsibilities involved in each job. A supervisor may have access to existing job descriptions; if such descriptions are not available, they can be developed with the assistance of higher-level managers or the human resources staff. Similarly, if a new job is created, the supervisor should determine its duties and responsibilities and develop an appropriate job description.

The supervisor may find it helpful to ask departmental employees to write down the tasks they perform during a given time period—say, a day or a week. This will provide the supervisor with considerable information from which to develop the content of a job description. Although the final form of the job description may be written by a human resources staff person, it is the supervisor's responsibility to determine what actually goes into it.[2] Figure 12-1 shows a step-by-step approach to developing a job description for the position of housekeeper that would be adaptable to many other types of jobs.

A supervisor should periodically (at least annually) compare each job description with what each employee does. As job descriptions become outdated, they may no longer fit the actual job duties and should be corrected. The supervisor may find that some of the duties assigned to a job no longer belong to it. They should be deleted or assigned elsewhere. Supervisors should not take the preparation of job descriptions lightly because they can be used to explain to applicants the duties and responsibilities

FIGURE 12-1

How to develop job
descriptions.

The following steps were developed for the preparation of a job description for the position of housekeeper in a hospital:

Step 1. Prepare a questionnaire to be sent to housekeeping employees and their supervisors, asking them to list what they feel are the major functions and subfunctions that must be performed to do their job effectively.

Step 2: Have several higher-level managers who are interested in housekeeping list what functions they feel should and should not be performed by housekeepers.

Step 3: Find out from others in the organization what they believe should be and should not be the functions of a housekeeper.

Step 4: Tabulate the results of each of the three sources given above.

Step 5: Reconcile the differences of the above three viewpoints with the objectives of your organization, and prepare a detailed list of activities to be performed.

Step 6: Classify activities as major and minor activities.

Step 7: Determine what each housekeeper needs to know, what qualifications are necessary to perform designated activities, and specifically why each activity is to be performed.

Step 8: Submit the results of Steps 5 to 7 to a committee of housekeepers and supervisors for their discussion and recommendations. At this point you may find that you have been asking employees to do more than could possibly be accomplished reasonably. Revise and finalize the job description and job specification as appropriate.

Step 9: Periodically—at least annually—review and revise the job description, following the eight steps listed above, when you feel that changes in products, equipment, the economic climate, or service demands necessitate a change in the job to be performed.

of a particular job. Job descriptions that describe the jobs accurately are useful in providing a realistic job preview, developing performance standards, conducting performance appraisals, and performing other staffing functions.

When the content of each job has been determined or reevaluated, a supervisor next should identify the knowledge and skills that are required of employees who are to perform the job. As discussed in Chapter 9, a written statement of required knowledge, skills, and abilities is referred to as a *job specification*. The process for determining what an employee needs to know is found in Figure 12-1, Step 7. Typically, the job description and job specification are combined into one document (see Figure 9-2 in Chapter 9).

Determining How Many to Hire

Supervisors are not frequently confronted with a situation in which large numbers of employees have to be hired at the same time. This situation occurs when a new department is created or when a major expansion takes place. The more usual pattern is to hire one or a few employees as the need arises. Of course, some supervisors constantly request additional employees because they feel pressured to get their work done on time. In many cases, however, a supervisor's problems are not solved by getting more help. In fact, the situation may become worse. Instead of problems being reduced, new problems may arise due to inefficiencies that accompany overstaffing.

Normally, a supervisor will need to hire a replacement when a regular employee leaves the department due to promotion, transfer, resignation, dismissal, retirement, or some other reason. There is little question then that the job must be filled. However, if major technological changes or a downsizing are anticipated, a replacement may not be needed. There are other situations in which additional employees have to be hired. For example, if new functions are to be added to the department and no one in the department possesses the required knowledge and skills, it may be necessary to go into the labor market and recruit new employees. Sometimes a supervisor will ask for additional help because the workload has increased substantially and the department is under extreme pressure. Before requesting additional help, the supervisor should make certain that the employees currently in the department are being utilized fully and that any additional help is absolutely necessary and within the budget.

Assistance in Recruitment and Selection

When supervisors have positions open in their departments, they normally ask the human resources department to recruit qualified applicants. Whether a particular job vacancy will be filled by someone from within the organization or someone from outside, the human resources department usually knows where to look to find qualified applicants. Most organizations try to fill job openings above entry-level positions through promotions and transfers. Promotions reward employees for past accomplishments; transfers can protect them from layoff or broaden their job knowledge. Internal applicants already know the organization, and the costs of recruitment, orientation, and training are usually less than those for an external applicant.

Generally, internal applicants can be found through the use of computerized skills inventories or job posting and bidding.[3] Information on every employee's skills, educational background, work history, and other pertinent data can be stored in a database that can be reviewed to quickly determine whether any employees qualify for a particular job opening. This procedure helps ensure that every employee who has the necessary qualifications is identified and considered. Most organizations communicate information about job openings by posting vacancy notices on bulletin boards or in newsletters. Interested employees apply or "bid" for the vacant position by submitting applications to the human resources office with a copy to the supervisor. Job posting creates a greater openness in the organization by making all employees aware of job opportunities.

The outside sources of job applicants will vary depending on the type of job to be filled. In all likelihood, a data entry clerk will not be recruited from the same source as a medical technologist. Advertising, public or private employment agencies, educational institutions, employee referrals, walk-ins, and contract or temporary help agencies are some of the sources that may be used.

To select from among job seekers, usually the human resources department first has applicants fill out employment application forms and then conducts preliminary interviews to determine whether the applicants' qualifications match the requirements for positions available. The human resources department also makes reference checks of the applicants' previous employment and background. For certain positions the department may administer one or more tests to determine whether applicants have the necessary skills and aptitudes. This may mean conducting statistical studies of tests that are used to determine whether they validly predict how an employee will perform on the job.[4] Eventually, applicants who do not have the required qualifications are screened out. Those who do have the qualifications are referred to the supervisor of the department where the job is open.

Supervisors Interview and Decide

After the human resources department has screened and selected qualified applicants for a job opening, the departmental supervisor normally interviews each candidate before any decision is made. The supervisor should make—or at least have the most say in making—the final decision to hire any candidate for a job within his or her department. Supervisors should not make staffing decisions without considering the legal ramifications of their decisions. It is easy to understand why supervisors are confused by the numerous laws, executive orders, regulations, and guidelines they may have heard or read about (see the Appendix at the end of this text for an overview of federal legislation). For example, Title VII of the Civil Rights Act of 1964 prohibits discrimination in employment. The Equal Employment Opportunity Commission (EEOC) was created to increase job opportunities for women and minorities and to enforce the law. The law prohibits employment practices that discriminate on the basis of race, gender, color, religion, and national origin. Laws protecting people who have physical and mental disabilities, Vietnam-era and other veterans, and older applicants and employees give a broader definition to the so-called "protected" classes.

Under equal employment opportunity and affirmative action programs, employers must make good-faith efforts to recruit, hire, and promote members of protected classes so that their percentage within the organization approximates their percentage within the labor market. While it is difficult to be current on all aspects of the law, effective supervisors should acquaint themselves with the Uniform Guidelines on Employee Selection Procedures because they apply to all aspects of supervisors' staffing responsibilities.[5]

In recent years corporate restructuring, or downsizing—the temporary or indefinite removal of employees from the organization—has created serious staffing concerns. Supervisors are being asked to do more with fewer employees. The consolidation of various job activities may not be a decision that the supervisor makes, but it is one that he or she must live with. Employees may be transferred from one

The human resources department makes the necessary reference checks of previous employment and past records of applicants.

job to another, or additional responsibilities may be added to existing ones. Some employees may even be involuntarily demoted from supervisory or staff positions. Unfortunately, supervisors may sometimes find themselves with little or no authority in staffing decisions. But, in general, the supervisor is the person who should make the decision to hire or not to hire.

Regardless of who makes the final hiring decision, selection criteria must be developed. **Selection criteria** are the factors that will be used to differentiate among the various applicants. Education, knowledge, previous experience, test scores, application forms, background investigations, and interpersonal skills often serve as selection criteria.

Selection criteria

Factors used to choose among applicants who apply for a job.

Discuss the selection process and the use of directive and nondirective interviewing in the process.

Selection

Process of choosing the best applicants to fill open positions.

THE SELECTION PROCESS

Selection is the process of screening applicants to choose the best person for a particular job. Once job applicants have been located, the next step is to gather information that will help determine who should be hired. Usually, the human resources staff or the supervisor reviews résumés or application forms to determine which applicants meet the general qualifications of the position. Then, qualified applicants may be given tests, reference or background checks, and interviews to further narrow the pool of applicants.

For supervisors, the most frequently used selection criterion—and often the most important part of the selection process—is the employee selection interview.[6] It is difficult to make an accurate appraisal of a person's strengths and potential from a brief interview. If there are several applicants for a position, the supervisor must ascertain which one is most qualified. This means trying to determine which applicant is most likely to perform best on the job and to stay with the company for the long term.

The employment interview plays a very important role in the selection process. Depending on the type of job, the applicant may be interviewed by one person or several members of a work team, but the applicant is also interviewing the organization (see Figure 12-2 for the goals of the applicant and the goals of the interviewer). How can one reconcile a major employer goal—to promote the organization—with a recent survey report that 20 percent of job applicants say they're "insulted" in job interviews.[7] The supervisor and/or the team members must properly prepare for the interview and remember that they are "selling" the organization. Interviewing is much more than a technique; it is an art that every supervisor must learn. Although our focus in this chapter is on the employee selection interview, over time every supervisor will conduct or be involved in other types of interviews that occur during the normal course of events. Among these are appraisal and counseling interviews, interviews regarding complaints and grievances, interviews regarding disciplinary measures or discharge, and exit interviews when employees quit voluntarily. The basic techniques are generally common to all interviewing situations.

Basic Approaches to Interviewing

There are two basic approaches to interviewing: directive and nondirective. These approaches are classified primarily according to the amount of structure imposed on the interview by the interviewer.

FIGURE 12-2   Goals of the selection interview.

GOALS OF THE APPLICANT	**GOALS OF THE EMPLOYER (THE INTERVIEWER)**
1. To obtain information about the job.	1. To promote the organization.
2. To obtain information about the organization.	2. To attract the best possible applicant.
3. To determine whether the job matches the applicant's needs.	3. To gather information about the applicant.
4. To determine whether he or she wants it.	4. To assess how well the applicant's qualifications match the job requirements.
5. To communicate important information about himself/herself.	5. To determine whether the applicant will fit in with the organization and other employees.
6. To favorably impress the employer (the interviewer).	

Source: Northeastern University's Career Services' "Successful Interviewing" web page provided the foundation for the development of this figure. Students may wish to visit www.dac.neu.edu/coop.careerservices/interview.html to obtain a preformatted copy of the Successful Interviewing Handout.

Directive interview

Interview approach in which the interviewer guides the discussion along a predetermined course.

Directive Interview.   In a **directive interview** the interviewer guides the course of the discussion with a predetermined outline and objectives in mind. This approach is sometimes called a "patterned" or "structured" interview. Using an outline helps the interviewer ask specific questions to cover each topic on which information is wanted. It also allows the interviewer to question and expand on related areas. For example, if a supervisor asks about the applicant's previous work experience, this may lead to questions about what the applicant liked and did not like about previous jobs. The supervisor guides and controls the interview but does not make it a rigid, impersonal experience. As a result of equal employment opportunity requirements, organizations are increasingly asking all applicants the same questions. This approach makes it easier to compare applicants since all have responded to the same questions.

Nondirective interview

Interview approach in which the interviewer asks open-ended questions that allow the applicant greater latitude in responding.

Nondirective Interview.   The purpose of a **nondirective interview** is to encourage interviewees to talk freely and in depth. The applicant has maximum freedom in determining the course of the discussion. Rather than asking specific questions, the supervisor may stimulate the discussion by asking broad, open-ended questions, such as "Tell me about your work in the computer field." Generally, the supervisor will develop a list of possible topics to cover and, depending on how the interview proceeds, may or may not ask them. This unstructured approach to interviewing allows for great flexibility, but it generally is more difficult and time consuming to conduct than are directive interviews. For this reason, it is seldom used in its pure form in employment selection.

Blending Directive and Nondirective Approaches.   Ultimately, the purpose of any interview is to promote mutual understanding—to help the interviewer and interviewee understand each other better through open and full communication. In employee selection interviews, the directive approach is used most often since supervisors find it convenient to obtain information by asking the same direct questions of all applicants.

However, at times supervisors should strive to blend both directive and nondirective techniques to obtain additional information that might be helpful in reaching a decision. Often, interviewers use situational questions to assess what the applicant would do in a certain situation. All applicants are given a specific situation to respond to. For example, the question "How would you assign daily work when two employees are absent?" allows the applicants to organize and express their thoughts about a realistic work situation. The supervisor may gain deeper insights about applicants' abilities to think and solve problems that could make the difference in choosing which applicant to hire.

Would it surprise you that "Can you type?" is one of the most commonly asked interview questions?[8] Regardless of the approach used, the initial questions about typing and computer skills should lead to the development of additional relevant job-related questions. For example, questions such as "What is your knowledge about a specific word processing package?" "Explain how you trained other employees in the use of the new software package," or "What are the steps involved in replacing a laser printer cartridge?" allow the applicants to reveal their knowledge and skills more clearly than could be ascertained from other sources. The supervisor should avoid using judgmental questions, such as "I believe that the information technology department is a detriment to our goals. What do you think?" Also, answers to questions that require a yes or no response, such as "Do you like to work with figures?" reveal very little about the applicant's ability to perform a particular job. It is better for the supervisor to ask why the applicant does or does not like to work with figures.

Preparation for an Employee Selection Interview

4
Describe how the supervisor should prepare for and conduct an effective selection interview.

Since the purpose of an employee selection interview is to collect information and arrive at a decision concerning a job applicant, the supervisor should prepare carefully for the interview. The supervisor must know what information is needed from the applicant, how to get this information, and how to interpret it.

As stated earlier, the directive interview is the most common approach used in selecting employees. Although most supervisors develop their own questions, some organizations have forms and procedures to guide supervisors in selection interviewing. For example, some firms require supervisors to fill out a detailed form on all applicants who are interviewed. Others use a standard interview form that more or less limits supervisors to asking only the questions that are included on the form. These interview forms sometimes are used to prevent supervisors from asking questions that might be considered discriminatory and in violation of government laws and regulations. Therefore, in preparing for an employee selection interview, the supervisor must know what can be and what should not be asked of job applicants during the interview. A general rule of thumb to follow is to seek information that is related to job qualifications and the candidate's ability to do the job.

Influence of Equal Employment Opportunity Laws. Legislation on equal employment opportunity has placed restrictions on the questions employers may ask job applicants. The overriding principle to follow in employee selection interviews is to ask job-related questions. Questions about topics not related to a person's ability to perform the job for which he or she has applied should be avoided. For example, asking an applicant for a position as data entry clerk about previous keyboarding experience would be directly related to the job. However, asking this applicant about owning or renting a home is of questionable purpose. Employee selection procedures also must ensure that legally protected groups such as minorities and women are treated fairly. Information that would adversely affect members of protected groups can be used only if it is directly related to the job. For example, the question "Who cares for your children?" is potentially discriminatory because traditionally it has adversely affected women more than men. On the other hand, the question "This job requires that you speak Spanish. Do you?" is legitimate because speaking Spanish is a job requirement. It would be wrong to ask the question selectively. It is essential that the same basic questions are asked of every applicant for a certain job. If the questions are different, then the selection criteria are different and the hiring decision cannot be justified, if challenged.

Figure 12-3 (see page 380) lists some of the most common areas of unlawful and potentially unlawful inquiry.

Application forms, tests, interviews, reference checks, and physical examinations must be nondiscriminatory and focus on job-related requirements. To determine whether or not a selection criterion is appropriate and complies with the law, one consulting firm has suggested the "OUCH" test.[9] OUCH is a four-letter acronym that represents the following:

O: Objective
U: Uniform in application
C: Consistent in effect
H: Has job relatedness

A selection criterion is objective if it systematically measures an attribute without being distorted by personal feelings. Examples of objective criteria include typing test scores, number of years of education, degrees, and length of service in previous positions. Examples of subjective criteria include a supervisor's general impression about a person's interest in a job or feelings that a person is "sharp."

A selection criterion is uniform in application if it is applied consistently to all job candidates. Asking a question such as "Would working on weekends conflict with your child-care arrangements?" only of female applicants is an illustration of not being uniform in application. However, it would be permissible to ask all applicants "Would you be able to meet the job's requirement to work every third weekend?"

A selection criterion is consistent in effect if it has relatively the same proportional impact on protected groups as it does on others. For example, criteria such as possessing a high school diploma or living in a certain area of town may be objective and uniformly applied to all job candidates, but they could screen out proportionately more members of minority groups. When a selection criterion is not consistent in effect, the burden of proof is on the employer to demonstrate that it is job related.

A selection criterion has job relatedness if it can be demonstrated that it is necessary in performing the job. For example, in most cases it would be extremely difficult

FIGURE 12-3   Areas of unlawful or potentially unlawful questions in application forms and employment interviews.

SUBJECT OF INQUIRY	UNLAWFUL OR POTENTIALLY UNLAWFUL QUESTIONS
Applicant's name	1. Maiden name. 2. Original name (if legally changed).
Civil and family status	1. Marital status. 2. Number and ages of applicant's children. 3. Child-care arrangements. 4. Is applicant pregnant or does she contemplate pregnancy?
Address	1. Foreign addresses that would indicate applicant's national origin.
Age	1. Before hiring, requests for birth certificate, baptismal certificate, or statement of age.
Birthplace (national origin)	1. Birthplace of applicant. 2. Birthplace of applicant's spouse, if any, and parents. 3. Lineage, ancestry, nationality.
Race and color	1. Any question that would indicate applicant's race or color.
Citizenship*	1. Country of citizenship if not United States. 2. Does the applicant intend to become a U.S. citizen? 3. Citizenship of spouse, if any, and of parents.
Disabilities	1. Preemployment physical examinations or questions about an applicant's physical or mental condition.
Religion	1. Religious denomination. 2. Clergyperson's recommendation or references. 3. Any inquiry into willingness to work a particular religious holiday.
Arrests and convictions	1. Numbers and kinds of arrests experienced.
Education	1. Nationality, race, or religious affiliation of schools attended. 2. Native tongue, or how foreign language skills were acquired.
Organizations	1. Is applicant a member of any association other than a union and/or a professional or trade organization?
Military experience	1. Type of discharge from the U.S. Armed Forces. 2. Did the applicant have military experience with governments other than the U.S. government?
Relatives	1. Names and/or addresses of any relatives.

*However, the Immigration Reform and Control Act of 1986 requires that employers determine that anyone they hire is a U.S. citizen or has a legal residency status.

to prove that a selection criterion such as marital status is job related. Job-related criteria should stress skills required to perform the job.

Supervisors may not always understand the reasons for some of the restrictions imposed on them by the equal employment opportunity policies of their organizations. They should not hesitate to consult with specialists in the human resources department for explanations and guidance in this regard.

Reviewing the Applicant's Background. Before interviewing a job applicant, the supervisor should review all available background information that has been gathered by the human resources office. By studying whatever is available, the supervisor can develop in advance a mental impression of the general qualifications of the job applicant. The application form will supply information concerning the applicant's schooling, experience, and other items that may be relevant.

When studying the completed application form, the supervisor should always keep in mind the job for which the applicant will be interviewed. If questions come to mind, the supervisor should write them down to remember them. For example, if an applicant shows a gap of a year in employment history, the supervisor should plan to ask the applicant about this gap and why it occurred.

A supervisor should also review the results of any employment tests taken by the applicant.[10] More and more organizations are administering job performance, integrity/honesty, and drug tests prior to the interview stage. Tests should be validated before they are actually used to assist in making hiring decisions.

The potential value of preemployment testing was illustrated in a study of 5,000 applicants for the U.S. Postal Service. Applicants who tested positive for drug use had a 59 percent higher absenteeism rate and a 47 percent higher involuntary turnover rate than applicants who did not test positive.[11] The selection criterion of preemployment drug testing was validated by the study—that is, the selection criterion bears a direct relationship to job success.

Human resources departments often administer job performance tests that measure skill and aptitude for a particular job as part of their normal procedures to screen out unqualified applicants. The human resources department must be able to document that these tests are valid, job related, and nondiscriminatory. This typically involves studies and statistical analyses by staff specialists—procedures that normally are beyond the scope of a supervisor's concern. Applicants whose test scores and other credentials appear to be acceptable are referred to the departmental supervisor for further interviewing. It is essential for the supervisor to understand what a test score represents and how meaningful it is in predicting an applicant's job performance. By consulting with the human resources department staff, the supervisor can become more familiar with the tests that are used and learn to interpret the test scores.

An additional source of information is references. Generally, telephone checks are preferable because they save time and allow for greater feedback. For the most part, information obtained from personal sources such as friends or character references will be positively slanted because applicants tend to list only people who will give them good references. Information from previous supervisors who were in a position to evaluate the applicant's work performance are best. However, because of emerging personal privacy regulations and potential damage claims, an employment background investigation is usually conducted by human resources department specialists. If possible, job references should be obtained in writing, should deal with job-related areas, and should be gathered with the knowledge and permission of the applicant. After reviewing all available background information, the supervisor should be able to identify areas in which little or no information is available and areas that require expansion or clarification.

Failure to Check Adequately Can Be Costly. It has been estimated that 85 percent of U.S. companies do not conduct any or do only minimal reference checks prior to hiring. This negligence has led applicants to omit or creatively explain the less positive aspects of their background. Even though job opportunities are plentiful, good jobs are still in relatively scarce supply. Some people will lie, cheat, and steal to get a great job.[12] Unfortunately, many employers will only say "John Jones worked here from such-and-such date to such-and-such date." In addition, applicants will only list references that will say good things about them. So is background checking fruitless? Consultant and author Bradford Smart recommends using TORC (threat of reference check). He suggests using the question, "If I were to ask you to arrange an interview with your last boss, and the boss were very candid with me, what's your best guess as to what he or she would say were your strengths, weaker points, and overall performance?" The interviewer will then gain insight into what makes this person tick and how they are apt to function in the job.[13]

The importance of verifying reference or application form data cannot be overemphasized. Various organizations have been charged with negligently hiring employees who later commit crimes. Typically, the lawsuits charge that the organization failed to adequately check references, criminal records, or general background information that would have shown the employee's propensity for deviant behavior. The rulings in these cases, which range from theft to homicide, should make employers more aware of the need to check applicant references thoroughly. It is suggested that the organization include on the job application a statement to be signed by the applicant stating that all information presented during the entire selection process is truthful and accurate. The statement should note that any falsehood is grounds for refusal to hire or for termination.[14]

Preparing Key Questions. In preparing for the interview, the supervisor should develop a list of key questions, which may include both directive and nondirective components.[15] Preferably, the supervisor should develop a list of key questions—perhaps 6 to 10 directive and nondirective questions—that are vital to the selection decision and are job related. It is important that all applicants be asked the same core set of key questions so that responses can be compared and evaluated. For example, the supervisor may want to know technical information about an applicant's previous work experience, why the applicant left a previous employer, and whether the applicant can work alternative shift schedules and overtime without difficulty.

Some organizations appear to have changed their focus from fixed job descriptions and job specifications to the competencies that differentiate average performers from the superior performers. Ron and Susan Zemke contend that "if you can identify the key skills, knowledge and personal attributes that make a master performer successful at a given job, then group these things into appropriate clusters, then you have a set of **competencies.** Link each of these broad competencies to a set of behaviors that answer the question, 'How do we know it when we see it?' and they can serve as sort of a blueprint to help you hire, train, and develop people."[16] Information in Figure 12-4 shows an illustration of how to use competencies to develop interview questions. By planning to ask such questions in advance, the supervisor can devote more attention to listening to and

Competencies

The sets of skills, knowledge, and personal attributes possessed by the superior performer.

Competency: Independent Judgment

Definition: Uses discretion in interpreting company procedures to make decisions in ambiguous situations.

BEHAVIORAL INDICATORS

- Performs well with minimal supervision.
- Tries to handle issues independently rather than passing them on.
- Uses supervisor as a resource but acts independently most of the time.
- Demonstrates ability to build learning and draw inferences from difficult experiences.

INTERVIEW QUESTIONS

- Describe a situation in which you had to arrive at a quick conclusion and take action.
- Tell me about a situation in which you had to make a decision on your own under pressure.
- Give me a time when you had to rely on your own judgment to make a decision.
- Tell me about the most difficult decision you've had to make in your job. What made it difficult?

Source: This example from Linkage Inc.'s Interviewing Skills Workshop appeared in Ron Zemke and Susan Zemke, "Putting Competencies to Work," *Training* (January 1999), p. 72. Reproduced with permission. © 1999. Lakewood Publications, Minneapolis, MN. All rights reserved. Not for resale.

observing the applicant, instead of having to think about what else should be asked. A thorough plan for the employment interview is well worth the time spent preparing it.

Conducive Physical Setting. Privacy and some degree of comfort are important components of a good interview setting. If a private room is not available to conduct an interview, then the supervisor should at least create an atmosphere of semiprivacy by speaking to the applicant in a place where other employees are not within hearing distance. This much privacy, at least, is necessary.

Conducting the Employee Selection Interview

The employee selection interview is not just a one-way questioning process since the applicant also will want to know more about the company and the potential job. The interview should enable the job seeker to learn enough to help him or her decide whether or not to accept the position if it is offered. The supervisor must conduct the interview professionally by opening the interview effectively, explaining the job requirements, and using good questioning and note-taking techniques.

Opening the Interview. The experience of applying for a job often is filled with tension for an applicant. It is to the supervisor's advantage to relieve this tension. Some supervisors try to create a feeling of informality by starting the interview with social conversation about the weather, the heavy city traffic, the World Series, or some other

Interviewing is much more than a technique; it is an art that every supervisor must learn.

Realistic organizational preview (ROP)

Sharing of information by an interviewer with a job applicant concerning the mission, values, and future direction of the organization.

Realistic job preview (RJP)

Information given by an interviewer to a job applicant that provides a realistic view of both the positive and negative aspects of the job.

topic of broad interest. The supervisor may offer a cup of coffee or make some other appropriate social gesture. An informal opening can be helpful in reducing an applicant's tensions; however, it should be brief, and the discussion should move quickly to job-related matters.

Many supervisors begin the employee selection interview with a question that is nonthreatening and easily answered by the applicant, but also contains job-related information that the supervisor might need. An example is "How did you learn about this job opening?"

The supervisor should avoid excessive informal conversation because studies of employee selection interviews have revealed that frequently an interviewer makes a favorable or unfavorable decision after the first five minutes of the interview. If the first ten minutes are spent discussing items not related to the job, then the supervisor may be basing the selection decision primarily on irrelevant information.

Explaining the Job.   During the interview, the supervisor should discuss details of the job, working conditions, wages, benefits, and other relevant factors in a realistic way. A **realistic organizational preview (ROP)** includes sharing complete information about the organization: its mission, philosophy, opportunities for the future, and other information that gives applicants a good idea of where the job under consideration will fit in and its importance. In discussing the job itself, a **realistic job preview (RJP)** informs applicants about the desirable as well as the undesirable aspects of the job. Because of eagerness to make a job look as attractive as possible, the supervisor may be tempted to describe conditions in terms that make it more attractive than it actually is. For example, a supervisor might "oversell" a job by describing in glowing terms what really is available only for exceptional employees. If the applicant is hired and turns out to be an average worker, this could lead to disappointment and frustration. Applicants who are given realistic information are more likely to remain on the job because they will encounter few unpleasant surprises.[17]

Effective Questioning.   Even though the supervisor will have some knowledge of the applicant's background from the completed application form and from information that the applicant volunteers, the need still exists to determine the applicant's specific qualifications for the job opening. The supervisor should not ask the applicant to repeat information already provided on the application form. Instead, questions should be rephrased to probe for additional details. For example, the question "What was your last job?" is likely to be answered on the application form. This question could be expanded as follows: "As a data entry clerk at Omega, what type of computer system did you operate?"

Some questions that may not appear to be directly job related nevertheless may be appropriate. For example, it may be important to know what an individual considers to be an acceptable income level. The salary limits of a position for which an applicant is interested may make it impossible for that person to meet existing financial obligations. This could force the individual to seek an additional part-time job to supplement income, thereby taking away some energy from the primary job. Or, in order to meet immediate financial needs, the applicant might accept a low-paying position in which he or she would be unhappy and continue to look for a higher-paying position with another firm. Problems of this nature, although not directly connected with job requirements, are relevant to the work situation and may be part of a selection decision.

A supervisor must use judgment and tact when questioning applicants. The supervisor should avoid "trick" or "leading" questions such as "Do you daydream frequently?" or "Do you have difficulty getting along with other people?" Questions such as these are sometimes used by interviewers to see how an applicant responds to difficult personal questions. However, these questions may antagonize the applicant. By no means should the supervisor pry into personal affairs that are irrelevant or removed from the work situation.

Taking Notes. In their efforts to make better selection decisions, many supervisors take notes during or immediately after the interview. Having written information is especially important if a supervisor interviews a number of applicants. Trying to remember what several applicants said during their interviews, and exactly who said what, is virtually impossible.

The supervisor should avoid writing while an applicant is answering a question. Instead, the supervisor should jot down brief summaries of responses after the applicant has finished talking. This is more courteous and useful. Although the supervisor does not have to take notes on everything said in the interview, key facts that might aid in choosing one applicant over the others should be noted.

Avoiding Pitfalls in Selection Interviewing and Evaluation

The chief problem in employee selection usually lies in interpreting the applicant's background, personal history, and other pertinent information. As normal human beings, supervisors are unable to eliminate their personal preferences and prejudices, but they should face their biases and make efforts to avoid or control them. Supervisors should particularly avoid making judgments too quickly during interviews with job applicants. Although it is difficult not to form an early impression, the supervisor should complete the interview before making any decision and should strive to apply the OUCH test to avoid the numerous pitfalls that can occur both during and after an interview.

Supervisors should avoid generalizations. The situation in which a supervisor generalizes from one aspect of a person's behavior to all aspects of the person's behavior is known as the "halo" or "horns" effect. In practice, this means basing one's overall impression of an individual on only partial information about that individual and using this limited impression as a primary influence in rating all other factors. This may work either favorably (the **halo effect**) or unfavorably (the **horns effect**), but in either case it is improper. For example, the halo effect occurs when a supervisor assumes that if an applicant has superior interpersonal skills, he or she will also be good at keyboarding, working with little direction, and so forth. On the other hand, if a supervisor judges an applicant with a hearing impairment as being low on communication skills and allows this to serve as a basis for low ratings on other dimensions, the horns effect prevails.

Halo effect
The tendency to allow one favorable aspect of a person's behavior to positively influence judgment on all other aspects.

Horns effect
The tendency to allow one negative aspect of a person's behavior to negatively influence judgment on all other aspects.

The process we have suggested does not guarantee that the supervisor will not form erroneous opinions. However, objectivity minimizes the chances of making the wrong choice.

Closing the Interview

At the conclusion of the employee selection interview, the supervisor likely will have a choice among several alternatives, ranging from hiring the applicant, deferring the decision until later, or rejecting the applicant. What the supervisor decides will be guided by the policies and procedures of the organization. Some supervisors have the authority to make selection decisions independently; others are required to check with either their managers or the human resources department. Still others may have the authority only to recommend which applicant should be hired. For purposes of brevity, we assume in the following discussion that the supervisor has the authority to make the final selection decision. Under these circumstances, the supervisor can decide to hire an applicant on the spot. All the supervisor has to do is tell the applicant when to report for work and provide any additional instructions that are pertinent.

If the supervisor wishes to defer the decision until several other candidates for the job have been interviewed, the applicant should be informed that he or she will be notified later. The supervisor should indicate a time frame within which the decision will be made. However, it is unfair to use this tactic to avoid the unpleasant task of telling an applicant that he or she is not acceptable. By telling the applicant that a decision is being deferred, the supervisor gives the applicant false hope. While waiting for the supervisor's decision, the applicant might not apply for other jobs, thereby letting opportunities slip by. Therefore, if a supervisor has made the decision not to hire an applicant, the supervisor should tell the applicant tactfully. Some supervisors deem it best to turn down the job seeker in a general way without stating specific reasons. This is often accomplished by merely saying that there was not a sufficient "match" between the needs of the job and the qualifications of the applicant.

The supervisor should keep in mind that an employment interview is an excellent opportunity to build a good reputation for the employer. The applicant realizes that other candidates probably have applied for the job and that not everyone can be selected. The last contact an applicant may ever have with the organization is with the supervisor during the employment interview. Therefore, even if the applicant does not get the job, the supervisor should recognize that the way the interview was handled will make either a good or a negative impression, sometimes a permanent one. Regardless of its outcome, an applicant should leave the interview feeling that he or she has been treated fairly and courteously. It is every supervisor's managerial duty to build as much goodwill as possible since it is in the organization's self-interest to maintain a good image.

Post-Interview Evaluation Form

Some organizations have the supervisor and other members of the interview team complete an evaluation form shortly after the interview—while the information is still fresh in their minds. Figure 12-5 is an adaptation of a form used by one retail store. Its ap-

POST-INTERVIEW EVALUATION FORM

Position	Major Job Requirements	
	(List Major Job Requirements Here.)	
Applicant's Name:	(Evaluate SKA's here)	(Total)
Strengths:		
Weaknesses:		
Applicant's Name:	(Evaluate SKA's here)	(Total)
Strengths:		
Weaknesses:		
Applicant's Name:	(Evaluate SKA's here)	(Total)
Strengths:		
Weaknesses:		

Instructions to Interviewers

1. The interviewer (s) may decide that some job requirements are more important than others. Thus, it may be appropriate to assign weights to those requirements to illustrate their relative importance.
2. Evaluate each applicant's skill, knowledge, or ability (SKA's) for each of the major job requirements:

    1 = unacceptable   2 = moderately acceptable
    3 = acceptable   4 = strongly acceptable

3. Total the rating for each applicant. (By totaling the ratings, the interviewer(s) will have a system by which to make a more objective choice.)
4. Record each applicant's strengths and weaknesses.
5. Retain the form as a means of documentation.

proach increases the likelihood that the same selection criteria are applied to each applicant. Other firms may require that supervisors submit a written evaluation which summarizes their impressions and recommendations concerning each job candidate.

The Hiring Decision

5
Explain the hiring decision and the importance of documentation.

The decision to hire can be challenging when the supervisor has interviewed several applicants and all of them appear to be qualified for the job. There are no definite guidelines that a supervisor can use to select the best-suited individual. At times, information from the application forms, tests, and interviews will indicate which of the applicants should be hired. However, there will be other times when available information is not convincing or perhaps is even conflicting. For example, an applicant's aptitude test score for a sales job may be relatively low, but the person has favorably impressed the supervisor in the interview by showing an enthusiastic interest in the job and a selling career.

This is where supervisory judgment and experience come into play. The supervisor must select employees who are most likely to contribute to good departmental performance. The supervisor may consult with the human resources staff for their evaluations, but in the final analysis it should be the supervisor's responsibility to choose. Before the final decision is made, the supervisor should evaluate each applicant against the selection criteria. By carefully analyzing all of the information available and keeping in mind previous successes and failures in selecting employees, the supervisor should be able to select applicants who are most likely to succeed.

Of course, hiring decisions always involve uncertainties. There are no exact ways to predict how individuals will perform until they actually are placed on the job. However, a supervisor who approaches the hiring decision in a thorough, careful, and professional manner is likely to consistently select applicants who will become excellent employees.

Employee Involvement in the Hiring Decision. The degree to which employees are involved in the selection process differs among organizations. Generally, subordinates, peers, or work team members meet with the applicant and give their impression to the ultimate decision maker. Members of employee work teams, for example, are generally most knowledgeable about particular job responsibilities and challenges. They can offer valuable insight into the employee selection process. Even without formal teams, some organizations allow employees to fulfill various roles, from assisting with the definition of job responsibilities to having a direct say in the final hiring decision. One such organization is General Motors's Saturn Corporation, which allows groups of 5 to 15 workers to perform various staffing tasks, including hiring.[18] However, it is important to note that the downside of employee involvement in the hiring decision is the possibility of favoritism and violation of EEO regulations. Supervisors need to be aware of company policies regarding **nepotism.** The practice of hiring relatives may eliminate others from consideration.[19]

Nepotism
The practice of hiring relatives.

Documentation. In recent years, many supervisors have been asked by higher-level managers and the human resources staff to document the reasons for their decisions to hire particular individuals from among the applicants interviewed. Documentation is necessary to ensure that a supervisor's decision to accept or reject an applicant is based on job-related factors and is not discriminatory. At times, a supervisor's hiring decision will be challenged; the supervisor must be able to justify that decision or risk being reversed by higher-level managers. Similarly, supervisors sometimes will be strongly encouraged by higher-level managers or the human resources staff to give preferential hiring considerations to minority or female applicants, especially if the organization is actively seeking such employees. Some supervisors resent this type of pressure, but they should recognize that the organization may be obligated under various laws to meet certain hiring goals. In general, if supervisors follow the approaches suggested in this chapter, they should be able to distinguish the most qualified people from among the applicants and also be prepared to justify their employment selections.

ORIENTATION OF NEW EMPLOYEES

6

Identify the characteristics of an effective orientation program.

When new employees report for work the first day, the manner in which the supervisor welcomes them and introduces them to other employees in the department may have a lasting effect on their future performance. The first days on the job for most new employees are disturbing and anxious. They typically feel like strangers in new surroundings among people whom they have just met. It is the supervisor's responsibility to make the transition as smooth as possible and to lead new employees in the desired directions. This initial phase is called orientation.[20] **Orientation** is a process designed to help new employees become acquainted with the organization and understand the expectations the organization has for them. In short, orientation helps the employee develop a sense of belonging to the organization and become productive as soon as possible.

Orientation

The process of smoothing the transition of new employees into the organization.

There are several approaches that a supervisor can use in departmental orientation of new employees. The supervisor may choose personally to escort the new employees around the department, showing them equipment and facilities and introducing them to other employees. Or the supervisor may prefer to assign new employees to an experienced, capable employee and have this person do all of the orienting, perhaps including instructing new employees on how to perform their jobs.

Using a Checklist

A useful technique to ensure that new employees are well oriented is to use a checklist. When developing an orientation checklist, the supervisor should strive to identify all the things that a new employee ought to know. Ask yourself the question: "In order to do the job well, what does a new employee need to know?" Without some type of checklist, the supervisor is apt to skip some important items. Figure 12-6 (see page 390) shows an orientation checklist prepared by an insurance company human resources department for use by supervisors.

Discussing the Organization

It usually is a good idea for the supervisor to sit down with new employees on the first day in some quiet area to discuss the department, the organization, and its policies and

| FIGURE 12-6 | Orientation checklist of an insurance company. |

WELCOME THE NEW EMPLOYEE. Meet the new employee at the door. Take the new employee to the reception area and try to make him or her feel at ease.

SHOW THE WORKPLACE. Briefly describe the group's work, and where his or her job fits in.

INTRODUCE THE NEW EMPLOYEE TO COWORKERS. It is important to create a sense of belonging right away.

GIVE A TOUR OF THE COMPANY. This can be done by one of your experienced employees. Show the coat closet, cafeteria, time clock, restroom facilities, areas where announcements are posted, and the other departments that will be pertinent to the new employee's job. Schedule video "President's Perspective" and vice president's chat.

ILLUSTRATE OUTSTANDING CUSTOMER SERVICE. Schedule with the employee a time to show the customer service video and group discussion.

TAKE THE NEW EMPLOYEE TO THE HUMAN RESOURCES DEPARTMENT. After a tour of the company, take the new employee to the human resources department to fill out the necessary employment papers.

EXPLAIN THE TELEPHONE SYSTEM. Take the new employee to the reception area, where a switchboard operator will explain the telephone system.

EXPLAIN THE COMPUTER SYSTEM. Take the new employee to the data processing area, where a staff member will instruct the employee in the procedures for computer usage, that is, password, log-on, and other shortcuts (the introductory two-hour session will be scheduled the first afternoon).

MAKE SURE THE NEW EMPLOYEE UNDERSTANDS THE FOLLOWING:
- Use of the time clock, and sign-out procedures.
- Starting and stopping times.
- Proper work clothes.
- Parking facilities.
- Identification requirements.
- Lunch period and break period.
- Restrictions on leaving the building during work hours.
- No smoking policy.
- Rate of pay and how it is figured.
- Overtime pay.
- Pay deductions.
- What to do about errors in paycheck.
- Probation period of 30 days.
- Performance evaluation. Discuss reward programs and career development opportunities.
- Reporting of absences.

CLARIFY JOB RESPONSIBILITIES. Set performance standards and clarify expectations. This is the first step in setting the stage so the new employee can get up to speed as quickly as possible.

ASSIGNMENT TO "STAR" EMPLOYEE. This employee will serve as the new employee's shepherd to help get him or her off to a good start.

REMIND THE NEW EMPLOYEE TO COME TO YOU FOR INFORMATION AND ASSISTANCE.

regulations. In some firms the human resources department provides booklets that give general information about the firm, including benefits, policies, and procedures. There may even be a formal class that provides this type of information to employees and takes them on a tour of the firm's facilities. In small firms it may be appropriate to introduce new employees to the owner or top-level managers. In larger firms this may not be practical, so sometimes these firms videotape an interview with the chief executive officer or other members of top-level management in which the managers present the vision for the future, corporate philosophy, market and product development, and the like.[21] Employees should receive an explanation of what they can expect from the organization. As discussed earlier in this chapter, realistic organization and job previews should clarify employee expectations. The key is that the information must be accurate and that all employees must receive the same information.

A common mistake made by some supervisors when orienting new employees is to give them too much information on the first day. Presenting too many items in a very short time may result in information overload. A new employee is not likely to remember many details if they are all presented in the first two hours of the first day. Consequently, the supervisor should spread different aspects of orientation over a new employee's first few days or weeks. Also, the supervisor should schedule a review session several days or weeks later to discuss any problems or questions the new employee might have.

Being Supportive

More important than the actual techniques used in orienting new employees are the attitudes and behavior of the supervisor. If a supervisor conveys sincerity in trying to make the transition period a pleasurable experience and tells new employees that they should not hesitate to ask questions, this in itself will smooth their early days on the job. Even when the human resources department provides formal orientation, it remains the supervisor's responsibility to assist each new person to quickly become an accepted member of the departmental work team and a contributing, productive employee.

Setting the Stage. Supervisory responsibility goes beyond passing out the employee handbook and distributing department work rules. The supervisor should inform the other employees that someone new is joining the group and let them know something positive about the new person. Imagine how difficult it would be for a person to be received into the work group if the employees had been told "we had to hire this person." The supervisor needs to set the stage for the new employee's arrival so that he or she is properly socialized into the work group.

Organizations that use work teams believe in spreading authority, responsibility, and accountability throughout the organization. For many employees this has meant learning to work more closely with others as team members and depending on each other for the completion of assigned tasks. Over a period of time, effective teams develop openness in communication and relationships. New employees need to understand the purpose of the work group, its goals, why the job is important, where it fits in, and so forth. They also need to understand the roles that various team members fulfill.

Supervisors must make certain that members of the work team understand it is their responsibility to communicate and contribute to this understanding.

Part of the orientation process is to shape the new employee's behavior in a positive manner. Since people observe and imitate others' behavior, it is not enough for a supervisor to simply state what is expected of the employee. People tend to act—both productively and counterproductively—like those with whom they closely identify. Effective work team members will model positive norms for the new employee. An effective technique is to place the new employee with an outstanding performer who acts as a coach or mentor. The reason for placing the new employee with an outstanding performer is to perpetuate excellent performance. Finally, as discussed in Chapter 4, all employees need positive feedback on performance, and an effective supervisor reinforces the new employee's early successes by giving sincere praise.

Mentoring. Since the publication of the 1978 classic *Harvard Business Review* article, "Everyone Who Makes It Has a Mentor," research during the past two decades has explored the role that mentors or sponsors play in an employee's development.[22] **Mentoring,** the process of having a more experienced person provide guidance, coaching, or counseling to a less experienced person, is deeply rooted in history, as illustrated by the story of Odysseus turning over the care and development of his young son, Telemachus, to Mentor. In the Middle Ages, guild masters were responsible for their protégés' social, religious, and personal, as well as professional, skills. Broadly defined, the mentor teaches "the tricks of the trade," gives the protégé all the responsibility he or she can handle, thrusts the protégé into new areas, directs and shapes the protégé's performance, suggests how things are to be done, and provides protection.[23]

Mentoring should be looked upon as one way to smooth the transition of new employees into the organization and develop them into productive employees. New employees can build a network of people who can collectively provide the many benefits of a mentor. The ultimate question for the new employee is "How do I attach myself to a role model who will shepherd and guide my career?" Professor Kathy Kram suggests, "Putting all your eggs in one basket is a mistake. I think people ought to think in terms of multiple mentors instead of just one. Peers can be an excellent source of mentorship."[24] Increasingly, the new employee is more and more responsible for his or her own career development. How does one go about selecting a mentor? Kram says, "Would-be mentors are most receptive to people who ask good questions, listen well to the responses, and demonstrate that they are hungry for advice and counsel. Mentoring is a chance for the mentor to revitalize their own learning."[25] Should the supervisor mentor? Yes, if he or she feels comfortable doing so. In Chapter 9, we discussed the concept of developing an understudy and in Chapter 14 we will further discuss delegation of authority. Broadly defined, both of these efforts by the supervisor to add to the employee's knowledge base can be considered to be a form of mentoring.

Mentoring
The guiding of a newer employee by an experienced employee in areas concerning job and career.

7
Explain approaches to training and the supervisor's role in employee development.

TRAINING AND DEVELOPMENT

In most job situations, new employees require both general and specific training. If skilled workers are hired, the primary training need may be in the area of company and departmental methods and procedures. If unskilled or semiskilled workers are hired, they will have to be taught specific job skills to make them productive within a short period of time. Methods of formal training vary among organizations and depend on the unique circumstances involved in each situation. At the departmental level, helping employees improve their knowledge, skills, and abilities to perform both current and future jobs is an ongoing responsibility of the supervisor.[26]

On-the-Job Training

Most training at the departmental level takes the form of on-the-job training. The supervisor may prefer to do as much of the training personally as time will permit. This has the advantage of helping the supervisor get to know the new employees while they are being trained in the proper methods and standards of performing the job. It also ensures uniform training since the same person is training everyone. If the supervisor does not have the time or the technical skills to do the training, then the training should be performed by one of the best current employees. The supervisor should give the training task only to experienced employees who enjoy this additional assignment and are qualified to do it. The supervisor should make periodic follow-up visits to see how each new employee is progressing.

When a supervisor does on-the-job training personally, it gives him or her the opportunity to get to know the new employee.

Off-the-Job Training

Many training programs for new as well as existing employees are conducted outside of the immediate work area. Some of these may be coordinated or taught by human resources staff or training departments. For skilled crafts involving, for example, electricians, machinists, or toolmakers, a formal apprenticeship training program may be established. Usually this requires the employee to be away from the job for formal schooling and work part of the time.

Increasingly, business firms are initiating college-campus-based programs for training their employees. Generally, college representatives and the firm's supervisors work together to develop a curriculum for employees. Employees attend classes on the campus during nonworking hours. Tuition is paid by the firm, and employees receive credit for taking classes related specifically to their jobs. One of the authors is familiar with an apprentice training program developed by representatives of a steel company and a community college. Employees were divided into two groups, each of which receives 640 hours of on-campus lecture and laboratory training pertinent to their craft. The groups alternate every four weeks, with one group assigned to the plant for hands-on experience while the other group receives classroom training. A continual process of curriculum review and assessment of employee on-the-job performance ensures that the program meets the firm's needs.

There also may be programs offered within the firm during or outside of working hours. For example, safety training meetings and seminars are commonly scheduled during working hours for supervisors and employees alike.

Ongoing Development of Employees

Supervisors should assess the skills and potential of employees and provide opportunities for ongoing development of their skills so that they can perform better both now and in the future. If a supervisor believes that training is needed that cannot be provided at the departmental level, the supervisor should go to a higher-level manager or to the human resources department to see whether there are existing courses outside the organization that can meet training needs.

Many organizations have tuition-aid programs to help employees further their education. A supervisor should be aware of available course offerings at nearby educational institutions and encourage employees to take advantage of all the educational avenues open to them. These learning experiences can help them develop knowledge, abilities, and skills that improve their performance and prepare them for more demanding responsibilities.

The Supervisory Role in Employee Development

The impetus for a training program can come from many directions, but generally, operating problems and nonaccomplishment of organizational objectives may highlight the need for training. The entire training activity must be based on the identification of the combined needs of the organization and the employees.

Training must be viewed as an ongoing developmental process, not a simple bandage for a short-term problem. Therefore, training must be relevant, informative, interesting, and applicable to the job, and it must actively involve the trainee in the process. As Confucius put it:

I hear and I forget;

I see and I remember;

I do and I understand.

Skills that employees need to perform the essential departmental tasks should be the initial training focus. However, in the current business environment, cross-training is becoming essential. Whether "reengineering," "reinventing the organization," "rightsizing," "downsizing," or whatever term is used, reductions in force have left hundreds of thousands of employees wondering what the future holds. Consolidation of job duties suggests that supervisors will need to identify jobs that are important to the ongoing performance of their departments and that can be learned by other employees. Employees will need to learn new skills that will make them more valuable to their organizations. Cross-trained employees will be called on to assume additional responsibilities.

In formulating an employee development program, supervisors should seek answers to the following questions:[27]

1. Who, if anyone, needs training?
2. What training do they need?
3. What are the purposes of the training?
4. What are the instructional objectives that need to be incorporated into the training program? (Instructional objectives are basically what the employee will know or be able to do upon completion of the training.)
5. What training and development programs best meet the instructional objectives?
6. What are the anticipated benefits to be derived from the training?
7. What will the program cost?
8. When and where will the training take place?
9. Who will conduct the training?
10. How will the training effort be evaluated?

Efficient and effective training should contribute to the achievement of organizational objectives. Development of instructional objectives is essential to the formulation of an evaluation plan. Training and development expert Donald Kirkpatrick formulated four levels of evaluation that can be used to measure the benefits of training: (1) employees' reactions to the training program, (2) their learning, (3) their application of learning to the job, and (4) the training's business results.[28]

Supervisory Training and Career Development

The need for training and development is not limited to departmental employees. Supervisors also need training and development to avoid obsolescence or status-quo thinking. By expanding their own perspectives, supervisors are more likely to encourage employees to improve their knowledge and abilities and to keep up to date.

Most supervisors will attend a number of supervisory management training and development programs, as well as courses in technical aspects of company and departmental operations. Supervisors may want to belong to one or more professional or technical associations whose members meet periodically to discuss problems and topics of current interest and share common experiences. In addition, they should subscribe to technical and managerial publications and read articles of professional interest.

The authors contend that today, moreso than at any other time, supervisors are responsible for their own destiny. In order to survive they must give some thought to their own long-term career development. The ambitious supervisor will find it helpful to formulate a career plan, writing down definite goals he or she would like to achieve during the next 5 to 10 years. Such a plan includes both a preferred pattern of future assignments and job positions and a listing of educational and training activities that will be needed as part of career progression.

In 1991, The Library of Congress crafted a list of the 25 books that have shaped readers' lives. The only business book on the list was Richard Bolles' *What Color Is Your Parachute? A Practical Manual for Job-Hunters and Career-Changers*. In a recent interview Bolles outlined his career development strategies: "Sending out resumes doesn't work. Neither does answering ads. Employment agencies? No way. What does work is figuring out what you like to do and what you do well—and then finding a place that needs people like you. Contact organizations you're interested in, even if they don't have known vacancies. Pester others for leads."[29]

What Call Did You Make?

It is vitally important for supervisors to verify references and confirm the accuracy of the information provided by applicants. Generally, human resources departments do this for the organization. The reluctance of firms to take the time to do reference checks has fueled applicant dishonesty.

The first thing that you, as Tom Garrett, must do is to realize that you do not have direct authority over Carrie Webster. After double checking the job description and job specifications for the accounting position, review Carrie's personnel folder and plan for your meeting with her immediate supervisor.

Carrie Webster is an above-average performer, and thus a college degree does not appear to be a necessary job qualification. You are right to assume that the human resources department advertised the position, screened initial applicants, and determined that their qualifications matched the job requirements. While this omission or falsification by Carrie Webster is not as bad as some possibilities (e.g., a fast-food restaurant hired a convicted child molester who later assaulted children in the restrooms), the position is that of an accountant, and Carrie did falsify her application to get the job. It has been said that in today's labor market "people will lie, cheat, and steal to get a job."

What do you do with Carrie? In practice, the accounting department supervisor will apply his or her own set of experiences and values to make the decision. Some supervisors will take the comfortable route; Carrie is doing a good job, and the time and cost involved in replacing her are not worth the effort. Others may rationalize that "everyone is doing it," while still others believe that if a person is dishonest in one aspect of the job, it will spill over into other aspects. The authors of this text believe that Carrie Webster should be removed from her position of trust. Not to do so would send the wrong message to your employees.

While the human resources department verified her past employment, you need to determine who, if anyone, had responsibility for the education background check. If someone had responsibility to do so and failed to check, that employee should be disciplined. The omission on both her application and résumé should have been a red flag to alert the human resources department and everyone who reviewed Carrie's application. This should have caused the interviewer(s) to ask a question like, "I see you graduated from Old Ivy University. What year did you graduate?" Not surprisingly, Mirage Resorts of Las Vegas (see this chapter's Contemporary Issue) checked applicants' job, school, and credit histories. It is well established that failure to do so can be costly. As vice president of human resources, you should ask each applicant to sign a statement that the information contained on the application form is true and that he or she accepts the employer's right to terminate the applicant's employment if any of the information is subsequently found to be false.

This "You Make the Call" asks you to develop safeguards to prevent the situation from recurring. You should begin by asking all supervisors to review the job descriptions and job specifications for all positions. You might want to designate someone in the human resources department to do the necessary background checks. Require written verification of work and educational experiences. Interview Carrie's immediate supervisor and all others that might have interviewed her. Get them to recall the selection interview they had with Carrie to ascertain the types of questions they asked. (If they took notes, this task will be easier.) It is often easy for people to place the blame on others, but you had responsibility for ensuring that all the bases of selection are covered. Someone once said that "we should learn from the mistakes of others because we will not live long enough to make them all ourselves." You should use this situation as a learning opportunity for all managerial and supervisory personnel. All personnel involved in the interview process should be reminded that they should ask open-ended questions that will allow them to detect the omissions or falsifications. They should remember to apply the OUCH test. The questions they ask should be related to the job. And what do you do about the two internal candidates that were denied an opportunity to interview because they did not have the requisite degree? Work with the accounting department supervisor to verify the job specifications for Carrie's position and then search internally to fill the vacancy.

SUMMARY

Managing human resources is the supervisor's most important activity. In fulfilling responsibilities for staffing, the supervisor can be substantially aided by the human resources department. Some organizations are using firms that supply temporary workers to do some of the staffing work.

There must be a balance of authority between line supervisors and human resources staff in staffing policies and decisions. Usually, the human resources department aids in recruitment—advertising the opening, recruiting a pool of applicants, screening, testing, checking background, and the like. The departmental supervisor then interviews applicants and either makes or has most of the say in the final hiring decision.

The pervasive presence of equal opportunity employment laws and regulations has resulted in the human resources staff's assuming much of the responsibility to ensure that an organization's employment policies and practices comply with these laws. Sometimes human resources departments take primary responsibility for hiring, interpreting policy, determining selection criteria, writing job descriptions and specifications, testing applicants, and the like. Supervisors should not release these staffing areas totally to human resources, although at times it might seem expedient to do so. A supervisor remains accountable for decisions even when relying on the advice of the human resources staff.

An ongoing process of the staffing function is determining how many employees and what skills are needed to accomplish various work assignments. Job descriptions indicate the duties and responsibilities of the job and must be reviewed periodically. Job descriptions that accurately describe the job are useful in providing a realistic job preview, developing performance standards, conducting performance appraisals, and other staffing functions.

Job specifications detail the knowledge, skills, and abilities an employee should have to perform a job adequately. Applicants are recruited and screened based on the job specifications.

Supervisors need to ascertain how current employees are being utilized before they make requests for additional help. If new functions are added to the department or the workload increases substantially, supervisors need to determine the number and types of employees needed.

Selection is the process of choosing the best applicant to fill a particular job. After job applicants are located, information must be gathered to help in determining who should be hired.

Supervisors are most likely to be involved in employee selection interviews. Two basic approaches are the directive interview and the nondirective interview. The directive interview is highly structured; the supervisor asks specific questions of each applicant and guides the course of the discussion. In the nondirective interview, the supervisor allows the applicant much freedom in determining the course of the discussion.

Regardless of the approach used, supervisors must develop job-related questions. Situational questions may be used to assess how the applicant would act in a given situation. Trick questions and questions that can be answered with a simple yes or no should be avoided.

It is vital for a supervisor to thoroughly prepare for the selection interview. A supervisor should be aware of equal employment opportunity concerns and applicable guidelines. Job-related questions that foster nondiscriminatory treatment should be used. Selection criteria should be objective, uniform in application, consistent in effect, and job related. Before conducting the interview, the supervisor should review the applicant's application form, test scores, and other available background materials. By having a list of key questions to ask, the supervisor should be able to cover the most important areas in which more information is wanted.

The supervisor may open the employee selection interview by using an approach that reduces tension, such as asking a question that is easily answered. The supervisor should explain the job, use effective questioning techniques, and take appropriate notes.

When evaluating an applicant, the supervisor should avoid such common pitfalls as making hasty judgments, allowing generalizations such as the halo effect or the horns effect to bias their judgments, or forming impressions based on his or her own personal bias and preferences. Application of the OUCH test will help the supervisor minimize judgmental errors.

At the conclusion of the interview, the supervisor should remember that the applicant is entitled to a decision just as soon as possible. The supervisor should strive to have the applicant leave with an impression of fair and courteous treatment.

The supervisor wants to select employees who will contribute to excellent department performance. A review of the selection criteria is critical in determining the best applicant. Depending on the organization, subordinates, peers, or team members may have a say in determining who is ultimately hired. This involvement varies from assistance in defining job duties to having a say in the final decision.

Documentation of the selection process is critical in helping to demonstrate that the process is based on job-related factors and is not discriminatory.

Effective orientation of new employees is a top supervisory responsibility. Orientation means helping new employees become acquainted with the organization and understand what is expected in the way of job duties. An orientation checklist can ensure that each new employee receives the same information. In most large organizations, the human resources department helps the supervisor with orientation. Effective orientation programs avoid information overload and generally look at orientation as a process rather than just the first day on the job. The supervisor's supportive attitude and the involvement of other employees are significant. Effective orientation shapes the new employee's behavior in a positive manner. Positive role models, coaches, or mentors should be used to perpetuate excellent performance standards.

On-the-job training is still another of the supervisor's major responsibilities. When a supervisor lacks the time or technical skills to do the training personally, she or he can delegate the task to an experienced employee with excellent job performance. Off-the-job training programs can also help employees perform better. Training and development is a continual process, not just a one-time effort.

Supervisors need to determine the skills employees need to do their jobs better. Factors such as failure to meet organizational objectives, operating problems, introduction of new machines and equipment, addition of new job responsibilities to a position, and the like can help the supervisor pinpoint training needs. The supervisor should constantly monitor who needs training and what training each person needs. Development of instructional objectives and a procedure for evaluating the effectiveness of training are essential.

Also, supervisors must recognize the need for their own training and development, and they should utilize whatever opportunities for career development are available to them. Supervisors should consider having career plans to help them chart and monitor their long-term career progression.

KEY TERMS

Selection criteria (page 376)
Selection (page 376)
Directive interview (page 377)
Nondirective interview (page 377)
Competencies (page 382)
Realistic organizational preview (ROP) (page 384)

Realistic Job preview (RJP) (page 384)
Halo effect (page 385)
Horns effect (page 385)
Nepotism (page 388)
Orientation (page 389)
Mentoring (page 392)

QUESTIONS FOR DISCUSSION

1. What are some of the major activities of the human resources department that can assist the line supervisor in the staffing function? What should be the primary responsibility of the human resources staff and of line supervisors for various employment and other staffing activities? Is there a clear dividing line of responsibility? Discuss.

2. Define some of the major laws and regulations that govern equal employment opportunity. Why have many organizations assigned to the human resources department the primary responsibility for making sure that their employment policies and practices are in compliance?

3. Discuss the differences between a directive interview and a nondirective interview. Does the employee selection interview tend to be directive or nondirective in nature, or both? Why?

4. Discuss how adequate supervisory preparation for an employee selection interview can be crucial to the interview's success.

5. Discuss each of the following aspects of conducting an employee selection interview:
   a. Opening the interview.
   b. Explaining the job.
   c. Using effective questioning techniques.
   d. Taking notes.
   e. Concluding the interview.

6. Identify several pitfalls that supervisors may encounter in evaluating job applicants both during and after an interview.

7. What guidelines can be suggested to improve a supervisor's decision making when hiring job applicants?

8. Why are supervisors and many employers now required to document why they did or did not hire applicants they have interviewed?

9. How is orientation of a new employee related to future performance? Discuss approaches that a supervisor may take in orienting a new employee.

10. What is mentoring? Discuss the advantages and disadvantages from the perspective of the person being mentored.

11. Why is on-the-job training most likely to be the type of training utilized at the department level? Enumerate other approaches for training and development that may be available.

12. Why should training programs be evaluated?

SKILLS APPLICATIONS

Skills Application 12-1: Successful Interviewing

You may have heard people say, "I know a good person when I see one." Look around the classroom and identify one person whom you do not know.

1. Based on your first impression—just by observing the person—make a list of adjectives that describe your impression.

2. Assume that you would be interviewing this person for an assistant store manager position at Sanders Supermarkets Store # 6. Using at least three different Internet resources, identify a list of questions that you might use for successful interviewing. At the time of the writing of this text, the following were found to be useful:

INTERNET ACTIVITY

www.wm.edu/csrv/career/stualum/intrvdir/question.html

This site identifies a list of questions that an employer might ask. Many were compiled from the list published in *The Northwestern Lindquist-Endicott Report.*

www.little.nhlink.net

Click on "Questions to Expect During Your Interview" for a list of questions that the interviewee might expect.

www.collegegrad.com/intv/intrview.html

This site contains an overview of the techniques for convincing the interviewer that you have the requisite skills for the job. Also see the current edition of the *College Grad Job Hunter* from Amazon.com (www.amazon.com).

www.dac.neu.edu/coop.careerservices/interview.html

This site provides excellent tips to guide both the interviewer and the interviewee.

3. Ask the person identified in question number 2 whether you may interview him or her for about three to five minutes. Use the questions you developed above as an outline for the interview.
4. How did your interview evaluation of this person compare with your first impression?
5. Summarize in a paragraph what you learned from this skills application.

Skills Application 12-2: The Choice

You are the newly appointed manager of the Wizards baseball team. Two players, Koss and Rivera, are vying for one open spot on the team—utility infielder. Player Koss has 10 hits in 39 at-bats against left-handed pitchers, for a .256 average, and 30 hits in 90 at-bats against right-handers, for a .333 percentage. The corresponding figures for Rivera are 16 for 60, or .266, against southpaws, and 20 for 58, or .345, against right-handed pitchers.

1. Develop a complete list of selection criteria for the position of utility infielder. (If your practical knowledge of baseball is insufficient, interview someone who can help you develop the list.) Compare your list with that of another student. Why are there differences?
2. If you could choose only one of the two players, Koss or Rivera, to keep on the squad who would it be? Why?

Skills Application 12-3: Ethical Issues

It is unlawful to ask certain questions of a personal nature prior to making an offer of employment. Legislation on equal opportunity employment has placed restrictions on questions employers ask job applicants.

INTERNET ACTIVITY

1. Using the Internet, identify a number of unlawful and potentially unlawful areas of inquiry.
2. Bill Barton (see this chapter's "You Make the Call") is interviewing Alan Hunter, who is confined to a wheelchair, for a data processing position in his store. Hunter has passed the usual selection criteria. Use the Internet to aid you in identifying a list of accommodations for Bill Barton to consider before he offers Alan Hunter the position.
3. Why is it important for supervisors to be up to date on legislation that affects staffing decisions?

Skills Application 12-4: The First Day on the Job

1. Ask your favorite college professor to reflect on his or her first day on the job.
2. How was this professor's formal orientation conducted? What could have been done to make it more effective?

3. Were the expectations clearly stated? Were the rules of the game, that is, what the professor needed to do to get promoted, tenured, and earn annual salary increases, clear?

4. Did the professor have a mentor? If so, how effective was the mentoring process? What could have been done to make the process more effective?

5. What insights did you gain from this skill application?

Skills Application 12-5: Real-Time Training

INTERNET ACTIVITY

Today's supervisors have a variety of resources to turn to for employee training and personal development. Online training is an option you might want to consider. Visit the following sites to see the types of training offered:

Learn2 (www.learn2.com)
Click2Learn (www.click2learn.com)

1. What resources can you find for an employee who needs to improve his or her presentation skills?

2. What resources can you find for a new supervisor who will be managing a team for the first time?

3. Take a 2torial (from Learn2.com) or a 2-Minute Tutor (from Click2Learn.com). What benefits do you see in online learning and training products like these? What disadvantages do you see?

SKILL DEVELOPMENT VIDEO

SKILL DEVELOPMENT MODULE 12-1: EMPLOYEE SELECTION AND INTERVIEWING PROTOCOL

This video segment shows Tony Roberts, accounting department supervisor at Lexicon Dynamics, who is faced with the challenge of finding someone to replace an employee who was recently promoted to another division within the company.

Questions for Discussion: The Ineffective Version

1. Discuss the selection mistakes Tony Roberts made.

2. Explain what procedures you'd recommend for finding someone for the staff accountant position.

3. Identify various reasons for not hiring a relative or a close friend for a subordinate position.

4. If you were Tony Roberts, the interviewer, what kinds of questions would you ask the applicant?

Questions for Discussion: The More Effective Version

1. Discuss the procedure that Tony Roberts followed in the selection and interview process.

2. What other questions should Tony ask the applicants to ascertain their suitability for the job? What questions should he not ask?

3. What else could Tony Roberts do to more effectively select the staff accountant?

4. Based on the conclusions you drew from watching the video, what might be reasons for hiring or not hiring Perry? Joann? Renee?

ENDNOTES

1. For a discussion of the role of human resources management, see Arthur W. Sherman, Jr., George W. Bohlander, and Scott Snell, *Managing Human Resources* (11th ed.; Cincinnati: South-Western College Publishing, 1998), Chapter 1.

2. See Figure 9-2 in Chapter 9 for an example of a combined job description and job specification. For a different point of view, see Cynthia D. Fisher, Lyle F. Schoenfeldt, and James B. Shaw, *Human Resource Management* (4th edition; Boston: Houghton Mifflin, 1999), pp. 154–155, ". . . some authors feel that to facilitate the flexibility required in today's rapidly changing environment, companies should do away with job descriptions." Noted author Tom Peters concurs, "It is imperative today that managers and non-managers be induced to cross 'uncrossable' boundaries as a matter of course, day after day. Standing on the formality of a written job description (as an excuse for inaction, or the reason you have to 'check up—and up and up—the line') is a guaranteed strategy for disaster." (see Peters, *Thriving on Chaos* (New York: Knopf, 1987), pp. 500–501.

3. Students may wish to see John Byrne, "The Search for the Young and Gifted: Why Talent Counts," *Business Week* (October 4, 1999), pp. 108+; *How to Find and Hire Stars: Roadmap to Success* (Boston: Fast Company, 1998); Dick Moore, "How to Hire Quality People," *Quality Digest* (December 1996), pp. 29–32; K. A. Lifson, "Hiring Stars . . . and Keeping Them Shining," *Discount Merchandiser* (May 1996), pp. 82–85; and David E. Terpstra, "The Search for Effective Methods," *HRFocus* (May 1996), pp. 16–17. For locating qualified internal candidates by computerized record systems, job posting and bidding, and the like, see Sherman, et al., *Managing Human Resources*, pp. 137–138. For information on using the Internet as a recruitment tool, see Sarah Fister, "Online Recruiting: Good, Fast and Cheap?" *Training* (May 1999), p. 26; and Shannon Peters Talbott, "How to Recruit Online," *Personnel Journal* (March 1999), pp. 14–17. Also see the three-part series, "How to Hire," *Inc.* (October 1998), pp. 36+; and Thomas Love, "Finding and Keeping Entry-Level Workers," *Nation's Business* (November 1998), pp. 28–29.

4. The resurgence of selection testing can be attributed in part to the positive results of the validity testing of the U.S. Employment Service. See "Is Preemployment Testing a Good Idea?" *Training and Development* (September 1993), p. 26; and Stephen L. Gunn, "Gain Competitive Advantage Through Employment Testing," *HRFocus* (September 1993), p. 15. For a discussion of validity, see N. Schmidt and F. J. Landry, "The concept of validity," in Neal Schmidt and Walter Borman (eds.) *Personnel Selection in Organizations* (San Francisco: Jossey-Bass, 1993), pp. 275–309; S. Messick, "Validity of psychological assessment," *American Psychologist* (50, 1995), pp. 741–749; and Scott Maxwell and Richard D. Arvey, "The Search for Predictors with High Validity and Low Adverse Impact: Compatible or Incompatible Goals?" *Journal of Applied Psychology* (June 1993), pp. 433–437. For an interesting approach to selection testing see Alessandra Bianchi, "The Character-Revealing Handwriting Analysis," *Inc.*, (February 1996), pp. 77–79.

5. A thorough discussion of equal opportunity and other antidiscrimination legislation and applications is the substance of Chapter 16. For an overview, see *Employer EEO Responsibilities* (Washington, D.C.: Equal Employment Opportunity, U.S. Government Printing Office, 1996). For a more comprehensive discussion on hiring the disabled, see John M. Williams, "Getting Answers On Hiring the Disabled," *Nation's Business* (November 1998), pp. 44+; and Williams, "Clearing Up Confusion on Hiring the Disabled," *Nation's Business* (December 1998), pp. 55–58.

6. For additional information on the preemployment interview, see Robert L. Dipboye, *Selection Interviews: Process Perspectives* (Cincinnati: South-Western Publishing, 1992); Diane Arthur, *Recruiting, Interviewing, Selecting and Orienting New Employees* (New York: AMACOM, 1991); Robert W. Eder and Gerald Ferris, eds., *The Employment Interview: Theory, Research, and Practice* (Newbury Park, CA: Sage Publications, 1989); and James M. Jenks and Brian L. P. Zevnik, "ABC's of Job Interviewing," *Harvard Business Review* (July–August 1989), pp. 38–42. While we discuss interviewing from only the employer's perspective in this chapter, interested students should consult the Internet for tips for the interviewee.

7. Frederic M. Biddle, "Work Week," *The Wall Street Journal* (September 28, 1999), p. A1.

8. An AMA study reported in "Testing . . . Testing," *Training* (September 1998), p. 14.

9. This concept was part of a training program developed by Jagerson Associates, Inc., for the Life Office Management Association.

10. Tests can be used as a selection criterion. For a discussion of employment testing, see Florence Berger and Ajay Ghei, "Employment Tests: A Facet of Hospitality Hiring," *Cornell Hotel and Restaurant Administration Quarterly* (December 1995), pp. 28–31; Daniel P. O'Meara, "Personality Tests Raise Questions of Legality and Effectiveness," *HRMagazine* (January 1994), pp. 97–100; Joyce Hogan and Ann Quigley, "Effects of Preparing for Physical Ability Tests," *Public Personnel Management* (Spring 1994), pp. 85–104; Gene Carmean, "Tie Medical Screening to the Job," *HRMagazine* (July 1992), pp. 85–87; and Jonathon A. Segal, "Pre-Employment Physicals Under the ADA," *HRMagazine* (October 1992), pp. 103–107. The 1991 report of the American Psychological Association cautioned employers to avoid honesty tests that lack validity documentation. Consult Tori DeAngelis, "Honesty Tests Weigh In with Improved Ratings," *The APA Monitor* (June 1991), p. 7.

11. Jacques Normand, Stephen D. Salyards, and John J. Maloney, "An Evaluation of Preemployment Drug Testing," *Journal of Applied Psychology* (December 1990), pp. 629–639.

12. "Reference Checking Limits Employers' Liability for Negligent Hiring," *Human Resources Management Issues and Trends* (June 23, 1993), pp. 102–103. Also see R. L. LoPresto, D. E. Mitcham, and D. E. Ripley, *Reference Checking Handbook* (Alexandria, VA: Society for Human Resource Management, 1993); J. Click, "SHRM Survey Highlights Dilemmas of Reference Checks," *HR News* (June 17, 1995), p. 13; "Recruiters Beware: Lying is Common among Applicants," *HRFocus* (October 1992), p. 5; and "Firms Face Lawsuits for Hiring People Who Commit Crimes," *The Wall Street Journal* (April 30, 1987), p. 29.

13. Bradford Smart as interviewed by Geoffrey Colvin, "How GE Topgrades: Looking to Hire the Very Best? Ask the Right Questions. Lots of Them," *Fortune* (June 21, 1999), p. 194. Also see Smart, *Topgrading: How Leading Companies Win by Hiring, Coaching and Keeping the Best People* (Englewood Cliffs, NJ: Prentice-Hall, 1999); and Michael Barrier, "References: A Two-Way Street," *Nation's Business* (May 1999), p. 19.

14. "Beware of Resumania," *Personnel Journal* (April 1996), p. 28; Marlene Brown, "Checking on a Resume," *Personnel Journal* (January 1993), pp. SS6–7; and T. Lammers, "How To Read Between the Lines: Tactics for Evaluating a Resume," *Inc.* (March 1993), pp. 105–107.

15. For lists of questions that might be asked during the employment interview, see op.cit., Colvin, pp. 192+; Michael Barrier, "Hire Without Fear," *Nation's Business* (May 1999), pp. 15+; Christopher Caggiano, "HR Red Herrings: Interview Questions," *Inc.* (August 1999), pp. 107–108; Caggiano, "What Were You In For? And Other Great Job-Interview Questions of Our Time," *Inc.* (October 1998), p. 117. In addition, visit the following Web sites: "Questions on Topics an Employer Might Ask" (originally published in The Northwestern Lindquist-Endicott Report by Victor R. Lindquist), www.wm.edu/csrv/career/stualum/intrwdir/question.html; "Questions to Expect During Your Interview," little.nhlink.net; and "Mastering the Interview," www.collegegrad.com/intv/intrview.html. The latter is an overview of *College Grad Job Hunter,* 1998.

16. Ron Zemke and Susan Zemke, "Putting Competencies to Work," *Training* (January 1999), pp. 70+. Also see Bruce Meger, "A Critical Review of Competency-Based Systems," *Human Resources Professional* (January–February 1996), pp. 22–25; Donald J. McNerney and Angela Briggins, "Competency Assessment Gains Favor among Trainers," *HRFocus* (June 1995), p. 19; and Edward E. Lawler, III, "From Job-Based to Competency-Based Organizations," *Human Resource Management* (1, 1994), pp. 51–74.

17. John P. Wanous, "Installing a Realistic Job Preview: Ten Tough Choices," *Personal Psychology* (Spring 1989), pp. 117–133. Also see Carol Hymnowitz, "How to Avoid Hiring the Prima Donnas Who Hate Teamwork," *The Wall Street Journal* (February 15, 2000), p. B1.

18. Aaron Bernstein, "Making Teamwork Work—And Appeasing Uncle Sam," *Business Week* (January 25, 1993), p. 101.

19. For a discussion of the pros and cons of hiring relatives, see Mary S. Yamin, "Think Long and Hard Before Hiring Relatives and Friends," *Capital District Business Review* (June 1998), pp. 26–27; Kevin Steel, "Nepotism is a Human Right," *Western Report* (June 15, 1998), pp. 17–19; Andy Cohen, "Does Nepotism Work?" *Sales & Marketing Management* (July 1998), p. 16; Douglas Massengill, "Not With Your Husband (or Wife) You Don't! The Legality of No Spouse Rules in the Workplace," *Public Personnel Management* (Spring 1997), pp. 61–76; and Sharon Nelton, "The Bright Side of Nepotism," *Nation's Business* (May 1998), p. 72.

20. For an expanded discussion of employee orientation, see M. Finney, "Employee Orientation Programs Can Help Introduce Success," *HRNews* (October 1996), p. 2; David K. Lindo, "Employee Orientation: Not a Self-Study Course, *Training* (November 1995), p. 16; Kaye Loraine, "How to Cut the Cost of Job

Orientation," *Supervision* (November 1994), pp. 3–7; and Paul Froiland, "Reproducing Star Performers," *Training* (September 1993), pp. 33–37. Students may wish to consult the classic articles by Walter D. St. John, "The Complete Employee Orientation Program," *Personnel Journal* (May 1980), pp. 373–378; and Edmund J. McGarrell, Jr., "An Orientation System that Builds Productivity," *Personnel Administrator* (October 1984), pp. 75–85.

21. In large companies, there may be other ways for top management to meet new employees. Christopher Caggiano, "Hot Tips," *Inc.* (June 1998), p. 106, reports on how one CEO meets a group of new employees for lunch and discusses the company's history, philosophy, and the like.

22. Franklin J. Lunding, "Everyone Who Makes It Has a Mentor," *Harvard Business Review* (July–August 1978), pp. 91–100.

23. Edwin C. Leonard, Jr., John B. Knight, and John L. Vollmer, "Mentoring: A New Look at an Old HRM Intervention," *Proceedings of the Midwest Society for Human Resources/Industrial Relations* (Chicago: 1994), pp. 229–236. General Electric, like many companies, has used mentoring programs for many years. Now its mentoring program has taken a strange twist. See Matt Murray, "GE Mentoring Program Turns Underlings into Teachers of the Web," *The Wall Street Journal* (February 15, 2000), pp. B1, B16. Jack Carew, author of *The Mentor* (Donald I. Fine Books, 1998) says "some of us have no mentors, and we have to figure it out for ourselves." A search of the Dow Jones Interactive Publications Library found over 200 recent articles on mentoring; see, for example, Pam Slater, "Careers Can Be Made or Derailed over Choice or Absence of a Mentor," *Knight-Ridder Tribune Business News: The Sacramento Bee* (August 9, 1999); and Mary Curtius, "Careers/Playing Politics: New Alliances Finding the Right Mentors—Inside and Outside Your Workplace—Can Be a Key to Success," *Los Angles Times* (August 10, 1998), pp. D2–8. For a systematic mentoring approach, see Beverly Kaye and Betsy Jacobson, "Reframing Mentoring," *Training & Development* (August 1996), pp. 44–47; or Denise Bolden Coley, "Mentoring Two-by-Two," *Training & Development* (July 1996), pp. 46–48.

24. From Karen Dillon, "Finding the Right Mentor for You," *Inc.* (June 1998), p. 55. Also see Edward O. Welles, "Mentors," *Inc.* (June 1998), pp. 48+; Kathy Kram, *Mentoring at Work* (Glenview, IL: Scott, Foresman, 1985); Julie Connelly, "Career Survival Guide," *Working Women* (April 1999), pp. 58–62; and Donna Brooks, *Seven Secrets of Successful Women* (McGraw-Hill, 1998).

25. Dillon, p. 55.

26. It is generally accepted that people learn in different ways. Increasingly, companies are using a variety of training methods to help employees learn and retain the information. "When you put your training hat on, you have to figure out what's most appropriate for the learner." See Kim Kiser, "Basic Training for SMEs," *Training* (April 1999), p. 45. For further discussion on training approaches, see Marc Adams, "Training Employees as Partners," *HRMagazine* (February 1999), pp. 64–70; Candice G. Harp, Sandra C. Taylor, and John W. Satzinger, "Computer Training and Individual Differences: What Really Matters?" *Human Resources Development Quarterly* (Fall 1998), pp. 271–283; Judith N. Mottl, "Online Training Gets Good Grades," *Internet Week* (October 5, 1998), pp. 35; and Suzanne Kapner, "Virtual Training Takes Foodservice into the Future," *Nation's Restaurant News* (April 15, 1996), p. 7. For information on the depth and breadth of training, see George Benson, "How Much Do Employers Spend on Training?" *Training & Development* (October 1996), pp. 56–58; and Valerie Freeze, "Workforce Growth Outpaces Training Spending," *Personnel Journal* (October 1996), pp. 23–24.

27. The questions were adapted from a list introduced by Edwin C. Leonard, Jr., *Assessment of Training Needs* (Chicago: Midwest Intergovernmental Training Committee, U.S. Civil Service Commission, 1975), p. 36.

28. George Kimmerling, "How is Training Regarded and Practiced in Top-Ranked U.S. Companies?" *Training & Development* (September 1993), pp. 29–36. For a detailed discussion of training program evaluation, see Donald L. Kirkpatrick, *Evaluating Training Programs* (Washington, D.C.: American Society for Training and Development, 1975); and "Four Steps to Measuring Training Effectiveness," *Personnel Administrator* (November 1983), pp. 57–62. Also see Dean R. Spitzer, "Embracing Evaluation," *Training* (June 1999), pp. 42–47.

29. Daniel H. Pink, "Richard Boles: What Happened to Your Parachute," *Fast* (September 1999), p. 241. For an expanded discussion, see the 30th anniversary edition of Boles's book (1999).

Performance Appraisal and Managing the Results: Coaching, Promoting, and Compensating Employees

You Make the Call!

You are Shane Wilson, the distribution center supervisor for Zimmer Wholesale Clubs. All of Zimmer's 36 stores are located east of the Mississippi River. The wholesale club concept of merchandising is very competitive.

You are 42 years old and have been with Zimmer for the past 12 years. When you were promoted to supervisor six years ago, there was no resentment on the part of your employees because they liked you and realized that you were the best person for the job. The employees hold tremendous respect for you and your ability to provide the distribution center with positive leadership. However, there is little possibility for advancement beyond your present position. A lateral move within Zimmer might be possible but you would hate to uproot your family.

Zimmer has just instituted a formal performance appraisal system. Three weeks from today, you will have to conduct a performance appraisal for all of your employees. You look forward to doing them with one exception—the one for Cheryl Iberra.

Cheryl was promoted to assistant supervisor about two years ago. Cheryl is 33 years old and is regarded as an effective supervisor. She is knowledgeable about the technical aspects of her job. She is a perfectionist about having the work done right. She gets along well with everyone and gets the work done in a timely fashion.

Cheryl will receive her degree from a local college at the end of this term, and you know that she expects to advance in the organization. She is the first person from her family to graduate from college, and she looks forward to the future.

Generally, her employees get the work done in an exceptional manner. She communicates extremely well with all her subordinates. She shares her technical knowledge with them and does a very good job of delegating. However, on occasions, she sides with the employees and openly complains about some of Zimmer's compensation and benefit policies.

Zimmer's sales have not been increasing. People in other area industries have been laid off. Zimmer does not want to lay off people but will reduce employment costs through normal attrition. The consolidation of duties has forced managers and supervisors to find creative solutions to problems and to do more with fewer resources. You know that Cheryl's performance stands out above the rest and that she very much wants to become a supervisor. In the near term, there is little likelihood that a position will be open. You are afraid that Cheryl will leave Zimmer. How will you approach her performance appraisal?

You Make the Call!

EMPLOYEE PERFORMANCE APPRAISAL

Define performance appraisal and clarify the supervisor's role in the process.

Performance appraisal
A systematic assessment of how well employees are performing their jobs, and the communication of that assessment to them.

From the time employees begin their employment with a firm, the supervisor is responsible for evaluating their job performance. **Performance appraisal** is a systematic assessment of how well employees are performing their jobs and the communication of that assessment to them. As discussed in earlier chapters, supervisors establish performance standards or targets that subordinates are expected to achieve. Performance appraisal includes comparing the employee's performance with the standards. Effective supervisors provide their subordinates with day-to-day feedback on performance. Regular feedback on performance is essential to improve employee performance and to provide recognition that will motivate employees to sustain satisfactory performance (see Figure 13-1 on page 408).

FIGURE 13-1

The effective supervisor avoids these comments by providing regular positive feedback on performance.

Most organizations also require supervisors to evaluate their employees' performance formally. These evaluations become part of an employee's permanent record and play an important role in management's decisions involving training, promoting, retaining, and compensating employees.

Supervisors should approach the appraisal process from the perspective that it is an extension of the planning, organizing, and leading functions. When employees understand what is expected of them and the criteria upon which they will be evaluated, and they believe the process is fairly administered, performance appraisal serves as a powerful motivational tool. While performance appraisals are most frequently used in determining compensation, supervisors also use information from performance appraisals to provide feedback to employees so that they know where they stand and what they can do to improve performance and develop to their full potential.

Another reason that supervisors need to keep accurate records of employee performance is to document fulfillment of equal employment opportunity regulations. The importance of documentation of personnel decisions cannot be overemphasized. It is becoming increasingly important for organizations to maintain accurate records to protect themselves against possible charges of discrimination in connection with promotion, compensation, and termination.

Although appraisal of employee performance is a daily, ongoing aspect of the supervisor's job, the focus of this chapter is on the formal system of performance appraisal. The purpose of the formal system is to evaluate, document, and communicate in understandable and objective terms the job achievements and the direct and secondary results of employee effort compared with the job expectations. This is done by taking into consideration factors such as the job description, performance standards, specific objectives, and critical incidents for the evaluation period. The evaluation is based on direct observation of the employee's work over a period of time.[1]

There is an emerging consensus that the long-term success of an organization is dependent to a substantial degree on the performance of its workforce. We've learned that to get employees to work smarter, they first have to know what is expected in the way of performance and then receive regular feedback on their performance. Effective supervisors should subscribe to the notion that "there is no substitute for daily feedback on performance." Unfortunately, some supervisors fail to either recognize performance problems or feel uncomfortable engaging employees in conversations about performance expectations and how to achieve them. The authors contend that most employees want to know how well they have performed in relation to the organization's expectations or performance standards. Generally, the supervisor should recognize and comment on a particular aspect of performance when it occurs. The supervisor may glean this information from direct observation of the employee's work or from other sources. Since it is impossible for a supervisor to actually observe everything an employee does, he or she must rely on performance feedback from other sources—customers, peers, attendance records, production (quality and quantity) data, sales data, and the like.

Regardless of the source of the information, it is essential that it be reliable. Imagine the situation where a percentage of your course grade is determined by your class participation. The instructor sometimes records attendance and sometimes does not. At the end of the course, the instructor uses his or her attendance data to determine your participation grade. As luck would have it, the only three days you missed class during the term were among those days that the instructor took attendance. Another student was rarely in attendance but was fortuitous enough to be there on the days that the instructor took attendance. Even though your test scores were similar, the other student received a higher grade in the course than you did. Obviously, from your point of view, this would not be fair. The instructor can reduce the probability of a grade appeal in several ways, including (1) making sure students understand from the start of the course that attendance will be an integral part in determining their course grade, and (2) by recording attendance on a regular basis—that is, all absences are recorded. (We've observed that many problems have occurred because some supervisors selectively record performance data.)

The Supervisor's Responsibility for Performance Appraisal

A performance appraisal should be done by an employee's immediate supervisor, who is usually in the best position to observe and judge how well the employee has performed on the job. There are some situations in which a "consensus" or "pooled" type of appraisal may be done by a group of supervisors. An example of this would be if an employee works for several supervisors because of rotating work-shift schedules or the organization has a matrix structure. Some organizations have implemented work team concepts that expand the supervisor's span of control, and some have become leaner and eliminated middle-level management positions. It is not practical for a supervisor to track the performance of 20, 30, or even 50 workers and evaluate their performance objectively. This restructuring of authority and responsibility could lead to grave inequities in the performance appraisal system. To ensure employees feel that the appraisal process is fair and just, each evaluator must understand what is necessary for successful job performance and be able to apply the standards uniformly. Supervisors should be trained in the use of the appraisal instrument.

Peer evaluation

The evaluation of an employee's performance by other employees of relatively equal rank.

Peer Evaluations. A **peer evaluation** is the evaluation of an employee's performance by other employees of relatively equal rank. Peers usually have a closer working relationship with each other and are more knowledgeable about an individual's contribution to the team effort than the supervisor. However, safeguards must be built in to ensure that peers are basing their evaluations on performance factors and not on bias, prejudice, or personality conflicts. Having an individual's performance evaluated anonymously by a team of peers is one way to encourage candid evaluation. To protect appraisees from prejudice or vendettas, the organization should establish an appeals mechanism to allow review of ratings by upper-level managers.

Generally, employees work cooperatively to achieve common goals. Consider the situation in which members of work teams evaluate other team members' performance. On the one hand, since a peer rating system uses a number of independent judgments, peer evaluations have the potential to be more reliable than supervisory evaluations. But on the other hand, when employees are forced to criticize their teammates via the performance appraisal system, their appraisals could have undesirable consequences for the cooperative culture and defeat the purposes of teamwork. Imagine what could happen to morale and spirit among team members when one worker gets a low evaluation

An employee's immediate supervisor is in the best position to observe and judge how well the employee has performed on the job.

from an unknown coworker and wonders who was responsible. To safeguard the peer rating process, supervisors can incorporate the input from all peers into a single composite evaluation. Thus, ratings that may be high because of friendship or low due to bias will cancel each other out. Safeguards to ensure confidentiality and minimize the potentiality of bias are critical to the effective use of peer evaluations.[2]

As the concepts of total quality management and self-directed work teams expand, performance appraisals are expected to take on a different role. Some speculate that appraisals will focus more on the future than on the past and will include input from a wide variety of sources. John F. Welch, CEO of General Electric, has developed a corporate culture that depends on shared values. Welch has stated that:

When you make a value like teamwork important, you shape behavior. If you can't operate as a team player, no matter how valuable you've been, you really don't belong at GE.

To embed our values, we give our people 360-degree evaluations, with input from superiors, peers, and subordinates. They are the roughest evaluations you can get, because people hear things about themselves they've never heard before. But they get the input they need, and then have the chance to improve. If they don't improve, they have to go.[3]

Increasing numbers of organizations are using a type of evaluation called a 360-degree evaluation. A **360-degree evaluation** is based on evaluative feedback regarding the employee's performance collected from all around the employee—from customers, vendors, supervisors, peers, subordinates, and others. These 360-degree evaluations provide employees with feedback on their ability, skills, knowledge, and job-related effectiveness from sources who see different aspects of their work.[4] This approach provides employees with a complete picture of what they do well and where they need to improve from various perspectives.

Self-Evaluations. Many effective supervisors find it appropriate to supplement their own judgments with a self-rating from the subordinate. About a week prior to the scheduled performance review, the employee is given a blank evaluation form to be used as a self-evaluation. Surprisingly, research has revealed that employees often rate their own work less favorably than do their supervisors.[5] The supervisor compares the two evaluations to make sure to discuss all important performance specifics in the appraisal meeting. As mentioned previously, if the supervisor has provided ongoing feedback to the employee, the employee's self-ratings should be very close to the supervisor's ratings. Widely divergent ratings could mean that the supervisor is not giving enough feedback throughout the year for the employee to have a clear picture of how well he or she is doing. Ideally, in a system of participative management, the formal appraisal should hold no surprises for the employee. Regardless of the approach used, the ultimate responsibility for completing the appraisal form and conducting the appraisal meeting lies with the immediate supervisor. If peer evaluations are used, the supervisor must still reconcile the appraisals and communicate the information to the employee. The formal appraisal meeting usually takes place at a set time each year and should summarize what the supervisor has discussed with the employee throughout the year.

Timing of Appraisals

Upper-level management decides who should appraise and how often formal appraisals should be done. Most organizations require supervisors to conduct formal appraisals of all employees at least once a year. Traditionally, this has been considered long enough to develop a reasonably accurate record of the employee's performance and short enough to provide current, useful information. However, if an employee has just started or if the employee has been transferred to a new and perhaps more responsible position, it is advisable to conduct an appraisal within the first three to six months.

In the case of an employee who is new to the organization, the supervisor may have to do an appraisal at the end of the employee's probationary period. This appraisal usually determines whether or not the employee will be retained as a regular employee. The performance evaluation of the probationary employee is critical. Employees are usually on their best behavior during the probationary period, and if their performance is less than acceptable, the organization should not make a long-term commitment to them. Consider the following illustration. A supervisor tolerated a probationary employee

---

360-degree evaluation

Performance appraisal based on data collected from all around the employee—from customers, vendors, supervisors, peers, subordinates, etc.

2

Explain how often performance feedback should be provided.

whose attendance record was not acceptable. Extensive efforts to develop better attendance habits failed. Even so, the supervisor felt that if the employee was terminated, the position might go unfilled and be lost. The supervisor's theory of "half an employee is better than none" cost the company dearly in the long run. The employee never became a satisfactory performer, and he eventually had to be terminated after the company had invested significantly in his training.

After the probationary period, the timing of appraisals varies. In some organizations, appraisals are done on the anniversary of the date when the employee started; in others, appraisals are done once or twice a year on fixed dates. If an employee exhibits a serious performance problem during the evaluation period, the supervisor should schedule an immediate meeting with the employee. This meeting should be followed by another formal evaluation within 30 days to review the employee's progress. If the performance deficiency is severe, the supervisor should conduct regular appraisals to completely document the performance deficiency and the supervisor's efforts to help the employee.

As stated before, performance evaluation should be a normal part of the day-to-day relationship between a supervisor and employees. If an employee is given ongoing feedback, then the annual appraisal should contain no surprises. The supervisor who frequently communicates with employees concerning how they are doing will find that the annual appraisal primarily is a matter of reviewing much of what has been discussed during the year. Figure 13-2 illustrates how regular feedback can reduce the natural apprehension surrounding performance appraisals by removing the uncertainty.

FIGURE 13-2   Regular feedback reduces the natural apprehension about appraisals.

Ongoing feedback throughout the year, both positive and negative, rewards good performance and guides improvement. Over time, ongoing feedback, as well as formal appraisals, can become an important influence on employee motivation and morale. Appraisals reaffirm the supervisor's genuine interest in employees' growth and development. Most employees would rather be told how they are doing—even if it involves some criticism—than receive no feedback from their supervisor.

Discuss the advantages of a formal performance appraisal system.

ADVANTAGES OF A FORMAL APPRAISAL SYSTEM

A formal appraisal system provides a framework to help the supervisor evaluate performance systematically. It forces the supervisor to scrutinize the work of employees from the standpoint of how well they are meeting previously established standards and to identify areas needing improvement.

Most firms use some type of formal appraisal system. Management scholar Douglas McGregor identified three reasons for using performance appraisal systems:

1. Performance appraisals provide systematic judgments to support salary increases, promotions, transfers, layoffs, demotions, and terminations.
2. Performance appraisals are a means of telling subordinates how they are doing and of suggesting needed changes in behavior, attitudes, skills, or job knowledge. They let subordinates know where they stand with the supervisors.
3. Performance appraisals are used as a basis for coaching and counseling of employees by supervisors.[6]

Organizations that view their employees as a long-term asset worthy of development adopt the philosophy that all employees can improve their current level of performance.

Employees have the right to know how well they are doing and what they can do to improve. Most employees want to know what their supervisors think of their work. This desire can stem from different reasons. For example, some employees realize that they are doing a relatively poor job, but they hope that the supervisor is not too critical and they are anxious to be assured of this. Other employees feel that they are doing an outstanding job and want to make certain that the supervisor recognizes and appreciates their services.

Formal appraisals usually become part of an employee's permanent employment record. These appraisals serve as documents that are likely to be reviewed and even relied on in future decisions concerning promotion, compensation, training, disciplinary action, and even termination. Performance appraisals can generate answers to questions such as the following:

- Who should be promoted to department supervisor when the incumbent retires?
- Who should get merit raises this year?
- What should be the raise differential between employees?
- Who, if anyone, needs training?
- What training do they need?

- I see this behavior has happened before. Does the employee need additional coaching, or is it serious enough for disciplinary action?
- An employee is appealing his termination. Do we have adequate documentation?

A formal appraisal system serves another important purpose. An employee's poor performance and failure to improve may be due in part to the supervisor's inadequate supervision. Thus, a formal appraisal system also provides clues to the supervisor's own performance and may suggest where the supervisor needs to improve. Even when designed and implemented with the best intentions, performance appraisal systems are often a source of anxiety for employee and supervisor alike. Formal performance appraisal systems can be misused as disciplinary devices rather than being used as constructive feedback aimed at rewarding good performance and helping employees improve. This chapter's first "Contemporary Issue" box presents some interesting perspectives on the formal appraisal process.

THE PERFORMANCE APPRAISAL PROCESS

Explain the concepts and techniques in using a written employee appraisal form.

Typically, a formal employee performance appraisal by a supervisor involves (a) completing a written appraisal form and (b) conducting an appraisal interview.

Completing a Written Appraisal Form

To facilitate the appraisal process and make it more uniform, most organizations use performance appraisal forms. There are numerous types of forms for employee evaluation. These rating forms are usually prepared by the human resources department with input from employees and supervisors. Once the forms are in place, the human resources department usually trains supervisors and employees in their proper use. Often supervisors are responsible for informing new employees about the performance appraisal process as part of their orientation.

Factors in Measuring Performance. Most forms include factors that serve as criteria for measuring job performance, skills, knowledge, and abilities. The following are some of the factors that most frequently are included on employee appraisal rating forms:

- Job knowledge
- Quantity of work
- Quality of work
- Timeliness of output
- Effectiveness in use of resources
- Positive and negative effects of effort
- Ability to learn
- Dependability (absenteeism, tardiness, work done on time)
- Amount of supervision required (initiative)
- Suggestions and ideas
- Conduct
- Cooperation (effectiveness in dealing with others)

- Safety
- Customer service orientation
- Aptitude
- Judgment
- Adaptability
- Appearance
- Ability to work with others

contemporary issue

For Decades, Many Have Criticized Performance Appraisals, But Everyone's Still Doing Them!

Most organizations have a formalized system of performance appraisal—a process by which the supervisor assesses the employee's performance over some specified period of time. Perhaps no aspect of human resources management is more discussed and cussed than the performance appraisal system. Quality guru W. Edwards Deming was one of the most vocal critics of the annual formal rite of appraisal: ". . . it nourishes short-term performance, annihilates long-term planning, builds fear, demolishes teamwork, nourishes rivalry and politics. It leaves people bitter, crushed, bruised, battered, desolate, despondent, dejected, feeling inferior, some even depressed, all unfit for work for weeks after receipt of rating, unable to comprehend why they are inferior."[1] He contended that performance appraisal is the number one American management problem. "It takes the average employee six months to recover from it."[2]

While agreeing in part with Deming's assessment of the downside of performance appraisal, Tom Peters suggests that "performance evaluation is essential—more than ever. It is a tool for directing attention to new targets."[3] Peters contends that successful appraisal requires four different sets of time:

1. day-to-day time spent giving constant feedback;
2. preparation time for the annual or semiannual evaluation;
3. execution time for the appraisal meetings, which should be spread out rather than bunched by the dozens in a single week; and
4. group time, during which fellow managers are consulted and appraisal criteria coordinated.[4] This last category not only provides the manager with input, but also engenders a sense of fairness and equity throughout the organization.[4]

Even noted management theorist Douglas McGregor (creator of the Theory X and Theory Y concepts discussed in Chapter 4) expressed his concern about the performance appraisal process when he said, "Managers are uncomfortable when they are put in the position of playing God."[5]

"No one likes to get a record card, and it's human nature to cringe from criticism, no matter how constructive," stated Martha Peak, group editor of *American Management Association's Magazines.* "When our firm instituted multirater (360-degree) feedback, I went through all the stages associated with refusal to accept reality: *denial* ("Why do I have to go through a 360 exercise?"), *panic* ("What if the results are lousy?"), and *hysteria* ("Who will see the information?") *before returning to my senses* ("Get a grip! Knowledge is obviously preferable to ignorance.").[6] Operating on the premise that people want to know how they're doing, effective supervisors will see performance appraisal as a powerful tool—for recognizing and rewarding performance that meets or exceeds expectations; for correcting deficient performance; and challenging employees to strive for stretching but attainable targets in the future.

Sources: (1) W. Edwards Deming, *Out of Crisis* (Cambridge, MA: Massachusetts Institute of Technology, 1982), p. 37. (2) Tom Peters, *Thriving on Chaos* (New York: Alfred A. Knopf, 1987), p. 495. (3) Ibid. (4) Ibid., p. 496. (5) Douglas McGregor, "An Uneasy Look at Performance Appraisal," *Harvard Business Review* (September/October 1972), p. 134. (6) Adapted from Martha H. Peak, "Consider the Source," *Management Review* (July/August 1997), p. 1.

Regardless of the factors used, they must be relevant to the employee's actual job. Factors that enable the supervisor to make objective performance evaluations rather than personality judgments should be used whenever possible. For each of these factors, the supervisor may be provided with a "check-the-box" choice or a place to fill in the achievement of the employee. Some appraisal forms offer a series of descriptive sentences, phrases, or adjectives to assist the supervisor in understanding how to judge the rating factors. Generally, the "check-the-box" forms are somewhat easier and less time consuming for supervisors to complete. Ideally, the supervisor should write a narrative to justify the evaluation. There should be no shortcuts to performance appraisal. Supervisors should give it as much time as it needs.

Figure 13-3 (see pages 418–419) is an example of a typical appraisal form.[7] The supervisor reads each item and checks the appropriate box. The supervisor identifies the outstanding aspects of the employee's work as well as specific performance characteristics that need improvement (weaknesses) and suggests several things that might be done to improve performance. The form provides space for additional comments about the various aspects of an employee's performance.

If the system calls for employee self-appraisal, the employee's form is usually identical to the regular appraisal form except that it is labeled as a self-appraisal. Self-appraisals give employees an opportunity to think about their own specific achievements and to prepare for the appraisal meeting.

Computerized Performance Appraisal Software Packages.   "Point and click" has become a way of life for many people. Various vendors have developed software packages designed to allow supervisors to effortlessly move though the performance appraisal form. While it is not our intent to go into great detail on the types of packages available, we do want to have the reader recognize that computerized performance appraisal systems will be an emerging trend in the new millennium.

Generally, the software program can import the company's existing evaluation form. For example, using the employee appraisal form shown in Figure 13-3, the supervisor chooses from the list of factors relevant for a given job, for example, personal efficiency, job knowledge, judgment, and the like. Each factor can be weighted according to its importance to the employee's job. Then the supervisor rates statements that appear on the screen that allow them to determine whether the employee has met, exceeded, or failed to meet the performance standard. According to freelance technology writer George Hulme, "The leading programs guide users through the process of performance appraisal, provide on-screen tutorials that answer frequently answered questions, and steer managers clear of potential legal problems. One such program, *Employee Appraiser 3.0,* helps the supervisor to write the evaluation. For example, if the text turned out by the program is more harsh or more flattering than what the reviewer intended, he or she can 'tune' the text with keystrokes to tone down the criticism or pump up the praise. The program's language scan feature locates potentially litigious phrases and words. Another program, *PerformanceNow!,* spots sensitive words and suggests alternatives."[8]

One of the authors is familiar with a company that decided to implement one of the software appraisal packages. After the first round of annual appraisals using the new system, employees were just as dissatisfied with the process and supervisors were more frustrated. Why? The software vendors contend that their systems should help make the appraisals more consistent, and able to withstand legal tests. In this case, the human resources manager assumed that the new approach would "magically" improve the appraisal process. What was forgotten was that for any annual appraisal to be effective, it must be built on factual information that is the culmination of the observed and reported incidents of the employee's performance over the time period covered. When the new computerized process was announced, some supervisors either quit keeping the "paper" record or failed to understand the importance of making a computer entry as the performance occurred. Nothing is more frustrating for any employee than to leave the appraisal feeling that the supervisor ignored certain outstanding performance incidents, or only covered the performance that occurred in the last few weeks. It should be obvious that supervisors must get in the habit of logging positive and negative performance information as they occur. As mentioned earlier in this chapter, the authors want to reinforce the notion that "there is no substitute for daily feedback on performance." Supervisors should document performance as it occurs so that there will be no surprises at annual review time.

Problems with Appraisal Forms. Despite the uncomplicated design of most performance appraisal forms, supervisors encounter a number of problems when filling them out. For one thing, not all raters agree on the meaning of such terms as "exceptional," "very good," "satisfactory," "fair," and "unsatisfactory." Descriptive phrases or sentences added to each of these adjectives are helpful in choosing the level that best describes the employee. Even so, the choice of an appraisal term or level depends mostly on the rater's perceptions, and this may be an inaccurate measure of actual performance.

Another problem is that one supervisor may be more severe than another in the appraisal of employees. A supervisor who gives lower ratings than other supervisors for the same performance is likely to damage the morale of employees, who feel they have been judged unfairly. One such supervisor stated that since no one is perfect, no one should ever be evaluated above average. Another supervisor felt that if he rated his employees too highly, someone would consider them for a promotion elsewhere in the organization and they would be lost to his department. Since he did not want to lose his people, he rated their performance much lower than it actually was. In the long run, the supervisor lost the employees' trust and respect or eventually lost them to other firms.

On the other hand, some supervisors tend to be overly generous or lenient in their ratings.[9] The **leniency error** occurs when supervisors give employees higher ratings than they deserve. Some supervisors give high ratings because they believe that poor evaluations may reflect negatively on their own performance, suggesting that they have not been able to elicit good performance from the employees. Other supervisors do not give low ratings because they are afraid that they will antagonize the employees and thus make them less cooperative. Some supervisors are so eager to be liked by their employees that they give out only high ratings, even when such ratings are undeserved.

Supervisors also should be aware of the problem of the halo effect or horns effect

Leniency error

Supervisors give employees higher ratings than they deserve.

FIGURE 13-3 A "check-the-box" type of performance appraisal form.

SANDERS SUPERMARKETS

Employee Appraisal Form

Employee's Name: _____
Occupation: _____

The following general definitions apply to each factor rated below.

Satisfactory: The employee's performance with respect to a factor meets the full job requirements as the job is defined at the time of rating. A satisfactory rating means good performance. THIS IS THE BASIC STANDARD FOR RATING ANY FACTOR BELOW.

Fair:	The employee's performance with respect to a factor is below the requirements for the job and must improve to be satisfactory.	**Unsatisfactory:**	The employee's performance with respect to a factor is deficient enough to justify release from present job unless improvement is made.
Very Good:	The employee's performance with respect to a factor is beyond the requirements for satisfactory performance for the job.	**Exceptional:**	The employee's performance with respect to a factor is extraordinary, approaching the best possible for the job.

Rate on Factors Below	Unsatisfactory	Fair	Satisfactory	Very Good	Exceptional
	☐	☐	☐	☐	☐
Personal Efficiency: Speed and effectiveness in performing duties assigned.	☐ Efficiency too poor to retain in job without improvement.	☐ Efficiency below job requirements in some respects.	☐ Personal efficiency fully satisfies job requirements.	☐ Super efficiency.	☐ Extraordinary degree of personal efficiency.
Job Knowledge: Extent of job information and understanding possessed by employee.	☐ Knowledge inadequate to retain in job without improvement.	☐ Lacks some required knowledge.	☐ Knowledge fully satisfies job requirements.	☐ Very well informed on all phases of work.	☐ Extraordinary. Beyond scope which present job can fully utilize.
Judgment: Extent to which decisions and actions are based on sound reasoning and weighing of outcome.	☐ Judgment too poor to retain in job without improvement.	☐ Decisions not entirely adequate to meet demands of job.	☐ Makes good decisions in various situations arising in job.	☐ Superior in determining correct decisions and actions.	☐ Extraordinary. Beyond that which present job can fully utilize.
Initiative: Extent to which employee is a "self-starter" in attaining objectives of job.	☐ Lacks sufficient initiative to retain in job without improvement.	☐ Lacks initiative in some respects.	☐ Exercises full amount of initiative required by the job.	☐ Exercises initiative beyond job requirements.	☐ Extraordinary. Beyond that which present job can fully utilize.
Job Attitude: Amount of interest and enthusiasm shown in work.	☐ Attitude too poor to retain in job without improvement.	☐ Attitude needs improvement to be satisfactory.	☐ Favorable attitude.	☐ High degree of enthusiasm and interest.	☐ Extraordinary degree of enthusiasm and interest.
Dependability: Extent to which employee can be counted on to carry out instructions, be on the job, and fulfill responsibilities.	☐ Too unreliable to retain in job without improvement.	☐ Dependability not fully satisfactory.	☐ Fully satisfies dependability demands of job.	☐ Superior to normal job demands.	☐ Extraordinary dependability in all respects.

FIGURE 13-3   *(Continued)*

Overall Evaluation of Employee Performance:	☐ Performance inadequate to retain in present job.	☐ Does not fully meet requirements of the job.	☐ Good performance. Fully competent.	☐ Superior. Beyond satisfactory fulfillment of job requirements.	☐ Extraordinary. Performance approaching the best possible for the job.

Use This Item Only If the Employee Is Still in the Learning Stage on the Job

Evaluation of Trainee Performance:	**Unsatisfactory**	**Fair**	**Satisfactory**	**Very Good**	**Exceptional**
Considering the length of time on the job, how do you evaluate the employee's performance so far?	Progress too slow to retain job. ☐	Progressing but not as rapidly as required. ☐	Making good progress. ☐	Progressing very rapidly. ☐	Doing exceptionally well. Outstanding rate of development. ☐

1. Outstanding abilities and accomplishments.

2. Weaknesses.

   Recommendation for Improvement:

3. General remarks concerning employee's performance.

4. Specific suggestions for further development.

Rated by: Date Reviewed by: Date

TO RATER: Initial and date this space when you have discussed this rating with the employee.

_____
SUPERVISOR

*Signature of Employee _____

*This signature merely verifies that this evaluation has been discussed with the employee, and it does not express approval or disapproval of the above.

(described in Chapter 12), which causes a rating on one factor to result in similar ratings on other factors. One way to avoid the halo or horns effect is for the supervisor to rate all employees on only one factor at a time and then go on to the next factor for all employees, and so on. This suggestion works only if the supervisor is rating several employees at the same time. If that is not the case, then the supervisor should pause and ask, "How does this employee compare on this factor with other employees?" The supervisor must rate each employee in relation either to a standard or to another employee on each factor.

The supervisor should ask what conditions exist when the job is done well. These conditions are **performance standards,** and are the job-related requirements by which the employee's performance will be evaluated. They should be described in terms of "how much," "how well," "when," and "in what manner." Effectiveness and efficiency measures are part of these standards. The positive and negative effects of performance should also be considered. Consider, for example, the most prolific salesperson in a store. His product knowledge and selling ability are second to none. However, he always expects the cashiers to set other orders aside and ring up his sales first. The cashiers are frustrated, and the other salespeople are not as able to give good service. In addition, he always has the stockroom personnel running errands for him. The salesperson receives accolades on selling, but every one of his sales is a rush project, and others are expected to juggle their schedules to accommodate him. While the salesperson is proficient in his own job performance, in the process of getting his job done he creates negative impacts elsewhere in the organization. The supervisor needs to broaden the performance standards to include more than product knowledge and selling.

Appraisal Should Be Job Based. Every appraisal should be made within the context of each employee's particular job, and every rating should be based on the total performance of the employee. It would be unfair to appraise an employee on the basis of one assignment that had been done recently, done particularly well or done very poorly. Random impressions should not influence a supervisor's judgment. The appraisal should be based on an employee's total record for the appraisal period. All relevant factors need to be considered. Moreover, the supervisor must continuously strive to exclude personal biases for or against individuals, which can be a serious pitfall in appraisal.

Although results of performance appraisal are by no means perfect, they can be fairly objective and serve as a positive force in influencing an employee's future performance.

The Appraisal Meeting

The second major part of the appraisal process is the evaluation or appraisal meeting. After the supervisor has completed the rating form, he or she arranges a time to meet with the employee to review the ratings. Since this meeting is the most vital part of the appraisal process, the supervisor should develop a general plan for carrying out the appraisal discussion. If poorly handled, this meeting can lead to considerable resentment and misunderstanding. The conflict that develops may not be repairable.

Performance standards
The job-related requirements by which the employee's performance will be evaluated.

5
Discuss the process of conducting a sound appraisal meeting.

The Right Purpose.   The primary purpose of the appraisal meeting is to let the employee know how he or she is doing. The supervisor formally praises the employee for his or her past and current good performance in the interest of maintaining the employee's good behaviors. The appraisal meeting is also used by the supervisor to help the employee develop good future performance. Emphasizing the strengths on which the employee can build complements the employee's career plans. The supervisor can explain the opportunities for growth that exist within the organization and encourage the employee to develop the skills needed. Finally, the supervisor uses the appraisal meeting to explain past behavior that needs correcting and the need for improvement. Even when improvement is needed, the supervisor should take the positive approach that he or she believes in the employee's ability to improve and will do everything possible to help. It is important that the supervisor has the right purpose for the appraisal meeting.

The Right Time and Place.   Appraisal meetings should be held shortly after the performance rating form has been completed, preferably in a private setting. It is a good idea for the supervisor to complete the rating form several days in advance and then review it a day or two before the meeting to analyze it objectively and to ensure that it accurately reflects the employee's performance. Privacy and confidentiality should be assured since this discussion could include criticism, personal feelings, and expressions of opinion.

The supervisor should make the appointment with the employee several days in advance. This enables the employee to be prepared for the appraisal meeting and to consider in advance what he or she would like to discuss.

Conducting the Appraisal Meeting.   Most of the discussion of interviewing included in Chapter 12 also applies to the appraisal meeting. Although appraisal meetings tend to be directive, in many situations an appraisal meeting can take on characteristics of a nondirective interview since the employee may bring up issues that the supervisor did not expect or was not aware of. It is easy for most supervisors to communicate positive aspects of job performance, but it is difficult to communicate major criticisms without generating resentment and defensiveness. There is a limit to how much criticism an individual can absorb in one session. If there is a lot of criticism to impart, dividing the appraisal meeting into several sessions may ease the stress. The manner in which the supervisor conducts the meeting influences how the employee reacts. After a brief informal opening, the supervisor should state that the purpose of the meeting is to assess the employee's performance in objective terms. During this warm-up period, the supervisor should state that the purpose of the performance appraisal is to congratulate the employee on his or her achievements and to help the employee improve performance, if necessary. The supervisor should review the employee's achievements during the review period, compliment the employee on those accomplishments, identify the employee's strengths, and then proceed to the areas that need improvement. A secret of success is to get the employee to agree on the strengths that he or she brings to the workplace because it is easier to build on strengths.

Unfortunately, not every employee performs at the expected level. Limiting criticism to just a few major points, rather than dumping a "laundry list" of minor transgressions on the employee, draws attention to the major areas that need improvement without being overwhelming. The supervisor must get the employee to agree on the areas that need correction or improvement. If there is agreement, then the supervisor and employee can use a problem-solving approach to jointly determine ways that the employee can improve performance. When dealing with an employee who is performing at substandard levels, the supervisor must clearly communicate to the employee that the deficiencies are serious and that substantial improvement must be made. The supervisor should mix in some positive observations so that the employee knows that he or she is doing some things right. The supervisor works with the employee to create an action plan for improvement with expectations and progress checkpoints along the way. It is important that the employee leave the meeting feeling capable of meeting the expectations.

Performance appraisals have been increasingly scrutinized by the legal system in recent years. It is essential that organizations ensure that their performance appraisal systems are legally defensible. Employees often disagree with negative aspects of the performance appraisal because the ratings affect their jobs later on. The supervisor must be certain that each employee fully understands the standards of performance that serve as the basis for appraisal. Also, the appraisal must accurately represent the employee's performance and be free of bias. The employee must know that the review is fair, is based on job performance factors, and is supported by proper documentation.

Most mature employees are able to handle deserved, fair criticism. By the same token, those who merit praise want to hear it. Figure 13-4 includes suggestions for relieving the uncertainty of the performance appraisal process.

During the appraisal meeting, the supervisor should emphasize that everybody in the same job in the same department is evaluated using the same standards and that no one is singled out for special scrutiny. The supervisor must be prepared to support or document ratings by citing specific illustrations and actual instances of good or poor performance. In particular, the supervisor should indicate how the employee performed or behaved in certain situations that were especially crucial or significant to the performance of the department. This is sometimes referred to as the *critical incident method*. To use this method, the supervisor must keep a file during the appraisal period of written notes describing situations when employees performed in outstanding fashion and when their work was clearly unsatisfactory. An example of a positive critical incident would be the following: "Shortly before closing on October 22, an employee realized that a customer had received an item of lesser value than she had paid for. The employee called the customer to verify that a mistake had been made, apologized for the error, and offered to either credit the customer's account or come to her residence to make the proper exchange. Identification and correction of the problem enabled the store to maintain customer confidence and develop a system to prevent recurrence." When the critical incident method is used, employees know that the supervisor has a factual record upon which to assess performance.

If the supervisor has chosen to use the employee self-rating approach mentioned earlier, the discussion primarily centers on the differences between the employee's self-ratings and those of the supervisor. This may involve considerable back-and-forth discussion, especially if there are major differences of opinion regarding vari-

FIGURE 13-4	Comprehensive checklist for performance appraisal.

☐ Supervisors are trained in the performance appraisal system:

☐ the forms ☐ providing feedback
☐ use of job standards ☐ rating scales & dimensions
☐ timing of appraisal ☐ linkages with personal decisions
☐ monitoring employee progress ☐ objective performance assessment
☐ contracting for performance ☐ documentation
improvement ☐ interviewing techniques
☐ using developmental methods & ☐ rewarding performance
action plans

☐ Both the supervisor and the employee understand the purpose of the appraisal process.

☐ The supervisor clarifies expectations for the employee (a job description with a listing of duties and responsibilities).

☐ Updated job descriptions serve as the foundation for the appraisal.

☐ The supervisor makes the employee aware of performance standards and specific areas of accountability.

☐ The supervisor provides ongoing feedback on performance. Example—"There is no substitute for daily feedback on performance."

☐ Supervisors give at least one official performance appraisal per year—within first 30 work days for new employees or transfers and as required for problem employees.

☐ As soon as a performance problem is observed, the supervisor openly problem solves with the employee to try to determine the cause of the problem and corrective action.

☐ The supervisor keeps a regular record of all unusual behavior—a critical incident file.

☐ The supervisor schedules the appraisal meeting several days in advance.

☐ The supervisor puts the employee at ease at the beginning of the appraisal meeting.

☐ The supervisor allows the employee to engage in self-evaluation. (The supervisor may have asked the employee to fill out the same evaluation form.)

☐ The supervisor reviews the written appraisal with the employee, stating both standards and/or objectives met or not met.

☐ The supervisor criticizes performance, not the person (tells the employee specifically what he or she did wrong.)

☐ The supervisor objectively emphasizes work behaviors rather than personal traits (the "O" of OUCH).

☐ The supervisor provides positive as well as negative feedback.

☐ The supervisor uses specific examples to illustrate the employee's accomplishments. (The employee knows that the supervisor is using factual information that is well documented.)

☐ The supervisor asks probing questions to get additional information, to seek clarification of misunderstandings or views that differ. This gives the employee an opportunity to bring forth mitigating circumstances or to discuss items of interest or concern (e.g., "What is my opportunity for advancement or specialized training?").

☐ The supervisor summarizes the discussion and overall rating.

☐ The supervisor allows the employee to summarize the interview in his or her own words.

☐ The employee knows that the organization has an audit procedure to review the supervisor's appraisal decisions in the event of disagreement, that is, the decision is audited to ensure that feedback is related to job performance (the "H" of OUCH).

☐ Personnel decisions are made consistent with the written results of the appraisal (the "C" of OUCH).

☐ The system is periodically reviewed to ensure that there is uniformity throughout the organization and that protected classes are not adversely impacted by the performance appraisal system (the "U" of OUCH).

☐ Performance ratings are linked to the achievement of organizational objectives.

At an appraisal meeting, the supervisor emphasizes an employee's strengths in order to help him or her develop good future performance.

ous parts of the appraisal form. Typically, however, this is not a major difficulty unless the employee has an exaggerated notion of his or her ability or feels that the supervisor's ratings were unjustified. The impact of downsizing and a tight job market may lead to greater disagreement over performance appraisal if there are now more people competing for fewer jobs. Conflict will be particularly likely if the employee perceives that the supervisor's appraisal may jeopardize his or her job.

Regardless of the way the supervisor approaches the meeting, he or she must include a discussion about plans for improvement and possible opportunities for the employee's future. The supervisor should mention any educational or training plans that may be available. The supervisor should be familiar with advancement opportunities open to employees, requirements of future jobs, and each employee's personal ambitions and qualifications. In discussing the future, the supervisor should be careful not to make any promises for training or promotion that are not certain to materialize in the foreseeable future. Making false promises is a quick way to lose credibility.

The evaluation meeting also should provide the employee with an opportunity to ask questions, and the supervisor should answer them as fully as possible. If the supervisor is uncertain about the answer, it is better to say, "I don't know but I'll find out and get back to you with an answer tomorrow." Employees lose trust in supervisors who evade the subject, are not truthful, and do not get back with answers in a timely fashion. In the final analysis, the value of an evaluation meeting depends on the employee's ability to recognize the need for self-improvement and the supervisor's ability to stimulate in the employee a desire to improve. It takes sensitivity and skill for a supervisor to accomplish this, and it is frequently necessary for the supervisor to adapt what is said to each employee's reactions as they surface during the meeting.

Difficult Responses During the Appraisal Meeting. Many supervisors try to avoid conducting appraisals. They believe the only thing they need to do is to fill out the form. With the increased demands placed on supervisors to do more with less, to increase productivity, and to find ways to continuously improve quality, many supervisors fail to find adequate time to evaluate the performance of their employees properly. As one manager recently stated, "We don't have time to evaluate around here. We're up to our neck in things to do." However, supervisors must evaluate their employees' performance.

People react to performance appraisals in different ways. Figure 13-5 lists some of the responses that have been encountered by supervisors conducting performance meetings. Difficult responses can cause headaches for a supervisor, but they should not cause the supervisor to ignore or short-circuit the appraisal process.

FIGURE 13-5

Difficult responses the
supervisor may encounter
during the appraisal
meeting.

1. "You hired me; therefore, how can I be so bad?"
2. "You're just out to get me!"
3. "You don't like my lifestyle. This has nothing to do with my on-the-job performance."
4. "This evaluation is not fair!"
5. "I didn't know that was important. You never told me that."
6. "Look, my job depends on getting good-quality material from others. I can't turn out quality work because I have to constantly inspect their work first."
7. "You never say anything nice to me. You just make me feel so bad," as the employee breaks into tears.
8. The employee fails to comprehend what you've said.
9. The employee refuses to talk about it, sits silently by, or fails to respond to your open-ended questions.
10. The employee rambles off the subject.
11. The employee explodes and vents deep-seated hostilities toward you, his or her spouse, a parent, a coworker, etc.
12. The employee accuses you of gender, racial, religious, age, or other bias.

Closing the Appraisal Meeting. In closing the appraisal meeting, the supervisor should be certain that the employee has a clear understanding of his or her performance rating. Where applicable, the supervisor and employee should agree on some mutual goals in areas in which the employee needs improvement. The supervisor should set a date with the employee—perhaps in a few weeks—to discuss progress toward meeting the new goals. This reinforces the supervisor's stated intent to help the employee improve and gives the supervisor an opportunity to praise the employee for progress made.

Many organizations request that employees sign their performance appraisal form after the meeting. If a signature is requested as proof that the supervisor actually held the appraisal meeting, the supervisor should so inform the employee. The supervisor should make sure the employee understands that signing the form does not necessarily indicate agreement with the ratings on the form. Otherwise, the employee may be reluctant to sign the form, especially if the employee disagrees with some of the contents of the appraisal. Some appraisal forms have a line above or below the employee's signature stating that the signature only confirms that the appraisal meeting has taken place and that the employee does not necessarily agree or disagree with any statements made during the appraisal.

Some organizations require the supervisor to discuss employee appraisals with a manager or the human resources department before the appraisal documents are placed in the individual's permanent employment record. A supervisor may be challenged to justify certain ratings—if, for example, the supervisor has given very high or very low evaluations to the majority of departmental employees. For the most part, if the supervisor has appraised employees carefully and conscientiously, such challenges will be infrequent.

The employer should have an audit or review process to review supervisors' appraisal decisions. The purposes of this audit are to ensure that evaluations are done fairly and to provide employees with a means of resolving conflicts arising from the appraisal process.

MANAGING THE RESULTS OF PERFORMANCE APPRAISAL: COACHING EMPLOYEES

Coaching

The frequent activity of the supervisor to provide employees with information, instruction, and suggestions relating to their job assignments and performance.

Effective supervisors use periodic performance evaluations as a way to develop their employees' competence. **Coaching** is the frequent activity of the supervisor to provide employees with information, instructions, and suggestions relating to their job assignments and performance. In addition to being a coach, the supervisor should also be a cheerleader and a facilitator in order to guide an employee's behaviors toward the desired results. If you want your people to be high performers (winners) than you need to help them get there (coach).[10] In this role the supervisor must identify activities that prepare employees for greater depth and breadth in their current or future jobs and reinforce the employee's positive behaviors and correct the negative behaviors in a positive way.

The supervisor's follow-up role in performance appraisal varies with the assessment. As a rule, supervisors use a coaching approach to help superior employees prepare for greater responsibility as well as to improve the performance of all employees. In both cases, the purpose of coaching is to help the employee become more productive by developing an action plan. Even though a plan may be jointly determined with the employee, the supervisor is ultimately responsible for providing the plan and the necessary instructions for carrying it out. The questions presented in Figure 13-6 may serve as guidelines for the supervisor's coaching effort.

Effective supervisors recognize that ongoing employee skill development is critical to the organization's success. Instruction, practice, and feedback are essential elements of development. Imagine playing golf without first receiving instruction and having a chance to practice the newly learned techniques. Most golfers seek instruction because they want to improve their game. Athletes such as Tiger Woods, who made a swift transition from amateur golf to the professional circuit and set records for wins and earnings, are gifted with fundamental ability, yet they continually seek advice from their coaches.

In business, as in sports, employees benefit from coaching. The coach observes the employee's current performance and communicates what went well and what specifically needs to be improved. The plan for improvement usually includes defining the expected level of performance, recommending specific steps for improvement, and observing performance. After developing the plan, the coach instructs the employee, allows time to practice the skills, and then observes the employee's performance, providing feedback about the effectiveness of the performance and offering further instruction and encouragement, if needed.

Generally, the employees who benefit most from coaching are the average performers, not the superstars. The former need to develop their skills and learn the fundamentals. The coach must provide constructive feedback on an ongoing basis. Remember, improvement does not occur overnight. Thus, the supervisor should be patient with the employee to allow for different learning styles and speeds.

FIGURE 13-6

Guidelines for coaching.

The effective supervisor should use the following guidelines to help the employee improve performance.

1. Have you identified specific areas of performance that need improvement?
2. Is it worth your time and effort to help the employee improve?
3. Does the employee understand that his or her performance needs improvement?
4. Does the employee know what is expected (standards of performance)?
5. Are there barriers beyond the employee's control that influence the current performance?
6. Does the employee know how to do the job?
7. Could the employee do the job if his or her life depended upon it? (If not, then training is necessary.)
8. What happens when the employee does the job well?
9. What do you do when performance is deficient?
10. Have you considered alternative courses of action?
11. Have you and the employee mutually agreed on a course of action to follow, such as setting specific objectives and a time table, developing improvement plans, identifying training program, etc.?
12. Have you provided information, instruction, and suggestions?
13. Does the employee fully understand the consequences if unacceptable performance continues?
14. What follow-up measures will you use and how will you measure the improvements?
15. How will you reward and reinforce improvement?
16. What will you do if performance does not improve?

Employee performance usually improves when specific improvement goals are established during the performance appraisal. It is important that the supervisor realize that he or she is responsible for improving the performance of a deficient employee. The supervisor must remember that an employee cannot improve performance unless he or she knows exactly what is expected. The supervisor should maintain close contact with the employee and provide instruction when needed. Supervisors also provide suggestions for improvement and serve as mentors. Performance improvements should be supported by positive feedback and reinforcement.

In rare circumstances when the action plan does not result in improved performance and unsatisfactory performance continues, termination may be necessary. Replacement of an employee is a very expensive proposition. Good coaching can avoid termination in many cases. The role of the supervisor in the positive discipline of less proficient employees is discussed in Chapter 19.

7

Identify the benefits derived from applying a policy of promotion from within.

MANAGING THE RESULTS OF PERFORMANCE APPRAISAL: PROMOTING EMPLOYEES

Given the proper encouragement, many employees strive to improve their performance and eventually be promoted. A promotion usually means advancement to a job with more responsibility, more privileges, higher status, greater potential, and higher pay.

Although the majority of employees want to improve or advance, this is not true of everyone. Some employees have no desire to advance any further. They may feel that an increase in responsibility would demand too much of their time and energy—which they prefer to devote to other interests—or they may be content with their security in their present positions. But employees who do not want to improve or advance tend to be in the minority. Most employees want promotions. For them, starting at the bottom and rising in status and income over time is part of a normal way of life.

Promotion from Within

Most organizations have policies for promoting employees. The policy of promotion from within is widely practiced, and it is important to both an organization and its employees. For the organization, it means a steady source of trained personnel for higher positions; for employees, it is a major incentive to perform better. If employees have worked for an organization for a long time, more is usually known about them than even the best selection processes and interviews could reveal about outside applicants for the same job. Supervisors should know their own people well, but they do not know individuals hired from the outside until those individuals have worked for them a while.

Occasionally a supervisor might want to bypass an employee for promotion because the productivity of the department would suffer until a replacement is found and trained. This kind of thinking is short sighted. It is better for the organization in the long run to have the best qualified people in positions where they can make the greatest contribution to the organization's success.

Similarly, there would be little reason for employees to improve themselves if they believed that the better and higher-paying jobs were reserved for outsiders. Additional job satisfaction results when employees know that stronger efforts on their part may lead to more interesting and challenging work, higher pay and status, and better working conditions. Most employees are better motivated if they see a link between excellent performance and promotion.

In considering promotion for an employee, the supervisor should recognize that what management considers a promotion may not always be perceived as such by the employee. For example, an engineer may believe that a promotion to administrative work is a hardship, not an advancement. The engineer may feel that administrative activities are less interesting or more difficult than technical duties and may be concerned about losing or diluting professional engineering skills. Such an atti-

Employee satisfaction increases when there are opportunities for advancement.

tude is understandable, and the supervisor should try to suggest promotional opportunities that do not require unacceptable compromises.

Also, the supervisor should be sensitive to employees who appear to be satisfied in their present positions. They may prefer to stay with their fellow employees and retain responsibilities with which they are familiar and comfortable. These employees should not be pressured by the supervisor to accept higher-level positions. However, if the supervisor believes that such an employee has excellent qualifications for promotion, the supervisor should offer encouragement and counsel which may make a promotion attractive to the employee for either current or future consideration.

Modifying a Promotion from Within Policy

Generally, it is preferable to apply a policy of promotion from within whenever possible. However, situations will arise in which strict adherence to this policy would not be sensible and might even be harmful to an organization. If there are no qualified internal candidates for a position, then someone from the outside has to be recruited. For example, if an experienced computer programmer is needed and no existing employee has programming expertise, the departmental supervisor will have to hire one from outside the organization.

At times, bringing a new employee into a department may be desirable since this person brings different ideas and fresh perspectives to the job. Another reason for recruiting employees from the outside is that an organization may not be in a position to train its own employees in the necessary skills. A particular position may require long, specialized, or expensive training, and the organization may be unable either to offer or to afford such training. Thus, to cover these types of contingencies, an absolute promotion-from-within policy must be modified as appropriate to the situation. This is why most written policy statements concerning promotion from within include a qualifying clause such as "whenever possible" or "whenever feasible."

Criteria for Promotion from Within

Typically, more employees are interested in being promoted than there are openings available. Since promotions should serve as an incentive for employees to perform better, some supervisors believe that employees who have the best records of production, quality, and cooperation are the ones who should be promoted. In some situations, however, it is difficult to measure such aspects of employee performance accurately or objectively, even when there has been a conscientious effort by supervisors in the form of merit ratings or performance appraisals.

Seniority

An employee's length of service within a department or organization.

Seniority. One easily measured and objective criterion that has been applied extensively in an effort to reduce favoritism and discrimination is seniority. **Seniority** is an employee's length of service within the department or organization. Labor unions have emphasized seniority as a major promotion criterion, and its use is also widespread among organizations that are not unionized and for jobs that are not covered by union agreements. Many supervisors are comfortable with the concept of seniority as a basis for promotion. Some supervisors feel that an employee's loyalty, as expressed by length of service, deserves to be rewarded. Basing promotion on seniority also assumes that an employee's abilities tend to increase with service. Although this assumption is not always accurate, it is likely that with continued service an employee's skills and knowledge do improve. If promotion is to be based largely on seniority, then the initial selection procedure for new employees must be careful, and each new employee should receive considerable training in various positions.

Probably the most serious drawback to using seniority as the major criterion for promotion is that it discourages younger employees—that is, those with less seniority. Younger employees may believe that they cannot advance until they, too, have accumulated years of service on the job. Consequently, they may lose enthusiasm and perform at only an average level since they feel that no matter what they do, they will not be promoted for a long time. Another serious drawback is that the best performer is not always the most senior. If seniority is the only criterion, then there is no incentive to perform well. Employees can be promoted for simply sticking around.

Merit and Ability.   Although labor unions have stressed the seniority criterion in promotion, seniority alone does not guarantee that an individual either deserves promotion or is capable of advancing to a higher-level job. In fact, some employees with high seniority may lack the necessary educational or skill levels needed for advancement. Consequently, most unions understand that length of service cannot be the only criterion for promotion. They agree that promotion should be based on seniority combined with merit and ability, and this type of provision is included in many union contracts.

Merit
The quality of an employee's job performance.

Ability
An employee's potential to perform higher level tasks.

Merit usually refers to the quality of an employee's job performance. **Ability** means an employee's capability or potential to perform, or to be trained to perform, a higher-level job. Supervisors often are in the best position to determine the degree to which merit and ability are necessary to compensate for less seniority. However, seniority is frequently the decisive criterion when merit and ability are relatively equal among several candidates seeking a promotion.

Balancing the Criteria.   Good supervisory practice attempts to attain a workable balance between the concepts of merit and ability on the one hand and seniority on the other. In selecting from among the most qualified candidates available, the supervisor may decide to choose essentially on the basis of seniority. Or, the supervisor may decide that, to be promoted, the employee who is most capable but who has less seniority will have to be far better than those with more seniority. Otherwise, the supervisor will promote the qualified employee with the greatest seniority, at least on a trial basis.

Because promotion decisions can have great significance, the preferred solution would be to apply all criteria equally. However, promotion decisions often involve so-called "gray" areas or subjective considerations that can lead rejected employees to be dissatisfied and file grievances. Realistically, unless there are unusual circumstances involved, it is unlikely that a supervisor will choose to promote an employee over other eligible candidates solely on the basis of merit and ability without giving some thought to seniority.

Discuss the supervisor's role in employee compensation and outline the goals of an effective compensation program.

MANAGING THE RESULTS OF PERFORMANCE APPRAISAL: COMPENSATING EMPLOYEES

Although it is not always recognized as such, a supervisor's staffing function includes helping to determine the relative worth of a job. Typically, of course, wage rates and salary schedules are formulated by higher-level management, by the human resources department, by union contract, or by government legislation or regulation. In this respect, the supervisor's authority is limited. Nevertheless, within such limitations the supervisor is responsible for determining appropriate compensation for departmental employees.

The question of how much to pay employees has posed a problem for many organizations. It is possible, however, to establish a compensation program that is objective, fair, and relatively easy to administer. The objectives of a compensation program should be to:

- Eliminate pay inequities to minimize dissatisfaction and complaints among employees.
- Establish and/or maintain sufficiently attractive pay rates so that qualified employees are attracted to and retained by the company.
- Conduct periodic employee merit ratings to provide the basis for comparative performance rewards.
- Control labor costs with respect to gains in productivity.
- Reward employees for outstanding performance or the acquisition of additional skills or knowledge.

Every supervisor has some responsibility in establishing standards for compensation that will attract and retain competent employees. Too often wage rate schedules simply follow historical patterns, or they are formulated haphazardly. At the departmental level, wage rate inequities often develop over time due to changes in jobs, changes in personnel, and different supervisors who use varying standards for administering compensation. However, when inequitable wage situations arise, they should not be tolerated. Nevertheless, inequities and concerns still exist (see this chapter's second "Contemporary Issue" box).

The Supervisor's Role in Compensation Decisions

Although a sound and equitable compensation structure should be of great concern to everyone in management, it is an area in which supervisors typically have little direct authority. However, supervisors should make an effort to make higher-level managers aware of serious compensation inequities at the departmental level. This can often be done when supervisors make their recommendations for wage and salary adjustments for individual employees.

Recommending Wage Adjustments. Unfortunately, too often supervisors automatically recommend full wage increases rather than seriously considering whether each

contemporary issue

Show Me the Money!

"Quitters never win." Or do they? According to some surveys, employers are offering job hoppers 10 to 20 percent raises over their current salaries. At the same time, employers are limiting raises to longtime employees to 4 percent, on average. The result—"it's not fair!" Longtime employees are finding that new hires make almost as much as they do or, in some cases, more. In addition, worker pay has not kept pace with other indicators:

	Percent increase 1991 through 1999
Average worker's wages	27%
Corporate profits	105%
Average CEO compensation (firms w/ >$10B in revenues)	163%
Standard & Poor's 500	218%[1]

A study by Steven Roach, chief economist at Morgan Stanley, points out that for 15 years in a row (through the end of 1997) employee productivity has climbed faster than real compensation. During this period, "There's been a lot of restructuring and cost-cutting, and labor has borne a disproportionate share. Shareholders have gotten the gains from it. Our society has chosen to reward the few for the labors of many."[2] For some employees, money has become the most important thing. It is the passport to a better way of life. However, when the typical factory worker reads that the average CEO of a major U.S. corporation makes $7.8 million, or 326 times more than he or she does, then it should come as no surprise that employees are dissatisfied with their compensation.[3]

To reverse this trend, managers should focus on three parts of the employee's anatomy: the head, the heart, and the pocketbook. The basics of using the head include using suggestion programs and other employee involvement programs to solicit employee ideas. Many employees are motivated by the sense of achievement that comes from seeing their ideas implemented. The basics of the heart come from empowering employees and getting them involved and enthused about their work. Based on interviews of more than 80 thousand managers and one million employees, the Gallup organization created a 12-question formula to determine the strength of a workplace. None of the questions dealt with issues like pay, benefits, or perks. Questions such as "Do my opinions seem to count?" and "Does my supervisor, or someone at work, seem to care about me as a person?" were used to identify the keys to higher levels of productivity, profit, employee retention, and customer satisfaction.[4]

What price is loyalty? A 1997 study found that "the amount of loyalty workers feel is directly related to the amount of compensation they receive." Eighty percent of employees would recommend their companies as the best place to work, but 40 percent would leave their current employers for only slightly higher pay.[5] So what's the answer? Author Curt Coffman contends that a *great manager* is someone who says, "You come to work with me, and I'll help you be as successful as possible; I'll help you grow; I'll help you make sure you're in the right role; I'll provide the relationship for you to understand and know yourself. And I want you to be more successful than me."[6]

Sources: (1) Kim Clark and Joellen Perry, "Why It Pays to Quit," *U.S. News & World Report* (November 1, 1999), pp. 74+. Also see Carol Hymowitz, "Managers Face Battle to Keep Salaries Fair in a Tight Job Market," *The Wall Street Journal* (March 21, 2000), p. B1. (2) Marjorie Kelly, "The Cruel Underside of 'Productivity,'" *Business Ethics* (July/August 1998), p. 6. (3) As reported in "CEOs Are Called Too Cozy with Pay Setter," *St. Louis Post Dispatch* (April 9, 1999), p. B1. (4) Mark Borden, "It's the Manager, Stupid!" *Fortune* (October 25, 1999), pp. 366–368 [An interview with Marcus Buckingham and Curt Coffman, authors of *First, Break All the Rules* (New York: Simon & Schuster, 1999)]. (5) Elaine McShulskis, "Well Paid Employees are Loyal Employees," *HRMagazine* (November 1997), pp. 22–24. (6) op.cit., Borden.

employee deserves such a raise. Here is where employee performance evaluation becomes crucial. If an employee's work has been satisfactory, then the employee deserves the normal increase. But if the employee has performed at an unsatisfactory level, the supervisor should suspend the recommendation for an increase and discuss this decision with the employee. The supervisor might outline specific targets for job improvement that the employee must meet before the supervisor will recommend a wage increase at a future date. If an employee has performed at an outstanding level, the supervisor should not hesitate to recommend a generous, more-than-average wage increase if this can be done within the current wage structure. Such a tangible reward will encourage the outstanding employee to continue striving for excellence.

Employee Incentives

Many organizations are attempting to get the "biggest bang" from their compensation program. While estimates vary on the number of organizations using performance-based or incentive compensation systems in an attempt to motivate employees to perform at a higher level, many organizations are attempting to link performance to pay.[11] In this section we present an overview of incentive systems.

Piecework. In a straight **piecework** system, the employee earns a certain amount of pay for each unit or piece produced. Difficulties arise when jobs are interdependent and the employee must rely on others to complete the assigned task.

Piecework
System in which the employee earns a certain amount of pay for each piece produced.

Pay for Performance. In **pay for performance,** compensation is awarded on the basis of achieving employee or corporate performance goals. Among these approaches are special cash awards, bonuses for meeting performance targets, team (departmental) incentive bonuses, profit sharing, and gain sharing for meeting production or cost-saving goals. **Gain-sharing plans** are group incentive plans. Group or team plans are normally used when the contribution of an individual employee is either not easily measurable or when performance depends on team cooperation. Employees share the monetary benefits (gains) of improved productivity, cost reductions, or improvements in quality or customer service. Most plans use an easy-to-understand formula to calculate productivity gains and the resulting bonus. One heralded gain-sharing program is that of Lincoln Electric Company.

Pay for performance
Compensation, other than base wages, that is given for achieving employee or corporate goals.

Gain-sharing plans
Group incentive plans that have employees share in the benefits from improved performance.

The 3,344 employees at the Cleveland, Ohio-based organization split approximately $64.5 million, or an average of $19,000 per employee in 1999. Lincoln employees are responsible for their own earnings. Production workers are paid on a piecework basis consistent with the average rate for a worker of that skill type in the Cleveland area. They must guarantee the quality of each piece they produce. If they do not produce a good piece, they are not paid for it. Employees are rated every six months on four factors: production output (quantity minus days of absence), quality minus the points they lose for customer rejections, dependability, and ideas and cooperation. An individual employee's share of the incentive is dependent on his or her performance rating.[12]

Skill-based pay

System that rewards
employees for acquiring
new skills or knowledge.

Skill–Based Pay. A **skill-based pay** or *knowledge-based pay* system rewards employees for acquiring additional skills or knowledge within the same job category. It does not reward the individual employee for the job he or she does. Employees are rotated through a variety of tasks associated with the job until they learn them all. The rewards are based on acquisition and proficiency in new skills, regardless of the employee's length of service.[13] Employees are rewarded in accordance with the number of skills they have mastered. Skill-based pay has become popular as a way to reward employees when promotional opportunities are scarce. Skill-based pay is most successful in organizations in which a participatory management philosophy prevails. The supervisor is usually the key to the success of a skill-based pay plan. Other attributes of a skill-based pay system are:

1. The need for deep commitment to training to achieve success.
2. The necessary use of job rotation.
3. The fact that the choice of plan is tied to business needs.
4. The support of supervisors.[14]

For a skill-based pay plan to succeed, the company must require and directly benefit from the skills it pays for. A closed-end questionnaire is used by employees to identify the activities, skills, knowledge, and abilities required by their jobs. All jobs are assigned a pay grade based on the value of their required activities, skills, and knowledge.[15] All employees now know what they must be able to do in order to be eligible for a promotion or a lateral transfer.

Suggestion Plans. In earlier chapters, we discussed the fact that employees may be motivated by the sense of achievement that comes from seeing their ideas implemented. Suggestion plans are one way to solicit employee ideas; typically employees are paid based on the value of their suggestions. Suggestion systems, however, may fail if they are evaluated on the basis of the savings alone.[16]

Incentive Plan Quandary. No incentive plan is immune from charges of "it's not fair." One critic, for example, is Linda Armbruster Milligan, executive vice president of Communications Workers of America Local 7777 in Englewood, Colorado. "The company (US West) is trying to introduce new and better ways to get people to perform better—to our minds, to speed up," Milligan says. The union isn't against financial rewards for performance. But, as she sees it, "US West's pay-for-performance plan is fatally flawed because it was built more to enhance the company's revenue than to improve customer service."[17] Getting input from the primary stakeholders (employees, first-line supervisors, and customers) before implementing the program will help to identify the "right things to measure." In the case of US West, there is a difference between "speeding up service" and "improving customer service," even though the two might be interrelated. For an incentive plan to be successful, management must clearly define what they want to reward. If it is customer service, then employees must understand what is to be measured and be able to impact those measures in their daily work. Team-based incentive plans are not without their problems. And these problems will continue to arise as team-based incentive plans grow in popularity because of the increasing use of teams.

A survey by Hewitt Associates found that only a few incentive pay plans met or exceeded their primary objectives. According to Ken Abosch, Hewitt's compensation business leader, "Unfortunately, a lot of companies don't know what they want the (compensation) plan to achieve; don't know how to monitor or measure plan performance; and, sometimes, don't want to know whether the plan is working because then they have to do something about it."[18] Regardless of the incentive compensation plan used, supervisors must fully comprehend the plan and be able to answer employee questions.

Employee Benefits

In addition to monetary compensation, most organizations provide supplementary benefits for employees, such as vacations with pay, holidays, retirement plans, insurance and health programs, tuition-aid programs, employee-assistance programs (EAPs), and numerous other services. Supervisors have little involvement in establishing benefits, but they are obligated to see that departmental employees understand how their benefits operate and that each employee receives his or her fair share.

When employees have questions about benefits, supervisors should consult with the human resources staff or higher-level managers. For example, a supervisor often has to make decisions involving employee benefits, as, for example, in scheduling departmental vacations or work shifts during the holidays. In these circumstances, the supervisor must be sure that what is done at the departmental level is consistent with the organization's overall policies, as well as with laws, union contract provisions, and the like.

Concerns for the Supervisor. It is common for employees to compare their own compensation to that of others. This becomes a serious motivational problem for the supervisor when the organization has wages or benefits that are lower than those for similar jobs at other firms in the community.

Two-tier wage systems and the use of contract employees are additional concerns for the supervisor in trying to maintain a perception of fairness. Depending on a firm's arrangement with a temp agency, the temporary employee may be paid more or less than regular employees performing the same job. In organizations using a two-tier wage system, new employees are paid less than present employees performing the same or similar jobs. Unfortunately, lower-paid employees can have feelings of inequity when working under these systems. Again, supervisors should make every effort to stay informed about their organization's compensation system and should consult the human resources or benefits office when questions arise. The best bosses are consistently honest. As easy as it might be to "blow off" employee concerns about their compensation, supervisors must recognize that this is an important area of concern for most employees. An employee survey reported what employees said was the most important information to them:

Employee benefit programs	82%
Pay policies and procedures	78%
Company's plans for the future	73%

How to improve work performance	65%
How my work fits into the total picture	61%[19]

We cannot emphasize enough the importance of communication. If the supervisor doesn't have the answer, the supervisor should say so, and strive to find out the answer to the employee's question. Moreover, supervisors should permit and even encourage employees to visit the human resources department—or the appropriate manager—for advice and assistance concerning benefits and compensation problems. This is particularly desirable when individual employees have personal problems or questions about sensitive areas such as medical and other health benefits and retirement and insurance programs.

What Call Did You Make?

As Shane Wilson, distribution center supervisor for Zimmer Wholesale Clubs, informal appraisals of employees such as Cheryl Iberra have probably been an accepted part of your normal supervisory routine. As an effective supervisor, you provide your employees with frequent feedback on performance.

Zimmer's new system will cause some employees to wonder, "Why are they instituting this system? Will it have something to do with who stays with the organization?" You are well respected by your employees, and to retain that respect you must have honest answers to any questions that arise during the performance appraisal process. You recognize that the success of Zimmer's newly inaugurated formal appraisal system will depend, in part, on how well you communicate the new system to your employees and how effectively you use it.

Hopefully, Zimmer will have training programs to clarify the new system and discuss the process so that it is employed consistently across and within departments. In communicating the new system to employees, begin by putting yourself in each employee's shoes and try to anticipate the questions they might ask you. Try to convey that the formalized system will make it easier for management to make important personnel decisions (e.g., compensation, training, promotion, retention, etc.).

In conducting the formal appraisals, remember to focus on job performance factors. Review the job descriptions, performance standards, and specific objectives that have been previously communicated to your employees. You will want to avoid making any of the various rating errors mentioned in this chapter. Focus on the job the employee is currently doing. Since you have provided your employees with regular feedback on performance, there will be no surprises with the new system. Positive feedback on performance is an effective tool for developing employees. Most of Cheryl's performance is very good. You should focus your attention on those factors. However, it appears that she sometimes displays an "antimanagement" attitude when it comes to company policy and compensation issues. You will need to address this area. If Cheryl believes that several policies are unfair, you can encourage her to develop a proposal and strategy for changing them. She may be correct; the policies might need revision. You want to get her to react in a proactive manner and make suggestions on how they can be improved.

The toughest part of the appraisal meeting will be when Cheryl asks you about the advancement opportunities at Zimmer. Since you have anticipated this question, you will have checked all possibilities with higher-level managers. Above all, you must be honest with Cheryl about the opportunity for advancement. If there are no openings anticipated at Zimmer, you must tell her so. As discussed in this chapter, some organizations are adopting a pay-for-skills program when advancement opportunities are limited. You may want to check with management about possibly setting up such a program to help retain good people like Cheryl. On the other hand, you might try to redesign her work in such a way that other rewards become more important than money and title. Certainly you would hate to lose a good assistant.

However, if Cheryl expects to be rewarded with a supervisory position upon completion of her degree and there are none at Zimmer, you might have to resign yourself to the fact that she will be happier working somewhere else.

SUMMARY

A formal performance appraisal system is the process of periodically rating an employee's performance against standards and communicating this feedback to the employee. Supervisors are responsible for appraising employee performance both on an informal, day-to-day basis and formally at predetermined intervals. Supervisors need to keep accurate records of employee performance.

To ensure that employees feel that the appraisal process is fair, each evaluator must understand what is necessary for successful job performance. Peer evaluations and 360-degree performance evaluations are ways to provide performance feedback from other perspectives besides the supervisor's, and they can contribute to a more complete performance picture. Including self-rating in the process can facilitate open discussion of an employee's own perceptions of his or her strengths and weaknesses.

Most organizations require formal performance appraisals at least once each year. In addition to formal appraisals, supervisors should provide their employees with frequent feedback on performance throughout the year. Because the decision to retain or not retain a new employee is critical, performance assessment of probationary employees should be done at the end of the probationary period. When there is a serious performance problem, the supervisor should provide immediate feedback. However, ongoing feedback, both positive and negative, should be a regular part of the supervisor's routine. If the employee is given ongoing feedback, then the annual appraisal should contain no surprises. It should be a review of what the supervisor and employee have discussed during the year.

If properly done, formal performance appraisals benefit both the organization and the employee. Organizations use performance appraisals as a basis for making important decisions concerning promotion, raises, terminations, and the like. Performance appraisals reward employees' good performance and inform them about how they can become more productive.

The major advantage of a formal system is that it provides a framework to help the supervisor systematically evaluate performance and communicate to the employees how they are doing. Formal appraisals can be an incentive to employees. They get positive feedback about their performance, and they know that the formal system provides documentation of their performance.

Much of the criticism of performance appraisals dwells on the fact that they often focus only on past accomplishments or deficiencies. Supervisors can overcome this criticism by emphasizing the developmental aspects of performance appraisal.

Appraisal forms may vary in format and approach, but they should allow supervisors to identify the outstanding aspects of the employee's work, specify performance areas that need improvement, and suggest ways to improve performance.

Supervisors should be consistent in applying the terms used to describe an employee's performance. Not all supervisors judge employees' performance accurately, and sometimes a supervisor can damage an employee's morale by giving lower ratings than the employee deserves. Additional perceptual errors include the leniency error, the halo and horns effects, and other personal biases.

When filling out the appraisal form, the supervisor should focus on the employee's accomplishments. The results should be described in terms of "how much," "how well," and "in what manner." Whatever the choice of appraisal form, it is important that every appraisal be made within the context of the employee's particular job and be based on the employee's total performance.

Although the appraisal meeting may be a trying situation, the entire employee performance appraisal system is of no use if this aspect is ignored or is carried out improperly. The supervisor should begin by stating that the overall purpose of the appraisal meeting is to let the employee know how he or she is doing. The supervisor should give positive strokes for good performance, emphasize strengths that the employee can build upon, and identify performance aspects that need improvement.

The meeting should be conducted shortly after the form is completed, and in private. How the supervisor conducts the meeting depends to a large extent on the employee's performance. Supervisors should direct criticisms to those areas that need correction or improvement. An employee performing at a substandard level must clearly understand that the deficiencies are serious and that substantial improvement is needed. An employee is more likely to agree with the appraisal when he or she understands the standards of performance and recognizes that the appraisal is free of bias.

The supervisor should emphasize that all employees in the same job are evaluated using the same standards and process. Supervisors may use a critical incident method for documenting employee performance that is very good or unsatisfactory. Employees should be given an opportunity to ask questions, and the supervisor should answer them honestly. The supervisor should anticipate questions, potential areas of disagreement, and difficult responses that may arise during the appraisal meeting.

The employee should clearly understand his or her evaluation. New objectives should be set and areas for improvement identified. Generally, the employee is asked to sign the appraisal form to prove that the meeting took place. Organizations should have an audit process to resolve conflicts arising from the appraisal.

Supervisors should fulfill the role of coach in the conduct of their daily activities. During the performance appraisal process, supervisors provide employees with information, instruction, and suggestions relating to their job assignments and performance.

Supervisors can use a coaching approach to prepare superior employees for greater responsibility as well as to improve the performance of all employees. Ongoing employee skill development is essential. Based on the performance appraisal, the coach develops a plan for improvement. Specific improvement goals are set. The employee receives instruction and is given an opportunity to practice. The coach provides feedback and encouragement.

Most employees want to improve and advance in the organization. Promotion from within is a widely practiced personnel policy that is beneficial to the organization and to the morale of employees. Supervisors know their employees' strengths and abilities; they do not know as much about individuals hired from the outside. If employees know that they have a good chance of advancement, they will have an incentive to improve their job performance. In short, promotion from within rewards employees for their good performance and serves notice to other employees that good performance will lead to advancement.

Strict adherence to a promotion-from-within policy would not be sensible. If internal employees have not received the necessary training, an external candidate may be preferred. Sometimes, an outsider may be needed to inject new and different ideas. However, organizations should promote from within whenever possible.

Since promotions should serve as an incentive for employees to perform better, it is generally believed that employees who have the best performance records should be promoted. Nevertheless, seniority still serves as a basis for many promotions. Seniority is easily understood and withstands charges of favoritism and discrimination. However, a promotional system based solely on seniority removes the incentive for junior employees who want to advance. Although it is difficult to specify exactly what should be the basis for employee promotion, there should be appropriate consideration of ability and merit on the one hand and length of service on the other.

The supervisor's staffing function includes making certain that employees of a department are properly compensated. Many compensation considerations are not within the direct domain of a supervisor.

Tangible monetary rewards serve, in part, to meet the needs of employees who perform at an outstanding level. Supervisors must become aware of other compensation arrangements that may better meet their employees' needs. Pay for performance, skill-based pay, suggestion systems, and other benefit plans could be considered.

Since supervisory responsibility and authority are limited in these areas, supervisors should work closely with the human resources staff to maintain equitable compensation offerings and to ensure that departmental employees are informed and fairly treated in regard to benefits and any bonus plans that may be available.

KEY TERMS

Performance appraisal (page 407)
Peer evaluation (page 410)
360-degree evaluation (page 411)
Leniency error (page 417)
Performance standards (page 420)
Coaching (page 426)
Seniority (page 429)

Merit (page 430)
Ability (page 430)
Piecework (page 433)
Pay for performance (page 433)
Gain-sharing plans (page 433)
Skill-based pay (page 434)

QUESTIONS FOR DISCUSSION

1. What are the purposes of a performance appraisal system? Do the purposes outweigh the criticisms?
2. What are the benefits of using peer ratings, 360-degree evaluations, and the employee self-rating approach?

3. What are some of the factors that most frequently are included on employee performance appraisal forms? Why should most performance appraisal forms include space for supervisors to write comments about the employee being evaluated?

4. How should the college or university deal with a professor who constantly grades students much below their deserved rating? Gives higher grades than they deserve?

5. Outline the major aspects of conducting an appraisal meeting. What are some of the major difficulties associated with this meeting?

6. What can a supervisor do to feel more comfortable in conducting performance appraisals?

7. Outline a coaching program for an employee who exhibits unsatisfactory behaviors. How will your program meet the needs of both the organization and the employee?

8. Why do some firms try to maintain a policy of promotion from within whenever feasible? Do most firms adhere strictly to this policy? Why or why not?

9. Discuss and evaluate the issues related to promotion based on seniority on the one hand and merit and ability on the other. Are there clear guidelines that a supervisor can use to ensure a workable balance between these criteria?

10. What are the reasons for the success of employee incentive plans? For their failure?

SKILLS APPLICATIONS

Skills Application 13-1: Effective Guidelines for Appraisal

1. Select a person who is currently employed and ask him or her the following questions:
   a. Briefly describe the circumstances under which a performance appraisal had positive effects on your morale or development.
   b. If you were a supervisor and had to conduct a performance appraisal of your employees, what one thing would you do to ensure that the appraisal has a positive impact on employee morale or development?

2. Compare your findings with those of several classmates. To what extent are your findings comparable?

Skills Application 13-2: Role-Play Exercise

1. Form into groups of three, with one person acting as the employee, a second as the supervisor, and the third as observer. The supervisor will evaluate the employee using the information contained in one of the situations listed below. The supervisor role will require you to use your imagination in providing feedback. It is suggested that you review the "check-the-box" appraisal form in Figure 13-3.

   The observer will observe the interview relationship using the Observer Recording Form (provided by your instructor) and provide feedback on the effectiveness of the interview process. At the end of each interview, the observer provides feedback on the effectiveness/ineffectiveness of the interview.

2. Rotate roles so that every person is in each of the three roles. Continue the exercise by switching roles until all have played each of the roles.

   Situation A: "Nowhere to Go." Alyn Adams is a very good/above-average performer with high potential for advancement. He is the produce department team leader for Sanders Supermarkets and was promoted to his current position three years ago. He won a supervisory management contest sponsored by the local college last summer. He has worked for Sanders for the past seven years. His strengths lie in personal efficiency, job knowledge, and dependability. On occasion, he is "too customer service oriented," for example, he makes substitutions of more expensive produce for a lesser price. You approach the interview knowing the following circumstances:

a. There are roadblocks ahead for the employee such that his opportunity for advancement is limited for the forseeable future.

b. There are several opportunities for advancement in the organization, but they require relocation or rotating shift work (both undesirable alternatives from the employee's perspective).

Situation B: "The Expert." Tony Becker had been a regional supervisor for Sanders Supermarkets. When the organization consolidated operations, Tony was demoted and transferred to an assistant's position at the Pridemore location. Tony has been with Sanders for over 30 years and is much older than his supervisor. Tony shows up for work early and stays late. Tony's knowledge of the supermarket industry is second to none. However, he is unwilling to share it with anyone. He is very angry about the demotion. In general, he is very difficult to work with. He is belligerent toward younger employees, resents your authority, and insists on doing things "Tony's way." He refers to the younger female employees and customers as "honey." You have constantly counseled Tony on his inappropriate behaviors and he reminds you that he started at Sanders before you were weaned. Some employees try to avoid him. Several have threatened to quit unless he changes his ways. Tony has made some serious errors in scheduling of deliveries. You approach the interview knowing the following circumstances:

a. Tony's performance is unsatisfactory on most factors.

b. You question whether he should be retained as an employee. Your perspective is clouded because you know that your immediate supervisor trained under Tony and has said on several occasions that Tony taught him everything he knows and that if Tony hadn't helped him back then, he wouldn't have such a great job.

Situation C: "Miss Cue." Mary Cue has an entry-level data processing position at Sanders Supermarkets. She has been on the job for six months and is generally performing at "less than a satisfactory level." She has an attendance problem. She usually misses work once every two weeks—either on a Monday or Friday. On five occasions, something happened that required her to leave work early to check on her elderly parents. She has a tendency to rush work, thus causing errors in payment, shipments, and the like. She is a great storyteller and she often can be found in other parts of the building describing her "late dates" to a very interested audience. You sent her to Windows 98 and WordPerfect Suite 2000 classes but she has trouble progressing beyond the basics of data entry. Her attention span is limited and she does not readily grasp new concepts. You approach the interview knowing the following circumstances:

a. Mary is a member of a "protected class."

b. Mary believes that she is underpaid for the work she is expected to do.

Source: The format for this role-play exercise was adapted from Don Harvey and Robert Bruce Bowin, *Human Resource Management: An Experiential Approach* (Upper Saddle River, N.J.: Prentice-Hall, 1996), p. 151. The situations were developed by Professor Leonard for use in this edition. The Observer Rating Form in the *Instructor's Manual* may be reproduced for use with Skills Application 13-2 only.

Skills Application 13-3: What Is the Right Way to Pay (Grade) Students?

Most colleges and university professors grade students based on their individual performance over the course of the term. Imagine the following situation.

The first day of a new term, you find yourself in Professor Jones' management class. Professor Jones, in order to provide her students a broader perspective of teamwork and encourage collaborative efforts, announces that she has decided to restructure the management class for the forthcoming term. She contends that as organizations restructure in favor of work teams, her students' ability to work effectively in teams is of vital importance. Groups of four to five students (randomly selected) will be given a "collaborative writing project"—this twenty-page paper complete with an exhaustive literature review will be due in six weeks and will constitute 50 percent of the course grade.

Your grade (total compensation) for the term will be computed from a base grade for performing individual core duties (pay for your individual performance on the midterm and final exam) and team grade (incentive pay for group achievement on the term paper). Professor Jones also believes in the notion of "share and share alike." Thus, each team member will receive the same grade on the term paper.

1. What are the advantages of Professor Jones' plan for your class? Are there any disadvantages to her plan?
2. Explain how a team-based compensation system might be developed for a college class.
3. Make a list of the different ways to evaluate student performance. What are the advantages and disadvantages of each?
4. Compare your responses with those of other students. What common views do you have? What are areas of difference? Discuss the basis for your differences.

Skills Application 13-4: 360-Degree Feedback

Many of today's companies are moving toward a 360-degree feedback process. Visit www.360-degreefeedback.com to learn more about this method of performance evaluation.

INTERNET ACTIVITY

1. What are the benefits of 360-degree feedback?
2. What steps are key in ensuring that the 360-degree feedback process is successful?
3. The 360-degree feedback is particularly valuable in a team environment. What unique issues do supervisors face when measuring the performance of a team? Make a list of issues and ways you might address these concerns. Visit the Zigon Performance Group (www.zigonperf.com) and check out their Performance Measurement Resources and Articles by Jack Zigon for helpful information.

SKILL DEVELOPMENT VIDEO

SKILL DEVELOPMENT MODULE 13-1: COACHING AND PERFORMANCE APPRAISAL

This video segment features Ken Foley, a production development specialist with Carson Products, as he tries to handle a situation with Jennifer Swanson, a systems designer, who comes to him for advice and guidance.

Questions for Discussion: The Ineffective Version

1. Discuss Ken Foley's coaching pitfalls.
2. In some organizations employees get to rate their supervisors. If you were Jennifer Swanson, how would you rate Ken Foley as a supervisor? Why?
3. How do you think Jennifer Swanson will continue to perform on the job? More effectively or less? Why?
4. If you were Ken Foley, what would you do to be more effective in helping Jennifer Swanson with her concerns?

Questions for Discussion: The More Effective Version

1. Discuss Ken Foley's appraisal and coaching technique.
2. How would you rate Ken Foley's performance as a supervisor? Illustrate with specific examples to support your rating.
3. If you were Ken Foley, what would you do to be even more effective in helping Jennifer Swanson with her concerns?
4. Why should Ken Foley strive to provide his employees with daily feedback on performance?

ENDNOTES

1. Many employees dislike performance reviews. See Michael Barrier, "Reviewing the Annual Review," *Nation's Business* (September 1998), pp. 32–34; Timothy D. Schellhardt, "Annual Agony: It's Time to Evaluate Your Work, and All Involved Are Groaning," *The Wall Street Journal* (November 19, 1996), pp. A1, A5; and Donna L. M. Mitchell and Esther Green, "Teaching Managers to Appraise Performances," *Nursing Management* (March 1996), pp. 48C–D.

   For an expanded discussion of performance appraisal, see Arthur W. Sherman, Jr., George W. Bolander, and Scott A. Snell, *Managing Human Resources* (11th ed.; Cincinnati: South-Western Publishing Co., 1998), Chapter 8; Carol A. L. Dannhauser, "How'm I Doing? Performance Reviews Don't Have to Be Painful," *Working Women* (December/January 1999), p. 38; Peter Barnes, "Making Appraisal Work in the New Millennium," *Management Services* (July 1997), pp. 14–16; Diane Arthur, "Face-to-Face with the Employee," *HR Focus* (March 1996), pp. 17–18; Polly A. Phipps, "Due-Process Performance Appraisals," *Monthly Labor Review* (March 1996), p. 34; John F. Milliman et al., "Companies Evaluate Employees from All Perspectives," *Personnel Journal* (November 1994), pp. 99–104; and Robert D. Bretz, Jr., George T. Milkovich, and Walter Read, "The Current State of Performance Appraisal Research and Practice: Concerns, Directions, and Implications," *Journal of Management* (June 1992), pp. 321–352.

2. For a discussion of peer appraisals, see "Multi-Rater Feedback and Performance Evaluation Programs Do Not Mix," *Supervision* (March 1998), p. 25; Daniel Kanouse, "Why Multi-Rater Feedback Systems Fail," *HRFocus* (January 1998), p. 3; David A. Waldman, "Predictors of Employee Preferences for Multirater and Group-Based Performance Appraisal," *Group & Organizational Management* (June 1997), pp. 264–287; Carol W. Timmreck and David W. Bracken, "MultiSource Feedback: A Study of Its Use in Decision Making," *Employment Relations Today* (Spring 1997), pp. 21–27; and Martin L. Ramsey and Howard Lehto, "The Power of Peer Review," *Training & Development* (July 1994), pp. 38–41. Also see Irene Buhalo, "You Sign My Report Card—I'll Sign Yours," *Personnel* (May 1991), p. 23; and G. M. McEvoy, P. F. Buller, and S. R. Roghaar, "A Jury of One's Peers," *Personnel Administrator* (May 1988), pp. 94–98.

3. John Welch as quoted in Stratford Sherman, "A Master Class in Radical Change," *Fortune* (December 13, 1993), p. 83. For an update, see A. Blanton Godfrey, "Black-Belt Careers: A New Training Model Extracts Talent from Within the Organization," *Quality Digest* (November 1999), p. 20; Hal Lancaster,

"Work Week," *The Wall Street Journal* (September 14, 1999), p. B1; and Matt Murray, "Can House That Jack Built Stand When He Goes? Sure, Welch Says," *The Wall Street Journal* (April 13, 2000), pp. A1, A8.

4. 360-degree appraisals are controversial. Dennis Coates says, "You can use 360-degree feedback for performance management, but not for performance appraisal. Why not? Because it undermines trust." (see Coates, "Don't Tie 360 Feedback to Pay." *Training* (September 1998), pp. 58–78. For an extended discussion of the pros and cons of 360-degree appraisals, see David A. Waldman and David E. Bowen, "The Acceptability of 360 Degree Appraisals: A Customer-Supplier Relationship Perspective," *Human Resource Management* (Summer 1998), pp. 117–129; Scott Wimer and Kenneth M. Nowack, "13 Common Mistakes Using 360-Degree Feedback," *Training & Development Journal* (May 1998), pp. 69+; Richard Lepsinger and Anntoinette D. Lucia, "360° Feedback and Performance Appraisal," *Training* (September 1997), pp. 62–70; Sabrina Salam, Jonathon F. Cox, and Henry P. Sims, Jr., "In the Eye of the Beholder: How Leadership Relates to 360-Degree Performance Ratings," *Group & Organizational Management* (June 1997), pp. 185–209; Stephanie Gruner, "Feedback from Everyone," *Inc.* (February 1997), pp. 102–103; Manual London and Richard W. Beatty, "360-Degree Feedback as a Competitive Advantage, *Human Resource Management* (Fall 1994), pp. 353–373; Brian O'Reilly, "360 Feedback Can Change Your Life," *Fortune* (October 17, 1994), p. 96; and Kenneth M. Nowack, "360-Degree Feedback: The Whole Story," *Training & Development* (January 1993), pp. 69–72.

5. Patricia J. Hewitt, "The Rating Game," *Incentive* (August 1993), pp. 39–41. Also see Michael Rigg, "Reasons for Removing Employee Evaluations from Management Control," *Industrial Engineering* (August 1992), p. 17.

6. Douglas McGregor, "An Uneasy Look at Performance Appraisal," *Harvard Business Review* (September–October 1972), pp. 133–134. For an expanded discussion on how supervisors can make more effective use of performance appraisals, see Charles N. Painter, "Ten Steps for Improved Appraisals," *Supervision* (June 1999), pp. 11–13. See also James McAlister, "Appraisal Interviews: Do's and Don'ts," *Supervisory Management* (April 1993), p. 12; and James Goodale, "Seven Ways to Improve Performance Appraisals," *HR Magazine* (May 1993), pp. 77–80.

7. There are many different types of performance appraisal formats. Among larger organizations, most use rating scales like that depicted in Figure 13-3. Other widely used forms include essays and MBO (see Chapter 6 for a discussion of comparing results against objectives). For a more detailed listing of formats, see Wayne F. Cascio, *Managing Human Resources* (Burr Ridge, IL: Irwin/McGraw-Hill, 1998), chapter 8; Arthur Sherman, George Bolander, and Scott Snell, *Managing Human Resources* (Cincinnati, OH: South-Western College Publishing, 1998), chapter 8; and Cynthia Fisher, Lyle F. Schoenfeldt, and James B. Shaw, *Human Resource Management* (Boston: Houghton Mifflin Company, 1999), chapter 11.

8. Excerpted and adapted from George V. Hulme, "Using Software for Worker Reviews," *Nation's Business* (September 1998), pp. 35–36. At the time of publication, PerformanceNow! can be obtained from KnowledgePoint in Pataluma, CA (1-800-727-1133) and Employee Appraiser 3.0 from Austin-Hayne Corp. (1-800-809-9920). Current issues of personnel and human resources management journals will periodically carry advertisements for other computerized software products. Check the following Web site for information on another product: www.avantos.com.

9. Barbara Holmes, "The Lenient Evaluator's Hurting Your Organization," *HR Magazine* (June 1993), pp. 75–77.

10. One of the supervisor's important roles is to coach—that is, help employees learn how to become better employees. For an enlightening discussion on the supervisor's role as a coach, see Clinton O. Longenecker and Gary Pinkel, "Coaching to Win at Work," *Manage* (February 1997), pp. 19–21; Don Shula and Ken Blanchard, *Everyone's A Coach* (New York: Harper Business, 1995); Jeremy Lebediker, "The Supervisor's Role as Coach: 4 Essential Models for Setting Performance Expectations," *Supervision* (December 1995), pp. 14–16; and Bill Halson, "Teaching Supervisors to Coach," *Personnel Management* (March 1990), pp. 36–53. Also see Marianne Minor, *Coaching for Development* (Menlo Park, CA: Crisp Publications, Inc., 1995). This book is self-instructional and forces the reader to get involved through a variety of exercises and problems.

11. In a 1997 survey of Fortune 1000 companies, benefits advisory firm Buck Consultants, Inc., reported that 70 percent of respondents were using, or were in the process of implementing, alternative pay strategies. These alternative compensation plans include skill and competency-based pay, group and team pay incentives, gain-sharing, lump-sum merit increases and broad-banding. There findings sup-

ported those reported by Hewitt Associates who reported that 72 percent of companies offer some type of variable pay. See Joanne Summer, "The Incentive Comp Quandary," *Business Finance* (December 1998), pp. 83–86. Also see Jeffrey Pfeffer, "Six Dangerous Myths About Pay," *Harvard Business Review* (May/June 1998), pp. 108–119; and Don Barksdale, "Leading Employees Through the Variable Pay Jungle," *HRMagazine* (July 1998), pp. 110–118. For additional information on compensation, see Patricia K. Zingheim, *Pay People Right* (San Francisco: Jossey-Bass, 2000); Edward E. Lawler III, *Rewarding Excellence* (San Francisco: Jossey-Bass, 2000); Glenn Parker, Jerry McAdams, and David Zielinski, *Rewarding Teams: Lessons from the Trenches* (San Francisco: Jossey-Bass, 2000); Milton L. Rock and Lance A. Berger, *The Compensation Handbook* (Columbus, OH: McGraw-Hill, 1998); and Jerry S. Rosenbloom, *The Handbook of Employee Benefits* (Columbus, OH: McGraw-Hill, 1999).

12. "Lincoln Electric Posts Record Earnings for 1998," *PRNewswire* (February 3, 1999) and Interview by one of the authors with Charlotte Filby, Lincoln's Corporate Relations Department (December 20, 1999).

13. For an expanded discussion of skill-based pay, see George E. Ledford, Jr., "Three Case Studies on Skill-Based Pay: An Overview," *Compensation Review* (March/April 1991), pp. 11–23; Richard L. Bunning, "Models for Skill-Based Plans," *HR Magazine* (February 1991), pp. 62–64; and Earl Ingram II, "Compensation: The Advantage of Knowledge-Based Pay," *Personnel Journal* (April 1990), p. 138.

14. Nina Gupta, Timothy P. Schweizer, and Douglas Jenkins, Jr., "Pay-for-Knowledge Compensation Plans: Hypotheses and Survey Results," *Monthly Labor Review* (October 1987), pp. 40–43.

15. R. Bradley Hill, "How to Design a Pay-For-Skills-Used Program," *Journal of Compensation and Benefits* (September/October 1993), pp. 32–38.

16. Pamela Bloch-Flynn and Kenneth Vlach, "Employee Awareness Paves the Way for Quality," *HR Magazine* (July 1994), p. 78; and John Allen, "Suggestion Systems and Problem-Solving: One and the Same," *Quality Circles Journal* (March 1987), pp. 2–5.

17. Extracted from Rebecca Ganzel, "What's Wrong With Pay for Performance?" *Training* (December 1998), pp. 34–40. After a bitter three-week strike in August 1998, the union did gain some say. Employee participation in the incentive program is voluntary.

18. Joanne Summer, "The Incentive Comp Quandary," *Business Finance* (December 1998), pp. 83–86.

19. W. H. Weiss, "Communication: Key to Successful Supervision," *Supervision* (September 1998), pp. 12–14.

Case

4-1

AN ETHICAL SELECTION DILEMMA

Charles Holmes is a supervisor in charge of pet foods production for a food processing firm located in the southeastern United States. In Holmes's earlier years at the company plant, he had relied on a fellow supervisor, Ellis Duvall, for assistance in learning many aspects of production and quality control and in meeting deadlines. Duvall subsequently became plant manager, and he now was Holmes's immediate boss.

Holmes was facing a difficult dilemma. Ellis Duvall had called, saying that his nephew, Rob Ling, had just graduated from college and was looking for a job. Duvall knew that Holmes's department had an opening for a quality control inspector. Holmes interviewed Rob Ling and found him to be a reasonably intelligent young man, but Ling had absolutely no experience to do the kind of work that Holmes required in an important area. To complicate the matter further, Holmes had found out that Rob Ling's father was a buyer for a large food store chain that was a major customer of the company.

Prior to meeting with Ling, Holmes had interviewed several applicants for the position. Three of the applicants were far more qualified than Rob Ling. The best qualified individual was Susan Wilson, who had excellent credentials and several years of experience as a quality control inspector. Holmes had almost hired Wilson on the spot, and now he wished he had.

Holmes decided to talk with Arleen Hunter, the human resources manager, about his dilemma. Hunter was not very helpful, stating that "I've seen jobs given as favors over and over again; you have to make up your own mind on this one. However, I would point out that your boss, Ellis Duvall, is on the management review committee, which currently is studying different ways of reducing supervisory and other managerial personnel. I think you've got a difficult choice to make."

As Charles Holmes left Arleen Hunter's office, he primarily wondered whether his job would be eliminated if he failed to hire Rob Ling.

Questions for Discussion

1. Could Charles Holmes lose his job by refusing to hire Rob Ling? Discuss.
2. What alternatives does Holmes have if he doesn't hire Ling?
3. Is it possible to do what's right for the company and what's right for yourself at the same time?

4. If Ling is hired and Susan Wilson discovers what has happened, could she file sex discrimination charges? What is the likelihood that she would win a sex discrimination case?

Case
4-2

HARRY BROWN'S DELICATE CHOICE

Harry Brown is the technical services supervisor for a regional accounting firm. The firm professes to be an equal opportunity employer. Brown coordinates and directs the job activities of six male staff members who provide technical assistance and advice to other departments within the firm and to outside clients. In a world seemingly overpopulated with consultants, the firm enjoys an excellent reputation for the quality of its advice.

The six men are bright, white, and mostly in their thirties. They were all hired immediately upon graduation from college; most have MBAs. Brown had created a working environment that made the group a "fun place" to work. Mutual trust and respect coupled with a high degree of caring, sharing, and celebrating successes marked the relationships between team members.

Shelly Klone, a 41-year-old single parent of two children, graduated in May from the local university. She was an honor student, president of the collegiate accounting society, and deemed by her fellow students as "most likely to succeed." However, because of her parental responsibilities, she was unable to engage in the school's accounting co-op or internship programs. She worked in the university bursar's office as a work-study student so that she could make use of the university's child-care services. She had many initial interviews through the campus placement office but no second interviews. Over a period of time, it seemed to her that accounting firms were unwilling to take on the challenge of hiring an older, mature graduate. Shelly had talked to several professors who confidentially told her that her chances were slim of receiving an offer comparable to offers made to classmates who were younger and who had lower grades.

Harry Brown was aware that he needed to hire another accountant who would be the best possible person to join his team. However, it had bothered him since he became supervisor several years ago that there had been an increasing number of older, single parents seeking entry-level accounting positions. He personally had no qualms about hiring a more mature person. His immediate manager, a partner of the firm, felt very strongly about the subject, saying, "I don't want us hiring any of those older people for entry-level accounting positions. They think they know everything. Besides, they'll never accrue the years of service to qualify for partner. My theory of hiring is to bring in the best young college graduates, work them to death over the first 6 to 10 years, and see where the cream rises to the top."

Questions for Discussion

1. What if Shelly Klone applied for a position with this firm and Harry Brown felt that Shelly Klone was the best candidate for the position he had? (Her recommendations from a reputable professor indicated that her accounting and analytical skills were "head and shoulders" above those of other recent graduates.) What should Brown do?

2. If Brown had full and final authority for the hiring decision, what should he do?

3. Describe what factors could affect Brown's final decision. Consider the legal implications as well as his boss's preferences.

4. If you were Harry Brown, what would you do, and why?

5. (*Optional*) Use the Internet to find reports, articles, and areas related to the problems faced by older workers in securing entry or reentry into the workforce. Write a brief report summarizing your findings as related to the circumstances described in this case. In particular, address the reasons why some individuals (e.g., Harry Brown's manager) hold such views about older people, and how these views can be changed.

INTERNET ACTIVITY

Case

4–3

FROM PART TIME TO FULL TIME?

Alice Toomer is supervisor of the clerical staff in the medical records department of a community hospital. She has the authority to hire and fire for her department, and is not affected by a union contract since the hospital has no union. She has seven employees working for her full time. Whenever a regular clerical employee does not show up, she calls Benton Temporary Services. Normally, she requests Helen Drew, who works as a relief person on an "as-needed basis." Drew expressed a preference for part-time work and liked the opportunity the hospital provided.

Toomer observed that whenever Drew came in to help out there seemed to be friction between the "temp" and the full-time employees. Apparently, the full-time employees did not like Drew's work habits. She had the ability to turn out ten hours of work in eight. Drew was older with college- and high-school-aged children. Most of the full-timers were young unmarried people in their early twenties. Toomer did not know whose fault it was, but there were numerous complaints about Drew from the other employees. Most common among these were that she didn't socialize with them during breaks or lunch hour, and that she didn't respond in a timely manner to requests for assistance. Toomer, however, was certain of the high quality of Drew's work and knew that everything she assigned her was done in a professional and timely manner.

Early one afternoon, Drew told Toomer that she would like to work full time since her youngest child would be in college next year and she could use the extra income.

This request came as something of a surprise and a problem to Toomer. Only the previous day Jody Williams had announced that she would be leaving to move to Dallas with her husband. Williams would be leaving within the next 10 days. Alice Toomer pondered whether she should offer this job to Drew. Of course, Drew would be very pleased to get this position, and it appeared that she knew it would be open. But Toomer was concerned about the reaction of the other employees in the department.

Questions for Discussion

1. When considering hiring a full-time employee, which is more important: (a) the work performance of the potential employee or (b) the way the individual will fit in with other employees in the department? Why is there seldom a clear answer to this question?
2. Did Toomer's failure to investigate the prior situation with Helen Drew and the other employees contribute to the current problem? Discuss.
3. Alice Toomer has to make an important decision. Should she seek advice of employees in the department and the human resources staff, or is this a decision she must make on her own? What should she do? Consider alternatives.

Case

4–4

THE STRESS INTERVIEW APPROACH

Bradley Distributors, Inc., employs 500 employees in its warehouse and retail outlets. Sterling Durbin, the director of human resources, has held this position for the past 17 years. He prides himself on his ability to conduct interviews effectively. When Patricia Sutton was hired as a new assistant human resources manager, Durbin took great pleasure in "breaking in" this recent college graduate on the practical aspects of effective interviewing.

"I can size anyone up in 10 minutes or less in an interview. My record shows how good I am at this, and I'll give you a few tips," Durbin told his new assistant. "We don't use written tests anymore because of EEOC hassles with them. It's just as well, because I didn't put much faith in what those tests showed anyway. As for personal interviews, we use several interviewers for important positions to get the effect of a group interview. All of the interviewers ask the questions that they feel are important, and they report to me anything outstanding or particularly negative that turns up. My interview with a prospective employee is the one that usually counts the most, though. I'm looking for 'hard drivers' and people who I think will succeed around here. In just a few minutes, I can tell by the way they look at me, the kind of clothes they wear, and their general confidence in themselves whether or not they're likely to be good employees. For example, you can tell a lot about a man by the kind of shoes he wears and how well they are polished. Also, I put a lot of stock in whether or not the applicants have finished the education they began, whether it's high school, junior college, or university. It shows that they can finish things and can stick to their tasks."

Durbin continued, "The best technique I've found to separate the poor applicants from those with real promise is to ask them how they would handle the following situation. I give them two alternatives to stop employees from arguing constantly with each other. First, the employees could be told either to work it out among themselves or to get a transfer out of the department. Second, the supervisor could sit down with the employees and work out the difficulties together. Whichever approach the applicant picks, I tell them that they are wrong. If they select the first method, I tell them that their job is to develop and help employees to perform better. If they select the second, I tell them they have more important things to do than to work out personal problems between employees. By doing this, I see how applicants handle stress and find out what they're made of. Good potential employees will stick by their guns and give me some good reasons why their approach should be followed. With all this information, I can usually make a good decision in a pretty short time. I've found that I am seldom wrong."

Questions for Discussion

1. Evaluate Sterling Durbin's interview techniques. What are the strengths and weaknesses of Durbin's system?
2. Is it possible to do an adequate job of interviewing in so short a time? Discuss.
3. How valid is the stress aspect of the interview?
4. What recommendations, if any, would you make to Durbin in regard to his interviewing?
5. What recommendations, if any, would you make to the new assistant, Patricia Sutton, concerning whether or not she should adopt the same interviewing approach as that of her supervisor?

Case

4-5

SANDERS SUPERMARKETS STORE #21: ORIENTATION OF A NEW EMPLOYEE

Max Brown was one of the most promising young applicants Nancy Brewer had interviewed and hired in months. As the employment manager of Sanders Supermarkets, she had instructed him on company policies, pay periods, rate of pay, and so forth, and had given him information about the union. He then left with his referral slip to report to Store #21, located in a suburban shopping center.

Before Brown went to his new job, he stopped at his favorite clothing store and bought new white shirts to conform with the company dress code described by Brewer. He then went to the barber shop for a haircut, his first since graduating from high school several months ago.

Upon arriving at Store #21, Brown introduced himself to Carl Dressel, the store supervisor. Dressel then told Brown to go over to aisle 3 and tell Sean Kelly, the head stock clerk, that he was to work with him. Brown walked into aisle 3, but no one was there. Not knowing what to do next, he just waited for someone to show up. About 20 minutes later, Kelly came into the aisle with a stock truck full of cases. Brown introduced himself and said, "Mr. Dressel told me to come and work with Sean Kelly. Is that you?"

"Yeah," said Kelly, "I was just going to lunch. Here's my case cutter and stock list. You can figure it out. I'll see you in 30 minutes or so."

Kelly then left the aisle with Max Brown standing there rather confused. "Some training program," he thought to himself. Nancy Brewer had said that there would be lockers in the store for his personal items, but he wondered where they were. Brewer had also told him about punching a time card, so he wondered where the time cards were. Since Kelly had an apron on to protect his clothes, Brown tried to figure out where he could get one, too. He thought he might look in the back room to see whether the answers to some of his questions might be back there. Walking into the back room, he introduced himself to a young woman who said that she was Evita Chavez, one of the store's produce department clerks. Brown asked her whether she knew where he could hang his coat, get a time card, and find an apron. Chavez responded, "For the most part, we just throw our coats on top of the overstock; the aprons are in the office, and so are the time cards."

"At last," thought Brown. "Now I'm getting someplace." On his way to the office, he saw several stock clerks working in aisle 1. He had seen four stock clerks so far, and only one wore a tie. Two had on plaid shirts, and the other had hair at least three inches below the collar. "I don't understand why Nancy Brewer was worried about the way I looked," he thought.

Finally, Brown found an apron and a time card. To find the time clock, he went toward the back room again and asked one of the meat cutters where the time clock was. He was given directions to go through the meat department to the other side of the store. He went through the door he was told to go through, which had a sign on it saying "Authorized Personnel Only." He was worried that he might not be an "authorized" person. He finally found the time clock, and, with a little difficulty, he figured out how to clock in. This done, he hurried back to aisle 3, where Carl Dressel stood waiting for him. "Where the hell have you been?" asked Dressel. "And where is Kelly?"

Brown explained that Kelly had gone to lunch and that he himself had been looking for an apron, the time clock, and a place to hang his coat. "You might as well learn right away that your job is putting up the loads of stock—and fast! I don't want to hear any more excuses. Now get to work," said Dressel.

As Brown started to open the top of the first box of cases, he thought to himself, "The only thing I know for sure right now is that Nancy Brewer has never worked in this store!"

Questions for Discussion

1. Identify and discuss several places where Max Brown's experiences in Store #21 could have been improved by proper orientation.
2. Although Carl Dressel's approach is certainly lacking, could some of the blame for Brown's poor orientation be attributed to Nancy Brewer? Why or why not? Discuss.
3. Outline a checklist or approach for orienting new employees in this type of work environment.

Case

4–6

PERSONAL HYGIENE

Armed with her two-year degree in hospitality management, Mary Johnson was hired as an administrative manager at Olympic Banquets and Catering, a dining and catering establishment. Her main duties were to assist the supervisors and the restaurant managers in reservations, private catering functions, and general activities as assigned.

Johnson had been employed for about six weeks when John Moore was hired to work in the food preparation area. Moore had been hired by Sue Shelby, the food preparation department supervisor, without even being formally interviewed. This was because Moore had been given a very high recommendation by Louise Knight, the director of the "Culinary Arts" program at the same school that Mary Johnson had attended. Knight had all of her students involved in a number of projects to enhance their learning experiences. If someone came out of Knight's program, one could be certain they had all the necessary skills to perform. Her enthusiastic "stamp of approval" that she gave concerning John Moore in a telephone conversation with Sue Shelby was sufficient for Shelby to make a job offer to Moore on the telephone.

John Moore's job training was to be under the guidance of Sue Shelby. During the first day of Moore's training, Mary Johnson noticed that after just a short period of observing his work, Sue had sent Moore off to work on a particular food item, and later he was sent to "read up" on certain recipes. Mary assumed this meant that Moore had rapidly grasped the requirements of his new job.

However, just before closing that evening, Andrea Burke, another food preparer, approached Mary Johnson and said, "We've got to talk about John Moore." Since other members had left for the day and Johnson was responsible for closing, they moved into the restaurant manager's office. Obviously upset, Burke closed the door and said, "I know that maybe this isn't your job, but something needs to be done about that man. He has the most foul odor about him. It was difficult to be in the same room with him. A couple of times I needed his help with certain items for a catering project, and I could only tolerate being near him for a few seconds. I had to go outside to get a breath of fresh air. Sue Shelby told me to work with him tomorrow morning on the ABC recognition luncheon we're catering at noon. I tried to tell her but she was off to a meeting. You've got to do something!" Mary Johnson recognized that this was a problem for which she had not received previous lessons at school.

Questions for Discussion

1. Why is Andrea Burke's concern a legitimate one?
2. If John Moore's personal hygiene does not essentially affect his job skills, should "something be done" as Andrea suggested?
3. Should Mary Johnson approach John Moore directly? If so, how?
4. If you were Mary Johnson, how would you handle the situation?
5. Should any effort be expended to discuss this matter with Louise Knight? Why, or why not?

Case

4–7

DEVELOPMENT, OR DUMPING?

Tom Simmons, the vice president of sales and marketing for Industrial Solutions Corporation (ISC), was asked by Marian Sharp, the human resources manager, if he could utilize the skills of Melissa Rogers. Rogers was originally hired through a temporary agency to assist another department with a project. The project had been completed, and Rogers had received an excellent review from the project leader. Simmons talked to his colleagues about Rogers, and he decided to hire her as a marketing research assistant in the sales and marketing department. Rogers was intelligent, ambitious, and had a degree in education. After student teaching in an urban school system, Rogers decided that teaching was not for her. She was so close to completing her education degree that she decided to "stick it out," and she completed the last two semesters of her course work rather than switch to another academic major.

ISC's corporate headquarters recently relocated to Atlanta after nearly three decades in Illinois. For Tom Simmons, it was a fairly simple decision. If he wanted to keep his job, he had to move. Twenty-seven managers and service support staff moved to Atlanta. Several of Tom's employees remained at the Illinois facility or were offered severance packages or jobs in other ISC divisions. Tom had been commuting between Atlanta and Illinois since he wore several hats in the corporation. He hoped that Rogers would be able to assume responsibility for some routine projects and tasks, which would allow him to work on building the southeastern and offshore customer base and other managerial functions.

Melissa Rogers accepted the position as marketing research assistant with the understanding that Tom Simmons would provide her with on-the-job training for the newly created position. However, after three months in the position, Rogers realized that her on-the-job training typically consisted of periodic five-minute conversations with her boss. Simmons only averaged three days a week in the Atlanta office, and he rushed from one project to another. Consequently, Rogers' workload was determined by the next "hot project." "Just get it done!" was the accompanying instruction. For several days at a time, Rogers would have nothing to do, and none of the other employees were helpful. When Simmons would drop another "hot project" on her, she worked long hours to get it done, almost to the point of exhaustion. Then she might go for days with little or nothing to do. Rogers enjoyed the work and the pay was good, but she resented the lack of direction and guidance.

One day Melissa Rogers decided to pour out her feelings at a luncheon she had with Lori Dell, a friend who worked as an administrative assistant in another firm in Atlanta. Rogers explained to Dell, "I work a lot of overtime to get his pet projects done, and he never tells me anything. The outside sales people and consultants get all the glory, especially when it comes to rewards and advancement. I thought the better I performed, the more good things would happen. I feel betrayed and ignored." Dell listened sympathetically and said, "You need to manage up! Get Bob Nelson's book *1001 Ways to Reward Employees,* and put it on your boss's desk."

Rogers was seriously considering resigning her position and looking for work elsewhere. Although she did not get a copy of the book recommended by Dell, several days later, Melissa Rogers asked Tom Simmons' secretary to schedule a meeting with Simmons which would take at least an hour of his valuable time.

Questions for Discussion

1. What is the distinction between "development" and "dumping" in training of new employees?
2. How should Melissa Rogers prepare for her meeting with Tom Simmons?
3. How should she handle the sensitive issues? (Suggestion: Review the ideas presented in Chapter 10 on managing meetings with the boss, or "managing up.")
4. How do you think that Tom Simmons will respond to Melissa Rogers' concerns?
5. If Simmons really wants to retain Rogers' services, what should he do to minimize the likelihood of this scenario recurring in the future?

Case

4–8

FEELINGS OF DEMOTION

Frank Schneider, plant superintendent of Central Metalworks Co., had just been informed that a young man named Kirk Bell had been hired from outside the firm for the position of vice president of manufacturing, a job that Schneider very much wanted to have. Bell was in his early thirties and had an undergraduate engineering degree, a master's degree in business administration, and some previous working experience.

Schneider is 50 years old. He has been with the firm for almost 30 years, working his way up from the bottom. Starting as a machine operator, he progressed to the positions of leadman, foreman of various departments, assistant superintendent, and his current job, which he has held for seven years. He has no formal education beyond high school, but he has a well-recognized talent for machines, tools, and anything associated with manufacturing metal parts. He also has an excellent ability to work with people, and he is well liked and respected by the employees.

When the president of the company, R. D. Allen, told Schneider who his new boss would be, Schneider replied, "I don't know whether I can work for a young man 20 years my junior, especially one who never dirtied his hands fixing or running a piece of machinery. What can a fellow like this possibly know about running a manufacturing plant?"

A few days later, Allen met with Bell in his office. "Kirk," said Allen, "I think you may have a serious problem with Frank Schneider. He's a good man, but his feelings are hurt, and he thinks he's been demoted. What would you propose to do to win him over?"

Questions for Discussion

1. Why would the president of the company choose a young man with an engineering degree and a master's degree in business administration over Schneider, who for seven years has been plant superintendent? Was this a prudent choice?
2. Is Schneider being unreasonable in his attitude toward his new boss? Discuss.
3. How should Bell approach the situation with Schneider? Should Allen assist Bell in trying to win Schneider over and soothe his hurt feelings? Consider alternatives open to them.

Case

4–9

SANDERS SUPERMARKETS STORE #13: WHO SHOULD BE PROMOTED TO HEAD STOCK CLERK?

Amanda Frazier is the store supervisor for Store #13 of the Sanders Supermarkets. Early one morning Jerry Stiffelman, stock clerk, approached her.

STOCK CLERK: Amanda, I hear that Tim Stapleton was promoted to head stock clerk. Why didn't I get a chance at the promotion? I've been working here eight years, and he's only been here six. Doesn't seniority count as long as two people are equally qualified?

STORE SUPERVISOR: Jerry, you were considered for the job at one time, but now I don't feel that you are qualified to handle the job. So you were passed over.

STOCK CLERK: What do you mean, I'm not qualified? I've done the job several times in the past when other head stock clerks were on vacation. You've never told me before that I couldn't handle it. It was my understanding that I'd get the next promotion on the basis of my seniority. Now you are telling me that I don't have the ability to do what I've already done before.

STORE SUPERVISOR: Nevertheless, that's our decision.

STOCK CLERK: That may be your decision now, but you'll think differently when the union contacts you. (And with that, Jerry walked away.)

Amanda Frazier started to think about what Jerry Stiffelman had said and remembered certain facts that she would bring out if the union did get involved. She considered Stiffelman a satisfactory stock clerk but certainly not above average. She believed that Stiffelman lacked the ability and dependability to handle the job of head stock clerk. On several occasions when Stiffelman had relieved other head stock clerks, the store had experienced out-of-stocks as a result of his poor job of ordering. Twice Frazier had received telephone calls from the police on the nights that Stiffelman had closed up the store and had accidentally set off the burglar alarm. She further noted that Stiffelman was frequently absent from work. During the previous year, Stiffelman had been absent 18 days, offering illness as the reason for his absences.

Several days later, Frazier was confronted by her boss, Susan Kennedy. As district manager, Kennedy was responsible for seven Sanders stores. The following dialogue took place:

DISTRICT MANAGER: Amanda, we have a grievance filed by the union on behalf of Jerry Stiffelman. The union claims that we should let him have the chance to prove he can handle the job. How well has he done as a temporary head stock clerk?

STORE SUPERVISOR: Terrible, Susan. The police woke me up two times because Stiffelman bungled the burglar alarm, and we had numerous out-of-stocks from his ordering.

DISTRICT MANAGER: Why didn't you tell me about this before? Did you talk to Stiffelman about these things?

STORE SUPERVISOR: I thought I did tell you, Susan, didn't I? But I think I did talk to him about it for sure. Customers were driving me crazy because we were out of toilet paper. He caused me a lot of headaches.

DISTRICT MANAGER: Well, according to his personnel file, he has never been written up. And as far as I can see, by seniority he was in line for a promotion. In response to the union grievance, I told the human resources department that we'd consider giving the head stock clerk position to Stiffelman on the basis of his seniority over Tim Stapleton.

STORE SUPERVISOR: That's a big mistake, Susan, because Stiffelman cannot handle it. Besides all that, he is absent too often.

DISTRICT MANAGER: What do you mean, absent too often?

STORE SUPERVISOR: Over the past year he has been "sick" 18 days.

DISTRICT MANAGER: There's no mention of any sick pay granted in his file. Was he paid for sick leave?

STORE SUPERVISOR: Darned if I know. I don't have time to pay attention to all these paperwork details.

DISTRICT MANAGER: Okay, Amanda. I guess we've got a real problem. Take a look at this provision of the union contract. It says that in making promotions we must give preference to the most senior employee, provided merit and ability are equal. What do you think we should do? The union business agent told me that if we don't promote Jerry Stiffelman, the union will take this case all the way to arbitration.

STORE SUPERVISOR: I think we should take a stand and stick with our original decision. Stiffelman just doesn't deserve the promotion, and I'll have nothing but trouble if he becomes a head stock clerk.

Questions for Discussion

1. Outline arguments that the union is likely to make in processing its grievance on behalf of Jerry Stiffleman.
2. Outline the arguments that the management of Sanders Supermarkets would take in defending its decision to promote Stapleton over Stiffelman.
3. What should the store's management do? Consider alternatives.
4. If the management should decide to acquiesce to the union grievance and promote Jerry Stiffelman, what should it do to determine that Stiffelman can properly handle the head stock clerk's job? Consider alternatives.

Case
4–10

WHAT DO I SAY TO HIM?

Jane McGraw sat at her desk, preparing for an evaluation session with one of her employees. McGraw is the advertising director in the marketing department of a major retail department store chain. She supervises 14 employees in her unit. Several days ago, McGraw completed a performance appraisal form for Art Gross, a copyediting employee. She was now waiting for Gross to come to her office for his evaluation interview.

McGraw was concerned about what she should say to Gross regarding his evaluation. She expected that there would be problems, because she again had rated Gross as "average" on most of the categories on the appraisal form. Only on "attendance" and "relationships with other employees" had she rated him as being "above average."

McGraw believed that Gross had not performed at anything other than a general or average level in most of his work responsibilities. In reviewing last year's appraisal form, she recognized that this was the same level that she had appraised Gross at that time. During her interview with him last year, Gross had disagreed strongly with her evaluation, because he thought he should have been rated "above average" or "excellent" on most factors. McGraw had tried to explain to him at that time why she had rated Gross as "average" on most categories and that she felt these were proper ratings. He had responded that her evaluation was unfair and that he felt it was discriminatory as compared to other employees. McGraw denied this, and she let the evaluation form stand as she had developed it. Gross refused to sign the form, since he was quite upset about it.

Now another year had gone by. McGraw recognized that she really had not given Art Gross any specific guidance as to how to improve his job performance. She also recognized that she had had only several conversations with him during the past year, most of which were about certain job situations and did not relate specifically to his performance. McGraw recognized that she should have kept much better records and developed some specific examples to discuss with Gross. But pressures of business and the responsibilities of supervising a large group of employees had kept her from keeping good records.

Now she wondered what would happen this time, and what she should say to him. Jane McGraw was convinced in her own mind that Art Gross was at best an average employee who had not improved over the last year. As she was pondering what she should say, Gross entered her office.

Questions for Discussion

1. Identify the errors made by Jane McGraw that are apparent in this case.
2. Is it possible that Art Gross is a better employee than McGraw believes? Discuss.
3. If you were in Jane McGraw's situation at the end of the case, what would you say to Art Gross in explaining your evaluation of his performance?
4. Outline a series of steps for Jane McGraw to follow in the future to prevent this type of situation from happening again.

Case
4–11

AIDS PHOBIA

Mid-States Financial Services Company has a strict confidentiality policy regarding employee performance appraisals, salary levels, and other personnel matters. Morgan Dennis, a 45-year-old employee, had open heart surgery about six years ago, and he had had several health-related problems during the past year. Even so, his work performance had been exemplary. Three months ago, Dennis had a complete physical examination. The health-case provider filed claims directly to the insurance carrier with carbon copies to the human resources department of Mid-States. An oversight in the provider's office allowed a copy of the health diagnosis and findings to accompany the copy of the medical claim to the human resources department. The report indicated that Dennis was infected with the HIV virus but he did not have acute symptoms of AIDS.

Lena Ables, a human resources department benefits clerk, noted the medical evaluation report and filed it appropriately. She later shared her knowledge of Dennis's medical condition with two of her closest friends. They proceeded, "in confidence," to tell others.

Upon return from a weekly progress and problem meeting, Mike Smith, information processing team leader, found five of his team members waiting for him in his office. They proceeded to inform him that they would refuse to work with Dennis on any future project. They reminded him of the company's responsibility to provide a safe workplace for all employees. They wanted their work stations located in another area and to have all work reallocated so they did not have contact with Dennis. Mike Smith was highly regarded as a team leader, but this information hit him like a ton of bricks. He asked the employees to have patience while he investigated the situation. As the employees reluctantly returned to work, one stated, "AIDS kills you, you know."

Questions for Discussion

1. Do you believe the employees' concern was valid? Why or why not?
2. How should Mike Smith educate his team members regarding AIDS/HIV and the Americans with Disabilities Act (ADA)? (Refer to the discussion concerning ADA in Chapter 16 for general information about this law.)
3. Assume the employees refused to work with Dennis on an important project. How should Smith handle the conflict?
4. Assume that Morgan Dennis became aware that several team members were reluctant to work with him. How should Smith deal with this in order to maintain an effective team?
5. What should the organization do with Lena Ables?
6. (*Optional*). Use the Internet to find current information on AIDS/HIV and the Americans with Disabilities Act. Then write a brief report that summarizes your findings and citations of recent cases and rulings that are relevant and interesting. Note: At the time of publication of this text, www.usdoj.gov/crt/ada/hirreprt.txt was an excellent source concerning the U.S. Justice Department's enforcement efforts to protect the rights of people living with HIV/AIDS under ADA. Information on enforcing ADA also could be found at www.usdoj.gov/crt/ada/aprjun99.htm.

INTERNET ACTIVITY

Case

4-12

WHAT WILL IT TAKE TO BECOME A SUPERVISOR?

Nelson Financial Group has 41 insurance and mortgage loan offices located throughout the United States. Becky Sanchez had worked as application processing clerk at the home office for three years prior to being promoted to group leader. Group leaders at Nelson Group were working members of the team who had responsibility for assigning work, training new employees, and the like. In a recent conversation with her supervisor, John Townsend, Sanchez expressed an interest in being considered for a supervisory position in the future.

Nelson Group used the services of a psychological testing firm to profile each supervisory and managerial candidate. Townsend sent Becky Sanchez to the human resources department to make arrangements to have her profiled. About a week later, Becky Sanchez spent a day at the premises of Psychological Diagnostics, a local consulting firm. She was given a battery of assessment tests and was interviewed by two of this firm's psychologists. Two weeks later, the following report was sent to Louise Gibson, human resources manager for Nelson Group.

Summary Assessment Profile for Becky Sanchez

She has average problem-solving and reasoning ability. Although learning ability is average, repetition may still be an effective training method, particularly if the work is complicated and technical. Management can assign Ms. Sanchez to special projects that will help her improve her problem-solving and reasoning ability. Any effort she makes to increase reading speed or enhance her memory skills should be encouraged.

Ms. Sanchez has had very little exposure to business terminology. Her observational skills are weak. She also may have a short attention span. Her language skills are below average but she is bilingual. When working under pressure, she feels much more comfortable relying on her Spanish vocabulary. Ms. Sanchez likes working with mechanical devices; she has obtained a great deal of computer literacy and appears to be able to fix most mechanical problems. She appears to be consistent and honest, yet flexible enough to handle emergencies. She is a fair and reliable individual who could easily win the trust of her coworkers.

Ms. Sanchez is a reserved person who does not feel comfortable around people she does not know. At first, others may find her distant and detached. As they become better acquainted, they will see that she is a good listener who has difficulty expressing herself around strangers.

Ms. Sanchez is very competitive and is prepared to meet or beat any challenge. She has an intense desire to excel and takes pride in her accomplishments. She was the first female in her family to complete high school. She is efficient and works hard to achieve her goals. However, she is not a team player and is often reluctant to contribute to a group project. She wants her work to stand on its own merits. Relationships with coworkers may suffer because of her strong desire to win. Ms. Sanchez does not handle criticism or rejection well. She oftentimes becomes discouraged for short periods of time. Ms. Sanchez becomes remotivated when the "right" rewards are offered. She will take risks if the potential for personal gain and recognition are evident.

John Townsend and Louise Gibson reviewed Becky Sanchez's performance appraisal results and the psychological assessment profile. Gibson commented to Townsend that, "with proper coaching," Becky Sanchez could be prepared for a group leader or supervisory position.

Questions for Discussion

1. What should John Townsend do to assist Becky Sanchez if she pursues a supervisory position?
2. Describe how Townsend should develop Sanchez's potential?
3. Applying the factors in determining training needs and the questions that supervisors should ask in formulating an employee development program, outline a development program for Becky Sanchez.

Case

4-13

THE ROUNDABOUT RAISE

Jon Everson is an area supervisor for Rite-Buy Qwik Marts. According to his manager, Al Perkins, he had done an exceptional job of helping the store supervisors increase sales, reduce inventory costs, and increase profit margins. However, due in part to the highly competitive nature of the industry and Rite-Buy's continued focus on fiscal austerity, Perkins was not able to increase Everson's salary. When Everson joined Rite-Buy several years ago, the human resources manager and other top-level managers had emphasized that "At Rite-Buy, we reward our supervisors based on their performance. The more money you make for us, the more money you will make!"

When Everson asked Perkins about a raise, Perkins praised his work. Everson's performance over the past 12 months had been superb. While the stores in Everson's area had done remarkably well, others did not. Perkins told Everson that the company's rigid fiscal austerity program would not allow for merit raises for the foreseeable future. However, Perkins then said, "I won't look too closely at the expense accounts for a while. I think you might see a way to help yourself, if you know what I mean."

Questions for Discussion

1. Should Jon Everson take this as an authorization to pad his expense account on the grounds that he would simply be getting the same money he deserved through a different route? Why or why not? (Suggestion: Refer to the "ethical tests" discussed in Chapter 5.)
2. What alternatives would Everson have if he didn't embellish his expense reports?
3. If Everson "pads his expense account" and top management discovers what happened, what is the likelihood that he will be terminated?
4. Discuss why the performance appraisal system and compensation system at Rite-Buy Qwik Marts probably failed to motivate employees such as Jon Everson to their fullest.

Case

4–14

THE ALTERED SUGGESTION

Allied Products Corporation, a nonunion metals manufacturing company, has a suggestion program that is administered by an all-employee committee. By saving money for the company, workers could improve their chances of getting bonuses at the same time they worked toward an individual award. Workers were encouraged to figure out ways to improve their workplace.

The winner of Allied's suggestion program was to be announced on a Friday morning in December. Although his own suggestion had been rejected by Allied, Mike Cooper wanted to know who had won and how much he or she had won. Cooper went to work early to read the notice announcing the winner on the company's bulletin board. The notice began, "George Monroe received $12,800 for his suggestion . . ." Cooper thought, "That is a lot of money!" Monroe worked in the quality assurance department. Cooper was even more surprised when he read the description of Monroe's suggestion. The winning suggestion was nearly identical to the one Cooper had submitted to Allied. Cooper could not believe it; the winning idea was the same as his, and someone else was claiming "his money."

Cooper had believed that a simple change in procedures would substantially reduce the amount of scrap metal created by his fabricating department. Cooper did not discuss his idea with anyone in the department other than his supervisor, Fred Wilson. Wilson seemed genuinely interested in the idea and had questioned Cooper extensively. Wilson encouraged Cooper to "bounce his idea" off Donald Page, the director of quality assurance. During a private discussion with Page, Cooper was encouraged to write his idea down and submit it to the company's suggestion program. About a week later, Cooper obtained a suggestion form, wrote his idea on the form, and placed it in the suggestion box. Cooper's suggestion was returned to him by the suggestion committee. A notation, "Similar suggestion submitted by another suggestor several days earlier," was written on the top of his suggestion form.

Subsequently, Cooper heard through the grapevine that George Monroe had given $5,000 of his award to Donald Page. Monroe told coworkers that he had given the money to Page for "his (Page's) help with writing up the suggestion." Cooper was incensed. Cooper knew that he had talked with his supervisor, Fred Wilson, for many hours about his idea and had only discussed the idea with Page at Wilson's suggestion.

Reflecting on these events and hoping for justice, Cooper told his supervisor, Fred Wilson, and asked for help. Cooper and Wilson met with the chairperson of the suggestion committee who referred them to the rules setting up the suggestion plan which stated that "decisions by the suggestion committee are final."

Fred Wilson told the vice president of Allied, Emil Brita, the facts he knew and asked him to revoke the award to Monroe and give the award to Cooper. The vice president refused and stated that the committee had complete authority to decide what suggestions were eligible for awards and the amount to be paid for the suggestions adopted.

Questions for Discussion

1. What should Mike Cooper do to support his claim that his idea was stolen by George Monroe and Donald Page?
2. What might be the effect if other employees learn of the way Cooper's idea was handled?
3. What should Fred Wilson do in an effort to correct the inequity?
4. What should Fred Wilson do to prevent this situation from recurring?

Leading

Supervisory Leadership and the Introduction of Change

You Make the Call!

You are Anita Mathews. You have worked in the accounting and data services department of Concord Community Bank for ten years, and about two years ago you were promoted to supervisor of a data processing section that sends bank statements to depositors. In a recent bank merger, Concord Bank acquired two smaller banks. The corresponding departments in the acquired banks were eliminated and your department was expected to handle the work without additional personnel. After integrating the different systems, your department still has an unusually large amount of work. Additionally, you have not gotten authorization to fill two vacant positions in your department. In order to get the work done, you decide to help in order to alleviate the situation. You now spend between two and four hours a day operating one of the machines to help get the statements out.

On a number of occasions you have asked employees—both individually and collectively—for their suggestions and opinions concerning what should be done. You have avoided giving direct orders and have tried to suggest to employees what needed to be done rather than spelling out the directions in detail. A number of years ago, your mentor suggested that your supervisory style should be one that "provides objectives and guidance rather than providing directions." Generally, the work performance of the fourteen employees is good and there is excellent camaraderie among the group members. However, just this morning, one of the employees, Nancy, expressed a complaint about the workload and questioned whether any relief was on the way. You understand how she feels and know that the chances of getting authorization to post or recruit for the two vacant positions are slim.

You have not neglected any of your supervisory duties, but while you are operating the machine, you are doing nothing else. This morning as you were op-

erating one of the machines, you thought to yourself, "I'm just swamped. This is our busiest time of the year. We're always behind and I don't know how much longer they can take the pressure." The continual battle of juggling family and work responsibilities has you looking haggard and exhausted. You have to put a *"good"* face on before you get to work.

Art Roberts, your supervisor, has just returned from a long out-of-town trip. He does not yet know of your decision to assist your employees by manning one of the machines. You had plans to discuss this with him two days from now, which was the soonest you could schedule a meeting with him. However, Roberts came looking for you only a few hours after he was back in the office because he wanted to discuss some problems with you. As a result, he found you operating a machine and not in your office. He became annoyed with you because of what you were doing, and he asked you into his office. He proceeded to lecture you, stating that it was a supervisor's job to get things done through and with people, and that did not mean you should be doing the work of the employees, even when the department was shorthanded. You listened patiently to Roberts's statements and pondered your response.

You Make the Call!

1
Discuss the leadership
component of
supervision.

LEADERSHIP: THE CORE OF SUPERVISORY MANAGEMENT

Although many supervisors are aware of the importance of motivation, there still is considerable misunderstanding concerning the supervisor's leadership role in influencing employee motivation and performance.[1] This misunderstanding often stems from a misconception regarding the meaning of leadership itself. Occupying a position of responsibility and authority does not necessarily make someone a leader that subordinates will follow.

The Test of Supervisory Leadership

Leadership
The ability to guide and influence the behavior of others.

Actually, it is not the supervisor's position alone that defines him or her as a leader. **Leadership** is the ability to guide and influence the opinions, attitudes, and behavior of others. This means that anyone who is able to direct or influence others toward objectives can function as a leader, no matter what position that person holds.

In the workplace, members of the work group often assume leadership roles. The direction of informal employee leadership can be supportive of or contrary to the direction the supervisor desires. For example, employee resistance to changes in work arrangements, work rules, or procedures is a common phenomenon. Such resistance usually is the result of some informal leadership within the work group itself.

Thus, leadership in the general sense is a process rather than just a positional relationship. Leadership includes what the followers think and do, not just what the supervisor does. The real test of supervisory leadership is how subordinates follow. *Leadership resides in a supervisor's ability to obtain the work group's willingness to follow, a willingness based on commonly shared goals and a mutual effort to achieve them.*

Leadership Can Be Developed

Supervisors often believe that any definition of *leadership* should include "basic traits" possessed by a leader. That is, they believe that effective leaders possess some special qualities, and they point to certain successful supervisors as being representative of outstanding leadership.

Does a person need to have certain natural qualities to become an effective leader? Generally, the ability to lead is something that can be learned: Leaders are made, not born. Many studies have shown that there is no significant relationship between one's

Supervisory leadership results in a work group's willingness to follow.

There is no significant relationship between one's ability to lead and characteristics such as age, height, weight, gender, race, and other physical attributes.

ability to lead and characteristics such as age, height, weight, sex, race, and other physical attributes. Although there are indications that successful supervisors tend to be somewhat more intelligent than the average subordinate, they are not so superior in intelligence that they cannot be understood. Intelligence is partially hereditary, but for the most part it depends on environmental factors such as amount of formal education and diversity of experiences. Successful supervisors do tend to be well rounded in their interests and aptitudes; they are good communicators; they are mentally and emotionally mature; and they possess a strong inner drive. Most important, they tend to rely on their supervisory skills to a greater extent than on their technical skills. These are essentially learned characteristics rather than innate qualities.

Author Peter Senge objects to the very notion of teaching leadership. "Teaching suggests that you have certain concepts you want to understand, and that's pretty useless in a domain like leadership. Leadership has to do with how people are. You don't teach people a different way of being, you create conditions so they can discover where their natural leadership comes from."[2]

Putting this in perspective, supervisory leadership is something that a person can develop if he or she has a real desire to be a leader and not just someone in charge of a group of people. Where can the novice gain leadership experience? As noted in Chapter 1, students can volunteer in a number of service or religious organizations, or seek an internship through their college placement office. Imagine the dynamics that can take place among a Boy or Girl Scout leader and a group of young scouts. Volunteer opportunities give the leader the opportunity to work on real projects in order to accomplish real objectives with real people. What you learn from such an experience is more than the cost of tuition. You can become a more effective leader if you earnestly strive to develop your managerial and human relations capacities and skills. Seize every opportunity to gain an advantage!

Effective Supervisory Leadership as a Dynamic Process

Harry S Truman, the 33rd president of the United States, once remarked that leadership is the ability to get people to do what they don't like to do and like it. It would be a tall order for someone without prior leadership experience to take on the task of scout leader. Good communication is the foundation of effective leadership—for example, getting the scouts to do things they have never done before. The ability to communicate, to keep the lines of communication open at all times, and to communicate in a way that meets workers' (scouts') expectations and needs is essential for any supervisor to be a leader.

The nature of the work environment, the size of the work group, and the type of people involved also are important. Generally, the larger the work group, the more important it is for the supervisor to be an effective planner, organizer, and coordinator of activities. The larger the work group, the more the supervisor will have to delegate authority. The smaller the work group and the closer the supervisor's physical location is to the employees, the more he or she must deal with the individual needs of those in the group.

Understanding the expectations of employees is vital in effective supervision. As discussed previously, today's employees want to participate in decisions concerning their jobs. However, sometimes a supervisor must exercise authority and make decisions that may not be popular with the work group. The ability to assess employee expectations and the demands of the job situation and then act appropriately is a skill that can be developed with experience and practice.

2

Identify and describe some of the elements of contemporary leadership thought.

CONTEMPORARY THOUGHTS ON LEADERSHIP

Contemporary writings concerning leadership are replete with many findings and some contradictions. However, there are several areas of agreement. One of the most noted writers on leadership, Warren Bennis, reported from his extensive research four things that people want from their leaders:

Direction—People want leaders to have a purpose. The leader has a clear idea of what is to be done. The leader loves what he or she does and loves doing it. Followers want passion and conviction from a strong point of view.
Trust—The ability to trust a leader is perhaps more important today than any time in recent history. Integrity, maturity, and candor are essential elements of building a relationship of mutual trust.
Hope—Leaders believe, and they kindle the fire of optimism in followers.
Results—Accomplishment of difficult tasks. Success breeds success.[3]

We often hear employees say "we don't trust *them*," obviously in reference to management. It is not uncommon to hear the words "us versus them" in the workplace. Conversely, few managers would admit, publicly, that they don't trust their employees. Yet trust is the foundation of effective supervisory relations. Some years ago, a customer placed a special order for a child's bedroom set at Souder's General Store. When told that it would be delivered in three weeks, the customer inquired, "Do you want me to give you some money as a deposit or sign something?" Owner Ed Souder said, "No problem. You told me you want it. If your word isn't any good, what good is your signature!"[4] As Bennis and others imply, "We want to be able to trust others and to have others trust us."

Stephen R. Covey, author of *Principle-Centered Leadership,* notes that:

Trust bonds management to labor, employees to each other, customers to supplier, and strengthens all other stakeholder relationships. With low trust, developing performance is exhausting. With high trust it is exhilarating. The principle of alignment means working together in harmony, going in the same direction, supporting each other. Alignment develops the organizational trustworthiness required for trust. And if personal trustworthiness and interpersonal trust are to mature, hiring, promoting, training and other systems must foster character development as well as competence.[5]

Noted leadership researchers James Kouzes and Barry Posner contend that "leadership is an observable, learnable set of practices. Given the opportunity for feedback and practice, those with desire and persistence to lead can substantially improve their abilities to do so."[6] After examining the experiences of managers who were leading others to outstanding accomplishments, Kouzes and Posner identified five practices and ten specific behaviors that can be learned and used by managers at all levels. The practices and corresponding behaviors include:

- Challenging the process (searching for opportunities, experimenting and taking risks)
- Inspiring a shared vision (envisioning the future, enlisting the support of others)
- Enabling others to act (fostering collaboration, strengthening others)
- Modeling the way (setting an example, planning small wins)
- Encouraging the heart (recognizing contributions, celebrating accomplishments).[7]

This chapter's "Contemporary Issue" box presents the thoughts of some industry leaders. Having reviewed the thoughts of several prominent writers and industry leaders, the next question is, What does a supervisor do to influence the behavior of subordinates? Most managers recognize that there is no one leadership style that is effective in all situations. There is no simple set of dos and don'ts that a supervisor can implement to achieve high motivation and excellent performance. Although leadership skills can be learned and developed, no one formula will apply in all situations and with all people. Considerable evidence suggests that an effective approach is contingent upon numerous factors in any given situation. **Contingency-style leadership** proponents advocate that these include considerations involving the supervisor, the organization, the type of work, the skill level and motivation of employees involved, time pressures, and the like.

Contingency-style leadership

No one leadership style is best; the appropriate style depends on a multitude of factors.

3
Identify prominent leadership theories.

LEADERSHIP THEORIES

While there is general agreement among researchers and theorists that leading is not the same as managing (see Chapter 2), there is still considerable debate regarding what the leader does and how the leader does it. A detailed discussion of various theories is beyond the scope of this textbook, but an overview can be found in Figure 14-1 on pages 474–475. Some approaches work better than others in promoting good performance.

The concept of leadership is one that has been studied and discussed for decades. One consensus flows from the discussion of leadership theories, and that is that *there is no one best style of leadership*. The lesson for practicing supervisors is that the most effective leadership depends on a multitude of factors, including the supervisor, the organization, the type of work, the employees involved, their ability and willingness to accomplish a particular task, the amount of time available to complete a task, and the particular situation and its urgency. In general, the authors have concluded that effective leaders need to be able to establish standards, develop a creative climate where people are self-motivated, and adapt to constant change. The effective leader provides direction, instruction, guidance, support and encouragement, feedback and positive recognition, and enthusiastic help when necessary.

contemporary issue

Ten Thoughts from Those in Charge

Pamela Barefoot, president of Blue Crab Bay Co.—"The first move toward implementing the communication skill was writing a mission statement that would clarify for the employees what the firm was all about. Once you've communicated your company goals to your employees, you must hold them accountable for how well they perform in striving toward those goals. They (her employees) know how I feel about things, and when I leave here they can run the business just as well as I can, because they know the way I want it done. That's trust."[1]

Colleen Barrett, executive vice president, customers, Southwest Airlines—"If I did have an ego, [this job] would be the most demoralizing thing. Everywhere I go, people say, 'Hi Colleen. Where's Herb?' Employees are really my first priority. If employees are happy, the customers will follow. I have no desire to be CEO, and I would not be a good CEO. I tend not to like to say no to people."[2]

Mark Cuban, president and cofounder, broadcast.com Inc. (Dallas, Texas)—"A leader's job is to recognize when a company is headed in the wrong direction and get it back on the right track. . . . Another part of my job as leader is to be clear that winning in this world is all about selling."[3]

Bill Capodagli—"Before Walt Disney would do anything, he would dream of things that had never been done before. After that, he would test those dreams against his beliefs and the beliefs of his company. Then he would dare to take the risks to make those dreams come true. And finally, he would put plans together to make those dreams become a reality. So dream, believe, dare and do are four things that anybody can do, whether you're in a large business or a small business."[4]

Julian Fifer, founder and president of the Orpheus Chamber Orchestra—"A founding principle of the orchestra was that we'd rotate seating and leadership. As a leader, a person learns what kind of support to expect from followers, and how to provide that support during his next stint as a follower. If you haven't been particularly attentive as a follower, what kind of support can you expect when your turn to lead comes?"[5]

Robert A. Lutz, Exide's CEO—"You have to have a sense of mission. The best leaders are usually humble, and that humility comes from a strong sense of self-confidence. Instead of creating destructive fear, a good leader will break down that kind of fear by talking to the troops. . . . I spent a lot of time on the shop floor. . . . When you banter with your employees and use self-depreciating humor, and take the blame for things that go wrong, you're establishing your credibility as a human being and a leader."[6]

Joe Mansueto, Morningstar founder—"We want to create a trusting environment where people can produce their best work. I also learned it's best to hire people you admire and want to be around. . . . We share information widely throughout the company in a way that is rare for private companies. By sharing information and communicating honestly, we develop an unusual degree of trust that's an important part of the Morningstar culture."[7]

Ruthann Quindlen, partner, IVP—"Leaders have to develop the chops for real-time decision making. I learned that from Bill Gates. He always said to me, 'I don't care if a manager makes five serious mistakes. At least that person is making decisions and learning from them.' If your instinct is to wait, ponder, and perfect, then you're dead."[8]

Rich Teerlink, chairman, Harley-Davidson, Inc.—"People are our only long-term competitive advantage. Therefore, a leader is responsible for creating an operating environment where people can do great things. That environment includes investing in capital and processes to support the efforts of the people. This investment starts our process, which identifies our key issues as quality, participation, productivity, flexibility, and cash flow. Note we focus on cash flow and not profits."[9]

Jack Welch, GE's CEO—"We have found that by reaching for what appears to be impossible we often actually do the impossible—and even when we don't quite make it, we inevitably wind up doing much better than we would have done."[10]

Sources: (1) Adapted and excerpted from Michael Barrier, "Leadership Skills Employees Respect," *Nation's Business* (January 1999), pp. 28–30. Blue Crab Bay Co. was recognized as a Blue Chip Enterprise in 1998. The program honors small businesses that have successfully weathered significant challenges. (2) Adapted and

A good manager uses delegation as a tool to develop employees' skills and abilities, not as a way to get rid of unpleasant tasks.

Discuss the delegation process and define its three major components.

Delegation

The process of entrusting duties and related authority to subordinates.

Accountability

The obligation one has to one's boss and the expectation that employees will accept credit or blame for the results achieved in performing assigned tasks.

THE PROCESS OF DELEGATION

Just as authority is a major component of the managerial job, so the delegation of authority is essential to the creation and operation of an organization. In the broadest sense, **delegation** gives employees a greater voice in how the job is to be done; the employee is empowered to make decisions. Unfortunately, some managers view delegation as a means to lighten their own workload. They assign unpleasant tasks to employees and subsequently find that the employees are not motivated to complete those tasks. The manager must look at delegation as a tool to develop employees' skills and abilities rather than as a way to get rid of unpleasant tasks.

The subordinate manager receives authority from a higher-level manager through the process of delegation, but this does not mean that the higher-level manager surrenders all accountability. **Accountability** is the obligation one has to one's boss and the expectation that employees will accept credit or blame for the results achieved in performing assigned tasks. When a manager delegates, he or she is still ultimately accountable for successful completion of the work.

excerpted from Diane Cyr, "Lesser-Sung Heroes," *Working Women* (April 1999), pp. 73–77. Barrett is Herb Kelleher's Number Two. Much of the credit for Southwest Airlines ranking as one of the best companies to work for in the United States goes to Barrett, who is charged with the care and feeding of all the company's employees. (3) As quoted in Polly LaBarre, "Leaders.com," *Fast Company* (June 1999), pp. 95+. Mark Cuban and Todd Wagner started broadcast.com in a spare bedroom in Cuban's Dallas apartment. Yahoo! bought Cuban's company for $5.7 billion. (4) As quoted by Bill Capodagli in the Third Thursday Forum at the Greater Fort Wayne (IN) Chamber of Commerce (June 17, 1999). Capodagli and Lynn Jackson co-authored "*The Disney Way: Harnessing the Management Secrets of Disney in Your Company.*" (5) "Case Study in C-Sharp Minor," *Training* (October 1998), p. 21. (6) David H. Freedman, Inc. (March 1999), pp. 51–58. Also see Lutz, *Guts: The Seven Laws of Business That Made Chrysler the World's Hottest Car Company* (John Wiley & Sons, 1998). (7) Christopher Caggiano, "Everything I Know, I Learned from Warren Buffett," *Inc.* (July 1999), pp. 85–90. (8) As quoted in Polly LaBarre, "Leaders.com," *Fast Company* (June 1999), pp. 95+. Ruthann Quindlen helped Microsoft and AOL go public. See Quindlen's *Confessions of a Venture Capitalist*, Warner Books (1999). (9) As quoted in "The Quotable Entrepreneur," *Inc.* (January 1999), p. 81. (10) Adapted from William M. Corley, "GE Implements $200 Million Program to Slash Number of Defects per Product," *The Wall Street Journal* (April 13, 1996), p. A4. Also see Jack Gordon, "My Leader, Myself," *Training* (November 1998), pp. 54–62.

FIGURE 14-1   Leadership theories: An overview.

MANAGERIAL GRID

Robert R. Blake and Anne Adams McCanse[1] refined the Leadership Grid® which identified various types of managerial leadership based on concern for production coupled with concern for people. While they consider the "team management" style of leadership to be ideal, they recognize that it may be difficult to implement in some work situations. Effective managers have great concern for both people and production. They work to motivate employees to reach their highest levels of accomplishment. They are flexible and responsive to change, and they understand the need to change.

CONTINGENCY THEORY

Fred Fiedler[2] developed a contingency or situational theory of leadership. Fiedler postulates that three important situational dimensions are assumed to influence the leader's effectiveness. They are:

- **Leader-member relations:** the degree of confidence the subordinates have in the leader. It also includes the loyalty shown the leader and the leader's attractiveness.
- **Task structure:** the degree to which the followers' jobs are routine as contrasted with nonroutine.
- **Position power:** the power inherent in the leadership position. It includes the rewards and punishments typically associated with the position, the leader's formal authority (based on ranking in the managerial hierarchy), and the support that the leader receives from supervisors and the overall organization.

PATH-GOAL THEORY

The path-goal theory postulates that the most successful leaders are those who increase subordinate motivation by charting out and clarifying the paths to high performance. According to Robert House's path-goal theory,[3] effective leaders:

- Motivate their followers to achieve group and organizational goals.
- Make sure that they have control over outcomes their subordinates desire.
- Reward subordinates for performing at a high level or achieving their work goals by giving them desired outcomes.

- Raise their subordinates' beliefs about their ability to achieve their work goals and perform at a high level.
- Take into account their subordinates' characteristics and the type of work they do.

LEADER-STYLE THEORY

The Vroom and Yetton Model[4] describes the different ways leaders can make decisions and guides leaders in determining the extent to which subordinates should participate in decision making. The expanded version of their model, the "Vroom, Yetton, Jago Model," holds that (1) organizational decisions should be of the highest quality and (2) subordinates should accept and be committed to organizational decisions that are made. The model presents methods for determining the appropriateness of leader style.

HERSEY AND BLANCHARD THEORY

Paul Hersey and Kenneth H. Blanchard[5] (a co-author of the *One Minute Manager*) identified a three-dimensional approach for assessing leadership effectiveness:

- Leaders exhibit task behavior (the extent to which leaders are likely to organize and define the roles of followers and direct the work) and relationship behavior (the extent to which leaders are likely to be supportive, encouraging, and the like).
- The effectiveness of the leader depends on how his or her leadership style interrelates with the situation.
- The willingness and ability (readiness) of an employee to do a particular task is an important situational factor.

This approach is easy to understand, offers suggestions for changing leadership style, and shows leaders what to do and when to do it. It focuses on the need for adaptability (the degree to which the leader is able to vary his or her style appropriately to the readiness level of a follower in a given situation).

TRANSFORMATIONAL LEADERSHIP

According to Bernard Bass,[6] transformational leadership occurs when a leader transforms, or changes, his or her followers in three important ways that together result in followers trusting the leader, performing behaviors that contribute to the achievement of organizational goals,

FIGURE 14-1   *(Continued)*

and being motivated to perform at a high level. Transformational leaders:

- Increase subordinates' awareness of the importance of their tasks and the importance of performing well.
- Make subordinates aware of their needs for personal growth, development, and accomplishment.
- Motivate their subordinates to work for the good of the organization rather than exclusively for their own personal gain or benefit.

Building on Bass's contributions, Tichy and Devanna identified the characteristics of transformational leaders as follows:

- They identify themselves as change agents.
- They are courageous individuals.
- They believe in people.
- They are value-driven.
- They are lifelong learners.
- They have the ability to deal with complexity.
- They are visionaries.

Sources: (1) Robert R. Blake and Anne Adams McCanse, *Leadership Dilemmas—Grid Solutions* (Houston: Gulf Publishing, 1991); and Blake and Jane S. Mouton, *The Managerial Grid III* (Houston: Gulf Publishing, 1985). (2) Fred E. Fiedler, "Research on Leadership Selection and Training: One View of the Future," *Administrative Science Quarterly* (June 1996), pp. 241–250; Fiedler, "Engineer the Job to Fit the Manager," *Harvard Business Review* (September-October 1965), p. 117; Fiedler, *A Theory of Leadership Effectiveness* (New York: McGraw-Hill, 1967); and Fiedler and Joseph E. Garcia, *New Approaches to Effective Leadership: Cognitive Resources and Organizational Performance* (New York: John Wiley, 1987). (3) Robert J. House, "A Path-Goal Theory of Leader Effectiveness," *Administrative Science Quarterly* (September 1971), pp. 321–328; and House and Terence R. Mitchell, "Path-Goal Theory of Leadership," *Journal of Contemporary Business* (Autumn 1974), pp. 81–97. (4) Victor Vroom and Philip Yetton, *Leadership and Decision Making* (Pittsburgh: University of Pittsburgh Press, 1973). Also see Vroom and Arthur G. Jago, *The New Leadership: Managing Participation in Organizations* (Englewood Cliffs, N.J.: Prentice-Hall, 1988). (5) Paul Hersey and Kenneth H. Blanchard, "Great Ideas: Revisiting the Life-Cycle Theory of Leadership," *Training & Development* (January 1996), pp. 42–47; and Hersey and Blanchard, *Management of Organizational Behavior* (Englewood Cliffs, N.J.: Prentice-Hall, 1993). (6) The concept of transformational leadership was developed by James MacGregor Burns, *Leadership* (New York: Harper & Row, 1978). Also see Bernard Bass, *Leadership and Performance Beyond Expectations* (New York: Free Press, 1985); Noel M. Tichy and Mary Anne Devanna, *The Transformational Leader* (New York: John Wiley & Sons, 1986); and Bass, "From Transitional to Transformational Leadership: Learning to Share the Vision," *Organizational Dynamics* (Winter 1990), pp. 140–148.

Delegation is a supervisor's strategy for accomplishing objectives. It consists of the following three components, all of which must be present:

1. Assigning duties to immediate subordinates.
2. Granting permission (authority) to make commitments, use resources, and take all actions necessary to perform these duties.
3. Creating an obligation (responsibility) on the part of each employee to perform the duties satisfactorily.

Unless all three components are present, the delegation process is incomplete. They are inseparably related in such a manner that a change in one will require adjustment of the other two.

Assigning Duties

Each employee must be assigned a specific job or task to perform. Job descriptions may provide a general framework through which the supervisor can examine duties in the department to see which to assign to each employee. Routine duties usually can be assigned to almost any employee, but there are other functions that the supervisor can assign only to employees who are qualified to perform them. There are also some functions that a supervisor cannot delegate—those which the supervisor must do. The assignment of job duties to employees is of great significance, and much of the supervisor's success will depend on it.

Granting Authority

The granting of authority means that the supervisor confers upon employees the right and power to act, to utilize certain resources, and to make decisions within prescribed limits. Of course, the supervisor must determine the scope of authority that is to be delegated. How much authority can be delegated depends in part on the amount of authority the supervisor possesses. The degree of authority is also related to the employees and jobs to be done. For example, if a sales clerk is responsible for processing items returned to the store, that clerk must have the authority to give the customer's money back with the understanding (limit) that the clerk should alert the supervisor if the returned item was obviously abused in some way. In every instance, enough authority must be granted to the employee to enable the employee to perform assigned tasks adequately and successfully. (For a review of empowerment, see Figure 4-7 on page 117.) There is no need for the amount of authority to be larger than the tasks assigned, but the authority granted must be sufficient to meet the employee's obligations.

Defining Limitations. Throughout the process of delegation, employees must be reassured that their orders and authority will come from their immediate supervisor. A supervisor must be specific in telling employees what authority they have and what they can or cannot do. It is uncomfortable for employees to have to guess how far their authority extends. For example, an employee may be expected to order certain materials as a regular part of the job. This employee must know the limits within which materials can be ordered, perhaps in terms of time and costs, and when permission from the supervisor is needed before ordering additional materials. If the supervisor does not state this clearly, the employee probably will be forced to test the limits and to learn by trial and error. If it becomes necessary to change an employee's job assignment, the degree of authority should be checked to make certain that the authority delegated is still appropriate. If it is less (or more) than needed, it should be adjusted.

Creating Responsibility

The third component of the process of delegation is the creation of an obligation on the part of the employee toward the supervisor to perform the assigned duties satisfactorily. Acceptance of this obligation creates responsibility; without responsibility, delegation is not complete.

The terms *responsibility* and *authority* are closely related. Like the concept of authority, responsibility is often misunderstood. Supervisors commonly use expressions such as "keeping subordinates responsible," "delegating responsibilities," and "carrying out responsibilities." Simply stated, however, responsibility is the obligation of a subordinate to perform duties as required by the supervisor. By accepting a job position or accepting an obligation to perform assigned duties, the employee implies acceptance of responsibility. Responsibility recognizes an implied agreement in which the employee agrees to perform duties in return for rewards such as a paycheck. The most important facet of the definition is that responsibility is something that a subordinate must recognize and accept if delegation is to succeed.

Supervisory Accountability Cannot Be Delegated

Although a supervisor must delegate authority to employees to accomplish specific jobs, the supervisor's own personal accountability cannot be delegated. Assigning duties to employees does not relieve the supervisor of the responsibility for these duties. Thus, when delegating assignments to employees, the supervisor still remains accountable for the actions of the employees in carrying out these assignments.

To reiterate, responsibility includes (a) the subordinate's obligation to perform assigned tasks, and (b) the supervisor's obligation to his or her own manager, or accountability. Thus, for example, when a higher-level manager asks a supervisor to explain performance within the department, the supervisor cannot plead as a defense that the responsibility for performance has been delegated to employees in the group. The supervisor remains accountable and must answer to the manager. Regardless of the extent to which a supervisor creates an obligation on the part of employees to perform satisfactorily, the supervisor retains the ultimate responsibility, along with the authority, that is part of the supervisor's departmental position. As illustrated in Figure 14-2,

FIGURE 14-2

Effective delegation requires an appropriate mix of task assignments and the authority and responsibility to accomplish the tasks.

effective delegation requires an appropriate mix of the assignment of tasks and the authority and responsibility needed to carry out those tasks.

That accountability cannot be delegated may be a worrisome thought for some supervisors, but the fact remains that responsibility for the work of others goes with the supervisory position. Delegation is necessary for jobs to be accomplished. Although a supervisor may use sound managerial practices, employees will not always use the best judgment or perform in a superior fashion. Therefore, allowances must be made for errors. Although accountability remains with supervisors, supervisors must depend on their employees. If employees fail to carry out their assigned tasks, they are accountable to the supervisor, who must then redirect the employees as appropriate. When appraising a supervisor's performance, higher-level managers usually take into consideration how much care the supervisor has taken in selecting employees, training them, supervising them, and controlling their activities.

Implied in the accountability concept is the notion that punishments or rewards will follow, depending on how well the duties are performed. However, the ultimate accountability to top-level managers lies with the supervisor who is doing the delegating. Supervisors are responsible and accountable not only for their own actions, but also for the actions of their subordinates.

DELEGATION BY THE SUPERVISOR

5

Discuss why some supervisors do not delegate and describe some benefits of delegation.

Every supervisor must delegate some authority to employees. This assumes, of course, that the employees are capable and willing to accept the authority delegated to them. Yet many employees complain that their supervisors make all of the decisions and constantly watch their work closely because they do not trust the employees to carry out assignments. These types of complaints usually describe a supervisor who is unable or unwilling to delegate except to a minimal extent.

Reasons for Lack of Supervisory Delegation

A supervisor may be reluctant to delegate for several reasons—some valid, some not.

Shortage of Qualified Employees.   Some supervisors cite a lack of qualified employees as an excuse for not delegating authority. Actually, such supervisors feel that their employees are not capable of handling authority or are not willing to accept it. If these supervisors refuse to delegate, employees will have little opportunity to obtain the experience they need to improve their judgment and enable them to handle broadened assignments. Supervisors must always bear in mind that, unless they make a beginning somewhere, they probably will never have enough employees who are capable and willing to accept more authority with commensurate responsibility.

Fear of Making Mistakes.   Some supervisors think it best to make most decisions themselves because, in the final analysis, they retain overall responsibility. Out of fear of mistakes, such supervisors are unwilling to delegate, and, as a result, they continue to overburden themselves. However, indecision and delay often are more costly than the mistakes they hoped to avoid by refusing to delegate. Also, these supervisors may make mistakes by not drawing on employees for assistance in decision making.

The "I'd Rather Do-It-Myself" Mentality.

The old stereotype of a good supervisor was that of one who pitched in and worked alongside the employees, thereby setting an example by personal effort. Even today, this type of supervision often occurs when a supervisor has been promoted through the ranks and the supervisory position is a reward for hard work and technical competence. By being placed in a supervisory position without having managerial training, this type of supervisor is faced with new problems that are difficult to comprehend. The supervisor therefore resorts to a pattern in which he or she feels secure by working alongside the employees. There are occasions when the supervisor should pitch in—for example, when the job is particularly difficult or when an emergency arises. With the trend toward eliminating management levels and consolidating operations, people will have to work together more closely. Under these conditions the supervisor should be close enough to the job to offer help. Aside from emergencies and unusual situations, however, the supervisor should be supervising and the employees should be doing their assigned tasks. Normally, it is the supervisor's job to get things done, not to do them.

Supervisors frequently complain that if they want something done right they have to do it themselves. They believe that it is easier to do the job personally than to correct an employee's mistakes. Or they may simply prefer to correct an employee's mistakes rather than to clearly explain what should have been done. Such supervisors may even feel that they can do the job better than any of the employees, and this may be true. But these attitudes interfere with a supervisor's prime responsibility to supervise others to get the job done.

A good supervisor occasionally shows how a job can be done more efficiently, promptly, courteously, and so forth. However, an employee who does the job almost as well will save the supervisor time for more important jobs—for innovative thinking, planning, and more delegating. Thus, the effective supervisor strives to see to it that each employee, with each additional job, becomes more competent. After a period of time, the employee's performance on the job should be as good as or better than what the supervisor would have done.

Other Factors.

Ineffective supervisors are afraid to let go. They may fear that if they share their knowledge with employees and allow them to participate in decision making, the employees will become so proficient at making good decisions that the supervisor will be unnecessary. The fear of not being needed can be partially overcome if the supervisor cannot be promoted unless someone has been prepared to take the supervisor's place.

Not everyone wants to take the responsibility for making decisions. The supervisor needs to identify those employees who need the opportunity to grow and who want to be empowered. Employees may be reluctant to accept delegation because of their own insecurity or fear of failure, or they may think that the supervisor will not be available for guidance. Many employees are reluctant to accept delegation due to past managerial incompetence. Everyone has heard of the "seagull manager." This manager, like the seagull, flies in, drops a load, and flies off. All too often, employees have had boring, mundane, and unpleasant tasks dumped on them from above. Oftentimes, a new employee will be given words of wisdom by one of the more seasoned veterans, "Don't volunteer for anything and if the boss gives you a new assignment, beg off."

It is difficult for supervisors to create an environment of employee involvement and freedom to make decisions when their own managers do not allow them the same opportunity. An environment for delegation and empowerment must be part of the organization's culture. Upper-level managers must advocate delegation at all levels.

Benefits from Delegation

Can supervisors realize benefits from delegation if they have only a small number of employees and there is no real need to create subunits within a department? This is the kind of situation that many supervisors face. Is delegation in this type of working situation worth the trouble and risks that it entails? In general, the answer to this question is a strong yes.

The supervisor who delegates expects employees to make more decisions on their own. This does not mean that the supervisor is not available for advice. It means that the supervisor encourages the employees to make many of their own decisions and to develop their self-confidence in doing so. This in turn should mean that the supervisor will have more time to concentrate on managing. Effective delegation should result in employees being able to perform an increasing number of jobs and recommending solutions that are workable and that contribute to good performance. As the supervisor's confidence in employees expands, the employees' commitment to better performance should also grow. This may take time, and the degree of delegation may vary with each employee and with each department. However, in most situations, a supervisor's goal should be to delegate more authority to employees whenever feasible. This goal contributes to employee motivation and better job performance.

Finally, it must be reiterated that there are some supervisory areas that cannot be delegated. For example, it remains with the supervisor to formulate certain policies and objectives, to give general directions for the work unit, to appraise employee performance, to take necessary disciplinary action, and to promote employees. Aside from these types of supervisory management responsibilities, however, the employees should be doing most of the departmental work themselves.

APPROACHES TO SUPERVISORY LEADERSHIP

6

Compare the autocratic (authoritarian) approach with the participative approach to supervision.

Most employees accept work as a normal part of life. In their jobs they seek satisfaction that wages alone cannot provide. Most employees probably would prefer to be their own bosses, or at least have a degree of freedom to make decisions that pertain to their own work. The question arises as to whether this is possible if an individual works for someone else. Can a degree of freedom be granted to employees if they are to contribute their share toward the achievement of organizational objectives? This is where the delegation of authority can help. The desire for freedom and being one's own boss can be enhanced by delegation, which in the daily routine essentially means giving directions in broad, general terms. It means that the supervisor, instead of watching every detail of the employees' activities, is primarily interested in the results they achieve and is willing to give them considerable latitude in deciding how to achieve these results.

Classifying Supervisory Leadership Styles

Organizational behavior and management literature are replete with numerous reported research studies and models that have sought to establish what style or styles of leadership are most consistently associated with achieving superior levels of performance from those being led and supervised. The magnitude of these are beyond the scope of this text, and the reported findings and concepts are not totally consistent or conclusive.[8]

Rather than debate the differences and nuances surrounding various leadership theories (see Figure 14-1), we believe that they can all be conveniently classified within two overall styles or approaches that face most supervisors and managers. These styles range from essentially autocratic, or authoritarian supervisory styles (based on Theory X assumptions) to variations of general supervisory styles (based on Theory Y assumptions). These two styles can be presented as being extremes along a continuum (see Figure 14-3). However, in actual practice a supervisor usually "blends" these approaches based on a number of considerations. These include the supervisor's skill and

FIGURE 14-3

Leadership style continuum.

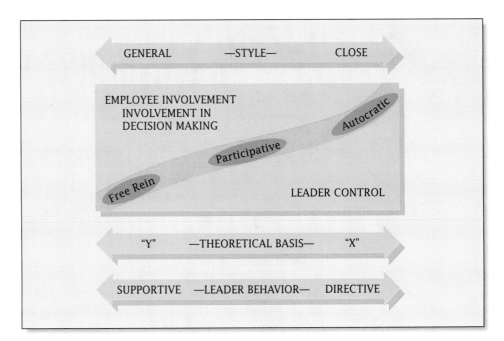

experience, the employee or employees who are involved, the situation at hand, and other factors. No one style of supervision has ever been shown to be correct in all situations. Consequently, every supervisor needs to be sensitive to the needs and realities of each situation and to accommodate his or her style as necessary to accomplish the objectives at hand.

In other chapters we introduced concepts of Theory X and Y, delegation of authority, and participative management. We expand these concepts in this chapter to relate them to a supervisor's day-to-day approaches to leading employees. While we primarily will focus on supervisory leadership, it should be recognized that not everything that influences employee behavior is in response to a supervisory approach.

Autocratic (Authoritarian) Supervision

Autocratic (authoritarian) supervision

The supervisory style that relies on formal authority, threats, pressure, and close control.

There are still many supervisors who believe that emphasis on formal authority, or **autocratic (authoritarian) supervision,** is the best way to obtain results. A supervisor of this type often uses pressure to get people to work and may even threaten disciplinary action, including discharge, if employees do not perform as ordered.[9] These managers sometimes are referred to by their employees as a "task-master" or "slave-driver." Autocratic supervision means close control of employees in which supervisors issue directives with detailed instructions and allow employees little room for initiative. Autocratic supervisors delegate very limited or no authority. They believe that they know how to do the job better than their employees, and that employees are not paid to think but to follow directions. Autocratic supervisors further believe that since they have been put in charge, they should do most of the planning and decision making. Since they are quite explicit in telling employees exactly how and in what sequence things are to be done, they follow through with close supervision and are focused on the tasks to be done.

Bureaucratic style of supervision

The supervisory style that emphasizes strict compliance with organizational policies, rules, and directives.

Autocratic supervision sometimes is associated with what has been called the **bureaucratic style of supervision.** This style emphasizes an organizational structure and climate that require strict compliance with managers' policies, rules, and directives throughout the firm. Bureaucratic managers believe that their primary role is to carry out and enforce policies and directives, and therefore they usually adopt an authoritarian approach in order to achieve this type of end result. Their favorite sayings are "It's policy," "Those are the rules," and "Shape up or ship out!"

Autocratic supervisors do not necessarily distrust their employees but they firmly believe that without detailed instructions, employees could not do the jobs required. Some autocratic supervisors operate from the premise that most employees do not want to do the job; therefore, close supervision and threats of loss of job or income are required to get employees to work (Theory X). These supervisors feel that if they are not on the scene watching their employees closely, the employees will stop working or just proceed at a leisurely pace.

When Autocratic Supervision Is Appropriate.   Under certain circumstances and with some employees, autocratic supervision is both logical and appropriate. Some employees do not want to think for themselves; they prefer to receive orders. Others lack ambition and do not wish to become much involved in their daily jobs. This is often the case when jobs are very structured, mechanized, automated, or routine, so that employees may prefer a supervisor who mainly issues orders to them and otherwise leaves them alone. Similarly, there are some employees who prefer an authoritarian environment and who expect a supervisor to be firm and totally in charge. For example, most passengers and flight attendants would prefer that the pilot use an autocratic style when faced with an "emergency in flight." The same is true in any organization when the situation requires immediate attention.

Probably the major advantages of autocratic supervision are that it is quick and fairly easy to apply, and that it usually gets rapid results in the short run. It may be appropriate when employees are new and inexperienced, especially if the supervisor is under major time pressures and cannot afford to have employees take time to figure out on their own how to get the work done.

Effects of Autocratic Supervision. For the most part, the autocratic method of supervision is not conducive to developing employee talents, and it tends to frustrate employees who have ambition and potential. They may lose interest and initiative and stop thinking for themselves because there is little need for independent thought. Those who believe in the sheer weight of authority and the "be strong" form of supervision tend to discount the fact that workers may react in ways that were not intended by the supervisor. Employees who strongly resent autocratic supervision may become frustrated rather than find satisfaction in their daily work. Such frustration can lead to arguments and other forms of discontent. In some cases employees may become hostile toward an autocratic supervisor and resist carrying out the supervisor's directives. The resistance may not even be apparent to the supervisor when it takes the form of slow work, mistakes, and poor quality of work. If the supervisor makes a mistake, these employees secretly rejoice over it!

Participative Management and General Supervision

Because of the potential negative consequences associated with autocratic and close supervision, most supervisors prefer not to use it or to apply it sparingly. Is one leadership style better than another? Research (review Figure 14-1) suggests that the effective supervisor tailors his or her leadership style to the situation at hand and to the abilities and motivation of subordinates. More effective supervisors who want to guide employees to higher levels of performance recognize that they cannot rely solely on managerial authority. **General supervision** means that the supervisor sets goals, discusses them with employees, and fixes the limits within which the work has to be done. Within this established framework, the employees have considerable freedom to decide *how* to achieve their objectives.

Participative management means that the supervisor who uses a participative approach discusses with employees the feasibility, workability, extent, and content of a problem before making a decision and issuing a **directive** (see Figure 14-4 on page 484). Regardless of one's preference for a particular leadership style, the supervisor must make sure that the assigned work gets done in an efficient and effective manner.

General supervision

The style of supervision in which the supervisor sets goals and limits but allows employees to decide how to achieve the goals.

Participative management

Allowing employees to influence and share in organizational decision making.

Directive

The communications approach by which a supervisor conveys to employees what, how, and why something is to be accomplished.

FIGURE 14-4

Characteristics of good directives.

Reasonable—The supervisor should not issue a directive if the employee receiving it does not have the ability, experience, and willingness necessary to comply.

Understandable—The supervisor should make certain that an employee understands a directive by speaking in words that are familiar to the employee and by using feedback to ensure understanding takes place.

Specific—The supervisor should state clearly what is expected in terms of quantity and quality of work performance.

Time-limited—The supervisor should specify a time limit within which the work should be completed.

Compatible with organizational objectives—Supervisory directives must comply with policies, regulations, and stated ethical standards of the organization.

Appropriate tone and working—Supervisors should make the request using a polite and considerate tone.

Whether assigning tasks to subordinates or helping them decide on how to do a particular task, the supervisor must provide directives. The degree to which the supervisor uses directives will, in part, vary with the task to be performed; the skill level, experience, and willingness of the subordinate; and the urgency of the situation.

A participatory style does not lessen a supervisor's authority; the right to decide remains with the supervisor and the employees' suggestions can be rejected. Participation means that a supervisor expresses personal opinions in a manner that indicates to employees that these opinions are subject to critical appraisal. It also means sharing ideas and information between supervisor and employees and thoroughly discussing alternative solutions to a problem, regardless of who originates the solutions. A high degree of mutual trust must be in evidence.

As presented throughout this text, the term *empowerment* has been used to describe an approach by which employees and work teams are given more responsibility and authority to make decisions about the jobs that they do. The essence of any empowerment approach is participative management since they both stem from the same model or philosophy of how to manage and supervise. Empowerment, like participative management, is a matter of degree. It is not some form of an absolute approach that involves

An effective supervisor expresses personal opinions in a way that lets employers know the opinions are open to critical appraisal.

the same amount of participation or empowerment for every individual and every situation.

More important than the exact approach is the supervisor's attitude. Some supervisors are inclined to use a pseudo-participatory approach simply to give employees the feeling that they have been consulted. These supervisors ask for suggestions even though they already have decided on a definite course of action. They use this approach to manipulate employees to do what will be required with or without their consultation. However, employees can sense superficiality and will usually perceive whether a supervisor is genuinely considering their ideas. If employees believe that their participation is fake, the results may be worse than if the supervisor had practiced autocratic supervision.

If participative management is to be successful, not only must the supervisor be in favor of it, but the employees must want it. If the employees believe that the supervisor knows best and that making decisions is none of their concern, then an opportunity to participate is not likely to induce higher motivation and better morale. Further, employees should be consulted in those areas where they are capable of expressing valid opinions and where they can draw on their own fund of knowledge. The problems involved should be consistent with the employees' experiences and abilities. Asking for participation in areas that are far outside the employees' scope of competence may make them feel inadequate and frustrated.

Advantages of Participative Management and General Supervision. Perhaps the greatest advantage of participative management is that a supervisor's directive can be transformed into a solution that employees themselves have discovered or at least into a decision in which they have participated. This normally leads employees to cooperate with more enthusiasm in carrying out a directive, and their morale is apt to be higher when their ideas are valued. Active participation provides an opportunity to make worthwhile contributions. Still another advantage is that participative management permits closer communication between employees and the supervisor so that they learn to trust and respect each other better. And, for the most part, the workplace can become more enjoyable with less tension and conflict to contend with. A number of companies utilize programs that call for active employee involvement in making and implementing decisions. The SunTeams highlighted in Chapter 15's "Contemporary Issue" box is one such example.

General supervision means permitting employees—within prescribed limits—to work out the details of their daily tasks and to make many of the decisions about how tasks will be performed. In so doing, the supervisor believes that employees want to do a good job and will find greater satisfaction in making decisions for themselves. The supervisor communicates the desired results, standards, and limits within which the employees can work and then delegates accordingly.

For example, a school maintenance supervisor might assign a group of employees to paint the interior walls of the school. The supervisor tells the group where to get the paint and other materials and reminds them that they should do the painting without interfering in the normal school operations. Then the supervisor suggests a target date for completing the project and leaves the group to work on their own. The supervisor may say that he or she will occasionally check back with the group to see whether they are encountering any problems or need help. The advantages of participative management/ general supervision are listed in Figure 14-5.

General supervision is not the same as what has been called **free-rein (laissez-faire) supervision.** A free-rein supervisor delegates virtually all authority and decision making to subordinates, perhaps even to the extent that he or she would not get involved in workplace decisions unless requested to do so. For example, employees would be given freedom to do whatever they decided was necessary to accomplish their tasks without violating laws or company policies. The perceptive reader should ask, "Since the supervisor essentially abdicates, why is there a need for a supervisor?" Free-rein leadership is typically not a viable approach given the true nature of most organizations.

For general supervision to work successfully, employees should be trained and know the routine of their jobs and what results are expected. But the supervisor will avoid giving detailed instructions that specify precisely how results are to be achieved. Further, general supervision also means that the supervisor, or the supervisor and employees together, should set realistic standards or performance targets. These should be high enough to represent a challenge but not so high that they cannot be achieved. Such targets sometimes are known as **stretch targets.** Employees know that their efforts are being measured against these standards. If they are unable to accomplish the targeted objectives, they are expected to inform the supervisor so that the standards can be discussed again and perhaps modified.

Participative Management and General Supervision as a Way of Life. When practiced simultaneously, participative management and general supervision are a way of

---

Free-rein (laissez-faire) supervision

Where a supervisor delegates virtually all authority to employees to decide and act without his or her involvement.

Stretch targets

Targeted job objectives that present a challenge but are achievable.

FOR SUPERVISORS:

- Frees the supervisor from many details, which allows time to plan, organize, and control.
- Gives the supervisor more time to assume additional responsibility.
- Instills confidence that employees will carry out the work and develop suitable approaches to making decisions on the job when the supervisor is away from the department.
- The decisions made by employees may be better than the ones made by the supervisor since the employees are closest to the details.

FOR EMPLOYEES:

- Are provided with a chance to develop their talents and abilities by making on-the-job decisions themselves.
- May make mistakes but are encouraged to learn from their own mistakes and the mistakes of others.
- Are motivated to take pride in the results of their own decisions.
- May feel that they have a better chance to advance to higher positions.

life that must be followed over a period of time. A supervisor cannot expect sudden results by introducing these types of supervision into an environment in which employees have been accustomed to authoritarian, close supervision. It may take considerable time and patience before positive results are evident.

Successful implementation of participative management and general supervision requires a continuous effort on a supervisor's part to develop employees beyond their present skills. Employees learn more when they can work out solutions for themselves rather than being given solutions. They learn best from their own successes and failures.

The participative supervisor spends considerable time encouraging employees to solve their own problems and to participate in and make decisions. As employees become more competent and self-confident, there is less need for the supervisor to instruct and watch them. A valid way to gauge the effectiveness of a supervisor is to study how employees in the department function when the supervisor is away from the job. This is the essence of real employee empowerment.

Although a supervisor may use participative management and general supervision whenever possible, from time to time he or she will have to demonstrate some authority with those employees who require close supervision. Participative and general supervisors must be as performance-conscious as any other type of supervisor. However, the style they use differentiates them from their more authoritarian counterparts.

The Proper Balance of Delegation

Although we have stressed the advantages of delegation that can be realized through general supervision, it is important to recognize that the process of delegation is delicate. It is not easy for a supervisor to part with some authority and still be left with the responsibility for the performance and decisions made by workers. There are numerous illustrations of how effective leadership requires sound judgment and skill. The supervisor must achieve a balance among too much, too little, and just the right amount in order to delegate without losing control. There are situations in which supervisors have to resort to their formal authority to attain the objectives of the department and get the job done. Supervisors at times have to make decisions that are distasteful to employees. Delegation does not mean that a supervisor should manage a department by consensus or by taking a vote on every issue.

7

Suggest approaches for introducing change to employees and for proposing change to higher-level managers.

INTRODUCING CHANGE

Change is expected as part of everyday life, and the survival and growth of most enterprises depend on change and innovation. Many books and articles have been written concerning the imperatives for change faced by most organizations. Indeed, it is recognized that the survival of a firm may depend on the abilities of its managers to make fundamental changes in virtually all aspects of operations while facing the risks of an uncertain future. The impact of change has become so commonplace that security and stability often are referred to as being concepts and practices related to the past.[10]

Making Change Means Supervisory Involvement

Despite all of the emphasis on change and changing, there still appear to be numerous problems and considerable resentment concerning both the introduction and effects associated with many organizational changes. There is an adage which says, "All progress is change, but not all change is progress." Too often, managers will look for a quick response in their organizations when making changes, and they become frustrated when expected results are not achieved. Mediocrity is then tolerated, and the net result is that the more things have changed, the more they have stayed the same.[11]

Our focus in the remaining part of this chapter is not to discuss comprehensive strategies for total organizational change.[12] Rather, it is to discuss the introduction and management of change from the supervisory perspective, which is another challenging aspect of a supervisor's leading function of management. As with so many other areas of concern, the introduction of change—such as a new work method, a new product, a new schedule, a new human resources policy, and the like—usually requires implementation at the departmental level. In the final analysis, whether a change has been initiated by higher management or by the supervisor personally, it is the supervisor who has the major role in bringing about the change. The success or failure of any change is usually related to a supervisor's ability to anticipate and deal with causes of resistance to change that usually are present.

Reasons for Resistance to Change

Some supervisors are inclined to discount the existence and magnitude of human resistance to change. What may seem like a trifling change to the supervisor may bring strong reaction from the employees. Supervisors should remember that employees seldom resist change just to be stubborn. They resist because they believe a change threatens their positions socially, psychologically, or economically. Therefore, the supervisor should be familiar with the ways in which resistance to change can be minimized and handled successfully.

Most people pride themselves on being up to date. As consumers, they expect and welcome changes in material things such as new automobiles, convenience items, electronic appliances, or computers. But as employees, they may resist changes on the job or changes in personal relationships, even though such changes are vital for the operation of the organization. If an organization is to survive, it must be able to react to prevailing conditions by making necessary adjustments.

Change disturbs the environment in which people exist. Prior to a change, employees become accustomed to a work environment in which patterns of relationships and behavior have reached a degree of stability. When a change takes place, new ideas and new methods may be perceived as a threat to the security of the work group. Many employees fear change because they cannot predict what the change will mean in terms of their own positions, activities, or abilities (Figure 14-6). It makes no difference whether the change actually has a negative result. What matters is that the employees believe that the change will cause negative consequences. For example, the introduction of new equipment is usually accompanied by employee fears of loss of jobs or skills. Even if the supervisor and higher-level managers announce that no employees will be laid off, rumors circulate that layoffs will occur or existing jobs will be downgraded. Employee fears may still be present months after the change has been in place.

FIGURE 14-6

Many people fear change because they cannot predict what the change will mean in terms of their own future with the organization.

For many years, noted author Tom Peters has advocated, "if it ain't broken, break it," and some organizations have continually adhered to his message. During the past decade, some organizations have been in constant change. Many examples come to mind but one sticks out. In the mid-1980s, two Fort Wayne, Indiana, banks—Indiana Bank and Peoples Trust Bank—merged. The resulting organization was called Summit Bank. Some branches were eliminated, tasks and functions consolidated, and early retirements proliferated. Since that time the following has occurred:

- Summit Bank was acquired by National Bank of Detroit (NBD) and the Summit Bank name was dropped.
- NBD and First Chicago entered a merger of equals and changed their signage to NBD/First Chicago.
- Bank One of Columbus, Ohio, then acquired NBD/Bank One to become the nation's fourth-largest bank.

At the time of publication of this text, with a depressed stock price and management turmoil, NBD/Bank One may become a takeover target itself. If you asked a veteran employee of the former Indiana Bank the question, "How many CEOs have you worked for?" their sarcastic response might be "All of them! My job has changed daily and every new manager keeps reinventing the wheel."

John B. McCoy, Bank One's former chairman and CEO, had, in the opinion of the authors, little problem initiating change. His problems, in part, came from the inability to sustain momentum that the original change(s) brought. All too often we have seen that new managers don't want to know the history of what's been done before, don't want to build on the successes of the prior change(s). The new group had to make its own mark—that is, "our way is the only way!"[13] In situations like these, many employees will begin to wonder "what does the future hold" or "will I be the next to go?"

Changes affect individuals in different ways. A change that causes great disturbance to one person may create only a small problem for another. A supervisor must learn to recognize how changes affect different employees and observe how individuals develop patterns of behavior that serve as barriers to accepting change.

Reducing Resistance to Change

Probably the most important factor in gaining employee acceptance of new ideas and methods is the personal relationship that exists between the supervisor who is introducing the change and the employees who are affected by it. If a relationship of confidence and trust exists, the employees are more likely to accept the change with minimal resistance.[14]

Provide Adequate Information. In the final analysis, it is not the change itself that usually leads to resistance. Rather, it is the manner in which the supervisor introduces the change. Thus, resistance to change, when it comes from fear of the unknown, can be minimized by supplying all the information that the employees consciously and subconsciously need to know.

Whenever possible, a supervisor should explain what will happen, why, and how the employees and the department will be affected by a change. If applicable, the supervisor should emphasize how the change will leave employees no worse off or may even improve their present situation. This information should be communicated to all employees who are directly or indirectly involved, either individually or collectively, and as early as appropriate. Only then can employees assess what a change will mean in terms of their activities. This will be facilitated if the supervisor has tried consistently to give ample background information for all directives.

Employees who are well acquainted with the underlying factors that surround departmental operations usually understand the necessity for change. They probably will ask questions about a change but they then can adjust to it and go on. When employees have been informed of the reasons for a change, what to expect, and how their jobs will be affected, they usually make reasonable adaptations. Instead of insecurity, they experience feelings of relative confidence and willing compliance.

However, if the change will involve closing certain operations and the loss of jobs, this should be explained openly and frankly. It is especially important to discuss which employees are likely to be affected and how the job cuts will be made. If higher-level managers have decided not to identify which individuals will be terminated until it actually happens, the supervisor should explain this as a reality and not try to hide behind vague promises or raise unrealistic expectations.

If a firm has 100 or more employees and it plans to close a plant or lay off major segments of employees, the firm must comply with the notification provisions of the 1988 Worker Adjustment and Retraining Notification Act (WARN). This law requires that employees must be given at least 60 days' prior notice before the closings or lay-offs are carried out. There are certain exceptions to this requirement. Compliance with this law is normally the responsibility of the firm's human resources or legal department, but supervisors may become involved in communicating the notifications to employees.

Encourage Participation in Decision Making. Another technique for reducing resistance to change is to permit the affected employees to share in making decisions about it. If several employees are involved in a change, group decision making is an effective way to reduce their fears and objections. When employees have an opportunity to work through new ideas and methods from the beginning, usually they will consider the new directives as something of their own making and give them their support. The group may even apply pressure on those who have reservations about going along with the change, and it is likely that each member of the group will carry out the change once there is agreement on how to proceed.

Group decision making is especially effective in changes in which the supervisor is indifferent about the details as long as the change is implemented. In these cases, the supervisor must set the limits within which the group can decide. For example, a supervisor may not care how a new departmental work schedule is divided among the group as long as the work is accomplished within a prescribed time, with a given number of employees, and without overtime.

Proposing Change to Higher-Level Managers

In many organizations higher-level managers complain that supervisors are too content with the status quo and are unwilling to suggest new and innovative ways of improving departmental performance. Supervisors, on the other hand, complain that higher-level managers are not receptive to ideas that they have suggested for their departments. There is probably some truth to both allegations. Early in the 1990s, Peter Senge introduced the concept of the "learning organization." Now he says that for big companies to succeed they need to start acting like gardeners: "I have never seen a successful organizational-learning program rolled out from the top. Not a single one. Conversely, every change process that I've seen that was sustained and that spread has started small. Just as nothing in nature starts big, start creating change with a pilot group—a growth seed."[15]

It should be clear that top-management's job is to pollinate those seeds (ideas) and help them to bear fruit. Unfortunately, that's not the way it works. If supervisors wish to propose changes, it is important that they understand how to present ideas not only to their employees, but also to higher-level managers. "Selling" an idea to a manager involves the art of persuasion, much as a good salesperson uses persuasion in selling a product or service to a reluctant customer. But what do I really do about my boss, if he or she is a tough sell? Cartoonist Scott Adams of *Dilbert* fame suggests that

Whatever you do, never use the so-called direct approach: "I have an idea. Let's do this." Dilbert would take exactly that approach, because he's an engineer and totally ignorant of the human condition. But the only way that a boss will respond to a reasonable suggestion is unreasonably—like with some of those great-idea-sinker questions: "If this is such a good idea, why isn't everybody doing it?" Or, "Have you asked everybody in the organization—all 1,000 of them—to buy into your idea?" The worst thing you can do is assume that your boss is a thoughtful person who will immediately recognize a good idea and take a personal risk to implement it. Instead, I suggest using the hypnosis approach. Lead your boss to your idea through subtle questioning—giving the impression that it was his idea in the first place.[16]

As silly as it may seem, at times, the supervisor must use various strategies to convince the boss that a proposal was actually the boss's idea!

Obtain Needed Information. A supervisor who has a good idea or who wishes to suggest a change should first ask, "What aspects of the idea or change will be of most interest to the boss?" Higher-level managers usually are interested if a change might improve production, increase profits, improve morale, or reduce overhead and other costs. It is important to do considerable homework to see whether a proposed change is feasible and adaptable to the departmental operation. By thinking through the idea carefully and getting as much information as possible, the supervisor will be in a better position to argue strong and weak points of the proposal. In addition, the supervisor should find out whether any other departments or organizations have used the proposed idea—either successfully or unsuccessfully. Doing this will impress the manager that the supervisor has invested time and effort in checking out the idea in other work environments.

Consult with Other Supervisors. To get an idea or proposal beyond the discussion stage, the supervisor should consult with other supervisors and personnel who might be affected and get their reactions to the proposed change. Checking it out with them gives them a chance to think the idea through, offer suggestions and criticisms, and work out some of the problems. Otherwise some supervisors may resist or resent the change if they feel they have been ignored.

If possible, it is helpful to get the tentative commitment of other supervisors. It is not always necessary to obtain their total approval, but higher-level managers will be more inclined to consider an idea if it has been discussed at least in preliminary form with knowledgeable people in the organization.

Formal Written Proposal. At times a supervisor may be asked by the manager to put the proposed idea in writing, so that copies may be forwarded to higher-level managers, other supervisors, or other personnel. This requires effort. The supervisor may have to engage in considerable study outside of normal working hours to obtain all the information needed. Relevant information on costs, prices, productivity data, and the like should be included in the proposal even if some data are only educated guesses. Highly uncertain estimates should be labeled as tentative, and exaggerated claims and opinions should be avoided. Risks, as well as potential advantages, should be acknowledged in the formal proposal.

Formal Presentation. If a supervisor is asked to make a formal presentation of the proposal, ample planning and preparation are required. The presentation should be made thoroughly and in an unhurried fashion, allowing sufficient time for questions and discussion.

A supervisor who has carefully thought through an idea should not be afraid to express it in a firm and convincing manner. The supervisor should be enthusiastic in explaining the idea, but at the same time be patient and empathetic with those who may not agree with it. A helpful technique in a formal presentation is to utilize some type of chart, diagram, or visual aid to dramatize it.

Acceptance or Rejection of Change by Higher-Level Managers

A supervisor who is able to persuade higher-level managers and other supervisors to accept a proposed change will feel inner satisfaction. Of course, any good idea requires careful implementation, follow-up, and refinement. Rarely does a change follow the exact blueprint suggested. Following up and working out the problems with others are important aspects of making a change effective.

However, despite a supervisor's best efforts, the idea may be rejected, altered greatly, or shelved. This can be frustrating, particularly to a supervisor who has worked diligently to develop an idea that he or she believes would lead to positive results. The important thing here is to avoid becoming discouraged and developing a negative outlook. There may be valid reasons why the idea was rejected, or the timing may not have been right. A supervisor should resolve to try again, perhaps to further refine and polish the idea for resubmission at a future date.

A supervisor who has developed an idea for change, even if it has not been accepted, usually will find that such efforts were appreciated by higher-level managers. Moreover, the experience of having worked through a proposal for change will make the supervisor a more valuable member of the organizational team, and there will be many other opportunities to work for the introduction of change.

What Call Did You Make?

As Anita Mathews in the opening vignette, you need to plan your communication carefully. Art Roberts may be upset at more than the fact that you are doing the work of employees. You need to try to understand what the real issue is. Does he understand that the department is shorthanded? Before you respond, think back to earlier conversations between yourself and Art. Has he communicated clearly what he expects from you? Have you felt free to disagree with Art when you talk? Is he aware of the problems you have in doing your job? What will the repercussions be if customers get their statements late?

You have fallen into one of the most common traps of supervision. When supervisors are asked the question, "What is the easiest and quickest way to get a job done?" they usually respond, "Do it myself!" It is natural to help out when you are needed. You feel comfortable doing the work, and in all likelihood you believe that your efforts in helping to get the work out on time will be appreciated. However, your supervisor, Art Roberts, does not like what you are doing. He believes that you should not do any of the work of the employees, even in extreme emergency situations.

Initially, you should have recognized the work backlog and talked to the employees about the problem. They could have helped you establish priorities if you must work alongside them for a period of time. You also could have called in temporary help to ease the backlog. However, you are uncertain about your au-

thority. Do you have the authority to call in temporaries? What budgetary authority do you have? These are issues that need to be clarified. It is your responsibility to clarify what is expected from you and what authority you have to get things done.

You should review the various leadership theories and leadership thought introduced in this chapter. These will provide insight on appropriate leader behavior. Ask yourself: What are the most important leadership activities that you should perform? In order to be a successful leader, you should assess a number of factors. Clearly, this particular situation and its urgency dictated the need for a different leadership style than normal.

On the other hand, maybe Art is trying to teach you something. Remember from Chapter 2 that we defined management as getting things done through others. Maybe he wants you to discover other ways to get the job done or to find ways to get your people to work smarter. Perhaps we are giving Art too much credit. In reality, he should be aware that the group is being asked to do the work that used to be done in three different facilities. In addition, he should realize that the survivors (those employees that remain since several vacated positions remain unfilled) need encouragement and support. It appears that you have implemented many of the suggestions found in this chapter.

Nevertheless, you will be uneasy telling Art how you feel since you are relatively new to the supervisory ranks. Pause and plan before you begin your discussion with Art. You want him to clarify his expectations. Ask specific questions that will elicit the answers needed to do the job. Recognize that perhaps now is not the best time to continue this discussion.

When you and Art discuss this issue, emphasize the importance of the customers and their expectation that their statements will be on time. Ask him what he would have done in similar circumstances. Clarify your authority. Above all, avoid conflict that could strain your long-term relationship with Art.

SUMMARY

1
Effective supervisory management means that supervisors must become leaders in the true sense of the word. Supervisory leadership primarily resides in the ability of the supervisor to influence the opinions, attitudes, and performance of employees toward accomplishing company goals. The test of supervisory leadership is whether subordinates follow willingly. Supervisory leadership skills can be developed.

2
Several different thoughts on leadership have been identified and discussed in this chapter. Warren Bennis categorized four things that people want from their leaders: direction, trust, hope, and results. Stephen Covey believes that the principle of alignment is essential for developing high trust. James Kouzes and Barry Posner believe that successful leaders exhibit a series of five practices—challenging the process, inspiring a shared vision, enabling others to act, modeling the way, and encouraging the heart. The "Contemporary Issue" box provides a variety of thoughts from industry leaders regarding leadership. The common threads are creation of a corporate vision, communicating honestly with employees, holding employees accountable, and engendering mutual trust and respect. In addition, managers must develop a culture in which subordinates buy into the organization's purpose and values.

3
Blake and McCanse's leadership styles are based on the degree of a manager's concern for people and for production. The more effective team manager successfully blends both concerns. The contingency or situational factors that influence leadership are identified in Fiedler's contingency theory, House's path-goal theory, Vroom and Yetton's leader-style theory, and Hersey and Blanchard's theory. Fiedler's contingency model stresses that the proper approach is contingent upon the factors in any given situation. Fiedler contends that leader-member relations, task structure, and leader position power are the important dimensions assumed to influence leader effectiveness. Effective leaders, according to House, are those who chart out and clarify paths to high performance. Situational factors that determine the extent of subordinate participation in decision making are the essence of Vroom and Yetton's theory. Hersey and Blanchard identify the readiness of a subordinate to do a particular task as an important situational factor.

Trust, self-awareness, and motivation are the core traits of transformational leadership. Although no one supervisory leadership style is universally acceptable, the need to establish standards, develop a climate where people are self-motivated, and adapt to constant change are the key traits of effective leaders.

4
The process of delegation is made up of three components: assigning a job or duties, granting authority, and creating responsibility. For delegation to succeed, supervisors must give employees enough authority and responsibility to carry out their assigned duties. All three components are interdependent in that a change in one requires a corresponding change in the other two.

5

6

7

The supervisor must be specific in telling employees what authority they have and what they can or cannot do. The supervisor delegates authority to employees to accomplish specific jobs, but the supervisor's own personal accountability cannot be delegated.

Included among the many reasons supervisors are reluctant to delegate are shortage of qualified employees, fear of making mistakes, the "I'd rather do it myself" mentality, fear of not being needed, reluctant employees, and lack of managerial support for decisions. "Seagull managers" have conditioned some employees to avoid receiving tasks from their immediate supervisor, who "dump" rather than delegate.

Effective supervisors see the benefits of delegation. Employees become more involved and gain knowledge and confidence in their skills. The supervisor benefits from greater flexibility, better decisions, higher employee morale, and better job performance.

Participative management and general supervision promote delegation because they provide employees with considerable involvement in making decisions and doing their jobs to meet departmental objectives. They offer many advantages to supervisors as well as employees. The supervisor saves time in the long term. By giving employees practice in making decisions and using their own judgment, the supervisor encourages them to become more competent and more promotable.

Some supervisors believe that autocratic supervision is more likely to get results from employees than general supervision. There are occasions when supervisors have to rely on their managerial authority. For the most part, however, these should be the exceptions rather than the rule.

The extent to which a supervisor uses the autocratic or general approach requires a delicate balance. The advantages of delegation are realized through general supervision. However, at times supervisors have to resort to their formal authority to attain departmental objectives.

To successfully cope with employees' normal resistance to change, supervisors must understand why resistance surfaces and what can be done to help employees adjust and accept necessary changes. A supervisor also should learn the principles of "selling" change to higher-level managers. Sometimes, supervisors may have to subtly convince their manager that the idea was his or hers in the first place. Regardless of the approach used, the supervisor must persuade all affected personnel that the acceptance of the proposed change will benefit them and the total organization.

KEY TERMS

Leadership (page 468)
Contingency-style leadership (page 471)
Delegation (page 473)
Accountability (page 473)
Autocratic (authoritarian)
  supervision (page 482)
Bureaucratic style of supervision (page 482)

General supervision (page 483)
Participative management (page 483)
Directive (page 483)
Free-rein (laissez-faire) supervision
  (page 486)
Stretch targets (page 486)

QUESTIONS FOR DISCUSSION

1. How might it be possible that an organization is criticized as "over-managed and under-led?"

2. Think of a time when someone got you to do something that you didn't like to do. You ended up liking it. What did the person do to motivate you to do it? Why are the motivation theories discussed in Chapter 4 at the heart of understanding leadership?
3. Why is trust a key ingredient in the leadership equation?
4. Review Kouzes and Posner's five practices and ten specific leader behaviors. Now review the thoughts of the leaders identified in this chapter's "Contemporary Issue" box. In what ways are the thoughts of Kouzes and Posner similar to those of the industry leaders?
5. Why are the concepts of responsibility, authority, and accountability closely related? Why can a supervisor's personal accountability not be delegated?
6. Why are supervisors reluctant to delegate? What benefits typically accrue to a supervisor who learns to delegate?
7. Distinguish between autocratic (authoritarian) supervision on one hand and participative management and general supervision on the other. What theoretical differences are implied in each of these approaches? Relate these to concepts concerning delegation of authority, motivation, and empowerment.
8. Is autocratic supervision always inappropriate? Are there situations in which a supervisor will have to rely on authority in order to receive high performance? Discuss.
9. Why is it inappropriate to assume that a leadership style that works best in one situation will be just as effective in another?
10. Assume that you are the night-shift supervisor in a fast-food restaurant. It has been difficult to hire qualified employees. On a typical shift, 20 percent of the scheduled employees are "no shows." Write a directive addressing the situation. Now compare your directive with the characteristics of good directives identified in this chapter. Are there better ways to get the message across?
11. Consider the following statement, "People don't resist change, they resist being changed." To what extent is the statement true? Discuss strategies for overcoming resistance to being changed.
12. Discuss the principles of proposing change to higher-level managers.

SKILLS APPLICATIONS

Skills Application 14-1: Delegation Practice

The following are some guidelines for effective delegation:
1. Make a list of your duties and responsibilities (tasks).
2. Identify regular tasks that could be delegated.
3. Make a list of your employees. Indicate their major strengths and weaknesses. What training opportunities do they need?
4. Match each task to the employee's abilities and needs.
5. Plan the communication; spell out specific objectives.
6. Provide training, coaching, and guidance as necessary.
7. Give employees freedom to do the task their way.
8. Monitor performance. Be available for assistance.
9. Make adjustments as necessary.
10. Provide reinforcement.

Your assignment:
1. **a.** Review what needs to be done for the next two weeks. Check those items you can assign or delegate to someone else.

    b. Using the guidelines cited above, develop a plan for assigning one of the tasks to someone else. (Note: This person may be a family member, roommate, or member of a group to which you belong.)

    c. Make a list of the important information that must be communicated to the other person.

    d. Determine how often and in what form you want progress reports.

    e. Practice by giving someone the assignment.

  2. Critique your approach. What could you have done better?

Skills Application 14-2: Delegating or Dumping?

The store manager stumbles on a card game being played in the employee lounge during the lunch hour. The employees are obviously playing for money. The store manager storms into the supervisor's office and bawls him out for letting this go on. "I don't care how you do it, but I want it stopped."

1. Is the store manager delegating or dumping? Explain your response.
2. Develop a way for the store manager to better handle the situation.
3. Compare your responses with those of an experienced supervisor and with other student responses.

What good ideas did you have that others did not? What ideas did others have that you would adopt?

Skills Application 14-3: Supervisory Styles

After reading each of the following scenarios, identify the type of supervisory style (i.e., authoritarian, participative, or general supervision) that you feel would be preferable, and why.

Scenario 1: You are the supervisor in charge of work crews who lay track for a railroad. Their basic duties are to remove old ties and rails, lay new ties, and secure the rails to the ties.

Scenario 2: You are the supervisor in charge of a cancer research project in a pharmaceutical firm. The duties of the personnel vary greatly due to the experimental nature of the project. The group you supervise are professionals—most have PhDs in pharmacy, chemistry, and biology.

Scenario 3: You supervise a work team in a call center. The employees answer customers' questions about their credit card accounts. Often customers are angry or have complaints about their accounts. The typical worker falls into two distinct groups—first full-time job for those just out of high school, or single mothers returning to the workforce. The work is periodically monitored by computer or other means of electronic surveillance. During the past year, you hired over 60 employees for the 14 positions. The hours are from 6:00 A.M. EST to 11:00 P.M. EST and the center is open seven days a week.

Scenario 4: You are a counselor at a YMCA camp. The middle school youngsters (ages 12 to 14) arrive on Sunday afternoon and leave the following Saturday at noon. During their stay they participate in a variety of learning, athletic, and social activities. In addition to being in charge of the swimming program, you are also the evening lodge counselor for 14 youngsters. The accommodations are a cottage consisting of a private counselor's room w/bath; seven bunk beds, a community bath and restroom facility, and a small reading/eating lounge.

Skills Application 14-4: The Most Admired Manager

1. Think of the manager you admire the most. List at least six things that the person did to make your most admired list.
2. Interview two persons who are employed full time—it is suggested that you interview one person who is a baby boomer (born between 1946 and 1964) and another who is a Gen-Xer (someone in their late 20s or early 30s). Ask them to think of the manager they admire the most. Develop a list of at least three things that this person did to make their most admired list.
3. Compare your list with those of the two people you interview. What are the similarities between the lists? What are the differences? What accounts for the differences? Write a brief paragraph describing what you learned from this skill application.

INTERNET ACTIVITY

Skills Application 14-5: Managing Change

Change is a constant in today's workplace. How will you manage it as a supervisor? Visit the Change Management Resource Library (www.change-management.org), the BPR Online Learning Center (www.prosci.com), or other sites dealing with "managing change" to learn more about effective change management. View a few of the articles you find in the Change Management Resource Library. You might also check out the Tutorials section of the BPR Learning Center.

1. Name at least five key elements that must be in place to affect change within your organization.
2. Create a list of strategies that you as a supervisor can use to help create and maintain change within your work group.

SKILL DEVELOPMENT VIDEO

SKILL DEVELOPMENT MODULE 14-1: DELEGATION

This video segment introduces Tony Roberts, the newly appointed supervisor in the Accounting Department at Lexicon Dynamics.

Questions for Discussion: The Ineffective Version

1. Discuss how Tony Roberts did not delegate and how it affected his department.
2. What should Tony Roberts do to be more effective as department supervisor?
3. Explain why good communication skills are important for effective leadership.
4. In your opinion, how has the upper-level management at Lexicon Dynamics failed Tony Roberts?

Questions for Discussion: The More Effective Version

1. Is Tony Roberts an effective supervisor? Why or why not?
2. How could Tony Roberts do a better job of leading his subordinates?
3. Which of the leadership theories presented in Figure 14-1 should Tony Roberts know more about? Why?
4. In your opinion, why would you like to work for a supervisor like Tony Roberts?

ENDNOTES

1. Students beginning a discussion of leadership should review Peter Drucker's article, "Not Enough Generals Were Killed!" *Forbes ASAP* (April 8, 1996), p. 104. Ronald A. Heifetz's *Leadership Without Easy Answers* (Belknap Press, 1994) is worth reading. For a more recent discussion of Heifetz's views on the future of leadership, see William C. Taylor, "The Leader of the Future," *Fast Company* (June 1999), pp. 130+.

2. Stratford Sherman, "How the Best Leaders are Learning Their Stuff," *Fortune* (November 27, 1995), pp. 90–102. Also see Peter Senge, *The Fifth Discipline: The Art and Practice of the Learning Organization* (Doubleday, 1990) and Senge, et.al., *The Fifth Discipline Handbook: Strategies and Tools for Building a Learning Organization* (Doubleday, 1994).

3. As reported in Gerald Graham, "Results among Four Traits Workers Want in Their Leadership," *The News Sentinel* (Fort Wayne, IN, July 8, 1996), p. 11b. Consistently, the literature is replete with the need for developing trust—the authors concur that building mutual trust and respect is the foundation of effective supervision. Also see Warren Bennis, "Learning to Lead," *Executive Excellence* (January 1996), p. 7; and Sherman E. Afholderbach, "Supervisory Techniques: A Supervisor's Perspective," *Supervision* (June 1998), pp. 11–13. Ram Charan and Geoffrey Colving, "Why CEOs Fail," *Fortune* (June 21, 1999), pp. 69–78, identified eight qualities that characterize successful CEOs. Not surprisingly, integrity was at the top of their list. Kevin Cashman, author of *Leadership from the Inside Out* (Executive Excellence, 1998), argues that there are three core qualities to leadership: authenticity, self-expression, and value creation.

4. Personal recollection by one of the authors of discussion with the late Ed Souder, owner of Souder's General Store in Grabill, Indiana. Souder's son, Mark, is currently a U.S. Congressman from the 4th Indiana District.

5. Stephen R. Covey, "Principle-Centered Leadership," *Quality Digest* (March 1996), p. 21. Authors Richard L. Daft and Robert H. Lengel, *Fusion Leadership* (Berrett-Koehler, 1998), describe a method for bringing people together to accomplish mutual goals based on shared vision and values. The principles of fusion (joining together) rather than fision (splitting apart) support individual employee growth and ingenuity.

6. A more complete discussion can be found in James M. Kouzes and Barry Z. Posner, *The Leadership Challenge: How to Get Extraordinary Things Done in Organizations* (Jossey-Bass, 1987) and *Leadership Practices Inventory (LPI): A Self-Assessment and Analysis* (available from Pfeiffer & Company, San Diego).

7. James M. Kouzes and Barry Z. Posner, *Credibility: How Leaders Gain and Lose It, Why People Demand It* (Jossey-Bass, 1993).

8. Ronald E. Merrill and Henry D. Sedgwick, in their article "To Thine Own Self Be True," *Inc.* (August 1994), pp. 50–56, identified six styles of entrepreneurial management—the Classic, the Coordinator, the Craftsman, the Team Manager, the Entrepreneur plus Employee Team, and the Small Partnership. Like the authors of this text, they contend that any one of them can be effective.

9. Much of this is based on personal observations of the authors and inferences drawn from articles like Sue Shellenberger, "The Care and Feeding (and the Avoiding) of Horrible Bosses," *The Wall Street Journal* (October 20, 1999), p. B1; Stanley Bing, "Hail and Farewell, Chainsaw Al! Don't let the door hit you on the way out, y'hear," *Fortune* (July 20, 1998), pp. 43–44; and Brian Dumaine, "America's Toughest Bosses," *Fortune* (October 18, 1993), pp. 38–50.

10. H. James Harrington, among others, asserts that "you can be certain that in the 21st century, change will accelerate even further." Harrington, "Master Change or It Will Master You," *Quality Digest* (February 1999), p. 22. Harry E. Chambers, "The Agencies of Leadership," *Executive Excellence* (August 1999), p. 12, states "you can't move forward while being immersed in the past" and offers suggestions for helping employees get off the fence. Also see Timothy Galpin, "Connecting Culture to Organizational Change," *HRMagazine* (March 1996), pp. 84–90; and Donald L. Kirkpatrick, "Riding the Winds of Change," *Training & Development* (February 1995), pp. 28–32.

11. Oren Harari, "Why Don't Things Change?" *Management Review* (February 1995), pp. 30–32. Author Jim Collins presents an interesting aspect of change. He says that while many experts say "'Change or Die,—the reason to get better is that bad things will happen to you if you don't.' Is that kind of fear a good motivator? Not for long." See Collins, "Fear Not," *Inc.* (May 1998), pp. 30–40.

12. For extensive overviews of strategic organizational change approaches, see Peter L. Brill and Richard Worth, *The Four Levels of Corporate Change* (AMACOM, 1997); Rick Maurer, *Beyond the Wall: Unconventional Strategies that Build Support for Change* (Bard Press, 1996); Peter Scott-Morgan, *Unwritten Rules of the Game: Master Them, Shatter Them and Break Through the Barriers to Organizational Change* (McGraw-Hill, 1994); and Price Pritchett and Ron Pound, *High-Velocity Change: A Handbook for Managers* (Pritchett Publishing Co., 1994). For information on bringing about quality improvement initiatives, see Don Harrison, "Accelerating Change," *Quality Digest* (December 1999), p. 33.

13. Based on observations and personal interviews with employees, including former Bank One Indiana Region president Tom Blume, during 1998–1999. Also see Joseph H. Cahill, "CEO McCoy Quits a Flagging Bank One," *The Wall Street Journal* (December 22, 1999), p. A3. Also see acting CEO Verne G. Istock's report to stockholders in *1999 Bank One Annual Report* (dated April 5, 2000), "Simply put, we did NOT manage the business as well as we could have."

14. For expanded discussions concerning building trust between supervisors and employees, see Lois P. Frankel and Karen L. Otzo, "Employee Coaching: The Way to Gain Commitment, Not Just Compliance," *Employment Relations Today* (Autumn 1992), pp. 311–320; or Parry Pascarella, "Fifteen Ways to Win People's Trust," *Industry Week* (February 1, 1993), pp. 47–51. Rick Maurer's "Put Resistance to Work for You," *HRMagazine* (April 1996), pp. 75–81, presents some basic suggestions for dealing with resistance to change.

15. Peter Senge as quoted in Alan M. Webber, "Learning for Change," *Fast Company* (May 1999), pp. 178+. Also see Senge's *The Dance of Change: The Challenges of Sustaining Momentum in Learning Organizations* (Doubleday/Current, 1999).

16. Scott Adams as quoted in Anna Muoio, "Boss Management," *Fast Company* (April 1999), pp. 91+.

Managing Work Groups: Teamwork, Morale, and Counseling

You Make the Call!

You are Charlie Graham, director of operations for Belmont Manufacturing. The 250 nonunionized employees manufacture plastic interior parts for the auto industry.

When Pandora Azuka joined Belmont five years ago, her supervisor at the time told her not to buy the most expensive pair of safety glasses because she wouldn't be with the company long enough to make the investment worthwhile. Azuka didn't listen. She bought the glasses. And she stayed, but it wasn't easy.

At one point, employee turnover at Belmont was over 75 percent. Belmont was scraping the "bottom of the barrel" when hiring employees. Some employees could barely read or write and had difficulty following basic instructions. The productivity problems alienated customers. Belmont was scrapping more product than they were shipping. That's when you and Elaine Knight, the new director of marketing, attended a total quality management seminar.

Upon your return, you and Knight began calling customers and vendors; visiting manufacturing plants known for their total quality commitment; and analyzing production processes, methods, and costs. Working with Bob Watters, the newly hired personnel manager, the three of you conducted an in-depth analysis of employee morale. This was followed with an identification of the costs, savings, and potential benefits of improving morale.

The trio and seven other employees formed the Belmont Excellence Team. Its mission was to make Belmont a better place to work. After several starts and stops, and a few glitches, the team came up with several ideas.

"The real key," you recalled, "was learning how to listen carefully to our people." They told us what they needed to be satisfied at work and in life. Additional data from the attitude surveys, exit interviews, and customer service indexes played a role in our restructuring. The personnel manager served as the conduit for all employee concerns. We instituted a basic literacy program for employees. We eliminated two management layers: plant superintendent and foreman. The removal of these positions showed that we were serious about the future—front-line workers would be empowered."

"When I came in here, corporate management had directed us to bring about improvement or they would close the plant. I knew from experience that there is no instant quality improvement program that would produce miraculous results overnight. We (Elaine, Bob, and I) had a commitment from top management that they would give us thirty months to show progress or the plant would be shut down. We had agreed among ourselves that we would follow Covey's "Law of the Farm" model—we must plow and plant in the spring and tend the crops during the summer, so we can harvest in the fall."

"We instituted job skills and process training. After the classroom training, all employees swung on ropes, climbed trees, and helped colleagues through a challenge course. It is common in a high output, just-in-time production plant for workers not to communicate with others outside their own work areas. The team training really helped to bring people from different departments together," said Knight. "As a result, other teams were formed to deal with specific projects—work processes, scrap, defects, productivity, and the like." Azuka volunteered to be on the first quality improvement team.

The plans resulted in a scrap rate less than the industry average; customer complaints were lowered from over 350 the year prior to your arrival to just 4 in the most recent quarter; individual productivity has jumped more than 50 percent; and overtime has been reduced to less than 8 hours during the past quarter.

You recounted, "People really want to come here and work. We now have a reputation as a good place to work. The cross-functional team members act like Belmont is their personal company. We've built a continuous improvement process into our culture. Increased employee wages and benefits have more than been covered by the savings generated through employee suggestions."

As director of operations, you know that more will be necessary. Where do we go from here? How can we sustain the momentum we've built up over the past four years?

You Make the Call!

1
Explain why work groups
form and function, and their
importance.

UNDERSTANDING WORK GROUPS AND THEIR IMPORTANCE

In Chapter 9, we presented an overview of the informal organization with particular reference to the supervisor's relationship with informal work groups and their leaders. We mentioned that informal work groups can exert a positive or negative influence on employee motivation and performance. Throughout this book we have emphasized that a supervisor's decisions must be concerned not only with employees as individuals, but also with how they relate to groups both within and outside the supervisor's own department.

An individual's motivations and clues to behavior are often found in the context of the person's associates, colleagues, and peers. On the job, an employee's attitudes and morale can be shaped to a large degree by coworkers, at times even more than by the supervisor or other factors in the work environment. Therefore, a supervisor should be aware of work groups and how they function. Moreover, a supervisor needs to develop a keen understanding of how morale influences employee performance and what can be done to maintain a high level of morale at the departmental level.

Why Work Groups Form and Function

There are many reasons why work groups form and function in work settings.[1] Among the most commonly identified reasons are:

1. *Companionship and identification.* The work group provides a peer relationship and a sense of belonging, which help satisfy the individual employee's social needs.
2. *Behavior guidelines.* People tend to look to others, especially their peers, for motivational guides to acceptable behavior in the workplace.
3. *Problem solving.* The work group may be instrumental in providing a viable means by which an individual employee may solve a personal problem.
4. *Protection.* The old adage of "strength in numbers" is not lost on employees, who often look to the group for protection from outside pressures, such as those placed by supervisors and higher-level managers.

Much behavioral research has focused on factors that make work groups tightly knit, cohesive, and effective. Work groups usually are most cohesive when:

1. The group members perceive themselves to have a higher status as compared to other employees, as, for example, in matters of job classification or pay.
2. The group is generally small in size.
3. The group shares similar personal characteristics, such as age, sex, ethnic background, off-the-job interests, and the like.
4. The group is located relatively distant from other employees, such as geographically dispersed work groups or groups located away from the home office.
5. The group has been formed due to outside pressures or for self-protection, such as a layoff or disciplinary action taken by management.
6. Group members can communicate with one another relatively easily.

Members of a cohesive work group enjoy their affiliation with the group.

7. The group has been successful in some previous group effort, which encourages the members to seek new group objectives.

Of course, a supervisor will never be completely aware of the kinds of forces that are most prevalent in the group dynamics of the department. However, a sensitivity to the considerations just described can help the supervisor deal with work groups more effectively.

CLASSIFICATIONS OF WORK GROUPS

2
Classify work groups and their meaning for supervisors.

Four major types of employee work groups can be identified in most organizations.[2] Groups can be classified as command groups, task groups, friendship groups, and special-interest groups. Since there is some overlap in these classifications, a supervisor should recognize that individual employees may be members of several such groups simultaneously.

Command group
Grouping of employees according to authority relationships on the formal organization chart.

Command Group. The **command group** is a grouping of employees according to the authority relationships shown on the formal organizational chart. Members of this group work together on a day-to-day basis to accomplish the regularly assigned work. For example, at the departmental level a command group consists of the supervisor and the employees who report to this supervisor. Throughout the organization there will be interrelated departments or divisions of command groups that reflect the formal authority structure.

Task group or cross-functional team
Grouping of employees who come together to accomplish a particular task.

Task Group or Cross-Functional Team. Consisting of employees from different departments, a **task group or cross-functional team** comes together to accomplish a particular task or project. For example, for a telephone to operate in a customer's home, the telephone company's employees and supervisors from a number of departments—such as customer service, construction, plant installation, central office equipment, accounting, and test center—may come into contact with one another to accomplish the job. Another example would be a hospital where numerous interdepartmental task relationships and communications take place among hospital personnel from departments such as admitting, nursing, laboratory, dietary, pharmacy, physical therapy, and medical records in order to care for a patient.

A more specialized subset of this group would be a customer satisfaction team. Members of this team will represent many different functions, and may include customer and supplier representatives. The team members come together to solve a specific problem and then disband upon initiating a solution. People are obviously the primary drivers in reaching customer satisfaction. In the true sense of self-directed project teams, members will develop the systems and the processes and, in turn, use them to perform their jobs. Organizations such as Sun Microsystems (see this chapter's first "Contemporary Issue" box) bring groups of people together so they can apply their combined talents to improve customer satisfaction.

Friendship group

Informal grouping of employees based on similar personalities and social interests.

Friendship Group. The **friendship group** is an informal group of people who have similar personalities and social interests. Many friendship groups are related primarily to common factors such as age, sex, ethnic background, outside interests, and marital status. Of course, the presence of command and task groups may be instrumental in bringing clusters of friendship groups together.

Special-interest group

Grouping of employees that exists to accomplish something in a group that individuals do not choose to pursue individually.

Special-Interest Group. The **special-interest group** exists to accomplish in a group something that individuals feel incapable of or unwilling to pursue individually. Such a group can be either temporary or permanent. A temporary special-interest group might be a committee of employees who wish to protest an action taken by a supervisor or management, to promote a charitable undertaking, or to organize an employee picnic. A labor union is an example of a more permanent special-interest group since it is legally and formally organized. A labor union brings together employees from different departments and divisions to unite them in striving for economic and other objectives.

As stated earlier, an employee may be a member of a number of groups in the workplace, and the supervisor who understands the nature of these different groups is more likely to be in a position to influence them. Some research studies have suggested that a supervisor has a better chance to influence an individual employee's behavior as a member of a work group than to deal with that employee individually (that is, without having the work group's influence in mind). Some concepts in this regard will be presented later in this chapter.

3

State some important research findings about work groups.

RESEARCH INSIGHTS FOR MANAGING WORK GROUPS

Numerous behavioral studies have been made of work groups and how they function. From these, a number of approaches for managing work groups effectively have been

contemporary issue

Self-Managed "SunTeams" Focus on Process Improvement Through Teamwork for Increased Customer Satisfaction and Loyalty

Since its inception in 1982, a singular vision, "The Network is the Computer™," has propelled Sun Microsystems, Inc., to its position as a leading provider of high-performance computer systems and solutions. The company is best known for the UNIX-based computer system and the Java programming language.

In 1995, the American Society for Competitiveness bestowed the coveted Philip B. Crosby Quality Award on Sun. Not content to rest on its laurels, Sun, as a part of a companywide quality improvement program, instituted a team improvement process. "One of the most important measures of quality is trust," says Jim Lynch, Sun Microsystems' director of corporate quality. "We earn a customer's trust by delivering products and services that meet customer expectations. And, just as we earn a customer's trust through quality, we build quality through the trust of our employees, partners, and suppliers."

The SunTeams program gives employees the power to improve the company's processes in order to increase customer loyalty, product quality, and employee collaboration and teamwork. A group of employees takes ownership of improving an internal company process in order to either reduce customer dissatisfaction or increase customer loyalty. This leads to the formation of a SunTeam.

All SunTeams compete for recognition at the annual companywide SunTeams celebration. At this event, the top teams present their improvements to the company's executives, who judge project outcomes on six criteria: teamwork and communication, project selection, analysis techniques, remedies, results achieved, and institutionalized improvements.

Another initiative, SunUp, is a collaborative effort between Sun employees, customers, and third parties to analyze, develop, implement, and manage services, infrastructure, and products that improve availability.

"The results have been phenomenal," says Lynch. "This year's 'best of the best' teams achieved goals including reducing specific product failures by 80 percent and cutting workstation manufacturing cycle times from 10 days to two days." "Employee morale has also increased as a byproduct of this process," added Marissa Peterson, director of U.S. manufacturing. "People are happier, and when they're happier, they perform better. We see performance improvements in terms of output, quality, and the efficiency we get from the operations. Motivated employees give us better ideas, and we see the results very quickly when those ideas are incorporated into production."

Lynch estimates that some 300 SunTeams will save the company $20 million through process improvement and innovation this year. "The SunTeams program not only positively impacts the bottom line, but also serves to attract and retain the best and brightest employees," explains Lynch.

Sources: Excerpted and adapted from "Teams Shine at Sun Microsystems," *Quality Digest* (May 1999), p. 10. For additional information about "Quality at Sun" including customer quality and loyalty indexes, SunTeams, SunUp, and other quality initiatives, visit Sun's Web site at www.sun.com, and see David P. Hamilton, "Sun Microsystems Basks in the Glow of Internet Aura," *The Wall Street Journal* (January 21, 2000), p. B4.

suggested. Although they are by no means certain to produce the desired results, they are consistent with behavioral research findings concerning work group dynamics and group behavior.

Insights from the Hawthorne Studies

Hawthorne Studies

Comprehensive research studies that focused on work-group dynamics as related to employee attitudes and productivity.

The work group studies that probably have had the most lasting influence during this century were conducted in the late 1920s and early 1930s at Western Electric Company's Hawthorne plant near Chicago, Illinois.[3] Known as the **Hawthorne Studies,** they remain a comprehensive and definitive source on the subject of work-group dynamics as related to employee attitudes and productivity.

A brief synopsis of two of the major experiments at the Hawthorne plant is given here. These are the relay assembly room experiment and the bank wiring observation room experiment.

Relay Assembly Room Experiment. In the relay assembly room experiment, a group of six female employees worked on jobs consisting of assembling electrical relay equipment. They were closely observed in a special room while being subjected to varying conditions. For about two years, researchers experimented with a number of scheduling arrangements, such as changes in rest and lunch periods, in workday arrangements, and in the workweek. Regardless of whether the changes instituted were favorable or unfavorable to the group, the outcome was that the employees' performance generally improved. By the end of this experiment, overall productivity had risen to about 30 percent over the pre-experiment level!

The researchers found that the primary reasons for the marked improvement in work performance were the attitudes and morale that had developed the employees into a solid, cohesive group. The employees became involved in the changes that were implemented, and felt that they were part of a team. The employees said that they felt that their supervision was much more informal and relaxed than they had experienced previously. Equally important was the fact that they considered the experiment to be an important part of a major project in the company. Since their work took on new importance, they developed their own norms for doing their jobs better. The research results clearly showed that a work group can be a positive influence on job performance if the group believes that it is part of a team and that what they are doing is important.

Bank Wiring Observation Room Experiment. A second group research experiment at the Hawthorne plant occurred a little later and lasted for almost a year. It involved 14 male employees whose work was to attach and solder banks of wires to telephone equipment. These employees and an observer were placed in a special room. The purpose of this experiment was to determine the impact of a series of wage incentive plans on employee productivity. The result of this experiment, however, revealed that a work group can have a negative influence on job performance. It turned out that the bank wiring observation room employees, as a group, developed an entirely different approach to their jobs than did the women in the relay assembly room experiment. The men decided to restrict output and keep it at a constant standard (or norm), which they referred to as the "bogey." It was learned from observation and interviews with the men in this group that there was strong pressure on the group members not to do anything more than the standard agreed upon by them. In effect, their approach was to maintain production at a level considered sufficient to keep the company "satisfied," but not nearly as much as the employees could do. In fact, the employees believed that if they increased production significantly, it would not mean higher wages but would instead lead to a management "speed-up" without additional compensation, and some employees might be laid off. Many of the lessons learned from the Hawthorne Studies are still applicable to supervisory practice today, giving support to the old adage that "the more things change, the more they stay the same."

Insights from Team Research

The Wisdom of Teams.   In a number of chapters we have mentioned various organized participative management programs. These have been called by many names—most prominently *quality circles, employee involvement,* and *total quality management.* Regardless of what they are called, they all have certain characteristics in common. For the most part, they try to build effective work teams that will foster continual improvement of work processes, project tasks, and service to customers. One of the most comprehensive surveys was conducted by Jon Katzenbach and Douglas Smith, two management consultants, who interviewed hundreds of team members in dozens of organizations that had utilized teams to address various types of problems. This research led them to identify common principles that were most associated with effective work teams. Among these were the following:

1. The members of the team must be committed to the group and the performance of the group.
2. Teams function better when they are small, usually 10 members or less.
3. Teams should be composed of individuals who have skills that are complementary and sufficient to deal with the problem at hand.
4. The team should be committed to an objective that is specific and realistic.[4]

Much can also be learned from the case studies reported in Steven Jones and Michael Beyerlein's *Developing High Performance Work Teams.* One such study describes Eastman Chemical Company's decision to move to a team management approach at its Kingsport, Tennessee facility. Based upon their findings, the authors concluded:

- Because supervisors must take on more responsibility and receive less recognition, they will feel threatened by the transition to teams. Therefore, it is essential that supervisors be coached, supported, and encouraged in their new roles.
- Team members must be held accountable for their actions to increase feelings of personal responsibility for the team's success.
- New team leadership roles for the supervisors include coaching and facilitating.
- Communication becomes ever more important. Team leaders must also be process oriented and have meetings to clarify team roles.[5]

The Importance of Team Members. At the start of the 20th century, commentators predicted what the next 100 years might bring. Who among them would have envisioned that participative management would be a topic of discussion a hundred years later? In Chapters 8 and 9, for example, we postulated about various types of organizational design. But there are many forces in the marketplace that can rapidly change even our best guesses. Nevertheless, we expect that teamwork will be as important tomorrow as it was yesterday—perhaps even more so.

When asked about effective teams, many illustrations from the world of professional and amateur sports come to mind. Why? Few organizations, their leaders, and members are as well-documented as sports teams. Most readers will recall that the New York Yankees, under manager Joe Torre, won back-to-back world championships in 1998 and 1999. But even the Yankees have stumbled from time to time. Did you know that in 1920, the Yankees bought Babe Ruth from the Boston Red Sox? Did this acquisition guarantee instantaneous success? No, it was not until Ruth's fourth season with the Yankees that they won their first World Championship. In the next 40 years they won 20 World Series. Astute baseball fans can recall some of the stars, but for every star there were dozens of unheralded role players. These role players show up for work every day, clearly understand their roles, are trained so they know how to perform and continuously improve their jobs, and want to feel they are making meaningful contributions to the effectiveness of their teams. As author Kenneth Turan said, "Team sports could not exist without, well, teams. Competent, superbly professional role players, the good soldiers who do what's asked of them and don't bask in anyone's attention, are the *sine qua non* of the organizations that win year after year."[6]

Teamwork

People working cooperatively to solve problems and achieve goals important to the group.

Collaborative workplace

Work environment characterized by joint decision making, shared accountability and authority, and high trust levels between employees and managers.

Collaborative Workplace. None of the great sports teams or business organizations of the 20th century could have been successful without **teamwork**—people working cooperatively to solve problems and achieve goals important to the group. Stated succinctly, a **collaborative workplace** means that throughout the organization there is shared authority for decision making between employees and management. Teamwork processes are utilized to promote trust and integrity and to build consensus and shared ownership in striving to achieve common objectives. Collaboration is based on a work ethic which recognizes that people want and need to be valued for their contributions, and that improvements and changes are best achieved by those who are responsible for implementing changes and committed to making them work.[7]

Noted quality writer and principal at Ernst & Young, H. James Harrington, writes:

The disadvantage with teams is that they are inwardly focused. They are small groups that, if functioning properly, strive to better other teams. Teams by their very nature are competitive. . . . In well-managed organizations, trust runs high and people are empowered to make decisions on their own. These organizations focus on promoting teamwork between individuals. It's an attitude of "How can I help?" "What can I do to make your job easier?" "How can we work together to produce more value for the whole organization?"[8]

Teams That Work. Another series of studies conducted among work teams in a large financial services company reached the conclusion that teams were most effective when

(1) the focus was on managing the team as a group and having the team manage its in- dividual members; and (2) the work teams were designed to be effective both in terms of improving productivity and in improving satisfaction of team members. These stud- ies emphasized that the success of teams was largely attributable to the careful design and focus of the teams at the outset.[9] Not all participative management programs have been successful. In fact, a considerable number of firms have abandoned these programs for a variety of reasons. Some problems were procedural or technical, such as cases in which teams were preoccupied with internal processes rather than focusing on external and targeted results. Perhaps the primary reason why organized participative manage- ment programs fail is because management is looking for a "quick fix." Stating this an- other way, a team concept will work only to the degree that top-level management gives its full support, effort, and resources over a period of time.[10]

Figure 15-1 summarizes the characteristics of effective work teams. While there is no one approach that will succeed in all situations, it is essential that the group know

FIGURE 15-1

Characteristics of effective work teams.

16 Keys to Effective Work Teams

- Group members agree upon team goals and objectives and are committed to those goals.
- All members participate actively in team meetings and discussions.
- Team rules, guidelines, and procedures are followed by all team members.
- All members are valued and treated with respect and dignity.
- Team members share vital information and ensure that everyone is fully informed on a "need-to-know" basis.
- Members express their ideas without fear of retribution—team members also feel free to express disagreement—the group grows with differences of opinion.
- The team uses a systematic problem-solving approach, yet, members are encouraged to think "outside the box"—i.e., alternative ways of thinking are encouraged.
- All members are included in problem-solving, developing alternatives, and institu- tionalizing the decision.
- Decisions are made by consensus—i.e., each team member gives his/her support to the decisions, even though they may not totally agree, therefore, every team member feels ownership for the team's decision and responsible for its success.
- The team is cohesive—openness, trust, support, encouragement is ever present.
- Conflict is viewed as healthy—conflict is brought out into the open and dealt with in a timely manner.
- Group members provide each other with honest feedback on performance—the con- structive feedback is used to improve performance.
- Team training and peer helping are essential elements of the team process. Peers help team members who may need individualized attention.
- The team continually evaluates its performance and uses the information as a basis for improvement.
- Pride in team accomplishments becomes a driving motivational factor for individual members.
- Members enjoy their affiliation with the team.

where it is going. Throughout this text, we have stressed the importance of setting goals and the notion that the supervisor must provide direction, not directives. As noted in Chapters 1 and 2, if supervisors want their work groups to perform at higher levels, there must be a shared purpose and values, and the supervisor must constantly strive to balance employee' needs with the organization's needs.

Self-Directed (Self-Managed) Work Teams: The "Ultimate" in Teamwork? In Chapter 9, brief mention was made of the growing phenomenon of self-directed (or self-managed) work teams, also known as autonomous work teams. In some respects, these could be considered the "ultimate" in efforts to maintain a collaborative workplace by having employees largely responsible for managing themselves and their work. Much has been written about self-directed work teams, and there are a number of approaches that organizations have taken. In general, these teams set their own targets or goals after consultation with higher management, and the team more or less determines how work is to be accomplished in order to achieve these objectives. In their most advanced form, teams may be given wide latitude to carry out the responsibilities that formerly belonged to supervisors and/or human resources department staff. These responsibilities include such areas as selecting and dismissing team members and leaders, assigning tasks within the group, training and appraising team members, allocating pay adjustments, conducting disciplinary actions, and scheduling work.[11] There have been few comprehensive studies concerning the effectiveness of self-managed work teams, but preliminary evidence—much of which is anecdotal—suggests that they can be very effective in improving efficiency, morale, and customer service.[12]

4
Discuss the importance of employee morale and its relationship to teamwork and productivity.

Morale
A composite of feelings and attitudes that individuals and groups have toward their work, their environment, their supervisors, top-level management, and the organization.

UNDERSTANDING AND MAINTAINING EMPLOYEE MORALE

Most definitions of morale recognize that it is essentially a state of mind. For example, Webster's dictionary defines the word morale as "the mental and emotional condition (as of enthusiasm, spirit, loyalty) of an individual or a group with regard to the function or tasks at hand." For our purposes we will consider **morale** as consisting of the attitudes and feelings of individuals and groups toward their work, their environment, their supervisors, top-level management, and the organization. Morale is not a single feeling but a composite of feelings and attitudes. It affects employee performance and willingness to work, which in turn affects individual and organizational objectives. When employee morale is high, employees usually do what the organization wants them to do; when it is low, the opposite tends to occur.

Numerous articles have suggested that today's employees are unhappier with many aspects of their jobs than were employees of earlier decades. Much of this lowered morale is attributed to a belief that many employers do not trust and are not loyal to their employees, and therefore employees do not trust and are not loyal to their employers. It has long been recognized and documented that the reasons why employees either stay with or leave an employer are more frequently attributable to factors other than pay.[13]

There should be little doubt that employee morale is an important supervisory consideration. Some supervisors simply believe that morale is something that employees either have or do not have. Actually, morale is always present in some form. It can be positive (high), negative (low), or a mixture. High morale, of course, is desirable. Employees with high morale find satisfaction in their positions, have confidence in their abilities, and usually work with enthusiasm and to the extent of their abilities. High morale cannot be ordered, but it can be fostered by conditions in the workplace that are favorable to its development. High morale is not the cause of good human relations; it is the result of good human relations. High morale is the result of positive motivation, respect for people, effective supervisory leadership, good communication, participation, counseling, and desirable human relations practices. The state of employee morale reflects to a large degree how effectively a supervisor is performing his or her managerial responsibilities.

Morale Should Be Everyone's Concern

Every manager, from the chief executive down to the supervisor, should be concerned with the morale of the workforce. It should be a priority concern to develop and maintain employee morale at as high a level as possible without sacrificing the company's objectives.

Workplace spirituality

Organizational efforts to make the work environment more meaningful and creative by relating work to employees' personal values and spiritual beliefs.

Because of widespread concern about deteriorating employee morale and alienation of many workers toward their employers, many firms have embarked on various programs and efforts that collectively have been called **workplace spirituality.** This essentially means organizational efforts designed to make the work environment more meaningful and creative by recognizing and tapping into people's deeply held values and spiritual beliefs. This chapter's second "Contemporary Issue" box describes a number of these types of efforts, what they are trying to do, and some of the perceived benefits from a renewed emphasis on spirituality and personal value systems in the workplace.[14]

Our concern in this chapter is not to analyze these and other organizationwide efforts aimed at improving morale. Rather, we primarily will discuss the role played by the first-line supervisor who probably more than anyone else influences the level of morale in day-to-day contact with employees.

Bringing morale to a high level and maintaining it there is a continuous process; it cannot be achieved simply through short-run devices such as pep talks or contests. High morale is slow to develop and difficult to maintain. The level of morale can vary considerably from day to day. Morale is contagious in both directions because both favorable and unfavorable attitudes spread rapidly among employees. Unfortunately, it seems to be human nature that employees quickly forget the good and long remember the bad when it comes to factors influencing their morale.

The supervisor is not alone in desiring high morale. Employees are just as much concerned with morale since it is paramount to their work satisfaction. High morale helps to make the employee's day at work a pleasure and not a misery. High morale also is important to an organization's customers. They usually can sense whether employees are serving them with enthusiasm or just going through the motions with a "care-less" attitude.

contemporary issue

Can Spirituality Make an Impact on Employee Morale and the Bottom Line?

Managers and employees at firms throughout the country are searching for ways to put their personal value systems into practice at the workplace. Because of widespread feelings of alienation, a spiritual movement has been emerging in the workplace as U.S. managers and employees attempt to connect and relate their work responsibilities to deeply held value systems and spiritual beliefs. Companies believe that an inward "search of a soul" can help create a sense of meaning and purpose at work. Such a connection between the company and its people may improve morale and go beyond just motivational benefits for employees. A recently completed study by McKinsey & Co. shows that when companies engage in programs that use spiritual techniques for their employees, productivity increases and turnover is greatly reduced.[1] Author Lewis Richmond points out that Buddha, himself, found enlightenment out of a "serious case of job dissatisfaction" as an Indian prince 2,500 years ago.[2]

Companies are approaching this in various ways. Some firms have discussion groups—at times led by the CEO—in which workers discuss spirituality and religious values. For example, S. Truett Cathy, an evangelical Christian and CEO of Chick-fil-A Inc., hosts a hymn-filled prayer service on Monday morning for those employees who want to take part. On Sunday, Cathy closes his 1,000+ fast-food shops because he believes in keeping the Sabbath.[3] Monsanto CEO Robert Shapiro meditates twice a day and has led three-day meditation retreats for top-level managers.[4]

Other firms hire consultants to lead discussion groups and meetings aimed at promoting spiritually based values to enhance teamwork and commitment. Still other firms incorporate spirituality sessions in traditional employee training and managerial development programs. Efforts are made to discuss commonly shared values that enable employees to make clear connections between what their company is or should be, what they are doing in their jobs, and their higher sense of service, worth, and growth as individuals. Even though Timberland's CEO Jeffrey B. Schwartz is one of his company's few orthodox Jews, he uses his religious beliefs to guide business decisions and, in some instances, company policy. Because community service is a foundation of Schwartz's faith, all Timberland employees get 40 hours a year to volunteer at the charity of their choice.[5]

According to India's spiritual leader, Sathya Sai Baba, "Fundamental human values such as concern for well being, responsibility, love, truth and inner peace provide the foundation to every major spiritual tradition."[6] He contends these fundamentals also directly support established business values.[7] Service-Master's CEO C. William Pollard formulated the companies guiding principles: To grow profitability; to pursue excellence; to help people develop; and to Honor God in all we do! Pollard contended, "Every person is created in God's image, ... He or she must be given dignity and worth regardless of the task. 'Empowerment' is a big word nowadays, but all it means is something we've practiced for a long time. It means every person is important and it is important to listen to everyone."[8]

Whether spirituality will remain a permanent part of U.S. business is an open question. Yet its importance was emphasized in one major study:

79% of Americans say they believe God exists and have no doubts about it.

78% of Americans say they feel the need in their life to experience spiritual growth.

60% of Americans say they have absolute trust in God.

51% of Americans say that modern life leaves them too busy to enjoy God or pray as they would like.

48% of Americans have had occasion to talk about their religious faith in the workplace in the past 24 hours.[9]

While there are those who believe that spirituality at work is an idea that does not fit into the business setting or that it is a form of "mind control," there is a belief that spirituality could improve employees' personal lives and mental outlook, and that this might translate into a better working environment.

Sources: (1) From *A Spiritual Audit of Corporate America* (Jossey-Bass, 1999) as reported in Michelle Conlin, "Religion in the Workplace: The growing presence of spirituality in Corporate America," *Business Week* (November 1, 1999), p. 153. (2) From Lewis Richmond, *Work as a Spiritual Practice: A Practical Buddhist Approach*

Relationships Among Morale, Teamwork, and Productivity

Teamwork is often associated with morale, but the two terms do not mean the same thing. Morale refers to the attitudes and feelings of employees, whereas teamwork primarily relates to the degree of cooperation among people in solving problems and accomplishing objectives. Good morale is helpful in achieving teamwork, but teamwork can be high when morale is low. Such a situation might exist in times when jobs are scarce and employees tolerate bad conditions and poor supervision for fear of losing their jobs. On the other hand, teamwork may be absent when morale is high. For example, employees working on a piecework basis or salespeople being paid on a straight commission basis typically are rewarded for individual efforts rather than for group performance.

Many supervisors believe that high morale usually is accompanied by high productivity. Much research has been done to study this assumption. Although there are many ramifications and some contradictions in research results, there is substantial evidence to suggest that in the long run high-producing employees do tend to have high morale. That is to say, well-motivated, self-disciplined groups of employees tend to do a more satisfactory job than those from whom the supervisor tries to force such performance. Furthermore, when supervisors are considerate of their employees and try to foster positive attitudes among them, there tends to be greater mutual trust, lower absenteeism and turnover, and fewer grievances.[15] Regardless of its other effects, there is little question that a high level of morale tends to make work more pleasant, particularly for the supervisor!

FACTORS INFLUENCING MORALE

5
Understand the factors that influence employee morale.

Virtually anything can influence the morale of employees either positively or negatively (see Figure 15-2 on page 516). Some of these are within the control of the supervisor; others are not. These factors generally can be classified as two broad types: external and internal.

External and Internal Factors

Influences outside the organization generally are beyond the supervisor's control. Nevertheless, they may significantly affect the morale of employees at work. Examples of external factors are family relationships, care of children or elderly parents, financial difficulties, problems with friends, a breakdown of the car, sickness or death in the family, and outside pressures. What happens at home can change an employee's feelings very

to *Inner Growth and Satisfaction on the Job* (Broadway Books, 1999) as quoted in Marci McDonald, "Shush. The guy in the cubicle is meditating," *U.S. News & World Report* (May 3, 1999), p. 46. (3) Conlin, pp. 152–153. (4) McDonald, p. 46. (5) Conlin, p. 154. (6) William C. Miller, "Spirituality, Creativity and Business," *The Inner Edge* (October/November 1999), pp. 20–21. (7) Ibid. (8) Jagannath Duashi, "God Is My Reference Point," *Financial World* (Fall 1994), pp. 36–37. (9) As reported in George Gallup, Jr. and Tim Jones, *The Next American Spirituality* (Gallup Organization: National Opinion Research Center, 2000).

quickly. An argument before leaving for work may set an emotional tone for the rest of the day. Even headlines in the morning newspaper may be depressing or uplifting.

Conditions within the company can also influence morale. Examples of internal factors are compensation, job security, the nature of work, relations with coworkers, working conditions, recognition, and so on. These factors are partially or fully within the supervisor's control. For example, when compensation is adequate, other factors may assume a more significant role. But even when wages are good, morale can sink quickly if working conditions are neglected. The critical factor here is whether or not the supervisor attempts to improve working conditions. Employees often will perform well under undesirable conditions and still maintain high morale if they believe that their supervisor is seriously trying to improve conditions.

Workplace Incivility. Many workers can relate to the playground bully of their childhood. In some instances, the playground bully has grown up and now works alongside us. The dilemma for many employees is "How can you expect me to get along with that jerk?" Two recent studies report that "rude behavior is on the rise in the workplace and can undermine an organization's effectiveness." The findings are summarized below.

- Incivility has worsened in the last ten years.
- Rude people are three times more likely to be in higher positions than their targets.

- Men are seven times more likely to be rude or insensitive to the feelings of their subordinates than to superiors.
- Twelve percent of the people who experience rude behavior quit their jobs to avoid the perpetrator.
- Fifty-two percent reported losing work time worrying.
- Nearly half of the respondents said they are sometimes angry at work.
- Twenty-two percent deliberately decreased their work effort as a result of the rudeness.
- One employee out of six reports being so angered by a coworker that they felt like hitting the person.[16]

Almost everyone has been on the receiving end of a rude person's temper or a bully's wrath. Whether the crude or impolite behavior takes place behind closed doors or out in the open, it directly affects the recipient and lowers group morale. Some organizations have conducted programs that have focused on the workplace behaviors that deter teamwork. Many books and programs are designed to provide guidance for people to successfully deal with difficult people. We will address several alternative coping mechanisms later in this chapter.

The Downside of Downsizing on Morale. According to a survey of about a thousand corporations employing more than 25,000 workers, a decade of downsizing has left a "legacy of fear" among workers. Some 46 percent of the employees surveyed indicated that they worried about being laid off, and 53 percent expressed concerns about the future of their firms. Both of these percentages were significantly higher than those from just four years previously. Further, only 40 percent of the surveyed workers indicated that they felt their companies valued long-term employees. These attitudes are understandable since millions of U.S. workers lost their jobs due to job cuts or company shutdowns during the decade of the 1990s.[17]

A more recent study found:

A worker's ability to form "best" friendships at work is among the most powerful of 12 indicators of a highly productive workplace. Workplaces with low turnover and high customer satisfaction, productivity and profitability also tended to be places where employees reported having a best friend present.[18]

It is apparent that downsizings force employees to sever workplace friendships. Also, those who remain suffer from what has been termed survivors' syndrome. Many studies support the notion that workplace incivility is on the rise, in part because of time and productivity pressures from managers trying to squeeze the most out of the survivors.[19] Most companies are not prepared to deal with widespread employee fears and insecurities. However, some firms have developed training programs and have provided counseling services in order to plan and implement job reductions and to assist remaining employees to cope with the aftereffects. Although a detailed discussion of these types of programs is beyond the scope of this text, among the recommended strategies are (1) early and ample communication with clear and specific details concerning which jobs have been eliminated and, more importantly, why, and (2) working with remaining employees to develop new short-term objectives to accomplish that will enable them to focus on activities and targets over which they have a semblance of control.[20] Here, too, first-line supervisors have a crucial role in influencing the direction of employee morale in these types of situations.

6

Discuss techniques to assess employee morale, including observation and employee attitude surveys.

ASSESSING EMPLOYEE MORALE

Although most firms believe that employee morale is important in the long run if the organization is to be successful, good measurements of employee morale are somewhat elusive. Some firms rely on statistical comparisons to assess the state of their company's morale. They look at data that compare their employees with industry standards for employee attendance, turnover, the use of sick leave, and other broad indicators.[21]

These comparisons are useful, but for supervisors they may or may not be relevant to the departmental situation. Some supervisors pride themselves on their ability to size up morale intuitively. However, most supervisors would be better advised to approach the measurement of morale in a more systematic fashion. Although it may not be possible to measure morale precisely, there are techniques for assessing prevailing levels and trends. The two most frequently used techniques are (1) observation and study, and (2) attitude surveys.

Observing and Studying Indicators of Morale

By observing, monitoring, and studying patterns of employee behavior, a supervisor can often discover clues to employee morale. The supervisor should closely monitor such key indicators as job performance levels, tardiness and absenteeism, the amount of waste or scrap, employee complaints, and accident and safety records. Any significant changes in the levels of these indicators should be analyzed because they often are interrelated. For example, excessive tardiness and absenteeism seriously interfere with job performance. The supervisor should find out why employees are often tardy or absent. If reasons are related to morale, are the causes within the supervisor's control, or should the employee be referred somewhere for counseling or assistance?

It is relatively easy to observe the extremes of high and low morale. However, it is quite difficult to differentiate among intermediate degrees of morale, or to assess when morale is changing. For example, an employee's facial expression or shrug of the shoulder may or may not reflect that person's level of morale. Only an alert supervisor can judge whether this employee is becoming depressed or frustrated. Supervisors must sharpen their powers of observation and be careful not to brush indicators of change conveniently aside.

The closeness of daily working relationships offers numerous opportunities for a supervisor to observe and analyze changes in employee morale. However, many supervisors do not take time to observe, and others do not analyze what they observe. It is only when an extreme, obvious drop in the level of morale has taken place that some supervisors recall the first indications of change. By then, the problems that led to this lowered state of morale probably will have magnified to the point where major corrective actions will be necessary. As so often is the case in supervision, an "ounce of prevention" would have been worth more than a "pound of cure."

Exit interviews

Interview with individuals who leave a firm to assess morale and reasons for employee turnover.

Many companies conduct exit interviews with individuals leaving their employment. **Exit interviews** are usually conducted by a human resources staff person, although sometimes, especially in a small firm, the supervisor may fill this role. The interviewer asks questions about why the person is leaving and about conditions within the firm as that person sees them. Results of exit interviews are used to assess the morale in the firm or in certain departments of the firm, as well as to identify reasons for employee turnover.

Employee Attitude Surveys

Attitude survey

Survey of employee opinions about major aspects of organizational life used to assess morale.

Another technique used to assess employee morale is an **attitude survey,** also called "opinion" or "morale" surveys. All employees—or a sample of the employees—are asked to express their opinions about major aspects of organizational life, usually in the form of answers to questions printed on a survey form. The survey questionnaire elicits employee opinions about such factors as management and supervision, job conditions, job satisfaction, coworkers, pay and benefits, job security, advancement opportunities, and so on.

Employee attitude surveys are rarely initiated by a supervisor. Usually they are undertaken by top-level management and are prepared with the help of the human resources department or an outside consulting firm.[22] The survey questionnaire should be written in language that is appropriate for most employees.

Attitude surveys, or questionnaires, may be completed on the job or in the privacy of the employee's home. Some organizations prefer to have employees answer these questionnaires on the job because a high percentage of questionnaires that are mailed are never returned. On the other hand, a possible advantage of completing the questionnaire at home is that employees may give more thoughtful and truthful answers. Regardless of where they are completed, questionnaires should not be signed so that they remain anonymous, although some surveys may request employees to indicate their departments.

Many attitude survey forms offer employees the choice of answering questions from a given list of answers. Other forms are not so specific and provide employees the opportunity to answer as freely as they wish. Since some employees may find it difficult to write their opinions in sentences or to complete started sentences, better results usually are obtained with a survey form on which the employees simply check the printed responses that correspond to their answers.

Follow-Up of Survey Results. Tabulation and analysis of questionnaires usually are assigned to the human resources department or to an outside consulting firm. Survey results are first presented to top-level and middle-level managers and eventually to departmental supervisors. In some organizations, survey results are used as discussion materials during supervisory training, especially when they provide clues about ways to improve employee morale.

Attitude surveys may reveal deficiencies that the supervisor can eliminate. For example, a complaint that there is a lack of soap in the washroom can be resolved easily. But frequently the responses are difficult to evaluate, as, for example, a complaint that communication channels are not open to employees. Such complaints raise more questions than answers and may necessitate a careful study of existing policies and procedures to see whether corrective actions are warranted.

If the attitude survey reveals a correctable problem at the departmental level—perhaps with an individual supervisor—the solution should be developed and implemented by the supervisor involved. On the other hand, a broader problem that requires the attention of higher-level managers should be reported to the appropriate manager for action. If supervisors and higher-level managers do not make needed changes as a result of a survey, the survey was a waste of time and money. In fact, if no changes materialize, or if changes are not communicated to the employees, a decline in morale may occur after the survey. Employees may feel that their problems and suggestions have been ignored. Thus, whenever possible, dissatisfactions expressed in an attitude survey should be addressed promptly by managers and supervisors. At a minimum, employees should be informed that management is aware of the dissatisfactions and what may be done to change things by some future date.

Organizational Development. Many companies follow up their attitude surveys with feedback meetings and conference sessions with groups of employees and supervisors. Typically these meetings are conducted by an outside consultant, or by a staff person from the human resources or some other department. In these meetings, results of attitude surveys are discussed and debated openly. The groups are expected to develop recommendations for improvement, which are forwarded anonymously to higher-level management for consideration and possible implementation.

This approach is often part of a broader concept that also has become widespread in many large enterprises. Known as **organizational development (OD),** "team building," or "process consultation," it usually involves having scheduled group meetings under the guidance of a neutral conference leader. The groups may consist of just employees, employees and supervisors, just supervisors, just higher-level managers, or whatever composition is appropriate. For the most part, the meetings focus on solving problems that may be hindering effective work performance or causing disruption, poor coordination, fouled-up communications, and strained personal relations. When there is frank discussion in a relatively open and informal atmosphere, individuals tend to open up about what really is on their minds and what might be done to resolve problems and reduce conflict. Organizational development can take numerous patterns that are beyond the scope of this text.[23] Suffice it to say, however, that many supervisors will be involved in organizational development efforts since these programs can contribute to the improvement of morale and organizational effectiveness.

> **Organizational development (OD)**
> Meetings with groups under the guidance of a neutral conference leader to solve problems that are hindering organizational effectiveness.

A supervisor's general attitude and behavior can result in good or poor employee morale.

7

Understand why counseling is an important part of the supervisor's job.

THE SUPERVISOR'S COUNSELING ROLE

All aspects of good supervision impact employee morale in relation to conditions on the job. However, perhaps the most significant day-to-day influence on employee morale is the supervisor's general attitude and behavior in departmental relationships. If a supervisor's behavior indicates suspicion about the employees' motives and actions, low morale will likely result. If the supervisor acts worried or depressed, employees tend to follow suit. If the supervisor loses his or her temper, some employees may also lose theirs. Conversely, if the supervisor shows confidence in the employees' work and commends them for good performance, this reinforces their positive outlook.

This does not mean that a supervisor should overlook difficulties that are present from time to time. Rather, it means that if something goes wrong, the supervisor should act as a leader who has the situation in hand. For example, supervisors often will be called upon to mediate conflict among their employees. The supervisor should demonstrate the attitude that the employees will be relied on to correct the situation and to do what is necessary to prevent occurrence of a similar situation.

Supervisors should not relax their efforts to build and maintain high employee morale. However, they should not become discouraged if morale drops from time to time because many factors beyond their control can cause this. Supervisors can be reasonably satisfied if employee morale is high most of the time.

Coaching is not the same as counseling. **Counseling** is an effort by the supervisor to deal with on-the-job performance problems that are the result of an employee's personal problems.[24] As mentioned in Chapter 13, an employee's performance problems may stem from a job-related personal problem such as failure to get a promotion, or from an off-the-job situation such as a financial crisis due to a divorce. If not addressed these problems can affect morale and the quality of work. Thus, the supervisor must

Counseling

An effort by the supervisor to deal with on-the-job performance problems that are the result of an employee's personal problems.

Counseling interview

Nondirective interview during which the supervisor listens empathetically and encourages the employee to discuss problems openly and develop solutions.

help get the employee back to being a productive employee. The most effective way to get an employee back on track is to counsel—the process of asking, listening, reflecting and encouraging. A **counseling interview** is essentially nondirective (as described in Chapter 12); the supervisor primarily serves as an empathetic listener, and the employee is encouraged to discuss his or her problem frankly and to develop solutions.

By being a good listener, the supervisor can find out what happened and may help the employee develop alternatives. For example, perhaps Laura is upset because of a sudden financial crisis, and her work performance shows a marked decline. She spends more of her time thinking about how to solve her financial problems than she does thinking about her work. In short, a counseling interview might begin when the supervisor addresses a performance problem: "Laura, I'm concerned about your performance. You were late for work two days last week and the Finegan report did not get done. Could you give me some explanation?" By identifying his concern about performance, the supervisor asks Laura for an explanation. The supervisor should listen carefully and without interruption in order to understand Laura's perspective on the issue. In Chapter 3, we discussed the importance of paraphrasing and reflecting to improve understanding. Paraphrasing involves expressing, in somewhat different words, Laura's response, "Let me see if I understand what you're saying. . . ." A follow-up question might be "Why do you feel that way?" By using the technique of reflection, the supervisor will help Laura talk about her feelings.

The supervisor may discuss with the employee the possible avenues to obtain financial assistance. The supervisor should not offer specific advice, which might bring unwanted repercussions. If the employee should feel dissatisfied with the results of following a supervisor's advice, she might blame the supervisor for her problems. This would only complicate a difficult situation. If the problem is beyond the supervisor's range of expertise, perhaps the supervisor can arrange for the employee to get help from a professional or refer the employee to the human resources department, where assistance may be available. For example, many employers provide various forms of assistance and referral services for employees who have personal problems. Many large employers also have employee assistance programs, which will be discussed later in this chapter. Regardless, the supervisor's job is to help the employee explore alternatives and choose the course of action that she thinks is best (see Figure 15-3).

Aside from a private counseling interview or referral of the employee to some source of assistance, there may be little else that the supervisor can do to cope with the factors that affect an employee's morale. The supervisor's main role is to help get the employee's performance back to an acceptable level.

Identify programs that organizations use to assist employees with personal and work-related problems, including workplace violence.

PROGRAMS FOR ASSISTING EMPLOYEES WITH PERSONAL AND WORK-RELATED PROBLEMS

As discussed previously, the supervisor may refer an employee to the human resources department or some designated management person who will hold the counseling interview and suggest possibilities for help.

FIGURE 15-3

Steps in the counseling process.

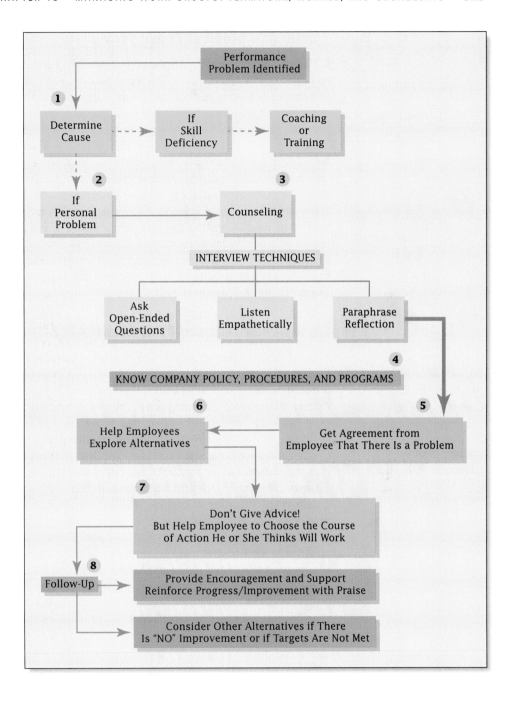

Family and Medical Leave Provisions

If the employee's problem involves a request for a leave of absence because of sickness or because of certain family considerations such as childbirth or caring for a seriously ill member of the immediate family, the supervisor normally should refer the request to the human resources department or higher-level managers. Many employers have developed policies for handling such requests in connection with the federal Family and Medical Leave Act (FMLA). Passed in 1993, the FMLA generally requires employers with 50 or more employees to grant up to 12 weeks of unpaid leave to workers for various reasons, including a serious medical problem experienced by the employee or his or her family, and the birth or adoption of a child. Paid sick leave or vacation time under a company policy may be substituted for the unpaid leave allowed by the FMLA.[25]

At the time of writing this text, revisions to the FMLA were proposed and several federal court decisions were on appeal. Thus, it is imperative that supervisors do not try to interpret its provisions but rely on the advice of the human resources department or the company's legal counsel. It is clear that the policy must be consistently and uniformly applied within the organization.

Employee Assistance Programs (EAPs)

Employee assistance program (EAP)

Company program to assist employees with certain personal or work-related problems that are interfering with job performance.

Many organizations—especially large corporations and major government agencies—have adopted **employee assistance programs (EAPs).** These programs typically involve a special department or outside resources retained by the firm to whom supervisors may refer employees with certain types of problems. Alternatively, employees may seek help on their own from the EAP, or they may be referred to the EAP by other sources such as their union. Most employee assistance programs provide help for alcoholism and substance abuse; marriage, child care, and family problems; financial questions; and other personal, emotional, or psychological problems that may be interfering with job performance. Figure 15-4 is a policy statement included in the EAP booklet provided to employees of a major corporation, which illustrates the typical elements of this type of program.

The supervisor's role in an EAP is essential for its effectiveness. The supervisor needs to be alert to signs that an employee may be troubled, even though the supervisor has tried to respond to the employee's work performance using normal supervisory procedures. For example, a supervisor may be concerned about an employee's recent poor attendance and low production while at work. The supervisor suspects that something is amiss, perhaps an alcohol-related problem or substance abuse. A recent study found the following:

- Among full-time workers, there were 6.3 million illicit drug users and 6.2 million heavy alcohol users.
- An average of 15–17 percent of employees in every U. S. company are substance abusers.
- They are 3 to 4 times more likely to be injured at work than nonusers.
- Substance abusers have 47 percent of serious workplace accidents.
- They are involved in 40 percent of fatal workplace accidents.

Employee Assistance Program

INTRODUCTION

The employee assistance program (EAP) was adopted to provide confidential, professional assistance to employees and their families. The program also provides managers and union representatives with a constructive way to help employees and reduce the adverse economic impact to the company that occurs when personal problems interfere with job performance.

HOW THE PROGRAM WORKS

There are essentially four ways that a person may enter the EAP—self-referral, management referral, union referral, or medical referral.

SELF-REFERRAL

Any employee or family member may call the EAP office for information or to make an appointment to discuss a personal problem. The contact, as well as what is discussed, is handled in strictest confidence.

MANAGEMENT REFERRAL

Managers and supervisors may suggest to an employee that he or she seek help when there is a noticeable decline in the employee's work performance that is not correctable through usual procedures or where there are specific on-the-job incidents that indicate the presence of a personal problem.

UNION REFERRAL

Official union representatives are encouraged to ask their members to make use of the services provided by the EAP. Union officials may call the EAP office and speak with the counselor or provide the employee or family member with the EAP office telephone number.

MEDICAL REFERRAL

Medical referrals to the EAP will be based either upon the identification of a medical symptom or disorder that is normally associated with a personal problem or upon a request from the employee for advice or assistance regarding a personal problem.

- They are 5 times more likely to file a workers' compensation claim.
- They are absent an average of 3 weeks more often than non-users.
- They are responsible for 50 to 80 percent of all internal thefts and loss.[26]

When talking with the employee, the supervisor should focus primarily on the person's poor or deteriorating job performance and then suggest to the employee the EAP services that might be of some help. Figure 15-5 (see page 526) is a procedural statement excerpted from a supervisory policy manual within a major firm's EAP. The procedural guidelines for supervisors in this policy are representative of types of approaches that most major organizations have adopted in their EAP efforts.

FIGURE 15-5

A firm's procedural guidelines for EAP case handling by supervisors.

SUPERVISORY PROCEDURES FOR EAP CASE HANDLING

The employee assistance program is for all employees—management and occupational—who want help with their personal problems. The EAP is prepared to accept referrals from many sources, including supervisors and union representatives, who believe that personal problems are causing an employee's job performance to deteriorate. Experience has shown that many employees will seek assistance once they realize that help is readily available. But the decision to seek help must always be the employee's, and actual counseling should be left to professionals.

The following procedures generally apply when trying to help an employee improve job performance:

Talk about job performance in an initial discussion with the employee. Only deteriorating job performance should be discussed. Opinions and judgments about possible personal problems should be avoided—leave that to the professional counselor. Specific instances of deteriorating job performance, such as unsatisfactory attendance, quality of work, or productivity, will be the basis for the initial discussion.

Employees who initiate discussion of personal problems with either supervisors or union representatives should be informed of the employee assistance program and encouraged to participate on a voluntary basis.

Describe the employee assistance program after job performance has been discussed. Tell the employee about the service available through the employee assistance program. Stress that EAP contacts are confidential; no information concerning the nature of the problem or the specific treatment will be revealed without the employee's consent. Usually, the employee will not be terminated for the unsatisfactory job performance until an opportunity to use EAP has been offered.

If the employee chooses to accept help, referral will be made directly to the EAP counselor to determine the nature of the problem and develop a course of action.

To help the EAP counselor, any information pertaining to the employee's job performance or behavior should be provided by the supervisor or union representative at the time of referral.

The EAP counselor may determine that outside resources are appropriate. If so, these referrals will be made as necessary.

The employee will be allowed a reasonable period to improve job performance with the aid of counseling and supervisory support.

If the employee rejects the offer of assistance and the job performance problems do not continue or recur, nothing further need be done.

If the offer is rejected by the employee and job performance problems continue or recur, appropriate action may then be taken in accordance with existing company policy and the union agreement for handling problems of deteriorating job performance.

Most EAPs emphasize the confidential nature of the services. Supervisors should discuss this with employees and assure them that no stigma will be associated with their seeking EAP help. However, the supervisor should inform an employee who refuses EAP assistance and whose work performance continues to deteriorate that such a refusal might be a consideration in a termination decision.

Wellness Programs

Wellness program

Organized efforts by a firm to help employees get and stay healthy in order to remain productive.

Another approach used by some firms, often where an EAP is in place, is what has been called a wellness program. A **wellness program** essentially is an organized effort by a firm designed to help employees stay healthy both physically and mentally and to reduce employer health costs. Programs are varied but they often focus on areas of recovery and staying free of certain problems such as stress, substance abuse, injury, and the like. Wellness programs can include providing exercise facilities, counseling, and other resources both on company premises or elsewhere. In some firms, corporate wellness programs are viewed as a type of employee benefit, but for the most part they are directed efforts by the firm to improve employee health and safety, which in turn should have a positive impact on morale and work performance.[27]

Dealing with Workplace Violence

In recent years, instances of workplace violence have increased dramatically both in large-scale enterprises and small businesses. Government statistics have estimated that some 100,000 or so incidents of workplace violence occur annually; of these, about

Wellness programs include providing exercise facilities, counseling, and other resources both on company premises and elsewhere.

1,000 involve homicides. Although experts agree that it is impossible to accurately predict violent behavior, some studies have identified certain behavioral problems that may portend serious problems on the job. Supervisors typically are in the best position to identify the warning signals, which include an individual's extreme interest in weapons or bringing weapons to the workplace; "paranoid" behavior such as panicking easily or perceiving that the "whole world is against me;" reacting to or failure to take any criticism either from a supervisor or a colleague; and unexplained dramatic changes in an individual's productivity, attendance, or hygiene.[28] Often, incidents of workplace incivility escalate into violent actions. Studies of violent acts in the workplace have shown that these typically start as a verbal dispute and involve persons who know each other. (See the "You Make the Call" segment at the beginning of Chapter 3.) Disputes may be over trivial matters or minor disagreements with supervisors or fellow employees.

The supervisor should immediately deal with problem behaviors before they escalate (see Figure 15-6 on page 529 for some strategies for dealing with workplace incivility).[29] A supervisor should be alert for those employees who have difficulty adjusting to their coworkers or to those who make the lives of others unbearable. By having a private counseling session with such an individual, the supervisor may be able to uncover the reasons for this behavior and take actions to help the individual stop the behavior. But, in many instances, the disagreement mushrooms and intensifies even in spite of the supervisor's "best efforts" to resolve the problem.[30]

Supervisors should be alert to these warning signals and report them to higher management, the human resources department, or the EAP staff if this type of service is available. Some firms have established oversight committees or programs—often in connection with security personnel—in order to have policies and procedures in place both to prevent and deal with work situations and individuals that have a potential for serious or violent consequences. In this connection, firms have developed specific policies and procedures that prohibit employees and others from bringing any weapons into the workplace.[31] Any situation that explodes into violence on the job can have a devastating impact on employee morale. Here, too, the sensitivity and actions of supervisors in coordinating efforts throughout the firm to prevent workplace violence are among the most important elements of a firm's response to this unfortunate but widespread problem.

Good Supervision Is the Foundation for Good Morale

All aspects of good supervision impact employee morale in relation to conditions on the job. However, perhaps the most significant day-to-day influence on employee morale is the supervisor's general attitude and behavior in departmental/team relationships. If a supervisor's behavior indicates suspicion about the employees' motives and actions, low morale will likely result. If the supervisor acts worried or depressed, employees tend to follow suit. If the supervisor loses his or her temper, some employees may also lose theirs. Conversely, if the supervisor shows confidence in the employees' work and commends them for good performance, this reinforces their positive outlook.

FIGURE 15-6

Possible strategies for dealing with workplace incivility.

1. **REMEMBER: YOUR PURPOSE IS:**
   ✔ To eliminate the problem behavior.
   ✔ To help team accomplish goals.
   ✔ To preserve team cohesion.
   ✔ To maintain self-esteem of team members.

2. **PAUSE AND EVALUATE WHAT WAS REALLY SAID (CONTENT, CONTEXT, TONE).**

3. **BE ASSERTIVE.**
   ✔ Stay in control when attacked; don't counterattack.
   ✔ Speak clearly, calmly, and choose your words carefully.
   ✔ Address the person by name.

4. **TAKE ACTION—PUT A STOP TO IT WHEN IT HAPPENS.**
   ✔ State how you feel: "David, when you do _____ I feel _____"
   ✔ State why you feel: "... because ... it may be discrimination, it may be harassment, it is inappropriate."
   ✔ State your expectations: "David, I expect this behavior to stop immediately! ..."
   ✔ Ask for commitment from individual to cease behavior.
   ✔ State repercussions if it happens again.
   ✔ Document discussion.

This does not mean that a supervisor should overlook difficulties that occur from time to time. Rather, it means that if something goes wrong, the supervisor should act as a leader who has the situation in hand. For example, the supervisor at times will be called upon to mediate conflict among the employees. The supervisor should demonstrate the attitude that the employees will be relied on to correct the problem and to do what is necessary to prevent the occurrence of a similar situation.

Supervisors should not relax their efforts to build and maintain high employee morale. However, they should not become discouraged if morale drops from time to time because many factors beyond their control can cause this. Supervisors can be reasonably satisfied if employee morale is high most of the time.

What Call Did You Make?

As Charlie Graham, director of operations for Belmont Manufacturing, you realize that you have accomplished much during the past four years. Since coming to Belmont, you are impressed with the many successes. The major problems have been eliminated or reduced. On the surface, it appears that you have been able to get most employees on board with the work team concept. Most of the concepts and principles discussed in this chapter were relevant to your success.

You, Elaine Knight, and Bob Watters (the management trio) need to review the characteristics of effective teams to ensure that Belmont's teams are still on track. Employee morale should be continually monitored. Questions such as "What can we do to enhance the success of your team? . . . your individual performance?" "What additional skills do you need or want to have?" "What can we do to help you be the very best employee?" should be asked of employees. It might be appropriate to implement a regular employee attitude and needs survey. Understanding employee needs and their perceptions about the workplace is critical. By tabulating and acting upon the information received, the management trio can ensure that success is sustained.

Finally, perceptive students will realize that even the best teams tend to get complacent. It is difficult to maintain and sustain the high performance over long periods of time. It would be a good idea to review the following chapters: Chapter 3 (Communication Skills), Chapter 4 (Motivation), Chapter 5 (Problem-solving), and Chapter 14 (Leadership); as all serve as foundations for Belmont's continual improvement.

In short, you can help your team become more effective by making sure that all employees know what is expected of them. The use of stretch targets is one approach. Hiring new employees who are or have the potential to be team players and having a senior employee (a high-performer) help them get acclimated is critical. Make sure that they know that it is "ok" to ask for help. It is important to recognize that all employees have off-the-job problems. Thus, if the firm does not have an employee assistance program (EAP), it should immediately consider implementing one. The teams should seek input from customers and suppliers to help identify problems, develop more efficient processes and procedures, and deal with issues in a timely manner. Last, but not least, you and the management trio must recognize the efforts of the teams—there is no substitute for daily feedback on performance!

SUMMARY

1

Work groups typically are formed to provide companionship and identification, behavior guidelines, problem-solving help, and protection. Various factors can contribute to the cohesiveness and functioning of the work group, such as the group's status, size, personal characteristics, location, and previous success. Work groups can exert significant influences upon employee attitudes and job performance, which supervisors must recognize and be prepared to deal with.

2

At any time, an employee may be a member of a command group, task group (cross-functional team), friendship group, or special-interest group. Command and task groups are primarily based on job-related factors; friendship and special-interest groups primarily reflect personal relationships and interests. There is an increasing use of customer satisfaction teams that may include customer and supplier representatives. Supervisors should be sensitive to all of these clusters and how they impact employee members.

3

The Hawthorne Studies demonstrated that work groups can have either a positive or a negative influence on employee performance. To influence work groups in a positive direction, supervisors should review the keys to building effective teams. Teams should be relatively small, and members must have the necessary skills and be committed to specific and realistic objectives. Work teams are called self-directed (or self-managed) if they are given wide latitude and autonomy for making decisions concerning workplace operations. Organized participative management programs primarily involve building effective teams to work on tasks that will improve work performance and customer service. For such a program to be effective, top-level and other managers must give their full support over a sufficient time period.

4

Employee morale is a composite of feelings and attitudes of individuals and groups toward their work environment, supervision, and the organization as a whole. Morale can vary from very high to very low and can change considerably from day to day. A concern for morale should be felt by everyone in the organization. Workplace spirituality is an effort to improve employees' personal lives and mental outlook. Morale and teamwork are not synonymous, but high morale usually contributes to high productivity.

5

Morale can be influenced by factors from outside the organization as well as by on-the-job factors. Workplace incivility, rudeness, and bullying have a negative effect on morale and can lead to turnover, dissatisfaction, and violent acts. Downsizing and corporate restructuring during the past decade has created a "legacy of fear" among workers. Supervisors need to be aware of employee needs, feelings, and perceptions that impact morale. In general, a supervisor's own attitude and behavior can significantly influence employee morale.

6

Astute supervisors can sense a change in the level of morale by observing employee behaviors and key indicators, such as absenteeism and performance trends. Another means of assessing levels of employee morale is to conduct an attitude survey. Supervisors and higher-level managers should—if possible—correct problems that have been brought to their attention through the survey. It is also desirable to discuss the results of an attitude survey in meetings with groups of employees and supervisors, and encourage them to recommend improvements.

7

Counseling is an effort by the supervisor to deal with the on-the-job performance problems that are the result of the employee's personal problems. If left unattended, these problems may decrease morale and eventually impact quality and productivity. The steps in the counseling process include identifying of the performance problem, asking questions, being an empathetic listener to the employee's concerns, and perhaps referring the employee to a source of assistance. The principles of interviewing and good communication practices are the foundation of the counseling process.

Supervisors need to be aware of the Family and Medical Leave Act and the company's policies in case an employee requests a leave of absence because of sickness or family medical considerations. To assist employees with personal and work-related problems that a supervisor would not be competent to handle, some organizations have employee assistance programs and wellness programs. EAP efforts typically assist employees to solve problems that detract from their job performance with the goal to restore them to full capabilities to meet acceptable work standards. Wellness programs aim at promoting and maintaining proper physical conditioning and other personal/health habits that will tend to keep employees healthy and on the job. Because of increased concerns about workplace violence, some firms have established programs and procedures to assist supervisors in recognizing symptoms displayed by problem employees that could lead to violent behavior, and what supervisors should do in such circumstances.

KEY TERMS

Command group (page 505)
Task group or cross-functional team (page 505)
Friendship group (page 506)
Special-interest group (page 506)
Hawthorne Studies (page 508)
Teamwork (page 510)
Collaborative workplace (page 510)
Morale (page 512)

Workplace spirituality (page 513)
Exit interview (page 519)
Attitude survey (page 519)
Organizational development (OD) (page 520)
Counseling (page 521)
Counseling interview (page 522)
Employee assistance program (EAP) (page 524)
Wellness program (page 527)

QUESTIONS FOR DISCUSSION

1. What are some of the most common reasons for forming work groups? What are some factors that make a work group cohesive? Is cohesiveness of a work group always desirable? Discuss.
2. Define each of the following classifications of work groups:
   a. Command group.
   b. Task group.
   c. Friendship group.
   d. Special-interest group.
3. Discuss the relevance of the Hawthorne Studies to modern supervision.
4. Would a team system like that initiated by Sun Microsystems work for a wide range of companies? in size? in different industries?
5. Identify several key elements of effective work teams and discuss the relationships among them.
6. Define the concept of employee morale. Evaluate the statement, "High morale is the result of good human relations."

7. Are workplace spirituality efforts desirable/realistic in most organizations? Discuss.

8. Differentiate between external factors and internal factors that influence employee morale. What should a supervisor do to minimize the influence of external factors on an employee's work? Discuss the impact of downsizing on employee morale and supervisory responses to its effects.

9. Why is it so difficult to adhere to the adage "Peace on Earth, Good Will to All?"

10. Discuss the use of employee attitude surveys in assessing employee morale. Why is follow-up on survey results vital if an attitude survey is to be worth anything? What types of follow-up can managers and supervisors utilize? Discuss.

11. Describe how you would counsel an employee who is habitually late for work. Why do some supervisors ignore this behavior rather than address it?

12. What should a supervisor do when an employee requests a family or medical leave?

13. Discuss the use of employee assistance programs (EAPs) and wellness programs.

14. Discuss what a supervisor should do if he or she is concerned that an employee is exhibiting behaviors that have been associated with subsequent workplace violence.

15. Mitch has just been assigned to your team. He has some skills and knowledge that are critical to your team's success. Within the first two days, three employees have complained to you about his behavior toward them. They have accused him of shooting numerous poisonous arrows (verbal assault) at them. The following morning during the team meeting, Mitch grabbed Carolyn's arm as she reached for a doughnut and said, "It looks like you've eaten too many of those already—you jelly belly!" A couple of employees laughed but most looked toward you in anguish. What should you do?

16. Why should employee morale be of concern to everyone in the organization? In this regard, discuss the relationships between (a) morale and teamwork and (b) morale and productivity.

SKILLS APPLICATIONS

Skills Application 15-1: Team Assessment

1. Describe the most effective team you have ever been associated with.
   a. Why were you (personally) able to perform successfully on the team?
   b. Provide specific examples to illustrate how team members used feedback to help you grow, develop, and improve.
   c. Compare your responses with those of a fellow classmate. What are the similarities? How do you account for them?

2. Contact two supervisors or managers who are willing to be interviewed. Ask them the following:
   a. Think of a time you experienced great pride or significant satisfaction from being associated with a particular team. What did you like most about being a member of that team?
   b. What did the team leader do to blend the different (diverse) team members into an efficient and effective group?
   c. What would have made you feel even better about your experience on that team?
   d. Compare the two supervisors' responses. To what degree are their responses similar? different? If there were major differences in the responses of the two supervisors, what do you feel are the reasons for this?

3. Write a one-page paper detailing what you learned from this skills application.

Skills Application 15-2: An Employee Attitude Survey

Following are data from an attitude survey taken among 150 employees in a small industrial plant. There were 15 team leaders in the plant. The question posed to employees was "What attention or emphasis is given to the following by your team leader, team (peers), or supervisor?"

	Too Much Attention	About Right	Too Little Attention	Does Not Apply
The quality of your work	32 (21%)	98 (65%)	16 (11%)	4 (3%)
Costs involved in your work	68 (45%)	57 (38%)	18 (12%)	7 (5%)
Meeting schedules	54 (36%)	62 (41%)	22 (15%)	12 (8%)
Getting your reactions and suggestions	28 (19%)	39 (26%)	80 (53%)	3 (2%)
Giving you information	24 (16%)	104 (69%)	20 (13%)	2 (1%)
Making full use of your abilities	23 (16%)	47 (31%)	68 (45%)	12 (8%)
Safety and housekeeping	38 (25%)	90 (60%)	12 (8%)	10 (7%)
Development of employees	40 (27%)	57 (38%)	48 (32%)	5 (3%)
Innovations, new ideas	26 (17%)	52 (35%)	70 (47%)	2 (1%)
Effective teamwork among employees	31 (21%)	102 (68%)	12 (8%)	5 (3%)

After reviewing the data, answer the following questions:

1. What overall observations would you make about the effectiveness of teams that generally is in place according to the survey data? Why?
2. What positive factors were revealed by the survey data?
3. What specific actions would you suggest to respond to potential problems revealed by the survey data?
4. What role could organizational development or other team training programs play in responding to the survey data?

Skills Application 15-3: Policies and Procedures for Employee Personal and Work-Related Problems

1. Contact two human resources department staff members who are willing to be interviewed concerning their firms' policies and procedures for handling employee personal and work-related problems. Preferably, one should be with an organization that has a formal employee assistance program (EAP); the other should be with a firm that does not have a formal program. In your interviews, ask the following:
   a. What are your policies/procedures for supervisors to follow when they suspect that an employee's personal or work-related problems are hindering job performance?
   b. Do you have any specific policies/procedures for supervisors regarding preventing/dealing with possible workplace violence?
   c. What company and other assistance services are available for referral?
   d. What are your policies/procedures regarding the time period and steps to be taken if the employee does not improve?
   e. How has the Family and Medical Leave Act changed the firm's policies/procedures concerning employee requests for leaves that are covered by this law?

2. Compare the responses of the HR staff members for similarities and differences. Were their policies/procedures more or less in line with the concepts and examples presented in this chapter? Why or why not?

Skills Application 15-4: Teamwork

INTERNET ACTIVITY

As a supervisor in today's workplace, it's likely you'll eventually lead a team of people. Visit the Center for the Study of Work Teams (www.workteams.unt.edu) and Teambuilding, Inc. (www.teambuildinginc.com) to learn more about managing teams.

1. Read through the "Abstracts and Lessons Learned" section of the Center for the Study of Work Teams Web site (click on the Free Articles and Links to find this). Create a list of dos and don'ts for supervisors based on the key learnings you find here.

2. Review several of the articles you find at Teambuilding, Inc. What are the specific challenges of teams for supervisors? What are some of the benefits? What do you think you would find most challenging about supervising a team?

ENDNOTES

1. For an expanded discussion of group processes in organizations, see Jennifer M. George and Gareth R. Jones, *Understanding and Managing Organizational Behavior* (Addison-Wesley, 1999), pp. 330–400.
2. See David H. Holt, *Management: Principles and Practices* (Prentice-Hall, 1993), pp. 351–352. Also see Natasha Calder and P. C. Douglas, "Empowered Employee Teams: The New Key to Improving Corporate Success," *Quality Digest* (March 1999), pp. 26–30 for a discussion of the types of empowered teams.
3. For discussion of the Hawthorne Studies and their impact, see Andrew J. Dubrin and R. Duane Ireland, *Management and Organization* (South-Western Publishing, Co., 1993), pp. 39–40.
4. Jon R. Katzenbach and Douglas K. Smith, *The Wisdom of Teams: Creating the High-Performance Organization* (Harvard Business School Press, 1993). Review chapters 6, 7, and 8 for useful checklists for building team performance, leading teams effectively, and overcoming team obstacles.
5. "From Supervisor to Team Manager" by Allen Ferguson, Amy Hicks, and Steven D. Jones is one of the case studies found in *Developing High-Performance Work Teams*, edited by Jones and Michael M. Beyerlein, (ASTD: Part 1, 1998 and Part 2, 1999). Also visit the Center for the Study of Work Teams (www.workteams.unt.edu) for additional information.
6. Kenneth Turan, "Tales From the Trenches: Role Players," *ESPN Sports Century* (December 12, 1999), p. 19.
7. See Edward M. Marshall, "The Collaborative Workplace," *Management Review* (June 1995), pp. 13–17.
8. H. James Harrington, "Beyond Teams: Teamwork," *Quality Digest* (August 1999), p. 20. Also see Harvey Robbins and Michael Finley, *Why Teams Don't Work: What Went Wrong and How to Make it Right* (Peterson's Pacesetter Books, 1995).
9. From Michael A. Campion and A. Catherine Higgs, "Design Work Teams to Increase Productivity and Satisfaction," *HRMagazine* (October 1995), pp. 101–107. Also see Ellen Hart, "Top Teams," *Management Review* (February 1996), pp. 43–47.
10. See Priscilla M. Elsass, "When Teammates Raise a White Flag," *Academy of Management Executive* (February 1996), pp. 40–49.
11. For a comprehensive review of what self-directed work teams do, see "1995 Industry Report," *Training* (October 1995), p. 72.
12. See Stephanie Overman, "Teams Score on the Bottom-Line," *HRMagazine* (May 1994), pp. 82–84.
13. See "Why I Do This Job," reporting survey data developed by William M. Mercer, Inc.—Yankelovich Partners, Inc., in *Business Week* (September 11, 1995), p. 8. Also see Jeffrey Pfeffer, *The Human Equation: Building Profits by Putting People First* (Harvard Business School Press, 1998); and Linda Grant, "Happy Workers, High Return," *Fortune* (January 12, 1998), p. 81.

14. In addition to the sources listed in the second "Contemporary Issue" box, the following are suggested: Edwene Gaines, "Four Spiritual Laws for an Abundant Life," *The Inner Edge* (June/July 1999), p. 20; Tom Brown, "Business Boards the Soul Train," *Management Review* (June 1996), pp. 6–7; Ellen Brandt, "Corporate Pioneers Explore Spirituality," *Business Week* (April 1996), pp. 83–87; Jennifer Laabs, "Balancing Spirituality and Work," *Personnel Journal* (September 1995), pp. 60–64; and Nancy K. Austin, "Does Spirituality at Work Work?" *Working Women* (March 1995), pp. 26–28.

15. For a comprehensive source on how to develop and maintain a positive work environment, see Jim Harris, *Getting Employees to Fall in Love with Your Company* (AMACOM, 1996).

16. In Kate N. Grossman, "Boys Behaving Badly: Men Mostly at Fault for Rising Incivility at Work," *Associated Press* (August 11, 1999). This news release summarized the work of University of North Carolina professor Christine M. Patterson, et.al., "Workplace Incivility: The Target's Eye View," presented at the Academy of Management's Annual Meeting (Tuesday, August 10, 1999). Alice Ann Love, "Survey Finds Workplace Angst: Colleagues, Communications Equipment Sources of Anger," *Associated Press* (September 6, 1999), reports on the Gallup Organization's telephone survey of workers for Marlin to assess the extent of workplace anger and stress. Also see Noa Davenport, Ruth Distler Schwartz, and Gail Pursell Elliott, *Mobbing: Emotional Abuse in the American Workplace* (Civil Society Publishing, 1999).

17. "Decade of Downsizing Has Left Its Mark," Associated Press story concerning a survey conducted by the International Survey Research Corporation, as reported in the *St. Louis Post-Dispatch* (December 26, 1996), p. 13D.

18. Sue Shellenbarger, "An Overlooked Toll of Job Upheavals: Valuable Friendships," *The Wall Street Journal* (January 12, 2000), p. B1.

19. Jim Owen, "Workplace Incivility: Bullying and Rudeness on the Rise," *Career Builder, Inc.* (1999). See also Rudy M. Yankrick, "Lurking in the Shadows," *HRMagazine* (October 1999), pp. 60–68.

20. Robert J. Grossman, "Damaged, Downsized Souls: How to Revitalize the Workplace," *HRMagazine* (May 1996), pp. 54–61.

21. From "Checking Your Firm's Morale," *Communication Briefings* (April 1993), p. 3.

22. See Elaine McShulkis, "Employee Survey Sins," *HRMagazine* (May 1996), pp. 12–13.

23. For a detailed explanation of OD, see Warren G. Bennis's classic, *Organizational Development: Its Nature, Origins, and Perspectives* (Addison-Wesley, 1969).

24. See Marianne Minor, *Coaching and Counseling: A Practice Guide for Managers* (Crisp Publications, Inc., 1989); and Arthur Sherman, George Bohlander, and Scott Snell, *Managing Human Resources* (South-Western College Publishing, 1998), pp. 550–553.

25. For additional information about the FMLA, see "Questions & Answers Employees May Ask About the FMLA," *Workforce* (January 1999) pp. 2–3; Stephanie Schroeder, Improving Family Leave," *Risk Management* (October 1999), p. 46; Faye Hansen, "Under the FMLA, Several Illnesses Combined May Constitute a 'Serious Health Condition,' " *Compensation and Benefits Review* (March/April 1998), p. 10; Mary-Kathryn Zachary, "Combined Ailments May Be FMLA's 'Serious Medical Condition,' " *Supervision* (November 1997), p. 17; Alicia Ault Barnett, "Fixing Dysfunctional Family Leave," *Benefits and Health* (March 1997), pp. 22–25; and Richard J. Reibstein, "The FMLA and Absenteeism," *HRFocus* (August 1996), pp. 3+;

26. Substance Abuse and Mental Health Services Administration (SAMHSA) press release (September 9, 1999). Also visit their Web site at www.rtwi.com/lc/substanceabusestats.html. The Drug-Free Workplace Act of 1988 requires companies receiving $25,000 or more in federal government contracts to maintain a "drug-free workplace," including establishing policies and conducting awareness programs to achieve this objective. See "Best Practices: How to Establish a Workplace Substance Abuse Program," U.S. Department of Labor, Internet site www.dol.gov. Also see S. L. Smith and Virginia Sutcliffe, "The Real Deal: Drugs in the Workplace," *Occupational Hazards* (September 1998), p. 23; Steve Bates, "An Expanded Push for Drug Programs," *Nation's Business* (July 1998), p. 51; Jane Easter Bahls, "Dealing with Drugs: Keep It Legal," *HRMagazine* (March 1998), pp. 104+ and "Drugs in the Workplace," *HRMagazine* (February 1998), pp. 80–87; John T. Adams III, "Addiction in the Workplace, Addiction on the Home Front," *HRMagazine* (February 1998), p. 8; and Melinda Ligos, "Are Your Reps High?" *Sales & Marketing Management* (October 1997), pp. 80+.

27. One study found that 85 percent of the surveyed companies offered wellness programs. See "Here's to Your Health," *HRFocus* (January 1996), p. 18; and Paul L. Cerrato, "Employee Health: Not Just a Fringe Benefit," *Business and Health* (November 1995), pp. 21–26.

28. See Sandra J. Kelley, "Making Sense of Violence in the Workplace," *Risk Management* (October 1995), pp. 50–57.

29. Many authors have applied their own terms to problem behaviors. Persons practicing incivility (bullying)in the workplace may be called: the atomic bomb, the unguided missile, backstabbers, jabbers, ridiculers, hotheads, showoffs, tyrants, Sherman tanks, hostile aggressives, and snipers, among others. If left unchecked this behavior will destroy the team. Underlying strategies for dealing with difficult people is the notion of self-esteem, assertiveness, and trust. See Michael Cole and Larry Cole, "Trust: An Integral Contributor of Managerial Success," *Supervision* (October 1999), pp. 3–4; Paula Jacobs, "How to Work with Difficult People," *Test & Measurement World* (June 1999), pp. 31–33; Cherie Carter-Scott, *Negaholics No More: You can survive . . . and transform . . . the negativity in yourself and your organization.* (National Press Publications, 1999); Rick Brinkman and Rick Kirschner, *Dealing With People You Can't Stand: How to Bring Out the Best in People at Their Worst.* (McGraw-Hill, 1994); Muriel Solomon, Working With Difficult People. (Prentice-Hall, 1990); and "Solving People-Problems on the Job," video available from *Communication Briefings.*

30. See Christine McGovern, "Take Action, Heed Warnings to End Workplace Violence," *Occupational Hazards* (March 1999), pp. 61–63; and John W. Kennish, "Violence in the Workplace," *Professional Safety* (November 1995), pp. 34–36.

31. See Anne Fisher, "How to Deal With Violent Co-Workers," *Fortune* (September 27, 1999), p. 300; Gus Stieber, "Crisis Intervention: Preventing Workplace Homicide," *HRFocus* (October 1999), p. 12; Jurg W. Mattman, "What's Growing in the Corporate Culture?" *Security Management* (November 1995), pp. 42–46; and Gregory G. Mathiason and Jodi L. Krugur, "Weapons in the Workplace: The Employer's Response," *Legal Report* (Spring 1996), pp. 5–8.

Supervising Diversity

You Make the Call!

You are Gail Williams, manager of Good n' Tastee Pizza, Waynedale location. Things had been going fairly well during your first three weeks on the job. Prior to assuming your current position, you had been in a six-month management training program and had previous managerial experience with a retail chain. During the past two days, you had two interviews that left you confused. This morning one of your fairly new wait-employees, Cindy Morris, came into your office and accused one of your shift supervisors, George Herring, of sexual harassment. She recounted the following:

"I worked yesterday from 10:30 A.M. to 3:30 P.M. I then went to class and shortly after I got home, around nine, I guess, my phone rang. I answered it like I usually do: 'Hello, this is Cindy.' The person said, 'Hi, Cindy—I just wanted to call and tell you how wonderful you are. You're the nicest looking thing I've seen in a long. . . .' I was startled and interrupted, 'Who is this?' The person said, 'You know—you know who this is. I can really make things great for you, if you know what I mean. I want to tell you how sexy I think you are. I would really like to get to know you better—if you know what I mean. When can we get together?' I slammed down the phone in anger. I was so embarrassed. It had to be George. Every time I see him, he seems to be staring at my body. I don't know what to do."

You asked her to allow you time to look into the situation and that you'd get back to her two days later—her next regularly scheduled day. As she left, you recalled yesterday's conversation with Ezel Barrett, an African-American employee, who had accused Herring of harassing her. According to Barrett, Herring continually criticized her for being unable to do her work in the way that he wanted it done. She claimed that Herring had joked about her weight and had used a number of obscene and sexual words when "yelling" at her to get the job done. Barrett stated that either it had to stop or she would file harassment and discrimination charges against the company.

About an hour later, you interviewed George Herring. His versions were quite different. He denied ever having used any sexual or obscene words toward Ezel Barrett. He acknowledged that he had not been satisfied with her work since she came to work in the store several months ago. However, he said he had gone to great lengths to help her whenever he could. Herring did not think that Barrett was able to handle the demands of the job, and he said that she had a poor attitude. Herring claimed that Barrett was simply out to get him in order to save her own job.

When asked about his impressions regarding Cindy Morris, Herring smiled and said, "Isn't she something? She's a divorcee, you know. I can't believe that any man would ever let her get away." Herring denied having called her or having made any suggestive comments to her.

You frankly don't know whom to believe. You believe that there may be some merit in the statements of both employees, but you don't know how to determine the truth. You know that your company has a strong policy prohibiting harassment that is similar to the policy statement shown in Figure 16-3 in this chapter. You don't know how to apply the policy in this situation. What should you do?

You Make the Call!

1

Recognize the importance of managing diversity as a reality and business necessity.

MANAGING DIVERSITY IS REALISTICALLY A BOTTOM-LINE CONCERN

In Chapter 1 we presented an overview of some of the principal demographic and societal trends that have an impact on organizations in general and supervision in particular. We mentioned that the increasingly diverse characteristics of people in the workplace have become a reality in organizational life that will continue to be among the major challenges faced by managers at all levels.

The reality of diversity in the workplace—sometimes referred to as the multicultural workforce—was summarized rather well in a management journal article:

Diversity is a reality. Just look around you. The American workforce is changing—in age, gender, race, national origin, sexual orientation and physical ability. So are customers and suppliers. Minority populations are increasing in every part of our country. In 50 of America's 200 cities with populations over 100,000, the so-called minority is the majority. Workers 55 and older are the fastest growing segment of the workforce. Communication and information technology is enabling more and more people with disabilities to enter the workforce.[1]

The value of diversity.*

Reproduced with permission of MetLife and Director of Licensing, Peanuts, 2000.

Because of these and other factors, the scope of diversity management now encompasses many considerations, including legal, demographic, economic, and political. The dimensions of diversity management touch virtually all aspects of a firm's operations, especially the supervisory level. Initiatives and efforts to better manage a diverse workforce are growing significantly, not just because of legal requirements or social considerations, but because there is a recognition that this has become an area of vital importance to a firm's long-term success and bottom-line results.[2] Figure 16-1 illustrates one company's recognition of the value of diversity.

2

Identify the major categories of legally protected employees and general guidelines for supervising diversity.

Protected-group employees

Classes of employees who have been afforded certain legal protections in their employment situations.

PROTECTED-GROUP EMPLOYEES AND SUPERVISION OF DIVERSITY

Throughout this book, we have stressed that employees are individuals shaped by a variety of forces from within and without the organization. In Chapter 15 we discussed how employees form groups and why supervisors should be aware of group dynamics. In this chapter we focus on the need for supervisors to develop a special awareness, sensitivity, and adaptability to protected-group employees, a term that we recognize in a legal sense but one that also has many human dimensions.

The identification of employees who have been afforded special legal protection comes primarily from civil rights legislation, equal employment opportunity regulations, and numerous court decisions. Various laws and regulations that govern employment policies and practices are listed in the Appendix. Areas of lawful and potentially unlawful inquiry during the selection process of job applicants were presented in Figure 12-3. For our purposes in this chapter, we will use the term **protected-group employees** to identify classes of employees who have been afforded certain legal protections in their employment situations. The underlying legal philosophy is that many individuals within these classes have been unfairly or illegally discriminated against in the past, or that they should be afforded special consideration to enhance their opportunities for fair treatment in employment.

A recent report by the U. S. Justice Department indicates that alleged discrimination in the workplace more than tripled during the past decade. Employment cases accounted for two-thirds of the increase. These are cases alleging employer discrimination in hiring, promoting, firing, pay and benefits, and opportunities for training because of a person's race, color, religion, sex, national origin, age, disability, or exercise of legal rights. Plaintiffs are allowed to win compensatory and punitive damages in certain job bias cases and have the right to a jury trail. Court decisions during the 1990s appear to have broadened the scope of employment practices deemed to be discriminatory.[3]

Since the requirements of employment discrimination laws at times can become quite complicated, we will not attempt to become too legalistic in our discussion.[4] Supervisors normally should refer questions that are of a legal or compliance nature to an appropriate human resources staff person. The human resources department usually will have the expertise to answer the supervisor's questions and give appropriate advice. At times, the human resources staff will seek legal counsel to determine what should be done regarding certain matters and to avoid legal difficulties.

Classifications of Protected-Group Employees

The protected-group employees that we will discuss in this chapter[5] are classified according to:

- Racial/ethnic origin
- Sex (gender, i.e., women)
- Physical or mental disability (i.e., disabled, handicapped)
- Age (i.e., over 40)
- Religion
- Military service (i.e., Vietnam-era or other veterans)

The supervision of protected-group employees by definition is part of a firm's efforts to manage diversity so as to benefit both the firm and the employees. Regardless of personal views, supervisors must be sensitive to possible illegal discriminatory actions and adjust their supervisory practices accordingly. More important, however, is that supervisors recognize the strengths and potential contributions of all employees and supervise in ways that will not limit their development for inappropriate reasons. Stated another way, effective supervision of a diversified workforce can be viewed as an opportunity to draw upon and utilize differences of people in a positive, productive, and enriching manner.[6]

As discussed in Chapter 15, incivility in the workplace is on the rise. It is a sad commentary on our society when certain inappropriate behaviors continue unabated. Perhaps it is an escalation of the old adage "the squeaky wheel gets the grease." But on the other hand, rude, obnoxious, and inappropriate behavior appears to get more attention in the popular press and on late-night television talk shows than other more important issues.[7] Harassment in the workplace has been unlawful for a long time; why is it still pervasive? This chapter's "Contemporary Issue" box sheds some light on the depth and complexity of discrimination and harassment in the workplace.

contemporary issue

**To some employees, it's harmless conversation or behavior.
To others, it's inappropriate and against the law.**

The decade of the 1990s began with daily news reports and nightly comments from Jay Leno and David Letterman about the Clarence Thomas—Anita Hill case. Then there was former Arkansas state employee Paula Jones' sexual harassment complaint against President Clinton. The case of B-52 pilot Lt. Kelly Flinn, who committed adultery with a married man, raised issues of morality and of double standards in the military. Many were shocked by the $176 million racial discrimination settlement that resulted from Texaco's alleged blatant acts of racism, including crude language by managers and employees. The highly publicized EEOC class action lawsuit against Mitsubishi Motor Manufacturing of America, Inc., alleging that hundreds of female employees at its Decatur, Illinois, plant had suffered abuse, was settled for $34 million. The $26.6 million judgment against Miller Brewing Co. in the so-called "Seinfeld" case was noteworthy. Thanks to the racy "Seinfeld" angle, the latter was broadcast on *Court TV*. Many forget that the lawsuit was brought by Jerold

MacKenzie, the alleged harasser, who successfully claimed he'd been wrongfully terminated. Other lesser profile cases are summarized below.

- **Circle K Corporation:** Four veteran managers, all of Vietnamese heritage, were fired for first-time events with no warnings, and it happened over a short period of time. The Court awarded the four former managers $18.2 million because it was determined they were fired because of their race rather than for job-related problems.[1]
- **Methodist Hospital Northlake:** A former male employee at the hospital who claimed he was fired for complaining about repeated sexual advances by female employees was awarded $2.8 million in a wrongful termination suit. He was hired in 1988 to work in the billing office with one other male employee and 13 female employees.[2]
- **Thomson Consumer Electronics:** The company agreed to pay 800 former employees $7.1 million to settle an age-discrimination lawsuit after the company closed one Indiana television plant and drastically cut staff at another one. The EEOC alleged that the company's policy of giving older workers less money in severance benefits was discriminatory and unlawful.[3]
- **Long Prairie Packing:** The Minnesota meat packing company agreed to pay $1.9 million to settle a same-sex harassment case. The EEOC claimed that three male workers were subjected to repeated sexual harassment by male coworkers. One worker also claimed coworkers taunted him because he is legally blind in one eye. This case was the EEOC's first settlement involving a case alleging a pattern and practice of same-sex and disability-based harassment in the workplace.[4]
- **National Steel:** A male employee claims that a female supervisor repeatedly threatened his job after their sexual relationship ended. Allegedly the two began their affair before she became his supervisor. The employee claims that after he tried to end the relationship, the supervisor began to harass him, required mandatory overtime, took him off larger customer accounts, and told him to change her company expense account sheets, adding personal mileage for extra trips not taken. The male testified that he began taking physician-prescribed medication for anxiety and depression because of the harassment. According to the lawsuit, company officials failed to take action to stop the alleged harassment after being notified, calling the man "just a jilted lover."[5]
- **'Babe':** This case involved a deposition hearing in a lawsuit by a woman seeking damages from a lawyer she said had given her genital herpes. As the woman left the room, Allen Harris, the lawyer representing the defendant, joked that the woman was going to meet another boyfriend. Susan Green, the woman's lawyer, complained about the remark, and asked: "You got a problem with me?" Harris answered, "No, I don't have a problem with you, babe." "Babe? You called me babe? What generation are you from?" Green replied. "At least I didn't call you 'bimbo'," Harris responded. "I've run into gender bias. However, I have never run into a situation where it has been so outrageous, so totally without provocation," Green said. The 69-year-old Harris later explained: "It's just a way my generation speaks. There was no offense intended, and it certainly was not meant to gain any advantage. It was just in the casual course of conversation." The court disagreed, ruling that Harris' behavior was a "crass attempt to gain unfair advantage through the use of demeaning language. . . . definitions of the word 'babe' are gender biased and derogatory."[6]

The following case provides an interesting approach for distinguishing between incivility and discrimination. Recently, "the U. S. Court of Appeals in Chicago upheld a lower court dismissal of a lawsuit in which a black female employee of S. C. Johnson & Co. charged a male coworker with sexual and racial harassment. Although the man had berated her with expletives—some with racial overtones—let a door slam in her face, and cut her off in the parking lot, the court found that the man 'treated all his coworkers poorly' and concluded that 'equal opportunity harassers' aren't guilty of discrimination."[7]

Management malpractice that allows such behavior in the workplace and employees who tolerate or condone such behavior share the blame for the rise of workplace incivility!

Sources: Adapted and excerpted from the following sources: (1) Jennifer J. Laabs, "Circle K Loses Multimillion Dollar Racial Discrimination Lawsuit," *Personnel Journal* (July 1996), p. 11; (2) Associated Press, "Jury Awards $2.8 Million," as reported in the Fort Wayne (IN) *Journal Gazette* (August 12, 1999), p. 1C; (3) Wire reports, "Thomson Settles Age Discrimination Lawsuit," as reported in the Fort Wayne (IN) *News Sentinel* (August 18, 1999), p. B1; (4) Wire reports, "Meat Packer Settles Same-Sex Harassment Case," as reported in the Fort Wayne (IN) *News Sentinel* (August 12, 1999), p. B1; (5) Associated Press, "Woman Is Hit With Sex Harassment Suit," as reported in the Fort Wayne (IN) *Journal Gazette* (June 4, 1999), p. 5C; (6) Associated Press, "Court: Female Lawyers Can't Be Called 'Babe,'" as reported in the Fort Wayne (IN) *Journal Gazette* (June 5, 1999), p. 2C; (7) Chris Lee, "The Death of Civility: Mean Streets and Rude Workplaces," *Training* (July 1999), p. 25.

The OUCH Test in Supervision of All Employees

The OUCH test, which we discussed in Chapter 12 as a guideline in selecting employees, also applies to day-to-day supervision. This test should remind supervisors that their actions should be:

O: Objective,
U: Uniform in application,
C: Consistent in effect, and
H: Have job relatedness.

For example, assume that an organization's policy specifies a disciplinary warning for being tardy three times in one month. The supervisor should give the same warning to every employee who is late the third time in one month, regardless of whether the employee is in a protected-group category. This supervisory approach would meet the OUCH test because tardiness is an observable behavior that is objectively measured for all employees. The penalty is the same for all employees, is consistent, and is clearly job related.

A myth occasionally voiced by some supervisors is that certain categories of employees cannot be disciplined or discharged because of government regulations (Figure 16-2). That view is false. Laws and regulations do not prevent a supervisor from taking disciplinary action against protected-group employees. However, they do require that such employees be treated the same as other employees whenever disciplinary actions are taken. Therefore, it is extremely important that supervisors be careful in meeting the

FIGURE 16-2

A myth occasionally voiced by some supervisors is that protected group employees cannot be disciplined or discharged.

OUCH test and in justifying their actions through adequate documentation. We discuss this in more detail in Chapters 17 and 19.

Explain issues involved in the supervision of racial/ethnic minority employees.

SUPERVISING RACIAL AND ETHNIC MINORITY EMPLOYEES

The most frequently identified racial and ethnic minority populations in the United States are African Americans (blacks), Hispanics, Asian Americans, and Native Americans. With the passage of major civil rights legislation, most employers have developed nondiscrimination and/or affirmative-action policies or programs for employment of people from racial and ethnic minority groups. A major thrust of these policies and programs is to ensure that minorities, as well as certain other protected-group individuals, receive special consideration in hiring and promotion decisions. The philosophy underlying affirmative action plans is to overcome the impact of past discriminatory practices and to provide greater opportunities for underrepresented groups to participate more fully throughout the workforce. The long-term goal is to have a fully diversified workforce in which all employees are hired and supervised solely on the basis of their individual capabilities and performance.

While most organizations recognize the importance of integrating their workplace, minorities still face substantial barriers. A recent SHRM survey indicated the following barriers for minorities: lack of role models, limited mentoring opportunities, exclusion from informal networks, stereotypes or preconceptions based on race or ethnicity, and the perception that the corporate culture favors nonminorities.[8] A review of the barriers warrants another question: Why should qualified minority applicants join an organization when they can look and see that in the past, no other minority has succeeded? Thus, the old "success begets success" circular effect takes place, that is, if the company is known as a great place for women and minorities, then it follows that other qualified minority applicants will be attracted to the company.

In recent years, a number of polls have indicated that a majority of Americans now oppose affirmative action because they believe that women and other minorities have made great progress in employment over the past several decades. At the time of writing of this text, both the philosophy and application of affirmative action have come under increasing criticism and political attack. Both opponents and proponents of affirmative action have engaged in extensive debate concerning the future direction of affirmative action both legally and as a viable practicality.

Effects of Previous Discrimination

Minority employees who have experienced prejudicial treatment may resent supervisors of different racial/ethnic backgrounds. The most common area of tension continues to be between black employees and white managers. Even though nondiscrimination laws have been in place for several decades, annual data compiled by the federal Equal Employment Opportunity Commission (EEOC) show that minority group members file tens of thousands of complaints about unfair treatment because of their race. Typically,

Supervisors must be sensitive about the effects of racial discrimination, both in past and present situations.

alleged discriminatory discipline and discharge have been the most frequent bases for these complaints.

Since responsibility for initiating discipline and discharge actions usually rests with supervisors, such decisions play a significant role in generating charges of discrimination. Investigations of charges require the extensive time, effort, and involvement of supervisors, human resources and legal specialists, and others. Thus supervisors must be sensitive to the feelings of minority employees who may have experienced discriminatory treatment in the past, or who believe that they currently have been discriminated against. Supervisors should not enter into racial debates with minority employees who display lingering resentment and suspicion. Rather, supervisors should always strive to be fair and considerate when making decisions that affect these employees. By demonstrating that minority employees will be supervised in the same manner as other employees, a supervisor can reduce the negative effects of past discrimination. In the event that a minority employee's feelings of resentment interfere with job performance or relations within the department, the supervisor should refer the employee to the human resources department or to an Employee Assistance Program (EAP) counselor if available.

Cultural Differences

A continuing debate about human behavior concerns how much heredity, as compared to environment, shapes an individual. Obviously, heredity is a major factor in the physical and ethnic makeup of a person. Moreover, because members of various races or ethnic origins often have different environmental experiences, unique subcultures have developed for each racial/ethnic minority group. For example, the ties that Native Americans have to their heritage reflect their subculture. People of Asian descent have distinctive values and traditions that reflect their heritage and cultures.

Unfortunately, differences in ethnic/cultural backgrounds can contribute to prejudicial attitudes and treatment of minority employees. For example, a minority employee's values regarding the importance of work and punctuality may be different from those held by a supervisor. If a minority employee has not grown up in an environment that stresses the importance of being punctual, especially in a work situation, the supervisor must be prepared to spend extra time explaining to that employee the reasons for punctual attendance and the consequences of tardiness and absenteeism. Regardless of what cultural differences exist, it is the supervisor's job to exert special efforts to reduce the effects of these differences. By so doing, the minority person can learn to accept the requirements of the work environment and meet the standards expected of all employees in the department.

Language Difficulties

Another consideration in supervising minority employees relates to different languages that may be spoken in a work environment. Some employers have held training programs to sensitize supervisors and managers to better understand minority language patterns, and to make them more knowledgeable about the cultural and language backgrounds of certain minorities. The training program focused on language expressions and speech habits with which people from other racial and ethnic backgrounds are generally not familiar.

The other side of the language problem has been addressed by some employers who sponsor English improvement and business English courses for minority employees. These programs focus on development of writing and speaking skills needed for job improvement and advancement.

At one time, some employers attempted to prevent employees from using their native languages at work. However, such restrictions today are viewed by courts and enforcement agencies with skepticism unless interpersonal communication is a critical part of the job. For example, a manufacturing company's refusal to hire a Spanish-speaking worker on an assembly line might be ruled as prejudicial since on this job communication skills may be much less important than manual dexterity skills. However, for a salesperson in a department store or for a nurse working in an emergency room adequate interpersonal language skills would be essential. In some parts of the United States, such as Miami, Florida, or San Antonio, Texas, a bilingual (Spanish-English) person would be a valuable asset. The large number of Spanish-speaking people in those areas represents a major pool of potential clients who could be better served by a bilingual person.

Fairness in All Supervisory Actions and Decisions

Many minority employees are clustered in entry-level or service positions for which they see little potential for advancement. Others find themselves in job situations where competition is keen for advancement to better-paying and more challenging positions. Tensions between majority and minority employees may be particularly noticeable at those times when a minority employee alleges discrimination or unfair treatment in a job assignment, promotional opportunity, or disciplinary matter.

For all employees—but especially when minority employees are part of the departmental workgroup—supervisors should endeavor to be scrupulously fair. In assignment of work, training opportunities, performance appraisals, disciplinary actions—in virtually all supervisory actions and decisions—supervisors must make every effort to decide on objective and job-related grounds. If a minority employee complains of harassment or discriminatory treatment by a fellow employee, supervisor, or some other person, the supervisor must treat that complaint as a priority concern. In most cases, the supervisor should listen carefully to the nature of the complaint and report it to a higher-level manager or the human resources department for further consideration and direction concerning what to do. In no way should a supervisor retaliate against the minority person, even if the supervisor believes that the discrimination or harassment allegation is without merit. The law protects a minority employee's right to challenge management decisions and actions that the person believes are discriminatory. The supervisor is responsible for making sure that this right is genuinely protected. In summary, supervising racial/ethnic minority employees requires understanding, sensitivity, and even "extra fairness" when the supervisor is not a member of that minority group.

Discuss factors that are particularly important when supervising female employees.

SUPERVISING WOMEN

Throughout the last several decades, both the number and the percentage of women in the labor force have increased dramatically. Among the reasons that have been cited most often are changed values regarding personal fulfillment through work, wider career opportunities, the feminist movement, higher educational levels, growth in single-parent and single-adult households, and economic pressures. At the time of writing this text, women comprised slightly under one-half of the U.S. labor force. Yet in many ways women are still "out of the loop." Consider that women represent only 11.9 percent of corporate officers in America's 500 largest companies, and men currently hold 93 percent of the high-profile jobs with profit-and-loss responsibility that often lead to the top spots.[9] While there is a general consensus that opportunities for women will increase during the first decade of the 21st century, there are still substantial barriers. These include the lack of females at the board level, male-dominated corporate culture, stereotypes or preconceptions about women, exclusion from informal networks, and lack of mentoring opportunities.[10]

Both men and women supervisors should be aware of a number of important concerns that affect the supervision of women. While not all inclusive, the areas to be discussed here represent a range of issues that supervisors should recognize and deal with appropriately.

Entry of Women into Many Career Fields

The combined effects of antidiscrimination laws, affirmative action programs, and the increasing number of women in the workforce have led to the movement of women into many jobs that were traditionally dominated by men. For example, in greater numbers than ever before, women are financiers, scientists, engineers, utility repair specialists, sales and technical representatives, accountants, and managers. However, a high percentage of women still work in clerical and service jobs.

The entry of women into jobs requiring hard physical labor and craft skills has been comparatively limited, but when women do assume craft or other physically demanding jobs, changes may occur. Experiences of a number of firms indicate that some equipment can be modified without excessive cost outlays. For example, there have been changes to the shape of some wrenches and other tools to accommodate women's smaller hands. Telephone companies have changed the mounting position for ladders on trucks used by outside repair employees to make them easier for women to reach and have bought lightweight ladders that are easier to carry. Also, special clothing and shoes were developed so that females could have the proper protective equipment.

Although women have successfully penetrated many of the barriers that previously limited their entry into male-dominated positions, there are still problems that occur, especially at the departmental level. A common supervisory consideration when a woman takes a job traditionally held by men is the reaction of the current male employees. Some of the men may resent and even openly criticize her. The supervisor should be prepared to deal with such attitudes to enable the woman to perform her job satisfactorily. The supervisor should first inform the men about the starting employment date of the woman so that her presence does not come as a surprise. Then the supervisor should make it clear to the men that disciplinary action will be taken if this woman—or any women employees in the future—is ignored or subjected to abuse or harassment. The supervisor should also make it clear that any woman taking a previously all-male job will be afforded a realistic opportunity to succeed based on her capabilities to perform the job.

When women assume a craft or other physically demanding job, some changes in equipment and procedure may be needed.

Issues of Sexual Harassment and Sexual Stereotyping

A growing number of civil rights and court cases in the United States have dealt with problems of sexual harassment. Sexual harassment usually means situations in which a female employee is subjected to sexual language, touching, or sexual advances by a male employee, male supervisor, or male customer. For example, if a female employee resists or protests such behavior by a male supervisor, she may fear retribution when the supervisor is considering pay raises or promotions. It is important to note that a female supervisor or female employee can be charged with sexual harassment of a male employee,[11] and harassment can also occur when both parties are of the same sex. However, sexual harassment of women by men has been the focus of most of the cases heard by federal agencies and the courts.

Guidelines issued by the Equal Employment Opportunity Commission (EEOC), which enforces the federal Civil Rights Act, define **sexual harassment** as sexual advances, requests for sexual favors, and other verbal or physical conduct of a sexual nature when:

- Submission to such conduct is made either explicitly or implicitly as a condition of an individual's employment.
- Submission to or rejection of such conduct by an individual is used as the basis for employment decisions affecting that person.
- Such conduct has the purpose or effect of unreasonably interfering with an individual's work performance or creating an intimidating, hostile, or offensive working environment.

Many firms have developed sexual harassment policy statements. Figure 16-3 is an example of such a statement by a printing company that defines the term harassment even beyond gender terms. The statement informs employees what to do if they encounter what they consider to be harassment.

Sexual harassment
Unwelcome sexual advances, requests, or conduct when submission to such conduct is tied to the individual's continuing employment or advancement, unreasonably interferes with job performance, or creates a hostile work environment.

FIGURE 16-3

No-harassment policy statement of a printing company.

NO-HARASSMENT POLICY

This company does not and will not tolerate harassment of our employees. The term "harassment" includes, but is not limited to, slurs, jokes, and other verbal, graphic, or physical conduct relating to an individual's race, color, sex, religion, national origin, citizenship, age, or handicap. "Harassment" also includes sexual advances; requests for sexual favors; unwelcome or offensive touching; and other verbal, graphic, or physical conduct of a sexual nature.

VIOLATION OF THIS POLICY WILL SUBJECT AN EMPLOYEE TO DISCIPLINARY ACTION, UP TO AND INCLUDING IMMEDIATE DISCHARGE.

If you feel that you are being harassed in any way by another employee or by a customer or vendor, you should make your feelings known to your supervisor immediately. The matter will be thoroughly investigated, and where appropriate, disciplinary action will be taken. If you do not feel that you can discuss the matter with your supervisor or if you are not satisfied with the way your complaint has been handled, please contact either the human resources director or the company president. Your complaint will be kept as confidential as possible, and you will not be penalized in any way for reporting such conduct.

Please do not assume that the company is aware of your problem. It is your responsibility to bring your complaints and concerns to our attention so that we can help resolve them.

Court decisions have generally held that an employer is liable if sexual harassment of employees is condoned, overlooked, or does not lead to corrective actions by management. Reprimand and discipline of offending employees and supervisors are recommended courses of action.[12] Supervisors should avoid and strongly discourage sexual language, innuendos, and behavior that is inappropriate in the work environment. Supervisors who use their positions improperly in this regard are engaging in conduct that is unacceptable and could lead to their own dismissal.

Because it is virtually impossible to monitor everything that happens in the workplace at all times, many firms have required their managers, supervisors, and employees to attend training programs or seminars designed to prevent and deal with sexual harassment. These programs typically are developed and presented by the human resources staff or by outside training consultants. Information and discussions focus on prohibited types of conduct, how employees can deal with offensive comments and behavior, and remedies that are available.[13] Such programs also may cover certain aspects of sexual stereotyping that can be problematical.

Sexual stereotyping

Use of language or judgments that demean someone, usually by men toward women.

Sexual stereotyping means the use of language or judgments to demean someone, usually by men toward women. For example, a department store supervisor may find that women buyers strongly resent being referred to as "the girls." Or a supervisor may imply that women are more emotional, less rational, and less reliable than men.

Many assertions about women employees as compared to men employees are inaccurate. For example, one large firm examined the absenteeism records of both their men and women employees. This firm found no significant difference in absentee rates between the two sexes and that their women employees with children had a lower absentee rate than single men. Thus, the supervisor should not make supervisory decisions based on sexual stereotypes.

Many job titles have been changed to avoid gender implications. For example, the job title "fireman" is now "fire fighter," a "mailman" is now a "letter carrier," a "stewardess" is now a "flight attendant," and so forth.

Training and Development Opportunities

Women employees should be offered equal access to available training and development activities, and those who have potential should be encouraged to develop their skills. This is especially important with regard to upgrading women to supervisory and other managerial positions.

A number of research studies have found that women employees often benefit from special training and development opportunities that focus on enhancing their self-esteem, communication skills, and career development. For women who already are managers and supervisors, many firms provide programs that include such topics as personal awareness, assertiveness training, managerial barriers to success, time management, delegation, and special problems encountered by women in managerial positions.

Despite the entry of women into supervisory and lower-level management positions, upward mobility for women in organizations still has been quite slow. A government report in the mid-1990s indicated that white males constituted less than half of the U.S. workforce but held some 95 percent of senior management positions. As mentioned in Chapter 1, the "barriers" to upward progression of women and minorities has been called the *glass ceiling*. Firms that make serious efforts to shatter the glass ceiling and bring more women and minorities into higher levels of management usually do so because their top management has a strong commitment to make this happen as part of the firm's diversity management initiatives within a strategic business plan.[14] Many firms find that a well-conceived and implemented mentoring program is essential. Mentoring efforts usually involve having senior-level managers—both male and female—serve as mentors or advisors for women and minority supervisors who have been identified as having potential for higher management positions. Mentors provide assistance in various ways, including feedback on job performance; career counseling; and networking with other mentors, advisees, and others to make them better known to people who can be influential in promotion and career decisions.[15]

Pregnancy and Family Care

The Pregnancy Discrimination Act of 1978, which amended the 1964 Civil Rights Act, requires that pregnancy be treated no differently from illnesses or health disabilities if an employer has medical benefits or a disability plan. Additionally, many states have laws that require certain pregnancy benefits for employed women. In response, most employers have policies that allow a pregnant employee to work as long as she and her physician certify that it is appropriate. These policies also grant the pregnant employee a leave of absence until she can return to work. To prevent abuse of pregnancy leaves— or other types of disability leaves—many employers require a physician's statement to verify a continuing disability.

In Chapter 15, we discussed the Family and Medical Leave Act. For employers covered by this law, a woman employee must be granted up to 12 weeks of unpaid leave related to the birth of her child. Health-care coverage must be continued during this period, and she must be returned to her former or a comparable position when she returns to work. Although the law makes these and other stipulations, an employer may go beyond these requirements—for example, by granting paid leave during the period of the employee's pregnancy or after childbirth.

Supervisors must see to it that pregnant employees are treated in a nondiscriminatory manner, although they are not required to give them easier job assignments. A more difficult problem for the supervisor is a pregnant employee's uncertainty about returning to work after her pregnancy leave is over. This affects supervisors in scheduling work and anticipating future staffing needs. Supervisors may have to hire part-time or temporary help, schedule overtime work, or take other temporary actions until the woman definitely decides whether and when she will return to work. This is not an unduly burdensome problem if a supervisor plans well in advance to accommodate the temporary absence of the employee.

One of the well-recognized major problems that accompanied the growth of women in the labor force has been the conflict between the job demands placed on women and their family responsibilities. Women with children often must cope with demanding responsibilities at home, which are not always shared equally by their hus-

bands. Moreover, many women head single-parent house-holds in which they are the primary provider for their families.

Because of concerns over this problem, many employers have adopted flexible policies concerning work schedules, leaves, and other arrangements in order to help employees—especially women—to meet their obligations.[16] The Family and Medical Leave Act also requires employers to grant unpaid leave to cover certain types of family-care situations, for example, to take care of a seriously ill child, spouse, or parent. There have been legislative proposals that would provide grants to assist in arranging child care for employees who must work and for whom no other care would be available. Regardless of the outcome of any future legislation, the tension between family and job responsibilities is one that employers and supervisors will have to address for many years to come. Supervisors should become familiar with their firm's policies regarding family- and child-care assistance and endeavor to resolve whenever possible those conflicts that interfere with the employee's capacity to carry out her or his job responsibilities.

Many employers have adapted their work scheduling, leaves, and other arrangements to alleviate the tension between family and job responsibilities.

Equity in Compensation

Statistically, the pay received by women employees in the U.S. workforce generally has been below that of men. Although estimates vary, the aggregate statistical median for women's compensation was about 70 percent of that for men.[17] This disparity exists even though the Equal Pay Act of 1963 requires that men and women performing equal work must receive equal pay. For example, a female bookkeeper and a male bookkeeper in the same firm who have approximately the same seniority and performance levels must be paid equally. Although equal pay has not always been interpreted to mean "exactly the same," a firm would probably be in violation of the Equal Pay Act if it paid the female bookkeeper $1 an hour less than her male counterpart. Yet disparities still exist. The issue of "equal pay" was raised in early 2000 when players from the U.S. women's World Cup champion national soccer team stated they would refuse to play in future games because of a contract dispute with the U.S. Soccer Federation. The women asked that their pay be raised to match the amounts paid to the men's team members.[18]

Comparable worth

Concept that jobs should be paid at the same level if they require similar skills or abilities.

A more complex reason for the disparity in the pay of men and women has been the issue of comparable worth. **Comparable worth** is a concept that jobs should draw approximately the same pay if they require similar skills and abilities. The issue arises when jobs that are distinctly different but require similar levels of skills and abilities have different pay scales—especially if one job is predominantly held by men and the other by women. For example, compare the job of medical technologist, which is held predominantly by women, with that of electrician, which is held mainly by men. Both jobs require licensing or certification, but medical technologists typically have more formal education. Now assume that the pay scales for medical technologists in a hospital are about one-third lower than those for electricians working in the same hospital. A comparison of these dissimilar jobs might suggest that unequal pay is being given for jobs of comparable worth.

However, a probable major cause for the difference in such pay scales is the labor market in the area. If unionized electricians are paid $24 per hour by other employers, the hospital would have to set its pay scale at this level in order to compete for electricians. Similarly, if the going rate for nonunionized medical technologists is $15 per hour, the hospital is likely to pay its medical technologists this rate. Also, the difference in pay may be attributable to numerous factors, including the supply or shortages of women in certain jobs. In the example cited, the reason why the job of electrician is predominantly held by men is that, in the past, few women sought or were permitted to become electricians. Only by providing training and entry opportunities for qualified women to become electricians will the disparity in pay be eliminated. Likewise, men with the appropriate interests and abilities could be encouraged to become medical technologists.

It is important for supervisors to understand the issue of comparable worth because it may become a major issue in the future. However, it is even more important for supervisors to identify and support qualified women to train and develop for higher-paying jobs that have been held predominantly by men. Supervisors should be willing to encourage, select, and assist these women as they progress into higher-paying positions of greater skill and responsibility.

SUPERVISING EMPLOYEES WITH DISABILITIES

5

Identify and discuss legal and other considerations involved in the supervision of employees with physical and mental disabilities.

For decades, many organizations have made special efforts to provide employment opportunities for people with physical and mental disabilities. Many of these efforts were made voluntarily and from the conviction that it was the proper thing to do. However, as a result of a number of laws and government regulations beginning with the Rehabilitation Act of 1973, people with disabilities were identified as a group that was to receive special consideration in employment and other organizational areas. The 1973 law used the term *handicapped* in defining individuals with physical or mental impairments, but the preferred usage today is "individuals with disabilities." This law requires certain employers doing business with the federal government and federal agencies to develop an affirmative action program and to make reasonable accommodation for the employment of such persons.

In 1990, the Americans with Disabilities Act (ADA) was passed. It is the most significant legislation dealing with legal protection for a group since the Civil Rights Act of 1964. The ADA applies to employers with 15 or more employees and identifies coverage for people who have disabilities. See Figure 16-4 for an illustration of one company's ADA policy.

The ADA requires that employers provide access to public spaces for people with disabilities and make necessary alterations to public accommodations and commercial facilities for accessibility by people with disabilities.

FIGURE 16-4

One company's ADA Policy.

We are firmly committed to providing every employee and every applicant an equal opportunity to succeed in the workplace and during the application process. The Company is committed to removing barriers and obstacles that inhibit employees and applicants from performing to the best of their ability, and providing them the opportunity to enjoy equal benefits and privileges of employment.

It is our policy to provide reasonable accommodations to any qualified applicant or employee with a disability requesting such accommodation to complete the job application process or to perform the essential functions of his/her position. Reasonable accommodation may include, but is not limited to, making facilities accessible, job restructuring, modifying schedules, reassignment to a vacant position, acquiring or modifying equipment, and/or providing interpreters.

The Americans with Disabilities Act (ADA) defines a qualified individual with a disability as a person qualified to perform the essential functions of a position, with or without accommodation, who:

- has a physical or mental impairment that substantially limits one or more of the person's major life activities;
- has a record of such an impairment; or
- is regarded as having such an impairment.

The company has developed, in cooperation with the Center for Independent Living, a Reasonable Accommodation Process to assist management and employees in handling reasonable accommodation issues. Additional information on this process can be obtained by contacting your Human Resources representative or the Center for Independent Living at 423-4810.

At the time of writing this text, the Supreme Court, by a 7-2 margin, had taken a restrictive view of what qualifies as a disability under the ADA. Generally, the court said the ADA doesn't protect from employment discrimination people with physical impairments such as poor eyesight or high blood pressure who can function normally when they wear glasses or take medication.[19] Nevertheless, supervisors should be familiar with major provisions of the ADA and, more importantly, its implications for supervision of employees with disabilities.

Who Is a Qualified Disabled Individual?

Qualified disabled individual

Defined by the Americans with Disabilities Act as someone with a disability who can perform the essential components of a job with or without reasonable accommodation.

To be protected under the ADA employment provisions, an individual with a disability must be qualified. A **qualified disabled individual** is someone with a disability who can perform the essential components of a job position with or without a reasonable accommodation on the part of the employer. This means that a person with a disability must have the skills and other qualifications needed for the job to receive employment protection under ADA.

The definition of a disabled person is very broad. By some estimates, about one in six Americans (or roughly about 45 million people) could be considered disabled under the statute's definitions. The law does exempt a number of categories from its definitions of disability, such as those who have an infectious disease and whose job includes food handling, homosexuals, and people who currently use illegal drugs. However, the definition of disability covers most major diseases, including cancer, epilepsy, diabetes, and HIV/AIDS.[20] The concept of making a reasonable accommodation for individuals with disabilities was established by the Rehabilitation Act of 1973. **Reasonable accommodation** means altering the usual ways of doing things so that an otherwise qualified disabled person can perform the essential duties of a job, but without creating an undue hardship for the employer. Undue hardship means an alteration that would require a significant expense or an unreasonable change in activities on the part of the employer to accommodate the disabled person.

Reasonable accommodation
Altering the usual ways of doing things so that an otherwise qualified disabled person can perform the essential job duties, but without creating an undue hardship for the employer.

Complying with the ADA

In order to comply with the provisions of the Americans with Disabilities Act, many employers have conducted training programs for supervisors who carry a significant responsibility in making the necessary adjustments. In the employment process, for example, an employer cannot require a pre-job-offer medical examination to screen out applicants (with the exception of a drug test) or make any type of pre-employment inquiries about the nature of an applicant's disability. Supervisors must be very cautious in talking about the requirements of a job and not bring into a pre-employment interview the possibility of an employee's disability or past medical record. However, an applicant may be given a medical examination after a job offer has been made to determine whether she or he is physically capable of performing the required components of the job. Most employers have reviewed their application forms to make sure that improper questions are not included. Many employers have revised their job descriptions to define the essential functions of each job.

Reasonable accommodation may take any number of forms. It typically means making buildings accessible by building ramps, removing barriers such as steps or curbs, and altering restroom facilities. Reasonable accommodation may mean that the arrangement of desks and widths of aisles have to be altered to allow people in wheelchairs access to job locations. It conceivably could include modifying work schedules, acquiring certain equipment or devices, providing readers or interpreters, and other types of adjustments.

In some situations, job duties can be altered to accommodate people with disabilities. For example, in one company an employee who assembled small component units was also expected to place the completed units in a carton at the end of an assembly process. Several times a day the full carton had to be carried to the shipping area. In order for an employee in a wheelchair to perform the subassembly job, the supervisor arranged for a shipping clerk to pick up completed component units at designated times each day. Thus, the supervisor made a reasonable accommodation so that a physically impaired employee could handle the subassembly job. Another supervisor added a flashing warning light to equipment that already contained a warning buzzer so that an employee with a hearing impairment could be employed safely.

Attitudes of Supervisors and Employees

The Americans with Disabilities Act is aimed at changing perceptions as well as actions in the workplace. The law encourages supervisors and employees to recognize the abilities rather than the disabilities of coworkers and others. As much as anything else, attitudes will play an important role in organizational efforts to accommodate people with disabilities.[21]

It is important that supervisors and employees recognize that the ADA is the law and that they believe it is the proper thing to do. Training programs are aimed at allowing an open discussion about different disabilities and opportunities to air questions and feelings of discomfort. Employees should be aware that certain words, although not intentional, may actually carry negative messages. For example, the ADA uses the term *disability* rather than *handicapped* because this is the preference of most people with disabilities. Some training programs have utilized simulated experiences in which nondisabled employees are required to experience certain types of mental, hearing, physical, or visual impairments. This includes sitting in a wheelchair and trying to maneuver through a work area. This type of training helps employees gain a better understanding of what it might be like to experience the difficulties of such a disability.

The type of disability an employee has may even affect the leadership style used by a supervisor. For example, employees who are mentally disabled may require somewhat close and direct supervision. However, a physically disabled employee who uses a wheelchair while working as a proofreader probably should be supervised with a more general and participative style.

Much research has shown that individuals with disabilities can make excellent employees provided that they are placed in jobs where their abilities can be adapted and utilized appropriately. As in so many other areas, the departmental supervisor is often the primary person to make this happen.

6
Discuss considerations involved when supervising older workers, employees of different religious views, and Vietnam-era and other veterans.

OTHER PROTECTED GROUPS AND THE SUPERVISOR

In addition to racial and ethnic minorities, women, and people with disabilities, there are a number of other protected-group categories with which supervisors should be familiar. A discussion of all the aspects of these categories is beyond the scope of this book. In this section we highlight some of the additional supervisory considerations applicable to employees who are older, those who have different religious beliefs, and Vietnam-era and other veterans.

Older Employees

At the dawn of the 21st century, anyone born when John F. Kennedy was elected president turned 40. They joined the growing number of the persons in the U.S. labor force 40 years of age and older. This large segment constitutes another legally protected group. The Age Discrimination in Employment Act, as amended, which applies to employers with 20 or more employees, prohibits discrimination in employment for most individuals beyond 40 years of age. Consequently, mandatory retirement ages (such as at age 70) are not lawful for most employees. Nevertheless, many workers do retire at age 65 or earlier. In part this is because of the existence of improved retirement programs and pension plans, including plans that allow early retirement. Some early-retirement plans permit employees who have 30 years of service to retire before age 60.

When making decisions to hire, promote, or discharge, supervisors should be aware of the legal protections afforded older workers. For example, selecting a 35-year-old person for a sales position instead of a 55-year-old with more selling experience might result in an age discrimination lawsuit. Laying off a 50-year-old engineer while keeping a 30-year-old engineer on the payroll during a reduction in force might be age discrimination unless the younger engineer is superior in abilities to the older one.

Supervisory decisions to demote or terminate older employees should be documented with sound, objective performance appraisals. Terminating a 62-year-old clerical worker simply for "poor job performance" might be discriminatory if this employee's work performance was not objectively measured and compared with all employees in the department. Some supervisors complain that greater costs and inefficiencies are incurred if they are required to "carry" older workers who no longer can do the job. Whether or not this complaint is valid, the supervisor must appraise the performance of all employees in an impartial, objective way before making decisions that adversely affect older workers. As emphasized in Chapter 13, performance appraisal is a significant part of any supervisor's job, but it is especially important when older workers are in the department.

It is not uncommon for supervisors to manage employees older than themselves.

Supervisors often express concern about older workers who show a decline in physical and mental abilities. While some older people do lose some of their former strengths on the job, they may be able to compensate by using their experience. Even with a decline in physical strength due to age, most firms report that older workers tend to have better quality, safety, and attendance records than do younger employees.[22]

Moreover, it may be possible, within certain limits, for supervisors to make special accommodations for some older employees. Supervisors should not disregard years of dedicated and faithful service. Adjustments in the older employee's workload, scheduling, and the like can be reasonable allowances that others in the work group can understand and accept, particularly those who are themselves advancing in years and who recognize that someday their capabilities might also diminish somewhat.

It is common for a newly elevated supervisor to be supervising persons old enough to be his or her parent—the proverbial "generation gap." Some older persons will reject the new supervisor and will resist changing old habits and learning new ways. In these situations, the supervisor must open the channels of communication, ask probing questions, avoid putting them on the defensive, listen actively to their ideas—most older employees have a wealth of experience and information—and involve them in the decision-making process. It is imperative that supervisors use common sense and sound supervisory practices in dealing with older employees.[23]

Older employees who are approaching retirement present another problem that requires sensitivity on the part of supervisors. Some employees who have worked for 30 years or more look forward to retirement as a time to enjoy a greater variety of leisure activities. However, others view retirement with anxieties about the security of a daily routine, steady income, and established social relationships.

Supervisors should be supportive and understanding as older employees near retirement. These employees should be encouraged to take advantage of pre-retirement planning activities that may be available in the company or through outside agencies. Some companies allow employees nearing retirement to attend retirement-related workshops during working hours without loss of pay. A member of the human resources department or a benefits specialist may spend considerable time with each employee nearing retirement to discuss pensions, insurance, social security, and other financial matters. Supervisors should also encourage recent retirees to attend company social functions and to maintain contact with their former supervisors and coworkers wherever possible. Such contacts are valuable aids in making the transition to retirement more comfortable.

Accommodation for Different Religious Views

Under the Civil Rights Act, most employers are required to afford nondiscriminatory treatment to employees who hold different religious views. Although EEOC and court decisions have not always clearly defined religious discrimination, two principles have evolved: (1) that employers must make reasonable accommodation for employees who hold differing religious beliefs, and (2) that an employee may not create a hostile work environment for others by harassing them about what they do or do not believe.[24] Employers generally may not discriminate in employment practices because of an individual's religious beliefs, and employers are obligated to prevent practices or actions that might constitute a "hostile environment" for someone because of his or her religion.[25]

Relatively speaking, charges of religious discrimination have been limited. Reasonable accommodation in holiday and other work scheduling has been the most recurring area where employers have had some problems of compliance. For example, employees who follow the orthodox Jewish faith consider Saturday as the day for their religious observance instead of Sunday. Requiring such employees to work on Saturday would be the same as requiring employees who are members of some fundamentalist Christian sects to work on Sundays. A supervisor might be able to accommodate the religious views of such employees by scheduling their workweeks in a way that takes into account their religious preferences. Allowing Jewish employees to take holidays on Rosh Hashana and Yom Kippur instead of Christmas and Easter is another example of accommodation, as is recognition of Ramadan for individuals of the Islam (Muslim) faith.

Supervisors may be confronted with situations in which it is difficult to accommodate all employees' religious preferences and still schedule the work. If this happens, a supervisor would be well advised to discuss the problem with his or her manager and with the human resources staff to determine whether scheduling alternatives are available that might accommodate the employees and yet not be too costly or disruptive.

Vietnam-Era and Other Veterans

Vietnam-era and other military veterans are another group that has been identified for certain employment protection. After the end of the Vietnam War and with many men and women released from military service, legislators and political leaders felt that Vietnam-era veterans were entitled to assistance to facilitate their return to the civilian labor force. The Vietnam-Era Veteran's Readjustment Act, which applies primarily to employers who have contracts with the federal government, requires employers to have affirmative action programs for the hiring and advancement of veterans. Other laws and regulations—particularly in public and government employment—provide for preferential hiring policies for veterans, including those who participated in Operation Desert Storm in the early 1990s.[26]

Supervision of military veterans usually involves few special considerations by comparison to supervision of other legally protected employees. Except for those veterans who experienced mental or physical impairment and who may continue to show some effects, most veterans cannot be distinguished from nonveterans. Consequently, after being employed and adjusting to the work environment, veterans generally should be supervised just like everyone else. Unless there is another major military happening, most employers will afford this protected group less special consideration in future years.

7

Recognize several pressures faced by supervisors who themselves are members of protected groups.

PROTECTED-GROUP SUPERVISORS

Thus far we have discussed how the supervision of legally protected employees requires both awareness and sensitivity to a variety of factors. Additional concerns can arise for supervisors who themselves are members of a legally protected category (e.g., minorities and women) and who may experience resistance and resentment in their supervisory positions.

For example, it is common to find a woman manager or supervisor whose subordinates primarily are men. Skepticism about the qualifications of the woman supervisor may be voiced in men's comments, such as "She didn't deserve the job" or "She got it because she's female." A woman supervisor in such a situation may feel that she has to accomplish more than a male supervisor might be expected to achieve in a similar job. However, past experiences of many women supervisors indicate that once they have proven their competence, most of this initial skepticism will fade away.

Another example might be an African-American production supervisor in a manufacturing plant who supervises black employees and who may be faced with a dilemma. Because the supervisor is of the same race, some employees may attempt to take advantage of the situation, perhaps by taking more extended break periods than allowed. On the other hand, the supervisor may put greater pressure on black employees to perform and to obey the rules so that no charge of favoritism can be justified.

Similarly, the woman supervisor who feels obliged to accomplish more than her male counterparts and who wishes to avoid charges of favoritism toward female subordinates may put greater pressure on women employees. This tendency has led some women employees to say that they would rather work for male supervisors because female supervisors are "tougher" on them than are men.[27]

On the other hand, it is recognized that, in general, supervisors tend to be able to communicate better with subordinates who are of the same race or the same sex. For example, an Asian-American supervisor is likely to better understand the culture, speech patterns, and attitudes of other Asian-American employees.

Problems such as those cited are not unusual, and they should even be anticipated by supervisors or potential supervisors. It is helpful if such issues are openly discussed in supervisory training and development meetings. In addition, protected-group supervisors—just like all other supervisors—must have performance expectations, policies, and decisions that are applied consistently and uniformly to all employees, regardless of race, gender, age, and other such considerations.

UNDERSTANDING REVERSE DISCRIMINATION

Explain the issue of reverse discrimination.

Reverse discrimination

Preference given to protected-group members in hiring and promotion over more qualified or more experienced workers from non-protected groups.

The reactions of employees who are not members of a legally protected group to hiring and promotion decisions represent another challenge to supervisors. These employees may view the promotion of a protected-group employee as reverse discrimination. **Reverse discrimination** may be charged when a more senior or qualified person is denied a job opportunity or promotion because preference has been given to a protected-group individual who may be less qualified or junior in seniority.

For example, in one U.S. Supreme Court case, a white male with higher seniority was denied admission to a company union training program because a specific number of openings were designated to be filled by black employees with less seniority. The Supreme Court decided that the white male had not been discriminated against illegally because the company and the labor union had negotiated a voluntary affirmative action program. Although the court indicated that there were times that such reverse favoritism might be unlawful, it did not identify those instances. Thus, the court upheld the idea of affirmative action but did not clearly rule for or against the issue of reverse discrimination.

Equal employment opportunity and affirmative action programs most often impact white male employees. Some white males feel that they do not have an equal or fair opportunity to compete for promotions or higher-paying jobs. They consider and interpret the existence of numerical goals in affirmative action programs as "quotas" that have to be met by hiring and promoting unqualified or less qualified women or minorities.[28]

Supervisors of integrated racial groups and male and female employees may be apprehensive about their situations. For example, supervisors may become reluctant to discipline anyone so as to avoid charges of favoritism or discrimination. Another difficulty is that conflicts and distrust among these various groups may arise that place stress on interpersonal relationships and may affect the performance of the department. Such problems are not easily overcome. However, communication between the supervisor and all groups of employees is absolutely essential, and the supervisor should try to correct misperceptions about any employee's abilities and qualifications as they occur. Whether reverse discrimination exists is not really important. Rather, what is important is the supervisor's response to the feelings of all groups and individuals in an understanding, fair, and objective manner.

GOOD SUPERVISION: THE OVERRIDING CONSIDERATION

Discuss the overriding concern in the supervision of all employees in a diverse workforce.

The issues discussed in this chapter will likely concern supervisors for years to come. Additional legislation and court decisions will specify or clarify other considerations for protected-groups that now exist and, perhaps, for other groups to be identified in the future.

Although the diversity and complexity of the workforce varies, a supervisor can take several steps to reduce the likelihood of litigation (see Figure 16-5). Supervisors must adapt their ways of managing their departments to meet the considerations afforded to legally protected employees. In this effort supervisors should always recognize that the best way to manage all employees in their departments—protected or not—is to constantly apply the principles of good supervision as presented throughout this book.

We stated at the outset of this chapter that management of a diverse workforce is a reality that affects most aspects of organizational operations and has an impact on a firm's bottom line.[29] Because of its importance, specialized training programs in diversity management are expanding.[30] But, in our view, supervision of diversity should not be viewed as something extra or separate. Supervision of diversity is and will continue to be an integral and significant component of good supervision that effective supervisors recognize as part of their ongoing responsibilities and challenges.

FIGURE 16-5 Steps to reduce harassment suits.

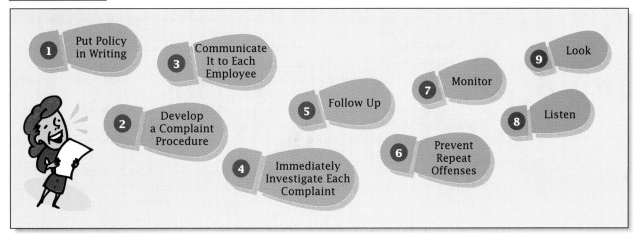

1. Put Policy in Writing
2. Develop a Complaint Procedure
3. Communicate It to Each Employee
4. Immediately Investigate Each Complaint
5. Follow Up
6. Prevent Repeat Offenses
7. Monitor
8. Listen
9. Look

What Call Did You Make?

As manager Gail Williams, you have found that life is complicated and becoming more so. You have just experienced a classic "she said, he said" situation where truth is difficult to ascertain. First interview other employees in the department to see whether any of them will back up either Cindy Morris's and Barb Barrett's allegations or George Herring's denials. In these types of cases, often no one else in the department will have seen or heard anything; or other employees do not want to get involved, so they refuse to say anything. Since you have been on this job for only a short period, you might want to check with your predecessor or others in higher management of Good n' Tastee Pizza to ascertain whether there have been past complaints about George Herring. If you are unable to get any further information that would support either version, you should immediately report the case to the human resources department or the manager who is responsible for handling issues of sexual harassment or discrimination Since this may have serious legal implications, further handling of the case probably should be left to those individuals.

However, as supervisor, you should again talk to George Herring and warn him to be very careful in what he says and does in relationship with employees. Tell him that you will be watching very closely to make sure that all employees are being treated fairly, and that no type of harassment will be tolerated. You also should talk, privately and individually, with Cindy Morris and Barb Barrett to tell them what you have done, but also remind them of the requirements of the job. Assure them that if they need any help, they should not hesitate to discuss their situation with you. In retrospect, you should have admonished George Herring when he answered his questions about Cindy Morris. It should have been obvious that Herring's comments were inappropriate. You should have stated assertively that comments of that nature about any employee will not be tolerated. Review the store's "no-harassment" policy. Make sure you and every employee understand the definition of harassment and what the company policy is. If you are uncertain, check with upper management or the human resources department. Finally, you should be sure that your future actions are consistent and fair toward all employees regardless of any protected-group status.

SUMMARY

The diverse nature of the U.S. workforce requires that supervisors are prepared to manage diverse people in the workforce to the firm's overall advantage and bottom-line results. Diversity management can impact virtually all aspects of a firm's operations and should be viewed by supervisors as both a challenge and an opportunity.

The major classifications of protected-group employees are by racial/ethnic origin, sex, age, physical and mental impairment, religion, and military service.

Supervisors need to be aware of legal protections that are afforded to protected groups and understand that this is part of supervising a diversified workforce. All employees should be supervised in a fair and objective manner that focuses upon their talents, abilities, and potential contributions.

When supervising racial/ethnic minority employees, supervisors should try to reduce the impact of past discrimination. Awareness of cultural factors and recognition of language differences are important aspects of a supervisor's sensitivities toward minority employees. Being scrupulously fair in all aspects of supervision and striving to prevent any type of discriminatory treatment toward minorities are essential.

Supervisors must try to ensure that women are provided fair opportunities as they move into a greater variety of career fields and positions. Avoidance of sexual harassment and stereotyping is mandatory. Human resources policies should stress training and development opportunities for women, nondiscriminatory treatment during pregnancy, flexibility in resolving family-care conflicts and problems, and equity in compensation.

The Americans with Disabilities Act prohibits discrimination in employment against individuals who have physical and mental disabilities. The ADA prohibits making certain pre-employment inquiries and physical examinations of job applicants. It further requires that employers make reasonable accommodations for otherwise qualified disabled individuals who are capable of performing essential components of a job. People with disabilities who are placed in job positions that are consistent with their capabilities and who are given a fair opportunity to perform by their supervisors typically become excellent employees.

The Age Discrimination in Employment Act prohibits discrimination against most employees over 40 years of age. When making decisions concerning older employees, supervisors should appraise their qualifications and performance objectively. Supervisors should try to adjust to reduced abilities of older workers, if possible. Also, supervisors should assist employees who are nearing retirement to prepare for it.

The principle of reasonable accommodation also should be followed when supervising employees of different religious beliefs. Reasonable adjustments in work scheduling should be afforded individuals who have certain religious requirements.

Vietnam-era and other veterans may be afforded special consideration when hiring decisions are made, but they usually require only regular supervision after they have adjusted to their work environment.

The supervisor who is a member of a protected group may encounter pressures from both protected-group and nonprotected-group employees. These typically involve questions about qualifications and fair treatment. The supervisor should act so that all employees are provided uniform and consistent/equal treatment and performance expectations.

Supervisors should be sensitive to the feelings of some employees—most often white males—about the issue of reverse discrimination. Employees may accuse the company of reverse discrimination if a protected-group person is hired or promoted over a more experienced or more qualified member of a nonprotected group.

9

No matter how future legislation and court decisions affect the issues related to protected groups, the best way to manage will always be to apply the principles of good supervision to all employees.

KEY TERMS

Protected-group employees (page 541)
Sexual harassment (page 550)
Sexual stereotyping (page 551)
Comparable worth (page 553)

Qualified disabled individual (page 555)
Reasonable accommodation (page 556)
Reverse discrimination (page 561)

QUESTIONS FOR DISCUSSION

1. React to the following statement: "Diversity based on characteristics people can see is the most worthless and superficial kind there is." Do you agree or disagree with this statement? Why?
2. Who are classified as protected-group employees? Does "protected group" mean the same as a "special or privileged group" of employees, especially in view of affirmative action requirements that may be present in a firm? Discuss.
3. Identify a particular racial/ethnic minority and discuss some cultural factors, language, and other differences that a supervisor might need to consider in supervising this group.
4. Discuss the following statement: "Racism, bigotry, and discrimination exist in the minds of people who are insecure and lack confidence in their own abilities. It is a result of ignorance and fear."
5. Discuss why and how employers have given women access to special training and development opportunities and/or moved them into jobs that might require the modification of existing tools or equipment.
6. Give an example of sexual harassment and describe what a supervisor should do to deal with it.
7. Discuss how women are affected by pregnancy and family-care situations and employer policies. What legal requirements are imposed, and not imposed, for employers in these areas?
8. Does equity in compensation for women mean that an employer must apply the principle of comparable worth in compensating all employees? Discuss.
9. How has the Americans with Disabilities Act (ADA) expanded legal protections for individuals with disabilities?
10. Discuss (a) the ADA's definition of a "disabled" person and (b) what is meant by "reasonable accommodation" for someone with a disability to perform the "essential functions" of a job. Why will these areas be difficult for supervisors to comply with in certain job situations?
11. What legal protections are afforded most employees who are beyond 40 years of age? Assume that a supervisor has a 60-year-old secretarial assistant whose performance has recently slipped. What considerations should affect the supervisor's actions toward this employee?
12. How does the concept of reasonable accommodation apply to employees of different religious persuasions? Are there limits to reasonable accommodation? Discuss.
13. Why does supervision of military veterans usually require few special considerations once they are employed and have adjusted to the job?

14. "Protected-group supervisors tend to be more demanding of employees who belong to the same protected group." Discuss this statement.

15. What is meant by "reverse discrimination?" Is it a valid concept, or a crutch used by some employees to justify their standing? How does it affect the practice of supervisory management?

16. Why should the application of the principles of good supervision be the overriding concern of a supervisor in charge of a department that is racially mixed, has both male and female employees, and has employees who have other legal protections?

SKILLS APPLICATIONS

Skills Application 16-1: Attitudes Toward People with Disabilities and the ADA

Below are a series of statements that relate to attitudes toward disabled people and the Americans with Disabilities Act (ADA). Mark each statement according to how much you agree or disagree with it, using the following scale:

Strongly Agree (SA)	Agree (A)	Disagree (D)	Strongly Disagree (SD)

_____ 1. Individuals with severe disabilities are not able to compete for jobs that require demanding physical and mental capabilities.

_____ 2. Under the ADA, an employer can expect just as much from a disabled person as from anyone else.

_____ 3. People with disabilities usually are more conscientious and reliable at work than other employees.

_____ 4. Most people with severe disabilities expect others to show sympathy toward them and provide them extra help to hold a job.

_____ 5. Employers will find that the ADA will be impossible to comply with in many situations without extraordinary costs and efforts.

_____ 6. The ADA will benefit attorneys far more than it will help people with disabilities.

_____ 7. Compliance with the ADA will cause considerable resentment toward people with disabilities.

_____ 8. The ADA is morally and ethically appropriate and will assist qualified disabled individuals to become more self-sufficient.

_____ 9. People with disabilities are usually more cheerful and enthusiastic on the job than other employees.

_____ 10. Reasonable accommodation under the ADA really means that special preferential treatment must be granted to people with disabilities.

After completing this survey, answer the following questions:

2. Why would awareness of attitudes toward people with disabilities and the ADA be important to supervisors?

3. Compare your responses to those of others. What common views do you have? What areas of difference? Discuss the bases for your differences of opinion.

3. If you were (are) a supervisor, how would you deal with negative attitudes toward people with disabilities and/or the ADA that might be held by other employees in a work group that includes a disabled person?

Skills Application 16-2: Sexual Harassment

Various actions may be perceived as sexual harassment, especially if they are objected to by someone of the opposite sex. Virtually everyone has experienced, heard of, or participated in actions that possibly could be viewed as sexual harassment. Respond to the following questions, and then compare and discuss your responses with others who have responded to these same questions.

1. Identify a situation of sexual harassment of which you have personal knowledge. Briefly describe.
2. How did you and others react to the situation?
3. What could or should be done to prevent similar situations in the future?

Skills Application 16-3: What Do Supervisors Know About Harassment?

1. Ask three supervisors—representing a variety of industries, for example, retail, manufacturing, health care, education, fast-food services, government, etc.—to respond to the questions listed below. Apply the following scale to each statement:

	Strongly Agree (SA)	Agree (A)	Disagree (D)	Strongly Disagree (SD)

_____ 1. Our company has a written policy on harassment that outlines steps to be taken if it occurs.

_____ 2. Our company should be held liable for harassment by an employee even if the employer didn't know it occurred.

_____ 3. Even if there are no formal complaints of harassment at a company, in all likelihood, it (harassment) still occurs.

_____ 4. Our company has educated all employees about harassment through written notices or workshops.

_____ 5. More harassment takes place on racial issues then on gender issues.

_____ 6. An employer should be held liable for harassment by an employee even though the company has a policy against it.

_____ 7. Our company has cautioned supervisors and managers about harassment through meetings, written notices, or workshops.

_____ 8. Harassment is an isolated occurrence at our company.

_____ 9. Our company has never had to warn, punish, or terminate an employee who engaged in harassment.

_____ 10. I think most people tolerate someone who tells a "raunchy joke" or makes an "ethnic slur."

2. Compare your findings with those of another student. Are there any differences in the perceptions? How do you account for them?
3. Write a one-page paper detailing what you learned from this skills application.

Skills Application 16-4: Another Night at the Movies: Can We Overcome Bias, Prejudice, and Stereotyping?

Go to your local video store and rent a copy of "Guess Who's Coming to Dinner." Sit down with a big bowl of popcorn and several friends and enjoy the movie. At the conclusion of the video, lead your group in a discussion of the questions below.

Synopsis: In this classic 1967 movie, Joanna (Katharine Houghton) returns home with her new fiance, John Prentice (Sidney Poitier), a distinguished black doctor. Christina Drayton (Katharine Hepburn, who won the Academy Award for Best Actress for her performance) accepts her daughter's decision to marry John. But Matthew Drayton (Spencer Tracy) and Prentice's parents are dismayed.

1. What appears to be the main problem? Why?
2. Define prejudice. List at least three statements or behaviors that illustrate bias, prejudice, or stereotyping.
3. Discuss the following statement: "In some cases prejudice is an entrenched attitude held by people who are afraid to change or admit they are wrong." How does this statement apply to the actors in this video?
4. Why do you think Matthew Drayton and Prentice's parents were intolerant of John and Joanna's decision to marry? Why was Christina Drayton more accepting of the couple's decision?
5. What steps did Joanna and John take to change their parents' perceptions?
6. Make a list of the steps that supervisors can take to reduce the negative effects of racial bias, prejudice, and/or stereotyping. Compare your list with those of others. What common views do you have?
7. Write a one-page paper describing what you learned from this skills application.

INTERNET ACTIVITY

Skills Application 16-5: Valuing Diversity

Today's workplace is characterized by significant diversity. As a supervisor, how will you manage diversity in your work group?

1. Visit the Department of the Interior Web site (www.doi.gov/diversity) to view their strategic plan for improving diversity. What is their vision for their workforce? What specific goals have they established to support their vision?
2. Review Figure 16-1. What do the "Peanuts" characters tell us about diversity?
3. Visit the Pitney Bowes Web site (www.pitneybowes.com) to view their corporate policies regarding diversity (link from Our Company, to About Pitney Bowes, to Diversity). How has this company promoted and managed diversity?
4. Using these as examples, develop your personal diversity vision statement for your work group. Then create a five-step plan for promoting and managing diversity as a supervisor.

ENDNOTES

1. Adapted from Genevieve Capowksi, "Managing Diversity," *Management Review* (June 1996), pp. 13–19. For a comprehensive overview see "Diversity Today: Developing and Retaining the Best Corporate Talent," Special Advertising Section, *Fortune* (July 1999), pp. S1–S28. For an interesting acticle on economic (disposable income) differences, see Margaret Olesen, "The Diversity Issue No One Talks About," *Training* (May 1999), pp. 46–56.

2. Don McNerny, "The Bottom-Line Value of Diversity," *HRFocus* (May 1994), pp. 22–23.

3. Associated Press, "Employee Bias Suits Triple in Past Decade," as reported in the Fort Wayne (IN) *Journal Gazette* (January 17, 2000), p. 3A.

4. See Robert M. Gault and Anne M. Kinnane, "Navigating the Maze of Employment Law," *Management Review* (February 1996), pp. 9–11. Historically, the courts have held that "employment must not depend on sexual favors—quid pro quo—and the workplace must not be a hostile environment. Two of the more recent cases—*Faragher vs. City of Boca Raton* and *Burlington Industries vs. Ellerth*—involved sexual harassment by supervisors. The March 1998 decision, *Oncale vs. Sundowner Offshore Services*, dealt with same-sex issues.

5. In this chapter we will not directly discuss emerging issues surrounding gender orientation, such as discrimination against homosexuals. To date, homosexuality has not been given a legally protected-group status nor is it considered to be a disability. Some firms have developed specific employment policies concerning gay and lesbian employees and their "domestic" partners.

6. See Lewis Brown Griggs and Lente-Louise Louw, *Valuing Diversity: New Tools for a New Reality* (McGraw-Hill, 1995).

7. See Chapter 15 for a more complete discussion of incivility in the workplace. Also see Karen A. Jehn and Elizabeth D. Scott, "Ranking Rank Behaviors," *Business & Society* (September 1999), pp. 296+; and Linda Micco, "Employers Mount Counterattack Against Abuse on the Job," *Bulletin to Management* (June 3, 1999), p. 175.

8. "SHRM Diversity Study Reveals Long Term Optimism," as reported in Special Advertising Section, *Fortune* (July 1999), pp. S17–18. Also see Geoffrey Colvin, "The 50 Best Companies for Asians, Blacks, and Hispanics," *Fortune* (July 19, 1999), pp. 53–68.

9. Genaro C. Armas, "More Women Break through Glass Ceiling," Associated Press as reported in Fort Wayne (IN) *Journal Gazette* (April 24, 2000), pp. 1C, 5C. Also see the February 2000 issue of the *Ladies Home Journal* for an assessment of the best places for women to live. The "Working it out" section ranked cities on five factors: the percentage of women-owned businesses, percentage of working women who are professionals or managers, salary gap between men and women, the number of reported cases of sexual harassment, and the number of reported cases of job discrimination based on gender. In 1979, Liz Nickles and Laurie Ashcraft began surveying women on what they saw in society (work) and felt in their own lives. For information on their Update, see Patricia Edmonds, "Now the Word is Balance," *USA Weekend* (October 23–25, 1999), pp. 4–6 or contact Nickles and Ashcraft at UPDATEWOMN@aol.com. Also see, Gary N. Powell (ed.), *Handbook of Gender and Work* (Thousand Oaks, CA: Sage, 1999); and Kay Koplovitz, "I Feel Passionate About Bringing Women Into the Mainstream," *Fast Company* (December 1999), p. 129.

10. Op. cit., "SHRM . . .", pp. S17–18.

11. See Anthony M. Townsend and Harsh K. Luthar, "How Do Men Feel?" *HRMagazine* (May 1993), pp. 92–96.

12. See Carole O'Blenes, "Harassment Grows More Complex," *Management Review* (June 1999), pp. 49–51; "Peter Brimelow, "Is Sexual Harassment Getting Worse?" *Forbes* (April 14, 1999), p. 92; Michael Barrier, "Sexual Harassment," *Nation's Business* (December 1998), pp. 14–19; Anne Fisher, "After All This Time, Why Don't People Know What Sexual Harassment Means?" *Fortune* (January 12, 1998), p. 156; and Gerald D. Bloch, "Avoiding Liability for Sexual Harassment," *HRMagazine* (April 1995), pp. 91–97.

13. See David Rubenstein, "Harassment Prevention is Now a Must for U.S. Companies," *Corporate Legal Times* (August 1999), pp. 31–32; Patricia M. Buhler, "The Manager's Role in Preventing Sexual Harassment," *Supervision* (April 1999), pp. 16–18; Rebecca Ganzel, "What Sexual Harassment Training Really Prevents," *Training* (October 1998), pp. 86–94; and R. Bruce McAfee and Diana L. Deadrick, "Teach Employees to Just Say 'No!' " *HRMagazine* (February 1996), pp. 86–89.

14. See "Glass Ceiling Report Is No Surprise to SHRM," *Mosaics* (April 1995), p. 4. For a rationale supporting the complementary balance of work and personal life, see Steward D. Friedman, Perry Christensen, and Jessica DeGroot, "Work and Life: The End of the Zero-Sum Game," *Harvard Business Review* (November/December 1998), pp. 119–129.

15. Today, more so than at any other time, it is appropriate for employees to have multiple mentors—"don't put all your eggs in one basket." See Anne Fisher, "Ask Annie: Readers Weigh in on Finding Mentors," *Fortune* (July 5, 1999), p. 192; Marilyn J. Haring, "Mentoring to Support Gender Equity," *Purdue Alumnus* (October 1999), p. 48; Amy Saltzman, "Woman Versus Woman," *U.S. News & World Report* (March

25, 1996), pp. 50–53; or Rose Mary Wentling, "Breaking Down Barriers to Women's Success," *HR Magazine* (May 1995), pp. 79–85.

16. See "Non Standard Hours Child Care Arrangements Becoming Hallmark of Today's Diverse Workplaces," *Mosaics* (March 1996), pp. 1–2.

17. Armas, "More Women Break through Glass Ceiling," p. 5C.

18. "Clinton Wants $27 Million for 'Equal Pay Initiative,' " *The Washington Post* (January 24, 2000), p. B1.

19. See Scott Carlson of *Knight Ridder Newspapers,* "The Door to the Working World has Grown Heavier for Some Workers with Disabilities," as reported in the Fort Wayne (IN) *News-Sentinel* (December 6, 1999), pp. 1B, 8–9B; and Teresa Burke Wright, "ADA & Punitive Damages Clarified," *Credit Union Magazine* (September 1999), p. 47. For a concise guide to compliance with the ADA, and interpretations, contact the EEOC Office of Communication and Legislative Affairs, 1801 L. Street N. W., Washington, D. C. 20507.

20. For an extensive discussion, see William F. Banta, *AIDS in the Workplace* (Lexington Books, 1993). Also see Milton Bordwin, "What to Do Before AIDS Strikes Home," *Management Review* (February 1995), pp. 49–52.

21. A research study conducted by one of the text's authors revealed considerable ambivalence and apprehension toward the ADA among human resources managers. See Raymond L. Hilgert, "Compliance With the ADA," *Proceedings of the Midwest Society of Human Resources/Industrial Relations* (March 1993), pp. 112–119. On the other hand, some companies see people with disabilities as a profitable marketing target. See Joshua Harris Prager, "People With Disabilities Are Next Consumer Niche," *The Wall Street Journal* (December 15, 1999), pp. B1, B6. Also see Sharon Nelton, "A Very Able Work Force," *Nation's Business* (October 1998), pp. 44–45; and Roberta Reynes, "When Workers Have Mental Disabilities," *Nation's Business* (December 1997), p. 50.

22. According to the U.S. Department of Labor Bureau Statistics, workers over 55 years of age are a third less likely than their younger associates to be injured at work seriously enough to lose work time. However, when they are seriously injured, older workers typically require two weeks to recover, about twice the amount needed by younger workers. From Glenn Burkins, "Work Week," *The Wall Street Journal* (May 7, 1996), p. A1. Yet Bob Violino, "The AGE Factor," *Information Week* (July 5, 1999), pp. 48–49 contends that "despite the serious shortage of qualified IT staffers, many candidates—particularly engineers and computer programmers—insist they can't get jobs in the field because of bias against older workers. For legal reasons, you're never going to hear anyone say, 'Sorry, you're too old.' But they'll say things like you're overqualified." See Janet Gemignani, Robert Shaw, and Doug Gunzler, "EEOC Hones Age Discrimination Rules," *Business and Health* (July 1998), pp. 9–10. (The EEOC issued new regulations that clarify the legal way to handle outgoing workers over 40. The new regulations take aim at the waivers employers ask those whose jobs are terminated to sign.) Also see Michael Verespej, "Time for Ageless Judgments," *Industry Week* (March 3, 1997), pp. 15–16. (The Supreme Court ruled in 1996 that even if someone 40 or older replaces a dismissed worker, age discrimination can still exist if the new worker is substantially younger than the dismissed worker.)

23. Carol Hymowitz, "Young Managers Learn How to Bridge the Gap With Older Employees," *The Wall Street Journal* (July 21, 1998), p. B1.

24. Michelle Conlin, "Religion in the Workplace," *Business Week* (November 1, 1999), p. 158.

25. See Lee Gardenswartz and Anita Rowe, "Responding to Religious Differences at Work," *Mosaics* (November 1995), p. 7; or "Religious Bias Examined," *Fair Employment Practices* (Bureau of National Affairs, Inc., September 7, 1995), p. 103. In March 2000, the EEOC charged Dalfort Aerospace LP of Dallas with illegally refusing to hire a member of the Seventh Day Adventists, a group whose Sabbath is Saturday. See Albert R. Karr, "WorkWeek: Religious Diversity Spurs Many High-Tech Firms to Allow Holiday Diversity," *The Wall Street Journal* (April 18, 2000), p. A1.

26. For example, the Uniformed Services Employment and Reemployment Rights Act of 1994 (USERRA) provides certain job protections for previously employed individuals who may be required to serve in the uniformed services on active-duty status, temporary active duty for training, full-time National Guard duty, and other categories. This act specifies reemployment and reinstatement rights for individuals when they return from service and the benefits to which a re-employed service person may be entitled. Eligibility for this act's protection is specified, as are provisions for enforcement and remedies available.

27. A 1996 Gallup poll survey on gender bias revealed that 46 percent of U.S. respondents preferred working for a boss who is a man. Only 20 percent indicated they preferred working for a woman, with the remainder expressing no opinion. Women were far more likely to resent working for a woman. Of women respondents, 54 percent said they would prefer a male boss; only 37 percent of men said the same. About two-thirds of the women who preferred to work for a male boss said it was easier to get along with men; that women tended to be "more uptight," or that women were "harder on other women." Barbara Brotman of the *Chicago Tribune,* "Women Gallup Away from Female Bosses," as reported in the Fort Wayne (Indiana) *News-Sentinel* (April 17, 1996), p. 2F.

28. See Michele Galen and Ann Therese Palmer, "White, Male, and Worried," *Business Week* (January 31, 1994), pp. 50–55.

29. Some research studies have statistically linked effective diversity management efforts by certain firms to positive economic results. For example, see Peter Wright, Stephen Ferris, Janine Hiller, and Mark Kroll, "Competitiveness Through Management of Diversity: Effects on Stock Price Valuations," *Academy of Management Journal* (January/February 1995), pp. 272–287.

30. See Iris Taylor, "Winning at Diversity," *Working Women* (March 1999), p. 36, for a discussion of what several organizations have done to create informal diversity plans. Also see "Diversity Training on the Rise," *Human Resources Forum* (December 1995), p. 3; or Alice Starke, "Diversity Training Program to Develop In-House Trainers," *HR News* (March 1996), pp. 21+.

Chapter 17

After studying this chapter, you will be able to:

1
Recognize that handling disagreements and conflicts in the workplace is a component of supervision.

2
Identify and contrast five styles that are inherent in approaches to conflict resolution.

3
Distinguish between supervisory handling of employee complaints in any work setting and grievances in a unionized situation.

4
Explain the major distinctions between grievance procedures, complaint procedures, and alternative dispute resolution (ADR) procedures.

5
Describe the supervisor's role at the initial step in resolving a complaint or grievance, especially the need for open and frank communication.

6
Identify guidelines for supervisors to resolve complaints and grievances in an effective manner.

Resolving Conflicts in the Workplace

You Make the Call!

You are Alfred Perry, a department supervisor in a plastics products plant. You have 14 employees in your department, all of whom are represented by the Independent Plastics Workers Union. You have supervised this department for about six months after having been transferred to this plant from another company plant. You have just received a written grievance signed by Allison Howard, union shop steward, on behalf of all department employees. The grievance protests the decision that you announced yesterday to stop the preparation of a pot of coffee in the department during working hours. The union grievance states:

The union protests your unfair decision to take away a privilege that has been in place for at least five years. Making coffee in our department only requires a few minutes of time by an employee each day. All costs are borne by the employees. Your decision violates Article 13, Section 3 of our labor–management agreement, which states: "The company shall not take away any privileges that are now enjoyed by the employees." We demand that you withdraw your decision, and that the long-established practice of having coffee brewed in our department be restored.

You are not too surprised by the union grievance, but when you made your decision you felt you had the right to do so. You relied on Article 2, Section 1 of the labor–management agreement, which states, "It is the responsibility of company management to maintain discipline and efficiency in this plant." Since becoming supervisor, you had warned the employees several times that making coffee, standing around drinking coffee, and other forms of wasting time in the department could not be tolerated. There are two other departments in the plant. Neither of these departments permits making coffee on company premises during work hours. However, employees can bring their own coffee in thermos bottles and drink it if it does not interfere with work. You felt it was time to put a stop to a practice that the previous supervisor had condoned. Now it is interfering with efficiency and production. You wonder how to respond to the union grievance.

You Make the Call!

DISAGREEMENTS AND CONFLICTS ARE A PART OF THE WORKPLACE

Recognize that handling disagreements and conflicts in the workplace is a component of supervision.

Substantive conflict

Conflict between individuals because of what should be done or what should occur.

Most of us grew up in a world full of conflict situations. Perhaps as children we fought with our siblings or with others over whose turn it was to play with a certain toy, or were in conflict with our parents over bedtime hours. These disagreements over what should be done or what should occur are referred to as **substantive conflict.**[1] Sometimes, through experience, we learned that conflict was good because we learned much by talking out our differences and settling on a course of action that met the needs of both parties. However, many of us grew up disliking disagreements unless we "won out in the end." Often we saw the dispute from only one point of view (ours), were unwilling to compromise or accommodate the other party, and as such the dispute escalated and the relationship between the two parties deteriorated. Growing up, we played games in which there could be only one winner. Sometimes, the winner arrogantly touted their prowess in winning. Other times, the loser pouted, ranted and raved, or cried. Someone may have countered, "you're a sore loser." The competitive nature of the our society—with a strong tendency to reward and revere "winners"—often carries over into the workplace.

What effect did the actions cited above have on the persons involved? For one, the winners still wanted to win—sometimes at any cost. Some of the losers lost interest in playing the game. Still others learned to intensely dislike the arrogance of the winner or the childlike behavior of the loser. They despised the "jerk." They bristled each time they saw that particular person. They argued for any reason or no reason just because they didn't like each other. **Personalized conflict** is emotionally laden. According to author Robert Bacal,

When conflict is personalized, each party acts as if the other person is suspect as a person. Problem solving rarely works, because neither party is really interested in solving a problem. In fact, in extreme cases, the parties go out of their way to create new problems, imagined or real. Personalized conflict almost always gets worse over time, if they cannot be converted to substantive conflicts.[2]

It appears to the authors that personalized conflict is on the rise. Since much of this is beyond the scope of this text, this chapter will discuss only some of the more important conflict, grievance, and complaint considerations.

Workplace Conflict Must Be Resolved

In the workplace, many supervisors become irritated and confused when they experience challenges to their authority in the form of employee complaints or grievances. Some find it difficult to function because they feel that disagreements with employees reflect on supervisory performance or perhaps that there is something wrong with them personally as supervisors. Further, supervisors at times have to act like referees to resolve conflicts between employees. Most supervisors do not like conflict because they may be drawn into the fray and they have to guard against losing their own tempers and getting themselves in deeper. If the conflict is handled improperly, what started out as an employee dispute can turn into anger and further conflict that is directed toward the supervisor.

Many events in the workplace can trigger complaints and conflicts (see this chapter's first "Contemporary Issue" box). Communication breakdowns, competition over scarce resources, unclear job boundaries ("That isn't my responsibility!"), inconsistent application of policies ("You didn't punish Joe when he was late, and now you're picking on me!"), unrealized expectations ("I didn't know that you expected me to do that!"), and time pressures ("You didn't give us enough notice!") are common events in the workplace that lead to irritations, disagreements, and complaints.

For these and other reasons, many supervisors view conflict in the workplace as being dysfunctional, that is, it distracts and does not contribute to completion of desired objectives. However, employee conflicts, complaints, and grievances should be viewed as an expected part of workplace relationships. Of course, it is not desirable for supervisors to have a constant flood of employee disagreements since this probably would indicate severe problems in the department. Yet supervisors should understand that as they carry out their managerial responsibilities, it is normal to expect that at times supervisory perspectives and decisions will conflict with those of employees and/or the labor union. Further, employees in the workplace are human beings who are prone to a variety of irritations and frustrations that inevitably can lead to some conflicts. Therefore, a supervisor should recognize that handling conflicts and resolving employee com-

Personalized conflict

Conflict between individuals that occurs because the two parties do not like one another.

contemporary issue

One Employee's Behavior Can Make Another Employee Cringe

"Good" conflict (sometimes, referred to as constructive conflict or functional conflict) is healthy for the organization and helps to improve performance. The needs of the individual employees and the organization are met. Other types of conflict are "bad" or "dysfunctional" for the organization and its employees. They are undesirable and, generally, limit the organization's ability to achieve its goals.[1] What type of conflict is the following example?

As a youth growing up in China, Selina Y. Lo learned to play mah-jongg with her family. The stakes were high: losers had their hands slapped 20 times by the winners. The game shaped the Alteon Web-Systems Inc.'s vice president of marketing's business philosophy. "I learned from

mah-jongg that you can't leave your opponents with even a breath because they may be able to revive," Lo says, "You have to take them out entirely."

During a production meeting, she jumped up yelling from her chair, banged her fist on the table, and shoved a finger in the face of a software engineer after he said he couldn't add a feature she asked for. The engineer quickly changed his mind. "I've left a few dead bodies behind me," Lo crows.[2]

While physical abuse does occur in the workplace, verbal abuse occurs much more frequently. Why? There are many reasons. Educator John Eldred contends: "The more change there is, the more the political quotient goes up. Dealing well with politics requires preparation and learned skills. Effective politics is about reaching mature compromises. Politics isn't about winning at all costs. It's about maintaining relationships and getting results at the same time."[3]

Sources: (1) There are many sources that discuss functional and dysfunctional conflict. See Stephen P. Robbins, " 'Conflict Management' and 'Conflict Resolution' Are Not Synonymous Terms," *California Management Review* (Winter 1978), p. 70+, for a discussion. (2) The information regarding Selina Y. Lo was excerpted and adapted from Andy Reinhardt, "I've Left a Few Dead Bodies," *Business Week* (January 31, 2000), pp. 69–70. (Sidebar: Would the engineer have every right to become angry with Lo's actions and eventually retaliate in some way? See Sandra Crowe, *Since Strangling Isn't An Option: Dealing With Difficult People—Common Problems and Uncommon Solutions* (Perigee Trade Paperback, 1999).) (3) The quotations attributable to John Eldred were adapted from Polly LaBarre, "The New Face of Office Politics," *Fast Company* (October 1999), pp. 80, 82.

plaints and grievances are a natural component of departmental relationships and the supervisory position.

2

Identify and contrast five styles that are inherent in approaches to conflict resolution.

Resolving Conflicts Successfully Requires Effective Communication

Our primary focus in this chapter will be on the effective handling of complaints and grievances that usually are the result of workplace disagreements or conflicts. However, before discussing the handling of complaints and grievances, it is appropriate to first identify in general terms some alternative approaches that are available and how communication is crucial to the effective resolution of conflict.

Although supervisors may approach conflict resolution in different ways, they should understand the five basic types of conflict resolution styles, also referred to as negotiation styles, that are depicted in Figure 17-1.

The horizontal axis on Figure 17-1 indicates degree of cooperativeness, ranging from low to high. A high degree of cooperativeness implies that one desires a long-term, harmonious relationship with the other party. A customer tells a sales supervisor that a competitor can provide the same services for a substantially lower price. The price is just slightly above the supervisor's break-even point. A conflict arises between what the supervisor is willing to sell the product for and what the customer is willing to pay. If the customer is a long-time purchaser of large quantities of the product, the supervisor would be "high" on the cooperativeness scale. On the other hand, if the customer purchased very little and only when others could not fill his or her orders, the supervisor might rate a moderate to low score on the scale. An important question can serve as a guide: When you have a conflict with someone else, ask yourself whether the relationship is worth saving. If the answer is yes, then you are at a higher position on the horizontal axis than if the answer were no.

Low to high concern for self, or degree of assertiveness, is found on the vertical axis of Figure 17-1. To determine location on this scale, the supervisor must ask: "What is really important to me?" For example, many supervisors have stated that employee safety and product quality are their top priorities. In other words, they will not compromise their high standards of quality and safety.

Various combinations of these concerns yield five **conflict resolution styles**:

- *Withdraw/avoid:* This approach may be appropriate when the issue is perceived to be minor and the costs of solving the problem are greater than the benefits derived. For example, a student leaves class and sees an altercation in the parking lot. Two students unknown to her are arguing. Withdrawal is probably the best strategy since potential costs to her outweigh the potential benefits. However, workplace conflict between two employees must be addressed if noticed by a supervisor. If left alone, conflicts have a tendency to fester. Thus, the supervisor needs to address the conflict because the costs in terms of declining performance are potentially great.
- *Accommodate/oblige:* The primary strength of this style is that it encourages cooperation. For example, Sam goes home this evening and is greeted by his wife, Mary, who says, "I thought we'd go out for dinner tonight. I would really like to go to the

Conflict resolution styles

Approaches to resolving conflict based on weighing desired degrees of cooperativeness and assertiveness.

FIGURE 17-1

Conflict resolution styles (also referred to as negotiation styles).

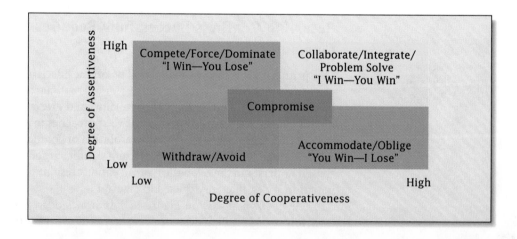

seafood restaurant." Sam had his mind set on having a quick dinner at home and watching football on TV. Sam decides to oblige Mary to preserve the relationship over the long term. This style is thought of as "You win—I lose." Since no one wants to lose all the time, this style implies the rule of reciprocity—that is, you give up something now to eventually get something of value in return.

- *Compromise:* This style is referred to as "Win some—lose some." Compromising styles can be traced throughout history, such as the story of King Solomon in the Bible.[3] Labor-management negotiations often use a compromise technique. Unfortunately, if one party knows that the other always compromises—that is, splits the difference—then they bring inflated demands to the bargaining table. Thus, valuable time is wasted trying to sort out what really are the issues.

- *Compete/force/dominate:* This style is characterized as "I win—You lose." This style may be appropriate in resolving the following type of conflict: Employees have not been wearing their safety glasses because in humid weather they are uncomfortable. The supervisor could force a decision on the employees, because the potential safety factor is deemed more important than their personal feelings. However, the question that arises is why the supervisor had to force the solution on the employees. If the supervisor had fostered an open and participative climate, then he or she could use good communication skills to gain understanding rather than decide by edict. The forcing style may foster resentment and cause long-term problems.

- *Collaborate/integrate/problem solve:* This style is usually characterized as "I win—You win." In essence, collaborative problem solving means that you first must seek to determine what the other person really wants; then find a way or show him or her how to get this; at the same time, you are able to get or attain what you want.

A collaborative problem-solving style means finding out what the other person wants, showing him or her how to get it, and also getting what you want.

Applying this style gives the supervisor an opportunity to ask questions of the other parties to ascertain their interests and needs. Joint problem solving leads all parties to understand the issues and restraints to be considered. Solutions are developed collaboratively, and mutual trust and respect can be a primary gain of this style. Although this style of conflict resolution is ideally the "best," it tends to be the most time consuming. Also, not every issue can be resolved as "win—win" solutions; in some conflict outcomes, there clearly will be winners and losers.

Communication in Resolving Conflicts. One of the first lessons students learn in school is that one does not have to shout to get attention. Yet, for example, suppose that a production worker comes to a supervisor and is really angry that the material handler let some inferior-quality material get through. The angry production employee is shouting. To defuse the employee's anger and to gain control of the situation, some communication experts advocate the following: Get the employee's attention by "shouting" right back, "You have every right to be angry, and I'm as angry as you are." Then continue in a normal tone of voice, "Now that we both agree this is a serious problem, what can we do about it and how can we prevent it from happening again?" This approach puts the employee back on track by focusing on the issues. The objectives of the organization and the needs of the employee then may be met through collaborative problem solving. See Figure 17-2 for suggestions for resolving conflict.[4]

In all of this, it should be apparent that the most effective communication and problem solving take place when people try to share common perspectives. If employees are on the same team and want to do a good job—and if supervisors are clear in their objectives and are working toward improving the human relations atmosphere—there is a better chance of making the organizational climate conducive to effective resolution of most complaints, grievances, and conflicts that will inevitably occur.

See this chapter's second "Contemporary Issue" box for an illustration of one company's effort to minimize complaints about pay inequities.

FIGURE 17-2

Suggestions for resolving conflict.

- Take responsibility for resolving the conflict—don't let it escalate.
- Identify the issue(s).
  - ✓ Explore all sides of the issue(s).
  - ✓ Become aware of each party's position, their needs, and feelings.
  - ✓ Ask more open questions—probe.
  - ✓ Use paraphrasing and reflective questioning to ensure understanding (see Chapter 3).
  - ✓ Establish ground rules for the discussional meeting (see Chapter 10)—e.g., everyone will have a chance to be heard; there will be no interrupting; feelings will be supported with facts, etc.
- Don't be too quick to use your authority or position power.
- Help parties to reach agreement on what the issue(s) (problems) are.
- Ask all parties for their commitment to work with you to solve the problem.
- Create a climate of open communication so that you can help the parties explore "win-win" alternatives.
- Develop fallback alternatives if the parties cannot reach consensus; you may have to use your authority or position power and force a solution if the participative approach doesn't work.
- Follow up to make certain the conflict has been resolved—or at the very least minimized.

contemporary issue

One Way to Minimize Pay Inequities

In an ideal world, everyone would march to the beat of the same tune and see things the same way. Unfortunately, that's not the way it is. Employee perceptions of what is "not fair" lead to complaints. Complaints over pay permeate many organizations. Romac Industries of Seattle, Washington, has worked to make sure every employee knows what every other employee makes—they post it for all to see.

The company manufacturers thousands of the tools and fittings necessary to keep municipal waterworks systems functioning. In 1974, company president Manford "Mac" McNeil surveyed employees to find out what they wanted. The answer: "I want a dollar's worth of praise . . . put it on my next paycheck." He initiated a system of "skill" and "voted" pay. Simply put, whenever an hourly worker wants a raise, his or her name, current pay rate, requested wage increase and its rationale, and picture go up on the company bulletin board.

Eligible employees include those who have been with Romac for at least one year and have received no written warnings for safety, personal conduct, or attendance concerns. The employee sits down with the supervisor and discusses the case. If the supervisor has some reservations, he or she will say "maybe you should wait. . . ." The employee is encouraged to do an in-depth self-assessment to consider his or her contribution to the overall welfare of the work group. If the employee decides to proceed with the case, the employee will submit the desired increase and the reasons why it should be granted. The

supervisor, team leader, all department members, and two people from outside the department who have access to what the employee contributes make up the departmental committee. The employee's case then goes to the wage committee—a group comprised of all the company's supervisors, the plant manager, and the human resources manager. Then the employee's case is voted on by all hourly employees. The vote used to be on an "all or none" basis, but after an employee survey the plan was modified. People wanted the ability to grant partial wages. A weighted average is used: supervisor's input (40%); department (25%); wage committee (20%); and company vote (15%) to determine the employee's increase. People closest to the employee—those who should know better than anyone else the contributions the employee is making—have the greatest input.

Are there problems with the system? President Jim Larkin and human resources manager Kim Kelly have heard the "popularity" and "favored employee" argument for years. "Sometimes the most popular employee gets more favorable consideration and the employee who is 'quiet' and shows up every day to do the job may not do as well," says Kelly. Larkin answers, "There's nothing wrong with giving employees a reason to get along better with their coworkers."

Does the system work? "Voted" pay has survived for more than a quarter century. Why? Because Romac has constantly surveyed their employees, and listened to and acted on what they had to say. Effective supervisors recognize that these techniques will be a critical component to managing conflict over a scarce resource—dollars available to pay employees.

Sources: The authors first became aware of Romac Industries's "voted" pay system through a PBS special featuring renown author Tom Peters. The material for this "Contemporary Issue" was acquired from a personal interview by one of the authors with Kim Kelly, Romac's human resources manager. Also see Christopher Caggiano, "Raises by Democracy," *Inc.* (April 1999), p. 105.

3
Distinguish between supervisory handling of employee complaints in any work setting and grievances in a unionized situation.

Complaints and Grievances in Supervision

For supervisors at the departmental level, resolving conflicts for the most part involves handling and settling employee complaints and grievances. The terms *complaint* and *grievance* are not synonyms. As commonly understood, a **complaint** is any individual or group problem or dissatisfaction that employees can channel upward to manage-

Complaint

Any individual or group problem or dissatisfaction that employees can channel upward to management, including discrimination complaints.

Grievance

A formal complaint presented by the union to management that alleges a violation of the labor agreement.

ment. A complaint normally can be lodged in any work environment, and the term can be used to include legal issues, such as a complaint of racial or sexual discrimination. Typically, a **grievance** is defined more specifically as a formal complaint involving the interpretation or application of the labor agreement in a unionized setting. This usually means that it has been presented to a supervisor or another management representative by a shop steward or some other union official.

In Chapter 11, we discussed at some length the terminology used in union–management situations and the important relationship between the supervisor and the union shop steward at the departmental level. The number and types of grievances that arise within a department can reflect the state of union–management relations. Of course, grievances can also be related to internal union politics, which usually are beyond a supervisor's control.

In this chapter, we will use the terms *complaint* and *grievance* somewhat interchangeably. Whether or not employees are unionized, every supervisor should handle employee complaints and grievances in a systematic and professional manner. It requires skills and efforts that are major indicators of a supervisor's overall managerial capabilities. The underlying principles for handling complaints and grievances are basically the same even though the procedures for processing them may be different. The supervisory approaches suggested here should generally be followed regardless of the issue involved or whether the work environment is unionized.

Explain the major distinctions between grievance procedures, complaint procedures, and alternative dispute resolution (ADR) procedures.

PROCEDURES FOR RESOLVING GRIEVANCES AND COMPLAINTS

Although procedures for resolving grievances and complaints are similar, there are some important distinctions that supervisors should understand. This section will discuss these distinctions.

Grievance Procedures

Grievances usually result from a misunderstanding, a different interpretation of the labor agreement, or an alleged violation of a provision of the labor agreement. Virtually all labor agreements contain a **grievance procedure,** which is a negotiated series of steps for processing grievances, usually beginning at the departmental level. If a grievance is not settled at the first step, it may be appealed to higher levels of management or the human resources department. The last step typically involves having a neutral arbitrator render a final and binding decision in the matter. Figure 17-3 is an example of a grievance and arbitration procedure within a labor agreement. It includes a provision for selecting and paying an arbitrator that is typical in many union–management labor agreements.

Grievance procedure

Negotiated series of steps in a labor agreement for processing grievances, beginning at the supervisory level and ending with arbitration.

Complaint Procedures

Many nonunion organizations have adopted formal problem-solving or complaint procedures to resolve complaints that employees bring to the attention of their supervisors.

FIGURE 17-3 Grievance and arbitration procedure in a labor agreement for a retail store's unionized employees.

ARTICLE 4-GRIEVANCES AND ARBITRATION

4.1 Should any differences, disputes or complaints arise over the interpretation or application of the contents of this Agreement, there shall be an earnest effort made on the part of both parties to settle same promptly through the following steps:

Step 1. By conference between the aggrieved employee, the union steward and/or business agent, or both, and the store manager or owner. Store management shall make its decision known within two (2) working days thereafter. If the matter is not resolved in Step 1, it shall be referred to Step 2 within two (2) working days.

Step 2. By conference between the business agent and the owner or a supervisor of the Employer. The Employer shall make its decision known within three (3) working days thereafter. If the matter is not resolved in Step 2, it shall be reduced to writing and referred within three (3) working days to Step 3.

Step 3. By conference between an official or officials of the Union and a designated representative of the Employer.

Step 4. In the event the last step fails to settle the complaint, it shall be referred within seven (7) working days to arbitration.

4.2 In any case in which an employee is aggrieved and the Union promptly notifies the employee that it does not intend to request arbitration after the Step 3 meeting, the time for requesting arbitration shall be stayed pending the employee's exhaustion of internal union appeals to the Union's Executive Board.

4.3 The Employer and the Union shall mutually agree to an impartial arbitrator to hear said arbitration case; however, if said arbitrator cannot be chosen within three (3) days, then the Federal Mediation and Conciliation Service will be requested to furnish a panel of seven (7) names from which the arbitrator may be chosen. The arbitrator will be selected within seven (7) days after the receipt of the panel by alternately striking names. The party striking first will be determined by the flip of a coin. The decision of the arbitrator shall be binding on both parties. The expenses of the arbitrator shall be paid for jointly.

Such arbitrator shall not be empowered to add to, detract from, or alter the terms of this Agreement.

4.4 The Employer may, at any time, discharge any worker for proper cause. The Union or the employee may file a written complaint with the Employer within seven (7) days after the date of discharge asserting that the discharge was improper. Such complaint must be taken up promptly. If the Employer and the Union fail to agree within five (5) days, it shall be referred to arbitration. Should the arbitrator determine that it was an unfair discharge, the Employer shall abide by the decision of the arbitrator.

4.5 Grievances must be taken up promptly. No grievance will be considered, discussed, or become arbitrable which is presented later than seven (7) days after such has happened.

4.6 The Employer shall have the right to call a conference with a Union steward or officials of the Union for the purpose of discussing a grievance, criticisms, or other problems.

4.7 Grievances will be discussed only through the outlined procedures; except that by mutual agreement between the Union and the Employer, the time limits may be waived.

4.8 There shall be no lockout or cessation of work pending the decision of the arbitrator.

Complaint procedure

A management-designed series of steps for handling employee complaints that usually provides for a number of appeals before a final decision.

A **complaint procedure,** which may be called a "problem-solving procedure" or by some other designation, is a management-designed procedure for handling employee complaints that usually provides for a number of appeal steps before a final decision is reached. A complaint procedure usually is explained in an employee handbook or a policies and procedures manual. Even when no formal system is spelled out, it usually is understood that employees have the right to register a complaint with the possibility of an appeal to higher-level management. A procedure for handling complaints differs from a union grievance procedure primarily in two respects. First, the employee normally must make the complaint without assistance in presenting or arguing the case; and second, the final decision is usually made by the chief executive or the human resources director rather than by an outside arbitrator.

Figure 17-4 is an edited excerpt of a problem-solving procedure that was established by a firm for its nonunion employees. Note that it involves a series of steps that begins at the supervisory level and ends with the company president or executive vice president.

Alternative Dispute Resolution (ADR) Procedures

In recent years, some companies have offered their employees assistance in processing complaints by providing a neutral person or counselor to serve an intermediary role. Others offer the services of a mediator—usually an outside "third party"—who facilitates communication but who has no direct authority to decide the outcome.

Numerous companies have adopted complaint procedures for employees that include a "jury" or "panel" of employees and managers who serve as a form of arbitration board at the final step in their complaint procedures. This approach is often referred to as peer review, and it can be adapted to resolve various types of disputes as an alternative to litigation.

Still other firms are using—or are experimenting with—the option of providing an outside arbitrator as the final step to resolve complaints, mostly in discharge and discrimination cases. Where utilized, all parties agree to abide by the arbitrator's decision. The arbitrator is a "third-party" neutral, and policies to cover the arbitrator's selection, fee, and hearing procedure must be specified and agreed upon prior to the hearing of the case.

Alternative dispute resolution (ADR)

Approaches to processing and deciding employee complaints internally as an alternative to filing a lawsuit, usually for disputes involving discharge and/or employment discrimination.

A number of firms have even adopted a combination of mediation and arbitration, called med-arb. Under med-arb procedures, the parties first attempt to resolve a dispute through some form of mediation. If mediation fails to achieve a satisfactory solution, then there is recourse to an outside arbitrator.[5]

Collectively, these types of approaches have been labeled as **alternative dispute resolution (ADR),** which generally means processing and deciding employee complaints internally as an alternative to filing lawsuits to resolve disputes, usually involving discharge and/or employment discrimination. The use of ADR approaches is definitely increasing, driven primarily by the desire of employers to expedite resolution of disputes and avoid the high costs of litigation.[6]

There eventually may be legislation to expand the availability of ADR to millions of workers who have no union or legal protection. In a major organizational policy

PROBLEM-SOLVING PROCEDURE

OBJECTIVE

It is our purpose to provide employees with an effective means to bring problems to the attention of management and get them resolved. A problem may be any condition of employment an employee feels is unjust or inequitable. Employees are encouraged to air any concern about their treatment or conditions of work over which the company might be expected to exercise some control.

NORMAL PROCEDURE

Step #1—The First-Line Supervisor—Problems are best resolved by the people closest to the situation. Employees are thus asked to first discuss their concerns with their immediate supervisor. Supervisors should, of course, seek a satisfactory resolution. If the employee feels that the supervisor is not the right person to solve the problem, he or she can ignore this step.

Step #2—The District Manager—If the problem is not resolved after discussion with the First-Line Supervisor, the employee should be referred to the District Manager (or Assistant).

Step #3—Higher-Level Divisional Management—If the problem has not been settled by either the First-Line Supervisor or District Manager, the employee should be referred to Higher-Level Divisional Management.

Step #3—Alternate—The Human Resources Staff—As an alternative, the employee can discuss his or her problem with a member of the Human Resources staff rather than Higher-Level Divisional Management.

Step #4—The President—If the matter is not adjusted satisfactorily by any of the foregoing, the employee may request an appointment with the President (or Executive Vice-President), who will see that a decision is finalized.

POLICIES

1. *Freedom from Retaliation*—Employees should not be discriminated against for exercising their rights to discuss problems. Obviously any retaliation would seriously distort the climate in which our problem-solving procedure is intended to operate.
2. *Prompt Handling*—A problem can become magnified if it isn't dealt with promptly. Supervisors are expected to set aside time to discuss an employee's concerns within one working day of an employee's request. Supervisors should seek to resolve a problem within three working days of a discussion.
3. *Fair Hearing*—Supervisors should concentrate on listening. Often, hearing an employee out can resolve the problem. Supervisors should objectively determine whether the employee has been wronged and, if so, seek a satisfactory remedy.

PRESIDENT'S GRIPE BOX

The President's "Gripe Box" is located on each floor of our Home Office buildings. Employees should feel free to use the "Gripe Box" to get problems to the President's attention expeditiously. Employees may or may not sign gripes. Written responses will be sent for all signed gripes.

statement, the Society for Human Resource Management (SHRM), a national organization of human resources professionals, has strongly endorsed ADR procedures that "provide employees a process that is accessible, prompt and impartial, and that results in reduced dispute resolution costs and more timely resolution of complaints as an alternative to costly litigation." In the same policy statement, SHRM has recognized that in order for ADR to be effective, certain standards of fairness and due process must be met. Included among these standards are:

- The opportunity for a hearing before one or more neutral, impartial decision makers;
- The opportunity to participate in the selection of decision makers;
- Participation by the employee in assuming some portion of the costs of the dispute resolution; and
- The opportunity to recover the same remedies available to the employee through litigation, and confidentiality of proceedings.[7]

A national legal commission, called the National Conference of Commissioners on Uniform State Laws, has proposed a new uniform employment statute that would permit terminated employees to take their cases before a neutral arbitrator. In addition, a number of states are seriously considering adopting this type of arbitration system; whether such a proposal will be widely adopted is a matter of conjecture. Most employers prefer that ADR be a voluntary process and not made compulsory by law. Regardless, a major question remains, "Does ADR work?" A recent government report cautioned that "no comprehensive evaluative data" exist on ADR's effectiveness.[8] A review of dispute literature, particularly arbitration decisions, indicates to the authors that many disputes could be prevented if supervisors would practice good communication skills and display genuine concern for employee problems. Our contention is supported by a recent study of employees:

- 56% said their employers fail to show concern for them.
- 45% said their companies failed to treat them fairly.
- 41% said their employers failed to trust them.
- 76% said they are not "truly loyal" to their company.[9]

In conclusion, if ADR is to be successful, companies must train supervisors on how to deal with conflict and ensure that fairness in the process prevails.

5

Describe the supervisor's role at the initial step in resolving a complaint or grievance, especially the need for open and frank communication.

THE SUPERVISOR AND THE SIGNIFICANT FIRST STEP IN RESOLVING COMPLAINTS AND GRIEVANCES

In the discussions to follow, we primarily will focus on the resolution of employee complaints and grievances with the role of the supervisor uppermost in mind. As in so many other areas, the supervisor's role in the handling of employee complaints and grievances is often the most crucial part in the eventual determination of the outcome. Supervisors also become involved in alternative dispute resolution (ADR) procedures and in the resolution of other types of conflict at the departmental level. Most of the principles involved in complaint and grievance handling are applicable in resolving virtually all forms of workplace conflict.

At the first step in a unionized firm, the departmental shop steward usually will present a grievance to the supervisor, and the aggrieved employee (or employees) may also be present.[10] The supervisor should listen to them very carefully. There is nothing to prohibit the supervisor from speaking directly with the employee in front of the shop steward. In other words, there should be frank and open communication among the parties. If the shop steward does not bring the employee along, the supervisor nonetheless should listen to the shop steward.

It is unusual for an aggrieved employee to present a grievance to a supervisor in the absence of the shop steward. However, if this should happen, it is appropriate for the supervisor to listen to the employee's problem and to determine whether it involves the labor agreement or the shop steward, or whether the union should be involved at all. Under no circumstances should the supervisor give the impression that he or she is trying to undermine the shop steward's authority or relationship with the employee. If the labor agreement or union interests are involved, then the supervisor should notify the shop steward concerning the employee's presentation of the problem.

If a grievance is not settled at the first step and if the shop steward believes that the grievance is justified, the grievance will proceed to the next step. The shop steward may carry the grievance further with some other objective in mind. In Chapter 11 we mentioned that the shop steward usually is an elected representative of the employees, is familiar with the labor agreement, and is knowledgeable in submitting grievances. The shop steward may be eager to receive credit for filing a grievance. By making a good showing or by winning as much as possible for the employees, chances of being reelected as shop steward at the next union election are enhanced.

If the firm is not unionized, some employees may be afraid to bring their legitimate complaints to their supervisor. They fear that complaining may be held against them, and possibly that there may be retaliation if they dare to challenge a supervisor's decision. At the other extreme are employees who resent supervisory authority and take every opportunity to gripe about matters that they do not like in the department. They even relish making the supervisor uncomfortable by bringing their complaints for attention. Since they do not have union representation, they may approach the supervisor as a group, believing that this approach gives them strength and protection.

The importance of the supervisor's handling of employee complaints at the first step cannot be overemphasized. Open and frank communication between all parties is usually the key element in finding an amicable resolution of the problem. If such communication does not occur, disagreement, resentment, and possibly an appeal to higher levels of management will be the likely outcome.

SUPERVISORY GUIDELINES FOR RESOLVING COMPLAINTS AND GRIEVANCES

6
Identify guidelines for supervisors to resolve complaints and grievances in an effective manner.

For the most part, the supervisor should take into account the same general considerations and use the same skills in handling both grievances and complaints. Regardless of the nature of an employee complaint or grievance, a supervisor should fully investigate details of the problem and determine whether it can be resolved quickly. It is always better to settle minor issues before they grow into major ones. Although there will be cases that have to be referred to higher-level managers or human resources staff (e.g., complaints involving charges of discrimination prohibited by law), the supervisor should endeavor to settle or resolve the issues at the first step. If many go beyond the first step, the supervisor probably is not carrying out his or her duties appropriately. Unless circumstances are beyond the supervisor's control, complaints and grievances should be handled within reasonable time limits and brought to a fair conclusion within the pattern of supervisory guidelines as discussed in the sections that follow.

Make Time Available

The supervisor should find time to hear a complaint or grievance as soon as possible. This does not mean that the supervisor must drop everything to meet immediately with the employee or shop steward. Rather, it means making every effort to set a time for an initial hearing. If the supervisor makes it difficult for a complaining employee to have a hearing as expeditiously as possible under the circumstances, the employee could become frustrated and feel resentful. A long delay could be interpreted to mean that the supervisor does not consider the problem important. It could even be interpreted as stalling and indifference on the part of management.

Listen Patiently and with an Open Mind

Often supervisors become preoccupied with defending themselves and trying to justify their own positions without giving the shop steward and/or the complaining employee ample time to present their cases. Supervisors should bear in mind that all the principles discussed in the chapters on communication and interviewing are applicable to complaints and grievances. All people involved should be encouraged to say whatever they have on their minds. If they gain the impression that the supervisor is willing to listen to them and wants to provide fair treatment, the problem may not seem as large to them as it did before. Also, the more a person talks, the more likely that person is to make contradictory remarks that weaken the argument. The person may even uncover a solution as he or she talks out the problem. Sometimes, the employee simply wants to vent frustrations, and after this is done the problem may be solved. Thus, by listening empathetically, the supervisor can minimize tensions and even solve some problems in the initial hearing.

Distinguish Facts from Opinions

Distinguishing facts from opinions means being cautious about relying on hearsay and opinionated statements. However, the supervisor should not try to confuse the employee or shop steward. The supervisor should ask factual, pointed questions regarding who or what is involved; when, where, and why the alleged problem took place; and whether there was any connection between this situation and some other problem. Frequently it is impossible to gather all the relevant information at once, making it inappropriate to settle the complaint or grievance immediately. Under such conditions the supervisor should tell the complaining employee or the shop steward that he or she will gather the necessary information within a reasonable time and by a definite date. The supervisor should not postpone a decision with the excuse of needing more facts when the relevant information can be obtained without delay.

Determine the Real Issue

In both union and nonunion work settings, there may be times when an employee complaint represents a symptom of a deeper problem. For example, a complaint about unfair work assignments may really reflect personality clashes among several employees in the department. Or a complaint that newly installed machinery does not allow employees to maintain their previous incentive rates may indicate that the employees are actually having a difficult time adjusting to the operation of the new equipment after years of operating old machines. Unless the real issue is clearly defined and settled, complaints of a similar nature are likely to be raised again in the future.

Check and Consult

Checking and consulting are perhaps the most important aspects of a supervisor's role in handling employee complaints and grievances. We cannot emphasize too strongly that the labor agreement, as well as company policies and procedures, must be administered fairly and uniformly. In a unionized setting, the supervisor may not be sure whether the grievance is valid under the existing labor agreement; or provisions of the labor agreement might be unclear in reference to the alleged violation. In no case should the supervisor make a decision until after carefully reviewing the company's manual on policies and procedures and the labor agreement.

As stated previously, grievances revolve around interpretation of the labor agreement, and complaints in nonunion settings may include questions of employment policies. Complaints that involve allegations of discrimination and other aspects of equal employment opportunity have legal implications. Therefore, whenever a grievance or complaint requires contractual, policy, or legal interpretation, the supervisor should tell the complaining individuals that it will be necessary to look into the matter and that an answer will be given by a definite date. Subsequently, the supervisor should consult with the human resources department and higher-level managers for advice and guidance on these matters.

Seeking assistance from human resources staff or higher-level managers is not buck-passing or revealing ignorance. Nor should it be considered by the supervisor as showing weakness, because the supervisor usually is not authorized or qualified to make the policy or legal interpretations necessary to respond to certain employee complaints and grievances.

Avoid Setting Precedents

The supervisor should consult records of previous settlements and make sure that any proposed decision is consistent with established practices. If a particular issue has not been encountered in the past, the supervisor should seek guidance from other supervisors or staff personnel who may have experienced similar but not necessarily identical problems. If circumstances require a departure from previous decisions, the supervisor should explain the reasons why to the employee or the shop steward. They also should be informed about whether any exception will constitute a new precedent.

Unless there is a valid reason, or unless there has been prior approval from higher-level management or the human resources department, the supervisor should avoid making individual exceptions to a policy. Making an exception is setting a precedent, and precedents often come back to haunt the supervisor and the organization. In labor arbitration issues, most arbitrators believe that precedents can become almost as binding on an organization as if they were negotiated in the labor agreement itself. Thus, a supervisor should be very careful about making an individual exception in a union grievance because a grievance settlement may become part of a future labor agreement.

Exercise Self-Control

Sometimes emotions, arguments, and personality clashes distort the communication between the supervisor and complaining individuals. The worst thing the supervisor can do in these situations is to engage in a shouting match or to "talk down" to the complaining employees. Emotional outbursts usually lead to little constructive thinking. Arguing and shouting may escalate a problem to far more serious proportions. Of course, there are limits to a supervisor's patience. If the employee or the shop steward persists in loud arguments, profanity, or the like, the supervisor should terminate the meeting at that point and schedule another, hoping that the problem can be discussed later in a calm and less emotional manner.

If the complaint or grievance is trivial or not even valid, the supervisor must be careful not to show any personal animosity toward the shop steward or the complaining employee. The supervisor should explain why a grievance has no merit. The supervisor cannot expect the shop steward to do the explaining since the steward is the employee's official representative.

Sometimes an employee or the shop steward may provoke an argument as a way of deliberately putting the supervisor on the defensive. Even this type of situation should not arouse open hostilities on the supervisor's part. If the supervisor does not know how to handle situations of this sort, he or she should consult with higher-level managers or the human resources department for assistance.

Minimize Delay in Reaching a Decision

Many labor agreements require a definite time period within which a grievance must be answered. The same principle should hold true in nonunion work situations. If an employee has raised a complaint, that employee should be entitled to know—within a reasonable time—exactly when management will make a decision concerning that complaint. If the complaint can be handled immediately and if it is within the supervisor's authority to do so, of course this should be done practically on the spot. But if the complaint involves an issue that requires consultation with higher-level managers or the human resources staff, the supervisor should close the hearing with a definite commitment as to when an answer or decision will be given.

Postponing a decision in the hope that the grievance will disappear can invite trouble and more grievances. However, arriving at a speedy settlement should not outweigh the importance of a sound decision. If delay is necessary, the supervisor should inform the parties and explain why, and not leave them thinking they are being ignored. Since waiting for a decision is bothersome to everyone, prompt handling is of utmost importance.

Explain the Decision Clearly and with Sensitivity

The supervisor should make every effort to give a straightforward, clear answer to the complaint or grievance as decided by management. In addition, the supervisor should communicate as specifically as possible the reasons for the decision, especially if it goes against the employee's case. It is frustrating for an employee just to get a "no" without any explanation other than that management "feels" that it does not have to do what the employee requests.

The supervisor should answer a complaint or grievance in a straightforward, reasonable manner.

Even when the complaint is not justified, the supervisor should not in any way convey to the employee that the problem is trivial or unnecessary. There are probably good reasons in the employee's mind for raising the complaint. Therefore, the supervisor's response should be sensitive to the employee's perspective.

If a written reply to a grievance is required under the labor agreement, the supervisor should restrict it to the specific grievance and make certain that the response is relevant to the case. References to provisions of the labor agreement or plant rules should be confined to those in question. The supervisor is well advised to first discuss the implications of a written reply with higher-level managers or the human resources department so that it will be worded appropriately.

Keep Records and Documents

Despite good-faith efforts of supervisors or higher-level managers to settle complaints or grievances, an employee may choose to appeal an adverse decision. If the complaint involves discrimination, the employee may file a formal complaint with a government agency for legal processing. If there is a union grievance, it may eventually go all the way to arbitration. In a nonunionized firm, the firm's complaint procedures may provide several steps for appeal. This is why it is important for a supervisor to maintain documentation of all available evidence, discussions, and meetings. In any appeal process, written evidence is generally superior to oral testimony and hearsay.

Many firms have policies to cover the confidential handling of certain employee records and documents. Supervisors must be careful to adhere to any such policies, especially where documents involve issues of employee job performance and company disciplinary actions.

Keeping good records is especially important when a complaint or grievance is not settled at the supervisory level. The burden of proof is usually on management to justify its position. Therefore, a supervisor should be ready to explain previous actions without having to depend solely on memory. Documentation can be very supportive in this regard.

Do Not Fear a Challenge

A supervisor should make every effort to resolve a complaint or grievance at the first step without sacrificing a fair decision. Unfortunately, supervisors at times are tempted to grant a questionable complaint or grievance because they fear a challenge or want to avoid a hassle. By giving in to an employee or the union just to avoid an argument, the supervisor may invite others to adopt the "squeaky wheel gets the grease" theory. That is, other employees or shop stewards will be encouraged to submit minor complaints because they feel that by complaining often and loudly they have a better chance of gaining a concession. Thus, a supervisor's "caving in" can establish a perception that may lead to even greater problems.

In efforts to settle a complaint or grievance, there will always be gray areas where a supervisor must use prudent judgment. The supervisor should be willing to admit and rectify mistakes. However, if the supervisor believes that a fair and objective decision was made, he or she should have the courage to hold to a firm decision even if the employee threatens to appeal. The fact that the employee appeals an adverse decision does not mean that the supervisor is wrong. Even if higher-level managers or an arbitrator should later reverse a supervisor's decision, this in itself does not imply poor handling by the supervisor. There will always be some decisions that will be modified or reversed during the appeal process for reasons that may go beyond the supervisor's responsibility.

For example, higher management—perhaps because of advice from the human resources staff or legal counsel—may decide to settle a case on terms more favorable to the employee than what the supervisor believes to be appropriate. This occurs because management is concerned about possibly losing the case in arbitration or litigation and incurring excessive extra costs in the process. Reversal of a supervisor's decision by higher management usually is not desirable since it can weaken a supervisor's position with departmental employees and cause resentment. But occasionally it will happen— sometimes for "political" reasons—and a supervisor should avoid becoming too frustrated or distressed by it.

Supervisors who generally follow the guidelines discussed in this chapter and who have done their best to reach an equitable solution will be backed up by higher-level management in most cases. At the very least, a supervisor normally should be able to handle a complaint or grievance in a professional manner and avoid having minor issues escalate into major ones.

In summary, handling employee complaints and grievances is another of the many skills of effective supervision. It requires sensitivity, objectivity, and sound analytical judgment—which are the same qualities that are required in most other areas of supervisory management.

What Call Did You Make?

As department supervisor Alfred Perry, you face a common dilemma in interpretation and application of a labor–management agreement, namely, which provision should prevail in determining a proper course of action. The union claims that a coffee-making privilege is protected under the labor–management agreement and cannot be changed unilaterally by a supervisor. However, you feel that the same agreement gives management the right to make necessary decisions to maintain discipline and efficiency. The grievance and the grievance procedure will test which view shall prevail.

Since interpretation of a labor–management agreement is at the heart of this grievance, you should consult the director of human resources for guidance. Virtually all of the principles included in this chapter may become applicable in the processing of the case. In particular, you should investigate thoroughly all aspects of the contested issue in your department and document all information that supports your position. Unless there is a settlement or compromise of some sort, the case conceivably could go all the way to arbitration for a final and binding decision.

Throughout the steps of the grievance procedure, you should argue your position in a straightforward manner, but do not attempt to belittle the union members' concern about retaining a privilege that they have had previously. Regardless of the final outcome of the grievance, you should understand that employees have the right to submit grievances, and the grievance procedure will eventually bring about a decision, hopefully in a fair and professional manner.

SUMMARY

1

As supervisors manage their departments, it is natural that their perspectives and decisions at times will conflict with those of employees and/or the union. Resolving employee conflicts and handling their complaints and grievances is part of each supervisor's job, and the supervisor's effectiveness in doing so is another indicator of a supervisor's overall managerial capabilities.

2

An understanding of the five conflict resolution (negotiation) styles can help supervisors in dealing with conflicts. The five styles are withdraw/avoid, compromise, accommodate/oblige, compete/force/dominate, and collaborate/integrate/problem solve. Different issues and individuals in the workplace may require supervisors to use all of these styles. The collaborative style is preferred in that a "win–win" mentality is developed. This style also aids in developing a climate of mutual trust and respect that is essential to attaining departmental and other objectives.

3

An employee complaint can occur in any work environment. Complaints may involve individual or group dissatisfactions that can be initiated with a supervisor and possibly appealed further. A grievance is normally identified as a complaint involving the interpretation and application of a labor agreement where employees are represented by a union.

4

Conflict resolution procedures have a number of steps beginning at the supervisory level. A grievance procedure in a unionized setting and a complaint procedure in a nonunionized setting differ in two major ways. In the nonunionized setting, the employee normally must make a complaint without any assistance; an employee who files a union grievance will have the assistance of a shop steward or some other union representative. Second, the final decision is usually made by the chief executive or the human resources director in a nonunionized firm, and some firms use other ways to resolve complaints. In a union grievance matter, an outside neutral arbitrator may make the final decision.

Alternative dispute resolution (ADR) procedures take a variety of formats, including mediation, arbitration, and "panel" (peer review) decision making. ADR is especially utilized in expediting and resolving discharge and discrimination cases in order to avoid high costs of litigation.

5

During the initial step in handling grievances, there should be open, frank communication between the supervisor and the complaining employee and the shop steward. If the grievance is not settled at this step, the shop steward probably will carry the grievance further, and it may eventually be submitted to an outside arbitrator. The same need for open and frank communication exists in hearing and resolving employee complaints at the supervisory level. Employee complaints should be settled in an amicable fashion by the supervisor whenever possible, rather than having them appealed and decided at higher levels.

6

Whether or not employees are represented by a labor union, the supervisor should follow the same general guidelines in resolving complaints or grievances. Among the most important supervisory considerations are the following: make time available, listen patiently and with an open mind, distinguish facts from opinions, determine the real issue, check and consult, avoid setting precedents, exercise self-control, minimize delay in reaching a decision, explain the decision clearly and with sensitivity, keep records and documents, and do not fear a challenge.

KEY TERMS

Substantive conflict (page 573)
Personalized conflict (page 574)
Conflict resolution styles (page 576)
Complaint (page 580)

Grievance (page 580)
Grievance procedure (page 580)
Complaint procedure (page 582)
Alternative dispute resolution (ADR) (page 582)

QUESTIONS FOR DISCUSSION

1. Why is it important for a supervisor to understand the difference between substantive and personalized conflicts? Before reading this chapter, what did workplace conflict mean to you? Do you view it differently now?
2. Why should employee conflicts, complaints, and grievances be considered a natural component of the supervisory position?
3. Define and discuss the five styles of conflict resolution.
4. Describe a conflict you are familiar with. How can you use conflict resolution techniques and good communication skills to resolve the conflict?
5. Imagine that your professor instituted a reward (grading) system similar to Romac Industries (see the chapter's second "Contemporary Issue" box). What would be the main advantages and drawbacks to such a plan? How might it lead to conflict?
6. How is a grievance defined in unionized firms? What are the major distinctions between a union grievance and an employee complaint in a nonunionized firm?
7. Distinguish between a union grievance procedure and a complaint (or problem-solving) procedure. What is meant by alternative dispute resolution (ADR)?
8. Discuss the shop steward's role in the grievance procedure. Why is it generally preferable that the supervisor listen to the shop steward and the complaining employee together?
9. Why is open and frank communication a key element in supervisory handling of a complaint or grievance at the initial meeting?
10. Why should most complaints and grievances be settled by the supervisor at the departmental level? Which should be referred to higher-level managers or human resources staff for decisions? Discuss.
11. Review and discuss each of the guidelines presented in this chapter for resolving complaints and grievances. Analyze the interrelationships among them. Why is the satisfactory handling of complaints or grievances a major component of effective supervisory management?

SKILLS APPLICATIONS

Skills Application 17-1: Conflicts! Conflicts! Conflicts! Or Teamwork?

On January 3, 2000, the last original daily "Peanuts" comic strip appeared in newspapers coast-to-coast. As the creator, Charles M. Schulz said in the finale, "I have been fortunate to draw Charlie Brown and his friends for almost 50 years. . . . Unfortunately, I am no longer able to maintain the schedule demanded by a daily comic strip, therefore, I am announcing my retirement. . . . Charlie Brown, Snoopy, Linus, Lucy . . . How can I ever forget them . . ." How can we ever forget "You're a Good Man Charlie Brown," or any of the other strips or television specials depicting the "Peanuts" gang?

INTERNET ACTIVITY

1. Using the Internet, find at least three Peanuts comic strips. (www.snoopy.com, www.peanutscollectorclub.com, and various other sites contain viewable strips)
2. What does a particular strip teach about conflict? . . . team work? . . . life?
3. Show one of the strips to a supervisor or manager. Ask them describe the extent to which the strip presents a realistic reflection of their workplace.
4. Compare your observations with one of your classmates. To what degree are your findings similar? If there are differences, how do you account for them?

Skills Application 17-2: Your Complaint

Everyone who has held a job has had work-related problems. However, many employees do not register complaints in nonunion situations. For this project, remember a situation in which you could have made a complaint to your supervisor but did not. Now is your opportunity.

1. State the nature of your complaint in one or two sentences and provide relevant background information.
2. What do you believe should have been done, assuming you had filed the complaint as part of the firm's complaint procedure?
3. What justification could the supervisor or higher-level managers cite for refusing to make any adjustments because of your complaint?
4. If a union had represented you, would you have filed a grievance in this situation? Why or why not?
5. How could a neutral arbitrator have helped in resolving your complaint?

Skills Application 17-3: The Discharge and the Union Grievance

The primary decision that usually must be made in a grievance situation is whether or not an action violated provisions of the labor agreement. The short case that follows is an abridged version of one that actually occurred. All names are disguised. Read the case and answer the questions that follow.

CASE

Midwest Meat Packers is located in an agricultural community with a population of 25,000. The plant employees are represented by the International Meat Packers Union. On Monday, October 8, Raymond Sanders left work with a bad toothache. Since he couldn't find his supervisor, he told Joe Teeters, a foreman with a subcontractor doing work at the plant, to notify Sanders's supervisor, Lewis Ranger. On Tuesday, October 9, when Sanders returned to work, he had no time card and he found a replacement working in his department. That day, the plant manager told Sanders he was terminated for violating Company Work Rule #6: "Walking off the job and leaving the plant without permission is a violation that will result in immediate termination of employment."

The union immediately filed a grievance on behalf of Raymond Sanders, claiming that the matter was not handled properly by the company and asking that Sanders be reinstated. The union claimed that the company did not have "just cause" to terminate Sanders as required by the labor–management agreement.

The company's written answer to the union grievance stated that Raymond Sanders had clearly violated Company Work Rule #6 and thus the company had just cause to terminate his employment.

At a grievance hearing held several weeks later, Raymond Sanders acknowledged that on October 8 he had left the plant at about 12:15 P.M. to go to lunch. He did not "clock out," and he did not return to work that afternoon. He did not ask for permission to leave work from any plant supervisor or the plant nurse, nor did he tell any of them that he was leaving. He admitted that it was a violation of the rules to leave work during his work shift without permission, but he stated that he did not think that it was a serious violation considering what had occurred.

Sanders stated that on that day he ate lunch with Joe Teeters, an independent electrical contractor. During lunch his wisdom tooth started hurting, and the pain became quite severe. He told Teeters that he was not going back to work and asked Teeters to tell his plant supervisor, Lewis Ranger, that he had gone home because of a toothache. Sanders claimed that several days later he saw Teeters. Teeters said he had told Dave Lillis, another plant supervisor, about Sanders leaving work.

Lillis was called from the plant to testify at the grievance hearing. Lillis claimed that he had no recollection of seeing or talking to Teeters on October 8; and further, if Teeters had given him a message for Raymond Sanders, he would have immediately passed it on to Lewis Ranger or the plant manager.

1. Why would the union pursue a grievance over this matter?
2. How does this case illustrate the importance of a grievance procedure?
3. What additional details would be useful before management could make a decision to deny the union grievance or to grant the union grievance and reinstate Sanders?
4. Assume that the case is pursued to arbitration and that you are the arbitrator. What would you decide and why? (Suggestion: Before deciding, read the concepts in Chapter 19 regarding the just-cause standard for discipline and discharge.)

Skills Application 17-4: Do People Work for You? Or With You?

1. Below are descriptive statements about your style, feelings, concerns, and interactions with others. Read each statement carefully; then rate yourself on how frequently you do the following when dealing with others.

Scale: Usually = 5		Sometimes = 3	Seldom = 1	
1. I fix ...	____	2. I show empathy ...		____
3. I protect ...	____	4. I encourage ...		____
5. I rescue ...	____	6. I share ...		____
7. I control ...	____	8. I confront ...		____
9. I carry their feelings ...	____	10. I am sensitive ...		____
11. I don't listen ...	____	12. I listen ...		____
I feel		I feel		
13. tired ...	____	14. relaxed ...		____
15. anxious ...	____	16. free ...		____
17. fearful ...	____	18. aware ...		____
19. liable ...	____	20. high self-worth ...		____
21. negative ...	____	22. positive ...		____

I am concerned with

23.	the solution.	_____
25.	the answers to problems.	_____
27.	being right.	_____
29.	details.	_____

I am concerned with

24.	relating to people.	_____
26.	feelings.	_____
28.	the person.	_____
30.	involving all who will be affected in solving the problem.	_____

31.	I direct people.	_____
33.	I am a manipulator.	_____
35.	I expect people to live up to my expectations.	_____

32.	I provide people with direction.	_____
34.	I empower others.	_____
36.	I believe that if I share myself others will have enough to make it.	_____

Total Left Hand Column   _____   Total Right Hand Column   _____

2. After completing the questionnaire, add the numbers in the two columns.
3. Is there a difference in the totals? Why do you suppose this is?
4. Retake the questionnaire. This time rate yourself in terms of how you would like to see yourself. Is there a difference? If so, what accounts for the difference?
5. (Supplemental Application): Often we think that we behave in a certain way, but, in reality, others see us differently. Therefore, we suggest that you select a handful of people who have worked with you or have observed you. Give them a copy of the questionnaire and have them rate you. (To ensure a realistic and candid response, have a third party tabulate the results.) Is there a difference in how others perceive you? In what specific areas do you need to modify your behavior?
6. Write a one-page paper describing what you learned from this skill application.

Source: The format for this skills application was developed by Professor Leonard for use in this application. The items contained in this Skills Application were originally developed by Dr. Beverly Wells, West Coast Institute, San Francisco, CA, and adapted with her permission.

INTERNET ACTIVITY

Skills Application 17-5: Communicating to Resolve Conflict

As a supervisor, how can you make conflict productive in your work group? Review several of the articles on conflict resolution at the Work911 Web site (www.work911.conflict.conart.htm), or other sites that deal with workplace conflict.

1. Create a list of ten communication strategies for resolving conflict in the workplace. Specifically, what can you as a supervisor do to manage conflicts?
2. Assess your own communication skills. Do you maintain a climate of open communication with your peers? In work situations? Do you practice cooperative communication? Are you a good listener? What steps can you take now to improve your communication and conflict resolution skills?

ENDNOTES

1. Adapted from Robert Bacal, "Conflict & Cooperation in the Workplace," *Institute for Conflict Prevention* (www.conflict.8m.com).

2. See Robert Bacal, "The Essential Conflict Management," *Resolution and Prevention Bookshelf* (Institute for Conflict Prevention, 1998).

3. See 1 Kings, Chapter 3 in the Bible for the story of King Solomon's approach in deciding which woman was the mother of the child.

4. For extensive discussions of various approaches to conflict resolution, the following are recommended: E. Wertheim, *Negotiations and Resolving Conflicts: An Overview* (Free Press, 1999); G. Richard Shell, "Negotiator, Know Thyself: Hone Your Negotiating Skills—With a Checklist Matched to Your Personality Type," *Inc.* (May 1999), pp. 106–107; and Shell, *Bargaining for Advantage: Negotiation Strategies for Reasonable People* (Viking Penguin, 1999). Also see Deborah DeVoe, "Learn to Resolve or Avoid Work Conflict," *InfoWorld* (August 23, 1999), p. 84; DeVoe, "Don't Let Conflict Get You Off Course," *InfoWorld* (August 9, 1999), p. 69; Patricia M. Fernberg, "Pulling Together Can Resolve Conflict," *Occupational Hazards* (March 1999), pp. 65–67; Mark Rowh, "How To Make Conflict Work for You," *Career World* (February 1999), pp. 24–27; Bernard Morrow and Lauren M. Bernardi, "Resolving Workplace Disputes," *Canadian Manager* (Spring 1999), pp. 17–20; and Dina Lynch, "Unresolved Conflicts Affect the Bottom Line," *HRMagazine* (May 1997), pp. 49–50.

5. From "Employers Resolve Worker Complaints Through Alternatives to Litigation," *Employee Relations Weekly* (November 25, 1991), pp. 1–2.

6. A survey of 500 human resources professionals revealed that about one-quarter of the represented firms had ADR procedures in place, and about another one-fifth were considering implementing them. Of the firms that had ADR procedures, the most common procedures mentioned were arbitration (44%), peer review (37%), and mediation (25%). Some firms used a combination of approaches. The majority of firms used third-party neutrals and paid the cost involved; about half permitted the employee to participate in the selection process. See "Alternative Dispute Resolution Gaining in Popularity," *Human Resources Management, Ideas and Trends in Personnel* (Commerce Clearing House, Inc., March 29, 1995), pp. 49–53.

7. See Dominic Bencivenga, "Fair Play in the ADR Arena," *HRMagazine* (January 1996), pp. 51–56.

8. Reported in Michael Barrier, "A Working Alternative For Settling Disputes," *Nation's Business* (July 1998), pp. 43–46.

9. The study by the Hudson Institute and Walker Information (Indianapolis, IN) as reported by Sue Shellenbarger, "To Win Loyalty of Your Employees, Try a Softer Approach," *The Wall Street Journal* (January 26, 2000), p. B1.

10. For extensive discussions of grievance procedures under a labor agreement, the following are recommended: *Grievance Guide* (BNA, 1995); Fred Whitney and Benjamin J. Taylor, *Labor Relations Law* (Prentice-Hall, 1995); and *How Arbitration Works* (BNA, 1985).

WHO NEEDS TQM?

Merrill Dawe, plant manager of a major food processing plant, had attended a meeting of an industry association in which he had been impressed by several presentations on total quality management (TQM) and labor–management participation teams. Dawe was convinced that such approaches would be very appropriate in his plant, since he felt they could help improve the employee relations climate and perhaps assist in improving productivity and reducing quality problems. Dawe decided to call a number of his supervisors, along with the local union president and several of the plant's union shop stewards, to his office to discuss his plans to implement TQM. At a meeting in his office, Dawe outlined what he proposed to do. He said that he planned to have TQM meetings on a periodic basis, probably once a month, in which various departmental employee groups and committees, along with their supervisors, would discuss production problems, quality problems, and any other problems that needed attention. Dawe emphasized that employees would be paid for the time they spent in these meetings and that any ideas and suggestions would be given open consideration and attention by supervisors and higher-level managers.

After listening patiently to Dawe's presentation, Jerry Bruno, the plant's local union president, responded as follows: "Mr. Dawe, our national and local union have heard about TQM and efforts of this nature. In general, we're skeptical about being part of them. We've heard that many companies simply use these as a way of trying to bypass the union contract and the grievance procedure. We feel that this can be just another tactic to lull employees into thinking that management is concerned about them. Frankly, I'd bet that TQM meetings will be little more than a place where the workers will say what's on their minds, and then company management will continue to ignore their concerns. Unless I'm convinced—and my fellow union representatives are convinced—that any such program in this plant will not be used to ignore the union and our labor agreement, we will not cooperate with you in this effort."

Dawe pondered what his response should be to Bruno's comments and whether he should seriously attempt to implement a TQM program.

Questions for Discussion

1. Evaluate how Merrill Dawe presented his ideas for a TQM program in the company plant. How might he have approached this in a way that would have gained greater support from the employees and the union? Discuss.

2. Evaluate the response of Jerry Bruno, the local union president. Why are these objections serious and difficult to overcome in a short period of time?

3. At the end of the case, what should Merrill Dawe do? On the assumption that Dawe decides to continue with the implementation of a TQM program, outline a series of steps or recommendations that would be helpful in overcoming union and worker opposition and making the program a worthwhile investment of time and management attention.

4. (*Optional*) Using the Internet, access at least two sites that will provide guidance on planning and implementing a total quality management (TQM) program. At the time of publication of this text, the following sites were recommended sources: www.iqd.com/quality, www.qualitydigest.com, or www.AQAPress.com.

INTERNET ACTIVITY

Then write a brief report in which you respond to the following questions:

a. What information could be used by Merrill Dawe to help convince Jerry Bruno of the value of a TQM program?

b. Discuss how various TQM educational materials could be used to give workers an appreciation of the importance of quality.

Case

5-2

THE "THEORY TRIPLE X" MANAGER

Otto Wood is an engineering technologist for Waite Conveyor Company. He was busy working on the final stages of the installation of a sophisticated computerized conveyor system in the Webster Department Stores. A sales engineer, Warren Clark, was in charge of the overall project from the time it was sold until it would be turned over to the Webster Department Stores. Clark had negotiated a deadline for installation, which was 10 days away. The sales contract provided for a severe price penalty in case of late delivery.

Wood's immediate boss is Will Meyers, head of the installation and inspection department. Last night, Wood phoned Meyers and told him that he was quitting immediately. He had had all he could take from Warren Clark, and he had decided to leave the firm. Wood told Meyers that Clark had been "breathing down his neck" continuously and that he had been pressuring him needlessly to get the job completed. Wood assured Meyers that he had been doing his best but that, in a sophisticated installation of this sort, many things create problems and interfere with getting quick results. Wood said that he didn't attempt to explain the problems to Clark because, in Wood's words, "Mr. Clark knows next to nothing about the intricate nature of the problems involved." The last straw was a threat from Clark to lock him in the building until the installation was operable, even if he had to bring him his food. Wood said he realized that Clark did not intend to do this; but Clark's threat, after everything else he had done, was too much to take. In Wood's view, Clark was a Theory Triple X manager all the way!

Meyers wondered what to do. He knew that people with Otto Wood's skills were hard to find. Particularly at this stage of the project, it would be next to impossible to get a replacement employee who could come in to pick up the installation where Wood had left off and complete the project on time. Meyers understood the meaning of a penalty for late delivery. The next morning he decided to meet with Warren Clark to discuss the situation.

Questions for Discussion

1. Is Warren Clark a "Theory Triple X" manager, or is he operating in a way that reflects the pressure of the job situation? Discuss.
2. Who should be in charge of meeting an installation deadline in a situation of this sort? Does Clark have the right to issue orders to Wood under the organizational setup in the Waite Conveyor Company? (Suggestion: Refer to the discussion in Chapter 8 on matrix-type organizational structure.)
3. What approach should Will Meyers take in meeting with Clark to discuss the situation? What approach should they both take in working with Wood to finish the project on time?
4. What should be done to avoid future problems of the types illustrated by this case? Consider alternatives.

Case

5-3

A GROUP DECISION BAFFLES THE SUPERVISOR

Shirley Rice is the supervisor of the packing department of Amcee Novelty Company. She supervises 15 employees, predominantly workers in their twenties, whose job it is to wrap finished products in tissue paper, put them into cardboard boxes, and then glue labels to the outside of the boxes. She is known as an experienced and firm supervisor. After observing and timing the operations frequently, she arrived at what she considered to be a fair standard of how many items each employee could box during an eight-hour day. However, this standard was seldom reached. In order to improve the situation, and after additional studies, she installed a different layout, rearranged the work benches, simplified the procedures, and did all she could to raise the output of the department. But output remained considerably below her expected standard.

As a last resort, Rice decided to try an idea that had greatly impressed her. During the last two months, the company had made it possible for all supervisors to attend a weekly series of classes given by a local university. These classes covered the basics of good supervisory management. During the last session, the professor had discussed the advantages of group decision making and group discussion, including the advantages of decisions reached by those who will be concerned with the outcome. The professor stated that, in such cases, the employees usually will do their utmost to carry their decisions through to a successful conclusion. He compared them with decisions handed down unilaterally by supervisors, which employees often only grudgingly complied with.

Rice decided to apply this method and called a meeting of the workers in the department. She told them that the current standard of output was too low and that a new standard of output had to be set. Instead of establishing the new production standard by herself, however, she wanted them to decide as a group what it should be. Of course, she hoped—but she did not say this—that they would arrive at a higher standard than the level at which they had been operating.

Several days later, much to Shirley Rice's amazement, the group arrived at a standard that was significantly lower than the current one. The group claimed that even with the new work arrangements, the current standard was too high. Shirley Rice realized that she now had a more serious problem than before.

Questions for Discussion

1. Analyze Shirley Rice's leadership style throughout this case in terms of McGregor's Theory X–Theory Y and any other leadership models. (See Chapters 4 and 14 if you need to review these concepts.)
2. How could Shirley Rice have avoided the outcome of the group's decision by another approach or approaches?
3. Why did the group set a lower rather than a higher production standard?
4. Why does Rice have a more difficult problem of getting group acceptance than she did before?
5. What should Rice do? What alternatives are open to her?

Case 5–4

LUNCHES WITH THE SUPERVISOR

Beth Conners is a recent electrical engineering graduate of a major university. She went to work for Wilcox Engineering Company, and she was assigned to work on projects designing electrical systems for automated and computerized equipment.

Beth was enjoying her work and developing a rapport with other engineers in the firm. The department supervisor was Terry Wells. Terry had been with the firm about six years, and he had been a supervisor for two years. He was 30 years old; like Beth, he was single.

Beth had been with the firm about four months when Terry Wells called her into his office to review her progress. Terry told Beth that she was doing a great job, and he was very pleased with her work performance. He discussed a few suggestions that he felt would further her development technically. When he was finished, he looked at his watch and said, "Wow, it is already lunchtime. Would you like to join me?" Hesitating at first, Beth agreed to have lunch with him at a local restaurant. Terry paid the bill for both of them.

Early the next morning, Beth was working on a computer-aided drawing system when Terry came into her office to chat. He made a lot of small talk, and then he asked her whether she again would accompany him for lunch. A little uncomfortable, Beth again agreed. Beth thought that this second luncheon offer was unusual, but she passed it off, thinking that maybe she was being overly sensitive.

However, Beth grew very concerned during the next several weeks when the invitations for lunch continued. Furthermore, on several occasions Terry asked her for dates for which she made up excuses to decline. Beth felt that she couldn't refuse the luncheon invitations since Terry was her supervisor. But she didn't want to have any kind of off-the-job relationship with her supervisor, even though she did like him personally.

The situation became very stressful when several of her colleagues told her at a coffee break that she was earning the reputation of getting special treatment from their supervisor. One engineer even asked, "Are you and Terry having an affair?"

Beth became even more distressed when one day Terry came into her office and made the following remark: "Beth, I don't know why you won't let me take you out some evening. I know we hit it off well at lunch, and I know we both are attracted to each other." Beth told Terry that she would think it over and let him know later.

Beth realized that the situation with Terry was getting out of hand, and that she had to do something. She knew the company had a policy on sexual harassment, but she didn't know whether this situation applied. She was concerned that if she reported this matter in confidence to the human resources director or to someone in higher-level management, it might jeopardize her position in the company. She pondered what she should do.

Questions for Discussion

1. Is this a situation of sexual harassment? Why or why not?
2. Should Beth Conners refuse any further luncheon invitations from her supervisor? Should she continue to refuse to date him, even if she genuinely likes him as a person? Discuss.
3. What options are open to Beth Conners? What would you recommend that she do?

Case

5-5

RESENTMENT TOWARD THE BLACK SUPERVISOR

"What's the matter with you, coming down so hard on me about my work? Why don't you get off my back and deal with the white employees in this department who are getting away with murder? You're worse than having a white boss!" These words, uttered by Sarah Washington, one of his African-American subordinates, worried the department supervisor, Walter Rawlins. The thought that other minority employees might resent his supervisory management position had disturbed him ever since he took over the department. Although no one had called him an "Uncle Tom" to his face, Rawlins knew that some of the employees thought this of him.

Walter Rawlins had graduated from a small southern college. He received a special fellowship for minority students that enabled him to complete an MBA degree at a midwestern university. Upon receiving his MBA, he accepted a position with a major department store chain in its accounting services division. After a year and a half in several staff positions, he was promoted to supervisor of the customer accounts department. Some 24 employees were in this department. All were women except for two male computer programmers. Eight of the employees were minorities.

Since he became department supervisor about a year ago, the human resources department had received several complaints from African-American employees about Rawlins's tendency to set higher standards for black employees under his supervision than for white employees. These complaints were passed on to Rawlins by May Carlins, the director of human resources. Rawlins had responded that the charges were not valid. He told Carlins, "I let everyone set their own pace. Some employees are going to come out ahead of others. I reward the ones who come out in front. That's my job."

The manager of accounting services, Rollie Dinkins, believed that Rawlins treated all employees alike. Dinkins evaluated Rawlins's overall performance as very good, and he was of the opinion that one of his strengths was fairness in dealing with employees.

This most recent comment was not the only occasion on which certain employees had suggested to him that the black employees in the department felt that they did not receive the same treatment as whites. These previous comments had involved the grapevine rather than a direct verbal confrontation.

Sarah Washington had begun her employment in the customer accounts department at an entry-level clerical position. Over a period of five years, she advanced through a series of promotions to one of the highest-level clerical positions in the department. Her job was complex, involving the maintenance and adjustment of billing records. The billing system had undergone a major transition to a state-of-the-art computerized system. During this transition a number of intermediate systems had been in use. Sarah Washington was one of the few people in the department who understood the intermediate systems and methods of adjusting records that occurred under each. She occasionally would try to impress Rawlins with her knowledge of adjustments to the billing system by asking him questions for which she knew he would not have the answers. She once asked Rawlins in front of several employees, "How do you expect to know in a few months what it took me five years to learn?"

Washington was an extremely ambitious young woman. On several occasions she had complained to the human resources department about being passed over for promotion into a supervisory position. Rollie Dinkins had passed her over for promotion to supervisor, because he said that she lacked the tact and interpersonal skills needed in a supervisory position.

Walter Rawlins decided that the time had come for some response on his part, but he pondered what it should be. At least, he knew that he must be prepared to respond to Washington's next insinuation.

Questions for Discussion

1. Why is a problem of this nature extremely sensitive for all individuals involved?
2. To what degree, if any, should Rollie Dinkins become involved in this situation? Should the director of human resources become involved?
3. Should Walter Rawlins approach this problem as a disciplinary matter, a racial matter, a performance question, or a work-group situation? Discuss.
4. What would you recommend that Walter Rawlins do?

Case

5-6

SEXUAL HARASSMENT IN THE ACCOUNTING OFFICE

Charlie Gillespie is office manager of a group of accountants and accounting clerks in the corporate budget office of a large publishing company. He is known to be a "happy-go-lucky" supervisor, who finds it very difficult to confront inappropriate behavior or take disciplinary action. Charlie normally tries to avoid conflict by looking the other way, pretending that he didn't observe inappropriate conduct.

On a number of occasions, Gillespie had observed one of his accountants, Oliver Olson, making crude and suggestive comments to a group of female accounting clerks in the department. Although Gillespie did not like what he heard and observed, he thought that most of the employees understood Olson for what he was and did not take him seriously.

However, one day an accounting clerk named Julie Lowe came to Gillespie's office. She claimed that Olson's comments were a form of sexual harassment. Lowe stated that she understood the company had a policy prohibiting sexual harassment and that, even though Olson had not made any direct sexual overtures to any of the female employees, his vulgar language and crude questions no longer could be tolerated by the women in the office. Gillespie responded that Olson was just a "good old boy," and that the women should ignore him and the problem would take care of itself.

Several weeks later, Lowe resigned her position with the company without giving an explanation as to why she had resigned. One week after she left her job, the company received a notice that Julie Lowe had filed charges with the Equal Employment Opportunity Commission, claiming that she had been discriminated against because of her sex. In her complaint, she had stated that there was an "atmosphere of sexual harassment in the office"; that because of this continued harassment the "hostile work environment caused her severe tension and distress," which she no longer could tolerate and which forced her to end her employment with the company.

Gillespie had received a copy of Lowe's discrimination and harassment charges from Pamela Richter, the company's director of human resources. Richter requested that Charlie Gillespie come to her office to discuss what the company's response to these charges should be.

Questions for Discussion

1. When do crude and vulgar humor and language become sexual harassment? Discuss.
2. What should Charlie Gillespie have done when he first observed Oliver Olson engaging in the undesirable behavior?
3. What should Charlie Gillespie have done when Julie Lowe complained to him about Oliver Olson? Evaluate his counsel that Olson was a "good old boy" who should be ignored.
4. What would you recommend that the company's response to the EEOC charges of discrimination and sexual harassment should be? Discuss.

Case
5-7

A WOMAN'S PLACE

Joni Jones is a production engineer at a unionized manufacturing plant of Gateway Corporation. She does not have any employees reporting to her, but she does coordinate the efforts of the tool room with production. The toolmakers report to the maintenance department supervisor Merton Sweeney, but they follow work directives from other supervisors in the plant, including Joni Jones. Jones relies particularly upon two toolmakers to keep tooling repaired and ready for production. All twelve employees of the tool room are male and over the age of 40. Jones, on the other hand, is just out of engineering school, single, and with only a year's experience in tooling and production. Jones has adjusted to working in a male-dominated environment and feels comfortable and confident about being the only woman in this part of the plant operation. However, when hired, Jones was warned by her boss and plant manager, Alvin Glanz, that some of the men in the tool room would have a "hard time" working with and taking orders from a woman.

During her first year in this position, Joni Jones, on several occasions, heard one of the toolmakers who took work orders from her, Fred Barnes, make questionable comments about the role of women in society. Barnes was very vocal about where his wife stood in their household and where all women should be. Barnes was critical about career women who neglected their homes and families. Because Jones had to work directly with Barnes, she disregarded his comments and tried to maintain a cordial working environment with him and the other men.

However, one day Jones was meeting with Barnes to discuss a problem with a production tool. It was essential that this tool be repaired as soon as possible as it was needed in production. During the course of her discussion with Barnes, Jones became irritated with his seeming indifference and lack of urgency. She told him in a rather stern voice to "stop joking" and to begin working on the tool "in a serious manner." Some words were exchanged, and the discussion ended with Barnes stating that, "This just proves why women belong in the kitchen and the bedroom!" Although Jones had heard Barnes make this type of comment before, it previously had not been directed at her. Jones felt something had to be done, but what?

Questions for Discussion

1. Do the comments made by Fred Barnes constitute sexual harassment? Why, or why not? (Suggestion: Review the criteria in Chapter 16 for defining sexual harassment).
2. Does the fact that Barnes is a member of the union change the way the situation should be handled? Discuss.
3. What options are open to Joni Jones?
4. If you were Jones, what would you do, and why?

Case

5-8

REACTION TO A VOICE MAIL MESSAGE

Dwayne Davis, vice president of manufacturing and plant manager at Elcon Corporation's Lakeview facility, a 250-person appliance assembly plant, had always been well known for his employee-involvement approach to management. He regularly sent employees cards for their birthdays, anniversaries, and other special occasions and handwritten notes congratulating them upon their achievement of performance objectives. Davis was generally admired and respected by most employees, supervisors, and managers.

Four major departmental managers reported directly to Dwayne Davis. They headed production, materials management (which included supplier contact, purchasing, and receiving), customer contact and shipping, and maintenance. Three other support staff departmental managers also reported to Davis; these were engineering and design, accounting, and human resources. Twelve first-line supervisors reported to the departmental managers.

Davis strongly believed that it was important for the plant to maintain strength and flexibility of operations by having a well-trained supervisory team. Consequently, the Elcon plant had for some ten years implemented a two-year rotation schedule policy for all of its production, materials management, and maintenance supervisors. This meant that each supervisor was required to rotate either shift or supervisory positions every two years. This policy had been followed without exception, even though some supervisors had "grumbled" about its value and fairness.

Peter Hilsinger, the materials management department manager, had asked to see Dwayne Davis in his office to discuss something he indicated was a very serious matter. Hilsinger began his conversation with a recap of the week's events. Hilsinger said, "Dwayne, I think you should know that Darius Simmons, the supplier contact supervisor, has been a real pain in my side for the last three months or so. He's African American, and he's got a chip on his shoulder about this with most of us. Well, last Monday I told him that he was being rotated to second-shift production supervisor. He voiced his objections to this rotation, but I reminded him that he should have been rotated three weeks ago. This was my fault, because with the new requirements from TMM, I just overlooked the timetable for his rotation. He was supposed to start his new position this afternoon, but he did not come in. On top of that, he left a pointed message on my voice mail."

Hilsinger had made a tape recording and played the message for Davis to hear. It said: "Peter! I'm not going to put up with this discrimination. You'll be hearing from my lawyer! You are a (expletives deleted) white SOB!"

Hilsinger continued, "Can I fire him?"

Davis said, "Slow down, Peter. Is he talking about the rotation, or does this have something to do with his race and interracial marriage?"

Hilsinger responded, "I talked to some of my employees before I asked to talk with you. They said that Darius had walked in on a conversation between two line technicians on the floor last Thursday that included a racial joke, and that Darius insisted that they finish it. When they did, he responded, 'I don't mind dumb racial jokes, but don't ever talk about my wife or I'll break your legs.' They said he spent the rest of the day complaining to anyone who would listen that Elcon allows bigotry and racial hatred. I'm tired of his 'the world is against me' attitude. He's been particularly belligerent the past three weeks. I've tried to talk with him about it. His performance has suffered, but he won't talk about it. I suggested he talk with HR or visit our EAP counselor. But he just clammed up. Can I fire him?"

Dwayne Davis responded, "Frankly, before we do anything whatsoever, we'd better talk with Tamika Massie, our human resources manager. She's a black woman, and she may have a different perspective about this than we do."

Questions for Discussion

1. Evaluate why this situation has developed. Who, or what, is most to blame? Discuss.
2. What might be Darius Simmons' basis for a racial discrimination charge?
3. Should Simmons be disciplined, irrespective of the racial discrimination charges that may be forthcoming? Why, or why not?
4. If you were Dwayne Davis and/or Tamika Massie, what would you do, and why?

Case
5–9

OVERTIME DENIED TO THE OLDER PAINTER

Local No. 134 of the Maintenance Workers' Union represented carpenters, painters, mechanics, and other workers employed by the Board of Education of the Hampton City School District. The district operated eight school facilities located in the suburbs of a major city in the northeastern United States.

A meeting was held at a school district office to hear a grievance filed by the union on behalf of Bernie Custolo, a painter. Present at the hearing besides Custolo were the union shop steward, Arnie Meredith; Evan Beechman, supervisor of the maintenance department; and Esther Jansen, director of human resources for the district. Custolo's written grievance alleged a violation of two provisions of the collective bargaining agreement between the union and the Board of Education. These provisions were as follows:

ARTICLE II
DISCRIMINATION

Section 2.1 There shall be no discrimination, coercion, or intimidation of any kind against any employee of the board for any reason whatsoever, including marital status, sex, race, creed, color, religious belief, age, disability, or union activity, by the board or by the union.

ARTICLE V
HOURS OF WORK

Section 5.8 All overtime shall be distributed equally in so far as this is possible on an annual basis among eligible employees in the school district.

According to Bernie Custolo, he had been denied overtime since he turned 65 years of age six months ago. Other painters had been assigned overtime work as needed, but Custolo was told by his supervisor that he would not be assigned any overtime in the future. Custolo's specific grievance related to a Saturday work situation when two younger painters were assigned to work an entire day on an overtime basis. This was despite the fact that Custolo had worked far less overtime hours prior to this situation than had the two younger painters, both of whom had fewer years of service with the school district than Custolo. Custolo claimed that this was discrimination based solely on his age, and it was a violation of the parties' bargaining agreement that required overtime to be divided equally among employees.

However, Evan Beechman, Custolo's supervisor, said that Bernie Custolo simply was not able to work as efficiently as did his coworkers. Beechman claimed that Custolo was slower and made more mistakes than any other painter in his crew, and this problem had become more serious during the last several years. Beechman said that allowing Custolo to work overtime would be a burden to the school district since the district was under great pressure to hold costs down. Taxpayers should not be required to pay time-and-a-half premium pay to workers who were not efficient. Beechman said that Custolo no longer had the energy to work an eight-hour work shift as he frequently became fatigued during the day. During the previous several years, Custolo usually refused overtime that had been offered to him, claiming that he was "burnt out." Beechman stated that it was not fair to other workers to be expected to "carry" Custolo even though Custolo had more seniority. Beechman further claimed that Custolo often had talked about retirement when he turned 65, but apparently Custolo had changed his mind and now wanted to continue to work indefinitely. As to the specific Saturday in question, Beechman stated that the two painters he assigned were the best and most efficient he had for the project. The project could not have been completed on Saturday if Custolo had been permitted to work overtime on that day.

After about a half hour of discussion, Esther Jansen, director of human resources, stated: "Let's adjourn the meeting. I need to discuss the case with the District Superintendent. We will have a reply to the grievance tomorrow by 10 A.M." Arnie Meredith, the union shop steward, responded: "Okay, Esther. We feel that your answer should go our way, or we are likely to take this case all the way to arbitration. I might add that Bernie also is thinking about filing age discrimination charges with the government, so you better keep that in mind when you make your decision."

Questions for Discussion

1. Was the school district obligated to assign Bernie Custolo to overtime work on an equal basis with other employees if Custolo in fact was much slower and made more mistakes in his work performance? Why or why not?
2. Could Bernie Custolo file an age discrimination complaint under provisions of the Age Discrimination in Employment Act (ADEA) in addition to filing a union grievance? Why or why not?
3. What should be the school district's response to the union grievance?
4. Discuss what the school district should do in order to prevent future complaints of age discrimination.

Case

5-10

THE DEPRESSED DESIGNER

Welcome Home, a full-service interior design and home furnishing firm located in a midwestern city, had been received exceptionally well since Louise Adams and John Charles formed a partnership 10 years ago. Their enthusiasm and hard work resulted in cooperative endeavors with general contractors, such as assisting contractors in showcasing their homes to prospective buyers.

Adams and Charles had been able to attract some of the best and brightest graduates of interior design programs. The firm enjoyed a reputation for outstanding quality. Employees were called "associates" and were expected to perform at an exemplary level. During peak times, they might work 60 to 80 hours per week. Welcome Home's associates were paid a base salary that was enhanced by a pay-for-performance plan, including bonuses for achieving certain performance goals. Additionally, associates participated in an end-of-the-year profit-sharing program. Since showcase projects were team efforts, associates often worked together to explore ways to lower costs and increase profitability. At this time, about 20 full-time and 10 part-time persons were employed by the firm.

Cheryl Brown

During her freshman year in college, the car Cheryl Brown was driving had been involved in a traffic accident that took the life of her fiancé. She received numerous facial cuts, and her sternum was badly bruised. However, periodic depression didn't stop her from completing her undergraduate degree at Old Ivy College. Louise Adams, based on the strong recommendation of a college professor she respected, offered Brown a junior associate position at Welcome Home. John Charles and Louise Adams had debated about this hire. Charles was concerned about "problems" that Brown might carry to work, since her résumé indicated that she had dropped out of school for two years. During a pre-employment interview, Cheryl Brown volunteered information about the accident and her in-patient and out-patient psychiatric treatment during that time. Brown asserted that she was fully recovered, and she was quite able to fulfill Welcome Home's expectations of junior associates.

After four years with the firm, Cheryl Brown was notified that her very good performance made her a candidate for a senior associate position. Several of the project teams that she worked with had received high commendations for their work. Carefully and with patience, Adams and Charles developed a plan for assigning jobs of greater importance and increasing Brown's responsibilities and authority. Six months ago she was promoted to senior associate and given responsibility for the Eagle Peak showcase project.

Medical Leave and the Return Proposal

Three months after receiving that assignment, Cheryl Brown asked to be excused from the increased responsibility. Adams and Charles told her that the Eagle Peak showcase project—a major subdivision with six model homes ranging in price from $250,000 to $600,000 and surrounding a prestigious golf course—was of critical importance. To make a change at this time would create significant problems for Welcome Home since the showing was less than 60 days away. Brown stated that she wasn't feeling well and that, "All this pressure has me very depressed."

When she called in the next morning, Brown told the secretary that she was ill. Brown sought medical attention, and she ended up taking two months of medical leave. She notified Adams and Charles that she had suffered a mental breakdown brought on by stress. When Brown was ready to come back to work, she met with Adams and Charles. She told them that she still suffered from stress and depression, and she was taking medication. However, she believed she could do the job of a junior associate if the firm made some accommodations for her. One proposal she suggested was to limit her work to a maximum of six hours per day and to permit her to take an additional day off every time she had to work a showcase weekend. Brown also proposed being assigned to a different senior associate. She contended that her breakdown, in part, was caused by a senior associate who did not maintain a supportive atmosphere. Cheryl Brown also asked Adams and Charles to guarantee her a satisfactory performance appraisal. She felt that since she had previously received high evaluations, she didn't want the stigma of mental illness to negatively impact her performance review.

Subsequently, Adams and Charles had two outside doctors evaluate Cheryl Brown. Both confirmed that she had the conditions she had reported. The doctors recommended that Brown could return to work if the firm made accommodations for her to reduce the stress of employment.

Louise Adams and John Charles believed that if Welcome Home provided the accommodations that Cheryl Brown requested, the firm's quality image might suffer. Further, some of her associates might feel that Brown was receiving preferential treatment. At the same time, if they didn't try to work out something for Cheryl Brown, other associates and perhaps customers might accuse them of being callous and indifferent to her situation. Adams and Charles also were concerned about possible legal ramifications if they should refuse to grant Brown's requests.

Questions for Discussion

1. Evaluate and discuss each of the following statements:
   a. Cheryl Brown, a salaried employee, is not entitled to protection under the Americans with Disabilities Act (ADA).
   b. Cheryl Brown should be discharged since she is unable to fulfill the essential functions of her job.

c. Louise Adams and John Charles should take specific actions to respond to Cheryl Brown's requests and to avoid legal problems.

2. In view of your responses to the statements above, how should Adams and Charles respond to Cheryl Brown?

Case

5-11

DISCIPLINE? OR DISABILITY?

Yolanda Alvarez is an employee working on Pinnacle Electronics' semi-automated assembly line, which produced a variety of small-volume electronic circuit boards. Yolanda had developed a habit of leaving her assigned workstation to chat with other employees in other areas of the plant. Bill Barker, her supervisor, had warned her that it was against written company policy to leave assigned work areas when not on break, and that she must stay in her work area or get permission to leave. He further explained that even though she claimed to leave her area only when work was slow or the line was stopped, leaving her work area just to talk with other workers was not permitted since it would hurt overall plant productivity.

Earlier this month, Yolanda Alvarez was given a written warning by Bill Barker after she was seen talking with a friend at another line when she should have been at her own workstation. Last week, Yolanda was again seen talking to an employee from another product line in a location distant from her own departmental area. This time, as the company disciplinary guidelines stated, Yolanda was taken in for a conference with her supervisor and Roberta McGarvey, the human resources manager. Alvarez was then given a second written warning. Barker and McGarvey explained to Yolanda that the next disciplinary step could be suspension or termination.

This morning, after taking a day off as a personal day, Yolanda Alvarez returned to work and asked Bill Barker if she could talk with him and the human resources manager. When Yolanda entered the human resources manager's office, she handed her an envelope. Inside was a letter from Yolanda's doctor stating that Yolanda had been diagnosed with attention deficit disorder syndrome (ADD), and this was logically the reason why she occasionally wandered away from her work area to talk with others. The doctor suggested that Yolanda should be allowed to do this from time to time. Further, because Yolanda's behavior was caused by her medical condition, the doctor stated that, in his opinion, disciplining her for her conduct was unwarranted and probably unlawful.

After Yolanda Alvarez had left, Bill Barker commented to Roberta McGarvey that he didn't think it would be appropriate to allow Yolanda to wander around the plant, because this was clearly a violation of a written policy. Further, he felt that other employees would be resentful if Yolanda would be given special privileges to roam as she pleased.

Questions for Discussion

1. Was Yolanda Alvarez protected under the Americans with Disabilities Act (ADA) as a disabled individual? Why or why not?
2. Was the doctor's suggestion and opinion to Pinnacle Electronics a reasonable one? Why or why not?
3. Should Barker and the human resources manager attempt to accommodate Yolanda's condition? If so, how?
4. Will special accommodation for Yolanda Alvarez mean that consistent treatment for other employees no longer is possible? Discuss.
5. (*Optional*) Special court cases have helped to define and expand upon the Americans with Disabilities Act. Using the Internet, find at least two cases, and write a report to explain their significance for helping Bill Barker and the human resources manager to define Yolanda's rights and the company's obligations under ADA, and what they might do in this situation.

INTERNET ACTIVITY

Case

5-12

AFFIRMATIVE ACTION OR REVERSE DISCRIMINATION?

Thompson Machine Company is a job shop that makes cylinders. It is a relatively small company with approximately 300 employees. Over 60 percent of its business comes from federal government contracts. The company was recently audited by the U.S. Department of Labor concerning affirmative action provisions required of federal government contractors. The Department of Labor informed Thompson Company that failures to meet previously established targets for employment and promotion of minorities and women could result in the loss of its contracts.

At about the same time, the setup worker in the lathe shop retired and a replacement was needed. This was the highest-paid job in the shop. Company policy was to promote from within when possible. Fred Saunders, the lathe department supervisor, believed that there were only two candidates to consider. These were Glenn Arbor, a 25-year employee with 16 years on lathes, and Jessica Stanley, a lathe operator with 7 years' experience. Saunders believed that the person with the most job knowledge, experience, and seniority should be selected. Although Saunders felt that Jessica Stanley had sufficient job knowledge and experience, Glenn Arbor had considerably more and he was the most senior employee by far. Therefore, Saunders thought this was an easy decision, and he contacted Brenda Moore in human resources to give her his recommendation.

After reviewing the situation, Brenda Moore felt that Fred Saunders hadn't considered the Department of Labor pressures. She called Saunders to her office for a meeting. Moore told Saunders about the affirmative action requirements, and she told him that top-level management had decided that Jessica Stanley should be awarded the position since she was an African-American woman. Moore explained that she knew it was a difficult situation, but she felt that Jessica Stanley was qualified for the position and a failure to promote Stanley could potentially result in major loss of business.

Fred Saunders informed Glenn Arbor and Jessica Stanley of the decision, and he then gathered the department together for the formal announcement. The news didn't sit well with most of the employees and particularly with Glenn Arbor. Arbor went to see Brenda Moore in human resources. He asserted that the only reason that he didn't get the position was because he was a white male. He said this was obvious reverse discrimination. Further, he said that if Thompson Machine Company had been unionized, the union wouldn't allow this because he had far more qualifications and seniority. Brenda Moore tried to explain the situation, but Glenn Arbor was still upset when he left her office.

Glenn Arbor continued working at Thompson, but with considerable resentment. The problem wasn't so much what he said and did; it was more what he didn't say and didn't do. He refused to assist Jessica Stanley whenever she asked for help, even to the point of allowing her to make errors that could have been avoided with his help. His negative attitude began to spread throughout the department. Jessica Stanley was finding it difficult to get the cooperation she needed from other employees for the efficient operation of the department. She brought the problem to Fred Saunders's attention. When Saunders told her it was her problem to solve, Jessica Stanley became angry. She told Saunders that it was his problem; if he didn't resolve it, she would resign and file sex and race discrimination charges against the Thompson firm.

Fred Saunders pondered what he should do next.

Questions for Discussion

1. Was management's decision to promote Jessica Stanley reverse discrimination, or was it a prudent economic decision made to preserve its business? Discuss.
2. Evaluate Glenn Arbor's assertion that this would not have occurred if a labor union represented the employees.
3. What should Fred Saunders do?
4. What should top-level management do?

Case

5-13

THE PROBLEM EMPLOYEE

Phyllis Walker, human resources manager at Marsh Electric Company, looked through her in-basket for a memo Steve Coster had mentioned briefly to her that morning. Steve, the contracts manager, was a relatively new, inexperienced supervisor, who had only been with the office for a few months. Happy that Steve had asked for guidance on how to handle what he had referred to as a touchy situation, Phyllis located the memo and read it immediately.

TO: Phyllis Walker, HR Manager
FROM: Steve Coster, Contracts Manager
SUBJECT: Stephanie Barkwell—Problem Employee

We've got a problem, Phyllis, and I need some advice on how to handle it. One of my department secretaries, Stephanie Barkwell, is beginning to act up. For the last couple of months she has been late to work almost a third of the time, and she regularly takes 45 minutes or more for lunch when the allotted time is only half an hour. Her frequent absences are disrupting office efficiency. Her 13-year-old boy is her usual excuse.

However, there are some recent unfavorable rumors that I've heard circulating through the department. I'm a bit uncomfortable mentioning them to you, although I have a gut feeling they might be true. The Tuesday before last, Stephanie called me at home around 9:30 at night, and she told me that she had some personal business to take care of and probably wouldn't be in the following day. She wasn't; nor did she show up at the office on Wednesday or Thursday. Friday she called and said she was too emotional to function at work, but she would be in on Monday.

On Monday she told me that her son was having trouble with the police. However, the rumor mill has it that Stephanie herself was arrested and held on drug charges. I've not discussed the issue with her; I would like your input first.

As a single parent, perhaps she has to deal with problems you and I don't face. However, we have a job to do here at Marsh, and people depend on Stephanie for secretarial support. When at work, Stephanie is very productive and pleasant to work with. Her prior work record apparently has been excellent. We're already shorthanded, and her recent absences and tardiness are now affecting the overall performance of my department. I've tried to be tolerant, but it is becoming a continuing problem. I've been getting complaints from her co-workers.

Let's sit down and talk about this soon, before I approach Stephanie. Please call me when you have had a chance to review her file, and we'll figure out the best way to handle this situation.

"Steve was not kidding," thought Phyllis as she completed her review of Stephanie's file. "It's a shame that this firm doesn't have an employee assistance program; in this case it might have been just the ticket."

Phyllis pondered the situation and wondered what the best course of action would be.

Questions for Discussion

1. If you were Phyllis Walker, what advice would you offer Steve Coster about how to proceed?
2. If Steve Coster determined that Stephanie Barkwell had a drug problem or some other type of serious personal problem, would the company be obligated to offer some form of personal assistance to her? Why or why not?
3. Once Steve Coster is fully aware of Stephanie's situation, how much information should he share with her coworkers?

4. Would you try to retain Stephanie Barkwell as an employee? Would it make a difference if the police are involved in this situation?
5. If you decided to keep her at this time, what steps would you take to ensure that her work performance improved?

Part 6

Controlling

Chapter 18

Learning Objectives

After studying this chapter, you will be able to:

1
Describe the nature and importance of the managerial controlling function.

2
Identify three types of control mechanisms based on time.

3
Explain the essential characteristics of effective controls.

4
Describe the essential steps in the control process.

5
Discuss the supervisor's role in controlling through budgets.

6
Discuss the supervisor's role in maintaining cost consciousness and in responding to higher-level managers' orders to reduce costs.

7
Identify additional control areas and explain how the controlling function is closely related to the other managerial functions.

Fundamentals of Controlling

You Make the Call!

You are Gil Pietro, accounting department supervisor for a manufacturing plant that employs approximately 600 people. Reporting to you are two accountants and four data entry clerks. All of your staff except one accountant are women. They work in an office area that is separate from other departments. Your department is involved in virtually all aspects of internal and external accounting responsibilities, although some work has been outsourced to local consulting firms.

Several new software packages had been successfully implemented within your department in the past. A new streamlined software system for processing accounts payable and receivable was a new project given top priority. It was so important that you decided to develop and carry out the project yourself. Your boss (the controller) specified a deadline date for completion, which was very tight. In developing the software package, you met with the data processing manager, the controller, and outside consultant representatives whom you hired to write the software package. Your staff, who will be the primary users, were only told recently about the project, the implementation date, and scheduled training sessions.

This morning (a day after the second training session), several members of your staff walked into your office quite upset. They claimed that the proposed implementation date was "totally unrealistic" and could not be met due to "serious flaws" in the new software package. They asserted that the new package would create more work than the old system, would be confusing to some customers, and would require much extra time that simply was not available with existing staff. Ellen Bond, a data entry clerk and one of the group, summed up their feelings by stating, "All of this could have been avoided if we had been part of the project planning right from the start!"

The group has just left your office, and you are rather distressed by this meeting. The scheduled implementation date is two weeks away, only one training session remains, and it would be impossible to rewrite the package in time. As Gil Pietro, how should you respond to your staff? What should you do to rectify the situation you are in? How could this type of issue be avoided in the future?

You Make the Call!

THE SUPERVISOR'S ROLE IN CONTROLLING

1

Describe the nature and importance of the managerial controlling function.

Although the word *control* often elicits negative reactions, control is a normal part of daily life. At home, at work, and in the community everyone is affected by a variety of controls, such as alarm clocks, thermostats, fuel and electronic gauges, traffic lights, and police officers directing traffic. Controls also play an important role in all organizations. Controls assure that results match what was planned. Every manager—from the chief executive down to the supervisor—must develop and apply controls that regulate the organization's activities to achieve the desired results.

Controlling

Ensuring that actual performance is in line with intended performance and taking corrective action, if necessary.

The managerial **controlling** function consists of checking to determine whether operations are adhering to established plans, ascertaining whether proper progress is being made toward objectives, and taking appropriate actions where necessary to correct any deviations from established plans. In other words, the supervisor takes action to make things happen the way they were planned. Controlling is essential whenever a supervisor assigns duties to employees because the supervisor remains responsible for assigned work. If all plans set in motion proceeded according to design without interference, there would be no need for the controlling function. As every supervisor knows, this is not the case in real life. Thus, it is part of the supervisor's job to keep activities in line and, where necessary, to get them back on track. This is done by controlling.[1]

Nature of the Controlling Function

Controlling is one of the five primary managerial functions. It is so closely related to the others that a line of demarcation between controlling and the other functions is not always clear. However, the controlling function is most closely related to the planning function. In planning, the supervisor sets objectives, and these objectives become standards against which performance is appraised. If there are deviations between performance and standards, the supervisor must carry out the controlling function by taking corrective action, which may involve establishing new plans and different standards.

Since controlling is the last managerial function discussed in this book, it might be perceived as something that the supervisor performs after all other functions have been executed. This might lead to the impression that controlling is concerned only with events after they have happened. It is true that the need for controlling is evident after a mistake has been made. However, it is much better to view controlling as a function that goes on simultaneously with the other managerial functions. As we discuss later in this chapter, there are control mechanisms that are utilized before, during, and after an activity.

Employee Responses to Controls

Employees often view controls negatively because the amount of control that exists within their department may determine how much freedom of action they have in performing their jobs. Yet most employees understand that a certain amount of control is essential to regulate performance. They know that without controls, confusion, inefficiency, and even chaos would result.

In a behavioral sense, controls and on-the-job freedom seem to conflict. However, when controls are well designed and properly implemented, they can be a positive influence on employee motivation and behavior. The supervisor should design and apply control systems that employees not only will accept without resentment, but also will be effective in monitoring performance in the department. Interestingly, some firms at times have loosened certain controls and given employees more freedom, only to be disappointed by the outcome and then have to either tighten up or go back to the original controls that had been discarded. This chapter's "Contemporary Issue" box illustrates this type of problem in regard to relaxation of workplace dress codes.

Controlling Should Be Forward Looking

There is nothing a supervisor can do about the past. For example, if work assigned to an employee for the day has not been accomplished, controlling cannot correct the day's results. Yet some supervisors believe that the main purpose of controlling is to blame someone who is responsible for mistakes. This attitude is not sound since supervisors primarily should look forward rather than backward. Of course, supervisors should study the past to learn what and why something happened and then take steps so that future activities will not lead to the same mistakes.

contemporary issue

Incivility May Mean Dress Codes Are Back in Style

Casual and informal dress in the workplace certainly has grown dramatically in recent decades. Based upon a belief that today's employees prefer more casual lifestyles and less formality, many companies have relaxed their dress and appearance codes, believing that this will contribute to morale and productivity. It is estimated that approximately half of the office workers in the United States are permitted to dress casually every business day, and 90 percent are permitted to wear casual clothes at work at least part of the time.[1]

However, excesses in casual dress appearance have led companies to reassess their policies and codes because many firms have become disturbed by seemingly "anything goes" attitudes by some employees. Attire such as halter tops, miniskirts, T-shirts with offensive slogans, provocative blue jeans, open-toed flat shoes, etc., are among the types of questionable attire that have shown up in many business offices. Anne Pasley-Stuart, president of a human resources consulting firm that advises corporate clients, stated, "As we dress more casual, our demeanor gets more casual, and work gets less professional." Similarly, Beverley O'Conner, office manager for Korn-Ferry International, one of the nation's largest executive search firms, stated, "We found that casual dress fostered a casual attitude. We found that instead of dressing as though it were a weekend night out, some people were dressing like it was a trip to the grocery store." Korn-Ferry has decided that its experiment in casual dress was

a failure, and the firm has reversed its code to return to more formal corporate attire and hopefully more professional on-the-job behavior.[2]

Further, there is some evidence that excessive office informality has been linked to growing problems of rudeness and aggressive behavior in the workplace. This has been described by some management researchers as fostering a "spiral of incivility." Professor Christine Pearson of the University of North Carolina, who has studied workplace violence, states, "You can start to lose control. The lack of formality that is implicit in the attire or in the organization may imply a lack of formality in terms of respect to each other, and in the general way we treat each other."[3]

Many firms are now trying to communicate and spell out specific guidelines to employees concerning what is acceptable and what is not acceptable. Sears Roebuck and Company recently installed two mannequins in its cafeteria, one modeling "appropriate" dress, the other "inappropriate." Federated Department Stores, the parent of Bloomingdale's and Macy's, issued a memo warning employees at its Cincinnati headquarters that "jeans, sweatshirts, and athletic caps are never appropriate."[4]

Most observers expect that casual work clothing and informality in appearance will remain as a benefit for many employees in the workplace. However, it would appear from a major survey of employers conducted by the Bureau of National Affairs that at many firms there will be periodic revisions of stated policies and rules governing workplace dress standards in order to more clearly specify management's expectations of what is acceptable.[5]

Sources: (1) Lauren R. Rublin, "Time to Go Short?" *Barron's* (August 17, 1998), pp. 25–28. (2) "Dress Codes Are Making a Comeback," *The Associated Press* as published in the *St. Louis Post Dispatch* (August 23, 1999), p. BP14. (3) Mary Kane, "Casual Workplaces Get a Dressing Down," *Newhouse News Service* as published in the *St. Louis Post-Dispatch* (October 20, 1999), pp. E1 and E4. (4) Wendy Bounds, Rebecca Quick, and Emily Nelson, "In the Office, It's Anything Goes," *The Wall Street Journal* (August 26, 1999), pp. B1 and B4. (5) Bill Leonard, "Survey Finds Most Employers Maintain Written Dress Policies," *HRMagazine* (March 1998), p. 12.

Since supervisors should be forward looking while controlling, it is essential that they discover any deviations from established standards as quickly as possible. Setting up controls within a process or within an activity's established time frame—rather than at its end—will enable the supervisor to take prompt corrective action. For example, instead of waiting until the day is over, the supervisor could check at midday to see whether a job is progressing satisfactorily. Even though the morning is past and nothing can change what has already happened, there may be time to correct a problem before the damage becomes excessive.

Controlling and Closeness of Supervision

Supervisors need to know how closely to monitor employees' work. The closeness of supervisory follow-up is based on such factors as an employee's experience, initiative, dependability, and resourcefulness. Permitting an employee to work on an assignment without close supervision is both a challenge and a test of a supervisor's ability to delegate. This does not mean that the supervisor should leave the employee completely alone until it is time to inspect the final results. It does mean that the supervisor should avoid watching every detail of every employee's work. By becoming familiar with each employee's abilities, the supervisor can develop a sensitivity as to how much leeway to give and how closely to follow up and control.

2

Identify three types of control mechanisms based on time.

TIME FACTOR CONTROL MECHANISMS

Before we discuss the steps of the controlling process, it is important to distinguish among three types of control mechanisms. These are classified according to time as (a) feedforward (or preliminary, preventive, anticipatory) controls, (b) concurrent (or in-process) controls, and (c) feedback (or after-the-process) controls.

Feedforward (Preliminary, Preventive, Anticipatory) Controls

Feedforward control

Anticipatory action taken to ensure that problems do not occur.

Since controlling has forward-looking aspects, the purpose of a **feedforward control** is to anticipate and prevent potential sources of deviation from standards by considering in advance the possibility of any malfunction or undesirable outcomes. A preventive maintenance program, designed so that equipment will not break down at the height of production, is an example of a feedforward control. The produce clerk who checks samples of bananas to ensure their acceptability is another example. The clerk selects a sample from the crates before the crates are unloaded and the merchandise is placed on display. Requiring assemblers to ascertain the quality of components prior to installation and to signify that they have done so is becoming increasingly commonplace. Other examples of feedforward controls include devices such as safety posters; fire drills; disciplinary rules; checklists to follow before starting up certain equipment; and the policies, procedures, and methods drawn up by managers when planning operations. Everyone uses feedforward control at one time or another. For example, a person who checks the tires, oil, and gas gauge before beginning a trip is using feedforward control.

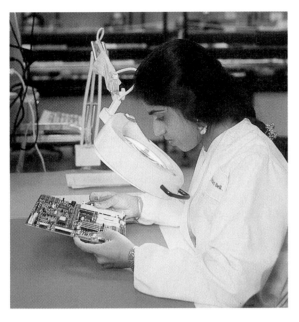

A worker at the Packard Bell factory inspects a motherboard for a computer for any deviations from company standards.

Concurrent control

Corrective action taken during the production or delivery process to ensure that standards are being met.

Feedback control

Actions taken after the activity, product, or service has been completed.

Concurrent (In-Process) Controls

A control that is applied while operations are going on and that spots problems as they occur is called a **concurrent control.** The traveler who notices that the fuel gauge is below half full or that the fuel warning light has just come on and pulls into the next gas station for a fill-up is using concurrent control. Examples of concurrent control mechanisms are on-line computer systems, numerical counters, automatic switches, gauges, and warning signals. To illustrate, suppose a retail store optically scans customers' purchases. The customer gets a printout of what was purchased and the price paid (the sales receipt). At the same time, the store's count of the number of items in inventory is automatically decreased by the number just sold. The store's computer records the items sold and stores the information. The computer has been programmed either to alert the purchasing supervisor or to automatically place a purchase order when the store's inventory reaches a specified level. Thus, the stock is replenished as needed and the store does not risk running out. Where these types of aids are not in place, supervisors monitor activities by observation, often with the assistance of departmental employees.

Even though feedforward controls have been set up, concurrent controls are still necessary to catch problems that feedforward controls were not able to anticipate. Consider the situation of the traveler who filled the fuel tank prior to the trip and estimated, based on past experience, that she should be able to travel the 300 miles to her destination without having to refuel. Unexpectedly, the weather turns unseasonably warm and the traveler experiences a lengthy delay due to a highway accident. For the convenience of the passengers, the traveler allows the car to run with the air conditioner on while they are tied up in traffic. The expected six-hour trip takes longer due to the delay, and the unexpected need for the air conditioner increases fuel consumption. Unless the traveler periodically checks the fuel gauge or is alerted by the low fuel warning light (concurrent controls), she will run out of fuel before she reaches her destination.

Feedback (After-the-Process) Controls

The purpose of a **feedback control** is to evaluate and, if necessary, correct the results of a process or operation when it is finished and to determine ways to prevent future deviations from standard. The traveler who calculates average miles per gallon and uses that feedback when planning the budget for the next trip is using feedback control. Other examples of feedback controls include measurements of the quality and quantity of units produced, various kinds of statistical information, accounting reports, and visual inspections. Since these controls are applied after a task, process, service, or product is finished, they are the least desirable control mechanisms if damage or mistakes have occurred. If no damage or mistakes took place, feedback controls are used as a basis for further improvement of the process or the finished product. Feedback controls are probably the most widely used category of controls at the supervisory level. Too often, however, they are used primarily to determine what went wrong and where to place blame rather than to prevent recurrence of the problem in the future.

CHARACTERISTICS OF EFFECTIVE CONTROLS

3
Explain the essential characteristics of effective controls.

For control mechanisms to work effectively, they should be understandable, timely, suitable and economical, indicational, and flexible. These characteristics are required of the controls used in all supervisory jobs—in manufacturing, retailing, office work, health care, government service, banks, and other services. Because there is such a diversity of activities in different departments, these characteristics will be discussed only in a general way here. Supervisors have to tailor control mechanisms to the particular activities, circumstances, and needs of their departments.

Understandable

All control mechanisms—feedforward, concurrent, and feedback—must be understood by the managers, supervisors, and employees who are to use them. At higher management levels, control mechanisms may be rather sophisticated and based on management information systems, mathematical formulas, complex charts and graphs, and detailed reports. At the top levels, such controls should be understandable to all of the managers who utilize them. However, controls should be much less complicated at the departmental level. For example, a supervisor might use a brief, one-page report as a control device. In a dry cleaning store, this report might show the number of different types of clothes cleaned and the number of employee hours worked on a given day. It is uncomplicated, straightforward, and understandable. If the control mechanisms in use are confusing or too sophisticated for the employees, the supervisor should devise new control systems that will meet departmental needs and be understandable to everyone who uses them.

Timely

Control mechanisms should indicate deviations from standard without delay, and such deviations should be reported to the supervisor promptly even if they are substantiated only by approximate figures, preliminary estimates, or partial information. It is better for the supervisor to know when things are about to go wrong than to learn that they already are out of control. The sooner a supervisor is aware of deviations, the more quickly the deviations can be corrected.

For example, assume that a project which requires the installation of equipment must be completed within a tight schedule. The supervisor should have regular reports (e.g., daily or weekly) showing where the project stands at that time and how this progress compares to the schedule. Potential roadblocks (e.g., missing parts or absences from work) that might delay the completion of the project should be included in these reports. The supervisor needs this type of information early in order to take corrective steps before the situation gets out of hand. This does not mean that the supervisor should jump to conclusions and resort to drastic action hastily. Generally, the supervisor's experience and familiarity with the job will be helpful in sensing when a job is not progressing the way it should.

Suitable and Economical

Controls must be suitable for the activity to be observed. A complex information system control approach that is necessary for a large corporation would not be applicable in a small department. The need for control exists in the small department, but the magnitude of the control system will be different. Whatever controls the supervisor applies need to be suitable and economical for the job involved. There is no need to control a minor assignment as elaborately as a manager would control a major capital investment project.

For example, the head nurse in a hospital will usually control the supply of narcotics with greater care and frequency than the number of bandages on hand. Or, in a small company with three clerical employees, it would be inappropriate and uneconomical to have someone assigned full time to check their work for clerical mistakes. It is better to make each employee responsible for checking his or her own work or, possibly, to make employees responsible for checking each other's work. However, in a large department involving the work of several hundred employees who are mass producing a small-unit product, it makes considerable sense to employ full-time inspectors or quality control specialists to check the results. Typically, this is done on a sampling basis since it is impossible to check every item that goes through the production process.[2] There are many in-between situations in which supervisors must use good judgment as to the suitability of the controls utilized.

Controls also must be economical; that is, they must be worth their expense, even though it may be difficult to determine how much a control system costs and how much it is worth. In such a situation, it is advisable to consider the consequences that could result if controls were not in place. For example, think of the value of an elaborate, expensive control system in a company producing pharmaceuticals as compared to an enterprise manufacturing rubber bands. Defective rubber bands would be an inconvenience, but defective drugs could kill people! The risks for the pharmaceutical company make elaborate controls worth the expense.

Indicational

It is not enough for controls just to expose deviations as they occur. A control mechanism should also indicate who is responsible for the deviation and where the deviation occurred. If several subassemblies or successive operations are involved in a work process, it may be necessary for the supervisor to check performance after each step has been accomplished and before the work moves on to the next workstation. Otherwise, if end results are not up to standards, the supervisor may not know where to take corrective action.

Flexible

Since work operations occur in a dynamic setting, unforeseen circumstances can play havoc with even the best-laid plans and systems. Therefore, controls should be flexible enough to cope with unanticipated changing patterns and problems. Control mechanisms must permit changes when such changes are required. For example, if an employee encounters significant changes in conditions early in a work assignment—such as an equipment failure or a shortage of materials—the supervisor must recognize this and adjust the plans and standards accordingly. If these difficulties are due to conditions beyond the employee's control, the supervisor also must adjust the criteria by which the employee's performance will be appraised.

Describe the essential steps in the control process.

STEPS IN THE CONTROL PROCESS

The control process involves three sequential steps. The first step (which usually is part of the planning function) begins with the setting of appropriate standards for what should be accomplished. Next, actual performance must be measured against these standards. If performance does not meet the standards, the third step is to take corrective action. These three steps must be followed in the sequence presented if controlling is to achieve the desired results (see Figure 18-1).

FIGURE 18-1

Steps in the control process.

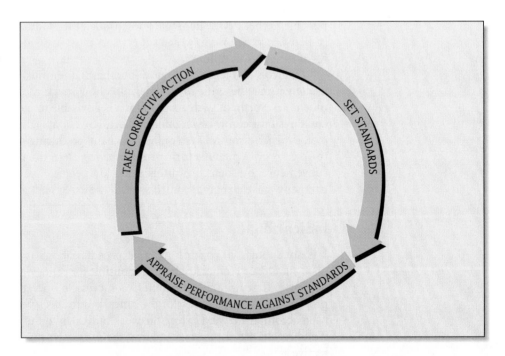

Setting Standards

Standards

Units of measurement or specific criteria against which to evaluate results.

Standards may be defined as units of measurement or specific criteria against which to judge performance or results. **Standards** indicate the targets that should be achieved; they are criteria against which performance will be compared for exercising control. Standards must be set before any meaningful evaluations can be made about a person's work, a finished product, or a service. In Chapter 6 we described the establishment of goals and objectives as foundations of planning. Objectives give specific targets for employees to aim for. However, just having specific targets does not mean they will be attained. The effective supervisor needs to follow up to ensure that the actions that are supposed to be taken are being taken and that the objectives are being achieved.

Tangible standards

Standards for performance results that are identifiable and measurable.

Intangible standards

Standards for performance results that are difficult to measure and often relate to human characteristics (e.g., attitude, morale, satisfaction, etc.).

Many types of standards can be established, depending on the areas of performance or results that need to be measured. **Tangible standards** are performance targets for results that are identifiable and measurable. For example, tangible standards can be set to measure such things as quantity of output, quality of output, market share, labor costs, overhead expenses, time spent in producing a unit or providing the service, and the like. (Tangible standards included on employee appraisal rating forms were identified in Chapter 13.) **Intangible standards** are targets for results that have no physical form; they may cover such areas as an organization's reputation, employee morale, and the quality of humane, loving care of patients in a health care center or nursing home. It is usually more difficult to establish intangible standards in numerical or precise terms.

The most frequent tangible standards that supervisors determine (or must follow) pertain to the operations of their departments. For example, in a production department, standards can be set for the number of units to be produced; the labor hours per unit; and the quality of the product in terms of durability, finish, and closeness of dimensions.[3] In a sales department, standards might be set for the number of customers contacted, the sales dollars realized, and the number and types of customer complaints.

In setting standards, a supervisor can be guided by experience and knowledge of the jobs to be performed. Through experience and observation, most supervisors have a general idea of how much time it takes to perform certain jobs, the different resources required, and what constitutes good or poor quality. By study and analysis of previous budgets, past production, and other departmental records, supervisors should be able to develop workable standards of performance for most aspects of their departments' operations.

Motion study

An analysis of work activities to determine how to make the job easier and quicker to do.

Motion and Time Studies.   A more thorough and systematic way to establish standards for the amount of work employees should accomplish within a given time frame is to apply work measurement techniques—preferably performed by, or with the assistance of, industrial engineers.[4] The most prominent techniques are motion and time studies. A **motion study** is an analysis of how a job currently is performed with a view to improving, eliminating, changing, or combining steps to make the job easier and quicker to perform. After a thorough study of the work motions and layout, the industrial engineer or analyst develops what he or she considers to be the best current method for doing this job.

Time study

A technique for analyzing jobs to determine time standards for performing each job.

Once the best current method has been designed, a **time study** is performed to determine a time standard for the job. This is accomplished in a systematic and largely quantitative manner by selecting certain employees for observation; observing the times used to accomplish various parts of the job; applying correction factors; and making allowances for fatigue, personal needs, and unavoidable delays. When all these factors are combined properly, the result is a time standard for performing the job.

Although this approach attempts to be objective, considerable judgment and approximations are part of the established time standard. A time standard is neither wholly scientific nor beyond dispute, but it does provide a sound basis on which a supervisor can set realistic standards.[5] Standards developed by motion and time studies can help the supervisor distribute work more evenly and judge each employee's performance fairly. Such standards also assist the supervisor in predicting the number of employees required and the probable cost of a job to be done.

Most supervisors work in organizations without industrial engineers. When a new job is to be performed in the department, the supervisor can set tentative standards based on similar operations in this or other departments. When no comparison standard is readily available, the supervisor should identify the key tasks necessary to accomplish the job and then directly observe the employees or ask them to record the time required to complete the tasks. From these data a reasonable standard can be calculated.

To illustrate, suppose a shift supervisor in a fast-food restaurant needs to determine how long it takes employees to prepare a new menu item. The supervisor lists all the steps necessary to complete the job. Then the supervisor can perform the task under several different circumstances and record the required time. The supervisor can also select several employees to perform the task under a variety of conditions. From among the several observations, the supervisor can determine the average time required to complete the task. Not only will realistic standards be established, but such an approach might also uncover better ways of doing the job.

There are, of course, numerous approaches for the measurement of workers' productivity that reflect the unique nature of a department's operations and the products or services involved. Some worker productivity standards may be expressed in relationship to overall sales volume, profitability, and other aggregate figures over which a supervisor has only limited or no control.[6]

Employee Participation.   Some employees resent standards, especially those arrived at through motion and time studies. This resentment is part of a longstanding fear that so-called "efficiency experts" and supervisors use motion and time studies primarily to speed up the workers' output. However, the main purpose for setting performance standards should be to create realistic targets—that is, objectives that can be achieved and that are considered fair by both the supervisor and the employees. Workers are more apt to accept standards as reasonable and fair if they have played an active role in the formulation of those standards.

One technique for having employees participate in establishing standards is to form a committee of workers to assist the supervisor and/or industrial engineer in carrying out a work measurement program. The employees selected for this committee should be those who, in the supervisor's judgment, consistently do a fair day's work.

In addition, the supervisor and industrial engineer should explain to all employees what is involved in motion and time studies, including areas in which judgment is involved. Employees should be given opportunities to challenge any standard that they consider to be unfair, perhaps even to have a job restudied and retimed if necessary. Most workers will accept performance standards if they feel that the supervisor has tried to help them understand the basis for the standards and has been willing to reconsider and adjust standards that appear to be unreasonable. A prominent example of employee participation in the workplace has been the Saturn plant of General Motors in Spring Hill, Tennessee. Not only are employees and their union (the United Automobile Workers) involved in setting productivity standards, they also participate in decisions regarding budgeting, pricing, product design, marketing, and sourcing. Among the major accomplishments attributed to this "workplace democracy" climate has been the plant's capability to reduce production line model changeover time from a number of weeks to essentially no lost time whatsoever.[7]

Strategic Control Points. The number of standards needed to determine the quantity and quality of performance may become larger as the department expands. As operations become more complex and as functions of a department increase, it becomes time consuming and impractical for the supervisor to constantly check against every conceivable standard. Therefore, the supervisor should concentrate on certain strategic control points against which overall performance can be monitored. **Strategic control points,** or **strategic standards,** consist of a limited number of key indicators that give the supervisor a good sampling of overall performance. There are no specific rules on how to select strategic control points. Because the nature of the department and the makeup of the supervisor and employees are different in each situation, only general guidelines can be suggested.

A major consideration in choosing one standard as being more strategic than another is its timeliness. Time is essential in control; therefore, the sooner a deviation can be discovered, the better it can be corrected. A supervisor needs to recognize at what critical step operations should be checked during a given process. For example, a strategic control point might be established when a subassembly operation is finished but before the product is put together with other parts and spray painted. A similar approach can be applied in the process of dry cleaning a soiled dress for a customer. A strategic control point is established shortly after the stain remover is applied. Imagine the costs incurred if all other operations had been completed and the stain was still present.

A supervisor should be careful that the selection of a strategic control point does not have a significant adverse effect on another important standard. For example, excessive control to increase the quantity of production might have an adverse effect on the quality of the product.[8] Likewise, if labor expenses are selected as a strategic control point, supervisors might try to hold down wage expenses by not hiring enough workers, causing both quality and quantity standards to deteriorate. To illustrate, a laundry department supervisor in a nursing home must not sacrifice the high standards set to prevent infections simply to achieve a goal of reducing the cost of laundering linen to a certain price per pound. Thus, decisions about strategic control points depend to some

---

Strategic control points (strategic standards)

Performance criteria chosen for assessment because they are key indicators of overall performance.

extent on the nature of the work performed. What serves well as a strategic control point in one department will not necessarily apply in another.

Another example of applying the concept of strategic control points is the supervisor who wishes to assess the quality of departmental employee relations. The supervisor might decide to use the following indicators as strategic control standards:

- Number of employees' voluntary resignations and requests for transfer.
- Levels of absenteeism, tardiness, and turnover.
- Accident frequency and severity rates.
- Number and types of employee grievances and complaints.
- Number and types of customer complaints.
- Amount of scrap and rejects, and unexplained losses of materials and inventory.

By closely watching trends and changes in these indicators, the supervisor should be able to spot problems requiring corrective action. If the trend of most or all of these selected indicators is unfavorable, major supervisory attention is needed.

Consider the example of a wire manufacturer that used simple statistics to track the productivity of machine operators. It was noted that during the preceding hour, scrap exceeded the acceptable standard by 10 percent. Using strategic control points in a timely fashion, the supervisor working with the operators and the maintenance department knew it was time to check the production process. A check of the diamond dies, pressure settings, and quality of the raw stock led to action so that scrap rates did not increase further and could be returned to their previous lower levels. Strategic control points should be established so that corrective action can be taken early in the production process.[9]

As mentioned previously, there are also areas of an intangible nature that should be monitored closely, even though it is difficult to set precise standards for them. For example, the state of employee morale is typically an important element of departmental operations that a supervisor may decide to appraise and assess as a strategic control standard. This particularly is important in an era where workplace anger and discontent among employees is reportedly widespread, and the potential for this erupting into violence is a real concern.[10] Techniques for measurement and evaluation of employee morale were discussed extensively in Chapter 15.

Checking Performance Against Standards

The second major step in the control process is to check actual performance against established standards. This is an ongoing activity for every supervisor. The primary ways for a supervisor to do this are by observing, studying oral and written reports, making spot checks, and using statistical sampling techniques. Figure 18-2 takes a lighthearted look at tracking performance.

Personal Observation. For monitoring employee performance, there is no substitute for direct observation and personal contact by a supervisor. The opportunity for inspection and close personal observation of employee performance is an advantage the supervisor has over top-level managers. This is because the farther removed a manager

FIGURE 18-2

After developing performance standards, the supervisor must be alert for any deviations from these standards.

is from where the employees actually carry out the organization's work, the more the manager will have to depend on reports from others. The supervisor, however, has ample opportunity for direct observation all day long.

When supervisors find deviations from expected standards, they should assume a questioning attitude but not necessarily a fault-finding one. It is possible that the problem is due to something outside of the employees' control, such as a malfunctioning machine or faulty raw materials. Supervisors should raise questions about mistakes in a positive, helpful manner. For example, instead of just criticizing what happened, a supervisor first should ask what caused the problem and whether there is any way in which he or she can help the employees do their jobs more easily, safely, or efficiently. Supervisors also should elicit suggestions from employees concerning what should be done to correct existing problems. When standards are stated primarily in general terms, supervisors should look for specific unsatisfactory conditions, such as inadequate output, poor quality work, or unsafe practices. It is not enough just to tell employees that their work is "unacceptable" or "not satisfactory." If the supervisor can point to specific instances or cite actual recent examples, the employee is more likely to acknowledge the deficiencies that must be corrected.

Also, supervisors can use personal observation and questioning to turn up causes of poor performance that are not the employees' fault, such as inadequate training, problems with work-flow design, or an unusual increase in workload. For example, if a retail store supervisor discovers that customers are not being processed through the cashier quickly enough, the reason may be that an unusually large number of customers

A supervisor watches an employee operate a laser machine and uses personal observation to assess her performance.

Exception principle
Concept that supervisors should concentrate their investigations on activities that deviate substantially from the standard.

entered the store at one time. Instead of chastising employees, the proper corrective action may be to open up another checkout lane. Also, the supervisor may need to find a better way to predict customer traffic or hire a backup cashier. The supervisor may include alternative ways of doing the job in future plans. Employees may have valuable ideas on how to prevent the problem from recurring.

Checking employee performance through personal observation does have limitations. It is time consuming, and it may require the supervisor to spend hours away from his or her desk. Also, it may not be possible to observe some important activities at critical times. There always will be some employees who perform well while being observed, but who revert to poorer, less diligent habits when the supervisor is not around. Nevertheless, personal observation still is the most widely used and probably the best method of checking employee performance at the supervisory level.

Oral and Written Reports. If a department is large, operates in different locations, or works around the clock, oral and written reports are necessary. For example, if a department operates around the clock and its supervisor has the overall responsibility for more than one shift, the supervisor must depend on reports submitted by employees to appraise the performance of shifts that occur when the supervisor is not present. When a department operates multiple shifts and different supervisors are in charge on different shifts, each supervisor should arrive early to get a firsthand report from the supervisor who is completing the previous shift.

Whenever reports are required, the supervisor should insist that they be clear, complete but concise, and correct. If possible, written reports should be submitted along with an oral presentation. Reports are more effective when they are substantiated with statistical or comparative data.

Most employees submit reasonably accurate reports even when they contain unfavorable outcomes. Report accuracy depends a great deal on the supervisor's reaction to reports and his or her existing relations with employees. If the supervisor handles adverse reports in a constructive and helpful manner, appreciating honesty instead of just giving demerits, employees will be encouraged to submit accurate reports even if the reports show them in an unfavorable light.

In checking reports, supervisors usually find that many activities have been performed according to standards and can be passed over quickly. As a result, many supervisors use the **exception principle** by concentrating on those areas in which performance is significantly above or below standard. Supervisors may even ask employees to forego reporting on activities that have for the most part attained the established standards and to report only on activities that are exceptionally below or above standard. If performance is significantly below standard, the supervisor will have to move to the third stage of the control process, taking corrective action. If performance is significantly above standard, the supervisor should praise the employees and study how such exceptional performance was achieved to determine whether what was done can be repeated in the future.

Spot Checks. If the employees' work routine does not lend itself to reports, the supervisor may have to rely on periodic spot checks. For example, a data systems supervisor who is responsible for a centralized computer department that works around the clock six days a week should occasionally come to work at varying times to see what goes on in the department during the different shifts. Supervisors who have little or no opportunity to perform spot checks usually have to depend on reports.

Sampling Techniques. Sampling techniques are really supplements to strategic control points and spot checks. In some firms, each part or product is inspected to determine whether it meets the prescribed standards. Inspecting every item is a time-consuming and costly process. While a detailed discussion is beyond the scope of this book, it is becoming increasingly crucial for supervisors, particularly in production facilities, to acquaint themselves with *statistical quality control (SQC)*. SQC is a method to help supervisors determine not only which products, product components, or services to inspect, but also how many of each to inspect.[11] **Sampling** is the process of inspecting some predetermined number of products from a batch to determine whether the batch is acceptable or unacceptable. To illustrate, suppose that a store manager has been concerned with the quality of produce received from a distributor. The store manager and the produce manager use SQC to determine how many of an incoming shipment should be inspected. Rather than inspecting the entire lot of produce, they compare random samples against a predetermined acceptable quality standard. If a certain number of the samples do not meet the standard, then they reject the entire lot. Note that if the distributor used this technique prior to shipping the produce, it would be feedback control. The same process used by the store manager would be feedforward control. While SQC saves time and money in inspection costs, the supervisor must ensure that the units inspected accurately represent the quality of all the units.

Sampling

The technique of evaluating some number of items from a larger group to determine whether the group meets acceptable quality standards.

Taking Corrective Action

When no deviations from established standards occur, the process of control is fulfilled by the first two steps—setting standards and checking actual performance against the standards. But if discrepancies or deviations have been noted through personal observation, reports, or spot checks, then the supervisor must take the third step of taking corrective action to bring performance back into line.

Prior to taking specific corrective action, the supervisor should bear in mind that there are various reasons why discrepancies or deviations from standards can occur in any job. Among these are the following:

1. The standards could not be achieved because they were based on faulty forecasts or assumptions or because an unforeseen problem arose that distorted the anticipated results.

2. Failure already occurred in some other job (or activity) that preceded the job in question.
3. The employee who performed the job either was unqualified or was not given adequate directions or instructions.
4. The employee who performed the job was negligent or did not follow required directions or procedures.

Therefore, before taking corrective action, the supervisor should analyze the facts of the situation to determine the specific causes for the deviation. Only after identifying the specific causes can the supervisor decide what remedial actions are necessary to obtain better results in the future. For example, if the reason for the deviation lies in the standards themselves, the supervisor must revise the standards accordingly. If the employee who performed the job was not qualified, additional training and closer supervision might be the answer. Or if the employee was not given the proper instructions, then the supervisor should accept the blame and improve upon techniques for giving directives. In the case of sheer negligence or insubordination on the part of the employee, corrective action may consist of a discussion with the employee or a verbal or written reprimand. At times, more serious forms of disciplinary action may have to be taken, including suspending or replacing the employee. Under such circumstances, the disciplinary procedures to be discussed in Chapter 19 should be followed.

<table>
<tr><td>

5

Discuss the supervisor's role in controlling through budgets.

</td></tr>
</table>

Budget

A financial plan that projects expected revenues and expenditures during a stated period of time.

Operating budget

The projection of dollar allocations to various costs and expenses needed to run the business, based on expected revenue.

BUDGETARY CONTROL

Among the tools for financial control, the budget usually is the one with which supervisors have the most frequent contact. A **budget** is a written plan expressed in numerical terms that projects anticipated resources and expenditures for a period of time, such as a month, a quarter, six months, or a year. Firms usually prepare a variety of budgets. Supervisors are most familiar with the operating budget. The **operating budget** is the projection of dollar amounts of various costs and expenses needed to run the business, given projected revenues. Operating budgets, which may be developed for every departmental unit, usually show how much is allocated for spending on inventory, salaries, supplies, travel, rent, utilities, advertising, and other expenses.

At times it is convenient to express budgets in terms other than dollars. Budgets pertaining to employment requirements, for example, may be expressed in numbers of employee-hours allocated for certain activities or numbers of workers needed for each job classification. Eventually, however, the various nonfinancial budgets are converted into monetary figures—an operating budget. This statement summarizes the organization's overall activities and serves as a foundation upon which managers can plan and control the use of financial and other resources.[12]

All managers, from the chief executive officer down to the supervisors, must learn how to plan budgets, live within their limitations, and use them for control purposes. The term *budgetary control* refers to the use of budgets by supervisors, accountants, and higher-level managers to control operations so that they will comply with the standards established by the organization in making the budgets.

Supervisory Participation in Budget Making

Budget making falls under the managerial function of planning, but carrying out the budget—or living within the budget—is part of the controlling function. As is true in so many other areas of management, the planning and controlling aspects of the budgeting process are quite interrelated. Preparing a budget, whether it is expressed in monetary or other terms, requires the budget maker to quantify estimates about the future by attaching numerical values to each budgeted item. The numerical figures in the final overall budget become the desired financial standards of the organization. Similarly, the numerical figures in the final departmental budgets become the standards to be met by each department and departmental supervisors.

Incremental budgeting

A technique for making revenue and expense projections based on previous history.

Zero-base budgeting

The process of assessing all activities to justify their existence on a benefit and cost basis.

Most annual budgets are projections for the following year based on the previous year's budget. This approach for making a budget is known as **incremental budgeting.** Another approach, which has gained some acceptance in recent years, is zero-base budgeting. If an organization practices **zero-base budgeting,** all budgets must begin "from scratch," and each budget item must be justified and substantiated. In zero-base budgeting, the previous budget does not constitute a valid basis for a budget being prepared for a future period. The advantage of zero-base budgeting, sometimes called *zero-base review,* is that all ongoing programs, activities, projects, products, and the like are reassessed by management in terms of their benefits and costs to the organization. This avoids the tendency of simply continuing expenditures from a previous budget period without much consideration. The disadvantage of zero-base budgeting is that it involves a large amount of paperwork and is very time consuming. Moreover, in actual practice it is difficult to apply the concept to some departments and types of operations.[13]

The budget that most concerns supervisors is usually the departmental expense budget, which covers the variety of expenditures to be incurred in the department. In the discussion that follows, we will presume that a firm uses incremental budgeting practices. To many supervisors, budgets have a negative connotation of arbitrariness, inflexibility, conflicts, and problems. If the budget is perceived in this manner, it will tend to breed resentment. To facilitate acceptance, expense budgets should be prepared with the participation and cooperation of those responsible for executing them. Preferably, supervisors should have an opportunity to participate in making their own departmental budgets. When they are allowed to do this, supervisors must be familiar with both general and detailed aspects of budget preparation. Even when a budget is just handed down to supervisors by higher-level management, supervisors must still understand the budget and the reasoning behind each budget figure.

To participate successfully in budget making, supervisors have to demonstrate the actual need for each amount they request and document their requests with historical data wherever possible. The final budget frequently will contain lower figures than those first submitted. A supervisor should not consider this as a personal rejection, because other supervisors also are making budget requests and having them cut. It is rarely possible for higher-level management to grant everyone's requests. Much will depend on how realistic the supervisors have been and how well their budget needs are documented or substantiated. Supervisors can only hope that the final budget will be close to what they requested and will give them sufficient resources to operate their departments efficiently.

Supervising Within the Budget

Supervisors must manage their departments within budget limits and refer to their budgets to monitor their expenditures during the operating period. When a budget is approved by higher-level management, the supervisor is allocated specific amounts for each item in the budget. Expenditures in the supervisor's department must be charged against various budget accounts. At regular intervals (e.g., weekly), the supervisor must review the budgeted figures and compare them with the actual expenses incurred. This comparison is usually reported to the supervisor by the accounting department. Many, if not most, firms utilize computer-based cost and financial control systems. Income and cost projections and reports are produced in the form of computer printouts, which may be prepared and distributed by the information systems department.

If the actual expenditures for a specific item greatly exceed the budgeted amount, the supervisor must find out what happened. Investigation could reveal a logical explanation for the discrepancy. For example, if the amount spent on labor in a manufacturing department exceeded the budgeted amount, this could be due to an unanticipated demand for the firm's product which required working overtime. If the excessive deviation from the budgeted amount cannot be justified, the supervisor must take whatever actions are necessary to bring the out-of-control expenditures back to where they should be, at least from that point on. Excessive deviations usually have to be explained by the supervisor to higher-level managers or the accounting department. To avoid this unpleasant task, a supervisor is well advised to make regular comparisons of actual expenditures with budgeted amounts and to keep expenses close to the budget.

Hopefully, a supervisor's budget will not be so detailed and rigidly applied that it becomes a burden. A budget should allow the supervisor some freedom to accomplish departmental objectives with a reasonable degree of latitude. Flexibility does not mean that the supervisor can change budget figures unilaterally or take them lightly. Rather, it means that the supervisor should not be led to believe that budget figures are carved in stone (see Figure 18-3). Budgets are guides for management decisions, not substitutes for good judgment.

To prevent a budget from becoming a straitjacket, most organizations provide for regular budget reviews by supervisors together with higher-level managers or the accounting department. These reviews should take place about every three months—or at least every six months—to ensure a proper degree of flexibility. If operating conditions have changed appreciably since the budget was established, or if there are valid indications that the budget cannot be followed in the future, a revision is in order. For example, unexpected price increases or major fluctuations in the general economic climate might be reasons for revising the budget. Usually there is enough flexibility built into a budget to permit common-sense departures to accomplish the objectives of the department and the total organization.

FIGURE 18-3

Budget flexibility means that the budget figures are not "carved in stone."

COST CONTROL AND THE SUPERVISOR

Discuss the supervisor's role in maintaining cost consciousness and in responding to higher-level managers' orders to reduce costs.

Competition from domestic companies and from abroad and the changing economic environment require most organizations to strive continuously to control their costs. Sooner or later most supervisors become involved in some way with cost control because higher-level managers expect them to control costs at the department level to help meet organizational cost goals. Thus, cost consciousness should be an ongoing concern of supervisors. Sporadic efforts to curtail costs, crash programs, and economy drives seldom have lasting benefits. Although many large organizations employ consultants trained in work efficiency and cost control, in the final analysis it remains the supervisor's duty to look at cost consciousness as a permanent part of the managerial job.

Sharing Information and Responsibility with Employees

While there have been many lists of companies that practice management excellence, author Robert Levering, from an examination of 20 top U.S. firms, concluded that managers can turn a bad workplace into a good one by granting employees more responsibility for their jobs. According to Levering, this means "establishing a partnership with employees rather than acting as adversaries."[14] In forging a partnership with its employees, a firm should be willing to share financial information with them. However, it is not enough for a firm just to share financial information with employees. Employees must have an understanding of what the financial data mean and have a basis for comparing their firm's current financial information with that of previous years and competitors.

An example of one such firm is Springfield Remanufacturing Company, a privately held engine rebuilder in Springfield, Missouri, that shares all of its financial information with employees. For many years, employees have been provided with weekly information on all aspects of the business, from revenue and purchasing costs to labor and management expenses. Every employee learns to understand the information; that part of their job is to move those numbers in the right directions; and how their day-to-day decisions and actions impact revenues, costs, and the bottom line.[15]

By having relevant financial data known to them, employees may act more conscientiously when making decisions that have cost consequences. Similarly, giving employees more responsibility to make choices about certain expenditures can also promote a sense of cost awareness that otherwise might not occur. For example, some firms are utilizing rather simplified approaches for controlling business expenses that rely upon the prudence and integrity of their personnel. Numerous firms are now using electronic on-line systems for travel expense filing that enable quick reimbursement payments to the employees rather than having long extended delays in processing and checking on expense vouchers.[16] Other firms are using per diem allowances for business meals which enable the employees to know in advance the expenditure limits that they can apply when travelling or entertaining business clients.[17]

Maintaining Cost Awareness

Because cost consciousness is of ongoing concern to the supervisor, plans should be made for achieving cost awareness throughout the department. Here is where planning and controlling again become closely interrelated. By setting objectives and defining specific results to be achieved within a certain time frame, cost priorities can be set.

In setting cost objectives, the supervisor should involve the employees who are in positions that will be most affected. Employees often can make valuable contributions. The supervisor should fully communicate cost-reducing objectives to employees and get as much input from them as possible. The more employees contribute to a cost-control program, the more committed they will be to meeting objectives. It may also be advisable to point out to employees that eventually everyone benefits from continuous cost awareness. Supervisors should help employees see cost containment as part of their jobs and as being in their own long-term interest. Firms that do not control costs cannot remain competitive, which could mean loss of jobs. Most employees will try to do the right thing and seek to reduce waste and costs if their supervisors approach them in a positive way.

Responding to a Cost-Cutting Order

Reducing costs is a natural concern of most organizations, and it is frequently brought on by competition. It is likely that within an enterprise, at one time or another, an order will come from top-level managers to cut all costs across the board by a certain per-

The more employees contribute to a cost-control program, the more committed they will be to meeting objectives.

centage. At first glance, such a blanket order could be considered fair and just; however, this may not be so since it could affect some supervisors much more severely than others. Some supervisors are constantly aware of costs and operate their departments efficiently, while others are lax and perhaps even wasteful. How should a supervisor react to such a blanket order?

There are some supervisors who will read the order to mean that everything possible should be done immediately to bring about the desired percentage of cost reduction. They might hold "pep rallies" with employees or, at the other extreme, engage in harsh criticism of employees and others. Some supervisors might stop buying supplies, leading eventually to work delays. Others might eliminate preventive maintenance work even though this eventually could lead to equipment breakdowns and interruptions of the work flow. Although these actions might bring about some cost reductions, they could be more expensive in the long run.

Other supervisors will merely follow the cost-cutting directive halfheartedly. They will make minimal efforts here and there to give the appearance that they are doing something about costs. Such efforts are not likely to impress the employees, who in turn will also make only a halfhearted effort. This type of supervisory response will not contribute adequately to a cost-control program.

An across-the-board cost-reduction order may present a hardship to the diligent, cost-conscious supervisor whose department is working efficiently. Nevertheless, this supervisor will strive to take some action by looking again at areas where there is still room to reduce expenses. This supervisor will call for suggestions from employees because they are the ones who can bring about results. For example, there may be some paperwork that can be postponed indefinitely. Or there may be certain operations that are not absolutely necessary even if they are performed efficiently. The supervisor should point out to the employees which are the most expensive operations and let them know what these actually cost. An employee might suggest a less expensive way of doing a job; if so, the supervisor should welcome the suggestion. The supervisor should be committed to the cost-reduction campaign and should set a good personal example whenever possible. Although it may be difficult to come up with large savings, at least the supervisor will have made a diligent effort to support the organization's cost-cutting drive. While supervisors play a key role in cost reduction, they cannot succeed without employee involvement and commitment.

Elimination of things that cost money is one way to save money. Effective supervisors are constantly on the lookout for ways to eliminate excess costs by questioning the necessity of everything that is done in their department.

Even if an organization does not have a formal suggestion program, supervisors can establish a climate of mutual trust and respect that encourages suggestions from their employees. The supervisor can use formal and informal encouragement during departmental meetings to emphasize the value of making suggestions. For example, if an employee or group of employees complains about a particular policy or practice, the supervisor might turn the complaint into a challenge for their thinking by saying, "You may be right. Why don't you do something about it? Perhaps we need a change. Think of a better way, and we'll take it to top management. Any credit for the idea will be yours." Whether for changing policies or controlling costs, employee suggestions can be a valuable source of ideas. Employees like to see their ideas put into effect and are more committed to goals they helped to set.

OTHER CONTROL AREAS

7

Identify additional control areas and explain how the controlling function is closely related to the other managerial functions.

In addition to accounting and budgetary controls, other areas of management control exist in many organizations. Typically, these control areas are supervised by specialized departments and are outside the realm of most supervisors' direct authority and responsibility. Nevertheless, supervisors should be aware of these control areas, and, if necessary, should familiarize themselves with the methods employed by the specialists who perform these control activities. Often such specialists are attached to the organization in staff positions.

Specialized Controls

Inventory control is concerned with keeping watch over raw materials, supplies, work in process, finished goods, and the like. Maintaining sufficient but not excessive inventory on hand, keeping status records of all inventory, ordering economic lot sizes, and many other problems connected with inventory policy are part of inventory control.[18]

Quality control consists of maintaining the quality standards set by a firm for its products or services. These must be continually monitored and improved to make certain that quality is maintained. As discussed earlier in this chapter, quality control of products is often accomplished by testing randomly selected samples to determine whether or not quality standards are being met. A commitment to *total quality man-*

agement, or TQM, as discussed in Chapter 6, means an overall effort to respond to customer needs by preventing defects/errors, correcting them when they occur, and continuously building better overall quality into goods and services as dictated by marketplace and other conditions.[19]

Production control usually consists of a number of activities to maintain overall operations on schedule. It involves routing of operations, scheduling, and, if necessary, expediting of the work flow. Elaborate charts and network analyses may be utilized. For example, the production control department may start with a Gantt chart, which is a diagram or pictorial representation of the progress and status of various jobs in production. If practical, this can lead to a computerized network analysis. Two of the most widely used analyses, PERT (program evaluation review technique) and CPM (critical path method), were discussed in Chapter 6.[20]

Controlling and the Other Managerial Functions

Throughout this book, we have discussed numerous aspects of effective managerial controls from different perspectives. At this point we will review several of them as they relate to the controlling function.

In Chapters 4 and 6, we discussed the system of MBO (management by objectives) in connection with motivation and planning. The MBO process involves setting objectives and standards, evaluating results, following up, and revising previous objectives if necessary. Evaluation of results, follow-up, and establishment of new objectives are elements of control.

Also in Chapter 4, we discussed the role of leadership and the importance of the acceptance theory of leadership. In general, this means that employees willingly accept and support the objectives and directions of management in guiding the organization. Often this is accomplished by programs and systems that involve employees in every phase of planning how best to meet customer needs. Employees are urged to search for new ways to help customers, and employees are furnished timely information concerning their performance accomplishments and any problems that require correction.[21] Such approaches, which are sometimes referred to as "commitment to excellence" programs, are consistent with the principles of control discussed in this chapter and with the principles of motivation discussed in Chapter 4.

In Chapter 6, we discussed standing (repeat-use) plans, such as policies, procedures, methods, and rules, primarily in regard to managerial planning. However, when standing plans are not working or are not followed, the supervisor must take the necessary corrective actions to bring the department's operations back in line. Thus, these types of standing plans may be seen as forward-looking control devices.

Performance appraisal, which we discussed under the staffing function in Chapter 13, also has a place as a control mechanism. During a performance appraisal meeting, the supervisor evaluates an employee's performance against predetermined objectives and standards. At the same time, the supervisor and the employee may agree on steps for corrective action, as well as on new objectives and standards. The element of supervisory control can be detected throughout a performance appraisal cycle. In Chapter 19, we will discuss employee discipline as part of the controlling function. If a supervisor takes disciplinary measures when established rules are not followed by employees, such measures serve as control techniques.

These managerial activities show how intrinsically related the controlling function is to all the other managerial functions. As stated previously, controlling typically is performed simultaneously with the other managerial functions. The better the supervisor plans, organizes, staffs, and leads, the better will be his or her ability to control the activities and employees in the department. Thus, controlling takes a forward-looking view, even though it has been discussed as the "final" managerial function in this book.

What Call Did You Make?

As Gil Pietro, you should not become angry or defensive in responding to your staff, but thoughtfully weigh their comments. One option is to call a staff meeting to discuss the situation. In preparation for the meeting, you should investigate the allegations of program flaws and increased workload. The meeting should be a discussional type meeting (see Chapter 10) during which you explain the reasoning behind the implementation decision, and then give your staff ample opportunities to express and discuss their objections about the new software. After this meeting and perhaps after further discussing the issues, decisions will need to be made. If the flaws and increased workload due to the software seem real, you could try to persuade your boss and upper management to delay the implementation date until the software is ready. If, however, you decide to go forward with the implementation plan for the new software, such a decision should be reported to management so that they know the implications and adjustments that may be required, such as approved overtime. If you believe that your staff's allegations are unfounded and are based on their resistance to change, you must try to reduce this resistance. As discussed in Chapter 14, this means to try to persuade them that it is a sound decision, and then involve your staff in decisions on how to proceed with the implementation. Without staff involvement and some support, the project may be doomed to failure, or at best be replete with problems and inefficiencies.

As for the future, learn from this experience and vow never to repeat its mistakes. Be sure to involve your staff in all of the planning phases of any project that will have a major impact upon their work situations. Then, as discussed in this chapter, there will be far less likelihood that such projects will be out of control and require major adjustments. The best form of *control* usually is a good *plan* in which all affected parties have participated and for which they are committed to its success.

SUMMARY

Controlling is the managerial function that determines whether or not plans are being followed and performance conforms to standards. Every manager must develop and apply controls that monitor the organization's activities to achieve the desired results. The controlling function is most closely related to the planning function. Supervisors set objectives and, in turn, these objectives become standards against which performance is checked. Well-designed controls can be a positive influence on employee motivation. Control should be forward looking since nothing can be done about the past. The closeness of supervisory control depends, in part, on the employees' experience, initiative, dependability, and resourcefulness.

Control mechanisms can be categorized as feedforward, concurrent, and feedback based on when they are implemented in the process. Feedforward, or preliminary, controls are used to anticipate and prevent undesirable outcomes. The person who checks the tires, oil, gas gauge, and the like before beginning a trip is using feedforward control. The traveler who notices that the fuel gauge is below half full or that the fuel warning light has just come on and pulls into the next gas station for a fill-up is using concurrent control. Feedback controls are employed after the fact—they are used as a basis for correction and further improvement. The traveler who calculates average miles per gallon and uses that information when planning the budget for the next trip is using feedback control. Generally, effective supervisors rely on all three types of control mechanisms to improve the process or prevent recurrence of a problem in the future.

To be effective, controls should be understandable to everyone who uses them and yield timely information so that problems can be corrected before the situation gets out of hand. Also, controls should be suitable and economical for the situation. The more serious the consequences of mistakes, the tighter the controls should be, despite the expense. Finally, controls should indicate where the trouble lies in the process and be flexible enough to adjust to changing conditions.

In performing the controlling function, a supervisor should follow three basic steps: setting standards, checking actual performance against standards, and taking corrective action if necessary. Standards may be set for both tangible and intangible areas. A supervisor's own experience and knowledge can serve to develop certain performance standards. More precise work standards can be accomplished through motion and time studies and the use of workflow charts. Employee participation in setting standards is crucial to their acceptance. Many supervisors focus their control efforts on selected strategic control points (or strategic standards) that provide major indicators of performance.

The supervisor should check performance against the established standards. In some instances, the supervisor has to depend on reports, but in most cases personal observation and inspection are appropriate for checking employee performance. At times, the supervisor may apply the exception principle, which means concentrating on areas where performance is significantly below or above the expected standards. Sampling can be used to help the supervisor determine whether or not products meet prescribed standards. When discrepancies from standards are revealed, the supervisor must take the necessary corrective actions to bring the performance back in line and to prevent future deviations.

The most widely used financial control device is the budget. The preparation of a budget is primarily a planning function. However, applying, supervising, and living within the budget are part of the controlling function. Supervisors should have an opportunity to participate in preparing budgets for their departments, regardless of whether the enterprise practices traditional or zero-base budgeting. Virtually all budgets need some built-in flexibility to allow for adjustments when necessary. When significant deviations from the budget occur, the supervisor must investigate and take whatever actions are appropriate to bring expenditures back in line.

Cost control and cost consciousness should be a continuing concern of all supervisors. When top-level managers issue cost-cutting orders, supervisors should avoid taking extreme measures that may in the long run be more costly than the reductions themselves.

7

Involving employees in cost-reduction efforts is one way that the effective supervisor can create cost awareness. Suggestion programs can be used to solicit ideas for potential areas of cost reduction. The supervisor should constantly be on the lookout for ways to eliminate excess costs. Periodically, the supervisor should look at the department "through the eyes of a stranger" and question the necessity of everything that is done in the department.

Many organizations have specialists who concentrate on inventory control, quality control, and production control. These types of control systems usually are not under the direct authority of most departmental supervisors but are handled by staff specialists. Other managerial concepts, techniques, and approaches used by departmental supervisors contain aspects of the controlling function. Among these are MBO, use of standing plans, maintenance of discipline, and employee performance appraisal. Thus, controlling is intimately interrelated with all the other managerial functions.

KEY TERMS

Controlling (page 619)
Feedforward control (page 622)
Concurrent control (page 623)
Feedback control (page 623)
Standards (page 627)
Tangible standards (page 627)
Intangible standards (page 627)
Motion study (page 627)
Time study (page 628)

Strategic control points
   (strategic standards) (page 629)
Exception principle (page 632)
Sampling (page 633)
Budget (page 634)
Operating budget (page 634)
Incremental budgeting (page 635)
Zero-base budgeting (page 635)

QUESTIONS FOR DISCUSSION

1. Define the managerial controlling function and discuss its relationship to the other managerial functions.
2. Why do many people view controls negatively?
3. If control should be forward looking, does this mean that looking backward is improper in the controlling process? Discuss.
4. Define and give examples of each of the following:
   a. feedforward controls
   b. concurrent controls
   c. feedback controls
5. In your experience, how bad is the problem of absenteeism in U.S. firms? How can the exception principle be used by supervisors to control it?
6. Define and discuss each of the primary steps in the control process:
   a. setting standards
   b. checking actual performance against standards
   c. taking corrective action
7. Why can a budget be described as a "projected financial statement"? What is meant by zero-base budgeting? How realistic is this approach in today's operating environment?
8. To what degree should supervisors be permitted to participate in the budget-making process? Discuss.

9. Discuss the supervisor's duty to take appropriate action when accounting reports indicate that actual expenditures are significantly above or below budget allocations?

10. Why should cost consciousness be of major concern to a supervisor? How should effective supervisors develop cost-reduction strategies?

SKILLS APPLICATIONS

Skills Application 18-1: Analysis of Examination Results

Think about your most recent test in the context of Figure 18-1. The test gave you a chance to appraise your performance.

1. What standards of performance did you set for yourself in the course?
2. Did the test results reflect your knowledge? Why or why not?
3. Look over the learning objectives (standards) listed in the textbook or presented by your professor. Did the test adequately cover the standards? Why or why not?
4. What corrective action might be indicated by the test results?

Skills Application 18-2: Effective Controls and Cost-Cutting at the College Level

Since your days as an undergraduate student at Old Ivy College, college tuition has increased dramatically. You have just been elected to membership on the college's board of governors. A recent threatened boycott of classes drew wide media coverage of the students' continuing concerns over the increasing costs of higher education and declining quality of instruction.

1. Your assignment is to determine whether or not the students' allegations are valid. What information would you need to collect? Where would you get the information?
2. If a review of the data indicated that costs have increased substantially, how would you design a cost-consciousness program that would instill in members of the academic community the need to control costs?
3. Assume that the college needs to reduce costs by 10 percent over the next two years. You are asked to advise the president on areas where costs can be reduced. What would be your recommendations?
4. Compare your responses with those of another student. What are the areas of similarity? Differences? Why?
5. Summarize, in 40 words or less, what you learned from this skill application.
6. (*Optional*) Design a control system to deal with the problem of escalating tuition costs.
   a. List the steps you would take to complete the assignment.
   b. What one thing should you do to ensure that your completed project is acceptable?
   c. Compare your responses with those of another student. Is there a single recommendation (feedback) that the two of you could make to the president? If so, what would it be?

Summarize, in 25 words or less, what you learned from this skill application.

Skills Application 18-3: Burger Control

You have been hired as a management efficiency consultant to advise the owner of Sycamore Hamburger and Shake Palace. At certain times during the day there are varying backlogs in the burger prep area. As a result, the flow of work slows down, waste increases, and customers complain about the wait or that their orders are not evenly warmed. Your assignment is to design a control system to deal with the problem.

1. List the steps you would take to complete the assignment. (Suggestion: If possible, visit a fast-food restaurant that features hamburgers, etc., and talk with a supervisor there for his/her ideas and suggestions.)
2. What recommendations would you make for Sycamore?
3. Compare your recommendations with those of another student. Is there a single recommendation that the two of you could make to Sycamore? If so, what would it be?
4. Summarize, in 25 words or less, what you learned from this skill application.

Skills Application 18-4: Poka-Yoke

INTERNET ACTIVITY

Shigeo Shingo was one of the industrial engineers at Toyota who has been credited with creating and formalizing Zero Quality Control (ZQC), an approach to quality management that relies heavily on the use of poka-yoke (pronounced POH-kah YOH-kay) devices. Poka-yoke is Japanese for mistake-proofing. Visit John Grout's Poka-Yoke Page (campbell.berry.edu/faculty/jgrout) to learn more about these quality control techniques.

1. Read the "Brief Tutorial." What are some key poka-yoke devices? How has poka-yoke been implemented in the workplace?
2. Now link to "Everyday Examples" and view the examples of mistake-proofing featured there. What other common problems can you think of that could be mistake-proof?
3. Compare your responses with those of another student.

Skills Application 18-5: Quality Improvement

INTERNET ACTIVITY

An article in the January 1999 issue of *Quality Digest* reported on three manufacturing firms that were winners of the 1998 Baldrige Award. The article detailed how these companies applied basic ideas of quality, planning, and control for measuring quality, improving customer service, increasing employee retention and loyalty, and opportunities for cost savings.[22]

Using either library information databases or the Internet, identify a "real-world" example of a firm that demonstrates the effective use of planning and control to improve quality. Answer the following questions to enrich your understanding of the interrelatedness of the management functions.

a. What is the relationship between quality improvement and everyone being part of a team?
b. How did the organization plan for quality?
c. If the organization has a labor union, how were partnership arrangements developed?
d. How did the organization manage information?
e. How did the organization identify possible sources of error?
f. If you were a manager at that organization, what else would you do to help the organization be more effective?

Tip on Using the Internet: A direct link to the National Institute of Standards and Technology (NIST) pages devoted to Baldrige Award winners is www.nist.gov. For a report on firms and organizations that submitted applications for a 1999 Malcolm Baldrige National Quality Award, refer to "Fifty-Two Businesses, Education, Health Care Organizations Try for Nation's

Top Award for Excellence" at www.nist.gov/public_affairs/releases/g99-82.htm. For a "1999 State Quality Awards Directory," refer to www.qualitydigest.com.

ENDNOTES

1. For expanded discussions on the nature of the controlling function, the following are recommended: John R. Schermerhorn, Jr., *Management* (6th ed.; New York: John Wiley & Sons, Inc., 1999), pp. 180–199; Ricky W. Griffin, *Management* (5th ed.; Boston: Houghton Mifflin Company, 1996), pp. 600–631; and David H. Holt, *Management: Principles and Practice* (3d ed.; Englewood Cliffs, N.J.: Prentice-Hall, Inc., 1993), pp. 546–625.

2. Often this is accomplished by some form of *statistical quality control (SQC),* which is discussed later in this chapter.

3. A major survey of over 700 manufacturing firms revealed that among the identified "leading" firms, the following areas of performance measurement were used by over 90 percent of these firms: manufactured/delivered costs per unit, inventory levels, worker productivity, manufacturing cycle time, and cost efficiencies in operations. See "Survey in Manufacturing" (survey conducted by American Management Association with the assistance of Ernst & Young), *Management Review* (September 1999), pp. 18–19.

4. For expanded descriptions of job design and work measurement techniques, see Richard B. Chase and Nicholas J. Aquilano, *Production and Operations Management: Manufacturing and Services* (7th ed.; Chicago: Irwin/McGraw-Hill, 1995), pp. 432–479; or Benjamin W. Niebel, *Motion and Time Studies* (9th ed., Homewood, Ill.: Richard D. Irwin, 1993).

5. See Rick Rutter, "Work Sampling: As a Win/Win Management Tool," *Industrial Engineering* (February 1994), pp. 30–31.

6. For a discussion of measurement of worker productivity, see Vida Scarpello, James Ledvinka, and Thomas Bergmann, *Human Resource Management: Environments and Functions* (2d ed.; Cincinnati: South-Western College Publishing, 1995), pp. 64–67. Also see Edwin R. Dean, "The Accuracy of Bureau of Labor Statistics (BLS) Productivity Measures," *Monthly Labor Review* (February 1999), pp. 24–34.

7. See Marjorie Kelly, "From Subjects to Citizens: The Role of Employees—and the Union—in Governance at Saturn Corp.," *Business Ethics* (June 1998), p. 4.

8. For additional information on productivity measurement, see Robert O. Brinkerhoff and Dennis E. Dressler, *Productivity Measurement: A Guide for Managers and Evaluators* (Newbury Park, Calif.: Sage Publications, Applied Social Research Methods Series, Volume 19, 1990). Also see Otis Port, "How to Tally Productivity on the Shop Floor," *Business Week* (November 23, 1998), p. 137.

9. In the major manufacturing survey mentioned in Endnote 3, manufacturers were asked to identify the "critical practices" they used to compare their operations with competitors. The five most often cited were cost efficiencies in operations, speed time to market, research and development, rapid supply from suppliers, and delivery logistics. See *Management Review, op. cit.,* p. 18.

10. See Evelyne Giradet, "Survey Shows a Lot of Anger in America's Workplaces," *Associated Press* as published in the *St. Louis Post-Dispatch* (August 11, 1999), pp. C1–C2. Also see Sherwood Ross, "Untrained Workers are Facing Greater Peril at Gunpoint," *Reuters News Service* as published in the *St. Louis Post-Dispatch* (September 13, 1999), p. BP4.

11. For expanded discussions on statistical quality control, see Roberta S. Russell and Bernard W. Taylor III, *Operations Management* (3d ed.; Upper Saddle River, NJ: Prentice-Hall, Inc., 2000), pp. 131–181; or James R. Chapman and Jacek Koronacki, *Statistical Process Control for Quality Improvement* (New York: Chapman & Hall, 1993).

12. For an expanded discussion on short-term financial analysis including budgets and budgetary control, see Stewart C. Myers and Richard A. Brealey, *Principles of Corporate Finance* (6th ed.; Boston: Irwin/McGraw-Hill, 2000), pp. 819–874. Sometimes even the best budgetary controls do not work. In December 1999, the Securities and Exchange Commission, frustrated by rising levels of corporate accounting fraud, announced plans to pursue criminal cases against any business executive involved in such behavior. How could employees ever trust top management if the accounting firm can't? Recently, PKMG

LLP quit as Rite Aid's outside auditors because it could no longer believe the drug-chain's management representatives. See Mark Maremont and Devon Spurgeon, "Rite Aid Faces Possible Criminal Probe of Accounting Practices," *The Wall Street Journal* (February 17, 2000), p. B2.

13. For a discussion comparing incremental versus zero-base budgets and several other budgeting approaches, see Stephen P. Robbins, *Managing Today* (Upper Saddle River, N.J.; Prentice-Hall, 1997), pp. 178–180.

14. From Beth Brophy, "Nice Guys (and Workshops) Finish First," *U.S. News & World Report* (August 22, 1988), p. 44. See Richard Osborne, "The World's 100 Best-Managed Companies," *Inc.,* (August 19, 1996), pp. 12–39, for a listing of the best of the best.

15. See John Case, "The Open-Book Revolution," *Inc.* (June 1995), pp. 26–43; David Whitford, "Before and After," *Inc.* (June 1995), pp. 44–50; John Case, *The Coming Business Revolution* (New York: Harper-Business, 1995); Willard I. Zangwill, "Focusing All Eyes on the Bottom Line," *The Wall Street Journal* (March 21, 1994), p. A12; and Timothy L. O'Brien, "Company Wins Workers' Loyalty by Opening Its Books," *The Wall Street Journal* (December 20, 1993), pp. B1 and B2.

16. See Michael Conlon, "Firm Offers Advance Pay for Travel Expense Accounts," *Reuters News Service* as published in the *St. Louis Post-Dispatch* (August 30, 1999), p. BP15.

17. See Tom Belden, "Suggestions for Controlling Costs of Meals on the Road," *Knight Ridder Newspapers* as published in the *St. Louis Post-Dispatch* (August 30, 1999), p. BP15.

18. For expanded information concerning inventory control, the following are recommended: Richard J. Tersine, *Principles of Inventory and Materials Management* (4th ed.; New York: North-Holland, 1994); or Jan B. Young, *Modern Inventory Operations: Methods for Accuracy and Productivity* (New York: Van Nostrand Reinhold, 1991).

19. For expanded information concerning quality control and TQM, the following are recommended: J. R. Evans and W. M. Lindsay, *The Management and Control of Quality* (3d ed.; St. Paul, Minn.: West, 1996); Bill Creech, *The Five Pillars of TQM: How to Make Total Quality Management Work for You* (New York: Truman Tally Books/Dutton, 1994); or Arnold Weimershirch and Stephen George, *Total Quality Management: Strategies and Techniques Proven at Today's Most Successful Companies* (New York: John Wiley & Sons, 1994).

20. For expanded information concerning production control, the following are recommended: Fred Aslup and Ricky M. Watson, *Practical Statistical Process Control: A Tool for Quality Manufacturing* (New York: Van Nostrand Reinhold, 1993); T. E. Vollmann, W. L. Berry, and D. C. Whybark, *Manufacturing and Control Systems* (3d ed.; Homewood, IL: Richard D. Irwin, 1992); E. M. Goldratt and J. Cox, *The Goal: A Process of Ongoing Improvement* (Great Barrington, MA: North River Press, 1992); or Donald W. Fogarty, John H. Blackstone, and Thomas R. Hoffmann, *Production and Inventory Management* (2d ed.; Cincinnati: South-Western, 1991).

21. For illustrations of outstanding customer service, see Susan Greco, "Real-World Customer Service," *Inc.* (October 1994), pp. 36–45.

22. See Elizabeth R. Larson, "1998 Baldrige Award Goes to Three Manufacturers," *Quality Digest* (January 8, 1999), p. 8. This same issue includes the "1999 State Quality Awards Directory," *Quality Digest* (January 8, 1999), pp. 59–64.

Positive Discipline

You Make the Call!

You are Linda Juarez, a departmental supervisor for a major aerospace firm. You currently manage a group of six accountants and financial analysts and a clerk who are responsible for maintaining all contract records for one of the company's aircraft programs. All of the accountants and financial analysts have bachelors' degrees and most are currently pursuing or have completed requirements for a master's degree. Over the past year, two of your employees left the company. Because the company was facing difficult times, these individuals were not replaced. Consequently, the remaining members of the department had to keep up with heavy workloads. Considerable overtime and Saturday work were necessary. About a month ago, higher-level management agreed to move an available person from another department to your department. This employee, Scott Stoner, had worked for the company for five years since graduating from college. During this time he completed his master's degree at a local university. He came to the department with excellent credentials, and he had a high recommendation from his previous supervisor in corporate accounting.

Thursday at 5:30 P.M. Kathy Florence, one of your financial analysts, comes into your office. This is what she has to say:

Well I don't really know where to start, Linda, so I guess I'll just jump right in. Quite a few of us in the department are upset with Scott. I don't know if you're aware of the situation or not, but the bottom line is he just doesn't do anything. He's great at reading The Wall Street Journal *and making weekend and evening plans. But when the rest of us are busting our tails to get the job done, it's a bit frustrating to watch him relaxing at his desk. He even went so far as to give out his office telephone number when he listed his car for sale. Then because he was on the phone all the time, most calls went to our department clerk, John. He was really angry, and I don't blame him. He has enough to do just supporting the rest of us. I know Scott's still pretty new in our department but the job here is not that different from the work he did in corporate accounting. Given how shorthanded we are, department morale is certainly going to drop further if he continues this way. One last thing. He's called in sick three days this month. None of us believes that he was sick since all of his absences were on Friday or Monday.*

The conversation continues just a bit longer. After Kathy leaves, you wonder how to handle the situation. You have never experienced a problem quite like this in three years of supervising this department.

You Make the Call!

THE BASIS AND IMPORTANCE OF POSITIVE DISCIPLINE

1

Discuss the basis and importance of positive discipline in an organization.

In earlier editions of the text, this chapter was included in Part 5 under the leading function of management. However, for the seventh edition and again for this edition, we decided that because the subject of discipline often is associated with the controlling function of management, the chapter would be placed within Part 6. We recognize that elements of discipline involve considerable overlap in these managerial functions, particularly at the supervisory level.

The term *discipline* is used in several different ways. Many supervisors associate it with the use of authority, force, or punishment. In this text, however, we prefer to consider **discipline** as a condition of orderliness, that is, the degree to which members of an organization act properly and observe the expected standards of behavior. **Positive discipline** exists when employees generally follow the rules and meet the standards of the organization. Discipline is negative (or bad) when they follow the rules reluctantly

Discipline

State of orderliness; that is, the degree to which employees act according to expected standards of behavior.

Positive discipline
Condition that exists when employees generally follow the rules and meet the standards of the organization.

or when they actually disobey regulations and violate the prescribed standards of acceptable behavior.

Discipline is not identical to morale. As discussed in Chapter 15, morale is a state of mind, whereas discipline is primarily a state of affairs. However, there is some relationship between morale and discipline. Normally there are fewer disciplinary problems when morale is high; conversely, low morale is usually accompanied by more disciplinary problems. Yet a high degree of positive discipline could be present in spite of low morale; this could result from insecurity, fear, or sheer force. However, it is unlikely that a high degree of positive employee discipline will be maintained indefinitely unless there is an acceptable level of employee morale.

Positive self-discipline
Employees regulating their own behavior out of self-interest and their normal desire to meet reasonable standards.

The best type of discipline is **positive self-discipline** in which employees essentially regulate themselves out of their own self-interest. This is based on the normal human tendency to do what needs to be done, to do one's share, and to follow reasonable standards of acceptable behavior. Even before they start to work, most people accept the idea that following instructions and fair rules of conduct are normal responsibilities in any job.

Positive self-discipline relies on the premise that most employees want to do the right thing and can be counted on to exercise self-control. They believe in performing their work properly; coming to work on time; following the supervisor's instructions; and refraining from fighting, using drugs, drinking liquor, or stealing. They know that it is natural to subordinate some of their own personal interests to the needs of the organization. As long as company rules are communicated and are perceived as reasonable, most employees will observe the rules.

Positive Employee Discipline Requires Supervisory Example

Unfortunately, there are always some employees who, for one reason or another, fail to observe established rules and standards even after having been informed of them. Direct employee theft from employers nationwide amounts to billions of dollars of loss annually.[1] When added to other forms of employee dishonesty—including habitual misuse or "stealing" of company time by unwarranted absenteeism and tardiness,[2] doing personal business, and socializing on company time—the cost of employee theft, fraud, and abuse to U.S. businesses has been estimated to be in the range of $400 billion annually according to the Association of Certified Fraud Examiners (ACFE). In a 1998 survey conducted by the ACFE, 80 percent of the respondents asserted that employees, supervisors, and managers were considerably more dishonest now than five years ago.[3] The problem of dishonesty is further accentuated by widespread misuse and abuse of e-mail and the Internet, which is the focus of this chapter's "Contemporary Issue" box.[4]

Despite such unfortunate statistics, supervisors should maintain a balanced perspective that employees at the departmental level will take most of their cues for self-discipline from their supervisors and managers (see Figure 19-1 on page 652). Ideally, positive self-discipline should exist throughout the entire management team, beginning at the top and extending through all supervisors. Supervisors should not expect their employees to practice positive self-discipline if they themselves do not set a good ex-

FIGURE 19-1

Self-discipline must exist at the supervisory level before it will exist at the employee level.

ample. As we have stated several times previously, a supervisor's actions and behavior are easy targets for the employees to either emulate or reject. Further, if the supervisor is able to encourage the vast majority of the employees in the department to show a strong sense of self-discipline, usually these employees will exert group pressure on the dissenters. For example, if a no-smoking rule is posted for a building, usually someone in the work group will enforce this rule by reminding smokers to leave the premises before lighting a cigarette. Thus, the need for corrective action by the supervisor is reduced when most employees practice positive self-discipline.

Oren Harari, a professor and management consultant, has commented that good employee discipline mostly depends on the supervisor's daily behavior and decisions being aligned in the same positive direction and with consistency of actions. He states: "Discipline is the daily grind that makes things happen and lets people know that you're worthy of your word. In short, it's about honor and integrity."[5]

IDENTIFYING AND CONFRONTING DISCIPLINARY SITUATIONS

2

Identify disciplinary situations that violate standards of conduct and discuss the need to confront them appropriately.

Because individuals do not always agree on what should be acceptable standards of conduct, top-level managers must define the standards for supervisors and employees. In many companies, standards are defined in statements of ethical codes and rules of conduct.

contemporary issue

Electronic Fun and Games: Employees Beware! Your Job May Be "On-The-Line"

There is little doubt that increasing access to e-mail and the Internet has magnified opportunities for various types of abuse and misuse. In a survey conducted by Elron Software of Cambridge, Massachusetts, 85 percent of the respondents indicated that they had used e-mail and the Internet at work for personal reasons. About half of them claimed that they had received inappropriate transmissions at work, such as pornography and sexist and racist materials. Already there have been numerous discrimination and harassment lawsuits because of the inappropriate use of e-mail. Some companies have paid huge damage claims because of the transmittal of extremely offensive material on their systems. Despite this, a survey by the American Management Association indicated that only about 20 percent of employers had software or other systems to track and review company e-mail.[1]

Because of these types of problems and concerns, as well as other concerns about the possible loss of trade secrets, sensitive financial data, and lost productivity, some companies are beginning to "clamp down" by electronically monitoring employees on the job. Software programs with such ominous names as "Little Brother" and "Message Inspector" are being sold to employers in order to keep track of employee e-mail and Website-viewing habits.[2]

Although the need for some surveillance seems obvious, it has brought about complaints and concerns regarding invasion of worker privacy rights. At the time of publication, there was no protection for employees who are monitored in regards to electronic communications on computer systems. According to Jeremy Gruber, an attorney with the American Civil Liberties Union, employers can go through an individual's e-mail, computer files, and Web-browsing history without being required to let employees know that this will be done. Only one or two states have a law requiring employers to inform employees if this type of monitoring will take place. Comments Mr. Gruber, "Under current law, if I were an employee I would be extremely hesitant to do any kind of personal business at work." Some companies do allow employees to "surf the Web" during lunch time and after hours provided they follow strict company rules concerning such activities during work hours and do not engage in pornographic, lewd, or offensive transmissions. It would appear that many more companies will have to specify more clearly what is and is not permissible. Regardless, employees should be cognizant that someone may be watching them electronically and to "keep their noses clean," or their jobs will be "on-the-line."[3]

Sources: (1) Bill Leonard, "E-Mail@Work: Ripe for Employee Abuse," *HRMagazine* (June 1999), p. 28. (2) Laureen Lazarovici, "Little Brother May Be Watching You," *America@Work* (AFL-CIO, September 1999), p. 11. (3) Michael Stroh, "Workers Beware: Big Browser May be Watching You," *Baltimore Sun* as published in the *St. Louis Post Dispatch* (August 18, 1999), pp. E1 & E4. (For a discussion of e-mail problems that raise various other legal issues, see Michael J. McCarthy, "Your Manager's Policy on Employees E-Mail May Have a Weak Spot," *The Wall Street Journal* (April 25, 2000). pp. A1 & A10).

Ethical Codes and Policies

In Chapter 5, we discussed "ethical tests" and guidelines to be applied in decision making, and we mentioned that many organizations have developed statements of ethical standards or ethical codes.[6] Such codes usually outline in broad, value-oriented terms the norms and ideals that are supposed to guide everyone within the organization. Figure 19-2 (see page 654) is an example of a corporate code of ethics. The nine principles within this code are expanded upon in a policy manual that provides guidance for employees concerning the meaning of the principles and compliance with them.

FIGURE 19-2

Corporate code of ethics.

CODE OF ETHICS

Integrity and ethics exist in the individual or they do not exist at all. They must be up-held by individuals or they are not upheld at all. In order for integrity and ethics to be characteristics of the corporation we must strive to be:

- Honest and trustworthy in all our relationships;
- Reliable in carrying out assignments and responsibilities;
- Truthful and accurate in what we say and write;
- Cooperative and constructive in all work undertaken;
- Fair and considerate in our treatment of fellow employees, customers, and all other people;
- Law abiding in all our activities;
- Committed to accomplishing all tasks in a superior way;
- Economical in utilizing company resources; and
- Dedicated in service to our company and to improvement of the quality of life in the world in which we live.

Merely having a code of ethics in place is no insurance that ethical conduct will always be followed. Some codes are documents that primarily outline legal requirements and restrictions, and they provide only limited guidance for resolving moral and ethical dilemmas at work.[7] In a 1998 survey of human resources professionals, over half of the respondents stated that during the previous year they had observed workplace conduct that was unlawful or that violated the employer's standards of ethical business conduct. Almost half of the respondents further stated that they had been pressured at times by other employees or managers to compromise their organization's business ethics standards in order to achieve business objectives.[8]

Because ethical standards and ethical behavior can be subject to varying interpretations, some firms have found it desirable to develop their ethical codes and policies with a major participative input from teams of employees and supervisors.[9] Further, some major firms have established so-called "hot lines" or ethics reporting systems by which employees are encouraged to report questionable situations or individuals whom they believe are acting unethically, improperly, or illegally. These firms may have a "corporate ombudsman" who investigates the allegations and takes appropriate action when justified. The person who reported the alleged wrongdoing, usually referred to as a *whistle-blower,* should be afforded anonymity. There is supposed to be no retaliation, regardless of whether or not the report is supportable by facts and evidence.[10] In this regard, it is generally recognized that a hot line or ethical reporting system requires top-level management's commitment to make the system credible, that is, both to deal firmly with wrongdoing when it is reported and, further, not to retaliate against a messenger who delivers an unwelcome message.[11] Of course, if someone has made an unfounded or false report with malice, this may require a disciplinary response by management.

Some firms also have developed statements and policies for dealing with "conflicts of interest;" these may be part of, or in addition to, their ethical codes. Conflict-of-in-

FIGURE 19-3

Excerpts from a "Conflicts of
Interest" policy statement.

CONFLICTS OF INTEREST

- Employees have the duty and the obligation to act—at all times—in the best lawful and ethical interests of Monsanto.
- Employees are specifically prohibited from using their positions with Monsanto for personal gain, favor, or advantage. For example, this specifically prohibits any unauthorized or personal use of the official stationery, news release masthead, logo, or any other forms, labels, envelopes, etc., bearing the name or logo of Monsanto Company *or* any of its subsidiaries.
- Employees are expected to avoid relationships which might interfere with the proper and efficient discharge of their duties—or which might be inconsistent with their obligations of loyalty to Monsanto. For example, if an employee, close relative, or any other person with whom the employee has a close personal relationship has a financial interest in an organization which does business or competes with Monsanto, a conflict of interest may exist. Also, there may be a conflict if an employee, or close relative or any other person with whom the employee has a close personal relationship, engages in certain transactions with, renders services to, or accepts payments, loans or gifts from customers, vendors, contractors or competitors of Monsanto.

terest statements usually define situations and employee behaviors that would be inconsistent with an individual's primary obligations to the employer. Figure 19-3 is an excerpted example of a major firm's statement on conflicts of interest.

In the final analysis, a firm's commitment to high standards of ethical behavior must go far beyond just codes and policy statements. It requires that everyone in the organization—especially those in management and supervision—show daily by word and deed that behaving ethically at work is not an optional extra. There is ample evidence that *good ethics means good business,* which was stated eloquently by Nicholas Moore, Chairman and Senior Partner of PriceWaterhouseCoopers, as follows:

When companies stand up for what's right, day in and day out, it has a positive impact. Positive in terms of who it attracts, because good people want to work in ethical environments. It simplifies decision making. We know what we won't even think about doing. And, in the process, we earn the respect of our competitors, our clients, and our people. In the long term, that's very, very important. So ethical behavior is at the core of the way we do business, and it's the only way we're going to do business.[12]

Rules of Conduct

Not every organization has a published code of ethics or conflict-of-interest statement. However, virtually every large firm, and probably the majority of other firms and organizations, have some formal statement or list of rules of behavior to which employees are expected to conform.

In Chapter 6, we discussed the need for policies, procedures, methods, and rules as standing plans that cover many aspects of ongoing operations. These are particularly vital in informing employees of what standards of behavior are expected and what types are not acceptable.

Most organizations provide employees with a written list of rules or codes of conduct. These are sometimes included in an employee handbook; otherwise, they are provided as a separate booklet or as a memorandum posted in each department. The supervisor must ensure that employees read and understand the general and departmental rules, which may include safety and technical regulations, depending on the activity of a department.

Written rules and regulations provide a common basis and standards that should assist the supervisor in encouraging employee self-discipline. Some organizations spell out very detailed lists of rules and infractions, and they may include classifications of the likely penalties for violations. Other organizations—probably the majority—prefer to list their major rules and regulations but without tying down the consequences for violations of various rules. An example of such a list is shown in Figure 19-4. Regardless of what type of list is used, the supervisor is the person most responsible for the consistent application and enforcement of both company and departmental rules. In fact, the degree to which employees follow the rules in a positive, self-disciplined way is usually more attributable to the supervisor's role and example than to any other factor.

Rules of conduct and policy statements in employee handbooks and manuals often are subject to review and change because of legal problems and interpretations. Al-

---

FIGURE 19-4

Partial list of company rules and regulations.

COMPANY RULES AND REGULATIONS

The efficient operation of our plants and the general welfare of our employees require the establishment of certain uniform standards of behavior. Accordingly, the following offenses are considered to be violations of these standards, and employees who refuse to accept this guidance will subject themselves to appropriate disciplinary action.

1. Habitual tardiness and absenteeism.
2. Theft or attempted theft of Company or other employee's property.
3. Fighting or attempting bodily injury upon another employee.
4. Horseplay, malicious mischief, or any other conduct affecting the rights of other employees.
5. Intoxication or drinking on the job; or being in a condition that makes it impossible to perform work in a satisfactory manner.
6. Refusal or failure to perform assigned work; or refusal or failure to comply with supervisory instructions.
7. Inattention to duties; carelessness in performance of duties; loafing on the job, sleeping, or reading papers during working hours.
8. Violation of published safety or health rules.
9. Possessing, consuming, selling, or being under the influence of illegal drugs on the premises.
10. Unauthorized possession of weapons, firearms, or explosives on the premises.
11. Requests for sexual favors, sexual advances, and physical conduct of a sexual nature toward another employee on the premises.

though review and revision of employee handbooks and the like are usually the responsibility of human resources staff, supervisors should be very familiar with the content of employee handbooks. Supervisors should not hesitate to offer suggestions for revisions when changes appear to be justified or needed for whatever reasons might be appropriate.[13]

Confronting Disciplinary Situations

Despite a supervisor's best efforts to prevent infractions, it is almost inevitable that he or she at times will be confronted with situations requiring some type of disciplinary action. Among the most common situations requiring supervisory disciplinary actions are (a) infractions of rules regarding time schedules, rest periods, procedures, safety, and so forth; (b) excessive absenteeism or tardiness; (c) defective or inadequate work performance; and (d) poor attitudes that influence the work of others or damage the firm's public image.

At times a supervisor might experience open insubordination, such as an employee's refusal to carry out a legitimate work assignment. A supervisor may even be confronted with disciplinary problems that stem from employee behavior off the job. For example, an employee may have a drinking problem or may be taking illegal drugs. Whenever an employee's off-the-job conduct has an impact on job performance, the supervisor must be prepared to respond to the problem in an appropriate fashion. In Chapter 15 we discussed a number of approaches by which employees with personal and work-related problems might be assisted.

Inevitably, every supervisor will be confronted with situations that require some type of disciplinary action.

Situations that call for disciplinary action are not pleasant but the supervisor must have the courage to deal with them rather than ignoring them, hoping they will go away. If the supervisor does not take responsible action when required, some borderline employees might be encouraged to try similar violations.

A supervisor should not be afraid to draw on some of the authority inherent in the supervisory position, even though it might be easier to overlook the matter or "pass the buck" to higher-level managers or the human resources department. A supervisor who finds it expedient to ask the human resources department to take over all departmental disciplinary problems is shirking responsibility and undermining his or her own position of authority.

Normally, a good supervisor will not have to take disciplinary action frequently. But whenever it becomes necessary, the supervisor should be ready to take the proper action no matter how unpleasant the task may be.

THE DISCIPLINARY PROCESS AND JUST CAUSE

3
Discuss the disciplinary process and approaches that ensure disciplinary action for just (or proper) cause.

Supervisors must initiate any disciplinary action with sensitivity and sound judgment. The purpose of a disciplinary action should not be to punish or seek revenge but to improve the employees' future behavior. In other words, the primary purpose of a disciplinary action is to prevent similar infractions in the future.

In this chapter we do not consider directly those situations in which union contractual obligations may restrict the supervisor's authority in taking disciplinary action. Special considerations involving labor unions were discussed in Chapters 11 and 17. Nevertheless, the ideas discussed here are generally applicable in most unionized as well as nonunionized organizations.

Disciplinary Action Should Have Just Cause

Just cause

Standard for disciplinary action requiring tests of fairness and elements of normal due process, such as proper notification, investigation, sufficient evidence, and a penalty commensurate with the nature of the infraction.

Most employers accept the general premise that disciplinary action taken against an employee should be based on "just cause." **Just cause** (or "proper cause") means that the disciplinary action meets certain tests of fairness and elements of normal due process, such as proper notification, investigation, sufficient evidence, and a penalty commensurate with the nature of the infraction. Figure 19-5 is a list of seven questions that arbitrators apply in union/management disciplinary-type grievance matters. A "no" answer to one or more of these questions in a particular case means that the just-cause standard was not fully met, and the arbitrator might then set aside or modify management's disciplinary action.

The overwhelming preponderance of labor union contracts specify a just-cause or proper-cause standard for discipline and discharge. Similarly, many cases decided by government agencies and by the courts have required employers to prove that disciplinary actions taken against legally protected employees (as discussed in Chapter 16) were not discriminatory but were for just cause. Even under various forms of alternative dispute resolution (ADR), which was discussed in Chapter 17, a just-cause standard—or something approximating it—typically is applied in resolving disciplinary

FIGURE 19-5

Seven tests for just cause.

> **SEVEN TESTS FOR JUST CAUSE**
>
> 1. Did the company give the employee forewarning or foreknowledge of the possible or probable disciplinary consequences of the employee's conduct?
> 2. Was the company's rule or managerial order reasonably related to (a) the orderly, efficient, and safe operation of the company's business and (b) the performance that the company might properly expect of the employee?
> 3. Did the company, before administering discipline to an employee, make an effort to discover whether the employee did in fact violate or disobey a rule or order of management?
> 4. Was the company's investigation conducted fairly and objectively?
> 5. At the investigation, was there substantial evidence or proof that the employee was guilty as charged?
> 6. Has the company applied its rules, orders, and penalties even-handedly and without discrimination to all employees?
> 7. Was the degree of discipline administered by the company in a particular case reasonably related to (a) the seriousness of the employee's proven offense and (b) the record of the employee's service with the company?

Source: These seven tests for just cause were originally suggested by arbitrator Carroll R. Daugherty. They are included in many texts and arbitral citations. See Raymond L. Hilgert, *Cases in Collective Bargaining and Industrial Relations* (9th ed.; Boston: Irwin/McGraw-Hill, 1999), pp. 205–206.

case matters.[14] For a number of years, some federal U.S. government offices have utilized a mandatory alternative dispute resolution system, and there have been legislative proposals to extend mandatory ADR for certain types of disputes in both the public and private sectors.[15] If this should take place, it would seem almost certain that a just-cause standard would prevail throughout most firms and organizations.

Although the ramifications of a just-cause standard for disciplinary action can be rather complicated, the guidelines presented in this chapter are consistent with the principles and requirements necessary to justify any disciplinary or discharge action. The supervisor who follows these guidelines in a conscientious way normally should be able to meet a just-cause standard, irrespective of whether it involves a unionized firm, a nonunionized organization, or a potential area of legal discrimination.[16]

Precautionary Questions and Measures

As a first consideration in any disciplinary situation, a supervisor should guard against undue haste or taking unwarranted action based on emotional response. There are a number of precautionary questions and measures that a supervisor should follow before deciding on any disciplinary action in response to an alleged employee offense.

Investigate the Situation. Before doing anything, the supervisor should investigate what happened and why. The following questions, while not comprehensive, might be used as a checklist as the supervisor considers what should be done.

1. Are all or most of the facts available and are they reported accurately? That is, can the alleged offense be proved by direct or circumstantial evidence, or is the allegation based merely on suspicion?
2. How serious (minor, major, or intolerable) is the offense? Were others involved or affected by it? Were company funds or equipment involved?
3. Did the employee know the rule or standard? Does the employee have a reasonable excuse and are there any extenuating circumstances?
4. What is the employee's past disciplinary record, length of service, and performance level? Does the offense indicate carelessness, absentmindedness, loss of temper, and so forth? How does this employee react to criticism?
5. Should the employee receive the same treatment others have had for the same offense? If not, is it possible to establish a basis for differentiating the present alleged offense from past offenses of a similar nature?
6. Is all the necessary documentation available in case the matter leads to outside review?

For certain gross violations, such as stealing, illegal substance use, and violence, an organization may call in law enforcement authorities to conduct an investigation and to take appropriate action. Some firms will employ a consultant to administer a polygraph test in an effort to determine who committed the violations, particularly in matters involving theft. The use of the polygraph, however, has been quite restricted as a result of a 1988 federal law. This statute prohibits random polygraph testing but permits an employer with "reasonable suspicion" of employee wrongdoing to use a polygraph if certain safeguards are met. Supervisors, for the most part, do not make the decision to use a polygraph; such a decision is made by someone in higher-level management, or the human resources staff, after consultation with legal counsel. There even may be situations where it is decided that investigation of possible wrongdoing requires some form of personnel surveillance. An outside private investigator may be hired to conduct electronic surveillance or perhaps become part of the workplace as an undercover "employee." The supervisor may or may not be informed that such surveillance is taking place.[17] However, a recent federal regulation requires that employers notify workers if the company intends to have an outside party investigate or probe alleged workplace or other wrongdoings. Such disclosure is required if an inquiry could lead to an adverse decision against an employee, such as discipline, termination, and job movement decisions.[18]

When an employee is injured on the job, many firms require the employee to take a drug and alcohol screening test. Such tests usually are given by a qualified person in the firm's first-aid room or by someone at an occupational health clinic where the employee is treated. Safeguards concerning employee privacy and test-result validation usually are followed, although the results may be utilized as part of management's investigation and decision-making process.[19]

Investigatory Interviews. As part of the supervisor's investigation of an alleged infraction, it may be necessary to question the employee involved as well as other employees who may have relevant information. In general, such interviews should be conducted in private and on an individual basis—perhaps with a guarantee of confidentiality. This is usually less threatening to an employee who otherwise may be reluctant to tell what he or she knows. This also helps prevent having what employees say be unduly influenced by another's versions and interpretations.

If a union employee is to be interviewed concerning a disciplinary matter, the employee may request that a union representative or coworker be present during the interview. Normally the supervisor should grant such a request. Under interpretations of federal labor laws, a union employee has the right to have a union representative present during an investigatory interview if the employee reasonably believes that the investigation may lead to disciplinary action.[20] However, a representative or coworker witness cannot disrupt an investigatory interview or answer questions in place of the employee being interviewed. Of course, if the employee is to have a witness present, the supervisor is well advised to have a fellow supervisor present to serve as a supervisory witness to the interview.

In conducting an investigatory interview, most of the principles of interviewing discussed in Chapter 12 are applicable. The supervisor should ask both directive and nondirective questions that are designed to elicit specific answers concerning what happened and why. Above all, the supervisor should avoid making any final judgments until all the interviews have been held and other relevant information has been assembled.

Maintaining Self-Control. Regardless of the severity of an employee violation, a supervisor must not lose self-control. This does not mean that a supervisor should face a disciplinary situation half-heartedly or indifferently. But if a supervisor feels in danger of losing control of temper or emotions, the supervisor should delay the investigatory interviews and not take any action until he or she calms down. A supervisor's loss of self-control or display of anger could compromise fair and objective judgment.

Generally, a supervisor should never lay a hand on an employee in any way. Except for emergencies, when an employee has been injured or becomes ill, or when employees who are fighting need to be separated, any physical gesture could easily be misunderstood. A supervisor who engages in physical violence, except in self-defense, normally will be subjected to disciplinary action by higher-level management.

Privacy in Disciplining. When a supervisor finally decides on a course of disciplinary action, she or he should communicate the discipline to the offending employee in private. A public reprimand not only humiliates the employee in the eyes of co-workers but also can lead to loss of morale in the department or even a grievance. If in the opinion of the other employees a public disciplinary action is too severe for the violation, the disciplined employee might emerge as a martyr in the view of every employee in the department.

Many union contracts require that employees who are to be disciplined for an infraction have the right to have a union representative present. If this is the case, it is desirable to have more than one management person present—for example, the supervisor, the supervisor's superior, and perhaps the human resources director. Thus, both management and the union have witnesses to the disciplinary action, even when it takes place in a private area.

Only under extreme circumstances should disciplinary action be taken in public. For example, a supervisor's authority may be challenged directly and openly by an employee who repeatedly refuses to carry out a reasonable work request. Or an employee may be drunk or fighting on the job. In these cases it is necessary for the supervisor to reach a disciplinary decision quickly—for example, by sending the offending employee home on suspension pending further investigation. The supervisor may even have to do this in the view of other employees in order to regain control of the situation and to maintain their respect.

Disciplinary Time Element. When a supervisor decides to impose a disciplinary action, the question arises as to how long the violation should be held against an employee. Generally, it is desirable to disregard minor or intermediate offenses after a year or so has elapsed since they were committed. Thus, an employee with a poor record of defective work might be given a "clean bill of health" by subsequently compiling a good record for six months or one year. Some companies have adopted "point systems" to cover certain infractions—especially absenteeism and tardiness. Employees can have points removed from their records if they have perfect or acceptable attendance during later periods.

There are situations when the time element is of no importance. For example, if an employee is caught brandishing a knife in a heated argument at work, the supervisor need not worry about any time element or previous offenses. This act is serious enough to warrant immediate discharge.

PRACTICING PROGRESSIVE DISCIPLINE

4
Define and discuss the application of progressive discipline.

Progressive discipline
System of disciplinary action that increases the severity of the penalty with each offense.

Unless a serious wrong, such as stealing, physical violence, or gross insubordination, has been committed, the offending employee rarely is discharged for a first offense. Although the type of disciplinary action appropriate to a situation will vary, many organizations practice a system of **progressive discipline,** which provides for an increase in the severity of the penalty with each offense. The following stages comprise a system of progressive disciplinary action: informal talk, oral warning (or verbal counseling), written warning, disciplinary layoff (suspension), transfer or demotion, and discharge. Figures 19-6 and 19-7 illustrate progressive discipline.

Early Stages in Progressive Discipline

Many disciplinary situations can be handled solely or primarily by the supervisor without escalating into a difficult confrontation. In the early stages of progressive discipline, the supervisor communicates with the employee concerning the problem and how to correct it.

Informal Talk. If the offense is relatively minor and if the employee has had no previous disciplinary record, a friendly and informal talk will clear up the problem in many cases. During this talk, the supervisor should try to determine the underlying reasons

FIGURE 19-6

Progressive disciplinary
policy for a hospital.

CORRECTIVE ACTION POLICY

Corrective action shall progress from verbal counseling to written reprimand, suspension, and termination. All actions taken shall include a reference to the specific policy or procedure that has been violated, the adverse consequence resulting from the violation, the type of behavior expected in the future, and the corrective action that will be taken if further violations occur. A copy of a written corrective action form shall be given to the employee. The following are guidelines for the corrective action procedure:

A. *Verbal Counseling*—A verbal counseling shall be given for all minor violations of Hospital rules and policies. More than two verbal counselings within the last 12-month period regarding violations of any rules or policies warrants a written reprimand.

B. *Written Reprimands*—Written reprimands shall be given for repeated minor infractions or for first-time occurrences of more serious offenses.

Written reprimands shall be documented on the Notice of Corrective Action form, which is signed by the department head or supervisor and the employee.

C. *Suspension*—An employee shall be suspended without pay for one to four scheduled working days for a critical or major offense or for repeated minor or serious offenses.

D. *Termination*—An employee may be terminated for repeated violations of Hospital rules and regulations or for first offenses of a critical nature.

FIGURE 19-7

A program of disciplinary
action often begins with an
informal talk. With repeated
offenses, penalties become
more severe.

for the employee's unacceptable conduct. At the same time, the supervisor should reaffirm the employee's sense of responsibility and acknowledge his or her previous good behavior.

Oral Warning. If a friendly talk does not take care of the situation, the next step is to give the employee an oral warning (sometimes known as *verbal counseling*). Here the supervisor emphasizes the undesirability of the employee's repeated violation in a straightforward manner. Although the supervisor should stress the preventive purpose of discipline, the supervisor should also emphasize that, unless the employee improves, more serious disciplinary action will be taken. In some organizations, a record of this oral warning is made in the employee's file. Or the supervisor may simply write a brief note in a supervisory log book to document the fact that an oral warning was given on a particular date. This can be important evidence if the same employee commits another infraction in the future.

At times, a supervisor may believe that the substance of the verbal counseling should be put in writing so that the message is documented and more likely to be impressed upon the employee. In such a situation, the supervisor may resort to what is called a *letter of clarification*. Such a letter should clearly state that it is not a formal disciplinary document, and that its primary purpose is to reiterate to the employee what was communicated verbally by the supervisor. In general, letters of clarification tend to be most applicable in dealing with minor employee infractions in the early stages of progressive discipline.[21]

If oral warnings and letters of clarification are carried out skillfully, many employees will respond and improve at this stage. The employee must understand that improvement is expected in the future, and that the supervisor believes the employee can improve and is ready to help the employee do so.

Written Warning. A written warning contains a statement of the violation and the potential consequences of future violations. It is a formal document that becomes a permanent part of the employee's record. The supervisor should review with the employee the nature of this written warning and again stress the necessity for improvement. The employee should be placed on clear notice that future infractions or unacceptable conduct will lead to more serious discipline, such as suspension or discharge.

Written warnings are particularly necessary in unionized organizations because they can serve as evidence in grievance procedures. Such documentation is also important if the employee is a member of a legally protected group. The employee usually receives a duplicate copy of the written warning, and another copy is sent to the human resources department. Figure 19-8 is an example of a written warning used by a supermarket chain. The form even provides space for the supervisor to note if the employee refuses to sign it.

Even at this stage in the disciplinary process, the supervisor should continue to express to the employee a belief in the employee's ability to improve and the supervisor's willingness to help in whatever way possible. The primary goal of disciplinary action up until discharge should be to assist the person to improve and become a valuable employee.

FIGURE 19-8

Example of a written warning used by a supermarket chain.

EMPLOYEE CORRECTIVE ACTION NOTICE

Employee's Name _____ Date of Notice _____

Store Address _____ Store # _____ Dept. _____ Job Classification _____

This notice is a: First Warning   Second Warning   Third Warning   Final Warning
                         ☐   ☐   ☐   ☐

Reason for Corrective Action: (Check below)

☐ Cooperation/Interest   ☐ Cash register   ☐ Insubordination
                                   discrepancy

☐ Quality/Quantity of work   ☐ Dress code   ☐ Time card violation

☐ Tardiness/Absenteeism   ☐ Disregard for safety   ☐ Other causes (Explain)

Explanation must accompany reason checked above:

_____

_____

_____

I HEREBY SIGNIFY THAT I HAVE RECEIVED A FULL EXPLANATION OF MY FAILURE TO
PERFORM AS EXPECTED. THE COMPANY AND I UNDERSTAND THAT FURTHER FAILURE
ON MY PART WILL BE DUE CAUSE FOR DISCIPLINARY ACTION UP TO, AND INCLUDING,
DISCHARGE.

_____   _____   _____   _____
Employee's signature   Date   Supervisor's signature   Date

                                          _____   _____
                                          Store Manager's signature   Date

REFUSAL OF EMPLOYEE TO SIGN THIS NOTICE SHOULD BE SO NOTED HEREON.

Note: Prepare original and four copies. Send original and one copy to the Human Resources Director. Send one copy to the Store Manager and one copy to the employee.

Advanced Stages in Progressive Discipline

Unfortunately, not every employee will respond to the counseling and warnings of the supervisor to improve job behavior. In progressive discipline, more serious disciplinary actions may be administered for repeated violations, with discharge being the final step.

Disciplinary Layoff (Suspension). If an employee has committed offenses repeatedly and previous warnings were of no avail, a disciplinary layoff would probably constitute the next disciplinary step. Disciplinary layoffs involve a loss of pay and usually extend from one day to several days or weeks. Because a disciplinary layoff involves a loss of pay, most organizations limit a supervisor's authority at this stage. Most supervisors can only initiate or recommend a disciplinary layoff, which then must be approved by higher-level managers after consultation with the human resources department.

Employees who do not respond to oral or written warnings usually find a disciplinary layoff to be a rude awakening. The layoff may restore in them the need to comply with the organization's rules and regulations. However, managers in some organizations seldom apply layoffs as a disciplinary measure. They believe that laying off a trained employee will hurt their own production, especially in times of labor shortages. Further, they reason that the laid-off employee may return in an even more unpleasant frame of mind. Despite this possible reaction, in many employee situations disciplinary layoffs can be an effective disciplinary measure.

Transfer. Transferring an employee to a job in another department typically involves no loss of pay. This disciplinary action is usually taken when an offending employee seems to be experiencing difficulty in working for a particular supervisor, in working at a current job, or in associating with certain other employees. The transfer may bring about a marked improvement if the employee adjusts to the new department and the new supervisor in a positive fashion. If a transfer is made simply to give the employee a last chance to retain a job in the company, the employee should be told that he or she must improve in the new job or else be subject to discharge. Of course, the supervisor who accepts the transferred employee should be informed about the circumstances surrounding the transfer. This will help the supervisor in assisting the transferred employee to make a successful transition.

Demotion. Another disciplinary measure, the value of which is open to serious question, is demotion to a lower-paying job. This course of action is likely to bring about dissatisfaction and discouragement since losing pay and status over an extended period of time is a form of constant punishment. The dissatisfaction of the demoted employee can also spread to other employees. Therefore, most organizations avoid demotion (or downgrading) as a disciplinary action.

Demotion should be used only in unusual situations in which a disciplinary layoff or a discharge is not a better alternative. For example, a long-service employee may not be maintaining the standards of work performance required in a certain job. In order to retain seniority and other accrued benefits, this employee may accept a demotion as an alternative to discharge.

Discharge (Termination). The most drastic form of disciplinary action is discharge (or termination). The discharged employee loses all seniority standing and may have difficulty obtaining employment elsewhere. Discharge should be reserved only for the most serious offenses and as a last resort.

A discharge involves loss and waste. It means having to train a new employee and disrupting the makeup of the work group, which may affect the morale of other employees. Moreover, in unionized companies management becomes concerned about possible prolonged grievance and arbitration proceedings. Management knows that labor arbitrators are unwilling to sustain discharge except for severe offenses or for a series of violations that cumulatively justify the discharge. If the discharge involves an employee who is a member of a legally protected group, management will have to be concerned about meeting appropriate standards for nondiscrimination.

In this regard, slightly over one-half of human resources professionals who responded to a survey in 1999 said that their firms had been named in one or more employment-related lawsuits. Overwhelmingly, these lawsuits had been filed by former employees who alleged that they were terminated or discriminated against unlawfully, which led to their exit or removal from employment.[22] Because of the serious implications and consequences of discharge, many organizations have removed the discharge decision from supervisors and have reserved it for higher-level managers. Other organizations require that any discharge recommended by a supervisor must be reviewed and approved by higher-level managers or the human resources department, often with the advice of legal counsel.[23]

Because of legal and other such concerns, the final termination interview with the discharged employee may be conducted by a human resources staff person. However, if the supervisor conducts the termination interview, he or she should be careful to focus on the reasons for the termination and be responsive to the questions of the person being terminated. The supervisor should not lose emotional control or engage in a heated debate about the fairness of the termination decision. Hopefully, the supervisor will be able to close the termination interview by suggesting avenues or options that the individual should consider for possible future employment elsewhere.[24]

All of the preceding considerations should generally be observed even by those employers who traditionally have had the freedom to dismiss employees at will, at any time, and for any reasons, except for unlawful discrimination, union activity, and the like, or where there are restrictions imposed by a contract, a policy manual, or some form of employment agreement. This has been called **employment-at-will,** and it still is generally considered applicable from a legal point of view.[25] Figure 19-9 is an example of an employment-at-will policy statement included in a bank's employee handbook.

Employers who primarily rely upon the employment-at-will principle for termination of employees may find themselves facing legal difficulties.[26] State and federal courts have found various exceptions to employment-at-will, and a number of states have passed laws or are considering legislation that would restrict the application of the at-will relationship in employment. As stated before, most employers recognize that a

Employment-at-will
Legal concept that employers can dismiss employees at any time and for any reasons, except unlawful discrimination or contractual or other restrictions.

FIGURE 19-9

Employment-at-will policy statement of a bank.

> **EMPLOYMENT-AT-WILL**
>
> Mercantile Bank is an at-will employer. This means that employees may resign from the bank if they choose to do so. Similarly, the bank may discharge an employee at any time, for any reason, with or without notice. Nothing in this handbook or any other manual or policy adopted by Mercantile in any way alters the at-will nature of employment at Mercantile.
>
> The separation decision is not one to be made without serious consideration by either the employer or employee. Generally an employee choosing to leave will give appropriate notice, and discharges are not likely to occur precipitously.

discharge action should have a rational basis, such as economic necessity, or should be for just cause or at least for *good cause* as it has been sometimes called.[27] When employers follow the principles of progressive disciplinary action coupled with good supervisory practices, they usually will not have to resort to employment-at-will to decide whether to terminate an employee who has not performed in an acceptable manner.

APPLYING THE HOT STOVE RULE

5
Explain the hot stove rule approach for disciplinary actions.

Hot stove rule

Guideline for applying discipline analogous to touching a hot stove: advance warning and consequences that are immediate, consistent, and applied with impersonality.

Taking disciplinary action may place the supervisor in a strained, difficult position. Disciplinary action tends to generate employee resentment, and it is not a pleasant experience. To assist the supervisor in applying the necessary disciplinary measure so that it will be least resented and likely to withstand challenges from various sources, some authorities have advocated the use of the **hot stove rule.** This rule compares touching a hot stove with experiencing discipline. Both contain four elements: advance warning, immediacy, consistency, and impersonality.

Everyone knows what will happen if they touch a red-hot stove (*advance warning*). Someone who touches a hot stove gets burned right away, with no questions of cause and effect (*immediacy*). Every time a person touches a hot stove, that person gets burned (*consistency*). Whoever touches a hot stove is burned because of the act of touching the stove, regardless of who the person is (*impersonality*). These four elements of the hot stove rule can be applied by the supervisor when maintaining employee discipline.

Advance Warning

For employees to accept disciplinary action as fair, it is essential that they know in advance what is expected of them and what the rules and regulations are. Employees must be informed clearly that certain acts will lead to disciplinary action. Many organizations use orientation sessions, employee handbooks, and bulletin board announcements to inform employees about the rules and how they are to be enforced. In addition, supervisors are responsible for clarifying any questions that arise concerning rules and their enforcement.

Some firms print their rules in an employee handbook, which every new employee receives. As part of orientation, the supervisor should explain to each new employee the departmental rules and the rules that are part of the employee handbook. Some organizations require employees to sign a document stating that they have read and understood the rules and regulations. For example, because of the numerous legal and performance problems associated with substance abuse, many firms provide their employees with detailed information concerning the firm's policies and procedures for dealing with employees who are discovered to have alcohol or controlled substances (i.e., drugs) in their systems. Such policies and procedures may specify information and warnings that spell out the firm's intentions regarding testing, treatment, and disciplinary responses including possible termination.[28]

It is important that employees be clearly informed that certain acts will lead to disciplinary action.

Unfortunately, in some organizations there are rules on the books that have not been enforced. For example, there may be a rule prohibiting smoking in a certain area that the supervisor has not previously enforced. Of course, it would be improper for the supervisor to suddenly decide that it is time to enforce this rule strictly and try to make an example by taking disciplinary action against an employee found smoking in this area.

However, the fact that a certain rule has not been enforced in the past does not mean that it can never be enforced. To enforce such a rule, the supervisor must inform and warn the employees that the rule will be strictly enforced from this point on. It is not enough just to post a notice on the bulletin board since not everyone looks at the board every day. The supervisor must issue a clear, written notice and supplement it with oral communication.

Immediacy

After noticing an offense, the supervisor should take disciplinary action as promptly as possible. At the same time, the supervisor should avoid haste, which might lead to unwarranted reactions. The sooner the discipline is imposed, the more closely it will be connected with the offensive act.

There will be instances when it appears that an employee is guilty of a violation, but the supervisor may be in doubt as to what degree of penalty should be imposed.

For example, incidents such as fighting, intoxication, or insubordination often require an immediate response from the supervisor. In these cases the supervisor may place the employee on temporary suspension, which means being suspended pending a final decision. The temporarily suspended employee is advised that he or she will be informed about the ultimate disciplinary decision as soon as possible or at a specific date.

Temporary suspension in itself is not a punishment. It protects both management and the employee. It provides the supervisor with time to make an investigation and an opportunity to cool off. If the ensuing investigation indicates that no disciplinary action is warranted, then the employee is recalled and does not suffer any loss of pay. If a disciplinary layoff eventually is applied, then the time during which the employee was temporarily suspended will constitute part of the disciplinary layoff. The advantage of temporary suspension is that the supervisor can act promptly. However, it should not be used indiscriminately.

Consistency

Appropriate disciplinary action should be taken each time an infraction occurs. The supervisor who feels inclined to be lenient every now and then is, in reality, not doing the employees a favor. Inconsistency in imposing discipline will lead to employee anxiety and create doubts as to what employees can and cannot do. This type of situation can be compared to the relations between a motorist and a traffic police officer in an area where the speed limit is enforced only occasionally. Whenever the motorist exceeds the speed limit, the motorist experiences anxiety knowing that the police officer can enforce the law at any time. Most motorists would agree that it is easier to operate in a location where the police force is consistent in enforcing or not enforcing speed limits. Employees, too, find it easier to work in an environment in which the supervisor is consistent in applying disciplinary action.

Because of numerous difficulties associated with inconsistencies in enforcing absenteeism and tardiness policies, many firms have adopted no-fault attendance policies, especially for blue-collar employees.[29] A **no-fault attendance policy** counts any unscheduled absence or tardiness as an "occurrence," and the accumulation of numbers of occurrences or assessed points during designated timeframes is used to invoke progressive discipline ranging from warnings, suspension, and termination. Supervisors often prefer a no-fault approach, since they do not have to assess or determine the legitimacy of an employee's unscheduled absence. A firm's no-fault attendance policy may have provisions for rewarding good attendance and may designate certain absence exceptions. These are all spelled out, so that employees and supervisors have a well-understood and consistent framework by which absences and tardiness will be evaluated and handled.[30] Figure 19-10 is excerpted from a manufacturing firm's "Absenteeism and Tardiness Policy," which is a no-fault system that applies to this firm's unionized plant employees.

However, being consistent in applying disciplinary action does not necessarily mean treating everyone in exactly the same manner in all situations. Special considerations surrounding an offense may need to be considered, such as the circumstances, the

No-fault attendance policy
Policy under which unscheduled absences and tardiness are counted as occurrences, and their accumulation is used in progressive discipline.

Absenteeism and Tardiness Policy

1. All employees are expected to report to work in sufficient time to receive job assignments as scheduled and to work their scheduled hours and necessary overtime. Employees will be charged with an "absence occurrence" when they fail to report for scheduled work hours. Employees will be considered tardy and charged with a "partial absence occurrence" when they report to work past their scheduled starting time. Similarly, workers who leave early will be charged with a partial absence occurrence.

2. "Partial absence occurrence" incidents will be combined so that for every three (3) "partial absence occurrences" an employee will be charged with one (1) "absence occurrence."

3. Each employee will be allowed two (2) nonchargeable absence occurrences supported by reasonable excuses in a 12-month period. To activate these allowances, the employee must notify the Personnel Office in advance.

4. Absences for which employees will be charged with an occurrence consist of failure to work a scheduled shift, except for the following exclusions: jury or military duty, work-related injuries or illnesses, scheduled time off for vacations and holidays, disciplinary suspension, temporary layoff, approved union business, court-ordered appearances, and authorized bereavement leave. Absences lasting several consecutive days due to nonwork-related illness and injury of the employee will be treated as one occurrence. Nonconsecutive partial occurrences related to the same medical or dental condition will also be treated as one partial occurrence with prenotification to the Company. The employer has the right to require workers to submit a doctor's note or undergo a physical examination to verify a claim of illness or injury.

5. Accumulation of four (4) occurrences in a 12-month period (not a calendar year) will result in an oral warning. The fifth (5th) occurrence will elicit a written warning, the seventh (7th), a one-day suspension, the eighth (8th), a three-day suspension, and the ninth (9th), a ten-day suspension. Employees who are charged with ten (10) occurrences within a 12-month period will be subject to discharge. The personnel department will provide counseling at each step of this progressive procedure, and will refer employees for outside counseling and assistance in dealing with medical, physical, or personal difficulties related to their attendance problems, if necessary. In order for an employee to offset "absence" and "partial absence" occurrences, each four (4) week attendance period in which that employee has no occurrences will entitle the employee to a removal of the oldest occurrence, whether a full occurrence or a maximum of three (3) partial occurrences, sustained in one attendance period during the prior 12 months from their attendance file.

employee's productivity, job attitudes, length of service, and the like. The extent to which a supervisor can be consistent and yet consider the individual's situation can be illustrated with the following example. Assume that three employees become involved in some kind of horseplay. Employee A just started work a few days ago, Employee B has been warned once before about this, and Employee C has been involved in numerous cases of horseplay. In taking disciplinary action, the supervisor could decide to have a friendly, informal talk with Employee A, give a written warning to Employee B, and impose a two-day disciplinary layoff on Employee C. Thus, each case is considered on its own merits, with the employees being judged according to their work history. Of course, if two of these employees had the same number of previous warnings, their penalties should be identical.

Imposing discipline consistently is one way a supervisor demonstrates a sense of fair play. Yet this may be easier said than done. There are times when the department is particularly rushed and the supervisor may be inclined to conveniently overlook infractions. Perhaps the supervisor does not wish to upset the workforce or does not wish to lose the output of a valuable employee at a critical time. This type of consideration is paramount, especially when it is difficult to obtain employees with the skill that the offending employee possesses. Most employees, however, will accept an exception as fair if they know why the exception was made and if they consider it justified. However, the employees must feel that any other employee in exactly the same situation would receive similar treatment.

Impersonality

All employees who commit the same or a similar offense should be penalized or treated in the same manner. Penalties should be connected with the offensive act, not with the

When a supervisor is imposing discipline, impersonality can help reduce the resentment the employee feels.

person or personality of the employee involved. It should not make any difference whether the employee is white or black, male or female, young or old, or a member of any other group. The same standards of disciplinary expectations and actions should be applied uniformly.

When a supervisor is imposing discipline, impersonality can help reduce the amount of resentment that is likely to be felt by an employee. At the same time, supervisors should understand that employee reactions to discipline will vary, just as individuals who get burned by touching a hot stove will react differently. For example, one person may shout, another may cry, another may reflexively inhale, or one may "push away" from the point of stimulus of pain with the opposite hand. Regardless of the individual, there will always be a reaction to being burned.

The optimal reaction to discipline would be the acceptance of responsibility for the wrongdoing and a change in behavior by the employee to the desired standards with no severe side effects—such as loss of morale, disruption of other employees, or a negative portrayal of the company to customers or external business associates. Making a disciplinary action impersonal may reduce the level of resentment felt by the employee, but it is difficult to predict each employee's specific reaction. Personality, acceptance of authority, the job situation, and circumstances of the offense will all factor into an employee's reactions. A supervisor may have to deal with an employee's reactions if these are of a detrimental nature. However, assuming that the employee's reactions are not severe, the supervisor should again treat the employee the same as before the infraction and disciplinary action, without being apologetic about what had to be done.

Discuss the need to document disciplinary actions and to provide the right of appeal.

Documentation

Keeping records of memoranda, documents, and meetings that are relevant to a disciplinary action.

Right to appeal

Procedures by which an employee may request higher-level management to review a supervisor's disciplinary action.

DOCUMENTATION AND THE RIGHT TO APPEAL

Whenever a disciplinary action is taken, the supervisor must keep records of the offense committed and the decision made, including the reasoning involved in the decision. This is called **documentation,** and it may include keeping files of memoranda, documents, minutes of meetings, and the like that were part of the case handling. Documentation is necessary because the supervisor may be asked at some future time to justify the action taken, and the burden of proof is usually on the supervisor. It is not prudent for the supervisor to depend on memory alone. This is particularly true in unionized firms where grievance-arbitration procedures often result in a challenge to disciplinary actions imposed on employees.

The **right to appeal** means that it should be possible for an employee to request a review of a supervisor's disciplinary action from higher-level management. If the employee belongs to a labor union, this right is part of a grievance procedure. In most firms, the appeal is first directed to the supervisor's boss, thereby following the chain of command. Many large firms have provided for a hierarchy of several levels of management through which an appeal may be taken. The human resources department may become directly involved in an appeal procedure. Complaint procedures in nonunion firms and grievance procedures in unionized organizations were discussed in Chapter 17.

The right of appeal must be recognized as a real privilege and not merely a formality. Some supervisors tell their employees that they can appeal to higher-level management but that it will be held against them if they do so. This attitude is indicative of a supervisor's own insecurity. Supervisors should not be afraid to encourage their employees to appeal to higher-level management if the employees feel that they have been treated unfairly. Nor should supervisors feel that an appeal threatens or weakens their position as departmental managers. For the most part, a supervisor's manager will be inclined to support the supervisor's original action. If supervisors do not foster an open appeal procedure, employees may enlist aid from outside, such as a union would provide. Management's failure to provide a realistic appeal procedure is one of the reasons why some employees have resorted to unionization.

In the course of an appeal, the disciplinary penalty imposed or recommended by a supervisor may be reduced or reversed by the higher-level manager. The supervisor's decision might be reversed because the supervisor has not been consistent in imposing disciplinary action or has not considered all the necessary facts. Under these circumstances, the supervisor may become discouraged and feel that the manager has not backed him or her up. Although this situation is unfortunate, it is better for the supervisor to be disheartened than for an employee to be penalized unjustly. This is not too high a price to pay to provide every employee the right to appeal. Situations such as these can be avoided if supervisors adhere closely to the principles and steps discussed in this chapter before taking disciplinary action.

DISCIPLINE WITHOUT PUNISHMENT

7
Explain the discipline without punishment approach as an alternative to progressive discipline.

Discipline without punishment
Disciplinary approach that uses coaching and counseling as preliminary steps and a paid decision-making leave for employees to decide whether to improve and stay, or quit.

A growing number of companies have adopted disciplinary procedures called **discipline without punishment.** The major thrust of this approach is to stress extensive coaching, counseling, and problem solving and to avoid confrontation. A significant (and controversial) feature is the paid "decision-making leave" in which an employee is sent home for a day or more with pay to decide whether or not he or she is willing to make a commitment to meet the expected standards of performance heretofore not met. If the employee makes a commitment to improve but fails to do so, the employee is then terminated.

In general, this approach replaces warnings and suspensions with coaching sessions and reminders by supervisors of the expected standards. The decision-making leave with pay is posed as a decision to be made by the employee, namely, to improve and stay, or quit.

Organizations that have implemented this approach successfully have reported various benefits, particularly in the area of reduced complaints and grievances and improved employee morale. It is questionable whether discipline without punishment programs will be adopted extensively since it is not clear that these programs are all that different in concept and outcome from progressive disciplinary action as discussed in this chapter. What is clear is that a discipline without punishment approach requires commitment from all management levels—especially from supervisors—if it is to be carried out successfully.[31]

What Call Did You Make?

As Linda Juarez, you recognize that following the principles discussed in this chapter is sometimes easier said than done. The situation in your department first requires investigation before you take action. You should make an extra effort to observe Scott Stoner to see if you can verify any of Kathy Florence's allegations. At the same time, you probably should talk with your own manager or the director of human resources for their suggestions on how to proceed. Then you should talk with several other employees in your department to get their versions of Scott Stoner's behavior to see how they compare with Kathy's report.

If they concur with Kathy's version, you should meet with Scott Stoner to inform him of the allegations and hear his side of the story, even if his explanation is primarily self-serving. If you believe that there is a major performance problem, you should go over the relevant rules of the department with Scott so that he is clear about your expectations concerning the rules, attendance, and work performance. You need to remind him of the importance of good work habits, including a specific admonition that most personal business should not be performed during work hours. Urge him to establish better relationships with his coworkers, and point out that if he does not, his contributions to the department will be minimal. Try to get him to agree to some specific target objectives for various components of his job which you then can evaluate more directly than otherwise might be the case. Tell Scott that he should consider this discussion as a verbal or informal warning and that you will be monitoring his performance closely in the weeks to follow.

Tell him that you hope his performance will improve considerably and that his relationships with his coworkers will foster teamwork. At the same time, make sure he understands that if similar complaints continue and his performance is not satisfactory, you will have to consider future disciplinary action. If he asks what such disciplinary action might be, do not be specific but be sure that he understands that it will be more than a verbal warning and that it even could result in his termination.

Finally, after your interview with Scott, write a memorandum that summarizes the interview. This memorandum should be kept confidential and in a safe place. It could be valuable as documentation if future disciplinary action becomes necessary.

SUMMARY

1

Employee discipline can be thought of as the degree to which employees act according to expected standards of behavior. It is likely that if employee morale is high, discipline will be positive and there will be less need for the supervisor to take disciplinary action. Supervisors should recognize that most employees want to do the right thing. Positive self-discipline means that employees essentially regulate their own behavior out of self-interest and their normal desire to meet reasonable standards. Supervisors should set a positive example for their employees to emulate.

2

Many employers have codes of ethics that describe in broad terms the values and ethical requirements of the enterprise. Ethical codes and conflict-of-interest policies usually include procedures for reporting possible violations.

3

Most organizations have written rules and regulations with definitions of infractions and possible penalties for infractions. Rules of conduct typically address areas of attendance, work scheduling, job performance, safety, improper behavior, and other matters. When infractions do occur, supervisors must take appropriate disciplinary action. If ignored, the problems will not go away.

When infractions occur, the supervisor should take disciplinary action with the objective of improving employees' future behavior. Before disciplining, the supervisor first needs to investigate the situation thoroughly. Disciplinary actions should be for just (or proper) cause. Emotional and physical responses should be avoided. The supervisor should determine whether there is sufficient evidence to conclude that the employee knew about the rule or standard and in fact violated it. The supervisor should consider the severity of the violation, the employee's past service record, and other relevant factors. If a disciplinary action is necessary, it normally should be administered in private.

4

A number of progressively severe disciplinary actions, ranging from an informal talk to a warning, a suspension, and discharge, are open to a supervisor as alternative choices, depending on the circumstances and the nature of the infraction. The supervisor's purpose in taking disciplinary action should be to improve the employee's behavior and to maintain proper discipline within the entire department. Progressive discipline is also desirable and applicable for at-will employees, even though it is not required.

5

Taking disciplinary action can be an unpleasant experience for both the employee and the supervisor. To reduce the distasteful aspects, disciplinary action should fulfill as much as possible the requirements of the hot stove rule. These are advance warning, immediacy, consistency, and impersonality.

6

Documentation of a disciplinary action is important in order to substantiate the reasons for the action taken by a supervisor. This is especially important if there is appeal of the disciplinary decision to higher-level management through a grievance or complaint procedure. In the interest of fairness, an appeal procedure provides the employee with a review process by which the supervisor's disciplinary decision may be sustained, modified, or set aside.

7

The discipline without punishment approach utilizes extensive coaching and counseling as preliminary steps. If there is no improvement, a paid decision-making leave may be given to the employee to decide whether he or she will make a commitment to improvement or be terminated.

KEY TERMS

Discipline (page 650)
Positive discipline (page 651)
Positive self-discipline (page 651)
Just cause (page 658)
Progressive discipline (page 662)
Employment-at-will (page 667)

Hot stove rule (page 668)
No-fault attendance policy (page 670)
Documentation (page 673)
Right to appeal (page 673)
Discipline without punishment (page 674)

QUESTIONS FOR DISCUSSION

1. Define the concept of employee discipline as a part of the working environment in a firm. In this context, differentiate between positive discipline and negative discipline.
2. Discuss the relationship between discipline and morale.

3. Evaluate the following statement: "The best type of discipline is positive self-discipline."
4. What are the differences between a code of ethics, a "conflict-of-interest" policy, and written rules and regulations? What are their purposes?
5. Why should supervisors not be afraid to confront disciplinary situations when they occur?
6. What is meant by the concept that disciplinary action should have just cause?
7. Discuss the importance of each of the following precautionary measures that supervisors must bear in mind when taking disciplinary action.
    a. Careful study and investigation.
    b. Considerations in conducting investigatory interviews.
    c. Avoiding emotional or physical outbursts.
    d. Privacy in administering discipline.
    e. Observing the time element.
8. Define and evaluate each of the following steps of progressive discipline.
    a. Informal talk.
    b. Oral warning (or verbal counseling).
    c. Written warning.
    d. Disciplinary layoff (or suspension).
    e. Transfer.
    f. Demotion.
    g. Discharge.
9. What should be the purpose of any disciplinary action?
10. Define and evaluate each of the following elements of the hot stove rule.
    a. Advance warning.
    b. Immediacy.
    c. Consistency.
    d. Impersonality.
11. Why have numerous firms implemented no-fault attendance policies in their efforts to control absenteeism and tardiness?
12. Discuss the following statement: "Discipline should be directed against the act and not against the person." Why is this sometimes difficult for a supervisor to accomplish?
13. Why should a supervisor document any disciplinary action that is taken?
14. What is meant by the right to appeal? How can this right be implemented in a nonunion organization? Discuss.
15. Is a discipline without punishment approach significantly different from regular progressive discipline? Discuss.

SKILLS APPLICATIONS

Skills Application 19-1: Employee Dress and Appearance Standards

Chapter 18's "Contemporary Issue" box focused upon some of the recent issues associated with widespread relaxed and informal dress and appearance standards in the workplace. Employee dress and appearance have been an ongoing concern and problem for supervisors for many years, and this has become one of the most difficult areas for disciplinary policies. This concern is especially important when employees deal directly with the public, such as in banks, retail stores, and restaurants. There also is concern about individual rights because of racial/gender/ethnic and other differences that often cause problems or potential issues of favoritism or discrimination.

1. Identify an organization that you are familiar with and write a dress/appearance code for employees as it might appear in an employee handbook.
2. Give at least two examples of attire and appearance for which some disagreements about acceptability could arise, and propose how you would handle such disagreements.
3. How would you propose handling repeated violations of the dress/appearance standards?
4. If possible, obtain the employee handbook for the organization you have used as your model. If this firm does not have a dress/appearance code, try to obtain such a code from another firm whose employees would be performing similar job duties as the one you identified. What were the similarities and differences between your dress/appearance code and your proposals for handling violations, and those of the firm? Can you explain the reasons for these differences?

Skills Application 19-2: Rules of Conduct

Reproduced below is a list of rules of conduct of Acme Co. as it appears in the company's employee handbook. The firm is not unionized. Review these rules and then answer the questions that follow.

RULES OF CONDUCT

Rules and guidelines have been established for the mutual benefit of Acme Co. and all employees. We ask your cooperation in following these rules. Our purpose is not to prohibit your rights but to help you be as productive and effective as possible.

The following list summarizes rule and policy violations subject to disciplinary action:

First Offense—Suspension or Immediate Discharge

1. Absence from work two consecutive days without authorization.
2. Intoxication and/or use of drugs.
3. Theft or unauthorized possession of Acme property.
4. Careless, negligent, or improper use of Acme property.
5. Falsifying employment application.
6. Refusal to work.
7. Abusive or threatening language to staff, supervisors, employees, or customers.
8. Fighting.
9. Falsifying work records or time cards.
10. Punching another employee's time card.
11. Releasing confidential information without proper authority.

First Offense—Verbal and/or Written Warning

1. Insubordination.
2. Unauthorized absence.
3. Excessive absenteeism.
4. Repeated tardiness.
5. Failure to report to work.
6. Failure to maintain satisfactory relationships with other employees.
7. Smoking in unauthorized areas.
8. Failure to punch the time clock.
9. Sleeping on the job.
10. Inefficiency; incompetency.
11. Disregard of personal appearance, dress.

12. Leaving assigned place of work without supervisory permission.

Second and/or Third Offense—Suspension or Immediate Discharge

Any of the above rule violations listed under "First Offense—Verbal and/or Written Warning" that occur a second or third time may result in a disciplinary suspension or immediate discharge.

The above rules of conduct are meant only to serve as a guide. Variations in disciplinary actions taken may depend on the severity and intent of the offense and other circumstances.

1. How does the list of violations illustrate a progressive discipline system?
2. Do you agree that the violations leading to possible immediate discharge after the first offense are appropriate? Why or why not? Which should be dropped, or what should be added?
3. Under a second and/or third offense, why might the vagueness of the process be both an advantage and a potential problem?
4. If you were to rewrite or edit this list of rules, what would you propose?

Skills Application 19-3: Disciplinary Action for Just Cause

1. From the materials in this chapter, develop a list of the requirements and considerations that you believe are the most essential for ensuring that a disciplinary action taken against an employee has a just cause basis.
2. **a.** Contact two practicing supervisors (or managers) who are willing to be interviewed. One supervisor should be in a unionized firm and have departmental employees under a union contract. The other should be in a firm whose employees are not represented by a union. Ask each supervisor to identify what he or she believes to be the five or more most important requirements and considerations when a supervisor takes disciplinary action against an employee. (Note: Do not use the term "just cause" in making your request.)
   b. Ask each supervisor to respond to the following hypothetical situation: "You discover an employee sound asleep at his or her work station, which is isolated from the view of other employees. It is 10:00 A.M. How would you proceed?"
3. **a.** Compare the supervisors' lists with your list. To what degree were these lists similar or different? If there were major differences, what do you feel would be the most likely explanation?
   b. Compare each supervisor's response to the hypothetical situation posed in question 2b. If there were major differences, how might they be explained?

Skills Application 19-4: No-Fault Attendance Policy

Locate a firm that has adopted and implemented a no-fault attendance policy. (This may require a number of telephone calls or networking conversations.) Then contact the human resources person who can describe and explain their policy. Request a copy of the policy in order for you to examine it and to suggest areas for analysis and explanation. Interview the human resources person so that you are able to answer the following questions.

1. What are the major features of the firm's no-fault attendance policy?
2. When and why did the firm implement it?
3. **a.** What are the primary advantages of this type of policy?
   b. What are the primary problems/disadvantages of this type of policy?

4. What is your overall evaluation of a no-fault attendance policy as compared with other approaches for controlling absenteeism and tardiness?

**INTERNET
ACTIVITY**

Skills Application 19-5: Rules of Conduct and Codes of Ethics

Many organizations today have published their own codes of ethics. Some, like Texas Instruments, have even established ethics offices. Visit Texas Instruments' Web site (www.ti.com) to learn more about the company's values and ethics.

1. How does the company work with employees to promote ethical conduct? What is the TI policy regarding positive discipline?
2. What is the company's "Ethics Quick Test?"
3. Search for other company codes on the Web [you'll find links to several at the Centre for Applied Ethics (www.ethics.ubcca/resources/business)]. Then write your own personal code of ethics for the workplace.

ENDNOTES

1. In a 1999 survey of almost 1,500 "anonymous employees" at 11 restaurant chains, respondents admitted stealing annually an average of $218 in food and property. This compared to an average of $96 a year earlier. Unauthorized meals for themselves or friends was the most frequently cited offense. See Richard Gibson, "Restaurant-Employee Theft Rises," *The Wall Street Journal* (September 14, 1999), p. A1.
2. Employee absenteeism reached a seven-year high in 1998, rising 25 percent from 1997. Some of this was attributed to burnout, work-family conflicts, and tight labor markets, which influenced workers to feel "more entitled" to take days off. See "Work Week," *The Wall Street Journal* (May 25, 1999), p. A1. Absenteeism in 1999 eased slightly (about a 7 percent reduction from the 1998 level). However, stress as a cause of absenteeism has tripled since 1995; as the reported reason for absenteeism, stress is now almost at the same level as physical illness. See Albert R. Karr, "Work Week," *The Wall Street Journal* (September 21, 1999), p. A1.
3. From Robert W. Thomson, "Fraud Costs Employers Dearly," *HRMagazine* (November 1998), p. 10. Also see Harrison Rainie, Margaret Loftus, and Mark Madden, "The State of Greed, *U.S. News & World Report* (June 17, 1996), p. 64.
4. For an expanded discussion of so-called Web abuses and what some employers are doing in response, see Bill Roberts, "Filtering Software Blocks Employees' Web Abuses," *HRMagazine* (September 1999), pp. 114–120. Also see Albert R. Karr, "Companies Crack Down on the Increasing Sexual Harassment by E-Mail," *The Wall Street Journal* (September 21, 1999), p. A1.
5. From Oren Harari, "U2D2: The Rx for Leadership Blues," *Management Review* (August 1995), pp. 34–36.
6. In a survey of large employers in the U.S., 60 percent of the surveyed companies indicated that they had a code of ethics in place, and a third of them provided training on ethical business conduct. See "Boost in Ethical Awareness," *HRMagazine* (February 1995), p. 19.
7. See Michael J. McCarthy, "An Ex-Divinity Student Works on Searching the Corporate Soul," *The Wall Street Journal* (June 18, 1999), p. B1. If a firm only gives "lip-service" to its ethics policies and its technical training for employees is minimal, the result may be worse than to have no ethics program whatsoever, according to a study conducted by Arthur Andersen's Ethics and Responsible Business Practices Group. See "Lip-Service Ethics Programs Prove Ineffective," *Management Review* (June 1999), p. 9.
8. From, "Many Workers Feel Pressured to Cut Ethical Concerns," *HRNews* (May 1998), p. 12.
9. See Mary G. Rendini, "Team Effort at Maguire Group Leads to Ethics Policy," *HRMagazine* (April 1995), pp. 63–66.
10. See Kate Walter, "Ethics Hot Lines Tap into More Than Wrongdoing," *HRMagazine* (November 1995), pp. 79–85.

11. For example, see Debra R. Meyer, "More on Whistleblowing," *Management Accounting* (June 1993), p. 26; and Marcy Mason, "The Curse of Whistleblowing," *The Wall Street Journal* (March 14, 1994), p. A14.

12. From Nicholas G. Moore, *Ethics: The Way to Do Business,* published pamphlet of his Sears Lectureship in Business Ethics at Bentley College (February 9, 1998), p. 9.

13. See "Review Employee Handbooks," *News You-Can-Use Letter* (St. Louis, MO: AAIM Management Association (February 1996)), pp. 4 and 6.

14. See Milton Bordwin, "Do-it-Yourself Justice," *Management Review* (January 1999), pp. 56–57.

15. See "Accountability Board Urges Greater Use of Dispute Resolution," *HRNews* (April 1999), p. 14.

16. For expanded information on grievance-arbitration procedures, particularly as related to discipline/discharge cases, see E. Edward Herman, *Collective Bargaining and Labor Relations* (4th ed.; Upper Saddle River, NJ: Prentice-Hall, 1998), pp. 316–331; or Arthur A. Sloane and Fred Witney, *Labor Relations* (9th ed.; Upper Saddle River, NJ: Prentice-Hall, 1997), pp. 243–272 and 445–450.

17. See James G. Vigneau, "To Catch a Thief . . . and Other Workplace Investigations," *HRMagazine* (January 1995), pp. 90–95.

18. See Albert R. Karr, "Some Employers are Alarmed About Disclosing Employee Investigations," *The Wall Street Journal* (June 1, 1999), p. A1.

19. Many companies also conduct random and other drug tests on their employees, especially federal government contractors and employers as mandated by the Drug-Free Workplace Act of 1988. Companies usually have policies and procedures that outline how tests will be taken, safeguards, and possible penalties for violations. See "Testing . . . Testing," *Business Week* (May 2, 1994). p. 6.

20. This is referred to as a unionized employee's Weingarten rights, based upon a U.S. Supreme Court decision. See Raymond L. Hilgert, *Cases in Collective Bargaining and Industrial Relations* (9th ed.; Boston: Irwin/McGraw Hill, 1999), pp. 115–116.

21. For an expanded discussion on the technique and applications of letters of clarification, see Paul Falcone, "Letters of Clarification: A Disciplinary Alternative," *HRMagazine* (August 1999), pp. 134–140.

22. See "Survey Reveals More Than Half of Employers Have Been Sued," *HRNews* (August 1999), p. 13.

23. See Francis T. Coleman, *Conducting Lawful Terminations* (Alexandria, Va.: SHRM Foundation, 1995).

24. See Dennis L. Johnson, Christie A. King, and John G. Kurutz, "A Safe Termination Model for Supervisors," *HRMagazine* (May 1996), pp. 73–78; and Gary Bielous, "How to Fire" *Supervision* (November 1996), pp. 8–10.

25. See Michael J. Phillips, "Toward a Middle Way in the Polarized Debate Over Employment at Will," *American Business Law Journal* (November 1992), pp. 441–483; or Kenneth Gilberg, "Employers Must Protect Against Employee Lawsuits," *Supervision* (November 1992), pp. 12–13.

26. "Loss of At-Will Job is Compensable," *HRNews* (February 1999), p. 8.

27. See Matt Siegel, "Yes, They Can Fire You," *Fortune* (October 26, 1998), p. 301.

28. See Jane Easter Bahls, "Drugs in the Workplace," *HRMagazine* (February 1998), pp. 81–87; or Louisa Wah, "Treatment vs. Termination," *Management Review* (April 1998), p. 8.

29. In a 1997–1998 survey of several hundred firms in the St. Louis, Missouri, metropolitan area, about one-third of the reporting firms indicated that they had a no-fault attendance policy for their production, maintenance, and service personnel. See *1997–1998 Personnel Practices Survey* (AAIM Management Association), p. 42.

30. For an expanded discussion on no-fault and other employee attendance policies, see M. Michael Markowich, "When is Excessive Absenteeism Grounds for Disciplinary Action?" *ACA News* (July/August 1998), p. 36–39.

31. For a thorough discussion of the pros and cons and applications of discipline-without-punishment approaches, see Dick Grote, *Discipline Without Punishment* (New York: American Management Association, 1995).

SANDERS SUPERMARKETS STORE #16: WHAT HAPPENED TO CONTROL?

Juan Sanchez is store supervisor at Store #16 of Sanders Supermarkets. For about three months he had been talking to his district manager, Sandra Greenberg, about a major renovation for the grocery section in the store. At last, Greenberg called Sanchez to tell him that a meeting at the corporate main office would be held to discuss the renovation project for Store #16.

The meeting was attended by supervisors from the sales department and the construction department, several district managers, and the corporate operations manager. By the end of the meeting, it was generally agreed that Store #16 should be reorganized (called "reset" in the language of the company), including relocating several main aisles. The supervisor of the reset crew and the construction supervisor were to submit final plans and a cost estimate at the next meeting of the group, which was scheduled for a week later.

During her next visit to Store #16, Greenberg told Sanchez about the meeting. Greenberg informed Sanchez about the plans for Store #16, although she added that nothing was finalized yet. She failed to mention that part of the reset would include moving some of the aisles.

The next week, completed plans and costs were submitted to and given a final approval by the corporate operations manager. Since new shelving had to be ordered and schedules made, the supervisor of the reset crew and the construction supervisor were assigned the job of putting the necessary paperwork into motion. Greenberg then called Sanchez and said, "The reset project for your store has been okayed. I'll let you know more as soon as I hear."

One month later, as Sanchez was driving to work, he made a mental note to call Greenberg to ask about the reset project. However, when Sanchez arrived at Store #16, he soon forgot about this plan. He walked into the store to find three major problems: the frozen food case had broken down, the floor scrubber was malfunctioning, and the grinder in the meat department had quit working. After some checking, he found that no maintenance calls had been made, because each of his two assistant supervisors, Jane Oliver and Wally Withers, had thought the other was going to do it. The floor scrubber had not worked well for three days, the frozen food case had broken down the previous afternoon, and the meat grinder had just conked out.

"It just doesn't pay to take a day off," Sanchez muttered to himself as he headed for the telephone. He called the maintenance department, explained what had happened, and requested immediate service. While waiting for the maintenance person, Sanchez called Jane Oliver and Wally Withers to talk to them about letting him and each other know about these kinds of problems and how to control them. "All it takes," he said, "is working together, communication, and follow-through to ensure that our customers get the best service available. We can't be out of merchandise, especially frozen food. And we have to make sure that when we are busy, as we will be this week, our customers aren't stepping over workers in the aisles."

At about that time, Sanchez was called to his office. When he arrived, he was greeted by five carpenters and laborers. "We just wanted to tell you we're here, and we'll get started right away," said the carpenter in charge.

"How come it takes this many people to fix a frozen food case?" asked Sanchez.

"We're not here to fix a frozen food case," said the carpenter. "We're here to move the shelving in the aisles and to reset the store."

"Today?" replied Sanchez. "Nobody told me that you guys were doing this today. I can't have you moving aisles during the day. What are my customers going to do?"

Sanchez then called Greenberg. "Sandy, did you know that they were going to start the reset project in the store today?"

"No," said Sandy, "I wasn't notified either."

"Why wasn't I consulted on this?" exclaimed Sanchez. "First of all, the first week of the month is always too busy a time for laborers to be working in the aisles. Second, this type of work must be done at night. Maybe other stores can handle this in the daytime, but my customers will not tolerate that kind of inconvenience."

"OK," said Greenberg, "it sounds like things are really out of control at your store right now. What are you going to do about it?"

"Sandy, don't you mean, what are we going to do about it?"

Questions for Discussion

1. Define various places where members of management did not plan in specific terms and then failed to follow through on their responsibilities.
2. Analyze Juan Sanchez's discussion with his two assistants, especially when he said that, "All it takes is working together, communication, and follow-through." Are these factors the essence of supervision, or does good supervision require something more? Discuss.
3. What should Greenberg and Sanchez do in regard to the immediate problem of the carpenters in the store?
4. Develop a series of general recommendations to improve planning and control procedures in the Sanders company.

Case

6-2

RESISTANCE TO A WORK SAMPLING PROGRAM

Debbie Quarter, a new staff engineer for C. W. S. Manufacturing Company, had been assigned the responsibility of administering the plant's work sampling program. This was the first assignment of this nature in her career. Her only knowledge of the program until this time came in the form of comments from friends working as plant foremen or supervisors. She recalled that they referred to the work sampling program as "bird dogging." They seemed universally to regard the program as unfair, a waste of time, and a personal affront. She realized that only the line superintendents supported the program, and even some of them regarded it as a necessary evil.

Details of the Program

The work sampling program, or ratio-delay as it was sometimes called, involved the statistical sampling of the activities of hourly production and maintenance department employees, which included approximately two-thirds of the plant's 2,000 employees. The sampling was conducted on a continuous basis by a full-time observer who walked through the plant via a series of randomly selected, predetermined routes. The observer's job was to record the activity of each worker as the worker was first observed. An activity could fall into one of seven categories, which in turn were subclasses of either "working," "traveling," or "nonworking." The data were compiled monthly, and results were charted for each group and sent to the various supervisors and superintendents.

The program had been in effect for about five years at the plant. At the time it was initiated, management stated the purpose of the program as threefold: (1) It was to be used as an indication of supervisory effectiveness; (2) it was to be of help in identifying problems interfering with work performance; and (3) it was to be a control measure of the effect of changes in work methods, equipment, facilities, or supervision.

Meetings on the Program

Realizing the widespread resistance to the program, Debbie Quarter began immediately to conduct informational meetings for all line foremen and supervisors. In these sessions she discussed the purpose of the program and the mechanics of conducting it. She also attempted to answer any questions raised. The foremen and supervisors were most vocal in expressing their negative opinions about the program, and after a few meetings she noted that certain comments were being repeated in some form by almost every group.

Most supervisory groups identified particular aspects of the sampling program that they thought biased its results against them. The most common complaint of this type was that the sampling was too often conducted during periods when work was normally lightest, that is, during coffee breaks and early or late in the day. Since the method of scheduling visits was quite complex, efforts to explain the concept of randomness and how fairness was ensured had never been accepted. Some basic statistical training had been attempted in the past but with little success— especially among the foremen who had traditionally come up through the ranks and had little technical background.

Another frequently repeated complaint was that activities normally considered as work were not recorded as such. Examples of this were going for tools or carrying materials. The reason for this, as had been explained to the foremen, was to allow identification of those factors not directly accomplishing work, since these were the areas where improvements could be made.

Several maintenance foremen complained that results were repeatedly used to pressure them to "ride" their workers. When they would tighten down, these foremen said, the workers would resist, and less was accomplished than before. One foreman quoted his boss as saying, "These figures (work sampling results) better be up next month, or I'm going to have three new foremen in here!" It was general knowledge that the superintendents placed quite a bit of emphasis on these results when appraising the supervisors and foremen.

Virtually no one at any level of supervision had a good understanding of how results could be affected by sample size. Small groups with few samples said they had experienced wide fluctuations in results that "just couldn't happen." This, of course, reinforced their distrust of sampling methods.

There had been few, if any, changes initiated by first-line supervisors as a result of work sampling results. Several staff projects had been generated—some of which were quite popular with the workers (for example, motorized personnel carriers)—but these were not generally associated with work sampling results.

After the first few sessions, Debbie Quarter wondered whether her meetings with the foremen and supervisors were perhaps doing more harm than good. The meetings seemed to get everyone upset, and anything that was learned was probably lost in the emotional discussion. She pondered what she should do next.

Questions for Discussion

1. Evaluate the work sampling program as described in this case.
2. Evaluate the work sampling program in view of the principles of a sound control system as outlined in Chapter 18.
3. Outline a course of action for Debbie Quarter.

Case

6–3

WHO'S TELLING THE TRUTH ABOUT QUALITY CONTROL?

Bartholomew Equipment Co. is a major manufacturer of complex electronic data processing equipment. The company has very strict delivery schedules, which have to be kept in order to preserve its good image with its customers. Currently, the company is involved in designing an extremely high-cost computer with specific data characteristics, which is to be submitted to one of Bartholomew's largest customers, the Kee Corporation.

Preparation of the Data Package

The project manager for the company, Ray Edwards, was responsible for gathering all the necessary data that would be incorporated into the final design data packages for various computers. Edwards had an engineer, Stan Neil, to whom he had assigned major responsibility for the Kee project. Neil had been with the company for only six months, but he had steadily gained knowledge of data packages and had carefully tried to understand what was required.

During the collection of various data, representatives of the Kee Corporation visited the Bartholomew plant to check on the progress of its data package. The representatives held meetings with Neil and Edwards, explaining what they wanted and various changes they required. Neil believed that these meetings had developed the full requirements for this customer's data package.

Inspection by Quality Control

Neil continued to gather the data in a timely manner. The deadline was drawing near, and some items were not complete. He felt that a major obstacle to completion on time could be the quality control department, which had the reputation of having been unable to meet scheduled inspection deadlines on other projects. To get the quality control people to recognize the urgency for meeting deadlines on the Kee project, he thought it might be beneficial to provide them with a portion of the data package that was already complete. He went to the quality control department to meet with Rebecca Chang, one of the inspectors. Chang accepted the drawings and data after being informed of the urgent requirements for the package. Chang said she would do all she could to expedite the matter.

Conflict Between the Departments

Neil went back to Edwards and told him that the quality control department would be entirely too slow in doing its work. He stated, "Rebecca Chang wants us to do work that the customer has not said is necessary. We'll never meet the delivery date if she continues to delay the inspection and approval of the data package!"

Edwards, who had not had a good working relationship with the quality control people in the past, took Neil at his word. Edwards complained to the company president about quality control's position and slow work. As a result, the company president, Marcus Finley, decided to call a meeting with Edwards, Neil, and Vic Johnson, the supervisor of the quality control department. These three people were notified to attend a meeting in Finley's office, although Finley did not inform them as to what the meeting would cover.

At the meeting, the trend of the conversation was directly aimed at quality control. Marcus Finley told Vic Johnson that his department was delaying the important Kee project, and this had to stop. Johnson became very defensive and told Finley, "I have no idea what is going on. I don't know who is responsible for this job or what the status of it is. You did not tell me what this meeting was going to cover. I feel very concerned about the way this meeting is being handled. I will not make any statements until I talk to my people about this job." At this point Johnson asked to be excused. He said he could be of more help after he had more of the facts.

Marcus Finley and Vic Johnson had a private meeting that afternoon. Finley apologized for the way the meeting was handled and asked Johnson to check into the problem.

Two days later, the Kee data package was approved by Rebecca Chang in quality control. However, Johnson sent a memo to Finley stating, "The engineering done on this data package was horrible." Johnson added that his department was not furnished the proper or complete drawings and data and that Edwards and Neil had been most uncooperative. He also mentioned Edwards and Neil specifically as having "very poor customer attitudes."

When Ray Edwards received a copy of this memo, he was beside himself. He considered whether he should write his own "poison pen" letter to tell his side of the story.

Questions for Discussion

1. Evaluate Neil's approach in trying to get the data package approved. Why did Neil report back to his manager, Ray Edwards, that the quality control department would hold up the project?

2. Evaluate whether Ray Edwards, the project manager for the company, was well advised to bring the president of the company into this problem situation. How might he have handled the situation otherwise?

3. Why would Vic Johnson send the memo to Finley complaining about the engineering on the data package and also complaining about Edwards and Neil? Was this a prudent move on his part?

4. If you were Edwards, what would you do?

Case
6–4

THE UNSAFE POLE

Henry Floyd was supervisor of a construction crew for Municipal Power and Light Company. The crew consisted of Roy McMillan, Howard Bierman, and Mel Shostak.

One morning, while out on the job, Floyd directed Bierman and Shostak to climb a pole and remove a number of tree limbs that had fallen on a main power line carrying some 7,000 to 8,000 volts. Senior lineman Roy McMillan said, "Henry, I don't believe it's safe to climb that pole with the wind blowing the way it is. You never can tell what will happen when you have broken limbs on a power line."

Floyd responded, "Oh, come on, Roy, we've done jobs like this on many occasions and we've never had any problems." Floyd proceeded to outline how McMillan should do the job to avoid an accident. McMillan then went back to the truck, where Bierman and Shostak were gathering their tools. Shortly afterward the three of them approached Floyd.

McMillan said, "Henry, we're not going to climb that pole. We think it's unsafe. Either we do it another day or we've got to have more men on the job in order to do it safely."

Floyd replied, "Now listen, fellows, we've been through this many times before. It's the supervisor who ultimately makes the decision whether or not a job is safe. We've done many jobs far more dangerous than this one without any problems."

McMillan went on, "We checked our union agreement, and the safety clause in it gives us the right to determine whether or not a job is safe." Floyd looked at the contract clause, which McMillan showed him. It read:

All employees have the responsibility for the safety of their fellow employees and others who are affected by their work. Safety engineering and other support personnel are responsible for assisting supervisors with their safety responsibilities.

All employees have the final responsibility for their own safety. They have the final control over their actions and the last possible chance of being aware of what can injure them and of doing their best to see that it does not. This is one of the job requirements for every employee of Municipal Power and Light Company.

Floyd said, "Yeah, but you're overlooking the fact that there's a clause that precedes it saying that supervisors have the direct responsibility!" With that he read the following clause:

Supervisors have the direct responsibility for safety. This means managers, superintendents, engineers, section heads, division managers, department heads, officers, and all supervisors are responsible for safety in their areas. This includes carrying out safety activities appropriate for their operations.

They continued to discuss the issue. Finally, Roy McMillan said, "Henry, we're simply not going to climb that pole. You can't make us. You can send us home if you want, but if you do we're going to file a grievance and we're also going to file an OSHA complaint for the company's failure to maintain safety standards!"

With that Henry Floyd pondered what he should do.

Questions for Discussion

1. Should the union and/or employees have the right to determine whether a job is safe or not? Should the safety of a job be the sole responsibility of management? Discuss.
2. If the union and management disagree concerning the safety of a particular job, should a neutral or third party be brought in to decide whether the job is safe? Discuss. What is the role of OSHA in this type of situation?
3. Suppose that Floyd ordered an employee to climb a pole that the employee felt was unsafe and the employee subsequently was injured. What are the ramifications of a supervisor's decision under such circumstances?
4. Why does a case of this sort have implications involving the ultimate authority of a supervisor to manage the department?
5. (*Optional*) Using the Internet, find information that would help Henry Floyd determine whether a job is safe or not. The home page of OSHA (at www.osha.gov/) provides OSHA standards and other aspects of workplace safety. The Index of Occupational Safety and Health Resources links to other pages on workplace safety.

   INTERNET ACTIVITY

   a. Many supervisors would like to find a reference source that would tell them exactly how they can determine whether a particular situation puts their employees in "harm's way." Discuss the role that Internet sites play in providing timely information.
   b. Briefly discuss any other ideas from a review of Internet sources that might be useful in helping Municipal Power and Light provide its employees with a safe working environment.

Case

6–5

THE SPEEDY STOCK CLERK

Gary Powell, age 19, had recently been hired as a stock clerk for a major discount department store in an urban center. Powell was African-American, and this was his first full-time job after graduation from high school. He was excited about being hired, since he felt that the job offered potential for future advancement if he did good work in his entry-level position.

Powell was assigned to work from 11:00 P.M. to 7:00 A.M., the so-called "graveyard" shift, as part of a group of some six other stock clerks. These stock clerks reported to a supervisor, Sylvia Prater. They were responsible primarily for replenishing and arranging merchandise throughout the store.

One evening about three weeks after Gary Powell had begun his job, he asked if he could talk with Sylvia Prater in her office. "Sylvia," said Powell, "I'm really upset about what has happened the last few evenings on the job. I've had several of my fellow employees tell me that I was working too fast, filling too many of the store's aisles, and that I was making the rest of them look bad. One employee even told me that if I didn't slow down that 'something might happen' that I wouldn't like, especially if I kept on making the rest of the clerks look bad."

"Why that's terrible," replied Prater. "Give me the names of the employees who talked to you in this fashion, and I'll put a stop to it immediately."

"Oh, I can't do that," replied Powell, "because then I'm sure that no one would have anything to do with me. I'm the only black stock clerk, you know, and it's tough enough trying to be accepted by my fellow employees as it is without giving you names of the ones who have been pressuring me to slow down. In fact, I'm sort of worried about coming to you with this in the first place. If the word gets back to the rest of the group that I've complained to you, things may get worse rather than better."

Prater realized that she had a problem. Powell seemed to be a conscientious employee who was being pressured by his fellow clerks about his good work performance. Yet she realized that she would have to be very careful in how she approached the problem so as not to make it worse than it already was.

"Thank you, Gary, for coming to me with your concerns," said Prater. "I'll think about it and see what I can do to straighten this problem out. In the meantime, Gary, keep working as you have been doing, the best you know how. And if someone says something to you again, just try to laugh it off and kid them about it rather than make an issue of it." With that, Gary Powell left Sylvia Prater's office.

Questions for Discussion

1. Should Gary Powell have told his supervisor his problem without being willing to reveal the names of the employees who were pressuring him? Discuss.
2. Evaluate the advice that Sylvia Prater gave to Gary Powell as to how he should handle the situation. What other advice might Prater have given to Powell in response to his complaint?
3. Outline a series of recommendations concerning how Sylvia Prater should approach the problem that has been presented to her by Gary Powell. Consider alternatives.

Case
6–6

PREFERENTIAL TREATMENT

George Mason is foreman of the production department of a small manufacturing company. Most of the time, he supervises eight to ten people. One of his employees is Paula Whisler, an African-American woman who is a widow with five small children. She is a very good worker, but she almost always is late for work in the morning. Mason had spoken to her numerous times about tardiness, but to no avail. She assured him that she tried hard to be at work on time, but she "just did not seem to be able to make it" at 7:30 A.M. since she had to get her children off to school and to the babysitter. She argued that she worked twice as hard as anyone else and that she stayed over in the evening to make up for the time she lost in the mornings. There was little doubt in Mason's mind that Whisler did produce as much as or more than anyone else and that she did stay later in the evening to make up the time she lost by being late in the morning.

One Thursday morning, however, Paula Whisler's tardiness was holding up a job that had to be finished by noon. Regardless of how hard she might work during the morning, it would be difficult to finish the job on time, since the production material had to dry for three hours before it could leave the department. Although some other worker could have performed the operation, George Mason felt that Whisler was most qualified to do it. But should she not come in at all or be quite late, again the entire production schedule would be thrown out of balance. All of this was going through Mason's mind when he heard one of the workers say to a coworker, "Whisler is getting preferred treatment. Why should a black be given any favors, like she's better than the rest of us?"

Sure enough, Paula Whisler arrived 45 minutes late. George Mason realized that the situation required action on his part, but he didn't know what it should be.

Questions for Discussion

1. Analyze how the principles of the hot stove rule discussed in Chapter 19 were not properly applied by George Mason in the circumstances of this case.
2. Should George Mason take into account Paula Whisler's home situation when trying to maintain departmental standards? Why or why not?
3. Can the conflict between organization demands and personal problems of employees be reconciled and still have the objectives of the organization accomplished? If so, how?
4. What action should Mason take? What alternatives are open if the problem is not resolved quickly?

Case

6-7

LONG LUNCH PERIODS AND THE SENIOR EMPLOYEE

Ries Company is a food processor that sells its product lines throughout the United States. One of the company's six plants is located in a large midwestern city, and it produces four of the eight major Ries products. In addition, it serves as a warehouse and distribution point for an area that includes most of the central United States.

The materials handling and shipping department has the task of storing products manufactured in the plant, as well as creating temporary storage facilities for products imported from other plants. Because of somewhat limited space in the warehouse, the supervisors in this department are under constant pressure to make maximum use of available space. To accomplish this, the department is responsible for loading as many boxcars each day as required to meet the company's shipping and space necessities.

The Supervisor's Problem

Tanya Roth was hired by the Ries Company after she received a business administration degree from a midwestern university. She was working as a trainee foreman in the materials handling and shipping department in order to obtain experience at the "grass roots" of the company. She hoped to advance to a department head position either at this plant or at one of the other company plants.

Since Roth believed that her advancement would hinge on how well she performed at her present job, she was now grappling with a serious problem concerning her work group of 15 people. The workers had been leaving for their lunch periods from five to ten minutes early each day. This disturbed her because she had always been quite liberal in enforcing the time allowed for lunch. Although the union contract provided a paid 30-minute lunch period, Roth and the other shift supervisors had always allowed the workers an extra ten minutes. The supervisors figured that this extra time was needed by the workers to get to the lunch room from their workstations and back.

A quick investigation revealed that one of the older workers, Mike Lange, usually left for his lunch period 15 to 30 minutes early. Since the other employees (most of whom were younger) observed this, they thought that they could do the same.

Lange had been employed continuously by the Ries Company for 28 years. He started working at the plant after graduating from high school. He unquestionably was the hardest working and most productive person in Roth's work group. Lange knew only one way to work—and that was to drive himself every minute he was on the job. He was very critical of most of the younger employees, often telling Roth that "the younger kids these days are lazy and would never have lasted in the old days."

Diana Royse, the director of human resources, told Roth of an incident that had taken place some years ago. In Lange's zest to complete a job in the shortest time possible, he drove his towmotor at rather reckless speeds around the warehouse. When the plant supervisor sternly reprimanded Lange about his work habits, Lange responded by organizing a work slowdown. As a result, everyone in the department worked at half speed for an entire week so that their output for that week was an all-time low in the department. The slowdown caused the warehouse to become so clogged that products from other plants could not be unloaded. This situation had brought considerable criticism from the home office.

From discussions with several older supervisors, Roth also learned that the slightest criticism could cause Lange to become very upset. Lange invariably would state that management didn't know how fortunate they were to have a person of his abilities still around.

The Supervisor's Alternatives

Roth felt that the output of the average worker in the department was already below standards. If she tried to force Mike Lange to observe the proper time to leave for lunch, she might lose Lange's extraordinary productive ability. Furthermore, Roth did not wish to contend with a work slowdown that Lange might instigate again.

On the other hand, Roth could allow the lunch period situation to continue in order to avoid alienating anyone. This action, however, would mean the continued loss of considerable work time.

Could Roth appeal to the union? She thought this action might be futile because Lange's seniority placed him in a privileged class among the union membership.

Roth preferred not to discuss this problem with her department head, as this might imply that she could not handle the job. She pondered what to do.

Questions for Discussion

1. Identify the problems in this situation that have contributed to Tanya Roth's loss of control.
2. Should a showdown with Mike Lange take place at this point?
3. Is Roth's attitude of not wanting to discuss the situation with her department head understandable? Is it desirable under the circumstances?
4. What alternatives are open to Roth? What should she do?

Case

6-8

UNDER THE INFLUENCE?

Carl Kloski had been employed as a laborer for eight years in the warehouse division of a wholesale appliance distributor. His record over the years indicated the following disciplinary actions:

> Three written reprimands for unexcused absences.
> One one-day suspension for reporting to work under the influence of alcohol.
> One five-day suspension for reporting to work under the influence of alcohol.
> One one-day suspension for failure to report to work.

On a Friday morning, Kloski reported to work at about 7:30 A.M. Sometime prior to the beginning of the shift, Kloski's lead person, George Ramsey, noticed that Kloski appeared to be under the influence of alcohol, since he was talking loudly and walking about in a confused manner. Ramsey reported this to his boss, the warehouse supervisor Steven Bell. Bell sent Ramsey and the rest of the crew out to perform their normal duties, but he ordered Kloski to stay behind to do cleanup work in the employee lunch room. About an hour or so later, Bell noticed that Kloski had done very little cleanup work. Bell approached Kloski and asked him why he had not followed his instructions. Kloski objected to this questioning, and he continued in a loud manner that the supervisor was always "picking on him" and "being discriminatory."

In response to these accusations, Bell took Kloski into his office to review his file for past performance appraisals and disciplinary actions. A lengthy discussion followed in which Kloski continued talking in a loud and angry manner. Both Bell and the office clerk, Marilyn O'Toole, believed that they could smell liquor on Kloski's breath.

Finally, Bell said, "Carl, I think you're under the influence of alcohol again, and with your past record, I ought to terminate you immediately!"

Kloski exploded, "What in the hell do you mean 'under the influence?' You assigned me to work over an hour ago, and you've got no proof whatsoever. You're just mad because I don't jump when you say, 'Jump!'"

Steven Bell pondered what his next response would be.

Questions for Discussion

1. What should Ramsey or Bell have done when they first believed that Carl Kloski might have been under the influence of alcohol? Discuss alternatives.
2. Was the decision to assign Kloski work to do, even though it was not his normal work, a questionable decision? Why or why not?
3. Discuss the response of Kloski to Bell to the effect that the company had no proof whatsoever that he was under the influence of alcohol.

4. To what degree is Kloski's past disciplinary record relevant to the decision Bell will have to make at the end of the case?
5. What should Steven Bell do? Consider alternatives.

Case
6–9

FEAR? OR EXAGGERATION?

For almost a decade, John Stephens had been the service department supervisor for Jentag Commercial Sales and Appliance Repair at its small office in Fort Wayne, Indiana. This office served as a regional office with its headquarters in Chicago. As a small office, Stephens was the only local company supervisor, and he reported to the manager of the sales and parts division in the Chicago office. Reporting to John Stephens was Karen Mullens, a service department dispatcher; Ben Griggs, the office's parts facilitator; and several appliance repairmen. Stephens' responsibilities usually were split between his supervisory duties and outside customer service tasks with large industrial users.

An integral part of the service department's success resided in having parts in stock to complete repairs in a timely fashion. Ben Griggs, the local office's parts man, had held this position for about five years. Griggs had always been rather quiet, but he had done a commendable job and most customers liked him. Stephens had told upper management that Ben Griggs had the ability and experience to be promoted to some larger office, but management had not as yet found another position for him.

Recently, Karen Mullens confided to Stephens that on several occasions when he (Stephens) was out of the office, she had heard Ben Griggs cursing customers and continuing to curse loudly when hanging up the phone. She said that she had seen Griggs physically throw small items in tirades. Mullens said she was worried that one day she might be the one "to light Ben's fire," and she could be physically harmed by him. Mullens also said that since she was the only person to have seen his tirades, if Griggs would be confronted about this, he would know who passed on the information. Stephens assured Mullens that he would look into it and take appropriate action.

Later, as John Stephens sat in his office privately, he reflected upon the fact that he knew that on some previous occasions, Mullens had a tendency to exaggerate problems and issues beyond their significance. However, he was concerned that something really could be amiss. Stephens had never seen Griggs "lose his cool" with anyone, and wasn't sure what he should do.

Questions for Discussion

1. As a supervisor, what should John Stephens do to investigate and correct this situation? How can he "weed out" the true facts?
2. Assuming that John Stephens determines that Karen Mullen's allegations are factual, what should he do to correct the situation?

3. Assuming that John Stephens determines that Karen Mullen's allegations are quite exaggerated, what should he do?
4. Should any or all of this be reported to higher corporate management? Discuss.

Case

6-10

LOCKER ROOM THEFT

For a number of months, Charlie Blair, the supervisor of a large warehouse servicing a major retail food distributor, had been concerned about reports of missing valuables from the lockers of employees in the employee dressing room in the warehouse. The company provided metal lockers for employees to use, but they had no locks. Employees shared these lockers on a rotating-shift basis, and the company never considered it necessary to assign lockers to individuals. The lockers were provided mainly for the convenience of employees to leave their clothing and other items while they were working in the warehouse.

Blair had reminded employees on a number of occasions about not leaving valuables in the lockers. He told the employees that the company assumed no responsibility for any loss, and he also told them that anyone found guilty of stealing a valuable that belonged to another employee would be immediately terminated for theft. This was in accordance with posted company rules in the warehouse.

However, for the last several months Blair had received reports of numerous items missing from employees' lockers. These reports included items such as a sweater, a lunchbox, food from several lunchboxes, and a baseball glove.

For a number of reasons, including several rumors that had been circulated to Blair, he was suspicious of a fairly new warehouse employee named Eric Raleigh. Raleigh was a young warehouse worker who operated a tow truck. He was about 22, and he had been employed by the company about six months previously. Coincidentally, the reports of missing items from the locker room seemed to have become more frequent the last several months.

On a Tuesday morning, Blair received a report from a warehouse employee named Willie Jeffries that a small transistor radio was missing from his locker. Jeffries stated that he had placed it in his locker when he reported to work at 7:30 A.M., and he noticed it missing when he came to his locker during his morning coffee break.

Upon receiving this report, Blair decided to conduct a search of Raleigh's locker while all the employees were in the warehouse working. At about 11:00 A.M., Charlie Blair went into the locker room and searched the locker where Raleigh had his clothing and lunchbox. At the bottom of the locker, underneath a number of magazines, Blair found a transistor radio. Blair returned to the office and summoned Jeffries to identify the radio. Jeffries identified the radio as his own; Blair did not disclose to Jeffries where he had found it.

Shortly thereafter, Charlie Blair asked Eric Raleigh to come to his office. Blair explained to Raleigh the nature of the report he had received, what he had done, and how he had found the missing radio in Raleigh's locker. Charlie Blair did not directly accuse Raleigh of theft; but he suggested that perhaps Raleigh might want to consider resigning from the firm because of the suspicions that had been circulating about his connection to the other missing items in the lockers.

At this point Raleigh became very angry. He stated that he would not resign because he was innocent; he felt that someone else had been stealing the items from the employee lockers and that whoever it was had planted the radio in his locker in order to place the blame on him. Raleigh insisted he was innocent, and he said that he would be willing to take a polygraph (lie detector) test to prove his innocence. He told Blair, "If the company decides to fire me for this, I'll get the union and a lawyer to sue the company for everything it has for false accusation and unjust termination." With that, Eric Raleigh left Charlie Blair's office and returned to his job.

Blair was somewhat taken aback by Raleigh's adamant denial of any involvement in locker room theft. Blair was not sure what he should do in this situation. He recognized that the union contract for employees in the warehouse required that any disciplinary action must be for "just cause." Charlie Blair decided that he would discuss the situation with Elaine Haas, the company's director of human resources.

Questions for Discussion

1. Evaluate the search of the locker by Charlie Blair. Was this an advisable course on his part?
2. What alternatives might Charlie Blair have utilized other than confronting Eric Raleigh in his office? Discuss.
3. Should Blair have suggested to Raleigh that he consider resignation? Why or why not?
4. At the end of the case, what should the company do?

Case

6–11

DISCHARGE FOR STRIKING A STUDENT

Gino Barsanti was employed as a maintenance worker at Midwest University, located in a small town in a midwestern state. Barsanti was considered to be a handyman who did every type of assignment ranging from manual labor to skilled carpentry and electrical work. He had been employed by the university for six years, and his work record was excellent. He had never received a reprimand, suspension, or any other type of disciplinary action during his six years of service at the university.

One day, Barsanti and two other employees were working on a broken fence adjacent to the baseball field. They were engaged in a heated discussion about religion and politics. Barsanti particularly was arguing that abortion was a terrible sin, to be condemned. Several students happened to be passing by and heard some of the comments being made by the employees. One of the students, Sidney Rose, decided that he would join in the conversation. Eventually Rose made several derogatory remarks about religion in general and the abortion issue in particular. Barsanti became angry that a student had entered into the conversation. Barsanti stated to him, "Who asked you to join in this discussion? Get out of here." At this point Rose responded, "There's no use trying to reason with a rigid religious nut!" Barsanti became enraged. He took two steps toward the student and hit him squarely on the jaw. Rose was bleeding from the mouth when he and his fellow students left the area.

Shortly thereafter, Barsanti was summoned to the office of the maintenance superintendent, Alex Higgins. Rose had reported what had happened, and Barsanti did not deny that he had struck the student. Barsanti was sent home for the rest of the day. The next morning Barsanti was notified by Higgins that the university had decided to terminate him for striking a student, which Higgins felt was in violation of the university's strict "no fighting" policy for employees while on campus and during work hours.

On the day following Barsanti's termination, the union business representative, William Kelford, filed a grievance on behalf of Barsanti, claiming that Barsanti's termination did not meet the requirement of "just cause" in the labor agreement for a discharge action to be taken against an employee. Kelford spoke with Higgins about the grievance and told him that no employee should be required to take the kind of abuse from a student to which Barsanti had been subjected. Further, in view of the fact that Barsanti had never had a previous disciplinary action against him and that no specific rule covered this type of event, Kelford argued that Barsanti should be reinstated immediately. Kelford also contended that the university's no-fighting policy for employees was never intended to be applied to circumstances like the situation that confronted Barsanti, and therefore discharge was extreme and not justified.

Alex Higgins told William Kelford that he would study the union grievance and make a decision within the next two days.

Questions for Discussion

1. Instead of striking the student as he did, what alternatives might Gino Barsanti have pursued in regard to the offensive remarks of the student Sidney Rose?
2. Given all of the circumstances of the case, was the university justified in discharging Gino Barsanti? Discuss.
3. At the end of the case, what should the university do? Consider this question from the standpoint of an arbitrator being asked to decide the case if the university refuses to rescind Barsanti's discharge and the union pursues the case to arbitration.

Case

6-12

DISCHARGE FOR DELIVERY OF A CONTROLLED SUBSTANCE

(This case presents the basic facts and contentions of the parties in a union grievance that was carried to arbitration for a final and binding decision.)

Bascomb Manufacturing Company had a major plant located in a midwestern city that manufactured parts for the automotive industry. Local No. 428 of the United Production and Maintenance Workers represented several hundred employees in manufacturing areas of the plant.

Kyle Craver, the grievant in this case, had been employed by the company for 22 years prior to his discharge. During that time, Craver had compiled a satisfactory work record; he had not received any major disciplinary warning or penalty during his employment.

In the fall of the year, Craver had been apprehended and charged by state law enforcement authorities with the "delivery of a controlled substance." In a plea bargain arrangement made with state prosecutors, Craver was placed on a special "probation/parole work release program." Through his union, Kyle Craver requested that he be returned to his job as a production line inspector while he served his three-month probation/parole work release program. The company's human resources director, Marjorie Florman, after consulting with higher management, refused to permit Craver to work under such an arrangement. The union filed a grievance complaining that the company was treating Craver unfairly since the company had previously allowed another employee to work on the job under a work release program following a drunken driving conviction.

After examining the situation further, the company discharged Kyle Craver stating that it had "just cause" to discharge him. The union then amended its grievance to include a protest against the company's "unjust discharge." After proceeding through the several steps of the grievance procedure, the company and the union agreed to submit the case to an arbitrator for a decision.

The following were the provisions of the parties' labor/management agreement relevant to the positions of the parties.

ARTICLE XIV—MANAGEMENT

Section 1. The Union recognizes the management of the plant and the direction of the working forces are exclusively the prerogatives of the Company. These prerogatives include but are not limited to:

* * *

C. The right to suspend or discharge for just cause; subject, however, to review thereof as provided in the grievance procedure contained herein.

* * *

Section 2. The Company agrees that in the exercise of management prerogatives, there shall be no violations of the terms of this Agreement.

ARTICLE XIX—SAFETY AND HEALTH

Section 7. Alcohol and Drug Abuse. Without detracting from the existing rights and obligations of the parties recognized in the other provisions of this Agreement, the Company and the Union agree to cooperate at the plant level in encouraging employees afflicted with alcohol and/or drug dependency to undergo a coordinated program directed to the objective of their rehabilitation.

Position of the Company

In the arbitration hearing, the company primarily contended that there was ample just cause to discharge Kyle Craver after he had publicly admitted his guilt to the delivery of a controlled substance. The company claimed that the plant operated within a larger community in which the company had a moral obligation to take actions which showed that the distribution or use of illegal drugs by employees would not be tolerated. The company claimed that there were many employees and generations of families and relatives of employees who objected to any form of drug use or condoning the sale or use of drugs.

If the company would retain Kyle Craver after he pleaded guilty of distributing drugs, this would be detrimental to the company's reputation and adversely affect employee morale and the company's business. The company further noted that it did business with federal government subcontractors who were obligated to comply with the provisions of the 1988 Drug-Free Workplace Act. The company said it would have a problem of credibility with customers if customers learned of the company's willingness to continue employment of someone who had been convicted of off-duty drug dealing.

In summary, the company claimed that Kyle Craver was guilty of a major felony. To continue his employment would cast a serious shadow on the company's reputation, employee morale, and the company's ability to deal with customers and the community at large. The company urged that the union grievance should be denied.

Position of the Union

The union, however, claimed that the company did not meet a proper burden of proof to support the claim that just cause existed for discharging Kyle Craver. The union claimed that there was no validity to the company's allegation that Craver's reinstatement would cause morale problems in the workplace. The fact that the union and union employees were supporting Craver's grievance showed that most employees felt that Craver should be returned to his job. This especially was in view of Craver's long years of good service with the company. The union further claimed that Kyle Craver had not violated any known work rule, policy, or provision of the collective bargaining agreement. He did make a mistake for which he paid an appropriate penalty. The union felt that there was no basis on which to terminate Kyle Craver since Craver's discharge involved something that happened off the job. The union also claimed that the company was inconsistent in having allowed another employee to work during a work release program while on probation and would not give the same consideration to Kyle Craver. The union urged that the arbitrator should reinstate Kyle Craver and make him whole for all lost pay, seniority, and benefits.

Questions for Discussion

1. Evaluate the contentions of the company in support of the position that the discharge of Kyle Craver was justified. Which do you find the most compelling and which do you find the least compelling?
2. Evaluate the contentions of the union in support of the position that the grievant, Kyle Craver, should be reinstated. Which of these do you find the most compelling and which do you find the least compelling?
3. If you were the arbitrator in this case, how would you decide? Explain the basis for your decision.
4. What are some of the broader implications of a case of this nature?

Appendix

———○———

PARTIAL LISTING OF FEDERAL EMPLOYMENT LEGISLATION THAT IMPACTS SUPERVISORS

1996 *Health Insurance Portability and Accountability Act.* Provides for certain flexibility in transferring health insurance from one employer to another when changing jobs. Other provisions cover aspects of group health plans and health insurance, including COBRA applications and limitations on preexisting condition exclusions by health insurance providers.

1996 *Small Business Regulatory Enforcement Fairness Act.* Requires federal agencies to listen to the business community before proposing new rules or significant changes in current regulations. Federal agencies must provide a cost-benefit analysis and describe steps taken to minimize the new regulation's impact on small business. Small business owners may challenge "unreasonable" federal agency rulings in court.

1994 *Uniformed Services Employment and Reemployment Rights Act.* Obligates employers to allow military service personnel to return to their job without loss of seniority or benefits. Protects employees against discrimination on the basis of military obligation in the employment process.

1992 *Family and Medical Leave Act.* Provides for up to 12 weeks of unpaid leave for certain personal and family health-related circumstances.

1991 *Civil Rights Act.* Amended five existing civil rights laws to extend their coverage and protection in employment situations. Increased damage awards to victims of discrimination up to $300,000 for corporations with over 500 employees. Reversed or responded to nine Supreme Court decisions.

1990 *Americans with Disabilities Act (ADA).* Prohibits discrimination based on physical or mental disabilities in places of employment and public accommodation. Modeled after the Rehabilitation Act of 1973 but applies to state and local governments, employment agencies, and labor unions, as well as private employers with 15 or more employees. In effect, employment discrimination is prohibited against "qualified individuals with disabilities."

1988 *Worker Adjustment and Retraining Act (WARN).* Requires firms employing 100 or more workers to provide 60 days advance notice to employees before shutting down or conducting substantial layoffs.

1988 *Drug-Free Workplace Act.* Requires companies receiving $25,000 or more in federal contracts to maintain a "drug-free workplace," including establishing and communicating policies to achieve this objective.

1988 *Employee Polygraph Protection Act.* Prohibits use of the lie detector in most employment decisions.

1986 *Consolidated Omnibus Budget Reconciliation Act (COBRA) as amended.* Requires that employers with more than 20 employees offer continuation of health care coverage for 18 to 36 months after an employee is fired, quits, or is laid off.

1978 *Civil Service Reform Act (Title VII).* Provides representation and collective bargaining rights to federal government employees.

1978 *Pregnancy Discrimination Act.* Requires employer to treat pregnancy, childbirth, or related medical conditions the same as any other medical disability if employer has a medical/hospitalization benefit program for employees.

1974 *Vietnam Era Veterans Readjustment Assistance Act.* Requires affirmative action among federal subcontractors for military veterans.

1974 *Employment Retirement Income Security Act (ERISA), as amended.* Covers most pension benefit plans of private employers; provides for vesting of pension benefits after certain number of years of service.

1973 *Rehabilitation Act, Section 503.* Prohibits job discrimination because of a disability. Employers holding $2,500 or more in federal contracts or subcontracts must set up affirmative action program. Enforced by Office of Federal Contract Compliance Programs (OFCCP).

1972   *Equal Employment Opportunity Act.* Extended coverage of Title VII of the Civil Rights Act to government employees, local employers, and educational institutions.

1970   *Occupational Safety and Health Act (OSHA).* Designed to protect the safety and health of employees. Employers are responsible for providing workplaces free from safety and health hazards. Created Occupational Safety and Health Administration to carry out provisions of the Act.

1967   *Age Discrimination in Employment Act, as amended.* Prohibits discrimination in employment on the basis of age to most employees over age 40.

1964   *Title VII of the Civil Rights Act, as amended.* Prohibits discrimination in hiring, promotion, discharge, pay, benefits, and other aspects of employment on the basis of race, color, religion, sex, or national origin. Equal Employment Opportunity Commission (EEOC) has authority to bring lawsuits against employers in the federal courts.

1963   *Equal Pay Act.* Requires equal payment of wages to women and men who perform substantially equal work.

1947   *Labor Management Relations Act (Taft-Hartley).* Amended the National Labor Relations Act (Wagner Act); specified unfair labor practices for unions, provided for Federal Mediation and Conciliation Service (FMCS) to assist in resolving labor-management disputes; and more clearly identified requirements for bargaining in good faith.

1938   *Fair Labor Standards Act (FLSA) as amended.* Established that employers covered by Act must pay an employee (1) at least a minimum wage, and (2) time and a half for all hours worked in excess of 40 in a given week. Classified a person working in a job that is not subject to the provisions of the Act as "exempt" from the overtime pay provisions. Most supervisors, professional staff, and outside salespersons fall in this category. (Note: At the time of writing of this text, legislation was pending in the U.S. Congress to permit compensatory time off to be substituted for overtime premium pay.)

1935   *National Labor Relations Act (Wagner Act).* Gave workers the right to unionize and bargain collectively over hours, wages, and other terms and conditions of employment. Specified five unfair labor practices for employers. Created National Labor Relations Board (NLRB) to (1) certify labor unions as the sole bargaining representative of employees and (2) investigate unfair labor practices.

1935   *Social Security Act, as amended.* Provided for old age and survivors insurance (pensions) and later established medical/hospitalization insurance for elderly.

Glossary

———o———

360-degree evaluation Performance appraisal based on data collected from all around the employee—from customers, vendors, supervisors, peers, subordinates, etc.

A

Ability An employee's potential to perform higher-level tasks.

Acceptance theory of authority Theory that holds that the manager only possesses authority when the employee accepts it.

Accountability The obligation one has to one's boss and the expectation that employees will accept credit or blame for the results achieved in performing assigned tasks.

Administrative skills The ability to plan, organize, and co-ordinate activities.

Alternative dispute resolution (ADR) Approaches to processing and deciding employee complaints internally as an alternative to filing a lawsuit, usually for disputes involving discharge and/or employment discrimination.

Arbitrator Person selected by the union and management to render a final and binding decision concerning a grievance.

Attitude survey Survey of employee opinions about major aspects of organizational life used to assess morale.

Authority The legitimate right to lead others.

Autocratic (authoritarian) supervision The supervisory style that relies on formal authority, threats, pressure, and close control.

B

Baldrige Quality Award U.S. Department of Commerce award to outstanding firms that exemplify world-class business quality standards.

Benchmarking The process of identifying and improving on the practices of the leaders.

Biological needs The basic physical needs, such as food, rest, shelter, and recreation.

Body language All observable actions of either the sender or the receiver.

Brainstorming A free flow of ideas within a group, while suspending judgment, aimed at developing many alternative solutions to a problem.

Budget A plan that expresses anticipated results in numerical—usually financial—terms for a stated period of time.

Bureaucratic style of management Style that emphasizes strict compliance with organizational policies, rules, and directives.

C

Chairperson Group leader who is responsible for guiding a meeting toward completion of its stated objectives.

Coaching The frequent activity of the supervisor to provide employees with information, instruction, and suggestions relating to their job assignments and performance.

Collaborative workplace Work environment characterized by joint decision making, shared accountability and authority, and high trust levels between employees and managers.

Command group Grouping of employees according to authority relationships on the formal organization chart.

Committee Group of people drawn together to solve a problem or complete a task.

Communication The process of transmitting information and understanding.

Comparable worth Concept that jobs should be paid at the same level if they require similar skills or abilities.

Competencies The sets of skills, knowledge, and personal attributes possessed by the superior performer.

Competitive advantage The ability to outperform competitors by increasing efficiency, quality, creativity, and responsiveness to customers and effectively utilizing employee talents.

Complaint Any individual or group problem or dissatisfaction that employees can channel upward to management, including discrimination complaints.

Complaint procedure A management-designed series of steps for handling employee complaints that usually provides for a number of appeals before a final decision.

Conceptual skills The ability to obtain, interpret, and apply information.

Concurrent control Corrective action taken during the production or delivery process to ensure that standards are being met.

Conflict resolution styles Approaches to resolving conflict based on weighing desired degrees of cooperativeness and assertiveness.

Contingency-style leadership No one leadership style is best; the appropriate style depends on a multitude of factors.

Contingent workforce Part-time, temporary, or contract employees who work schedules dependent primarily upon employer needs.

Controlling Ensuring that actual performance is in line with intended performance and taking corrective action.

Cooperation The willingness of individuals to work with and help one another.

Coordination The synchronization of employees' efforts and the organization's resources toward achieving goals.

Corporate culture Set of shared purposes, values, and beliefs that employees hold about their organization.

Counseling An effort by the supervisor to deal with on-the-job performance problems that are the result of an employee's personal problems.

Counseling interview Nondirective interview during which the supervisor listens empathetically and encourages the employee to discuss problems openly and develop solutions.

Critical path The path of activities in the PERT network that will take the longest time to complete.

Cumulative-trauma disorder Workplace injury caused by repetitive motions usually of the hand or arm.

D

Decentralization When decision-making authority is widely delegated downward and throughout organizational levels.

Decision criteria Standards or measures to use in evaluating alternatives.

Decision making Defining problems and choosing a course of action from among alternatives.

Decision-making process A systematic, step-by-step process to aid in choosing the "best" alternative.

Decisional meeting People gathered together to make decisions on a particular problem or task for which the group has been granted some decision-making authority.

Delegation The process of assigning duties and related authority to subordinates.

Department An organizational unit for which a supervisor has responsibility and authority.

Departmentation The process of grouping activities and people into distinct organizational units.

Directive The communications approach by which a supervisor conveys to employees what, how, and why something is to be accomplished.

Directive interview Interview approach in which the interviewer guides the discussion along a predetermined course.

Discipline State of orderliness; that is, the degree to which employees act according to expected standards of behavior.

Discipline without punishment Disciplinary approach that uses coaching and counseling as preliminary steps and a paid decision-making leave for employees to decide whether to improve and stay, or quit.

Discussional meeting People gathered together to participate in a discussion with the group leader by offering their opinions, suggestions, or recommendations.

Diversity The cultural, ethnic, gender, age, educational level, racial, and lifestyle differences among employees.

Division of work (specialization) Dividing work into smaller components and specialized tasks to improve efficiency and output.

Documentation Keeping records of memoranda, documents, and meetings that are relevant to a disciplinary action.

Downsizing (restructuring, right-sizing) Large-scale reduction and elimination of jobs in a company that usually results in reduction of middle-level managers, removal of organizational levels, and a widened span of management for remaining supervisors.

E

Electronic meeting Group meeting via electronic transmissions in which participants are not physically together in one location.

Emotional intelligence skills The ability to intelligently use your emotions.

Employee assistance program (EAP) Company program to assist employees with certain personal or work-related problems that are interfering with job performance.

Employment-at-will Legal concept that employers can dismiss employees at any time and for any reasons, except unlawful discrimination or contractual or other restrictions.

Empowerment Giving employees the authority and responsibility to accomplish their and the organization's objectives.

Equity theory Explains how people strive for fairness in the workplace.

Ethical "tests" Considerations or guidelines to be addressed in developing and evaluating ethical aspects of decision alternatives.

Exception principle Concept that supervisors should concentrate their investigations on activities that deviate substantially from the standard.

Exit interview Interview with individuals who leave a firm to assess morale and reasons for employee turnover.

Expectancy theory Theory of motivation that holds that employees will perform better if they believe such efforts will lead to desired rewards.

External stressors Causes of stress that arise from outside the individual, such as job pressures, responsibilities, and work itself.

F

Feedback The receiver's verbal or nonverbal response to a message.

Feedback control Actions taken after the activity, product, or service has been completed.

Feedforward control Anticipatory action taken to ensure that problems do not occur.

Filtering The process of omitting or softening unpleasant details.

Fishbone technique (cause-and-effect diagram) Cause-and-effect approach to consider potential interrelatedness of problem causes in decision making.

Flexible workforce Employees are trained in a variety of skills to perform multiple tasks.

Flextime Policy that allows employees to choose their work hours within stated limits.

Forecasts Predictions of future events upon which plans are based.

Free-rein (laissez-faire) leadership Where a leader delegates virtually all authority to employees to decide and act without his or her involvement.

Friendship group Informal grouping of employees based on similar personalities and social interests.

Functional approach School of management thought that asserts that all managers perform various functions in doing their jobs, such as planning, organizing, staffing, leading, and controlling.

Functional authority The right granted to specialized staff people to give directives concerning certain matters within their expertise.

G

Gain-sharing plans Group incentive plans that have employees share in the benefits from improved performance.

Gantt chart A graphic scheduling technique that shows the activity to be scheduled on the vertical axis and necessary completion dates on the horizontal axis.

General supervision The style of supervision in which the supervisor sets goals and limits but allows employees to decide how to achieve the goals.

Glass ceiling Invisible barrier that limits advancement of women and minorities.

Glass walls Invisible barriers that compartmentalize or segregate women and minorities into certain occupational classes.

Grapevine The informal, unofficial communication channel.

Grievance A formal complaint presented by the union to management that alleges a violation of the labor agreement.

Grievance procedure Negotiated series of steps in a labor agreement for processing grievances, beginning at the supervisory level and ending with arbitration.

Groupthink Phenomenon that occurs in meetings when group members do not express dissenting views in order to avoid conflict rather than realistically appraise alternatives.

H

Halo effect The tendency to allow one favorable aspect of a person's behavior to positively influence judgment on all other aspects.

Hawthorne effect The fact that when special interest is shown in people, this may cause them to behave differently.

Hawthorne Studies Comprehensive research studies that focused on work-group dynamics as related to employee attitudes and productivity.

Hierarchy of needs Maslow's theory of motivation, which suggests that employee needs are arranged in priority order such that lower-order needs must be satisfied before higher-order needs become motivating.

Horizontal corporation Where a firm is restructured by customer process and organizational structure is very flattened.

Horns effect The tendency to allow one negative aspect of a person's behavior to negatively influence judgment on all other aspects.

Hot stove rule Guideline for applying discipline analogous to touching a hot stove: advance warning and consequences that are immediate, consistent, and applied with impersonality.

Human relations movement/behavioral science approach Approach to management that focuses on the behavior of people in the work environment.

Human relations skills The ability to work with and through people.

Human resources department Staff department that provides advice and service to other departments on human resources matters.

Human resources management (HRM) Organizational philosophies, policies, and practices that strive for the effective use of employees.

Hygiene factors Elements in the work environment that, if positive, reduce dissatisfaction but do not tend to motivate.

I

Incremental budgeting A technique for making revenue and expense projections based in previous history.

Informal organization Informal groupings of people, apart from the formal organizational structure, that satisfy members' social and other needs.

Informational meeting People gathered together to hear the group leader present information.

Innovative duties Creative activities aimed at finding a better way to do something.

Intangible standards Standards for performance results that are difficult to measure and often relate to human characteristics (e.g., attitudes, morale, satisfaction, etc.).

Internal stressors Pressures that people put on themselves, such as feeling a need to be outstanding in everything.

ISO 9000 A rigorous series of manufacturing quality standards created by the International Organization for Standardization.

J

Jargon The use of words that are peculiar to a particular occupation or specialty.

Job description Written description of the principal duties and responsibilities of a job.

Job enlargement Increasing the number of tasks an individual performs.

Job enrichment Job design that helps fulfill employees' higher-level needs by giving them more challenging tasks and more decision-making responsibility for their jobs.

Job rotation The process of switching job tasks among employees in the work group.

Job sharing Policy that allows two or more employees to perform a job normally done by one full-time employee.

Job specification Written description of the personal qualifications necessary to perform a job adequately.

Just cause Standard for disciplinary action requiring tests of fairness and elements of normal due process, such as proper notification, investigation, sufficient evidence, and a penalty commensurate with the nature of the infraction.

Just-in-time (JIT) inventory control system A system for scheduling materials to arrive precisely when they are needed in the production process.

K

Kanban Another name for a just-in-time inventory control system.

Knowledge management Systematic, storage, retrieval, dissemination, and sharing of information.

L

Labor agreement (union contract) Negotiated document between union and employer that covers terms and conditions of employment for the represented employees.

Labor agreement negotiations The process of discussion and compromise among representatives from labor and management leading to an agreement governing wages, hours, and working conditions for union employees.

Labor union (labor organization) Legally recognized organization that represents employees and negotiates and administers a labor agreement with an employer.

Lead person Employee placed in charge of other employees who performs limited managerial functions but is not considered part of management.

Leadership The ability to guide and influence the behavior of others.

Leading The managerial function of guiding employees toward accomplishing organizational objectives.

Leniency error Supervisors give employees higher ratings than they deserve.

Line authority The right to direct others and to require them to conform to decisions, policies, rules, and objectives.

Line department Department whose responsibilities are directly related to making, selling, or distributing the company's product or service.

Line-and-staff-type organizational structure Structure that combines line and staff departments.

Line-type organizational structure A structure that consists entirely of line authority arrangements with a direct chain of authority relationships.

M

Management Getting objectives accomplished with and through people.

Management by objectives (MBO) Participative management System through which jointly set objectives are used for performance evaluation.

Managerial authority The legitimate right to direct and lead others.

Matrix-type organizational structure A hybrid structure in which regular functional departments co-exist with project teams made up of people from different departments.

Mentoring The guiding of a newer employee by an experienced employee in areas concerning job and career.

Merit The quality of an employee's job performance.

Method A standing plan that details exactly how a single operation is to be performed.

Mission statement A statement of the organization's basic philosophy, purpose, and reason for being.

Morale A composite of feelings and attitudes that individuals and groups have toward their work, their environment, their supervisors, top-level management, and the organization.

Motion study An analysis of work activities to determine how to make the job easier and quicker to do.

Motivation A willingness to exert effort toward achieving a goal, stimulated by the effort's ability to fulfill an individual need.

Motivation factors Elements intrinsic in the job that promote job performance.

Motivation-hygiene theory Herzberg's theory that factors in the work environment primarily influence the degree of job dissatisfaction, while intrinsic job content factors influence the amount of employee motivation.

N

Nepotism The practice of hiring relatives.

Networking Individuals or groups linked together by a commitment to shared purpose.

No-fault attendance policy Policy under which unscheduled absences and tardiness are counted as occurrences, and their accumulation is used in progressive discipline.

Noise Obstacles that distort messages between people.

Nominal group technique (NGT) A group brainstorming and decision-making process by which individual members first identify alternative solutions privately and then share, evaluate, and decide on them as a group.

Nondirective interview Interview approach in which the interviewer asks open-ended questions that allow the applicant greater latitude in responding.

Nonprogrammed decisions Solutions to unique problems that require judgment, intuition, and creativity.

O

Operating budget The projection of dollar allocations to various costs and expenses needed to run the business, based on expected revenue.

Operational plans Short-range plans of supervisors to cover specific areas and activities of accountability.

Optimizing Selecting the "best" alternative.

Organization Group structured by management to carry out designated functions and accomplish certain objectives.

Organizational development (OD) Meetings with groups under the guidance of a neutral conference leader to solve problems that are hindering organizational effectiveness.

Organization chart Graphic portrayal of a company's authority and responsibility relationships.

Organization manual Written description of the authority and responsibilities of managerial and supervisory positions as well as formal channels, major objectives, and policies and procedures.

Organizing Arranging and distributing work among members of the work group to accomplish the organization's goals.

Orientation The process of smoothing the transition of new employees into the organization.

P

Participative management Allowing employees to influence and share in organizational decision making.

Pay for performance Compensation, other than base wages, that is given for achieving employee or corporate goals.

Peer evaluation The evaluation of an employee's performance by other employees of relatively equal rank.

Performance appraisal A systematic assessment of how well employees are performing their jobs, and the communication of that assessment to them.

Performance standards The job-related requirements by which the employees' performance will be evaluated.

Permanent (standing) committee Group that meets on a more or less permanent basis to deal with recurring issues or problems.

Personal power Power derived from a person's skill, knowledge, or ability and how others perceive them.

Personality The knowledge, attitudes, and attributes that combine to make up the unique human being.

Personalized conflict Conflict between individuals that occurs because the two parties do not like one another.

PERT activity A specific task to be accomplished.

PERT event The beginning and/or ending of an activity.

Piecework System in which the employee earns a certain amount of pay for each piece produced.

Planning Determining what should be done in the future.

Policy A standing plan that serves as a guide to thinking when making decisions.

Political skills The ability to understand how things get done outside of formal channels.

Position power Power derived from the formal rank a person holds in the chain of command.

Positive discipline Condition that exists when employees generally follow the rules and meet the standards of the organization.

Positive self-discipline Employees regulating their own behavior out of self-interest and their normal desire to meet reasonable standards.

Principle of compulsory staff advice (service) Situation in which supervisors are required by policy to consult with specialized staff before making certain types of decisions.

Principle of organizational stability Principle that holds that no organization should become overly dependent on one or several key "indispensable" individuals.

Procedure A standing plan that defines the sequence of activities to be performed to achieve objectives.

Program A major single-use plan for a large undertaking related to accomplishing the organization's goals and objectives.

Program evaluation and review technique (PERT) A flowchart for managing large programs and projects showing the necessary activities with estimates of the time needed to complete each activity and the sequential relationship among them.

Programmed decisions Solutions to repetitive and routine problems provided by existing policies, procedures, rules, and so on.

Progressive discipline System of disciplinary action that increases the severity of the penalty with each offense.

Project A single-use plan for accomplishing a specific nonrecurring activity.

Protected-group employees Classes of employees who have been afforded certain legal protections in their employment situations.

Q

Qualified disabled individual Defined by the Americans with Disabilities Act as someone with a disability who can perform the essential components of a job with or without reasonable accommodation.

Quantitative/systems approaches Field of management study that uses mathematical modeling as a foundation.

R

Realistic job preview (RJP) Information given by an interviewer to a job applicant that provides a realistic view of both the positive and the negative aspects of the job.

Realistic organizational preview (ROP) Sharing of information by an interviewer with a job applicant concerning the mission, values, and future direction of the organization.

Reasonable accommodation Altering the usual ways of doing things so that an otherwise qualified disabled person can perform the essential job duties, but without creating an undue hardship for the employer.

Recentralization Reducing or revoking delegated authority when realigning functions or responsibilities.

Re-engineering Concept of restructuring a firm on the basis of processes and customer needs and services, rather than by departments and functions.

Regular duties The essential components of a supervisor's job, such as giving directives and checking performance.

Relationship management Coordinated efforts to communicate and build trust with customers.

Reverse discrimination Preference given to protected-group members in hiring and promotion over more qualified or more experienced workers from nonprotected groups.

Right to appeal Procedures by which an employee may request higher-level management to review a supervisor's disciplinary action.

Routine duties Minor tasks, done daily, that make a minor contribution to achievement of objectives.

Rule A directive that must be applied and enforced wherever applicable.

S

Sampling The technique of evaluating some number of items from a larger group to determine whether the group meets acceptable quality standards.

Satisficing Selecting the alternative that minimally meets the decision criteria.

Scenario-based forecasting Developing a range of alternative forecasts that could impact a firm's future.

Scheduling The process of developing a detailed list of activities, their sequence, and the required resources.

Scientific management approach School of management thought that focuses on determining the most efficient methods to achieve greater output and productivity.

Security needs Desire for protection against danger and life's uncertainties.

Selection Process of choosing the best applicants to fill open positions.

Selection criteria Factors used to choose among applicants who apply for a job.

Self-directed (self-managed) work teams When employee groups are given wide latitude and considerable authority to make many of their own job-related decisions.

Self-fulfillment needs Desire to use one's abilities to the fullest extent.

Self-respect needs Desire for recognition, achievement, status, and a sense of accomplishment.

Semantics The multiple meanings of words.

Seniority An employee's length of service within a department or organization.

Sexual harassment Unwelcome sexual advances, requests, or conduct when submission to such conduct is tied to the individual's continuing employment or advancement, unreasonably interferes with job performance, or creates a hostile work environment.

Sexual stereotyping Use of language or judgments that demean someone, usually by men toward women.

Shop steward Employee elected or appointed to represent employees at the departmental level, particularly in grievance processing.

Single-use plans Plans developed to accomplish a specific objective or to cover only a designated time period.

SKAs Skills, knowledge, and abilities that a person has.

Skill-based pay System that rewards employees for acquiring new skills or knowledge.

Social needs Desire for love and affection and affiliation with something worthwhile.

Span of management principle There is an upper limit to the number of subordinates that a supervisor can manage effectively.

Special duties Tasks not directly related to the core tasks of the department, such as meetings and committee work.

Special-interest group Grouping of employees that exists to accomplish something in a group that individuals do not choose to pursue individually.

Staff authority The right to provide counsel, advice, support, and service in a person's areas of expertise.

Staff department Specialized department responsible for supporting line departments and providing specialized advice and services.

Staffing The tasks of recruiting, selecting, orienting, training, appraising, and evaluating employees.

Standards Units of measurement or specific criteria against which to evaluate results.

Standing plans Policies, procedures, methods, and rules that can be applied to recurring situations.

Status Attitudes toward a person based on the position he or she occupies.

Stereotyping The perception that all people in a certain group share common attitudes, values, and beliefs.

Strategic business partners Staff personnel collaborate with line managers to continuously improve overall organizational performance.

Strategic control points (Strategic standards) Performance criteria chosen for assessment because they are key indicators of overall performance.

Strategic planning The process of establishing goals and making decisions that will enable an organization to achieve its long- and short-term objectives.

Strategic plans Long-range overall plans developed by top management.

Stress A person's nonspecific bodily reactions to demands and conditions that he or she encounters.

Stretch targets Targeted job objectives that present a challenge but are achievable.

Substantive conflict Conflict between individuals because of what should be done or what should occur.

Supervisor First-level manager in charge of entry-level and other departmental employees.

T

Tactical plans Annual or intermediate-range plans developed by middle managers and staff specialists.

Tangible standards Standards for performance results that are identifiable and measurable.

Task group or cross-functional team Grouping of employees who come together to accomplish a particular task.

Teamwork People working cooperatively to solve problems and achieve goals important to the group.

Technical skills The ability to do the job.

Telecommuting Receiving and sending work to the office from home via a computer and modem.

Temporary (ad hoc) committee Group that meets only for a limited time and for a specific purpose.

Theory X Assumption that most employees dislike work, avoid responsibility, and must be coerced to do the job.

Theory Y Assumption that most employees enjoy work, seek responsibility, and are capable of self-direction.

Time study A technique for analyzing jobs to determine time standards for performing each job.

Total quality management (TQM) An organizational approach involving all employees in the effort to satisfy customers by continual improvement of goods and services.

Two-tier wage systems Paying new employees at a lower rate than more senior employees. (Also used to define disparities associated with high executive compensation.)

U

Underemployment Situation in which people are in jobs that do not utilize their skills, knowledge, and abilities (SKAs).

Understudy Someone who can assist the supervisor and is able to run the department in the supervisor's absence.

Union business representative Paid official of the local or national union who may be involved in grievance processing.

Union shop A labor agreement provision in which employees are required to join the union as a condition of employment, usually after 30 days.

Unity of command principle Principle that holds that each employee should report directly to only one supervisor.

V

Virtual corporation Where companies link together on a temporary basis to take advantage of marketplace opportunities.

Visioning Management's view of what the company should become that reflects the firm's core values, priorities, and goals.

W

Wellness program Organized efforts by a firm to help employees get and stay healthy in order to remain productive.

Work sampling Inspecting a sample of work from an entire job to determine areas for improvement.

Working supervisors First-level individuals who perform supervisory functions but who may not be legally or officially part of management.

Workplace spirituality Organizational efforts to make the work environment more meaningful and creative by relating work to employees' values and spiritual beliefs.

Z

Zero-base budgeting The process of assessing all activities to justify their existence on a benefit and cost basis.

Index

Photo Credits

———o———